FORTHCOMING BOOKS IN THE SERIES

North America

Europe

Asia

{ SHARE }

**Conversations about
Contemporary Architecture**

– The Nordic Countries –

TODD SAUNDERS & JONATHAN BELL

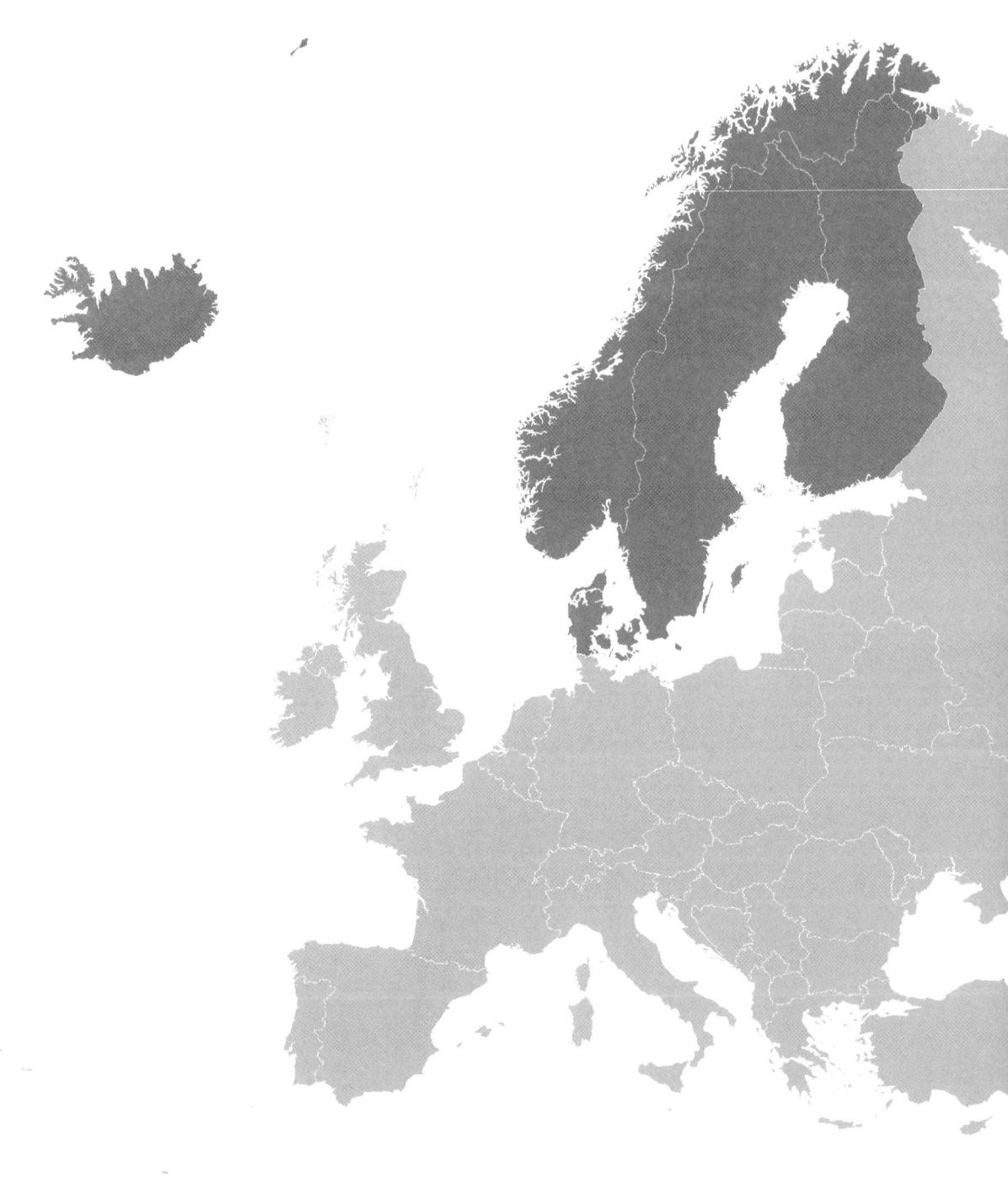

The Nordic Countries

8	Introduction	84	Vandkunsten
16	Ninety nine questions about practice		*Copenhagen*
		94	3XN
			Copenhagen

DENMARK

FINLAND

20   THE STATE OF MODERNISM
By Professor Katrine Lotz

106   A DOZEN YEARS IN FINNISH ARCHITECTURE
By Kristo Vesikansa

24   BIG – Bjarke Ingels Group
Copenhagen

110   ALA Architects
Helsinki

38   Henning Larsen Architects
Copenhagen

122   Avanto Architects
Helsinki

50   Marianne Levinsen Landskab
Copenhagen

132   K2S Architects
Helsinki

60   Norrøn
Copenhagen

72   Studio dominique + serena
Copenhagen

146   OOPEAA
Helsinki

158	Planetary Architecture *Helsinki*		NORWAY
172	Studio Puisto *Helsinki*	236	A SHARED PROCESS *By Joakim Skajaa*
		240	Gartnerfuglen Arkitekter *Oslo*
	ICELAND	250	Haugen/Zohar Arkitekter *Oslo*
184	DIALOGUE WITH NATURE *By Hildigunnur Sverrisdóttir*	264	Helen & Hard *Stavanger*
188	A arkitektar *Reykjavik*	278	Jensen & Skodvin *Oslo*
200	Basalt Architects *Reykjavik*	290	Reiulf Ramstad Arkitekter *Oslo*
210	PK Arkitektar *Reykjavik*	302	Rintala Eggertsson *Oslo*
222	Studio Granda *Reykjavik*	314	Snøhetta *Oslo*

330	Vardehaugen *Oslo*	410	Acknowledgements
		413	Biographies
		415	Image credits
		416	Colophon

SWEDEN

344 IN A STATE OF BECOMING
By Malin Zimm

350 Claesson Koivisto Rune
Stockholm

362 Förstberg Ling
Malmö

372 Johan Dehlin
Stockholm

384 Tham & Videgård
Stockholm

398 Wingårdhs
Stockholm

{ SHARE }

INTRODUCTION

{ BY }

TODD SAUNDERS

Architecture can be a very insular way of life. Despite being a profession that requires years of study and a willingness to absorb ideas and theories from a colossal amount of collected knowledge, the actual practice of architecture can easily descend into a solitary pursuit, a journey in a tunnel. Unlike the world of the student, the working architect is often only aware of the destination, not the landscape they are travelling through. But what is architecture without dialogue and interaction? One of the fundamental tenets of the profession is that a successful building should be engaging on many different levels, socially, culturally, physically, environmentally. Good architecture does not exist in isolation. Yet all too often, architects find themselves – whether inadvertently or otherwise – trapped in a bubble of their own making.

When I came up with the idea for this book, my motivations were probably quite selfish. Saunders Architecture, the firm I established in 1998 in Bergen, had reached something of an impasse. After working on approximately 175 projects in over 15 countries around the world, I felt like I had reached a crossroads in my career. A disproportionate amount of my time was spent travelling to meet new clients and visit sites. The landscape and outdoor life I had grown up with in Canada had been replaced by the sterile, over-familiar landscape of airports and plane interiors, all processed air and identikit views. I saw a chance to take another path and make a change.

I decided to re-focus the practice and concentrate my creative energies on projects that would make a difference or offer something new. It was a radical change. In the process, it raised a lot of questions about the practice of architecture. I gradually realised that these were questions that might benefit the wider profession. By reaching out and asking these questions, we could open up the insular nature of architectural practice and re-establish the connections that had closed off over time. We wanted to create a book that set out the realities of architectural practice, the kind of "how-to manual" that simply didn't exist when I started studying architecture. Hence the title of the book, Share.

Two important framing devices determined the shape of this book. The first was the decision to focus on the Nordic countries. I have practiced in Norway my entire career and have always felt a strong affinity with the culture and landscape, and the ways in which architecture mediates between them. This book includes conversations with architects, young and old, from Denmark, Sweden, Finland, Iceland and, of course, Norway. Even as an "outsider", I am aware of the strong sense of cultural unity in the Nordic regions, one that transcends borders without diluting key characteristics of each region. I have crossed paths with many of the people in this book over the years, at conferences or workshops, at dinner parties or Biennales, or judging alongside or competing against. There's a strong sense of having grown up together in a profession that – in Scandinavia at least – often feels like a shared community.

The second element was the shortlist of 99 questions about architectural practice that forms the core of each conversation. Over the years, I have asked myself many questions about the work that I do and haven't always had a satisfactory answer to hand. It struck me that most – if not all – architects must feel the same way. We approached a selection of some of the best-known and most promising architects working today and asked them if they would value this kind of insight. The vast majority said yes, selecting the questions they felt best equipped to answer. The result is a book that explores the shared values of contemporary architectural practice in a unique way, as a series of conversational enquiries about architects' hopes, fears and aspirations, as well as the challenges of running a practice in the 2020s.

A book that was conceived and started in 2020 could hardly ignore the Covid-19 pandemic. A number of cultural shifts have taken place over the course of our research, interviews and writing that have had a huge bearing on the world of work, and how architects have responded to it. We have chosen not to let the pandemic dominate the conversations, but there are some inescapable conclusions that came out of the upheaval. As I had personally discovered, architecture can be an all-consuming profession to the detriment of anything else. It's fair to say that living your job as if it were your life is no longer seen as a positive statement; it's not valuable or even realistic to be on hand 24/7. The slowdown created by Covid might only be temporary, but for many people it forced a reset of their relationship to time and speed. It feels right for a reassessment.

On a more practical level, almost every interview in this book ended up being conducted over the internet, rather than face to face as originally intended. What was originally supposed to be the perfect opportunity for a series of architectural road trips ended up being the epitome of digital collaboration. Some questions were therefore framed differently. Most importantly, physical buildings became peripheral to the discussions, rather than a focus, since site visits were impossible.

Throughout the project, my initial premise remained relevant; this would be the perfect book for newly qualified architects to read just as they were starting their careers. Common threads emerged, understandably, as did points of difference. It was noticeable that many architects considered themselves to be rule breakers, going against conventional wisdom or expectations. It also felt subversive to ask practitioners what they would have done differently, or what – in their opinion – they now considered to be mistakes.

Share *is not about re-framing practice for a new era, for there is no universal approach to a topic as infinitely diverse as architecture. The architects in this book have worked on a broad spectrum of projects, from modest single-family homes to winners of international competitions for major new public buildings. Instead, it is a conversation, a place to find common ground and uncover points of difference.*

Share was born out of a desire to reassess and rediscover the things that made architecture important to me in the first place. This is by no means everyone's story. Architecture is a profession that defines its practitioners and shapes their outlooks. We are architects all the time, whether at the dinner table, in the queue at the grocery store, driving on the highway or lying in bed at night. Most architects, I suspect, wouldn't have it any other way. By asking questions about what matters and why, I hope this book starts a conversation about the processes behind architecture, and how different outlooks translate into the work that we do and the way we achieve it. As one of the interviewees said to me, architecture "is a beautiful, amazing profession, but it's a matter of finding the points where at least you feel like you can make a change."

Todd Saunders

INTRODUCTION | TODD SAUNDERS

NINETY NINE QUESTIONS ABOUT PRACTICE

{ NOW }

1. Can you tell us about a current project that you are really excited about?

2. What opportunities and constraints are you facing now?

3. Can you describe your career in a few sentences?

{ PERSONAL }

4. Can you tell us something about your beginnings in architecture?

5. Did you give anything up in order to practice architecture (a hobby, another career, etc.)?

6. Did you have any false beliefs as a younger professional that do not hold true any more?

7. Were there any memorable "rites of passage" in your career?

8. Seeing, listening or drawing – which is your biggest strength? Which sense do you use most?

9. Do you believe you are different from other architects? If so, why?

10. What is the role of conversation and public speaking in your daily life?

11. What makes architecture such a worthwhile profession for you?

12. Describe some qualities in people or architecture that inspire you to forge onwards.

13. Have you ever thought of quitting or changing professions? If yes, describe.

14. Which century, beside the 21st would you prefer to be an architect in?

15. What would make you quit architecture? What would you then do?

16. Do you think you have achieved a good work/life balance?

{ PROCESS }

17. How does your design process typically begin?

18. Are there any unconventional professions or people you collaborate with?

19. What are the challenges of designing for urban and rural sites in Scandinavia?

20. Do you ever recycle old ideas or advance upon them? Can you give an example?

21. In what ways has your work evolved since you started your career?

22. How are the key design principles expressed in your buildings?

23. What is unique about your process of making architecture?

24. What are some things you think you need now to make your architecture evolve and be better?

25. What are some of your daily/weekly rituals in your office that have made your architecture better? Describe the ideal day of work. Include some of your routines.

26. How do you inspire your team to help them reach their potential?

{ LEARNING }

27. What are some industries or movements outside of architecture that you are curious about?

28. Is your work related to academia in any way?

29. Are books and journals important to the way you work?

30. Do you do pro bono or philanthropic work? How did it help others and how did it help you?

31. Do you manage to keep on learning? Is this important, or not?

32. How do you ensure that you keep learning, evolving and growing as a professional?

33. What are the ways in which you learn best?

34. What do you want to learn now at this point in your life and career?

35. Can you tell us about something you didn't initially know how to do when you started as an architect but are glad you took the time to learn later in life?

36. Which project taught you the most? How? Can you tell a story?

37. What was the most important lesson learned during your education?

38. Do you believe creativity is due to nature or nurture?

39. How much of making architecture is an intrinsic talent and how much can be taught and learned? Can you share your views on this?

40. Can you tell us about a few "a-ha" moments you have experienced as an architect?

41. Does your office do design and build? If so, what have you learned from working this way?

{ PEOPLE }

42. Architecture cannot be practised alone; who are the key people who have helped your practice?

43. Which architect was most influential to your understanding of architecture?

44. Who, outside of your studio, do you get architectural advice from?

45. Do you have people that you discuss the business side of architecture with? How have they helped?

46. Do you think the people in your studio share certain character traits?

{ ATTITUDE }

47. In your opinion, what makes a building a good piece of architecture?

48. What advice would you give your 10, 20, 30, 40, 50, 60, 70, 80-year-old self, or another person in your profession? You can pick any of these ages.

49. What makes your work useful to the world? What makes it real?

50. Do you believe your architectural approach is truly personal? Why?

51. Is architecture your hobby or profession? Or both?

52. Do you welcome resistance or conflict? If so, how does it help your architecture?

53. Describe a complex problem you have faced and how you solved it.

54. Is daydreaming important?

55. Have you ever made any past mistakes that you subsequently learned from?

56. Which of your projects do you believe is the most provocative?

57. What are the enduring qualities of your approach to architecture?

58. What is your take on the relationship between vernacular and contemporary architecture?

{ PRACTICE }

59. How does your studio reflect the values of your practice?

60. Which tools or specific architectural knowledge is invaluable to you and your studio?

61. How do you instigate change on a macro or micro scale in your practice?

62. What professional and creative challenges have you overcome and/or are you facing? Do difficult moments generate more creativity?

63. Can you tell a story of one of your projects that has become known as a great success?

64. Are there any "projects that got away"? Do you still think about them and why?

65. Can you explain a small change in your studio that made a big difference?

66. Are you able to control which clients and projects find you?

67. Can you tell us three ways you get new businesses? Any secrets you can share?

68. Do you find it easier to work in the office or elsewhere?

{ EMOTION }

69. Can you describe an emotion you experienced when visiting a site for the first time?

70. How do you use intuition in your practice?

71. Have you ever been asked a question that made a big impact on you? What was it?

72. Is there a place for emotion in architectural practice?

73. What are the character traits of the clients that you work with best?

74. Would you have worked on any of your projects free? Can you explain the reasons why?

75. Do you have a favourite or a worst project? No need to name it but can you describe why?

76. What is one project you really want to do before you finish being an architect?

77. Have you ever been emotionally moved by a building? What about one of your own projects?

78. Do you find architecture creatively satisfying?

{ PLACE }

79. How does your architecture make the world a better place?

80. Can you list any ways in which your work is different because of where you live and work?

81. Are there any important differences or similarities with your local peers?

82. What is one building in your city that you love and why?

83. Does the opportunity to work in other countries and cultures influence your work?

84. Does your location influence your architecture? Would it be different if you were elsewhere?

85. What is the most important value that architecture can bring to communities?

86. Can you describe an ideal architectural project for your local community?

{ TIME }

87. Can you explain whether speed or slowness was ever a benefit in your process?

88. Can you share your thoughts about the changing pace of creating architecture?

89. Is solitude a useful or essential part of your working process?

90. Do you need to protect yourself from distractions in order to find time to create? How?

91. What is the role of tenacity, grit and stamina in your past and current practice?

92. How much does the impact of time weigh upon your design approach?

{ ETHICS }

93. Can you explain what you do and what you do not do?

94. Is there something you want to say with your architecture?

95. What are your basic criteria or set of values to help you decide how to proceed with a project?

96. What things do you say "yes" or "no" to in life and work?

97. What do you think people in your community will remember about you and your architecture?

98. How are the impacts of time important to your work?

99. Is there a particular kind of project you would like to complete before you retire?

{ ESSAY }

THE STATE OF MODERNISM

{ BY }

PROFESSOR KATRINE LOTZ

Head of Department at the Institute of Architecture, Urbanism and Landscape at the Royal Danish Academy

Architectural culture changes over time. Not just the conditions that the architecture profession and the building trades work in, but also the self-consciousness of the architects themselves. The present generation of young Nordic architects appear to be anything but arrogant. Instead, they are extremely strong in their professional approach, and their projects are driven by a remarkable sense of responsibility informed by the perspective of the imminent climate and biodiversity crises. They are not afraid to couple scientific knowledge with super-refined aesthetics and to let them cross-fertilise.

As an architect, researcher and writer on architecture, I have been interested in the relationship between architecture and the ongoing development of the Danish welfare state. It is obvious that Denmark can boast a rich tradition of design and architecture, but I am most interested in the implications of the current changes in the welfare systems to architecture, and how we perceive of space and "the good life". The roles of the architect are still afforded importance and prestige within Danish society, and also in the other Nordic countries that have similar cultures. Wherever you turn, you'll meet an architect; they are with clients, advisers, in the municipalities, in the supporting foundations, in research and so forth. Even if they're not your traditional architect with a capital "A", their work is acknowledged as seminal for the whole culture of architecture. Of course, architecture and planning is often disputed and controversial, but an engaged public debate on a high level is also an important support to architecture.

The development of the Danish welfare state saw the country's architects participate vigorously in the creation of the spaces and institutions of a new society in the interwar years, and the values of "the functionalist tradition", originally coined as a kind of local translation of the international modernism that in many ways still resonates. Caring for the design of common spaces, striving for comfort and for democratic accessibility, a certain degree of modesty coupled with high ambitions of compositional and tectonic clarity and significance, are all prominent traits also in the most current works of younger architects. Danish architecture was never a closed system, and since the '90s, the bolder, perhaps more media-friendly architecture inspired by Dutch architects has contributed to the discourse especially. I find it particularly interesting that this seemingly pragmatic but also very programmatically driven architecture has been tempered and refined artistically over the past few decades.

I would also like to point to the importance of a number of philanthropic foundations that have either architecture in the narrower sense or the built environment as a whole as their purpose. They come in many different sizes and economic abilities, but in the last 20 years their impact on the possibilities for developing architecture and high-quality urban development outside of the increasingly larger mainstream architectural bureaus can hardly be overestimated. Look at how Dreyers Fond offers support for younger offices to get a foothold in the industry and increase their business awareness. Also, there is Realdania, with its huge financial ability to support municipalities and others in pursuing ambitious strategies for architecture and urban planning. We can discuss their strategies, and if the "activistic philanthropy" that they have introduced is always the most appropriate approach to support, but their importance to architecture and the built environment is indisputable.

Perhaps this is a uniquely Danish condition. Our welfare state and also civic society, with its ongoing quest for social equality and an emphasis on universality, still holds features that can point towards the next levels of sustainability we need to obtain, even if it is still challenged by forces like international competitions and undemocratic movements, as we also see in the rest of Europe.

Many of the younger generation of Danish architects are now wrestling with the challenges of the circular economy, as well as the struggle of transitioning from small-scale projects to major works without compromise. Even then, despite the best intentions of various collaborators, the existing systems and dynamics that shape the country's real-estate market, from land prices to local legislation, all act as barriers that must be surmounted.

The Danish architecture education system is also changing, as it recognises the need to invent radically new ways of engaging with nature, not only through sustainable development in terms of climate and resources, but also by sustaining biodiversity. I think we have no other option than to put ourselves at the forefront of these changes, and to see ourselves as important drivers for them. We need new concepts of sustainability that are tangible, understandable, relatable and which present actual alternatives to the ways things are currently done. They must be scalable and realistic – developing a convincing alternative to concrete, for instance – or providing answers to how we can increase urban density without losing our quality of life. Architects also need to engage with public debate and the bodies of knowledge that feed into decision-makers and the political classes. The profession needs to reinvent itself just as the earlier generations of "welfare architects" did before and after the Second World War.

BIG – Bjarke Ingels Group

Bjarke Ingels was born in 1974 in Copenhagen, and studied architecture at the Royal Danish Academy of Fine Arts and then the Escola Tècnica Superior d'Arquitectura in Barcelona. He then spent three years working at the Office for Metropolitan Architecture in Rotterdam, where his projects included the design of the Seattle Library. In 1998 Ingels co-founded PLOT Architects with another OMA alumnus, Julien De Smedt, before setting up BIG, the Bjarke Ingels Group, in 2006. The acclaimed practice now has offices in Copenhagen and New York and has a high-profile presence on the global architecture scene. From housing projects through to major cultural works, BIG has won many awards. Ingels himself was awarded the Knight's Cross of the Order of Dannebrog and appointed Knight of the French Ordre des Arts et des Lettres in 2018 and 2019 respectively. In constant demand as a lecturer and teacher, he combines his practice with publishing and writing, bringing a holistic, global approach to improving and emphasising the role of architecture in addressing issues like climate change and sustainability.

big.dk

Previous page: Tirpitz, Blåvand, Denmark

This page: VIA West 57, New York, USA

TODD SAUNDERS: Hi Bjarke, what are you working on at the moment?

BJARKE INGELS: Among other things, we're working on 3D-printed housing in Mexico. We also used the technology for an orphanage for Cambodian girls, which was part of the Vancouver condo project. Everyone who bought a condo in Vancouver also effectively bought one small house. We didn't design them, but the project obviously contributed to the creation of around 350 mini homes and then we designed the school for them.

TS: You have so much responsibility with BIG, but what would you personally like to focus on over the next few years?

BI: It's been a year of remote collaboration, right? I have to say it's driving me insane. I have offices in Barcelona, London, Copenhagen and New York and it's been forever since I've seen most of them. And I think that kind of human longing is beginning to impact the satisfaction of the work. A day of Zoom calls is like a vampire for the soul. There's a lot of travelling you don't need to do and Zoom meetings can be great for a lot of things. But it also shows that we're just not ready for a virtual existence. We're physical human beings.

TS: What are the benefits of not travelling for you?

BI: At the beginning, it was a great break for me and my family. I got to be incredibly present in my young son's life. But what's great about coming home is that you've been away. And with travelling you depart from your home and you see something different and then you come back with that new experience.

The only way to see yourself is to understand how others do it differently. I think the back and forth of travelling is a meaningful dialogue with the world that I'm missing. We're now doing a few remote projects where we haven't even been to the site.

TS: I remember seeing the world differently when I moved to the Rhode Island School of Design as an exchange student at the age of 21. I realised that by travelling, I can experience much more and get my cultural biases wiped out and grow into a different person.

BI: A hundred per cent. I moved to Barcelona when I was 21 for a year. I met a lot of Erasmus people from many countries in addition to the Catalans. It was before anyone had email or a cell phone, so I had to create a whole new habitat there. I had grown up on the outskirts of Copenhagen and I'd never really left my habitat. My surroundings didn't leave me much space to evolve or grow. It's a bit like it's hard to see your children as anything other than your children.

TS: What type of energy do you need around you from people in the firm?

BI: I have, like, 22 partners in the business, and you end up interfacing differently with different people. There is a creative hierarchy at BIG – it's the only way to run it. Of course, I enjoy communicating directly with the people that hold the X-Acto knife and the people that programme the laser cutter because you need that. If I need help with something specific, I'll remember someone's exceptional presentation and then I'll end up spending more time with that person than any of the partners or the CEO, and

I get to know that person incredibly well. If you get isolated in an ivory tower in your own organisation, then you've lost it.

TS: When you're isolated, you're like a dead branch on the tree. Do you have anyone who works for you who just showed up one day? One guy knocked on my door one Friday afternoon and just said he was an industrial designer – he wasn't even an architect. And he's been spectacular – he worked on all the Fogo projects. Some people just come into your life and make a huge difference.

BI: Half of our partners started off as interns. In many cases they were just these kids who were very smart and who ended up growing tremendously with the company. Employee number one, our very first professional architect, he's also a partner and is ten years my senior.

TS: They all appreciate that you grew up together in a way.

BI: A lot of these guys I've known for 20 years now.

TS: Where are you right now?

BI: I'm in this nature reserve in Mexico and it's empty because of Covid. Every other day, we all pick up the garbage at the beach – not the stuff that's been left by people, but the rubbish which comes in from the Caribbean. Even the most untouched places are full of garbage these days. The only places that have a chance to appear like they're untouched nature have people actually clearing them up all the time. If we don't take on all of Earth as our responsibility, then the absence of our planning and intervention will make it drown in trash. We used to be able to say, Let's leave some places on Earth completely untouched, but that's no longer an option. The most untouched places will drown in trash and will suffer from acidic oceans or heightened temperatures, etc. The absence of a masterplan for the planet is having consequences on a planetary scale.

TS: Can architecture still be specific and distinct though in those situations?

BI: At different scales, you have different ways of providing meaningful input, right?

TS: But can you make architecture specific at a larger scale? Should it be?

BI: If you make a masterplan for Earth, you're not going to produce building designs. Maybe you can dive down or zoom in. One of my partners and I once talked about redrawing a world map based on regions rather than countries. Someone – I forget who – wrote about how as animals get bigger, they become more productive and more energy efficient. The same is true for cities and for companies – they increase productive output with scale. When you pass the Dunbar number of 150 people, which is the amount of people that you can engage with on a personal level, there's a taxation on the increase in productivity. That's not true for countries – they're artificial constructs. But perhaps with the advent of the internet, we're approaching a situation where you can facilitate exchange and communication and coordination either on a planetary scale, or as locally and specific as possible.

TS: That's what I like, the idea of being local and specific.

Below: Kistefos – The Twist (KIS), Jevnaker, Norway

There's this easy dichotomy between the idea of collaboration being essential and the idea that it's all about individual genius. It's all about individual contribution and it's all about collective collaboration at the same time.

— Bjarke Ingels

Above and right: Kistefos – The Twist (KIS), Jevnaker, Norway

BI: This means you render the nation scale obsolete. Of course, there's cultural heritage, but that is always porous across borders. Back in the medieval Europe of city states, language was like a gradient. If you hiked from Stockholm to Seville, the dialect would change a tiny bit from town to town, not a dramatic change from one language to another.

TS: I once saw a lecture about Ian McHarg, who talks about planning based on rivers and watersheds. In a way, that's how I grew up – my grandfather was a fly fish guide, and everyone tended to be connected and took responsibility for their little bit of nature, their watercourse. The dialect might be different to the next river and stuff like that. The idea of erasing man-made borders and going back to natural borders is becoming more relevant. How can such ideas evolve?

BI: We often mislabel things revolutions when they are in fact evolutions. I think a revolution is catastrophic and costly. The patient often dies. That's why a mutation that is dramatic and fundamental in Darwinian evolution will often be so catastrophic that the host organism dies from it. When you burn down churches or behead the elite then you lose such an amount of information, culture and capability. Revolutions often lead to a regime that is more repressive and more rigorous than the one it sought to replace. Napoleon in France. The Ayatollahs in Iran. In Denmark, at least the royal family – maybe out of fear or out of some idea of consensus – ended up handing over power voluntarily instead of being beheaded. The way evolution works is by constantly testing way too many ideas, way too many variants and constantly upvoting with various means the ones that have slight benefits.

TS: This is where it crosses into my territory because I've experienced monocultures with no cultural diversity, as well as places like Vancouver where you can hear 15 different languages walking down the street.

BI: It's important to understand that evolution and experimentation is constant. Our challenges are so complex that the solution is not something you can think through. I noticed one of your questions was if you had any false beliefs as a younger professional? I used to be much more arrogant about my ability to dream up things and had much more faith in pure concepts. I've learned how to think with my hands and how to think with the hands of others. When you do that, you have to relinquish the pride that you hold in being great.

TS: You get out of your own way.

BI: It's a huge motivator, to come up with the most brilliant idea, but you have to recognise that we are all pursuing these eureka moments and they won't necessarily originate from you. There's this easy dichotomy between the idea of collaboration being essential and the idea that it's all about individual genius. It's all about individual contribution and it's all about collective collaboration at the same time.

TS: I've talked about collective emotions with other architects. Have you ever experienced that with all the partners in BIG, where everyone came together with a shared emotion?

BI: Our discipline is that every six months we all meet, all 23 of us, which of course we haven't been able to do this year. It's hard to get together, but it always ends up being this revitalising experience where we somehow rediscover what incredible friends we are and what an incredible adventure we have come through and so we plot a course for the years ahead.

TS: What's one of those favourite trips you've had?

BI: In the late fall of 2019, we went through to these cabins upstate, in the snow. It was where I formulated this idea: to apply architectural thinking and master planning on the scale of the entire planet. One of our partners did a presentation looking at greenhouse gas emissions and sustainable habitation in general. By using architectural methods of visualising complex information, we made this seemingly insurmountable complex situation into something that you could grasp. It was so invigorating. I'm an architect with a capital A, so I love designing the shit out of something. In the context of the climate crisis, the things that would make a difference are not necessarily practical within the confines of our profession. However, we can still think holistically and address complex situations with an understanding, but also with a capacity for action and intervention. We recently created BIG Leap – Landscape, Engineering, Architecture and Product design – all under the same umbrella. It allows us to be more informed in a broader spectrum of our practice. It's about creating a framework for a way of working, creating concept designs that are necessarily incomplete, but you know that it's not final and that it can be modified until it evolves into something that everybody can accept.

TS: In the past, nobody really accepted that humanity was just one big unit. Nobody knows the answers just yet, but we need to commit to larger thinking and yet still find space to be specific. It's about stepping back and forth constantly, big and small.

BI: A hundred per cent. Public discussion tends to be extremely polarised, which makes it more difficult. I believe the way forward is probably more like a fractal, that the closer you zoom in, the more you see that in the middle between left and right, north and south, whatever it is, the more infinite possibility there is. It's so easy to talk about enemies, to say that economic growth is the source of all the misery. For sure, our environmental challenges are, to a large degree, a by-product of the success of humanity. There are always unanticipated side effects. Buckminster Fuller said that all waste is simply valuable resources that haven't been identified yet. It's important you don't end up in this unproductive dichotomy of saying economy is bad, ecology is good, because there's nothing more economical than nature. All living things take resources from their environment and use those resources to resist entropy and maintain life. We want to keep making life better for more, but there are still detrimental side effects that need addressing.

TS: What did you learn from Bruce Mau? His Massive Change exhibition seemed to make a huge difference to you.

BI: For sure. I met him first when I was at OMA working on the Seattle Library. He was very influential to us, especially how he ran his studio. Also, the idea of thinking about design as form giving, in the fullest possible way. Not just about beautifying something, but potentially orchestrating all aspects of life in a way that is more meaningful.

Above and right: Copenhill – ARC, Copenhagen, Denmark

DENMARK | BIG

TS: What about another Canadian figure, Douglas Coupland?

BI: I am a huge admirer of his writing – I think I faithfully read every book. He's become a really good friend. He lives in Vancouver – as does William Gibson. My two favourite writers. I started architecture school at 18, and the average age of a first-year student back then in Copenhagen was 23. There was a healthy level of pretentiousness. I was straight out of high school and although I was good at drawing and quite smart I didn't really know how to channel it. I wasn't governed by anger or trauma – I didn't potentially feel like a revolutionary. And then I found this quote from Coupland that I felt made him the smartest, the most insightful guy on the planet: he was the child of the "middle, middle, middle, middle, middle, middle class". I was like, thank you! A massive part of his work is about contemplating the everyday with such scrutiny that you end up uncovering the meaningful in the mundane. Everyday life is airports and gas stations and parking lots and all that shit.

TS: I'm convinced that there's so much stuff out there, so many little niches of information that everything will become more specific. There's probably a hundred Couplands or Bruce Maus out there, thousands of great architects. And they're all connected and they're all different.

Below: OCEANIX, Busan, South Korea

DENMARK | BIG

Right: BIG workshop, Copenhagen, Denmark

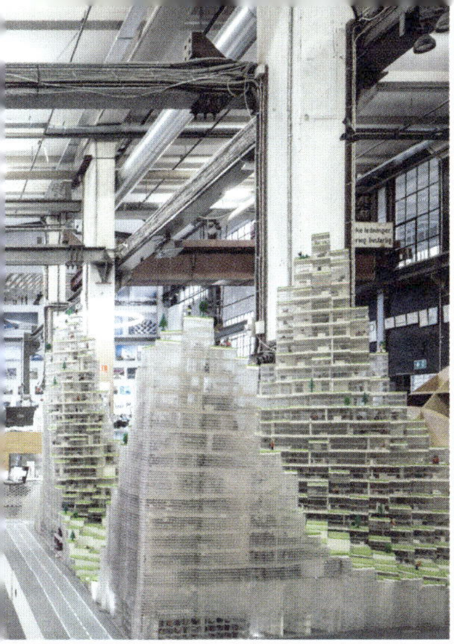
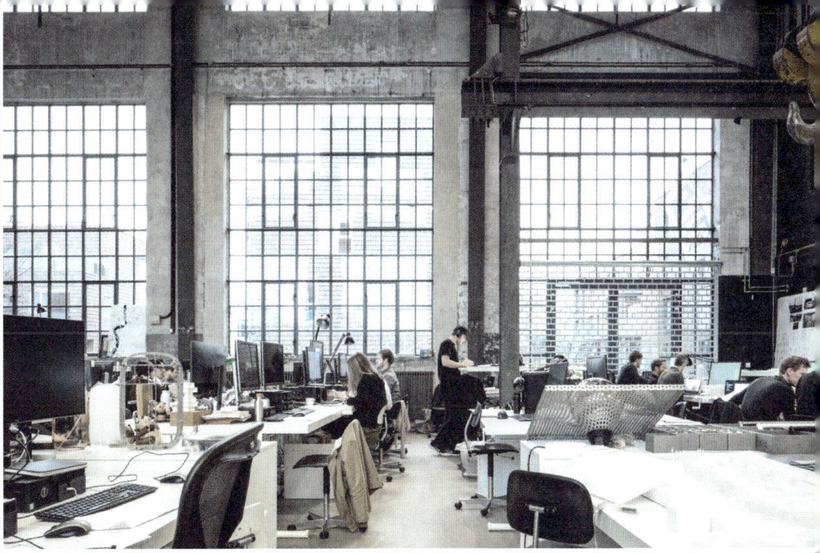
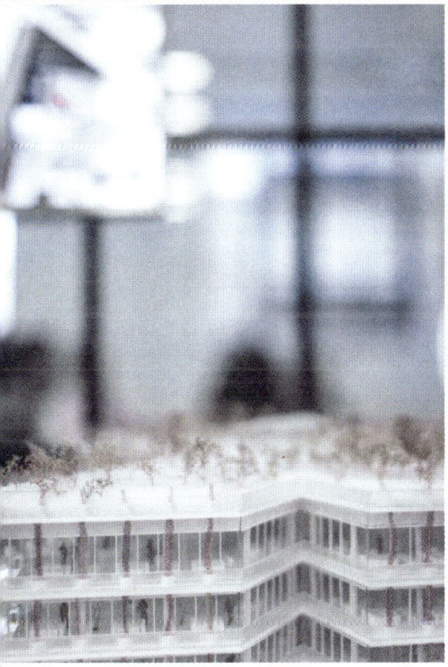
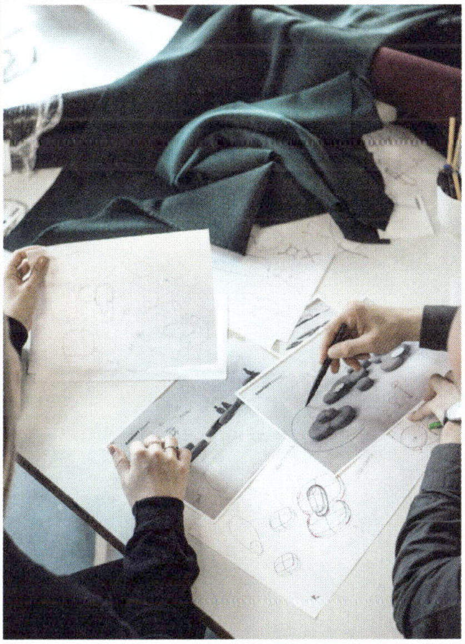
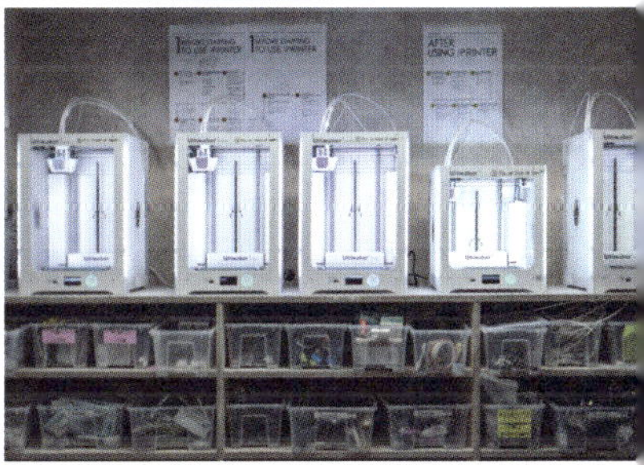
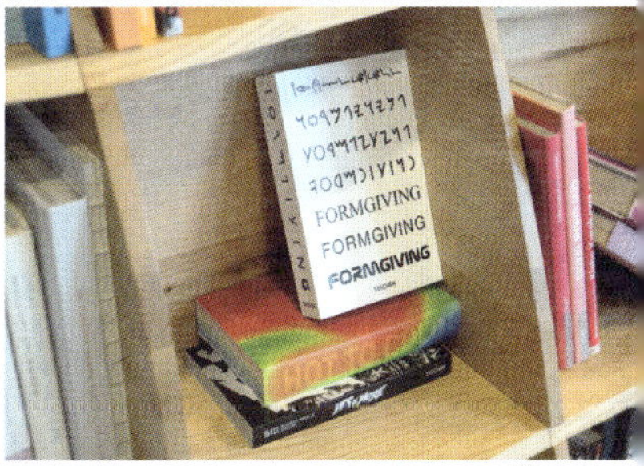
FORMGIVING
FORMGIVING
FORMGIVING
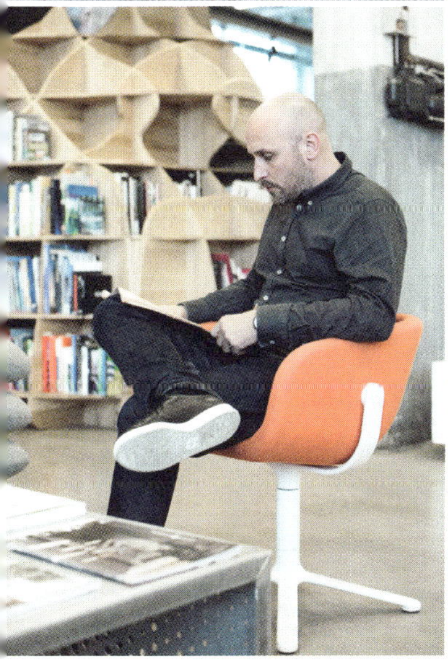
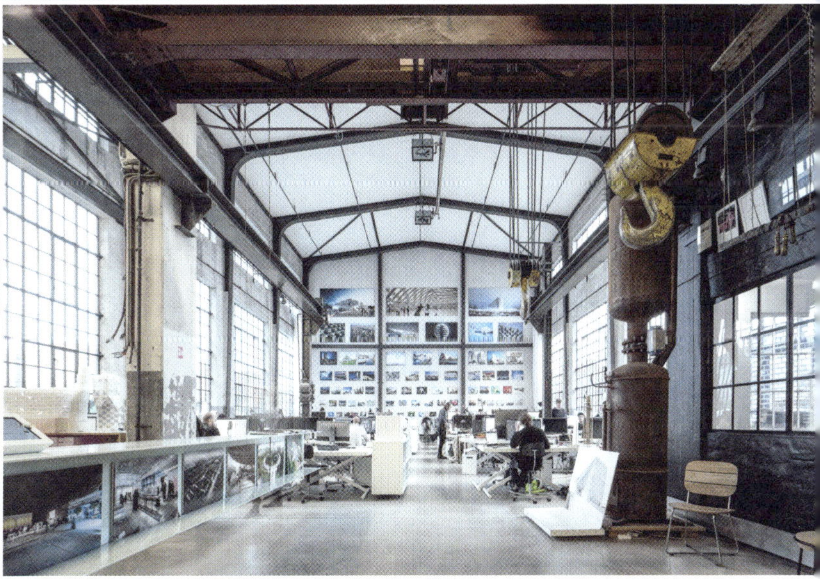

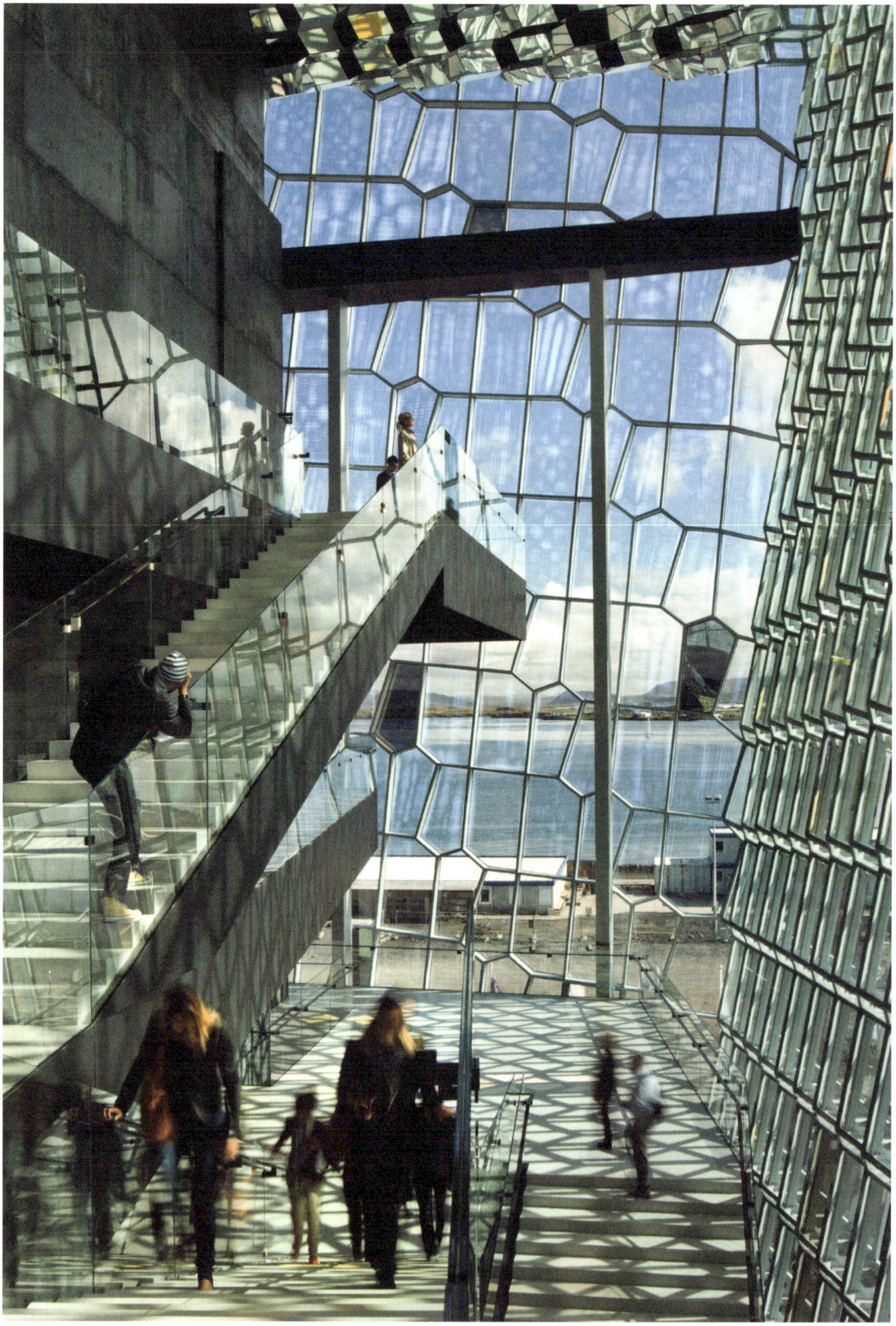

Henning Larsen Architects

Danish architect Henning Larsen (1925–2013) founded his eponymous architecture firm in 1959. Often described as the "master of light", his work was rooted in the Scandinavian design tradition, but also developed a way of "merging the present with the timeless". Larsen once reportedly said that the best architecture was "about making something with qualities that are difficult to talk about: materials, proportions, lighting, sizes, rhythms. That is what is important in each style, in each period – that is something that remains constant through time, and therefore has nothing to do with time." Part of the Ramboll Group since 2019, the studio continues Larsen's ethos with an emphasis on co-creation and collaboration. Sustainability has also become a central pillar of the practice's work, and major projects like the Siemens HQ in Munich, the Harpa Concert Hall in Reykjavik and the city hall for the new city of Kiruna in Sweden, exemplify the firm's large-scale fusion of architecture, cityscape and topography. Louis Becker joined Henning Larsen in 1989, and is now Global Design Principal. He combines his role with a teaching position at the Aalborg University Institute of Architecture, Design and Media Technology. In 2011, Louis's contribution to Danish architecture was recognised when he was awarded the Eckersberg Medal by the Royal Danish Academy of Fine Arts.

henninglarsen.com

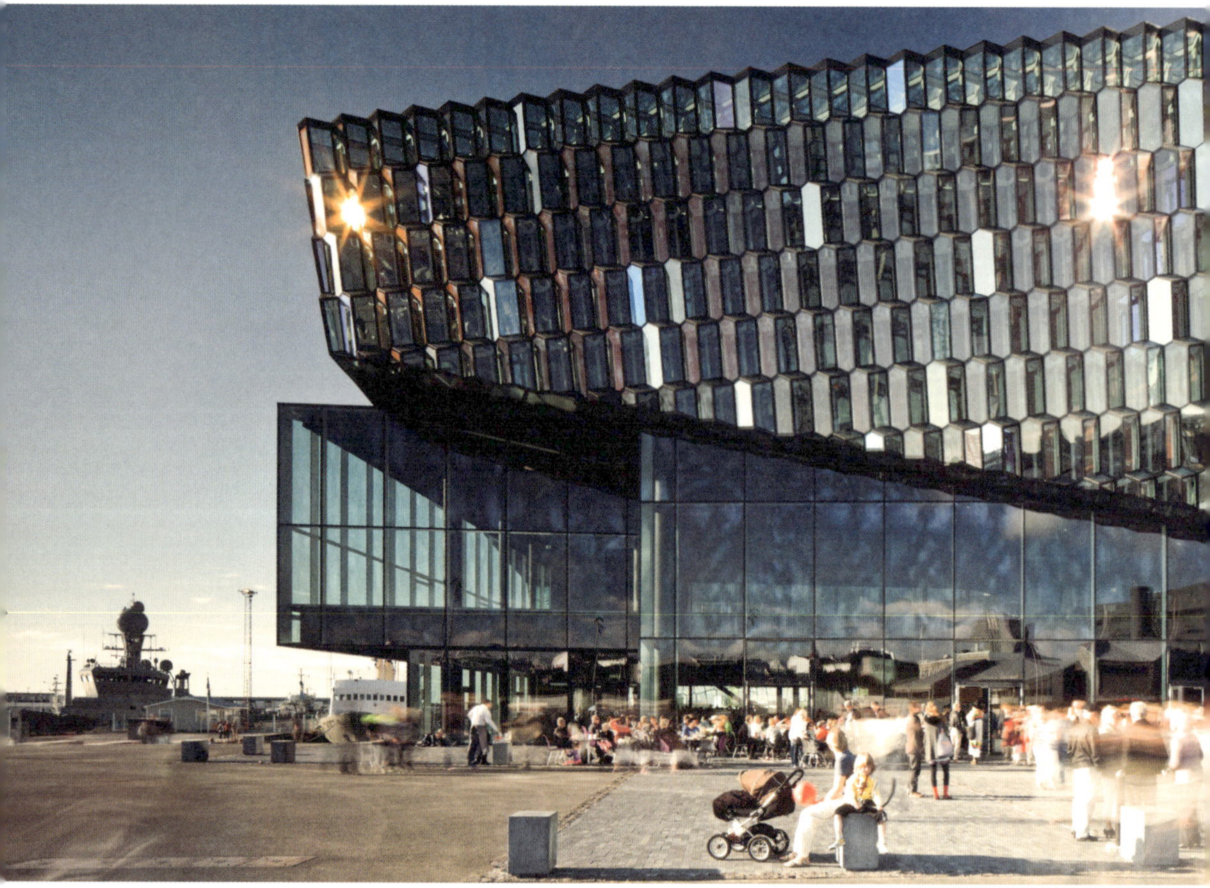

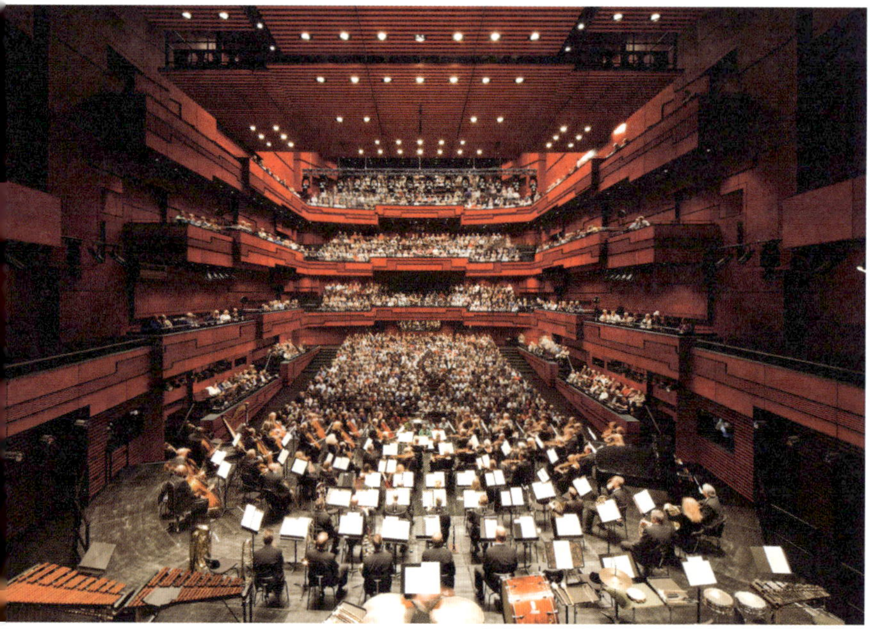

Previous page and opposite: Harpa Concert Hall and Conference Centre, Reykjavik, Iceland

Todd Saunders: How has 2020 been for a company as big as Henning Larsen?

Louis Becker: It's been hard. We now have over 600 people and haven't even physically met a lot of them yet.

TS: I saw that the firm recently became part of the Ramboll Engineering Group.

LB: Yes. We had become too big to be small, and too small to be big. We thought, "Either we want to buy somebody and be even bigger, or we'll be bought or merged." It was a scary process.

TS: I have the opposite problem. Every time we grow, I get pushed up to managing, which doesn't interest me.

LB: This happens all the time. Suddenly, the systems run you, rather than you run what you want to do.

TS: We don't necessarily have control, but we do have quite a bit of freedom.

LB: Our deal is a bit different. Rather than us becoming part of Ramboll, we have taken over Ramboll's architecture division. We are two different companies because design culture is so different from engineering culture. Even so, I'm surprised at how much time and effort it has taken. With the size of our operations now, it's important that younger designers can still feel empowered.

TS: How are things structured now?

LB: The business is part of a foundation and part of a long-term investment that really values quality [over a quick return]. It's also good for our research projects to be in a foundation-owned environment because they're so dependent on grants.

TS: What are you building now that you're really excited about?

LB: The Visa credit card headquarters in San Francisco is under construction. But also two interesting projects in Germany. One is a big project with Volkswagen, an innovation centre in Wolfsburg. It's a whole section of the city, 280,000 square metres, all built using wooden structure. Wolfsburg is based around an enormous factory where 73,000 people go to work. This innovation centre is all about attracting young talent. These days, the car companies are in competition with Google, Amazon and Tesla. We're also doing the global brand headquarters for Volvo in Gothenburg.

TS: Were they both competition projects?

LB: Yes, almost all the work we do now is from competitions. All our current projects are enormous – partly why we had to do this merger. The risk profile was too big. The other big project is in Berlin, a new neighbourhood to the west near Spandau.

TS: It must be amazing to work in Berlin.

LB: It's really good. This project is about a beautiful medieval city which has kind of fallen asleep on the outskirts of Berlin. We have to find out the place's core qualities and translate them to the 21st century. We're also working a lot with mobility, because of Volvo. It's interesting what's happening now with self-driving cars.

TS: I think it's going to be the biggest ever change in town planning. We can all start walking again. You're doing two projects in Germany, and one in Sweden. What do you think Henning Larsen offered these places?

LB: In Germany, we took an eye-level perspective on the projects, and more than design, we discussed what we wanted to experience as people. We didn't divide it up and say, "This is Volkswagen, and this is the city." We just said, "It's all the city." Of course, the design and wooden structures were different but ultimately it was about understanding the perspective of the location. Many of the other entries just followed the existing masterplan which was basically one block repeated 11 times. It just didn't work. Our in-house engineers realised that it was creating a really, really bad microclimate situation with a very cold spring and fall. So we used the way the medieval city was organised, trying to catch the warm sun in the spring, stuff like that. We were the only competitors that broke the masterplan.

TS: What makes a city is creating the places that people go to, outside of the factory.

LB: We're also working with another car company right now. You know that Amazon is doing a car now? We're in competition to do an 800,000 square metre campus in Europe for them.

TS: How do you keep people aligned during your design process?

LB: We've developed a strict design method over the past 15 years. But how you work within it can be freer. You cannot do anything before you know what's on the table, so the first thing is data collection. Every project starts with a workshop looking at all the available information; political, environmental, economic, etc. Then we do analytics and see where this data leads us. This results in what really makes a difference, a strategic concept. This is a text and drawing and diagram all in one, a one-pager, that typically talks about the aspirations; the site, the budget and what it means for that place. When we did the Carl H Lindner College of Business at the University of Cincinnati, we could see that the budget was not enough to build what they wanted. Our analysis also revealed that they were asking for far more space than they needed. So we could reduce the buildings to meet the budget, and have the same personality, perhaps even better, with smaller auditoriums. This strategic concept is a guiding rule for everybody. And after that, we do three concept designs and pick one with the client.

TS: When clients come to us, we always try to break down the differences between their wants and needs.

LB: Exactly. However, in Cincinnati, we also asked the clients to sign off this strategic concept. So whenever they went off track, we said, "Guys, you signed this. This is what we do, and this is what you're asking now. It's not what we do." The idea was that the building should be a home for students from other faculties, who could bring ideas from mechanics or medicine or whatever and develop it in the business school with the business students. We designed something we called the marketplace. Of course, once we had this space, lots of other people on campus were asking if they could have an office there. "No, no, you cannot."

This page: The Biotope, Lille, France

DENMARK | HENNING LARSEN ARCHITECTS

TS: How old is this strategic concept process – is it from Henning Larsen's time?

LB: No. It began when we started to have different studios, and we could not find an easy way to discuss projects. We have researchers in-house, so we learn from these people in academia. It was not something we learned in architect school, so it was a steep learning curve for us. Also, we had lost ten competitions in a row, which was serious for us. So we sat down and looked through each entry. They all looked fine. But then we read the briefs carefully, and we looked at the sites, and we found out that all our proposals were answering a different question than we were asked. We invented our own reality, basically. At the time, we thought that the clients were stupid and didn't understand a thing. But the world changed, and the clients were not as impressed as they were in the old days, where the architects were the artists. Today, we have a much better understanding of the client. They're often trying to ask a question but it's difficult for them to ask difficult questions, especially in a huge organisation. So with this method, 75–80 per cent of our jobs come through winning competitions.

TS: When I visited your studio, I saw that even the competitions had a really rigorous six-week process, with all that research. We've also had

Left: French International School, Tseung Kwan O, Hong Kong

> Every project starts with a workshop looking at all the available information; political, environmental, economic, etc. Then we do analytics and see where this data leads us. This results in what really makes a difference, a strategic concept. This is a text and drawing and diagram all in one, a one-pager, that typically talks about the aspirations; the site, the budget and what it means for that place.
>
> — Louis Becker

to learn to get good at asking questions before we even pick up a pen. Maybe more architects need researchers to go in and dig up things first.

LB: We have anthropologists who go to client interviews and presentations. They take the clients to three different workgroups and we developed three different narratives together with them.

TS: As well as the research you do in-house, do you get any personal inspiration from travelling and different cultures?

LB: The diversity in Canada is something we should learn from, I have to say. And I think the way you have an acceptance of that, is something that we really could learn from.

TS: Canadians accept things and commit to changing. It's not just superficial.

LB: We're doing something like five projects in Canada, right now. We're doing this city hall in the western part of Toronto. I'll never forget, we did a public presentation to win the project and there were more than 500 people in the room. The jury was sitting in the first row, and they were really responsive to what they heard behind them. The architects had to win over the people as well.

DENMARK | HENNING LARSEN ARCHITECTS

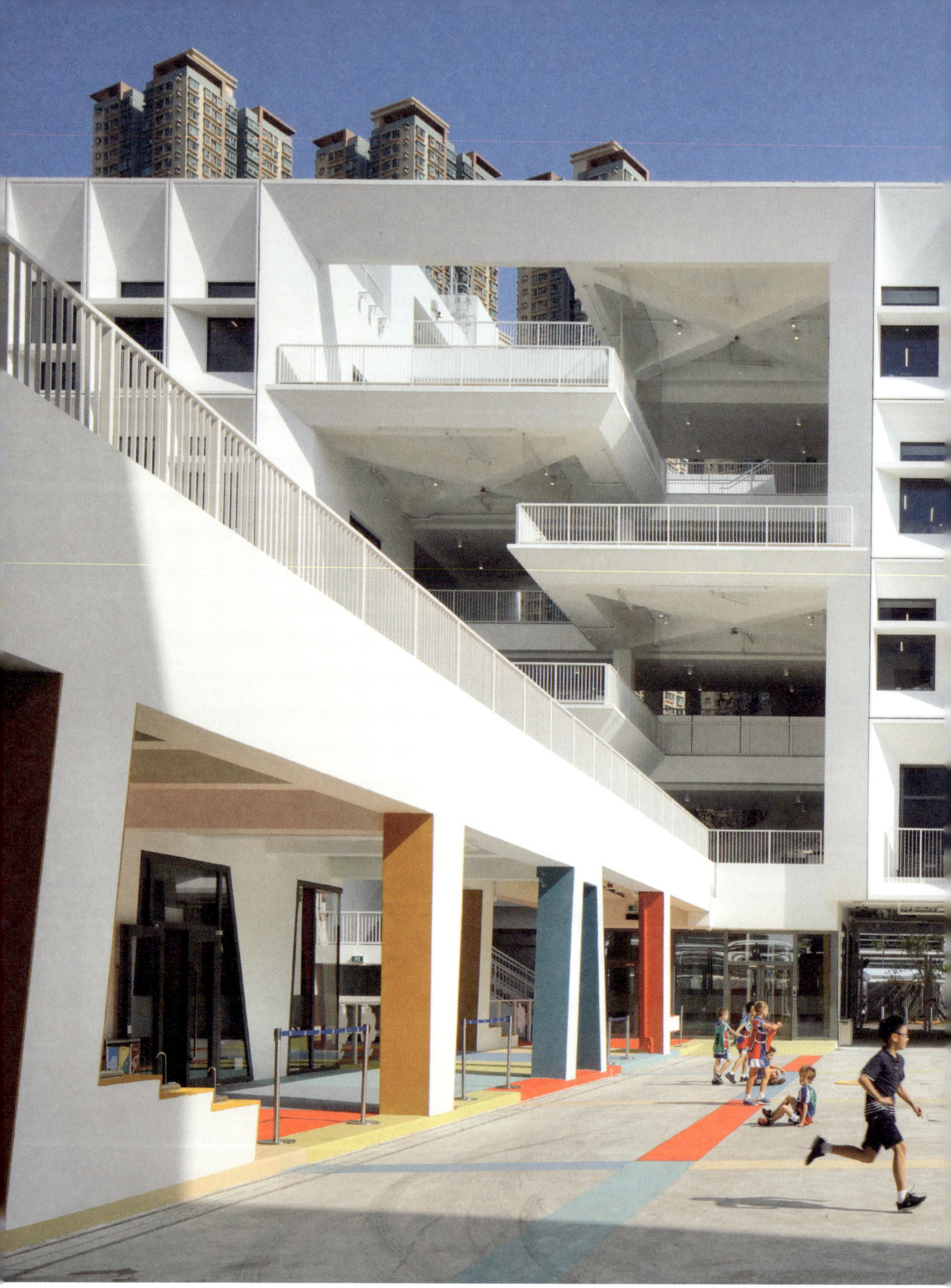

DENMARK | HENNING LARSEN ARCHITECTS

Previous pages: French International School, Tseung Kwan O, Hong Kong

Right: Henning Larsen Architects, Copenhagen V, Denmark

Give it away instead of wasting it

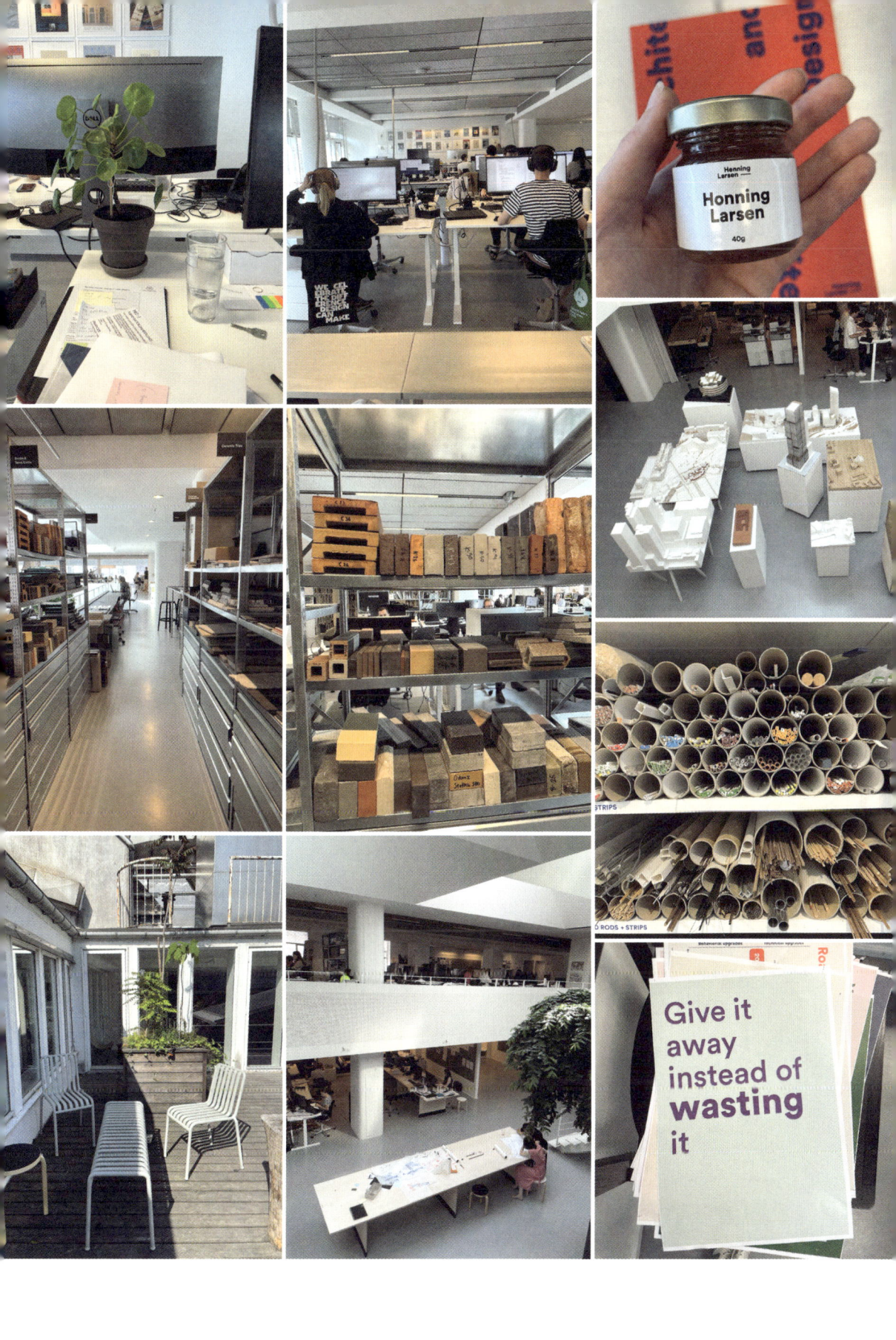

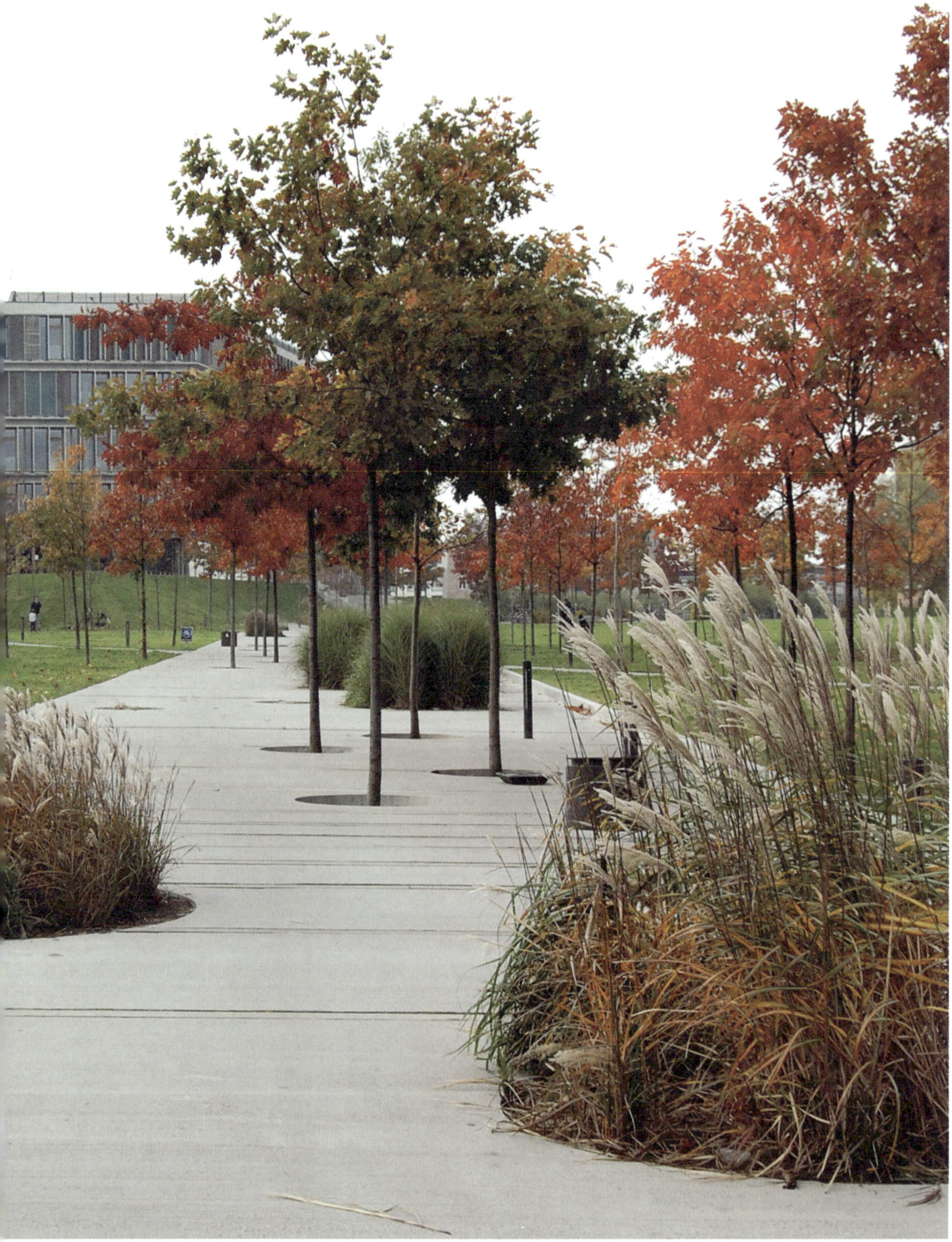

Marianne Levinsen Landskab

Marianne Levinsen is one of the most prominent Danish landscape architects of her generation. Her design office is based in Copenhagen and focuses on developing a strong awareness of the environmental and social challenges of urban spaces. Her work has comprehensively highlighted the power and importance of landscape design as a generator of place and human interaction, while the office is also directly involved in the effects of climate change and global warming, exploring strategies for mitigating change and repairing damaged landscapes.

After working as a tapestry weaver for Jette Gemzøe in her early twenties, Levinsen studied at the Royal Danish Academy of Fine Arts, graduating in 1995. She then taught, alongside working in the studio of landscape architect Professor Sven-Ingvar Andersson.

Marianne Levinsen Landskab ApS, established in 2002, has collaborated with many leading architects, including Dorte Mandrup Arkitekter, Vandkunsten, and COBE, on projects in Denmark, Norway, Sweden and Germany. Levinsen herself has received honorary awards from Nationalbankens Jubilæumsfond, the Henning Larsen Fund, and Dreyers Fond, and received the Eckersberg Medal from the Royal Danish Academy in 2012. She has worked closely with the public art department at The Danish National Arts Foundation for many years.

mariannelevinsen.dk

In landscape architecture, we always speak about time as the fourth dimension, because we do things that grow. We plant things that will grow long after we are dead, so we always have this perspective in our architecture.

— Marianne Levinsen

Previous page: CBS Campusplan, Frederiksberg, Denmark

Opposite: Vadehavscentret, Ribe, Denmark

Todd Saunders: It seemed natural to include you in this book as you're one of the best-known landscape architects in the region. You set up your office 20 years ago – how do you ensure that you keep learning, evolving and growing as a professional?

Marianne Levinsen: This one is quite easy for me to answer, because besides my own practice, I do a lot of other activities, like judging in competitions. In fact, most of my work I get through competitions. We are currently starting one in Norway, for the Lillehammer Art Museum.

TS: You won the Whale Museum project on Andøya island in collaboration with Dorte Mandrup Architects, didn't you?

ML: Yes, that was really engaging. We've also just won a competition with Lundgaard & Tranberg Arkitekter for the new Archäologisches Landesmuseum in Rostock, and we also worked with them on the Danevirke Museum in South Schleswig, Germany, which is due to open in 2024. It's a very beautiful project, not so much about what we did, but more about what we didn't do. It was about reading and understanding the landscape and then emphasizing its history. Doing very little but doing it very precisely. There's more and more work in Germany for Danish architects.

TS: Are competitions important to your practice?

ML: Yes, because they're a way of continuing to learn. I've also overseen student projects in Copenhagen for many years. I'm on several grant committees, as well as being a member of the National Art Council, first in the visual arts department, and now with the architecture department. These things give me a good insight into the architectural scene. In Denmark, we've had a state art organisation since the early 1950s, with a law that the state must spend money on artists, starting with visual artists, then music, literature, architecture, and film, etc. We grant over 12 million kroner each year, just in our department. Other departments have more.

TS: When I first moved to Norway, I received a grant because I was designing playgrounds for children and helping their parents build them.

ML: I got a similar grant many years ago when I started my studio. It's such an important organisation.

TS: We pay a lot of taxes in Scandinavia, but then you see things like this as a result. It makes such a big difference when you allow people to be free and creative for a few years without any pressure.

ML: And also funding things like travelling, publishing books. It's a strong system. I hope it will last forever. Norway has a good system as well – we often refer to it. It's most helpful for young people who have been working for many years in a larger company and want to start up on their own. More and more offices in Denmark are getting very large, and there have been a lot of examples of architecture firms selling their name to an engineering company.

TS: It was like that in Sweden, and Norwegian firms have started doing this as well. Henning Larsen are now part of Ramboll, for example. But back to the question: do you think being on these committees give you an insight into how what younger architects are doing?

ML: Absolutely – it really is a way to keep on learning and stay in touch. After I graduated, I spent ten years teaching, although I stopped in 2005.

TS: One of our questions was originally about how to become happy, but it seems that "happiness" is a bit of an illusion. You really become happy through growth and learning.

ML: And engagement.

TS: Exactly. Even though it's a tough profession, ensuring you can grow and learn is what gives them support. How do you balance your time with work and all these committees?

ML: The only way I could answer is just… It's work, work, work.

TS: I've discussed the idea of the "art life", which is something the director David Lynch wrote about. If you're involved in a creative profession, then that's your whole life because you're always thinking about it. I don't think that a balance is the goal – it's to learn and always be engaged.

ML: You have to be engaged all the time. I think that the only time you're not working, is when you close your eyes.

TS: Is there one that got away – a project you regret not doing?

ML: Our "big fish" was not really a "fish", but more like a very important part of a project. In 2008, there was a competition for a new national and high security prison in Denmark. We worked hard on placing the prison within the landscape, as well as the areas inside the prison itself. It was a ten-year project.

We worked with Ramboll and C F Møller Architects, as well as all the security specialists and representatives from the Department of Justice and prison employees. At the end of the process, only two people in the project group had been there since the outset: myself, and the Chief of the Justice Department, who retired immediately afterwards. There were so many things to negotiate. Imprisonment has two functions; on the one hand it's a punishment because there's no question that we need prisons in society. But at the same time, it's also about rehabilitation. There's no benefit to society if inmates finish their sentences as worse people than when they went in. So it's about creating meaningful activities, whether it's education or sports, or other things.

TS: There's also the question about the impact of time, which must be relevant.

ML: It is very important. In landscape architecture, we always speak about time as the fourth dimension, because we do things that grow. We plant things that will grow long after we are dead, so we always have this perspective in our architecture. In this prison, time has another perception. Your perception is limited by the walls, and the passing of time is slow and monotonous. You have no spatial perception. From the beginning, that was the focus on my engagement on the project. We spent many years developing the idea of prison gardens, kitchen gardens, sports fields, a garden for the prison chapel, even playgrounds for the children that visited. One element that was very important to me was a working apple orchard. The region was very well known for apple production, so you needed to have gardeners, and harvesters, and then all the production system for making apple juice. It took a huge amount of time to develop, and we worked

This page: Lindevangsparken, Frederiksberg, Denmark

DENMARK | MARIANNE LEVINSEN LANDSKAB

closely with the justice department – every question was about security.

TS: So there were security cameras everywhere?

ML: The planting had to be arranged to frame the view of video cameras. The apple varieties had to be very difficult to turn into alcohol, for example. So there were so many things to think about, and we had all these ideas about seasons, about time, about meaningfulness, about humanity.

TS: How many apple trees were there?

ML: I think it was 700 or 900 – it was huge. But right at the end of the project, there were some budget cuts. The space for the orchard was reduced, so the whole idea was no longer viable. Everything was fixed. Everything was decided. But for me, it's a project that got away.

It was a simple element which could have been a very important element of the prison – there were so many dimensions.

TS: One reason I have so many questions about time: many architects forget their buildings might last 300 years, but landscape architects always know their work is going to survive long after they're dead.

ML: We are always site specific. We always need to go deep into a site because we have to know about the type of soil and the origins of the landscape. In Norway, you have mountains. In Denmark, we have this flat landscape on a base of chalk which is sometimes very near the surface. Chalk and sand and gravel. And these create very different conditions, particularly because we are surrounded by water.

TS: Is there a project you did early in your career that you still have a relationship with?

Opposite: K.B. Hallen, Frederiksberg, Denmark

ML: Not so much yet, because I'm too busy. When you finish one, you go straight on to the next one. However, I will follow and go back to a project I did with a Swedish sculptor, Anders Krüger. It was a memorial in Trondheim to the victims of the 22 July attacks, an important and special task. We finished it in 2018. I am sure I will go back to it. There's a museum in Lund, the Skissernas Museum – the Museum of Sketches for Public Art – and they have our sketches and a plaster model. They also have the project by Jonas Ståhlberg, the Sørbråten Memorial that cut into the island. That was never made.

TS: That was a very nice project. I like that landscape architects can work on a really large scale. Is there a project you would love to do for a community or one you have done that made a difference?

ML: Every project can be very exciting, even if you didn't originally think it was interesting. Engagement doesn't always come directly from the subject. We've always been very conscious of biodiversity and the need to work with the climate. But one thing that's interesting is working with water, although we've always worked with it to some extent. We are putting more emphasis on rainwater. Back in 2016, we did a park in Fredriksberg in Copenhagen which took rain from buildings, pumped it beneath a big road and then made it visible and useful and part of the landscape.

TS: Are other landscape architects working in this field as well?

ML: I think everyone now works with a focus on biodiversity and climate. It's obvious that there are very big problems to solve but it doesn't always need to be big science. There are ways of treating landscape to restore it. Sometimes it's not what you do, but what you don't do. Some of these questions can be answered in a very simple way – just by leaving land alone. It's not a new question in landscape architecture. In Denmark we had Gudmund Nyeland Brandt, one of the pioneers of landscape architecture. He designed the Mariebjerg Cemetery, among other things, and he also lectured at the Danish Academy of Fine Arts. I often go to Mariebjerg, not because I have family there, but because it's a very, very strong piece of spatial architecture. One of Brandt's main points was how to decide what we control and what we let free. The balance between the very straight and the natural, between controlled and uncontrolled.

TS: Where I usually practise in Norway and Canada there is some resistance to building in this wild landscape. I think the way ahead is to have areas where you just let things grow wild and then learn how nature repairs itself.

ML: Denmark is a flat country, a farmer's landscape. For so long, the question has been how to make it efficient farmland, usually by draining the water away. But what would happen if you didn't do this? We would probably have some very strong, nice wetlands, which could still absorb water while also having lots of biodiversity. Farmers are very strong politically in Denmark, so change will take a long time. As landscape architects, we can plan and draw as best we can, but we can never predict everything precisely, because as soon as you dig into the soil you find something – and you are always surprised. This relates back to your question about how we keep on learning over time – because we understand the value of time.

DENMARK | MARIANNE LEVINSEN LANDSKAB

Right: Marianne Levinsen
Landskab, Copenhagen K,
Denmark

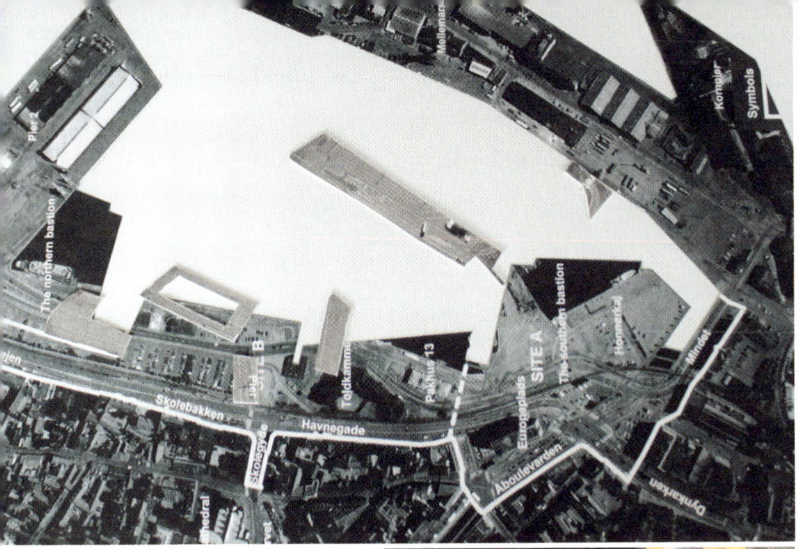
Pier 2
The northern bastion
Skolebakken
Havnegade
Pakhus 13
SITE A
The southern bastion
Europaplads
Aboulevarden
Dynkarken
Mindet
Kompier
Symbols

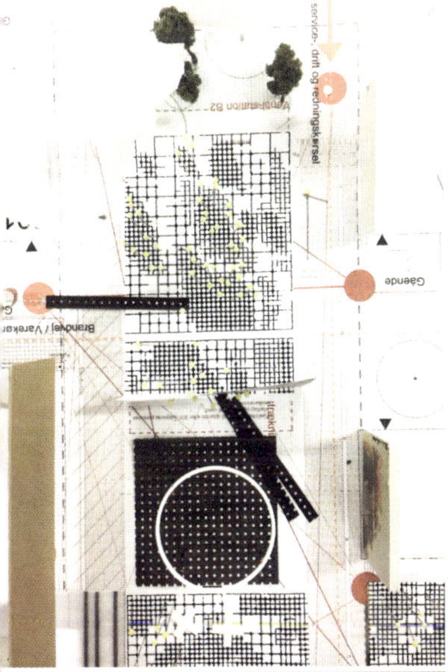
Gående

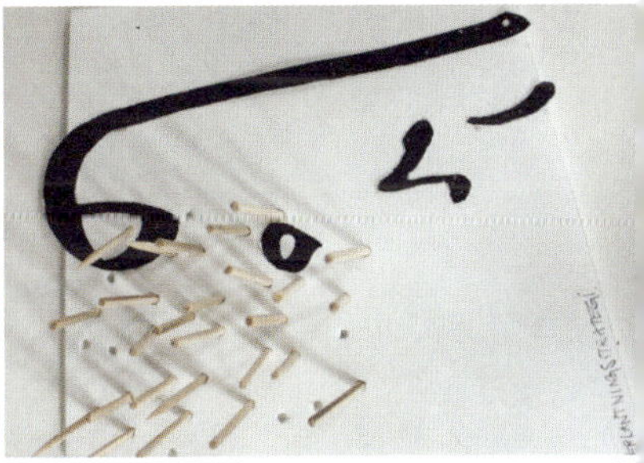

3018

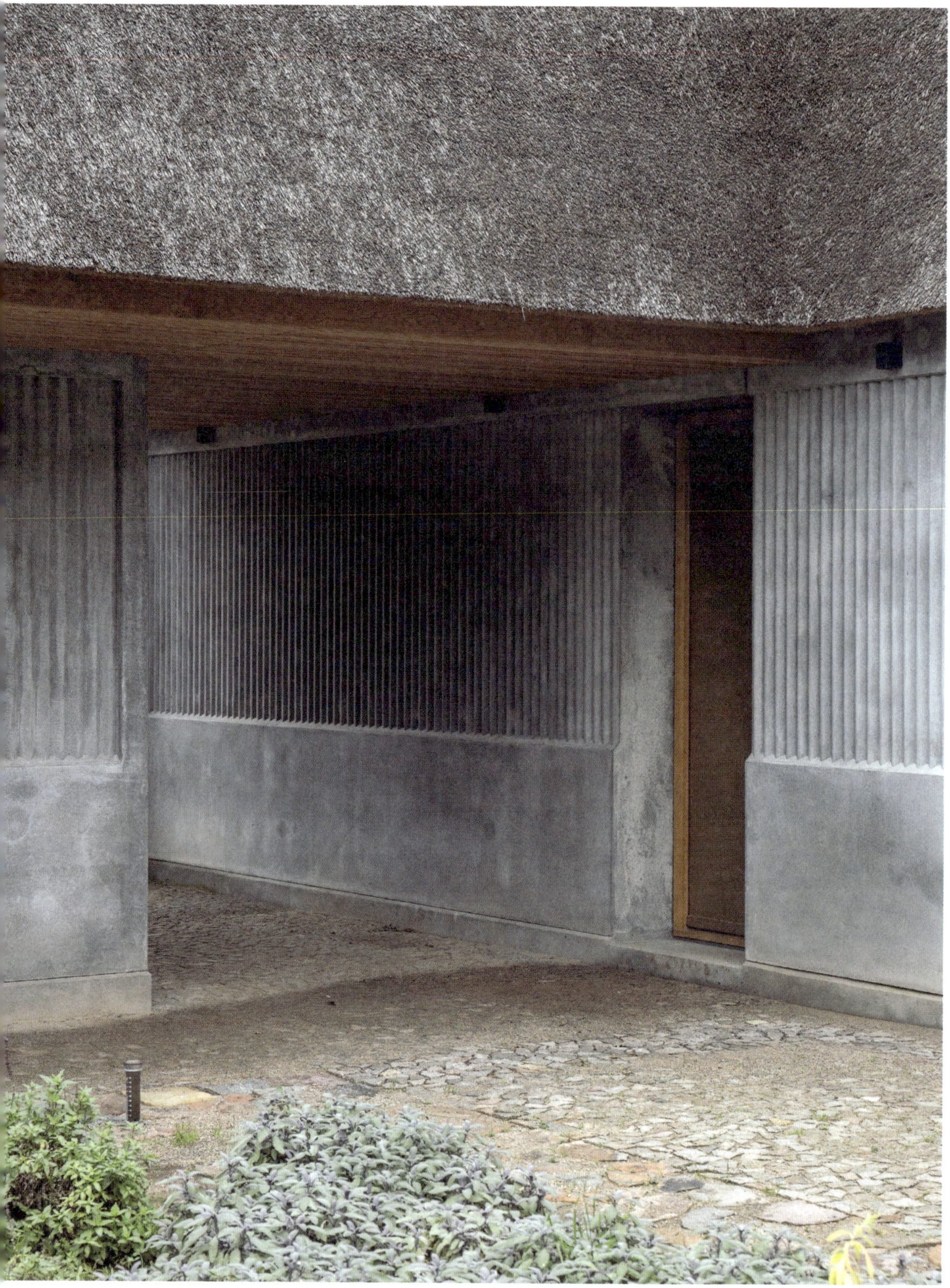

Norrøn

Founded by Marco Berenthz and Poul Høilund in 2014, Norrøn is a Copenhagen-based architecture studio that specialises in developing destinations, using architecture as a central part of a narrative that celebrates past and present, while anticipating the future. Berenthz and Høilund work within this experience economy across the Nordic countries, in Denmark itself and increasingly in Greenland. "Destination development is about what makes the individual place special, but just as much about what binds an area together," they write, stressing that, through sensitive but progressive architectural interventions, communities can be strengthened, both socially and economically. Working closely with clients, residents and other stakeholders, their approach is narrative-driven, with an emphasis on authenticity and inclusivity.

norroen.dk

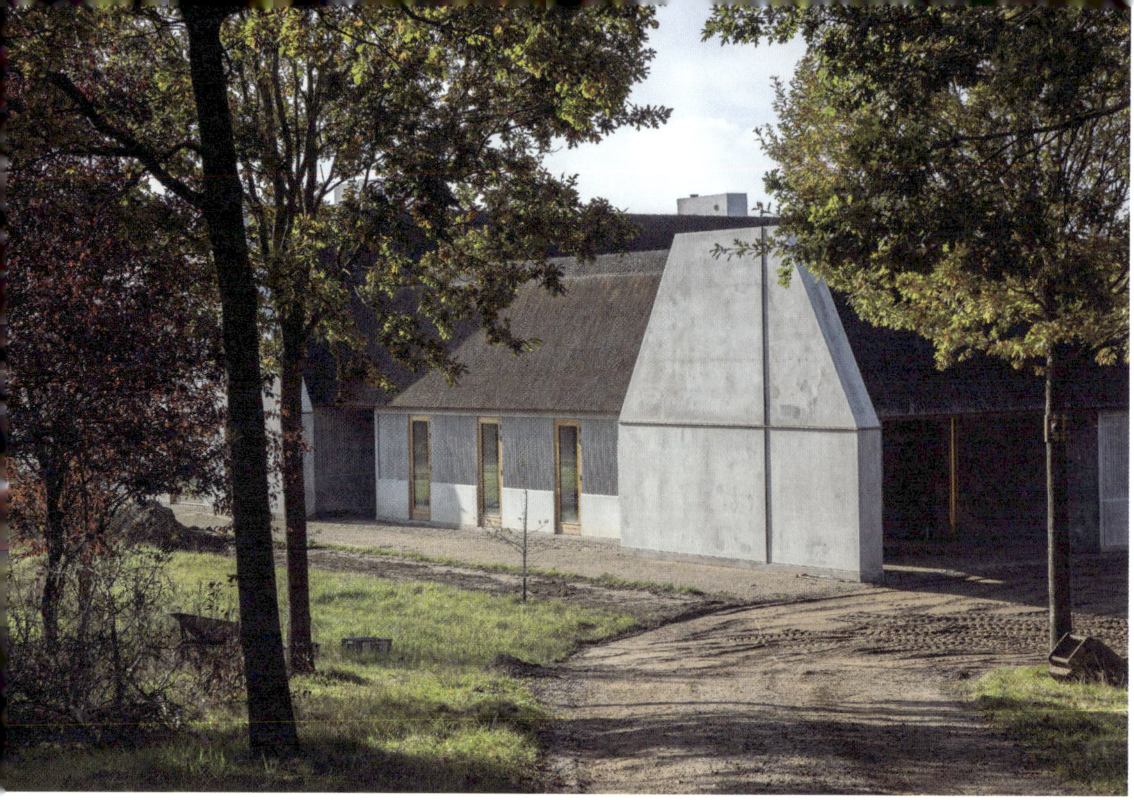

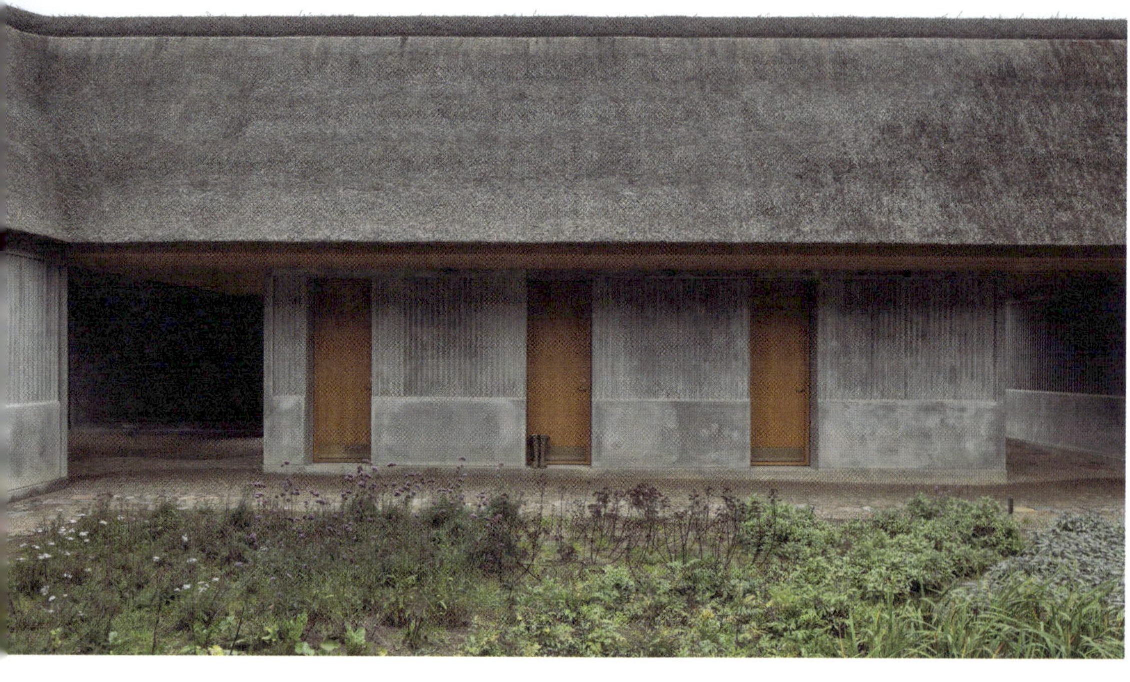

Previous page and opposite: Åstrup Have, Haderslev, Denmark

Todd Saunders: Where are you in your studio's journey?

Marco Berenthz: Our office has just turned seven. In pop cultural slang, it's time for the next jump, like the "Madonna curve", when she re-invented herself once again. So we're discussing our next chapter.

Poul Høilund: Being an architect is such a broad discipline, not just what you're taught in school. Maybe you're only spending 1 per cent of your day on things you really want to do, because you need to solve so many other problems. And if you don't stop sometimes, you end up only solving these problems and nothing else. From the start we realised that it takes as long to do a bad project as a good one.

MB: It takes the same number of years out of your life, so you had better be picky.

PH: The more you learn about architecture, the more critical you get. Now, something has to be really good to excite me.

TS: What do you think makes your work useful to the world?

MB: We didn't start with a big project or competition – we just wanted to have an office together and do something different from our colleagues, 95 per cent of whom were working on developer housing. For us, it wasn't just about what our architecture should look like, but what it should do. This helped us initiate the field of "destination development". Even though it's a broad subject, we are still considered as somewhat specialised. Both Poul and I grew up in rural areas and came to the capital. We saw that those rural areas were not investing in planning and creating beautiful and poetic places. So we started to look for a different industry that could work with them, and that was tourism. Through this we discussed regional development as a purpose, and architecture as a tool. That established us. It's taken us to many different places.

PH: You asked if there's a place for daydreaming and emotion in architectural practices. For me, the best architecture creates some kind of longing and belonging. Longing for being in a certain place, and given time to just be in a faster world. Creating that sort of place is when our architecture becomes really useful.

TS: When I was growing up in Newfoundland, they didn't ask you where you were from, they asked you, "Where do you belong?" In small rural communities, you usually feel like you belong to a place. But there's a generation who have moved from these areas to the city and they don't feel like they belong any more. Are there any projects where you created a sense of belonging for a small community via architecture?

MB: When we're done with a project, it should taste of something that people locally can recognise, but they couldn't have made it themselves. But we're also exploring the issues of tourism more scientifically and working out how we can fix them. For instance, generic investments in tourism that alienate local people is one of the biggest issues with the industry. The important thing with cultural exchanges is to get people to understand something.

PH: It's like finding some kind of language from a specific place that you can emphasise and highlight in a new, valuable way.

Opposite: Åstrup Have, Haderslev, Denmark

MB: I love that reaction when we present a proposal, and all the things that define a place – literature, poems, cultural history or the nature of the landscape – have been made into something new. Then people understand the project is part of them as well as opening it up to the future. This balance between longing and belonging that Poul mentioned is important; it needs to be interesting enough for you to want to go there, but it also needs to capture the soul of a place.

TS: A lot of your language is very emotional. When you present a project do you see these emotions in your clients?

MB: Yes – it's a big privilege of working in this field. Maybe a century ago, all architects enjoyed this privilege, because it was such an exclusive profession tasked with handling substantial investments. Today, many of our peers working in urban development, for example, are being told to cut surplus and scale things back. This field of experience economy has allowed us to always ask our clients whether they want to cut the cost at the sake of the experience. I feel our best projects have this understanding with our clients that emotions and experiences are more than something physical, but the physical act is to create that experience. We have clients who acknowledge the need to not cut that away. Otherwise, the competition will take the future customer.

PH: Longing is searching for something, and belonging is something you can be proud of. We're a little flame that keeps a fire alive. Maybe this explains why we're not so interested in doing residential work in Copenhagen, because we just don't see the same values in those outcomes.

TS: You have a different motivation for making architecture.

MB: Obviously there's a ton of stuff in that field that needs solving, but we've always been clear about our chosen field of work. We began by only doing rural projects. Now we've done a few urban projects as well, but we're still working on cultural exchanges, especially with World Heritage Sites where they're showcasing different cultures. You're less likely to conflict with something that you've taken time to understand, and those are the projects we keep coming back to. Ultimately, you don't get to do that many projects in your lifetime, so doing something inspirational is more interesting than simply building more projects.

TS: Almost like passing the torch to the next generation. When longing and belonging align, it's a magical feeling. It happened at the Aurland Lookout for the Norwegian National Tourist Routes project. People were initially uncertain – they thought these young architects were going to come and do something new and strange to this beautiful site. But now it's the first thing that a visitor is shown when they come to the town. It's powerful when you can make that alignment.

PH: We've likened it to building temples. As the world's population grows, we should move from "I should buy a new flat screen", or "I should buy a new table", towards buying an experience. We use the word "temples" to signify the idea of creating a place that gives unforgettable experiences.

MB: We use physical parts to hopefully create a memory. There are three phases of visiting a place: the expectation of going, the actual experience and then the memory. However,

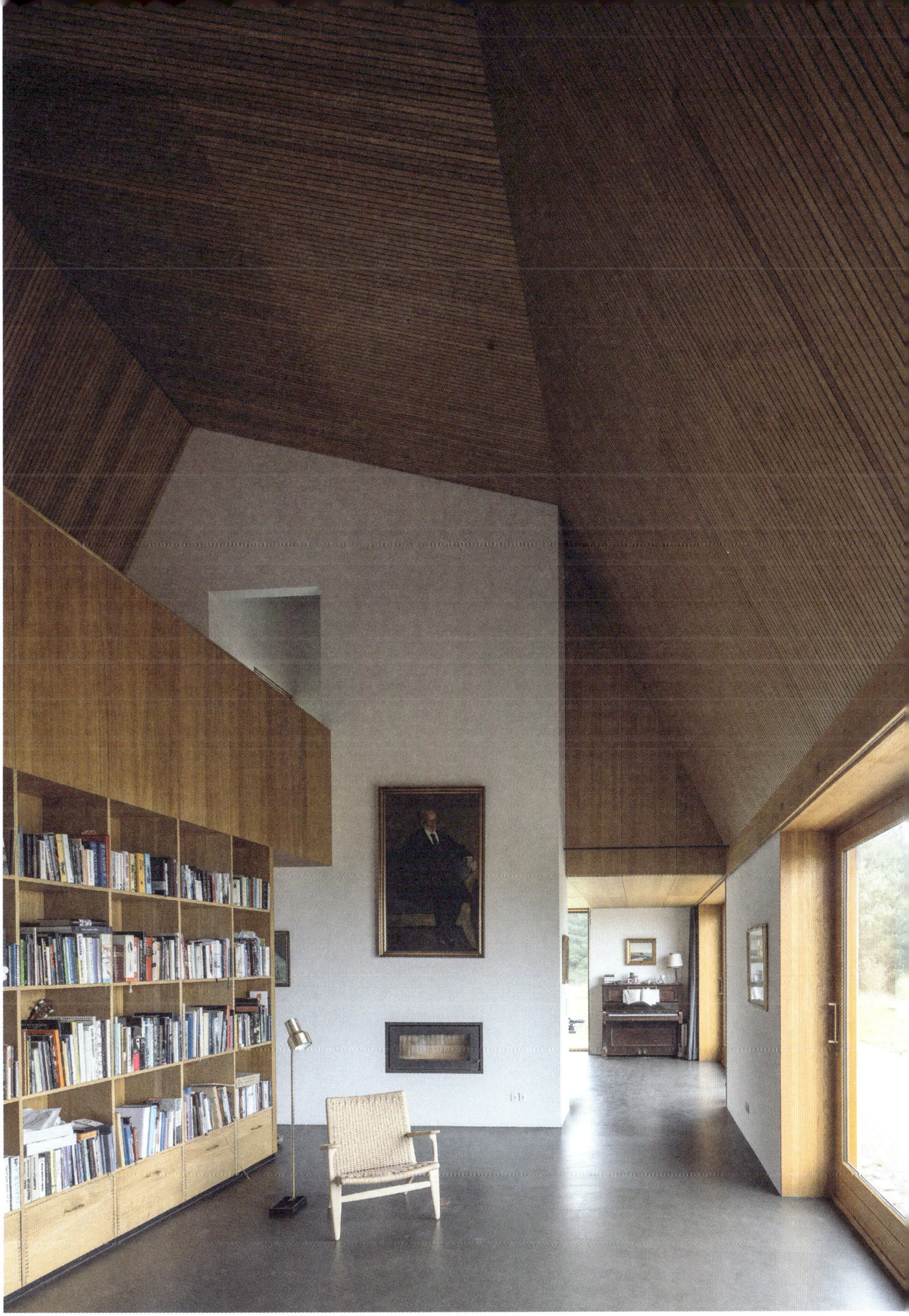

This page: Åstrup Have, Haderslev, Denmark

For me, the best architecture creates some kind of longing and belonging. Longing for being in a certain place, and given time to just be in a faster world. Creating that sort of place is when our architecture becomes really useful.

— Poul Høilund

all three need resources to create them. The global middle classes are at a point where they all want the same level of consumption. It's not unlikely that they'll choose unforgettable experiences over material things, but we must create something to do that. We like that we are playing on the immaterial side of the table, potentially competing with the absorption of global resources.

TS: Are there any examples of this transition from material to immaterial that you really admire?

MB: In Denmark, the experience economy is still young, so we're looking at things like the Norwegian routes you just described, and Naoshima Island in Japan. The main thing is to ask people what matters to them, and they'll often mention their memories of important experiences.

TS: Maybe tourism highlights a beauty that people don't realise they have. I only realised how beautiful Newfoundland was after I'd visited over 100 different countries in 20 years. Which is your favourite of your tourism-related projects?

MB: We finished the first phase of one project about six months ago that I can't get out of my mind. We started working strategically with Greenland about 18 months ago because they have investments in big infrastructure projects and the tourism industry. We helped a client with an existing hotel. Instead of expanding their seasonal offering, we ended up creating an Arctic spa that gave them a winter season. It was a socioeconomic shift from something part-time to all year round, yet still on a local scale. We also got to work with the local geology, the local red sandstone. It was a temple for the ice, socioeconomically viable but the client was on board. It also told a story: what was important for the whole area. I really loved that process.

TS: Are you doing other projects in Greenland?

MB: I think we have five architecture projects and a master plan for sustainable tourism in the capital, Nuuk. As well as the spa, we're looking at how to harness melt water for energy and we're doing a UNESCO dog sled centre, an art centre and boutique hotel. Some are private; some are communal, run by the city.

PH: Many of our projects use architecture to bring people together and make a place dare to dream of something bigger than what they expected. Architecture is a tool.

TS: How easy is it to fund these projects?

MB: Think about architecture as a slow profession and then add some. The subtitle to our practice name is "Territory for Dreaming" and the way we express and present ourselves also helps attract dreamers. I'm sure our hit rate of built projects is lower than if we only did straightforward commissions. But creating those fragile dreams on initial project stages is what we do. Many foundations finance the cultural building scene. We help our clients understand the political climate of what can be funded philanthropically.

TS: How do you approach a project like the Statens Museum outpost?

MB: We did a competition for a project called Cold Hawaii Inland, a surfing community on Denmark's west coast – great waves but

Opposite: Åstrup Have, Haderslev, Denmark

obviously very cold. It started as a way of bringing people into a deprived part of the country and we're now working on ten different coastal facilities. Meanwhile, we were able to convince the municipality and the Statens Museum to let us look at their satellite gallery project. The original level of ambition wasn't high enough, so we helped develop it so these foundations could help fund it.

PH: The project evolved from being just a few paintings displayed in an old building. We explored how you can tell a good story with these buildings.

TS: When you work with these communities, are there any tools you use, like workshops, to create an area for daydreaming, so they don't just tell you all the things they don't like?

PH: We do questionnaires and workshops, and they bring up their likes and what has potential. But equally importantly, they can say what they don't want.

TS: I do this thing where you lay out a map of the whole area and get people to make a heart on the places they love. It's fun to watch and it opens up possibilities because then I can ask questions about why they love that particular place.

MB: Only in the last couple of projects have we really started to understand how big the process side is. The complexity of the process also depends on the client. It's important for us to retain those first dreams within the process as well.

PH: If you don't understand the people around you, no matter what you do in terms of design, they won't like it unless they feel they have been consulted as part of the process. Designing is not just about shapes and textures and colours. Sometimes it is about finding this cross functionality within a new building to make people love it more.

MB: There's always a balance because you often have a democratic agenda in some places, but I don't think this necessarily turns out good buildings. For me it comes down to not giving people what they say they want, but what they mean. It's about getting strategic input – because we have something that's architecturally satisfying – but also the clients get something they wouldn't otherwise have been able to do themselves.

TS: Is your approach about getting to the core of what the client needs?

PH: Yes – the importance of daydreaming, and the importance of being able to facilitate other people's daydreaming. What makes this process new and useful is how we can transform a dream into a reality.

DENMARK | NORRØN

Right: Norrøn, Copenhagen N, Denmark

70 | 71

TERRITORY FOR DREAMING

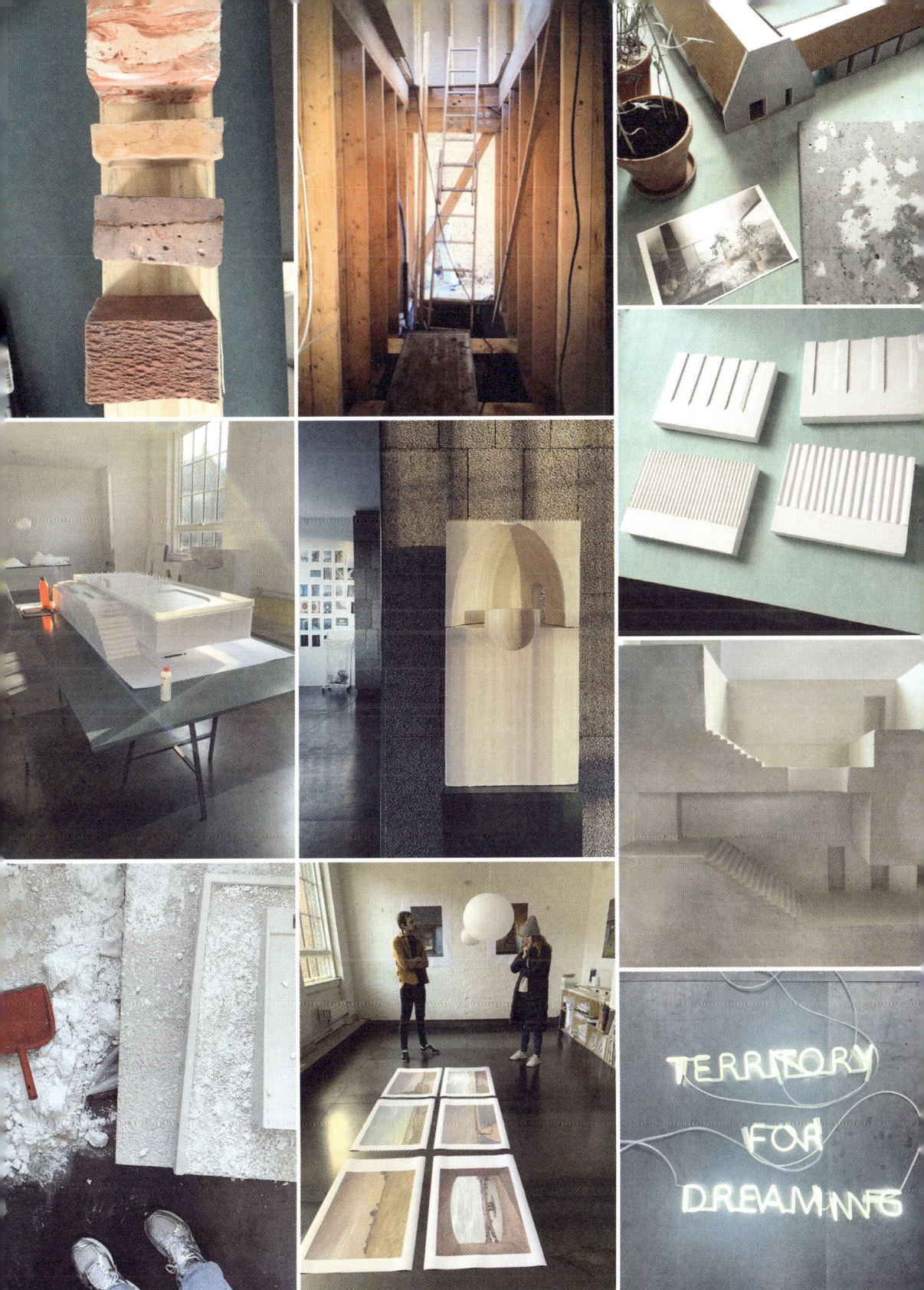

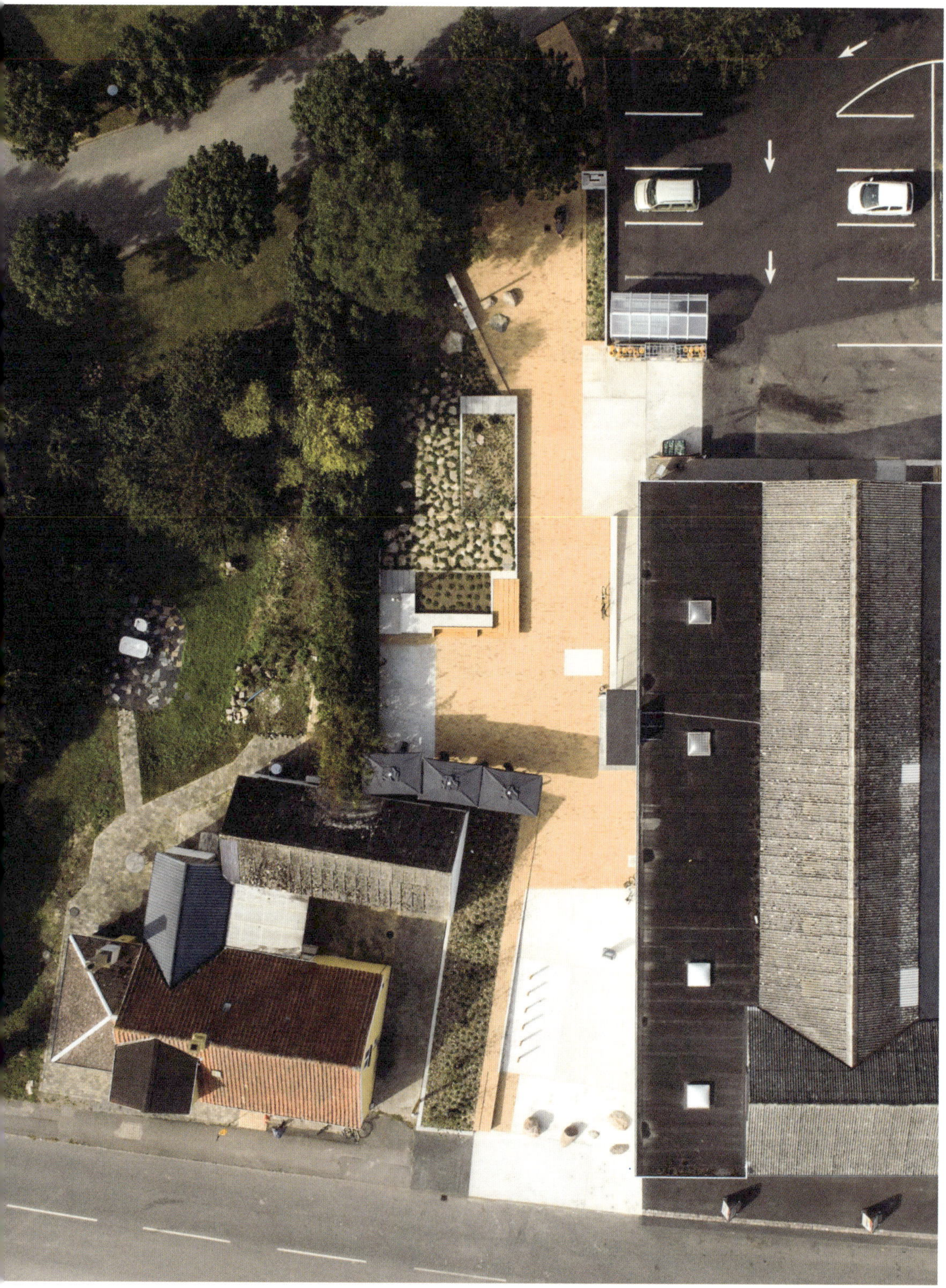

Studio dominique + serena

dominique + serena was founded by German-Polish architect Dominique Hauderowicz and Danish architect Kristian Ly Serena. Their studio is based in Copenhagen and their work emphasises the connections between architecture, art and politics, with a special focus on age-inclusive projects. As well as public and private commissions, the studio has also undertaken several self-initiated projects, highlighting the importance of dialogue at all stages of the design and construction process. "We don't worry too much about the boxes that different fields of spatial practice are usually divided into," they say. dominique + serena has also taken a conscious decision to stay small to allow for hands-on engagement with every project. "We are deeply engaged in the process of realisation and the gritty work that comes with that," they write. "Over the years we have built a network of colleagues and partners within a variety of fields that we trust and love to work with." Recent work includes a case study for an age-inclusive urban space development in a small town on the southern Danish island of Møn, and a series of pieces of mobile urban furniture for a market square in the Municipality of Næstved.

dominiqueserena.dk

> The Age-Inclusive Cities project is about understanding an ageing population as a catalyst for urban development.
>
> — Dominique Hauderowicz

Previous page and opposite: Age-inclusive public space, Vordingborg, Møn, Denmark

TODD SAUNDERS: Did you meet at architecture school or art school?

KRISTIAN LY SERENA: Architecture school, yes. At The Royal Danish Academy of Arts, School of Architecture

TS: And do you teach there now?

DOMINIQUE HAUDEROWICZ: We taught for a couple of years after we graduated. Then the school underwent major structural changes. We left after a couple of years and have since been teaching shorter workshops. Now we have more contact with the Aarhus School of Architecture, not the Copenhagen School of Architecture. We also taught there a little bit. Aarhus is maybe a little bit more open and dynamic than Copenhagen. It's a very Scandinavian student body – lots of Norwegians, Swedes and Icelandic people. We have mostly taught in Denmark. Our short workshops are more intensive but are also self-contained and you can set the themes yourself.

TS: I like workshops better as well. They're a hybrid of designing and building. It's like you said, it's very contained. When you're finished, it's done. It can be very intense, but in a good way.

DH: Teaching takes a lot of energy if you want to do a good job. It can be quite draining, as well.

TS: What kind of projects are you focusing on now?

DH: Last year we published a book – just in time for the pandemic! It's called *Age-Inclusive Public Space*. We initiated the project, as well as writing and editing it.

We invited contributors from different fields – psychologists, anthropologists, philosophers. The book asks what it means to design public space that is age-inclusive and tries to come at that topic from many different angles.

KLS: We wanted it to be quite concrete – how does this perspective impact on the stroke you're about to draw on your drafting table? What does it mean for a given shape? What does it mean for organising space? One part of the project was to build a case study, and it forced us to explore how considerations towards people of all ages fit with everyday planning processes and so on. We are currently developing more landscape and building projects that deal with this theme, as well as projects that look at the social potential of architecture.

DH: In addition to commissioned work, we initiate projects and jobs that interest us. Then we go and find funding, find interesting partners and say, "Can we explore these things together?" Trying to be more proactive. The field of age inclusion is very interesting. We've always been intrigued by the Scandinavian welfare model and how it has spatial implications for the city. For instance, you have institutions that are designed to cater to the "unproductive" citizens in society, mainly children and the elderly. What does this mean for the way that the city organises itself and how does it contribute to a divided city? The Age-Inclusive Cities project is about understanding an ageing population as a catalyst for urban development. We have three case cities now in Denmark.

TS: Did the inclusive design process also involve getting people involved in the making of the landscape project?

KLS: We have done this, to some extent, in the projects we're talking about. Next spring, we'll initiate some temporary installations together with local residents. We try and involve local residents in all the public work we do.

TS: Is this landscape project self-initiated, based on what you learned in the book?

DH: When we defined the project for the book, we wanted it to have two components: building and academic. We wanted the process of building and that of writing the book to inform each other.

TS: Are there other examples of public spaces in Denmark that work well across the multi-generational spectrum, from age eight to 80?

KLS: In the book, we point out examples that showcase this exact approach. That's not to say they're perfect. Sometimes, they prove to be valuable in an unintentional way. For instance, rather than using examples as something that can be transferred from one context to the next, we like to use them as means to emphasise or illustrate specific points or approaches. This is all about how to host differences between people as well as differences in one person over time. Dealing with how human beings change is something that the modern city has just totally abandoned. So this is our aim when we are making buildings and when we are making or writing about landscapes.

DH: We also went on quite a long study trip to Japan before the writing process and include some interesting examples of buildings that work with the spaces in between institution and public space and care and landscape.

TS: Did you notice any big differences between the Japanese and Scandinavian ways of using public space?

DH: In Japan, I think they would say, themselves, that they don't have public space in the same way that we do – but there are quite inspirational examples of a relationship between local community and caretaking, which can be applied to a Scandinavian context. In the Nordic countries, care is very formalised. We used to say that, in Denmark or in Norway, you pay your taxes as a gesture of love to your neighbour, right?

TS: I grew up in a very small island community in Canada where you felt very safe because you knew someone was watching out for you. Nobody locked their doors. When I came to Scandinavia, it was almost as if architecture was too "perfect" – as if it put lines between people but didn't open doors. It was strange, as a foreigner, because there seemed to be no opportunities for chance meetings. It's different in Copenhagen, or downtown Bergen, still with those public spaces where people can meet by coincidence. I like the idea of space without a formal title.

DH: We're especially interested in these heterogenic public spaces where everyone actually feels welcome. These days spaces are programmed and targeted at certain age groups, and so are only super interesting to a tiny fraction of the population. Through the book we argue for other ways of designing with an age perspective, to open up new ways of considering the design process.

TS: You mentioned that the book took a long time – was there a lesson to be learned from the speed of the process?

This page: Vordingborg, Møn, Denmark

DENMARK | STUDIO DOMINIQUE + SERENA

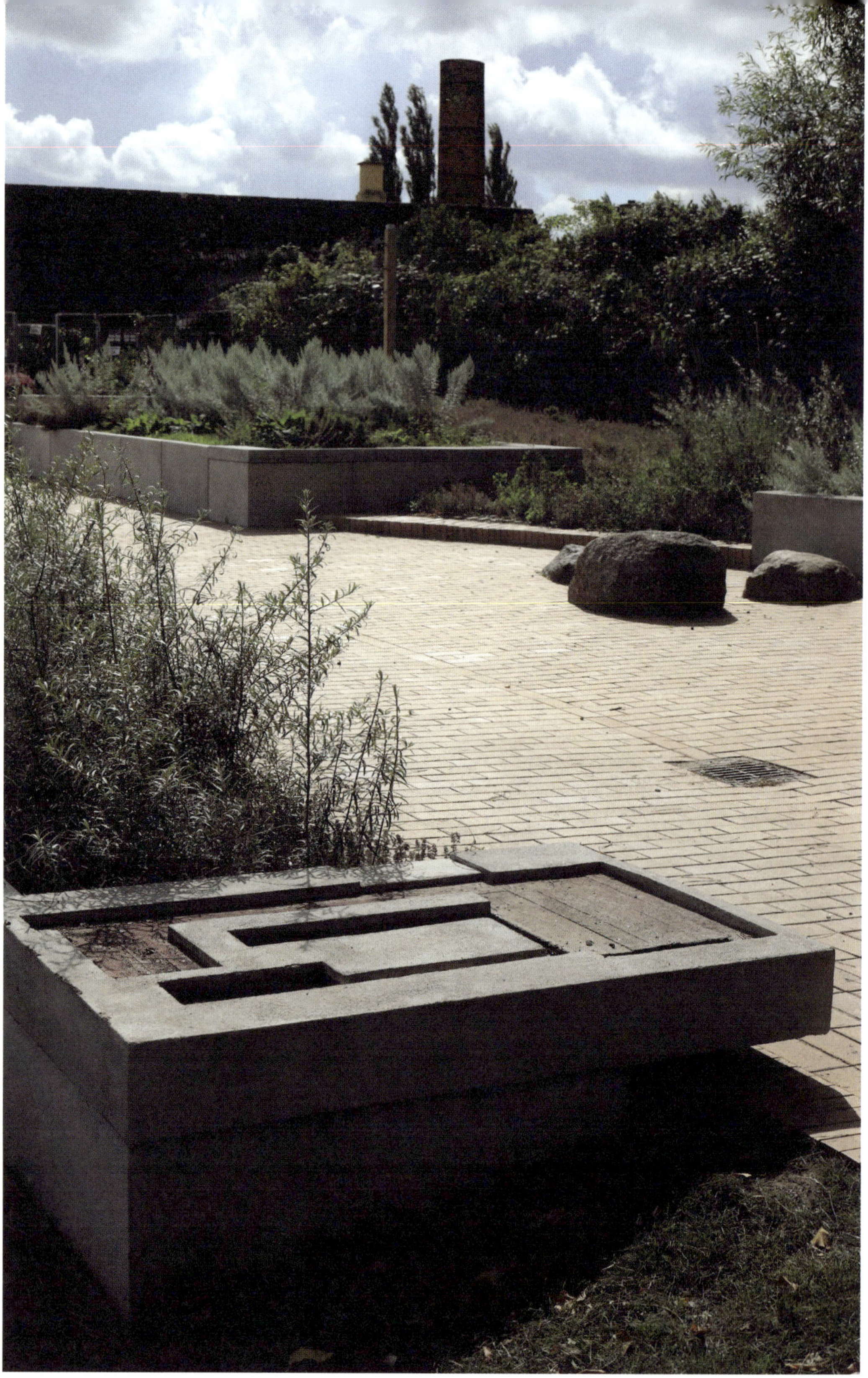

Opposite: Vordingborg, Møn, Denmark

DH: It's the kind of thing that you only do once because you go into it completely unaware of what you're about to do. It was interesting, but also labour-intensive. Many of the contributors are senior to us, academics and professors within their own professions and fields, and we were coming in as outsiders. But I don't think speed and slowness is inherently bad or good. Different things happen in different time spans, right? We value speed in the first stages of our design process, perhaps because of the value of intuition – but some projects and themes that interest us have a time span of many years. For instance, our installation for the Oslo Triennale in 2019 expanded on some of the ideas in the book, although in a completely different medium, such as an exhibition. We like that ideas can develop and take different shapes over time; some of our current work was first mentioned in competitions we did five or six years ago. Regardless of the media, ideas can be like a stock for a stew.

TS: It gives you a flavour and a basis to work on, and something to go back to. Had you worked in other offices before setting up dominique + serena?

KLS: We started the company the day we graduated.

TS: Tell me about your research trip to Japan for the book. Where did you go?

DH: It was centred around Tokyo as well as a brief tour to Kyoto. I'd been to Japan before, but this time we had a hyper-narrow focus, a grant to go and see architecture for care institutions for the elderly. We also travelled with our two-year-old son, so it was quite disarming as we appeared as a family as much as researchers.

TS: How do you ensure you keep learning and evolving? I think I can hear the answer in your responses already, but is this a conscious approach?

KLS: We try to avoid all kinds of style discussions. When we walk around the city, we also get inspired by extremely ugly things. Another architect might close their eyes and cry, but if a building is doing something good in the way it's made and shaped, it's interesting. We're quite old-fashioned in this way. This approach came to us through our interests, our research, things we've touched on in small projects or competitions. If you cycle around Copenhagen and just look a little bit closer, then you can get inspired but also see these problems that are not talked about a lot– the age-segregated city, for instance. It's frustrating that we just keep on taking this approach to the city that, in some regards, does not work.

TS: Are there too many rules in architecture in Scandinavia? In town planning, for example?

KLS: Some new planned dwellings only facilitate an extremely narrow way of life – they pre-suppose a certain idea of the city dweller that shops around like a nomad. It is not set up to cater to other kinds of people, age groups, family constellations, etc. Maybe we should ask how we can do some of these things differently?

DH: You need a language and reflection about how to make space and create situations that aren't just the archetypal reproduction of existing typologies. Reinterpreting a spatial idea or programme pushes us to do things in a new way. Herman Hertzberger is very clear about the importance of social relationships in architecture and giving this a very precise

Right: A New Theory of Love Installation for The Library, Oslo Architecture Triennale, Sverre Fehn Pavilion, National Museum, Oslo, Norway, 2019

architectural form. Hertzberger calls it "inviting form, a space that invites someone to do something or sets the stage for a meeting". Other academics, environmental psychologists for example, already have a language for some of these things. Many architects do not.

TS: I feel there are too many rules in architecture, but doing pop-up, temporary architecture is more forgiving in showing the value of architecture. Have you done any projects like that?

KLS: Prototyping is part of our process of creating something permanent. Ultimately, we would like to abandon the idea of a "finished" project.

DH: Copenhagen will be the world architecture capital in 2023. I really want to convince the organisers to create "building" playgrounds, inspired by the *Byggelegepladser* adventure playgrounds of the 1950s. If we could install these in prominent parts of the city, it could highlight the value of ephemeral life and play. Things are not static.

TS: I was once quoted as saying, "Everything I learned about architecture was before I was 12 years old," talking about building cabins. I don't think there's many opportunities for kids to do that any more.

DH: This idea of children as autonomous citizens is something we'd like to work with more, as well as the world of play and playgrounds.

KLS: You could say we're trying to provide a more playful kind of inhabitation.

TS: I think it's important for kids to have freedom and mystery in their environment, where everything isn't necessarily predictable. Maybe there needs to be less architecture in these public spaces.

DH: The last section of the book is called "Undesigning". I think that's a really good word. Leave some pockets of space for people to create this sense of agency over their surroundings. That is tremendously important. It's something we're not very good at in Scandinavia, actually.

TS: Maybe that's your contribution to architecture, to create spaces where you're not allowed to design. Let things just happen there instead.

DH: We like approaching design as if it were botany. This idea of natural propagation so that things that can grow. Like a garden, you set the conditions for something, but what comes up can also surprise you and surpass whatever you thought it might be. There's also a more intimate relationship between humans and environment. Your question as to why architecture is such a worthwhile profession is important – it frames everything from the most intimate moments of people's lives through to societal concerns and the environment.

TS: You mentioned you looked at Hertzberger in the Netherlands but do non-architects also inspire you?

DH: As Kristian mentioned earlier, how people in general do things, how they inhabit places, how they make space their own, is fascinating.

KLS: Someone like Lina Bo Bardi, an architect who's always seen as very modernist. When she drew her houses, her sketches included the lives of people – what the inauguration party would look like, a table laid with food, etc. Somehow, she creates this intense atmosphere of welcomeness that you can just bathe in when you visit the projects. You can never reduce these feelings to only formal discussions and drawings. What does architecture mean to the life that's lived there?

TS: The worst thing about modern architecture is that you never see humans. So maybe prioritise humans over architecture before making decisions?

KLS: The architect and educator Mark Rakatansky describes how in other forms of art, like cinema, people have no problem acknowledging that they express a certain culture of life, a way of life.

DH: He concludes by saying that you shouldn't regard architecture as a container of life, but as an expression of life and culture itself.

TS: Architecture as a platform for humanity, a way of opening up possibilities instead of creating walls to block them out.

DH: I see the same thing with this some of the Instagram architecture that we have nowadays. It's like looking through a window onto something motionless, nothing to do with people's reality or experience. We're back to talking about "undesign" and being anti-formal. There is huge variation in architecture. You can go at it from every angle and from every scale.

DENMARK | STUDIO DOMINIQUE + SERENA

Right: Studio dominique + serena workshop, Solrød Strand, Denmark

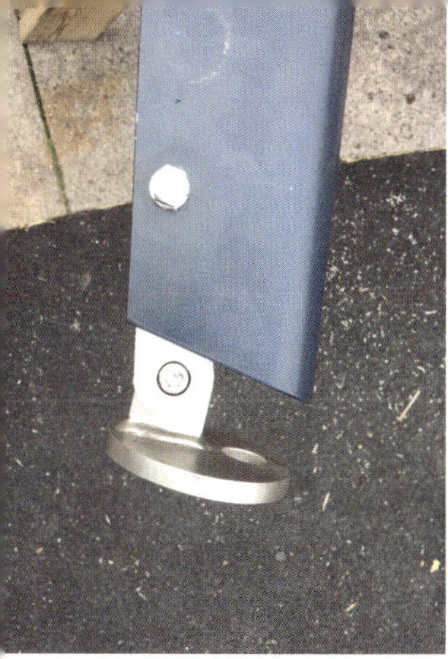

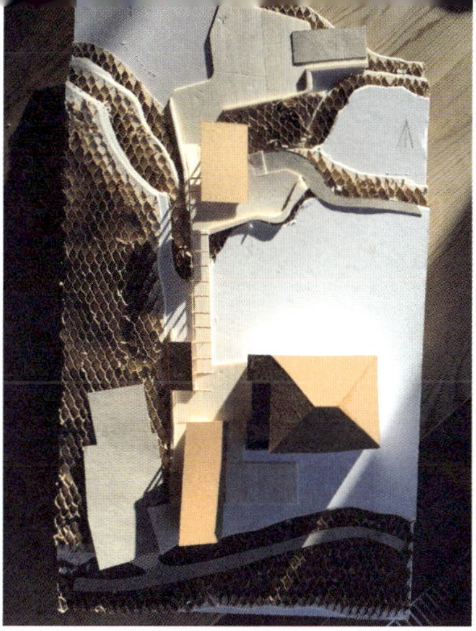

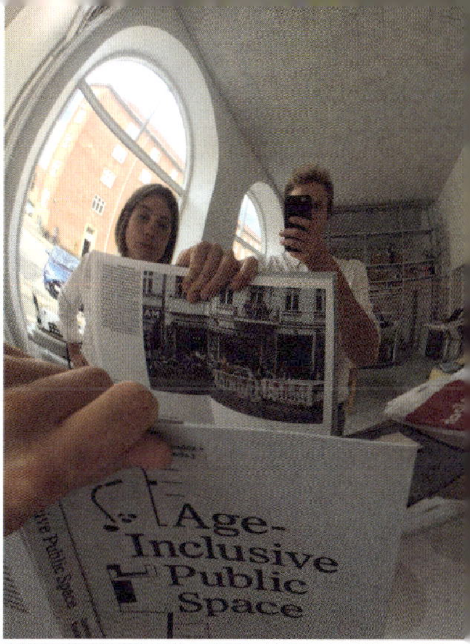
Age-
Inclusive
Public
Space

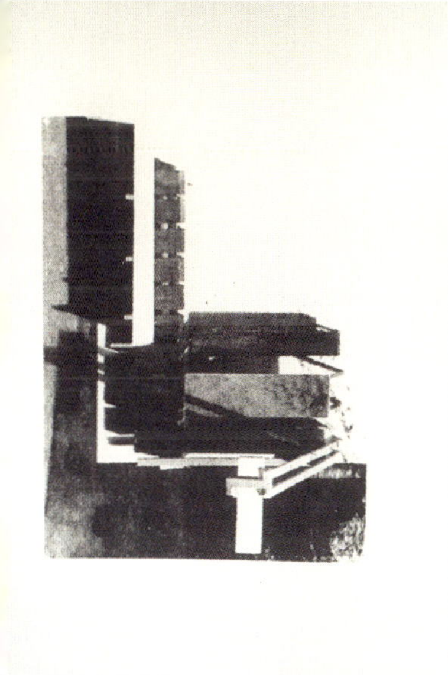

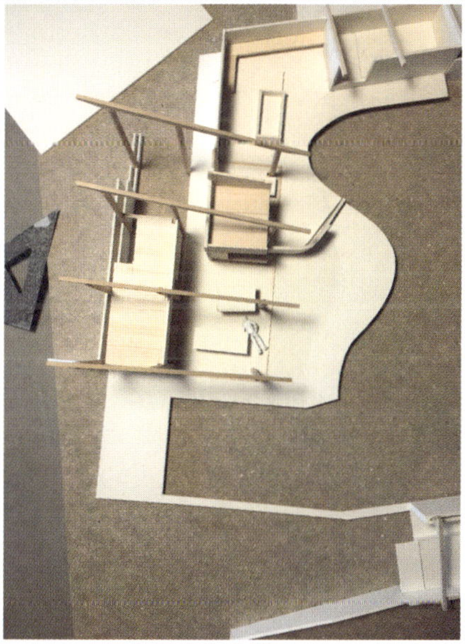

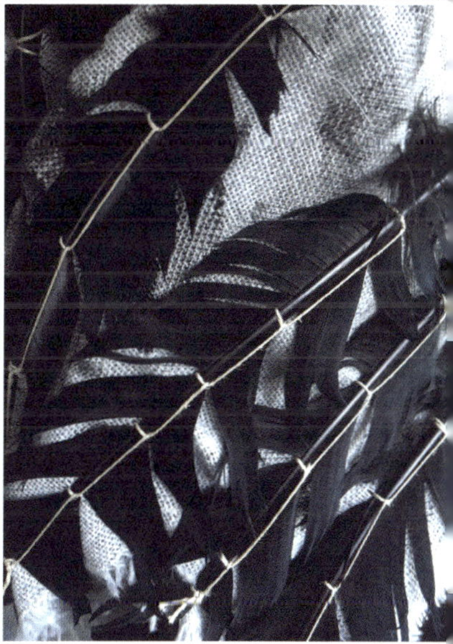

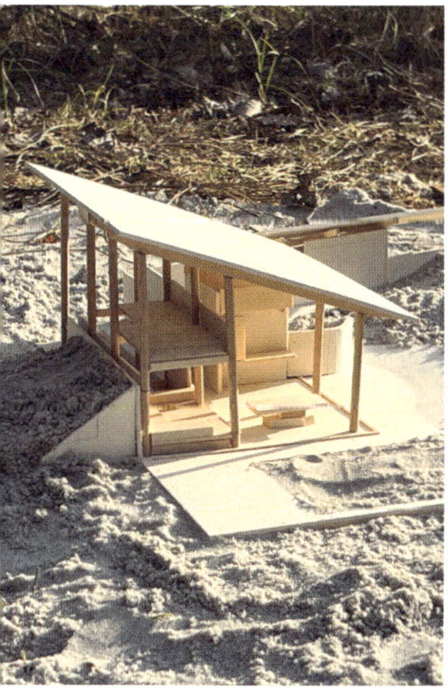

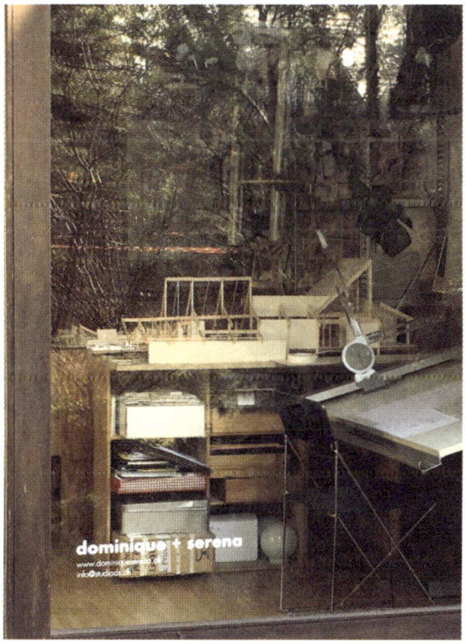
dominique + serena

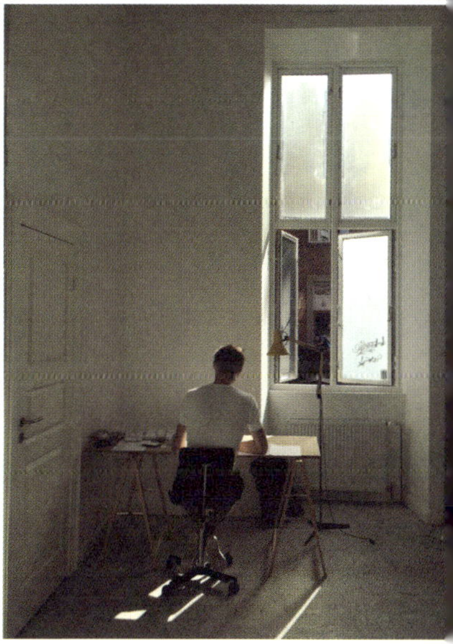

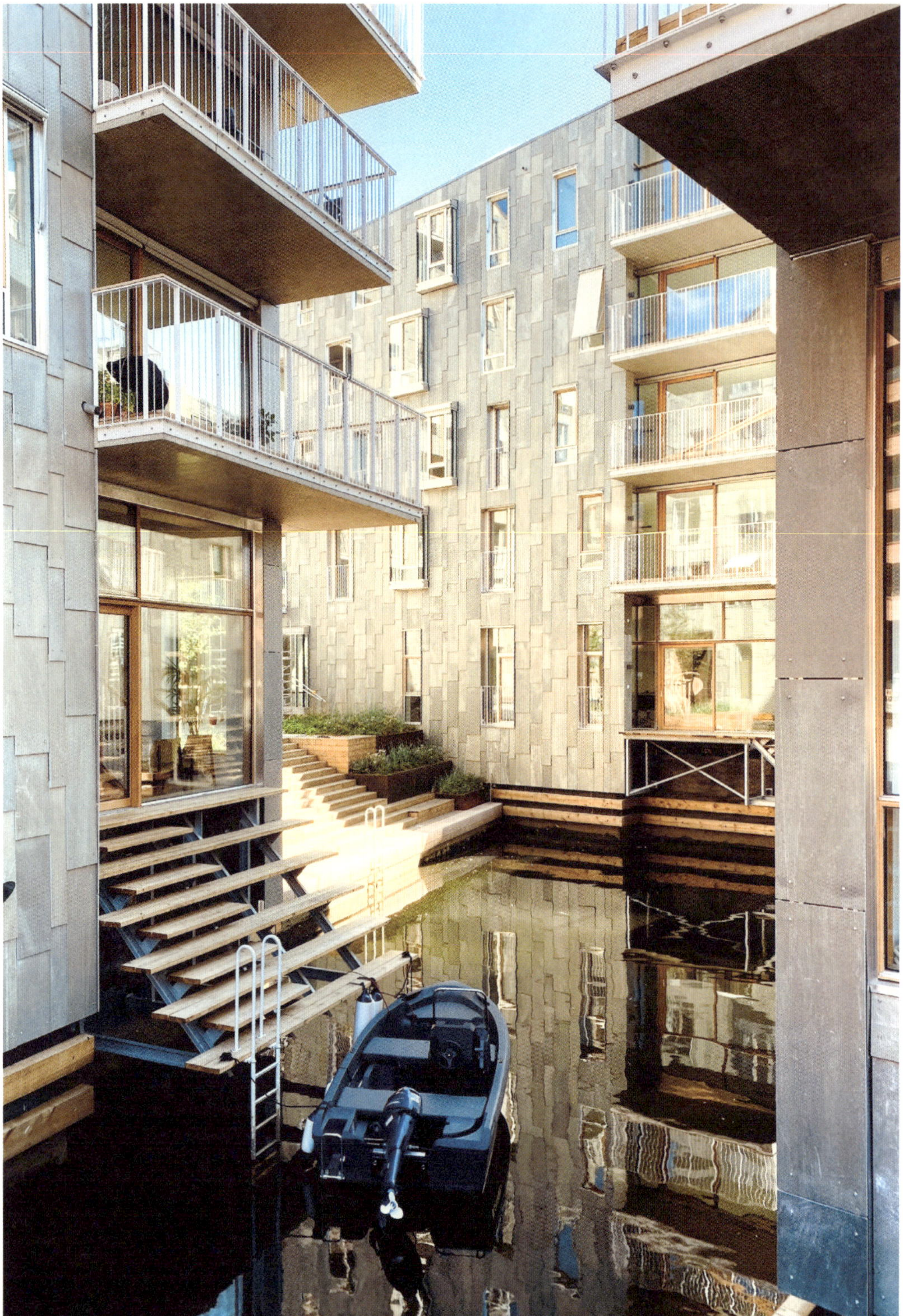

Vandkunsten

Vandkunsten was founded in 1970 by Michael Sten Johnsen, Svend Algren, Jens Thomas Arnfred and Steffen Kragh. It is a non-hierarchical architectural studio collective with strong opinions and attitudes. Its team of around 80 employees work – among other projects – with a focus on community-led buildings, designed to enhance the lives of the people who use them. The focus is on people and places, not "architecture" that draws attention to itself. "We only design projects we believe in," the practice states. "But once the work is done, the architecture is not ours. It belongs to the community." This approach challenges the conventional structures that shape architecture, whether economic, social or cultural, using pre-existing conditions to help create each building.

Based in a converted workshop building at the city of Copenhagen's Quintus battery on Holmen islet, Vandkunsten's workspace is arranged around a large, long table for communal eating; conversation and debate are an essential part of the design process.

Pernille Schyum Poulsen joined the practice in 1990 and now specialises in masterplan competitions. She has taught at and is currently censor at The Royal Danish Academy of Fine Arts, and in 2015 she was awarded the Eckersberg Medal with Jan Albrechtsen for their work on progressive masterplanning.

vandkunsten.com

Previous page: Housing in Bispevika, Oslo, Norway

Below left and below right: Balancen senior co-living, Ry, Denmark

Bottom: The City Houses (Byhusene), Islands Brygge, Copenhagen

Todd Saunders: Tell me about Vandkunsten and how the office works.

Pernille Schyum Poulsen: We work like a collective. I began my career studying political sociology and economics, but it wasn't a very social course. I had a boyfriend who was an architecture student. He took me to his school, and there were all these big rooms with people drawing, drinking coffee and smoking and I thought that looked very nice. So I ended up at the school of architecture, almost by accident. I became a student worker at Vandkunsten in 1990, so I have been here for 32 years, the first three years as a student.

TS: Did you only study architecture at college?

PSP: I started with architecture before studying landscape for two years, and then I went back to architecture, which is when I met Michael Sten Johnsen. Sadly, he died in March 2022, although he hadn't been active in the company for some years.

TS: I'm very sorry to hear that.

PSP: He had a beautiful funeral in the church at Bagsværd made by Jørn Utzon. Although we see ourselves as a collective, he was very much part of the company's DNA. Vandkunsten is 52 years old, and its fundamental principles still apply.

TS: What's still the most important thing for the studio?

PSP: Sustainability. How we work has always had a sustainable foundation. Of course, on the social side we're most concerned about everyday community life. We haven't built big theatres or museums, or whatever. It's about everyday life for – I hate to say "normal people" – everybody.

TS: That's what I noticed about your work. It's an architecture about the people. It's very rarely about the buildings – the people are always put at the front.

PSP: That's how I see it. Another thing – we've always considered everything when we do a plan, from the parking spaces to the dustbins. This focus on everything is also a very sustainable view. We consider the physical environment; can we use something in the surroundings, for example? It sounds banal, but we don't cut down an old tree if we could use it to create better quality space. We have to re-use whatever we can.

TS: When I visited the Dianas Have housing in Hørsholm with Claus Bech-Danielsen, I experienced all these things that you're describing. I noticed the care and love that was put into everything. That project really made a big impression on me. Have you ever been moved emotionally by a piece of architecture or a building, whether by your firm or someone else?

PSP: Of course, many times. It can be unconventional architecture without architects, like an old barn in the countryside with a rusty metal roof, an image that inspired us to use rusted metal in one of our projects. One of the great inspirations at Vandkunsten is to see how cheap materials age over time. Beauty sometimes happens by accident, as well as through simple building traditions. At the other end of the scale, I remember being fascinated as an architecture student by Le Corbusier. He had this playful game between structure, intuition and art, putting things together in a very unsystematic way. Seeing some of his work was an important experience, although I'm obviously not the first architect to say this.

Opposite: Fællesbyg Køge Kyst, Køge, Denmark

TS: Ronchamp is a true example of architecture and art blending into each other. Which is your favourite Le Corbusier building?

PSP: Sainte Marie de La Tourette near Lyon. And the Unité d'Habitation in Marseilles. His way of finding a balance between both the modernistic, systematic way of doing things, and playfulness, made a big impression on me. You also ask this question of our own projects. Some buildings I didn't work on myself still have a big impact on me, like the Tinggaarden housing in Herfølge from 1978. I still get touched that people are so happy to live there, and that the common houses are still working well, with its flexible shared rooms. The Jystrup Savværk co-housing project is also important to me, although it's a bit more radical than Tinggaarden.

TS: Do these projects still offer useful lessons?

PSP: Yes. We have to be more sustainable and live in less space. We must share more and change our behaviours.

TS: This architecture truly belongs to the community, it seems. I've heard other architects talk about visiting projects 10 years or so after completion and finding that they've changed unexpectedly for the better. It's as if you've created a framework for things to happen that are totally out of your control, but it makes life better for the people.

PSP: It's obvious in Tinggaarden that the people who chose to live there probably wanted to live that way. But now it's 40 years old, the physical surroundings and environment still support this. I guess you are not lonely when you live there, because loneliness is another big human problem.

TS: What about a recently built project that you've been excited about?

PSP: The Fællesbyg project in Køge, a proactive housing project that "one to one" tries to show another way of developing. It's very sad that housing has become a financial product – a lot of housing is built for somebody to earn a lot of money. It's all about getting it done fast and cheap so you can get the most profit. We're keen to find other ways to build housing. We visited the *baugruppen* in Tübingen in Germany, for example, and although it's uncommon to make *baugruppen* in Denmark, what was fascinating about Tübingen was that you could feel a much stronger civil society being created because people had come together to build. Some residents even built affordable accommodation specifically for refugees. It's not just an important part of a good society, but also about living in a more sustainable way. We have to be able to do things together. Most of all, we're trying to find alternatives to profit-oriented housing.

TS: How did that project take shape?

PSP: We worked with the Selskabet for Billige Boliger fund and the Køge Kyst Development Company. We advertised in the local paper and invited interested people to meet with us. It was a long process, but it succeeded. Ultimately, half of our time was spent discussing financing, even though there was very strong political will in the city. Political and financial structures need to support other ways of doing things.

TS: How many people live there now?

PSP: There are around 45 apartments. Perhaps it was a little too big for the small banks in

It's not just an important part of a good society, but also about living in a more sustainable way. We have to be able to do things together. Most of all, we're trying to find alternatives to profit-oriented housing.

— Pernille Schyum Poulsen

DENMARK | VANDKUNSTEN

This page and opposite: Housing in Bispevika, Oslo, Norway

Denmark, who are keen to work on collective projects, but they were nervous about the scale. We're also having to change the culture in the financial sector, because we need their support.

TS: It's important to show that other housing models are possible. Sadly, there are too many profit-driven buildings that don't appear to be good places to live or look at. I think Danish architects have a lot to teach the world about co-housing. What else did you learn from that project?

PSP: We initially wanted to use a wooden structure but as prices went up it became uneconomical. When you build low, one or two storeys, you have a kind of freedom. But with a higher density like the project in Køge, there's structure and services to consider. You also have a great responsibility with this kind of client, because they have spent so much time assembling their group. The most important thing was to give everyone a sense of ownership and involvement. The strong façade colours helped, because we wanted to shout a little, and each colour represents an apartment, so there's a certain liveliness or happiness to it – it has strength. Of course, it's not aesthetic in a classical way.

TS: What about other recent projects?

PSP: Our housing project in Bispevika in Oslo takes a completely different approach. I think they're the most expensive apartments in Oslo, in that way it's not very Vandkunsten-like. But I like that, with this project, instead of just building a block of private space for rich people, it opens up the waterfront to the public. The public spaces work very well, because you can now easily get to the fjord from the back streets of the city. All the other projects along the waterfront are very private and closed.

TS: What are the different opportunities you see in urban and rural areas?

PSP: There's a very big responsibility to the site, wherever it is. At Vandkunsten, we talk a lot about "knitting" new projects together with the old. We do a lot of work analysing the existing city, for example trying to support small shops instead of relying on big shopping malls. Masterplanning is so complex, with so many layers, and it's about finding the balance between every layer. We believe that the spaces between buildings create the city, because these spaces are where it's nice to be and where you can meet each other. They have an architectural and spatial quality because they are the physical framework of the city. We need diverse cities, where people from different walks of life can meet; they might not talk to each other, but they can see each other and walk through each other's spaces. Look at, for example, London or Oslo, places that are so expensive that teachers and police officers can't live in them. These things have a huge impact on society and how we live together.

TS: I like how, in Vandkunsten, you ensure that people and their needs are the most important thing in any project. I've had students who talk about architecture as a series of objects, not the people who actually use buildings. The city is such a complex thing, from the developer's profit to the city's need for taxes, to play spaces, to urban loneliness.

PSP: We have to make a nice, liveable city out of all this complexity. And with the climate crisis, you have to try and keep what you already have – a new layer that is quite interesting.

TS: There's a new generation of architects that is very idealistic and enthusiastic about saving and recycling, so I'm hopeful. Now Vandkunsten is 50 years old, do you also feel there's a generational shift? Are there any aspects of your practice that could be passed on to other firms?

PSP: It's not about building a "masterpiece" that doesn't consider its surroundings or anything else. You must be interested in society and what happens politically. Of course, architecture is extremely important in our office. We spend a lot of time finding the right proportions to make buildings beautiful, but bringing these things together should be a part of every architect's work. At Vandkunsten, we do all this as a collective, coming together to solve problems that affect everyone.

Right: Vandkunsten,
Copenhagen, Denmark

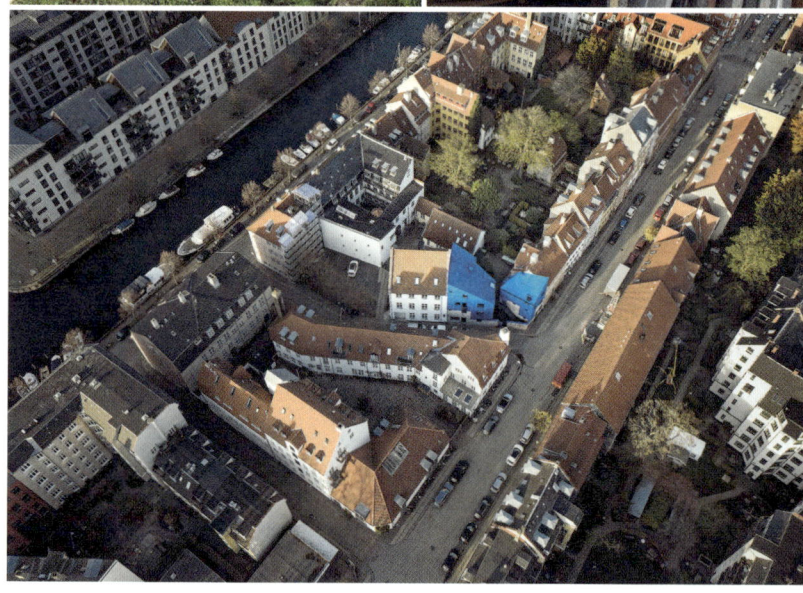

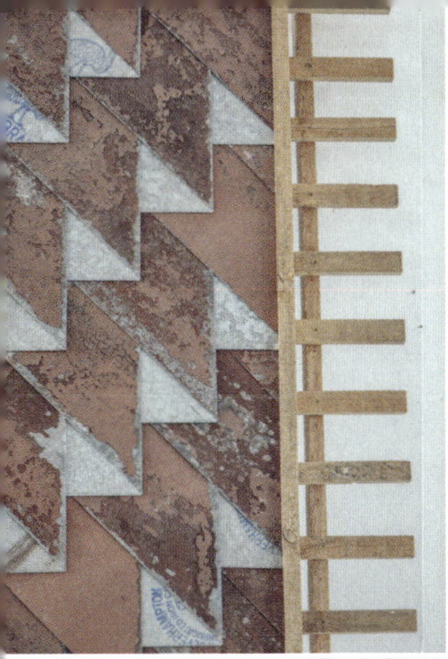
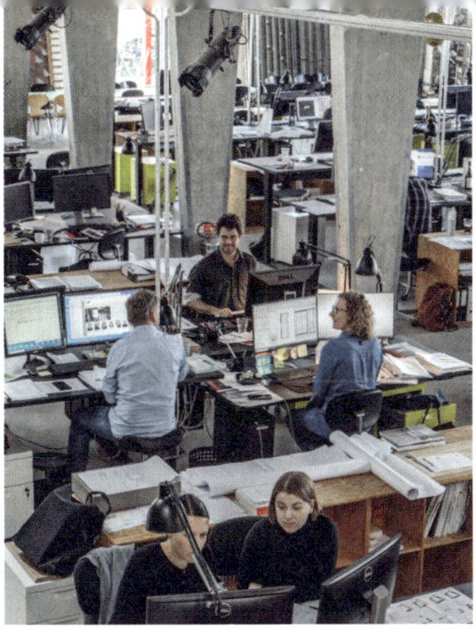
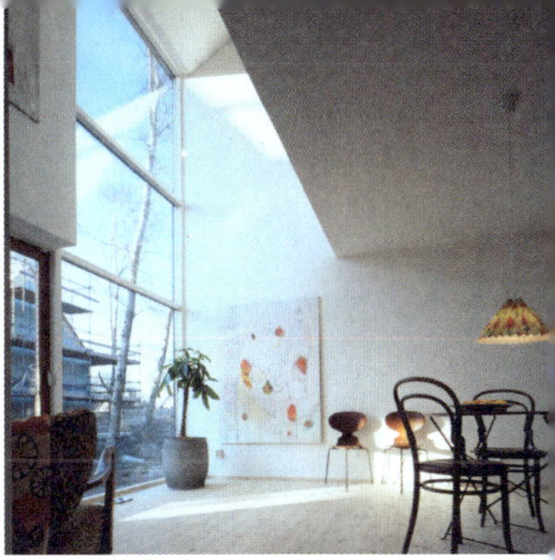
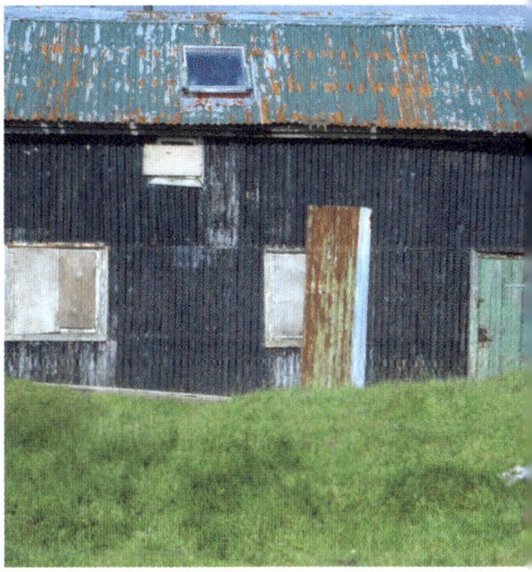
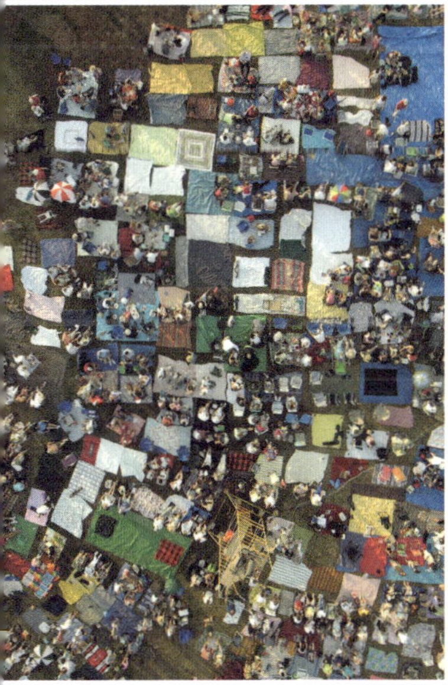
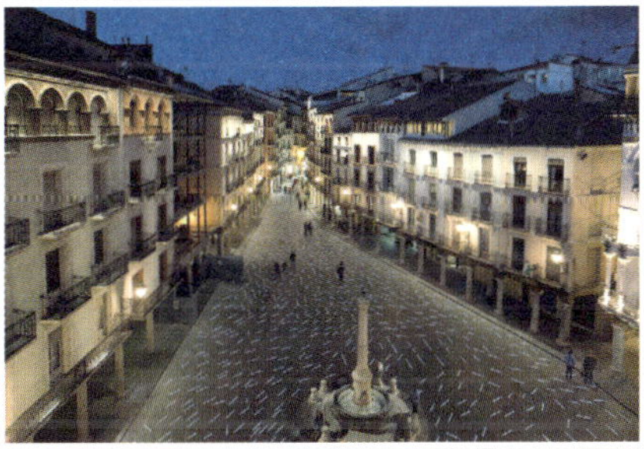
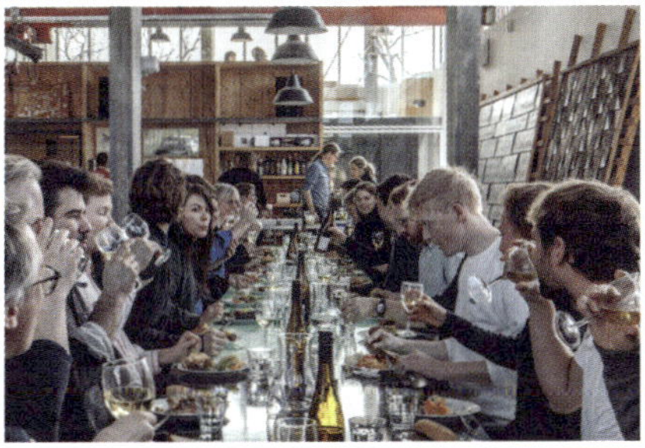
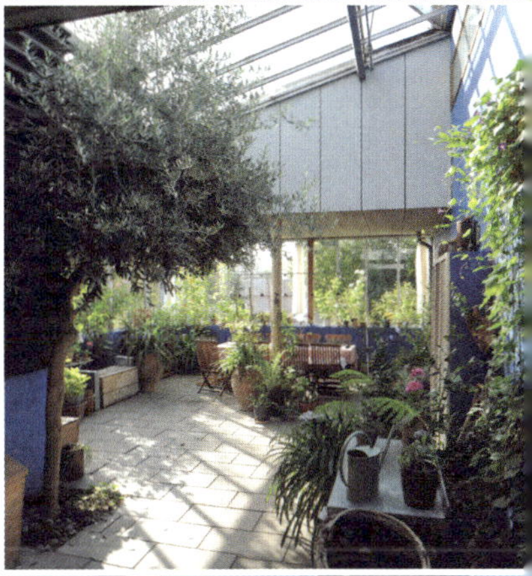
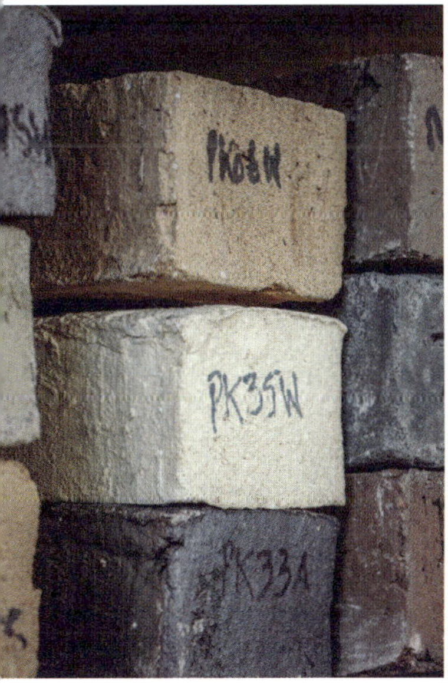
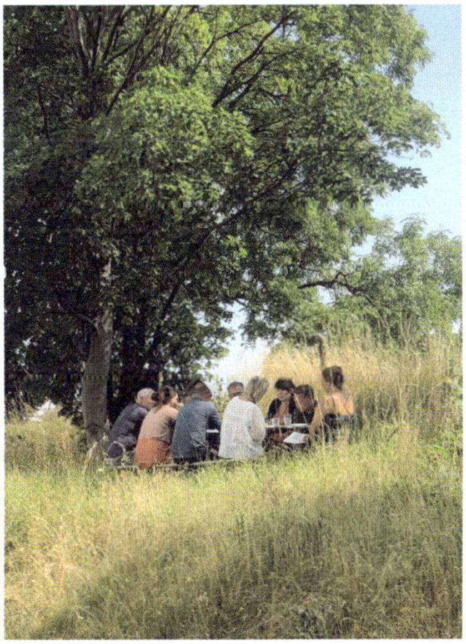
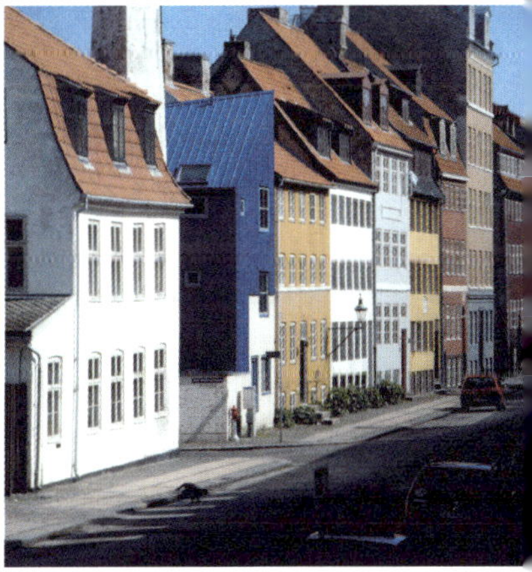

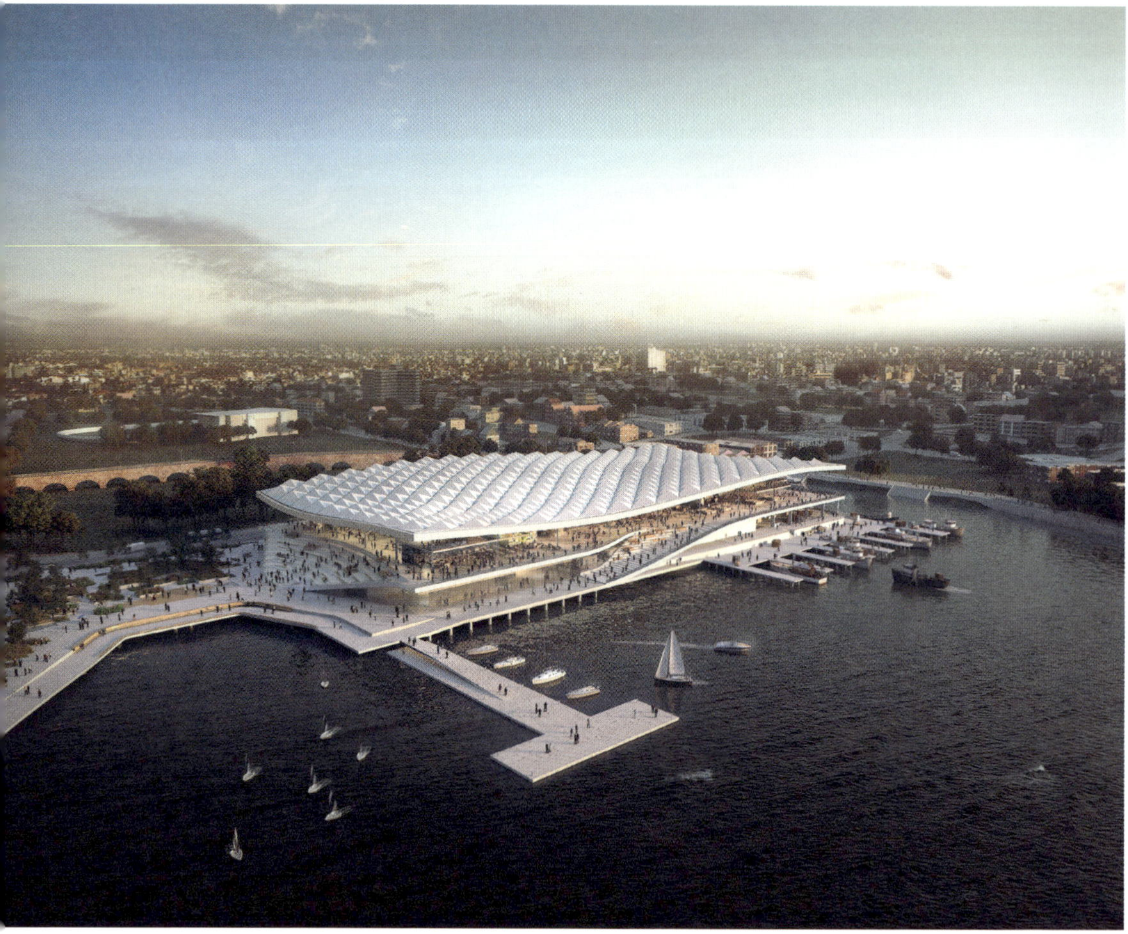

3XN

3XN was founded in Aarhus, Denmark in 1986 by Kim Herforth Nielsen, Lars Frank Nielsen and Hans Peter Svendler Nielsen. Together, they established an architectural approach that combined theory with aesthetics. The studio grew rapidly and now stands at nearly 180 people, drawn from 25 nationalities around the world, and spread across five offices. "We work on a global scale but take pride in our history and Scandinavian roots, all bound by humanistic values," they write. "This allows us to reinvent tradition with a clear understanding of some of the most exciting and pressing challenges of the 21st century." A research and innovation unit, GXN, was set up in 2007 to support the design team, as well as explore new innovations in digital processes, materials and behavioural science. Audun Opdal is a Senior Partner and Head of Design at 3XN, having joined the company in 2008. 3XN is currently working on major projects in Copenhagen, London, Munich, Shenzhen, Sydney and Toronto, among others. Major works include Copenhagen's Royal Arena, and the IOC Headquarters in Lausanne.

3xn.com

It's important that we talk about experience, emotions, aesthetics, and what it means to the people that are in or around our buildings. If there's not a place for emotion, then there's probably not a place for human beings.

— Audun Opdal

Previous page, above and right: Sydney Fish Market, Sydney, Australia

Todd Saunders: Tell me about a project that was a real rite of passage for you.

Audun Opdal: For my first few years at 3XN I mainly did competitions, and by chance I did this competition in Toronto. We won it and that was a big turning point for me. Canada was a very inviting culture – I became friends with my clients. I wanted to go there because of the building, to see the people, and work together for a common goal. It also taught me that even though you might come from a small country like Denmark, exchanging ideas can have a massive impact on other people and places. I've translated this into our work in Australia, Greece, London, as well as in Sweden. Every single country is different, but there are also similarities.

TS: What you just said made me a bit homesick for Canada. I realised how much I grew up with that level of hospitality – people are inclusive, friendly, always inviting you home to dinner.

AO: Maybe it helps being a foreigner as well. When I started doing architecture, I was all about the buildings. These days I appreciate the process and the connections that I get through my work just as much as the final product. I learned that in Canada. If you have fun while you're doing it, the product will always reflect that.

TS: How many countries have you worked in now?

AO: I don't keep count. At least 12 in Europe, as well as Canada, the States, Japan, Australia. There are elements of luck in all these things. Strange things come together that can shape your professional and personal life.

TS: So where do you get your energy from?

AO: I've always been very keen to stay connected with where I came from and where I studied. These days, I mentor on a couple of courses here in Copenhagen. I run two sessions each semester with master's students, giving feedback on their projects. It allows me to be part of their process and I think they learn something from practice as well. I believe in a strong connection between academia and practice. In Denmark this is sometimes lacking. 3XN is doing a lot of complex buildings and it can be overwhelming for students to understand how to even start such a project. It's the same design processes as if you were working on a small residential project or whatever, you know? I get a lot out of this link.

TS: Were you a student when you started at 3XN?

AO: No. I had already started a job before I finished my master's, which was fortunate. I went back to Norway to work as the very first intern at DARK Arkitekter in Oslo. The first thing they asked was "Can you archive a little bit?" I think I said that I'm really bad at archiving and then I turned in sick for a day. But after that it changed and it was a pretty cool experience.

TS: How else are you expanding the firm's interaction with students?

AO: We have four architects doing mentoring. It's a really good way to get your staff to do something else than just doing project-related stuff. It's also one way for us to get new staff. The connection is important. Our innovation

Opposite: Astoriahuset and Nybrogatan 17, Stockholm, Sweden

company, GXN, has four industrial PhDs in their office right now. I've been introducing those guys into our projects. In our current London project, GXN is an external consultant to work on futureproofing the scheme. It's about connecting our more academia-oriented people to the practice-based world.

TS: How many employees do you have now?

AO: I think we're 160 in 3XN and maybe 15 in GXN. As well as our headquarters in Copenhagen, we have offices in London, New York, Stockholm and Sydney.

TS: Can we talk about your recent buildings? I was really interested in three projects: the Cobot Hub building in Odense, the Sydney Fish Market and the climate-positive hotel in Bornholm.

AO: Of course. Both the Cobot Hub and the Fish Market buildings are trying to have more than just one single function. Many waterfront or harbour cities are replacing all their older industrial functions with high-end residential. Instead, Sydney Fish Market is intended to remain a working, industrial building. We wanted to connect industry with public and recreational activities. This building combines this industrial marketplace with a more open public-oriented function in the form of a retail floor.

TS: Is it like a big kitchen or living room for the city?

AO: Exactly. What is a market? It's a place that's open to the air, it has daylight and it needs to feel like part of the public realm. All these things inform the design. We kept wanting to extend this working space out onto the waterfront. There were so many stakeholders – I think more than 80 different wholesalers and retailers. They all need to live together under that roof. On the floor above are the restaurants. Ultimately, it's much more than just a fish market. It's a public plaza as well as an extension of the waterfront promenade.

There's a little bit of this approach in the Cobot project in Denmark. It's completely different, a factory and an office building, a place where two companies develop and test robots. However, we tried to create a structure that could accommodate all these different activities within just one kind of framework. The building can adapt itself to become workspaces or testing areas or lab space for the robots… The use is the design driver.

TS: So is it a combination of mechanical logistics, then people mixed on top of it?

AO: Yes, a mixed approach. With the hotel in Bornholm, we started out knowing that this was to be a prefab timber building that had to be built in just six months. It's a small extension to the existing hotel, 22 rooms or so, but the approach was to use the construction framework as a design tool. We knew we had to challenge ourselves in terms of materials to reduce the carbon footprint. It's always interesting to use these kinds of constraints.

TS: Have you used this construction approach anywhere else?

AO: The Cobot Building is also made from a kit of parts. It's timber, fastened together with mechanical components. The site is an old industrial space, with high ceilings and natural daylight.

DENMARK | 3XN

Above and left: Olympic House – IOC Headquarters, Lausanne, Switzerland

TS: But that kind of building will go in the garbage when it gets ripped down. The building you're designing can be taken apart, packed down, moved and put up again. I'm interested in the benefit of timber.

AO: Our clients there know they will probably expand. And they know they'll need to reconfigure their building in a few years. So we needed a system that can allow for the entire building to both be more or less just workplaces, or more or less just warehouses. You never know. The fish market solved this by adopting a single, fixed roof structure that addressed many technical and environmental issues such as rainwater harvesting, energy production and air flow, while sheltering a series of very flexible spaces below.

TS: Were they all built at the same time?

AO: Both the hotel and the Cobot Hub we did more or less under Covid restrictions. I don't think there's any production facility for robots built in a similar way. Some tech companies are doing a similar thing, but they don't usually have production or testing facilities at a similar scale.

TS: The smaller companies we've interviewed often emphasised the role of emotions in their architecture. Are there emotions at work in large offices like 3XN's?

AO: I would say so. There is a necessity to address emotions in all the projects we do, large and small. It's important that we talk about experience, emotions, aesthetics and what it means to the people that are in or around our buildings. If there's not a place for emotion, then there's probably not a place for human beings. Even if you're building 100,000 square metres or 100 square metres, people will still be occupying the buildings and their emotions will be affected by the space they're in. In the first big project I did, an HQ for Swedbank in Stockholm, if we hadn't dared to discuss the emotions of that space, we would probably have ended up with a soulless factory. An efficient building, but not for the people who work there.

TS: There's a theory that if someone – whether a private client, community or company – falls in love with a building, then the building will last longer.

AO: It's interesting and it links back to academia. When I present these projects to students, they might think at first that they're all about money. But really, it's about the people who work on that project, whether it's the client, engineer or contractor. If you do not consider the emotional component for everyone, you'll probably end up not making a good project. We try to always remember that what we create will affect people, not only by its function, but also its appearance and spatial experience.

TS: What's one public building you would love to do?

AO: The Fish Market is probably the one. It was so good. You could imagine having design meetings with fishermen in rain cloaks in the morning after they'd been working all night. It was the most interesting clash of cultures and a project – that as a fisherman myself – I enjoyed most of all.

Right: 3XN, Copenhagen K, Denmark

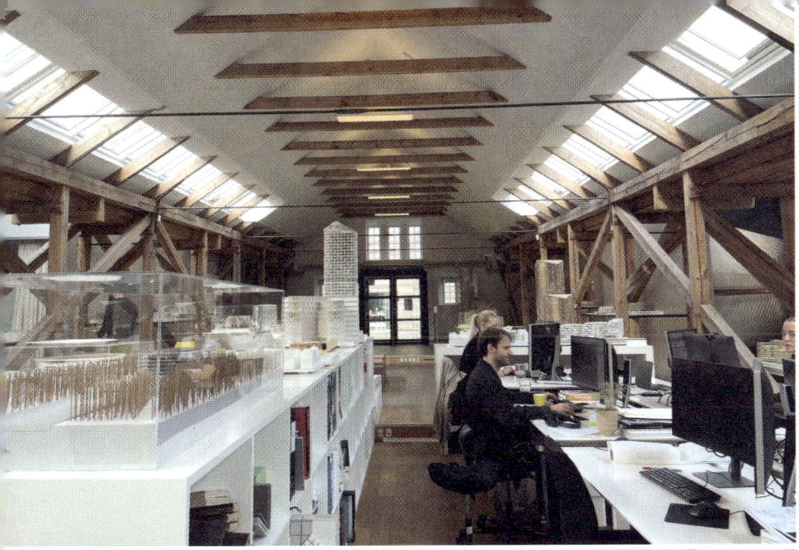
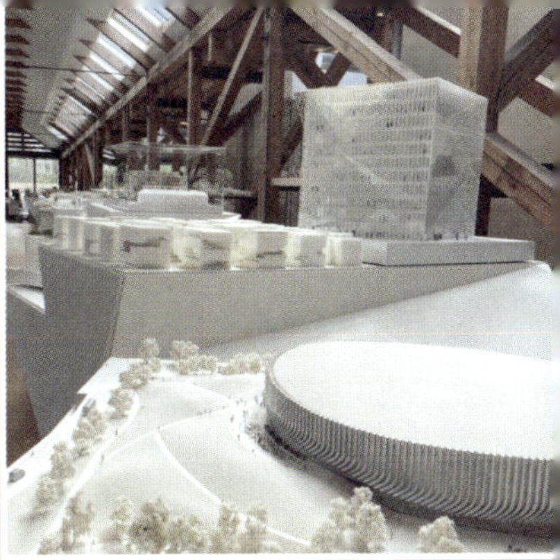
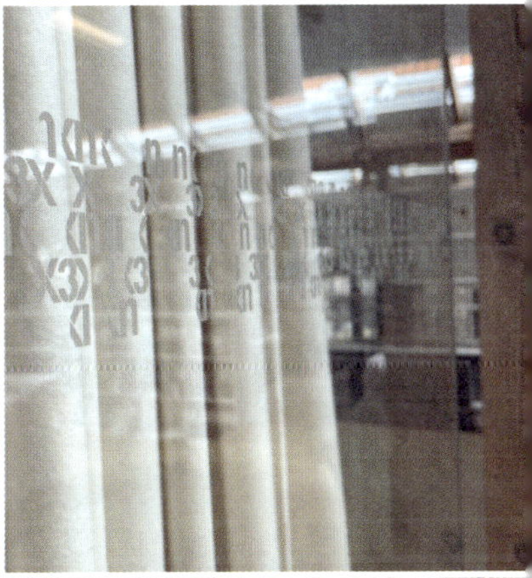

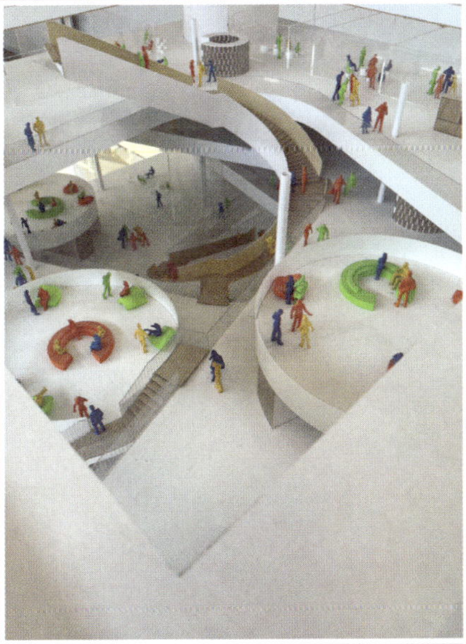
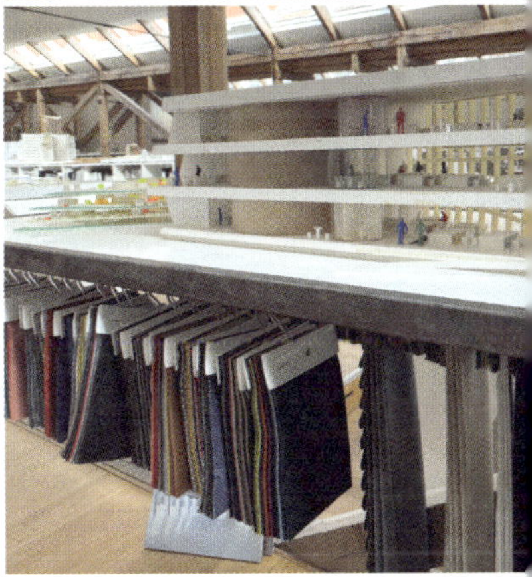
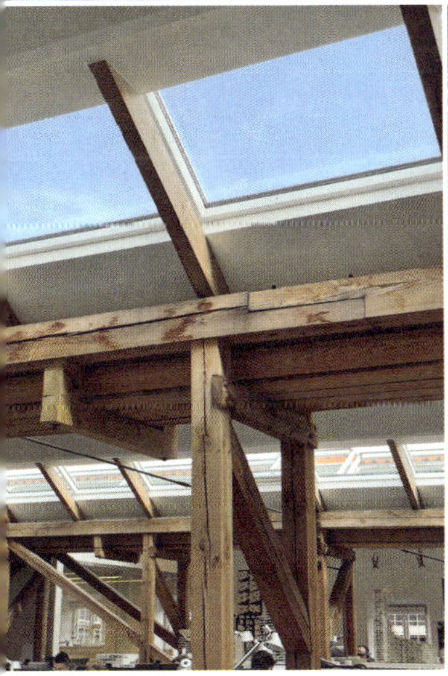
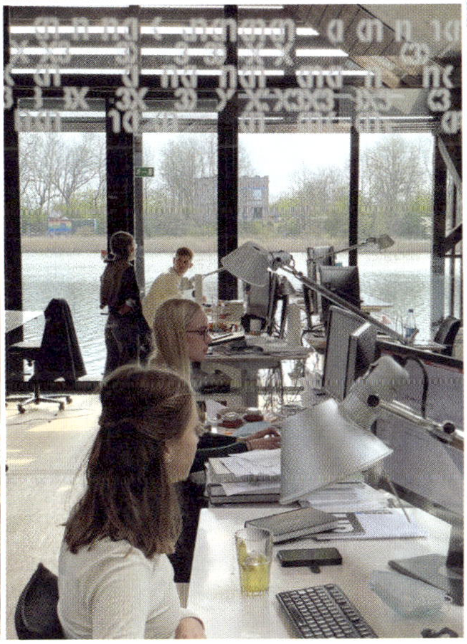
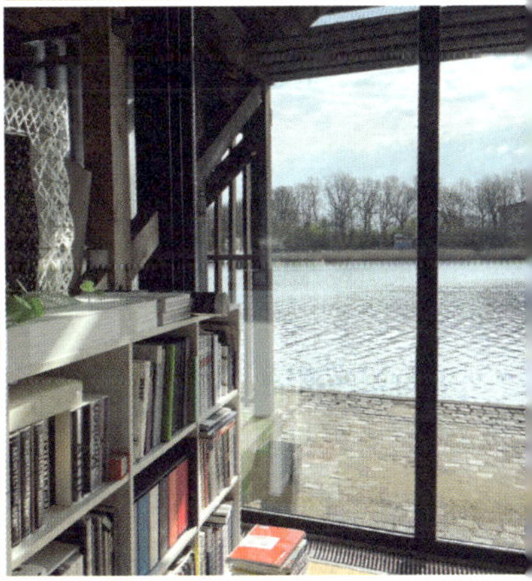

FINLAND

{ ESSAY }

A DOZEN YEARS IN FINNISH ARCHITECTURE

{ BY }

KRISTO VESIKANSA

Editor in Chief at Finnish Architectural Review ARK

In 2009, nine recently established Finnish architectural offices, including ALA, Avanto, K2S and Lassila Hirvilammi, produced a travelling exhibition and a publication called *Newly Drawn – Emerging Finnish Architects*. Most of these offices had been set up after they had won an open architectural competition – as has been typical for successful Finnish offices for more than a century. At the time, most of the offices were still in the process of implementing their first major projects, but in the 13 years since they have all completed numerous landmark buildings. ALA, Anttinen Oiva and Verstas have grown into large firms for Finland, while Avanto, for example, has continued to work as a studio, focusing on smaller projects. Some of these architects have also become full-time teachers.

The architects involved in the *Newly Drawn* project had all received a relatively uniform education at the Helsinki and Oulu Schools of Architecture in the 1990s, but they also belonged to the first generation of Finnish architects with extensive opportunities to study abroad. A few of them had also worked for well-known foreign architectural firms, such as OMA and Sauerbruch Hutton. The works of these architects are therefore both rooted in the Finnish tradition of modernism as well as being open to international contemporary architecture in its various forms.

This dichotomy is most evident in the way these architects have approached irregular sculptural forms. They were, of course, a major international trend in the early 2000s, influenced by rapidly evolving information technology, post-structuralist theories, and iconic buildings by Frank Gehry, Zaha Hadid, Daniel Libeskind, et al. From the Finnish point of view, however, the undulating lines could also be seen as references to the organic forms within Alvar Aalto's and Reima Pietilä's architecture. This national interpretation was further strengthened by the use of natural wooden surfaces in many buildings, such as the Kamppi Chapel (K2S, 2012), Löyly restaurant and sauna (Avanto, 2016) and the Oodi Library (ALA, 2017).

In 2009, the *Newly Drawn* group represented the new generation of Finnish architecture. In subsequent years, competition has arisen from younger architects with different ideals and practices. For example, the Uusi Kaupunki collective (now Nordic Works) was founded in 2013 and made user-centred urban development chronicled by a popular TV show. This book includes one of the collective's affiliates, Studio Puisto, which has found its own specialisation in high-end tourist buildings. AOR and Opus, on the other hand, have profiled themselves with a highly disciplined, semi-classical architecture that can be seen as a reaction to the sculptural forms favoured by the previous generation. Such severe designs have also become popular among well-established offices and developers.

Over the past decade, the need for sustainability, carbon neutrality and recyclability have forced architects to re-evaluate many of their values and approaches. This also shattered the long-cherished myth that Finnish modern architecture has a special relationship with nature. The organic buildings of Aalto and Pietilä were designed for a single use, with difficult-to-repair structures and synthetic materials, and cannot serve as a basis for a sustainable approach. For this reason, many architects today study traditional building techniques with ancient histories, such as solid masonry, logs and clay. Natural ventilation is attracting interest for the same reasons. The Ylivieska Church (K2S, 2021) with its steep medieval roofs, shows that such construction methods often result in a rather archaic design language.

However, the large-scale introduction of these traditional construction techniques does not seem very likely at present, as it would require radical reforms in building regulations and processes. Engineered wood products, such as CLT and LVL, could instead provide an easier way to replace concrete and steel with lower-carbon products. These products have spread rapidly to the construction of schools and day-care centres, with good examples being the Tuupala school (Alt, 2018) and the Hopealaakso day-care centre (AFKS, 2021). However, a breakthrough in the multi-story residential buildings is yet to be achieved, despite several high-level prototypes, such as Puukuokka (OOPEAA, 2018).

The pursuit of sustainability has also made the refurbishment and reuse of existing buildings an increasingly important task. As Finland's building stock is younger than in other Nordic countries, many of these operations concern Modernist buildings. The most spectacular renovation project in recent years has been the Helsinki Olympic Stadium, undertaken by K2S and NRT and completed in 2020. The stadium, which served as the main venue of the 1952 Summer Olympics, is now considered a national monument, and the architects have upgraded it into a contemporary multi-purpose arena without spoiling the original atmosphere. ALA, on the other hand, has specialised in repairing unique buildings designed by Raili and Reima Pietilä.

So what does the future of Finnish architecture look like? Many young architects and students today feel that the profession has not taken climate change and species extinction seriously enough. To promote these issues, they have formed new collectives, such as Vapaa and You Tell Me, producing exhibitions, seminars and articles on the subject, although it is still too early to assess what kind of architecture will emerge from these ideas. Indications can be found in a few competition entries, such as Heljä Nieminen's and Havu Järvelä's third-prize nomination for the Sara Hildén Art Museum. Based on that, the Finnish architecture of the future looks quite monumental, absolutely modular and a bit decorative.

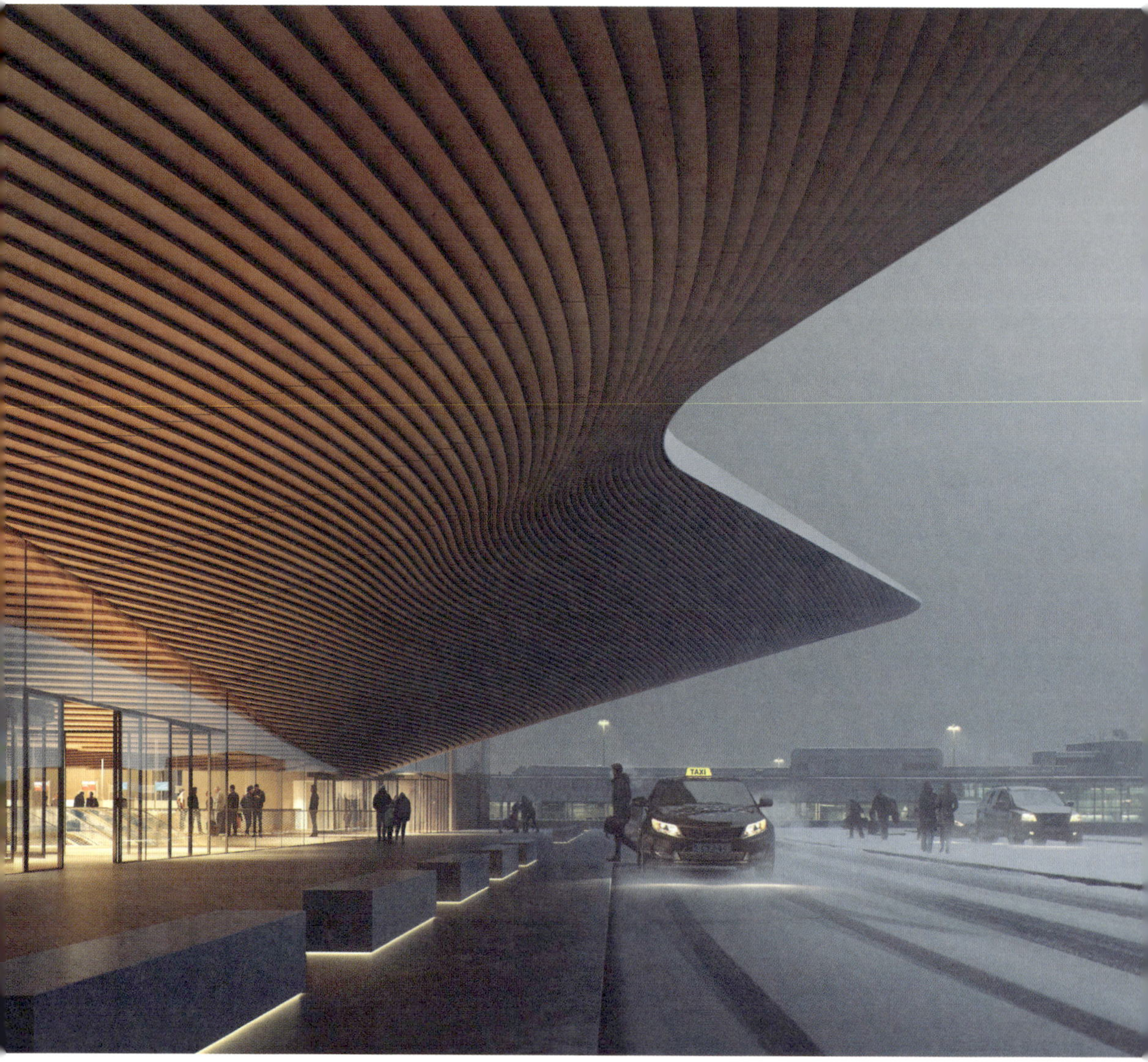
TAXI

ALA Architects

ALA Architects was founded in 2005 by Juho Grönholm, Antti Nousjoki, Janne Teräsvirta and Samuli Woolston. That year, they won an open international competition for a new concert hall in Kristiansand, Norway, and the project was the focus of the practice's early years. The Kilden Performing Arts Centre opened in 2012, one of a number of arts and cultural projects that have since come to characterise ALA's work. The 45-strong studio is based in Helsinki and is now run by Grönholm, Nousjoki and Woolston. Recent projects include the renovation of the Finnish Embassy in New Delhi, the Helsinki Central Library and the Courtyard Tampere City hotel, as well as a substantial expansion of Helsinki Airport. Other works include the western extension of the Helsinki Metro and a forthcoming university library in Lyon, France, one of several educational buildings in their portfolio. All three partners teach in Finland, as well as at Columbia and Washington University in the US. Eschewing straight lines in favour of flowing forms, the architects describe their approach as a search for beauty, "achieved by combining the intuitive and the analytical, the practical and the extravagant, the rational and the irrational." The firm received the Finnish State Prize for Architecture in 2012.

ala.fi

Putting a personality aside is one aspect of making architecture. But what separates us from a larger company is we really put our personalities into our projects.

— Juho Grönholm

Previous page: Helsinki Airport arrivals and departure building, Helsinki, Finland

This page: Kilden Performing Arts Centre, ALA Architects with SMS Arkitekter, Kristiansand, Norway

Todd Saunders: What did you learn about working in Norway on the Kilden Performing Arts Centre?

Antti Nousjoki: That was the first project we did as an independent office so in a way we learned everything. Later, we had to relearn things that were specific to the Norwegian project. Of course, one can't separate Norway from the project so perhaps we feel that a Norwegian quality might be specific to only this building and this place.

Juho Grönholm: We learned to speak Norwegian, to argue in a foreign language, to fight for architecture, to negotiate. Every day we needed to justify decisions – everything had to be sorted democratically. Architecture had no power to overrule things.

AN: We learned to handle tremendous pressure on a personal and organisational level. We currently have a troublesome project but this is nothing compared to our first five years. So it was useful in a way – pretty tough training, a demanding client, and of course the language issues.

JG: Maybe it took ten years off our lives, or maybe we ended up super strong. I don't know – it's almost impossible to imagine winning that sort of competition now.

TS: Perhaps it gave you a different kind of experience at a high level?

JG: It definitely showed in our later work. There are similar qualities of scale and maybe even style, certainly with the library. But we were all professionally and emotionally ready to take difficult steps. It also helped us push the library to pretty extreme levels in terms of structure. Ultimately, we could complete the project on our terms. Our authority was present in every meeting, and in the finished building.

AN: There were negative things as well. Maybe Kilden also left some scars.

TS: I've read that the reason you won the Helsinki library was because you knew the place so well. I've just done my 12th building in Canada and although I haven't lived there for 20 years, when I was there working on these projects there was this natural feeling that I knew the place. Can you describe a similar feeling of knowing a site so well?

JG: It was not only about knowing the site, because it has changed a lot in our lifetime, but also knowing the history of Finnish architecture and competitions – how they are part of a larger story about the monuments of the country's architecture, like the Parliament building and music hall.

AN: A couple of hundred other teams, and the people of Helsinki, knew all this as well. However, after our slightly strange experience in Norway, we also had the experience of being almost "foreign" architects and working outside of that immediate Finnish context. We could step back and look at the wider context. In many countries, architectural language can be influenced by recent competition. We disregarded this and focused on local narrative.

TS: You mentioned that the library was about "doing, learning and meeting". Now that it's open, which of those three is the most successful?

JG: The programme dictated that the ground level was about meeting up and sharing information. Most of the interviews and lectures we've given have been about the "doing". That's what the hype is about – "You have a 3D printer there?!" However, the best feedback we got is about the top level, the traditional library level. The landscape and the roof. It's beautiful up there and people love this magnificent space. You have the books and a 360-degree panorama across the hills of Helsinki.

AN: The success of this top level is perhaps because there aren't any worktables or 3D printers and large auditoriums. This is where the traditional library functionality goes, even though the lower levels are more architecturally complex. Here, you are almost liberated from the need to constantly produce content.

JG: When the project was still on paper, I thought that the entrance would be mind-blowing and beautiful, with its dynamic cantilever. But nobody talks about it. They just talk about the library level.

TS: I was in the Calgary library by Snøhetta and it was amazing. Almost like a giant living room for the city. One of the best contemporary public buildings I have experienced in the past ten years.

AN: The aesthetic quality of a space is linked to the functionality. Architectural beauty is connected to function in an emotional way. The library becomes part of the narrative of the history of the project – the locals recognise that it is the result of a public conversation that went on for decades. Its functionality will evolve, just as the content of a library changes.

TS: You're doing Helsinki airport as well as the library. Is there an ideal project you'd like to do in the city, to make it a better place to live?

JG: Now that the airport is nearly complete, perhaps the next dream project would be to work with a completely new, different typology. Right now, we are on a shortlist of four architects for a new central library in Macau. It's a very different context to Helsinki. Thinking about how our design would work in that culture is interesting.

AN: So far, our big projects have been prescriptive buildings, so in a theatre, for example, you can describe the audience's route minute by minute, metre to metre. You enter there, leave your coat there, sit there, have a cognac, etc. An airport is the same, it's predictable. A library, though – people are free to use it any way they want. It would be interesting to approach a public project that wasn't somehow pre-written. Perhaps a more commercial project that could be experimental and adaptive.

It would be great to build an aquatic centre in Helsinki. We need more swimming pools and have an interaction with the sea as well. There is a physicality about such buildings and it would be good to play with these forms. It's not just about walking on one level – you have a different interaction with the users.

TS: You've done an airport, concert hall, library and an embassy. If you created a town in Finland that incorporated all these buildings, what would that look like?

JG: Apart from Helsinki, the other cities in Finland are not exactly thriving in terms of urbanity and architecture. Tampere is

Below: Keilaniemi metro station, ALA Architects with Esa Piironen Architects, Keilaniemi, Finland

FINLAND | ALA ARCHITECTS

Left: Kuopio City Theatre renovation and extension, Kuopio, Finland

Opposite: Lappeenranta City Theatre, Lappeenranta, Finland

growing a lot – there's an open art museum competition there at the moment. But it feels like the opportunities in Finland are mostly in Helsinki.

TS: With good public infrastructure, these smaller cities have a good advantage. It's a good time for architects doing public architecture to turn towards rural areas. We did some micro public buildings on Fogo for example. Let's talk about competitions. You've said you've done 150 competitions. What if you didn't win half of them – would you still do them?

AN: We were almost 30 years old when we won the Kilden competition. The last chance to do something on our own. Financially difficult but an adventure. We had the skills and education to make something exciting. There's a lot of chance and coincidence in life as well, which is obvious in our profession.

TS: Perfect timing for you.

AN: Totally. We had a backs-against-the-wall mentality that we carried over into the project. It was all or nothing. Maybe that was part of the inspiration.

TS: Is there a project that got away?

AN: For me, I think it was the UPM Headquarters, next to the library site.

JG: I don't care about that one at all! [laughter] It was a great entry, but I don't really have regrets that it didn't happen. I forget past competitions quite soon.

AN: He speaks the truth. It's harder for me to get over these. Especially the ones where we clearly had the best entry. We should have definitely won the Oslo Museum of

Modern Art, but that turned into a complete nightmare project for the winner. It's easy to say, thank God we didn't get into that process.

TS: You dodged a bullet. In your office, are there things that you guys do to prevent burnout? It's a very demanding profession. Is there a balance, or is it like David Lynch says, and there's a sort of "art life" you have to live?

AN: From the very beginning we kept our working hours close to normal – much closer to our North American or central European colleagues. All three of us have quite similar family setups, and our responsibilities as husbands and fathers are quite similar because our children are all the same age. And as three partners, we share the stresses of the whole office, and the highs and lows of the emotional load.

JG: Work/life balance is good. The office is big enough that it doesn't make a huge difference if I work 6 or 8 or 10 hours a day. Our effective hours are the same.

AN: If you work ten hours a day, six days a week for 15 years you're not going be very communicative and clear-thinking, but a bit bitter and hostile. Many of our successes come from being able to make smart decisions and to have conversations and criticism. People who work a lot often feel they deserve more reward and recognition. But it's still an increasing challenge to keep ourselves functional and curious. One great thing about this profession – because the processes take so long, technologies change. When we start a new project it feels like we can try new things.

TS: That point really struck me – I sit alone with all my risk and all my victories. How does

Right and below right: Helsinki Central Library Oodi, Helsinki, Finland

the conversation and curiosity keep going between the three of you?

AN: We are by no means close to the level of architects who constantly travel and are never at the office, but we did systematically, constantly, visit some interesting places, often together. We had a shared experience of seeing buildings.

JG: We are curious about our opinions, not only on our designs but on the work of others. Less perhaps about art, literature or music. We have a slightly problematic relationship with contemporary art, it's difficult to talk about. But our focus is very much on architecture, not to copy it, but to understand its deeper flows.

TS: You use these visits to align your values?

AN: Yes, that's true. We're individuals and we have our personal opinions. We used to get into intense arguments about super stupid stuff. Because when working on a design, you have to put that individuality on hold and try to act more as a team. Our method is that personal opinions are not a driving force behind our office's design. But it results in relationships with certain buildings, like MVRDV's work in the Netherlands. Together we've become quite knowledgeable of their first 20 years of work, actually visiting some really obscure small buildings – like a greenhouse in the courtyard of a hospital. We had trouble finding it and trouble getting in. MVRDV do delightful things as well like the market hall, which is a real shared sense of joy for everyone. We are looking forward to getting back to that method. Hopefully next summer.

JG: Putting a personality aside is one aspect of making architecture. But what separates us from a larger company is we really put our personalities into our projects.

TS: When you start aligning your values through visiting other people's architecture, the aim is to find the common values.

AN: It's hard to imagine being three painters who are creating one painting, and also visiting art shows and looking at other people's paintings and being inspired by them. Architecture is a source that can be used in multiple ways. We don't really get inspired by images – we don't work in Pinterest-board-reference-image type of fashion. It's more about a shared experience that we can refer back to in conversations.

FINLAND | ALA ARCHITECTS

Right: ALA Architects, Helsinki, Finland

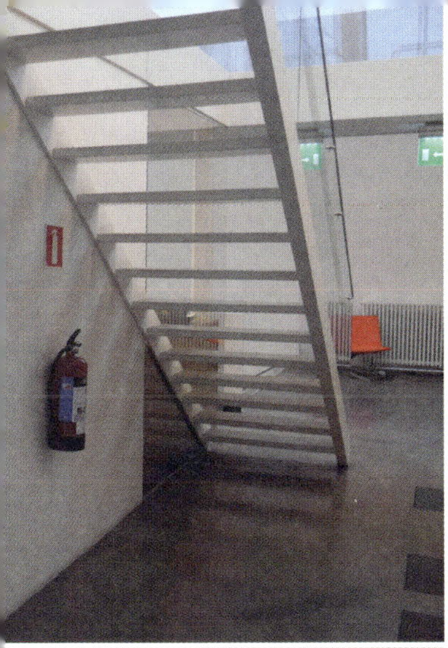
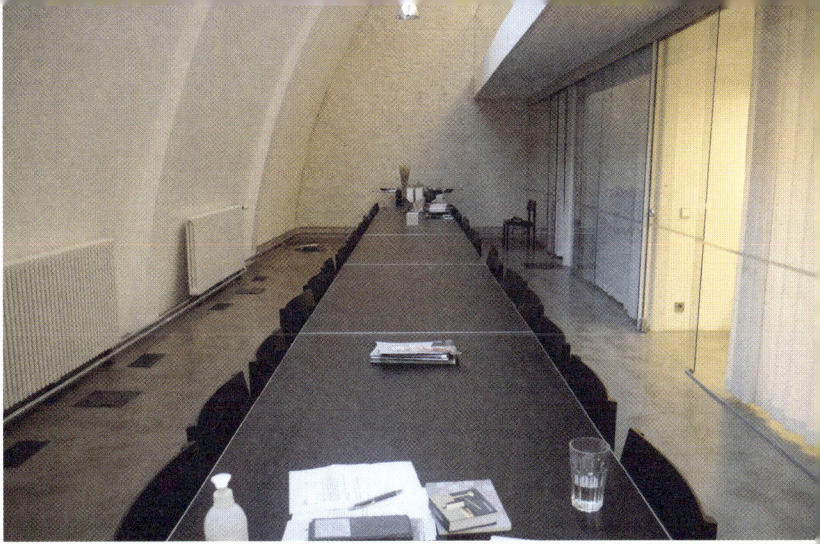
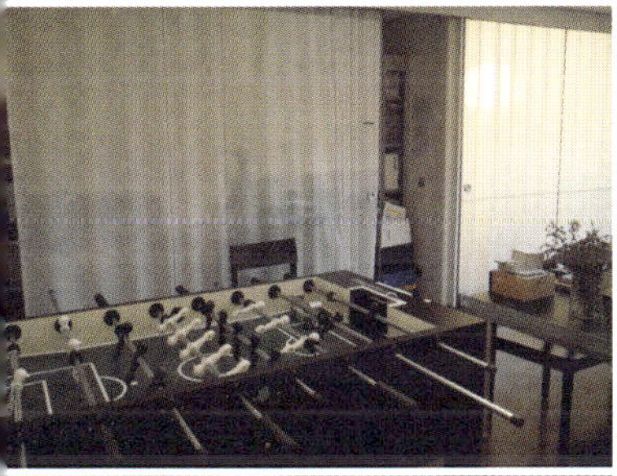
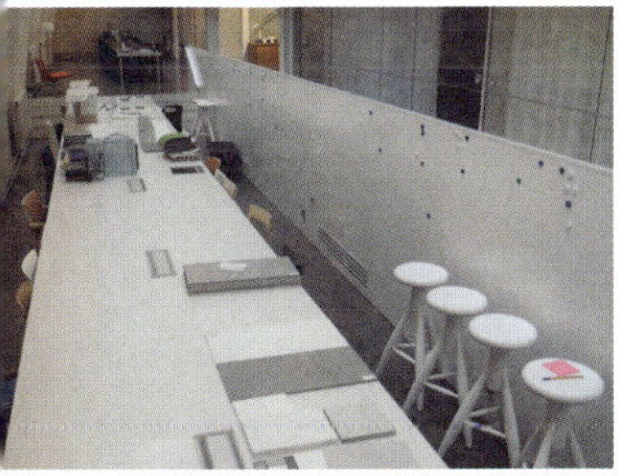
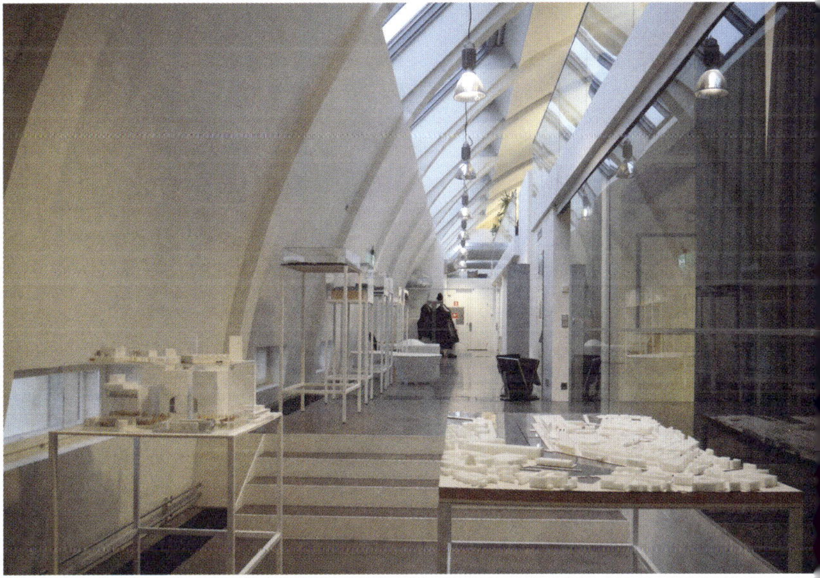
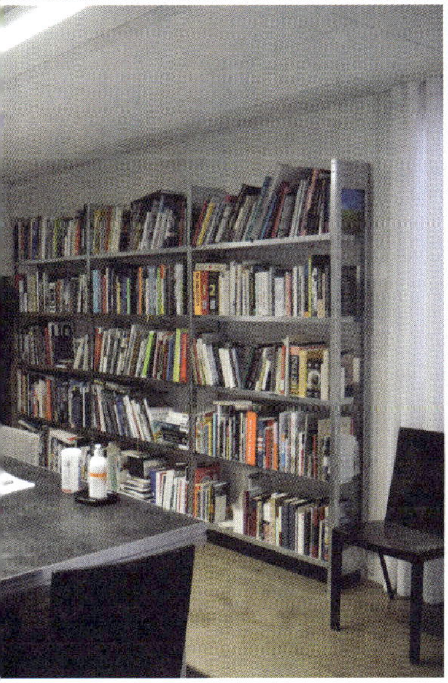
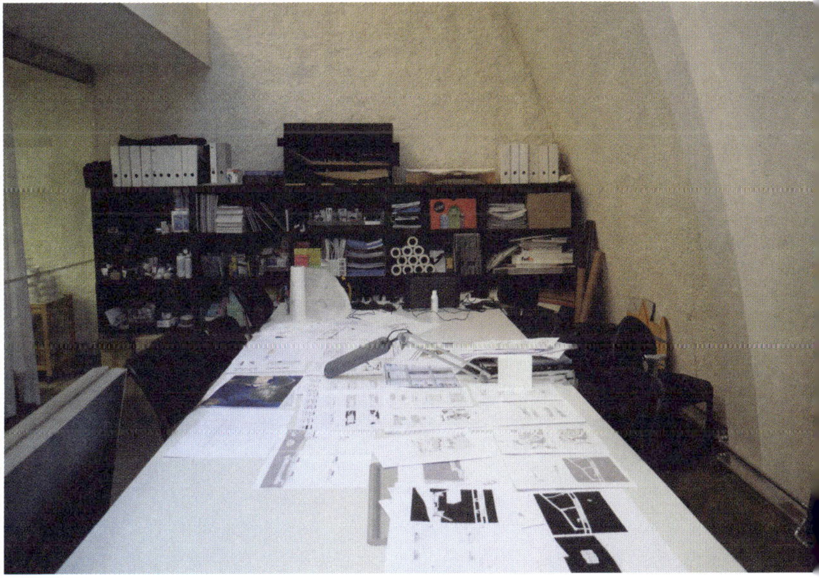

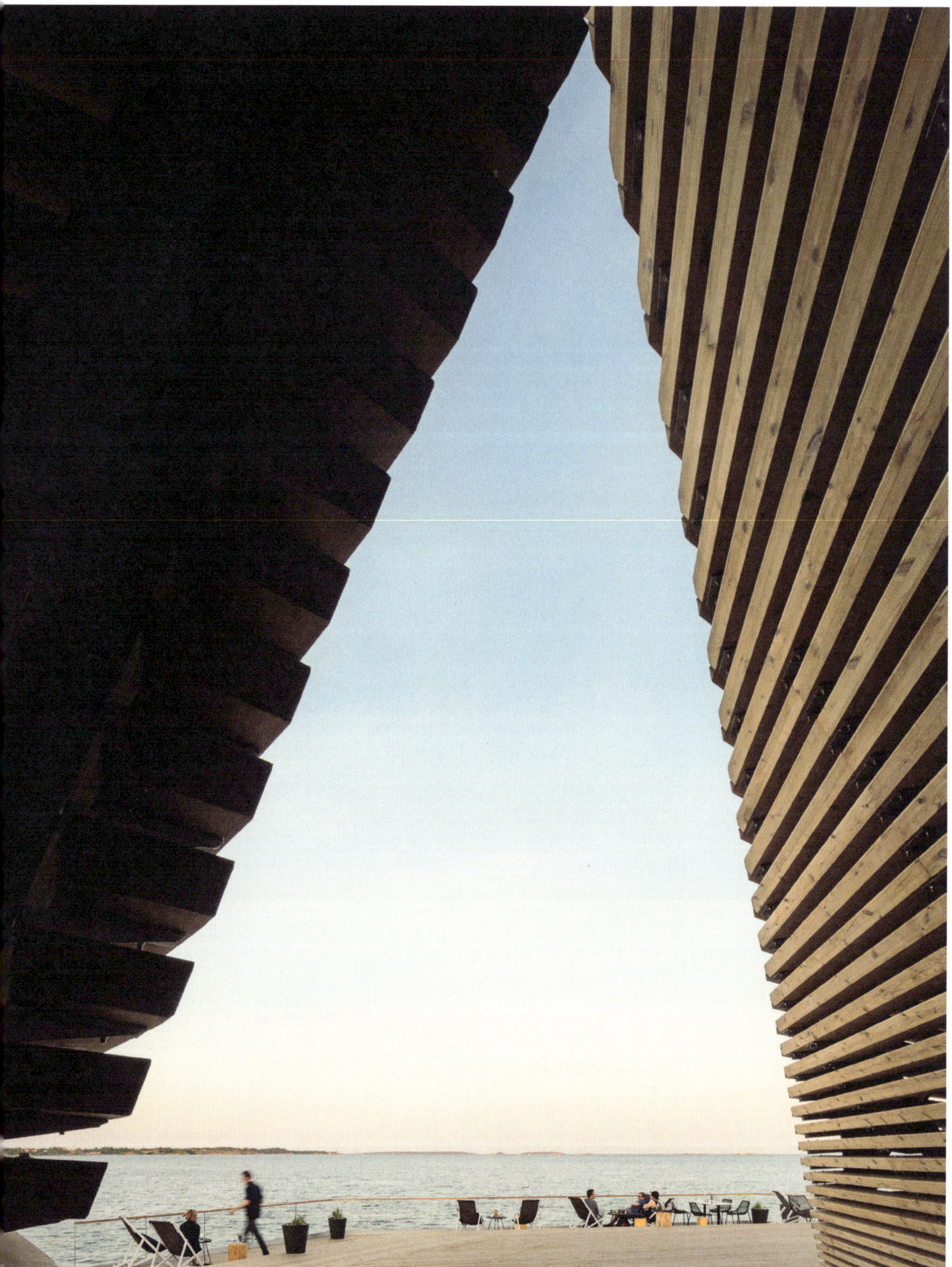

Avanto Architects

Co-founded by Anu Puustinen and Ville Hara in 2004, Avanto Architects is based in Helsinki, Finland. The studio has since grown in size and influence to become one of the country's most prominent architecture firms. Named after the Finnish custom of winter bathing – the name "Avanto" means "hole in the ice" – the partners wanted to create buildings that delivered the excitement and invigoration of this experience. Avanto is resolutely multidisciplinary, offering clients a complete service from small-scale product design to large-scale urban design. The practice is multi-award winning, including the 2018 Chicago Athaneum International Architecture Award and an IOC IAKS Award Silver medal in 2017. Projects have also been recognised for their innovative use of materials, particularly wood and concrete. Puustinen and Hara describe their approach as "creating new type of places where design, sustainability and personal experience are the key elements."

avan.to

Todd Saunders: Your studio works on very large projects, but can you tell us whether there's a different attitude behind some of your smaller recent projects?

Ville Hara: We're struggling with that question quite a lot at the moment. We started our office when we were quite young with the Chapel of St Lawrence in Vantaa, a project most architects would dream about doing. We were very fortunate. Anu was still a student and I had only just graduated. The Chapel project took ten years, and we needed to find other projects in the interim, so we worked on single family houses to develop our architecture and ideas. Challenging because there's a lot of competition in that market. You get maybe 10,000 euros and work for two years. It's almost like giving a gift to those clients. So we mostly do these today when we're inspired by a client's personality and they give us the freedom we need. We don't see any point in working on a standard one-family house – it's two years of your time on one project that serves only one family. We see architecture as very important within society. To bring people happiness and joy with urban design or public buildings is more rewarding.

TS: We also started with a tiny cabin, then won the competition for the Aurland Lookout. We've done about 30 houses now and it takes a lot of emotional energy. Our criteria is: do we learn something? Is it advancing our architecture? Is it financially viable? Do you have any examples of small public architecture, like the look-out towers, or the Kyly Sauna?

VH: In 2010 we created the Green shed range for Kekkilä Garden, a combination of greenhouse and storage space. It was a big success because nobody had done it before, and it was rewarding although it was a small-scale project because it was mass produced so the price could be lower. The project was intense but went on for many years. We had to do all the installation instructions, with all the different combinations – all things that architects never normally do! It took more than a thousand hours, if I remember rightly.

TS: We're also finding that smaller projects are more like products than a one-off idea. Was it worth it for you?

VH: Yes, definitely. We also worked in a group with other designers, which was refreshing.

TS: Were you the client?

VH: No. We had quite a strong client who challenged her company to do more lifestyle gardening projects, like tools and equipment. It worked well as they got a lot of press coverage. People in the city who were alienated from the soil really loved it. The do-it-yourself aspect was also really important.

TS: What did you believe when you were students that you don't believe any more, and vice versa?

Anu Puustinen: In Finland at that time, it wasn't a very encouraging atmosphere. There was more or less only one style of architecture. We are very pragmatic and the way of teaching here was as well. You could almost not speak about conceptual ideas because education was simply about designing buildings. For me at least it was very refreshing to be abroad in the Netherlands and find another way of working. I was at Delft for a year. It's good to see Finland from outside at one point in your life.

Previous page, left and below: Löyly, Hernesaari, Helsinki, Finland

We see architecture as very important within society. To bring people happiness and joy with urban design or public buildings is more rewarding.

— Ville Hara

FINLAND | AVANTO ARCHITECTS

Above and left: Löyly, Hernesaari, Helsinki, Finland

As a student I also had this turning point: I understood the difference between our view of architecture in Scandinavia versus the view in the Netherlands, where the landscape is almost entirely man-made. We have a natural landscape. Our architecture comes out of this landscape and an understanding of how to treat it. Then you understand why Dutch architecture wants to shout. We wanted to consider nature first. Nature is almost dominant. You are secondary.

TS: Many of the projects we work on are also based on geological time, not human time. When the building is gone the landscape still stays the same.

AP: After I lived in Rotterdam, I understood that the Dutch are more or less creating landscape when they create architecture. In Finland, architecture has always been very serious, and not playful at all.

TS: That's strange, because Aalto was very playful.

AP: Yes, but our teachers there were so serious. When we designed the Chapel, we had been abroad, but the project was still coming from a very traditional modernist background. There was a lot of symbolism, referencing earlier Finnish and Scandinavian cemetery chapels. The project doesn't try to hide that tradition. It is timeless, rather than contemporary.

TS: Always have one foot in the past – we're searching for the future, rather than creating a big gap with the past.

AP: Even that was too radical for some of the conservative people in the church.

TS: What things differentiate Finnish architects from other architects?

VH: It's very hard for us to be objective. For a start, it is also still a privilege to live in Northern countries. In 2017, on the hundredth anniversary of Finnish independence, we created a Finnish sauna in the city centre of Hong Kong for the people there. We felt like the city's quality of life wasn't that great, as there is so much stress and noise, so it seemed like a great idea. But it didn't work because people were given just five minutes to do the sauna ritual – they didn't even have time to change clothes and they just put a bathrobe on top of their normal clothes, went to the benches and took a selfie. I was disappointed at first because I wanted the project to be about peace and being present at the moment. But you cannot teach people how to live their lives. There is no right way.

TS: How does speed work as part of your process? I feel that your buildings invite people to take a pause – do you use the rhythm of life in your architecture?

VH: In architecture, with big gestures you can understand what a building is all about very quickly. We think ourselves into the building and go through the spaces, exploring the smell, the haptics, the acoustics and echoes all the senses are involved. Our culture is so dominated by visuality and it's very fast-paced. We did a competition for a sauna project to create a meditative space within a very defined volume. We divided the already small space into a series of spaces that become more and more intimate as you move from one space to another. The project was selected as a finalist, it was built at a design fair and it became a real place of retreat in the middle of a fair hall full of noise and visual disturbance. It was wonderful to see people reclined backwards on the sauna room bench, almost melting even though the heat wasn't on. Exactly as we had envisioned it. The power of architecture is huge, and we want to believe that we can use it to, say, comfort people who have lost somebody when they visit chapel.

TS: I feel that your architecture touches on emotions.

AP: Generally, the Finnish are not small talkers. However, we think emotions are very, very important, especially when you put yourself in the position of a user. The sequences of space, and how you move from one space to another is always a question. How do you guide people?

TS: When I first came to Scandinavia, I found this quietness very curious, but I really appreciate it now. I read somewhere that people can experience as many as 52 different emotions, and some of them are non-verbal. It seems that in Finland there's a real benefit to architecture that can explore these non-verbal emotions. You seem to have the best churches, the best saunas.

VH: Being silent has different meanings in different cultures. Here it means you are at ease, and comfortable and trusting of other people. But it's changing all the time.

TS: How are things different now to when you started out?

VH: I think we have lost some of our idealism. When young and naïve you think everything is possible – in a positive way. And sometimes we find out that our clients don't share our values.

A building is just something they build – they don't care how long it lasts or if it's ecologically sound, or if the people inside an industrial building even have basic things like windows.

As architects I think it's important for people to understand that buildings should last for a long time. Maybe the initial investment is a bit higher. If we only work with people who share our values, then we just operate in a bubble. We're more effective when our clients think in a different way. Some battles you lose, some you win. But it's more valuable to be where people don't understand the value of architecture.

We're more interested in quality than quantity, so our office isn't huge. I also hate speaking about sustainability because so much is spoken about it but so little is done. There's a lot of greenwashing around. We should be climate neutral by now, but our generation has to solve all these big questions. And architecture has a big responsibility – but also a lot of potential.

TS: If you could only do one more project, what would you build?

VH: It's possible to make something extraordinary out of very different typologies, whether a simple garden shed, or a cemetery chapel – we're very proud of that project as we've met so many people who have lost their loved one and they have told us that they have got comfort from the building in this very difficult moment.

AP: I was born in northern Finland – it's a beautiful part of the country – and I would love to bring something back to the community there. I'm not sure exactly what – perhaps a pilgrimage destination where you can have a quiet sauna or a dip into a clear lake. Something sustainable and very high quality.

This page: Löyly, Hernesaari, Helsinki, Finland

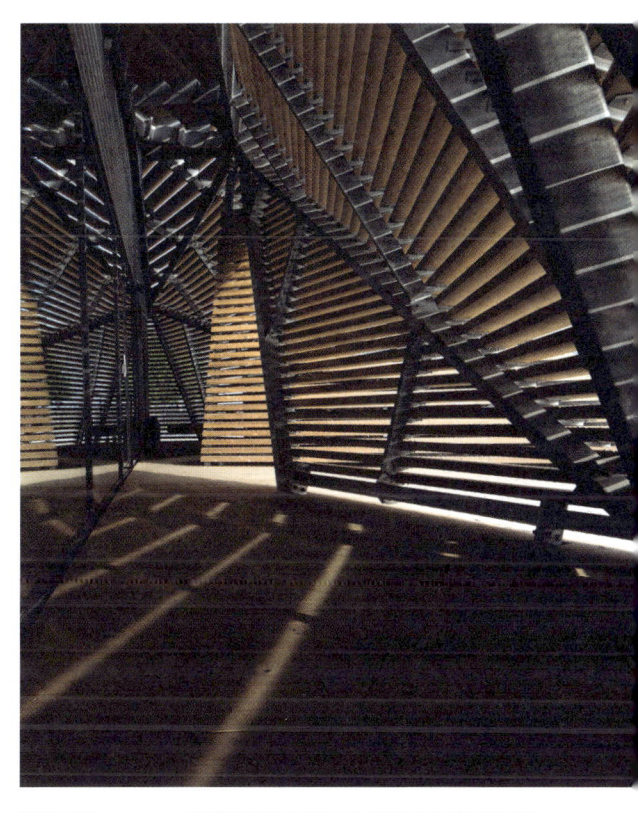

FINLAND | AVANTO ARCHITECTS

Right: Avanto Architects, Helsinki, Finland

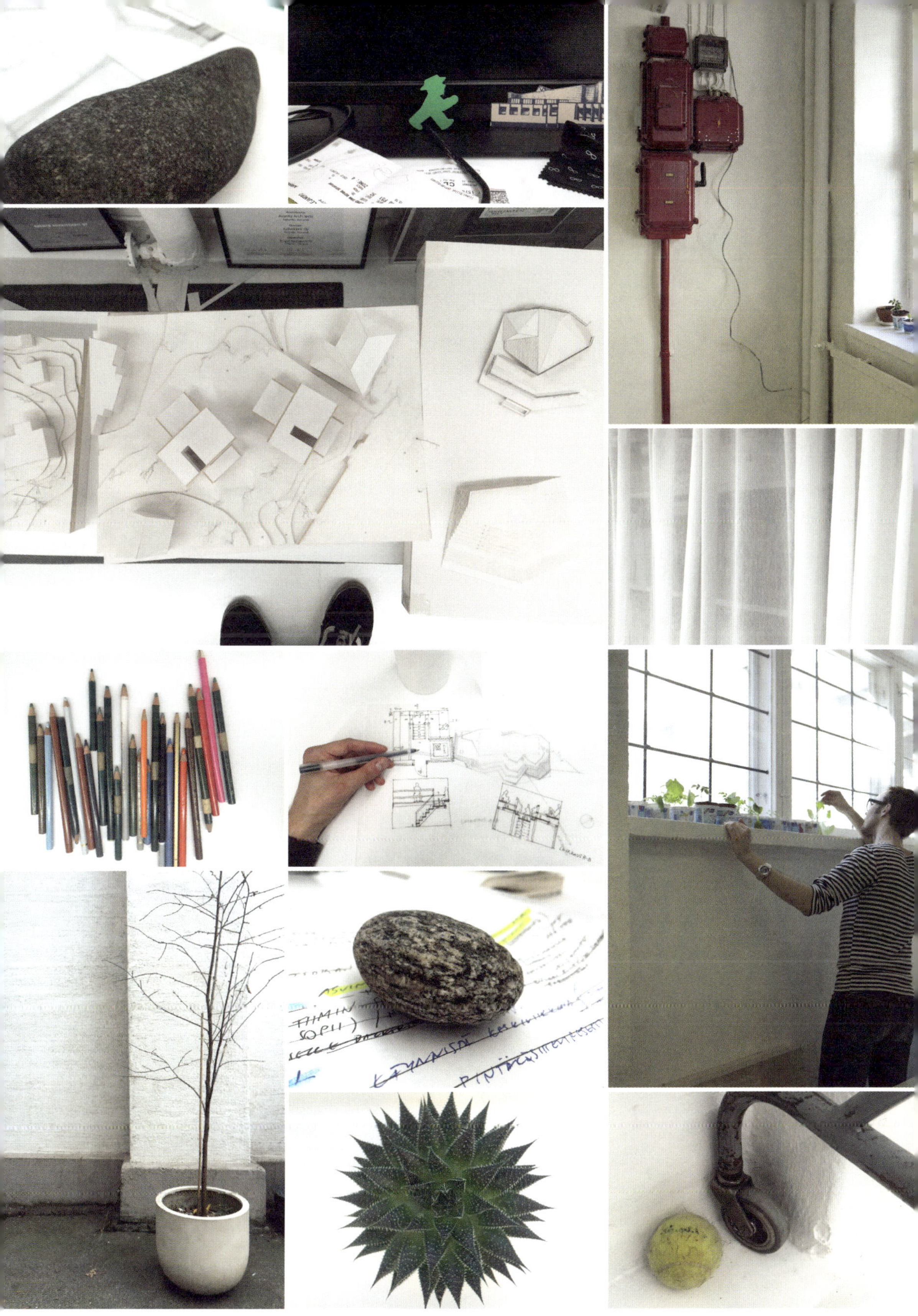

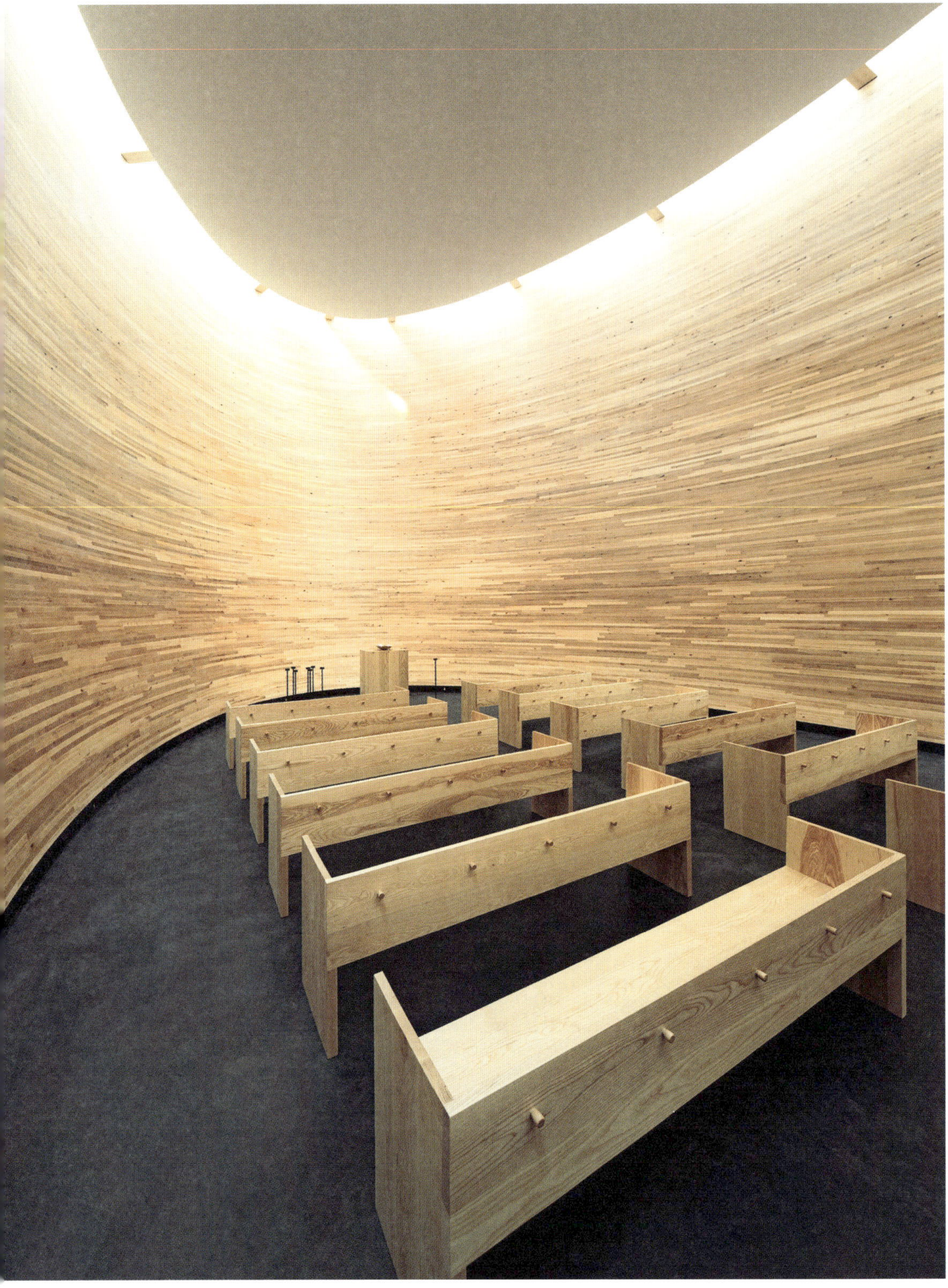

K2S Architects

K2S was founded by partners Kimmo Lintula, Niko Sirola and Mikko Summanen. Long-standing colleagues and friends, the trio also share a professorship at Aalto University in the Greater Helsinki region, combining teaching with practice. Their Helsinki studio has won more than fifty prizes and awards to date, making it one of the most acclaimed Finnish architecture practices. The firm describes its work as "resilient architecture with Finnish roots", carrying on the country's modernist tradition while also incorporating innovative new approaches and careful detailing. They bring a deep contextual understanding to every project, as well as diverse use of materials. Collaboration with other creatives, including architects and manufacturers, is also a key part of the K2S approach. The resulting buildings demonstrate a pleasant, warm functionality as well as unique spatial experiences. "K2S makes landmarks that embody Nordic wellbeing."

k2s.fi

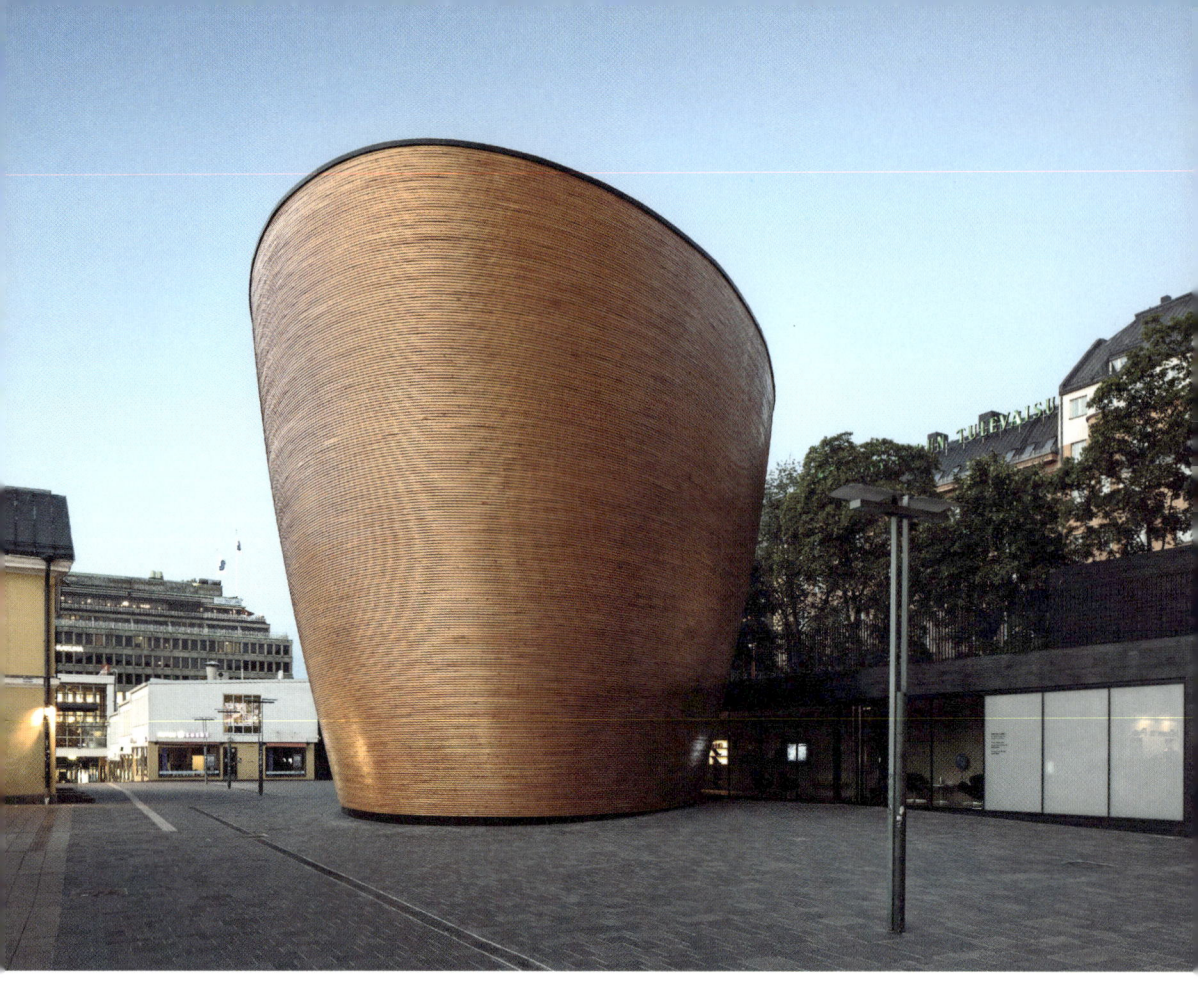

It has taken a long time to create a working environment where shared emotions can take on a physical presence, so they are a natural part of the creative process.

— Mikko Summanen

Previous page, left and below: Kamppi Chapel, Narinkkatori Square, Helsinki, Finland

TODD SAUNDERS: I'd like to start by asking how your firm deals with time. Do you manage your time well?

MIKKO SUMMANEN: Not always. But we share this professorship between the three partners in the office, which makes it a bit easier. It's unusual to share a professorship, but the university administration is very progressive in that respect.

TS: Did you study there?

MS: I studied in Tokyo for a year on an exchange programme, but I did my degree at the Helsinki University of Technology, which is now Aalto University.

TS: It seems like there's a lot of respect between Finnish architects for each other. Is there enough work there for everyone?

MS: Yes and no. There's a lot of competition for the best commissions.

TS: Let's discuss the Chapel in Kamppi. It's one of the best buildings I've ever visited.

MS: That was the first sacral building we completed. In that small building we realised many things that were important to us. We wanted to create an atmosphere of safety and contemplation – a secure, comfortable place for a human within a very hard, commercially orientated city. We can write down words or establish numbers and facts, but you have to be able to bring in the unexplainable, the emotional, the magical. To me, that's what architecture is about – and in the interior of the Chapel we feel we were able to materialise that feeling.

TS: Architectural education prioritises the technical, but our successful projects tend to touch on emotions. We try to find out the core of what a client needs, but sometimes it is unexplainable, an intuition that you can't teach.

MS: It is difficult to define. It's the essence of the creative process in our office which happens mainly between myself, Kimmo Lintula and Niko Sirola. It comes from a very long friendship with great mutual respect. It has taken a long time to create a working environment where shared emotions can take on a physical presence, so they are a natural part of the creative process. Of course, it is so much easier to discuss things that are concrete and mathematical and from the world of engineering and science. There is a gut feeling that something feels good and you can communicate it together, but it is difficult to analyse – how does that happen?

TS: When I've interviewed architectural duos and partnerships, everyone speaks of being in a place where partners have to align emotionally. Are there any buildings that you have visited together which gave you that shared feeling?

MS: It can come from a moment: in a bar when somebody's playing a certain song, or a snowfall in front of the office, or a shared everyday meal. When it comes to architecture, we might get that feeling and talk about it afterwards, although I'm not going to name any particular building.

TS: What about buildings of your own?

MS: We love construction sites, the smell of concrete and the scent of wood. There is an anticipation when the main space at a site is starting to take physical form. There's always some kind of a surprise – you might already have it in your head, but the space has to be experienced. About a year ago, we completed our longest-running project, the refurbishment and extension of the Helsinki Olympic Stadium. The first contract we signed was in 2003. Architecture is a patient person's discipline.

We had designed a canopy for the stadium – it was our first open competition victory. Seventeen years later we finally went to the stadium to see how the canopy looked when it was completed. It was a very powerful shared moment.

TS: How much does time weigh upon your design approach?

MS: Time is a twofold thing in my opinion. We recognise the enormous weight of responsibility, understanding that architecture exists for a long time. The longer a building exists, the more successful it is, and we should aim for that for obvious reasons of sustainability. Even more interesting is the great opportunity. Some of our most interesting projects are done in an already powerful context – all we are doing is writing the next chapter. For example, the Olympic Stadium or the Paasitorni Hotel. In virtually every case there is something old and valuable which we have to carefully analyse and understand.

TS: It's like philosophy. One philosopher gets to one point and then they die and the next person has to build on that.

MS: You might assume that the Kamppi Chapel is a tabula rasa – that we just built something new and contemporary on that site. But we're building on traditions, not just the tradition of wooden sacral buildings in the Finnish context. There are also traditions of philosophies, proportions, the use of light and material and the understanding of spatial relationships.

TS: Where are you on the line between contemporary and architectural tradition? Do you get a sense of doing a transition from one generation to the next?

MS: Maybe it's easier to answer if you're looking from outside. But when you talk about philosophers building on previous philosophies, that's sort of what we're trying to do: understand what was valuable before us and find out how to continue that story. Not by copying, but by adding our own point of view to that long narrative. From project to project there are different roots to the past.

TS: Which of your buildings do you feel will last the longest?

MS: I really haven't thought about it. We are constructing a new church in brick and wood in northern Finland which will be completed early next year. The lifespan of that building is meant to be 200 years, but I hope and believe that it will live for longer.

TS: It's a fantastic feeling going into these old stave churches – 800, 1,200 years old – in Norway. They're very simple, handmade and not so perfect.

MS: In Finland people are leaving the Church and then perhaps at some point in the future, they might not even be a house for a Christian God any more. Good architecture is versatile

This page: Fazer Experience Visitor Centre, Vantaa, Finland

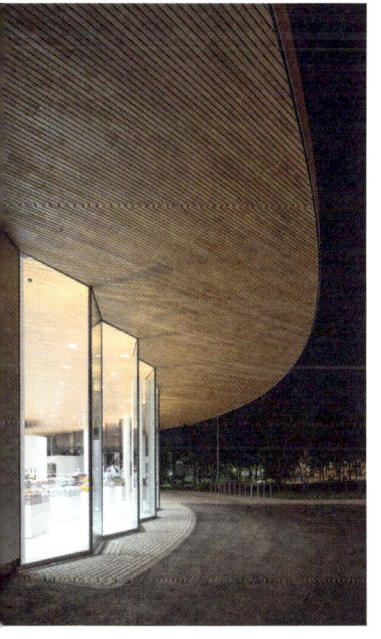

FINLAND | K2S ARCHITECTS

Above and left: Helsinki Olympic Stadium, Helsinki, Finland

– even with drastic functional changes, it can still have a future.

TS: What other types of building programme need to last a long time?

MS: If you design a building with very specific functions then it won't be very flexible or versatile. We want to create flexible spaces with an identity, with a soul. If people don't have a real emotional attachment to a building, then I don't believe it will last long, however flexible it is.

TS: What's the benefit of having three partners in your process?

MS: We got to know each other as students because we all played in the same band. Three of us formed K2S Architects and the other two members of the band went into the film industry, one as a director and one as a set designer. Playing in a band is a good metaphor for playing together in an architecture firm. You know your strengths and weaknesses and you know your role, yet you can sense what the other guys are playing.

TS: I miss playing ice hockey with the 17 guys I grew up with, from the age of 4 to 15. I could pass the puck to someone and just know they'd be there.

MS: I play ice hockey too, so I know that feeling. But with music, I play keyboards, Niko is a guitarist and Kimmo plays the drums. It was the early 1990s, so we were a surf rock grunge type of band.

TS: Apparently there's a model maker in Helsinki who was a well-known rock star. There are a bunch of bands who studied architecture and design. Talking Heads met at the Rhode Island School of Design.

MS: Pink Floyd too. Nick Mason, Roger Waters and Richard Wright all studied architecture. At K2S, we know each other well, but when we were younger there was too much conflict, not progressive conflict, and several years later we realised that this would not lead to anything good.

TS: Reaching that point of shared emotion must have felt fantastic. For single practitioners like me, with a boss and a team, it feels like there's always a glass wall somewhere.

MS: Usually the glass wall doesn't come from the boss, but from the people who work for you. We're trying to get rid of the wall to get the most out of people. However, sometimes it feels like they put that wall there as they can't lose the idea of a hierarchical situation.

TS: How do you look for new work?

MS: We have some direct commissions, as well as work we get through competitions. And then there's everyday work. Now we have the city of Helsinki as a client, as well as an energy company. There are also smaller commissions that probably won't be published but they're good, honest work.

TS: Do you feel like you're in the place you want to be at your age? Have you met your expectations as a company?

MS: If this was my last day as an architect – which it could be, you never know – then I feel that yes, I've achieved enough that I'd be content. But there's still a lot of hunger for things you want to do.

TS: Have you discussed these things in the office?

MS: Oh yes. Last summer one of our former clients invited us to a sauna. He does it every summer and it's always a night when we reflect on the past year. This client asked exactly the same question.

TS: It can be hard to define a finish line with work. When I did my own house I was the worst client I ever had. Have any of you designed your own house or office?

MS: No, our office is located in an old apartment building from the 1930s. We've been talking about building something together for several years. We're looking for a nice industrial space which we could transform. It's expensive to buy anything in Helsinki, though. But my question to you is: How were you able to reach the finish line and decide that had to be built?

TS: It took two years, but basically my family needed a home. I'm quite used to building my own projects though – I also have a series of summer houses on a peninsula near Bergen. It's a slow project but it's helped me slow things down in general.

MS: It sounds like it's a fantastic R&D project for yourself and the office.

TS: Aalto had a summer house as well, where he experimented with his architecture.

MS: Yes, an experimental summer house as well. But the biggest reason for that was he got a lot of tax deductions because he called it an experimental house. So it was also a financial decision for Aalto.

TS: Can you tell me a bit more about your floating office project for Arctia?

MS: This was a direct commission from the shipping company who run Finland's icebreaker fleet. Finland is the only country whose ports freeze during the winter – every other country has some open ports but if the Baltic freezes, then we don't have any ports. It's a lifeline for Finland to have a good icebreaker fleet. A couple of years ago the shipping company called as they wanted their own headquarters right next to the icebreakers on the docks. We started by locating the office on the docks, but it was too hard to build there. So we suggested making it a floating office building, as if it were one of the ships in their fleet. The architecture grew from those ships, with their black hulls. We made custom aluminium façades like abstract ice particles. The interiors are clad in wood, which references traditional ships with their soft geometry, and then there's a more rigid steel hull on the outside. The structure is kept level by a ballast tank at each corner. It was very convenient to work with a shipping company as they had all the right connections – it was actually more like shipbuilding than architectural construction.

TS: It sounds like you're experienced at using experts from outside architecture.

MS: I think that's really a lifeline for a small architect office, to connect and cooperate with all the best specialists in every field. We also cooperate with other architecture offices to stay versatile and small. We're only 12 people in the office. Everybody knows each other.

TS: How do you work with other companies?

Below and bottom: Helsinki Olympic Stadium, Helsinki, Finland

FINLAND | K2S ARCHITECTS

Above, left and opposite:
Helsinki Olympic Stadium,
Helsinki, Finland

MS: It depends on each project. We recently won second prize in an urban planning competition. We worked very democratically with another architect office and we could say that both offices share authorship. Maybe with a single building it would be more challenging.

TS: Your work still feels fresh, that you're still growing. What would be your dream project?

MS: Even small or "insignificant" projects are adventures. I'd like to complete my own summer house. We have a small island on a lake in Finland which contains several old buildings. I've drawn up plans for a small house with a sleeping cabin for my daughters, a work room for me and my wife, who designs sportswear. And a place to practice Gyotaku, a Japanese graphic method of recording the fish you caught. I have 20 or 30 different sketch versions of the house, so that's the one building I need to complete.

Right: K2S Architects, Helsinki, Finland

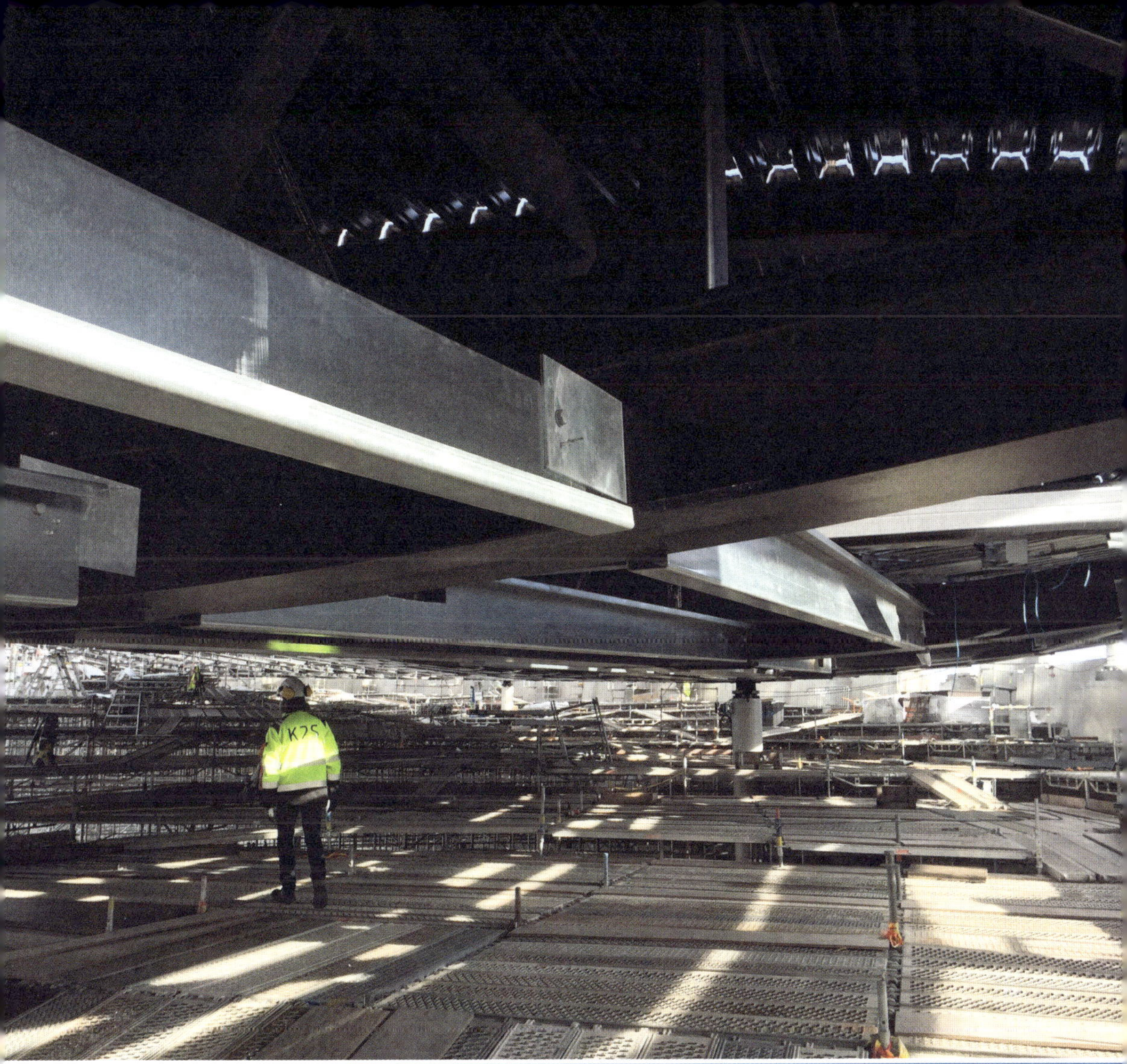
K2S

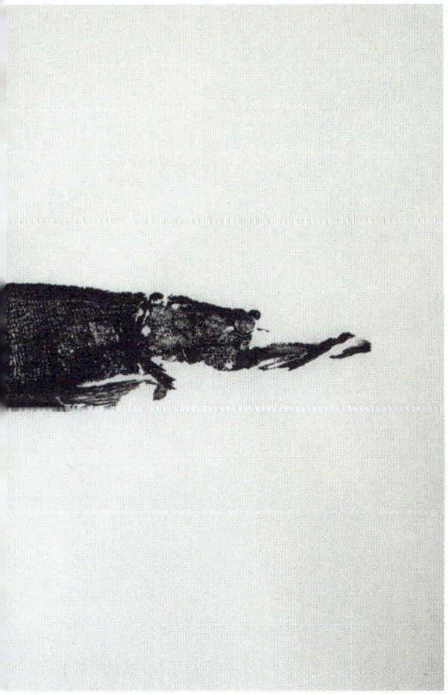

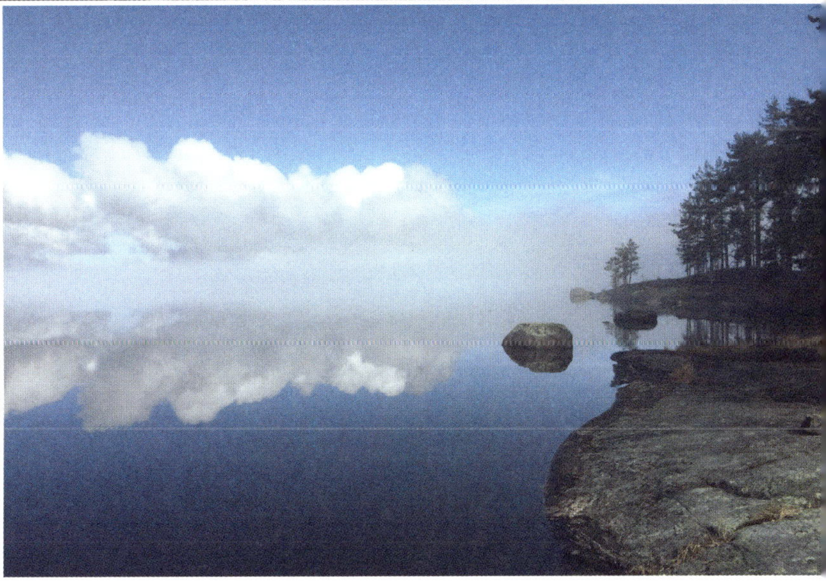

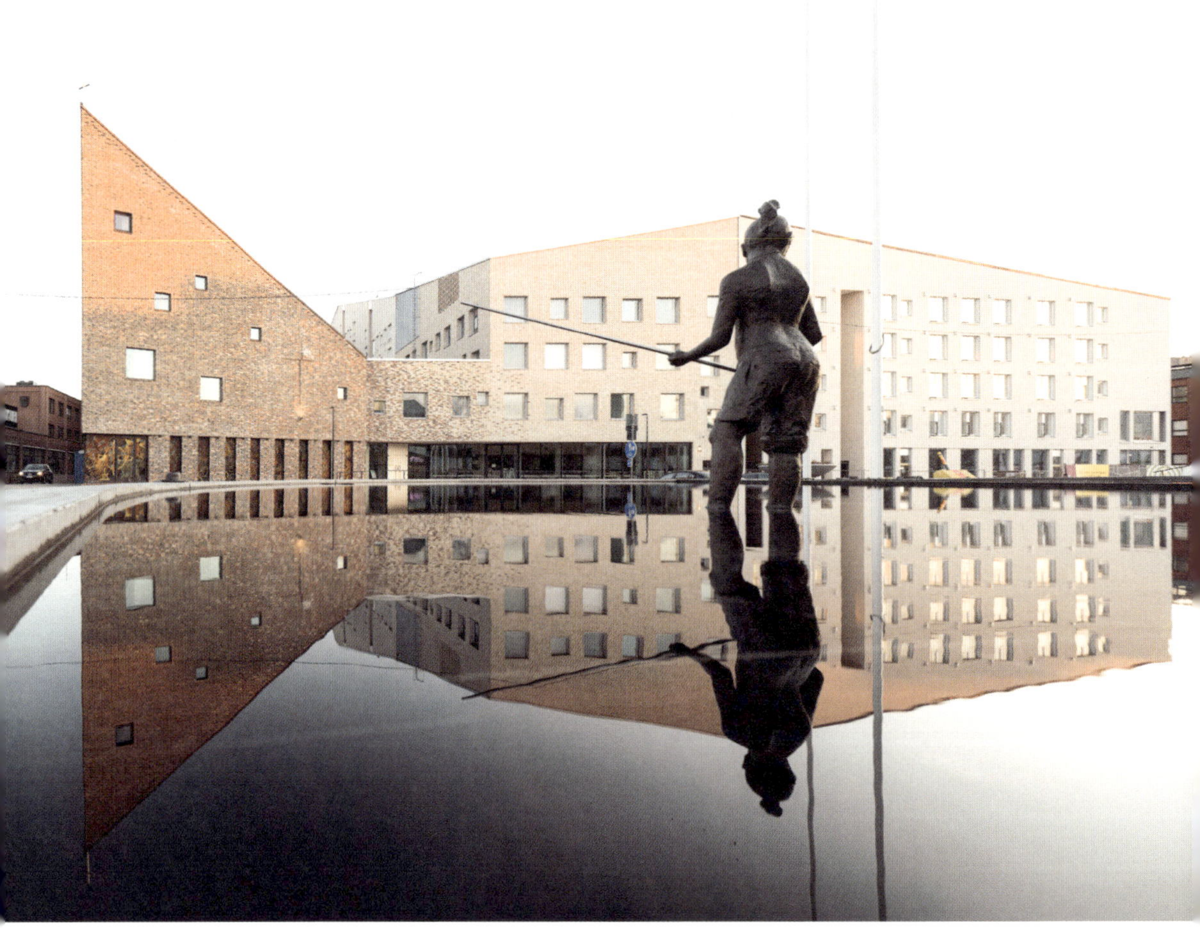

OOPEAA

The OOPEAA Office for Peripheral Architecture was set up by Anssi Lassila in 2001, who was still a student when the studio's breakthrough project, the Kärsämäki Shingle Church (2004), won in a competition. At first the office operated under two different names, and since 2014 it has had the name of OOPEAA. The practice's work explores the limits of materials, new solutions and ways of working, without losing sight of traditional processes and methods. Experimentation with wood has become a key part of the studio's aesthetic, from highly hand-crafted projects through to developing new custom modular systems. OOPEAA has used traditional methods in projects like the Kärsämäki Church and the Lonna Sauna, along with Cross Laminated Timber in its urban housing projects. The team is composed equally of women and men, with around one-third of staff coming from abroad. The studio breaks projects down into teams and is based in two locations, Helsinki and Seinäjoki. In 2015, the studio won the Finlandia Prize for Architecture and the Wood Architecture Award and has been shortlisted for the European Union Prize for Contemporary Architecture Mies van der Rohe Award on a number of occasions.

oopeaa.fi

Previous page: Tikkurila Church and housing, Tikkurila, Vantaa, Finland

This page: Villa Koivikko, Espoo, Finland

> Yeah, nature is my church in a way. It's a really good way to escape from the architecture.
>
> — Anssi Lassila

Todd Saunders: You and I are from roughly the same generation – we're effectively halfway through our careers. This is a chance to look back and see what we learned, and see what we're going to do next. As well as practising, you teach at the University of Oulu, is that right?

Anssi Lassila: Yes, I'm a professor of practice in contemporary architecture at the architecture school. It's great to see the young generation and communicate with them. It's a fresh experience to be teaching.

TS: Have you ever employed students that you've taught?

AL: Not yet, because I just started. But it is a good way of attracting talented people to come to work with you.

TS: When I look at your Instagram pages, and how you draw, I see all these hand sketches. Whereas I always have my iPad right next to me. I use this program called Morpholio Trace – like using tracing paper.

AL: Yeah. I use a tracing program these days. I also downloaded this 3D program, but I don't really use it much.

TS: I use Shapr3D. It's really good – I learned it in over three evenings by myself. I discovered if I spend one hour in that program it saves my staff eight hours.

AL: I suppose because it's easier to create 3D models? If you just make hand drawings for people to model from, there's almost always some kind of misunderstanding or catch. But sometimes a misunderstanding can be a good way to develop a solution, because we are not perfect.

TS: No one is. I agree – a team sometimes reinterprets things in their own way and sometimes nice surprises come out of it.

AL: Misunderstandings and mistakes can be good ways of working towards the solution. They are just different ways of thinking.

TS: Are you open to talking about mistakes in public and with your staff?

AL: Of course. We try to share things so we don't repeat the same mistakes every time. It's not easy when you have a small office and draw everything, handling all the details and communicating with the contractors. When the office grows bigger and you get older, it can be very stressful and hard to be responsible for everything.

TS: So you run the office by yourself?

AL: Yes. I'm the only partner in the office.

TS: Same as me. When you have more than one partner, someone can have a bad day and it's okay. But for me and you, when we're alone, it's very hard for us to have a bad day at the office.

AL: It is not easy to have a rest or get some distance when you're responsible on your own without the possibility to share responsibilities with someone else. It's easier if you have a partner.

TS: What do you like about working the way you do?

AL: I started my office in 2001. At first, there was my partner with me, and we built our first building after I won the church competition. But after that I wanted to keep going in a different direction. It happened quite naturally. But you must be very honest with yourself, and the people working around you. It's a straight and honest way to work, to be responsible for everything. But it's also hard that way because it is difficult to get distance. And somehow the office becomes a part of you when you are the sole owner.

TS: The director David Lynch has something called "The Art Life", where his life and his work feel like they are moulded together. I think you have a balance – you take time out to go skiing, and you seem to be honest when you need to take time in nature.

AL: Yeah, nature is my church in a way. It's a really good way to escape from the architecture. You don't even see any buildings – it's a little bit like people who sail for the whole summer.

TS: They just get away from it all.

AL: Yes. Before the pandemic, we were all travelling a bit too much – you get more and more invitations, you might have a project in another country. And you don't stop travelling at all. But even during that time, when I could get into nature, I felt, "Okay, now I have some force again."

TS: Tell me about your use of wood. I never considered myself a wood specialist, but it seems most of my work uses wood. In Finland, it seems wood is the main material.

AL: It is available and cheap, and you can also find people with skills to do almost anything using wood. For us, it's more natural to make a wooden building than to use concrete or any other material.

TS: With the Kärsämäki Shingle Church though, were you involved in building it yourself? Because it was all handmade and carved, it was really beautiful.

AL: Well, it was a student competition in university. It had to be handmade and use local materials. At first, I thought it was an awful brief, because you couldn't do fancy new architecture using those things. But when I started drawing and thinking and resourcing and trying to understand it, my thinking changed completely. You can do everything if your people just build by hand and use the material in a very clever way. There are no limitations.

TS: I was so fascinated with that building, because it was modern, and handmade. Have you done any other buildings like that?

AL: The church was a unique case. We're still trying to find ways to combine manufacturing with hand processes. We're currently building a villa extension in the east of Finland, a structure that dates from 1900, the Russian era. We have built an extension next to this super decorated wooden villa. The primary structure is CLT but the exterior walls are handmade red panels of shingles. This kind of combination is more typical than a purely handmade building. We did a sauna project that was totally handmade. But usually it's only for unique situations and rich people.

TS: How do you slow things down without it becoming very expensive?

AL: I use great carpenters and I have connections with amazing furniture makers and joiners. You just need to have a client who can afford to do that kind of thing over time. It's the only way to make a very interesting product.

FINLAND | OOPEAA

Previous page, above and right: Puukuokka housing block, Jyväskylä, Finland

Opposite: Kärsämäki shingle church, Kärsämäki, Finland

TS: We have had a couple of clients build their own projects. Maybe this also happens in Finland? Many Norwegians can build things themselves, when they have time and money. It is fantastic to watch a client build their own house because they can put in a lot of love. Typically, our projects take one year to build, but these self-built projects can run for three years.

AL: That also happens in Finland. Many of the generation born in the '40s and '50s have built their own houses. But it's becoming rarer in our generation and the generations that followed. Today I think people want to use their time in a totally different way. And they no longer have those kinds of skills.

TS: It's a bit sad in a way.

AL: There are different kinds of skills. Today, we have experts who work with a computer rather than by hand. That's just what happens between generations.

TS: The architect Juhani Pallasmaa used to talk about the relationship between the hand and architecture. Are you still getting projects that require a level of handicraft?

AL: For our first few years, it was possible with small-scale projects to really make things and communicate directly with the makers and do very nice detailing. This doesn't happen on a large scale because things become more and more pragmatic. It's different to simply needing more skilled work.

TS: In Scandinavia, everyone I speak to seems to have a different approach. I thought many firms would have some little things in common.

AL: In my office we have architects who studied in Japan and elsewhere. When they come to Finland, they initially think the whole of Scandinavia is very similar, but there are quite big differences between the cultures.

There are very different histories, for example, and all this is reflected in the buildings and construction methods.

TS: What do you feel will be your personal contribution to architecture?

AL: What we do isn't really about big change. When I was young, of course I thought our work would be much more revolutionary.

TS: What do buildings actually change? If anything, it's slow change, I think.

AL: Here's an example. I also have an office in the west of Finland, in Seinäjoki. It's sort of in the middle of nowhere with very simple, beautiful period buildings. There was a competition to extend the library, maybe ten years ago, and it was won by a firm from Helsinki. I was interviewed when it was finished because they wanted to see how this one building might influence the local architecture. Would it evolve and become better? What would happen? In the end? One building alone will not change much. However, if you build something that is contextual and of high quality, it will influence people by making them feel better about themselves in these places. So ultimately the meaning of architecture is that it is for the people who use the buildings.

TS: The church you designed made a big impact on me and I was only there for a few minutes. It was enough to see that we can still make modern, handmade architecture and it took me a long time to get to that point. It was almost like you set the standard and gave me hope.

AL: I think that's almost the only meaningful thing that architects can do – have a positive influence on how we perceive places.

Left and below: Kärsämäki shingle church, Kärsämäki, Finland

Right: OOPEAA, Helsinki and Seinäjoki, Finland

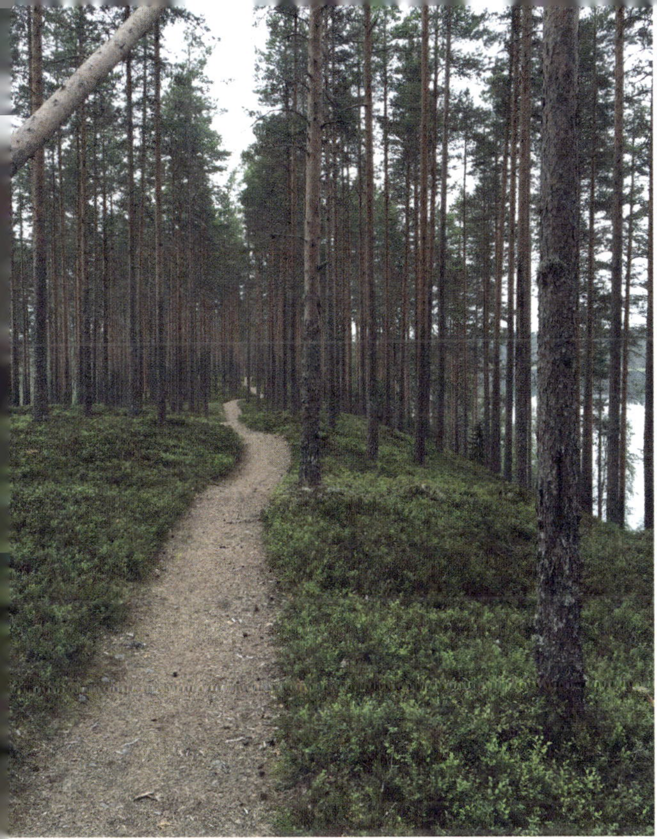
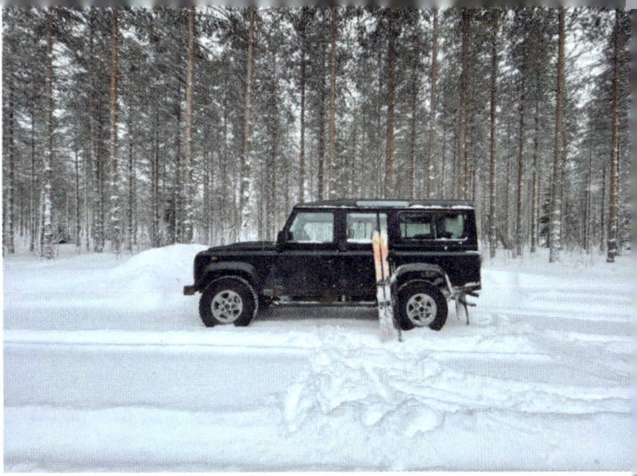
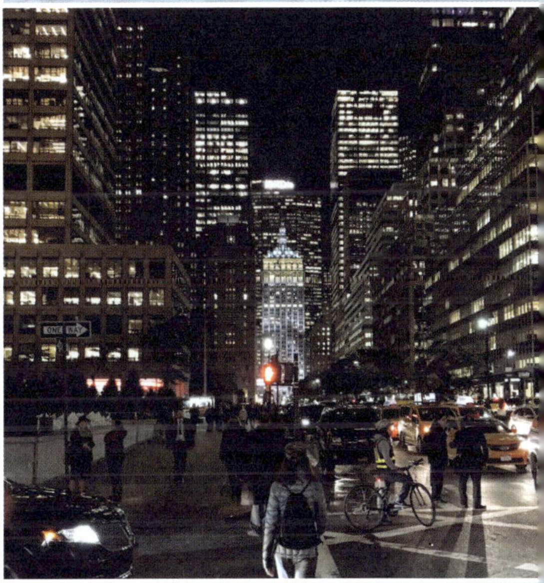
ONE WAY
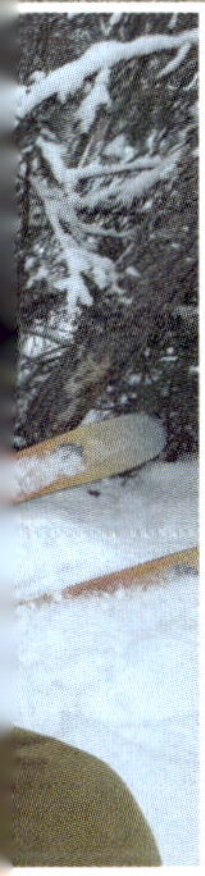
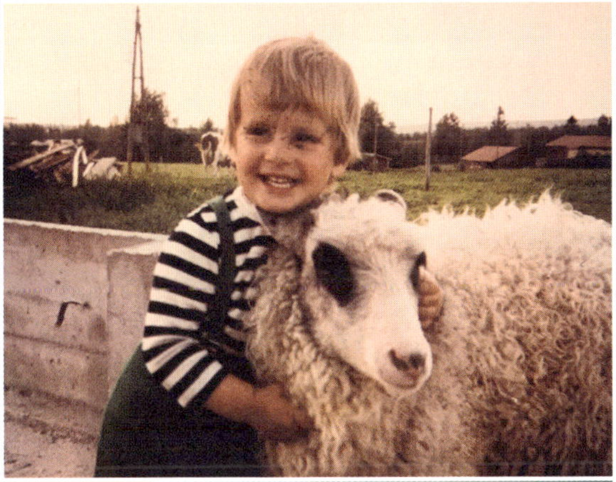
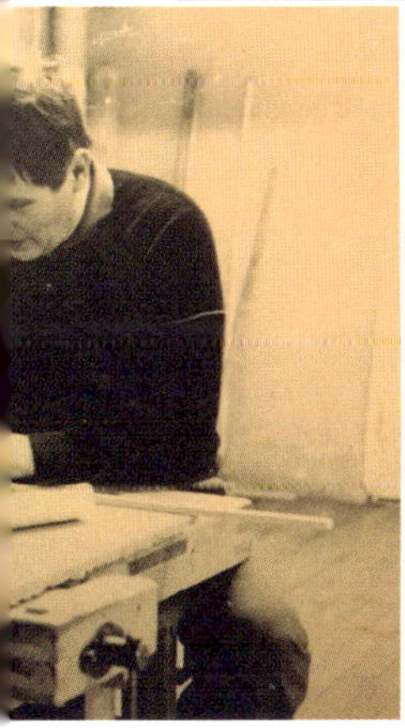
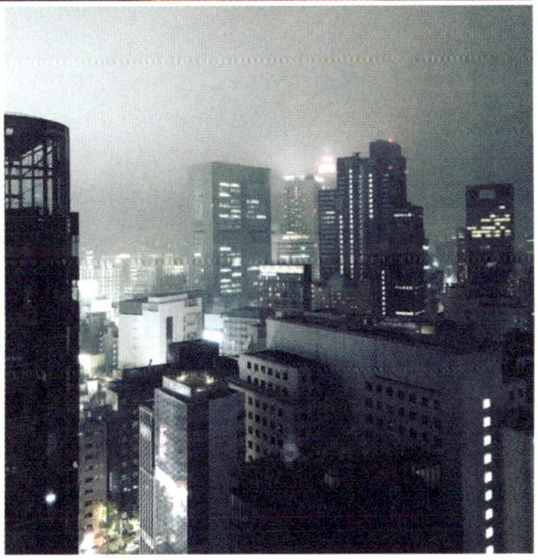
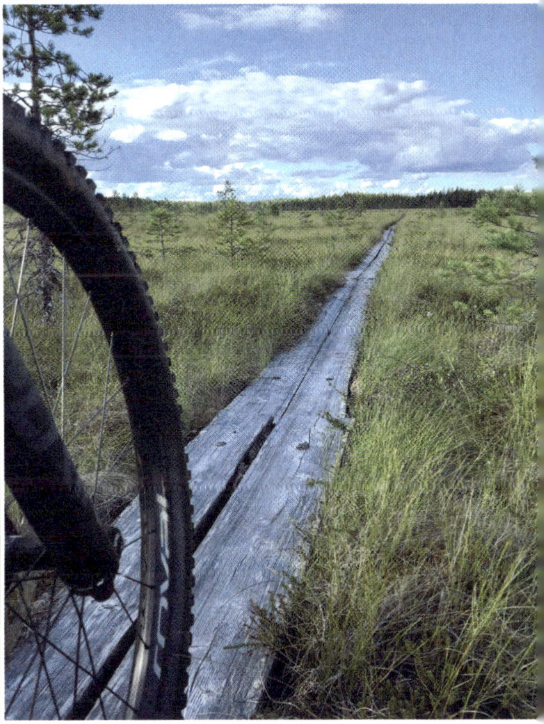

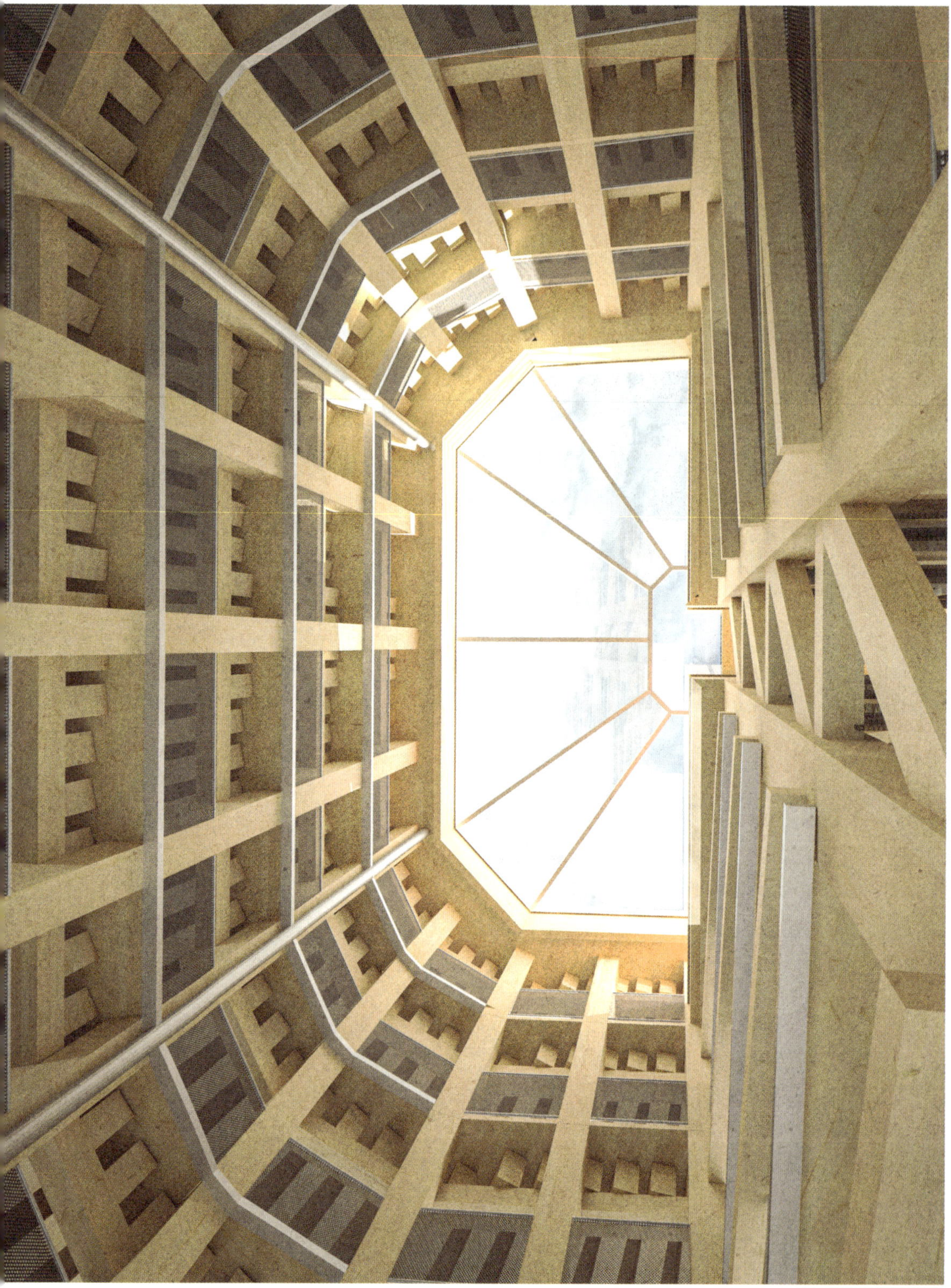

Planetary Architecture

Finnish architect Pekka Pekkanen founded Planetary Architecture in 2019, after 11 years as a partner in Huttunen-Lipasti-Pakkanen Architects. He began his career at Nurmela-Raimoranta-Tasa Architects in Helsinki, before spending a year at Atelier Peter Zumthor as a project architect. Since 2002, he has been teaching in the Departments of Building Technology, Landscape Architecture and Timber Architecture at the Aalto University in Espoo. He also writes and curates, with a special focus on new technology for timber architecture. "In every project we see our planet as one of the clients," says Pakkanen, and the studio's work explores not just the structural potential of timber, but also architecture's role in creating a zero-carbon circular economy. Current projects include the Serlachius Museum Gösta in Mänttä, and the Versowood Headquarters in Vierumäki.

planetary.fi

Previous page: Modular timber parking garage system, Helsinki and Vantaa, Finland

Below and bottom: VIS hybrid house design concept, 2021

TODD SAUNDERS: Can you tell me about your new firm?

PEKKA PEKKANEN: I started a new office two years ago and we are still quite small. Half of us are online working from home. I hated lockdown. The video calls kill all the creativity. But I'm in an exciting new phase. In our previous office, architecture was always about style – trying to find the answer for each programme and plot and for each case. That worked well for over a decade, but then I felt like I hit a wall.

TS: I can relate to that.

PP: I was the chief designer of a long, difficult project in downtown Helsinki, the Allas Sea Pool. The client never had enough money for it, and then it was split into different phases. And each phase, the constructors and other designers left. The client was really challenging, so I had a lot of responsibility. It was low-budget and hard work for about three or four years. After that, I felt I had nothing to give to anybody. So I just had to leave, but I had no Plan B.

TS: Had you been thinking about leaving for a while?

PP: It was dramatic, but sometimes in life the worst things become the best. In Silicon Valley, there's a school called the Singularity University, which looks at where artificial intelligence becomes wiser than human intelligence and examines how exponential growth can be utilised in different areas. My wife entered the X Prize Visioneering competition called Feeding the Next Billion, and was invited to take it further so we went to California and worked together on it for seven or eight months. We gathered a team of scientists from Finland and from and Silicon Valley. I was sure that they would tell us at some point, "You don't know anything about this stuff. Just go home." But in the end, we won the whole thing.

TS: Congratulations.

PP: It was a huge thing. We were looking at how to feed the global population increase of one billion over the next 12 years. Most agricultural land is already used so you cannot really grow more crops. Something completely different must happen, and we suggested using soil-less tech food production techniques. You recycle the water and the nutrients. These methods were always really energy intensive, but today solar power prices are coming down, so the curves will meet. The whole point of our entry was how to produce proteins – vertical farms are always about salads and herbs. The whole field is changing dramatically.

TS: What are the best plant-based proteins for that system?

PP: Soy is of course one of the best for protein. There are also techniques where people can grow either meat cells or proteins as themselves in the laboratories. One of our most exciting projects has been with a Finnish startup called Solar Foods. They capture CO_2 from the air, and then cook it with bacteria to get protein as a powder that can be put into any food. Our starting point for architecture is similar in a way. We figure out what needs to be done, and then we find the team and the players and then keep it conceptual as long as is needed. And also accept that it might never turn into a project. But we are trying.

TS: There's a lot of joy in that. We're at a time of our lives – we're about the same age – where existential crises are quite common. Kierkegaard said something like the existential crisis has to happen in order to become a wiser and more evolved person.

PP: You need to have meaning. I was fortunate to drop into this world outside architecture. Every morning when I'm coming to work, I've been loaded with energy.

TS: How did you use your architecture tools in that project?

PP: In the Xprice Visioneering it was about defining the meaningful questions, and also an architect can basically do many things – we can survive in chaos that for many people would be really stressful. The learning process is reading a lot, then mixing and matching and picking the right pieces. It was like architecture but not so visual.

TS: Like picking apart a problem, breaking it down and approaching it in different ways?

PP: As well as a team of experts I used the usual skills of any project management, working on different tasks and then coming up with conclusions that would feed the big picture.

TS: When the Norwegian State Oil Company built their headquarters in Oslo, they didn't use the standard construction industry tender and building process. Instead, they used the same method they had for building oil refineries. It was built much faster and on budget. This hybrid approach is super exciting.

PP: I used to worry about how to stay excited. When you're younger, the world is about typologies – airports and apartment buildings, shops and service stations. But that's really limited. Now new things have opened up. One project I'm currently working on is promoting the use of wood and trying to find different ways to use it – it's like opening a door to a new world.

TS: Our biggest strength as architects is to ask questions. Today's most successful businesses didn't even exist 15 years ago. What happens when you don't use the standard typologies?

PP: Exactly. How do you build for a fast-changing world? How do you prepare for the unknown?

TS: My interest now also incorporates the social entrepreneurship side of things. How can a building make money for a community rather than taking from it?

PP: That sounds so good.

TS: Then the question is: How do you do that? And where are you putting your knowledge to work?

PP: If you can't push and make that change, then what do you have? Every project is always a new adventure anyway, so you might have something built or you might have an interesting concept, or you might not have anything. But it's all about just trying, trying and trying, and keeping your own mind excited.

TS: The curiosity is the effort. The learning from mistakes. It's like a building in a magazine is just a picture. It does not tell you anything. The process of getting there tells you it all.

Below: Removable sauna

Below: Design concept for Solar Foods, 2020

Every project is always a new adventure anyway, so you might have something built or you might have an interesting concept, or you might not have anything. But it's all about just trying, trying and trying, and keeping your own mind excited.

— Pekka Pekkanen

That's where I feel architecture isn't honest enough yet.

PS: In the Helsinki architecture scene it often feels that showing your inner feelings might demonstrate weakness or lack of knowledge. But if you just show the final project and you don't open up, your building is a wrapped package that is semi-meaningless for most of us.

TS: Eero Koivisto of Claesson Koivisto Rune Architects in Stockholm told me that he now only buys architecture books if they're about one building. There's a need for more honesty and depth and sharing your experiences in architecture.

PP: Those are the most valuable learning experiences, when you get hurt the most.

TS: Architects have a high tolerance for pain. We're like push, push, push. You can't really break someone who's gone through architectural education.

PP: The most painful moments are out of your control. How much of your impact is outside of the work you do? Through your teaching, for example.

TS: I'm teaching at Yale this Fall [2021] and the topic will be: How can architecture instigate change? How do you personally do it through teaching?

PP: I'm teaching about wood in architecture, its material qualities. I think understanding systems help to get somewhere and make an impact. But you have to choose your battle. We're also looking at renewables and recycling. There are so many rules and regulations that are against it happening, as well as the logistics and the general economy. The projects that we're working on are about deeper systems. We're doing a parking house in Helsinki.

TS: The whole thing is in wood?

PP: Yes, but all the joints are mechanical so you can make extensions, make it smaller, relocate the whole thing. How do you work with architecture that is not built for a specific plot? Then it's just a matter of not building it in this engineering, logical sense but really putting a soul into it. The oldest surviving examples of architecture are there because they're loved. So how can you build a system that will end up being loved?

TS: So people will take care of it?

PP: Exactly.

TS: With that parking house you're creating, if you can persuade people to love that, then it's easier to get them to love other buildings.

PP: I see similarities between your Fogo project and the vernacular architecture on the island that was purely functional. There was nothing else but function.

TS: Yes, it was all about needs.

PP: So how can the fair, clean but functional design of contemporary architecture also have soul? This is a vital question for our era. Every structure is using some system, so you could turn that system to the gain of the users.

TS: If you look at a hammer or an axe for example, those have been tools for thousands of years. That's our goal – to make things that

Opposite: Timber tower for a ski resort

really work, are really useful, and that function well.

PP: If you give a damn, then somebody else will as well.

TS: I think that's why we got so much leverage on Fogo – it was a functional building and a functional idea, both in terms of economics. But there was also care. How do you know that a building is made with care?

PP: If you visit a piece of architecture, you feel immediately in your guts if it has been made with special care.

TS: I felt it with places in Norway, for example, and in Morocco. With handmade buildings, if you sense that someone took the effort to cut down a tree and put a building together, you have a respect for the craft and history.

PP: It's about respect for the material. On an intellectual level we should be aware we're overusing material at the moment. But you should value every piece of material that has been produced at some point. There's potential for the next approach to architecture. How do you mix together the pieces that exist so that you come up with, unseen, something unique?

TS: It's like your idea of changing systems. Maybe there should be legislation that parking houses will only be made from wood from now on, not concrete. Wood therefore never becomes garbage – it has to be reused.

PP: Thinking about a circular economy is rising dramatically as we speak. Change is so slow in construction so it will take some decades before it happens, although I'm sure it is inevitable. Personally, I welcome it. It offers us possibilities to find new ways of using existing materials.

TS: When you take a standpoint on something, interested clients come to you. We should be more decisive.

PS: The beauty of architecture is that you are free to use any material for any place. This is my path now.

TS: What's the biggest barrier to using wood instead of concrete?

PP: Fire protection, although this has been solved. Originally, we wanted to find out cost, whether it would be equal to concrete. There are no real reasons why you should not use wood for parking houses. Our cost calculations are only for construction – they don't consider the lifespan. If you look at that, then wood wins 1,000 to zero. I've also been wondering about typologies of wooden buildings. It's getting more popular to do large housing projects in wood. Some typologies are always built of concrete, for technical reasons. We're working with researchers who are developing wood products to be used underground for foundations. We're working on this off-grid house that is built of wood, half the house is underground. It's producing its own oxygen. It's growing its own food and most of the baring structures are of wood.

TS: What typologies do you think are easy to do in wood right now?

PP: Daycare centres, schools. That's a no-brainer. They're being produced already and there are several techniques that can be used for those. For housing there are all sorts of semi-temporary buildings.

FINLAND | PLANETARY ARCHITECTURE

Below: Vertical Natura house

Bottom: Removable sauna in use

TS: What are you teaching next semester?

PP: We have a module on recyclable and reusable projects so students can come up with their own programme and transform it into something else or relocate it. Next autumn it will be under the umbrella of timber architecture. The results were really good.

TS: Before, architects just wanted to get the nice photos and get out of there. Now you have to consider the life cycle of your building. Remember all the phases from sketch project to construction documents and then as-built drawings? Perhaps there should be a phase that asks, "What's happening to this building in 100 years?"

PP: It's a natural continuation of the design phase. Usually, the magical images that represent architecture in magazines and online, are taken before anybody moves in and starts using the building. It's a moment that does not exist. It would be more interesting to follow the life of a building.

TS: Maybe that's a challenge for your students. How will your building get better? How can it be used in another place? All the questions that are not asked after the as-built drawings are finished.

PP: Once you've asked those questions, then you'll also define architecture in the new meaningful sense. It's not about design, but something greater. As an architect, what are you most afraid of?

TS: I came to Bergen with nothing, no money. Now I speak Norwegian, I have friends and contacts but that fear of having nothing is still real. I learned the value of money, that you don't need that much. So in a way my career has not been based on wants, more on needs. That fear is going away now.

PP: Is your plan to enjoy it or are you still planning to push yourself?

TS: I'm too curious to take it easy. But I think it's time to focus on one thing at a time and to slow down a bit.

PP: Most fears are unreal. Maybe every now and again experiencing a real fear – like with ice climbing – puts the fear of failure into perspective.

TS: Bruce Mau said something about "make mistakes faster". I used to think mistakes sounded too negative, but now I see them as situations to learn from. Fear is normal. In architecture, you have to accept that there is risk.

PP: Do you ever have to mentally prepare yourself to be strong to make a point, whether it's a meeting with a client or contractor or somebody?

TS: I have a couple of techniques. Before the meeting, I write down what important things I want out of it, so it's very clear from the beginning. It's tested all the time, but if you know what you need and want out of a project it's a bit easier.

PP: There is often sort of trading in these situations. Like in politics, you have to figure out what are you after. In some cases, you have to slide it in from a side door.

TS: I don't mind having straight up conversations. I think people relate to you better if you are very clear.

PP: Maybe the client, but with some manufacturers or when somebody's selling you something, if they know what makes you tick, then the most important thing can suddenly become quite expensive. In our previous office, one client was a construction company. They were sort of nightmarish, no interest or understanding for architecture. You had to be strong to counter them and I had a technique of being a "power animal". You go into a meeting and decide that you are a moose. Nobody fucks with a moose!

TS: Nobody messes with a moose, but a moose is slow and quiet.

PP: But it also can make random moves. That worked for me, deciding to be this large animal. When I would say something, people would listen.

TS: I've noticed some of my successful older clients don't go in aggressively and powerfully. They're low and calm but they know what they need, and they stick to that. That's why I want to do this architecture and philanthropy part, because the clients have the right motivations. It sounds like you want to have clients that think about architecture in the long term.

PP: I have had a career of doing what I was asked to do. Now this is where it turns meaningful.

TS: My way of working has evolved into being the person that pursues what they want and how they can contribute to architecture.

PP: I certainly feel relieved now that the world inside my head is becoming more intellectual than physical.

Right: Planetary Architecture, Helsinki, Finland

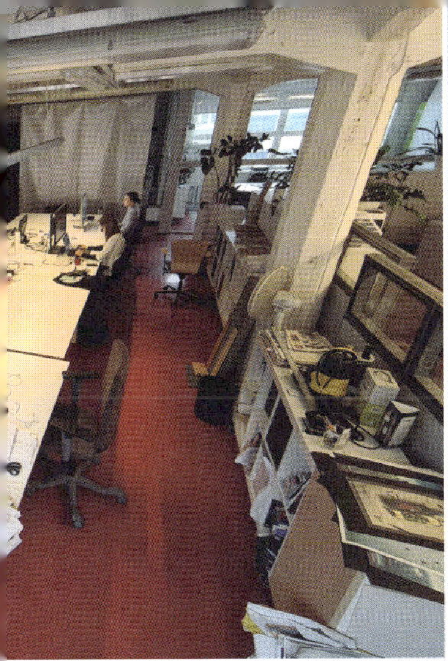

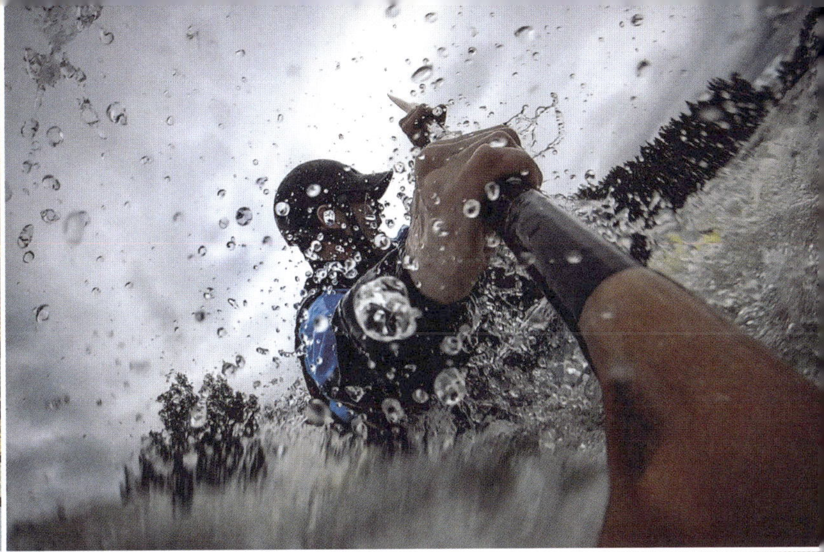

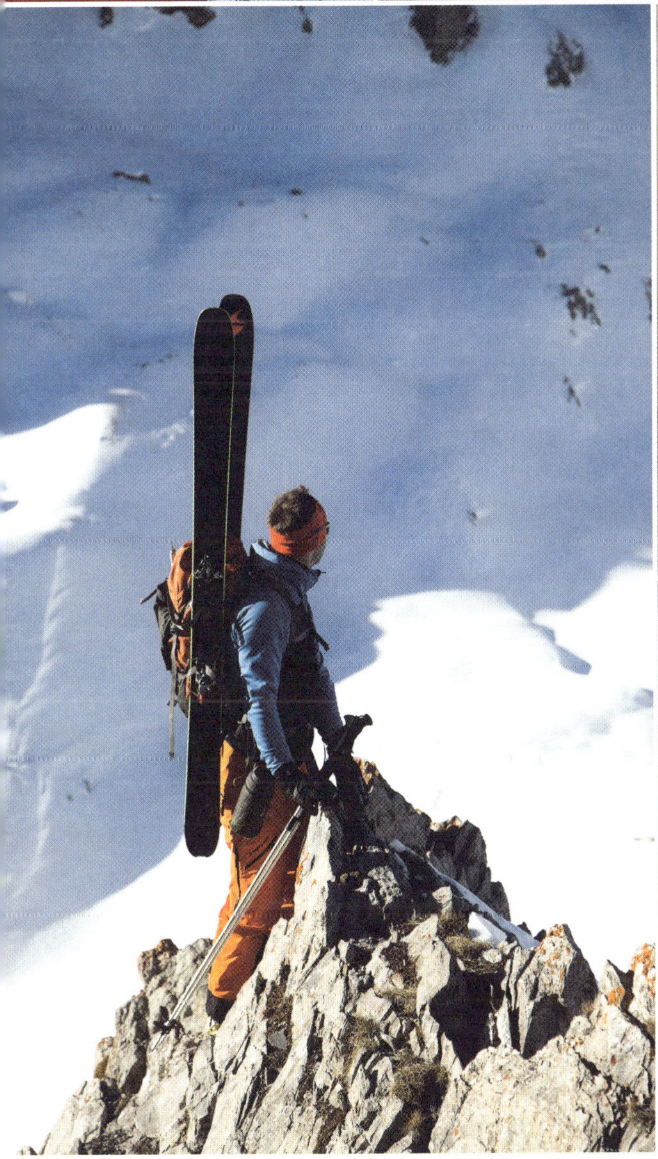

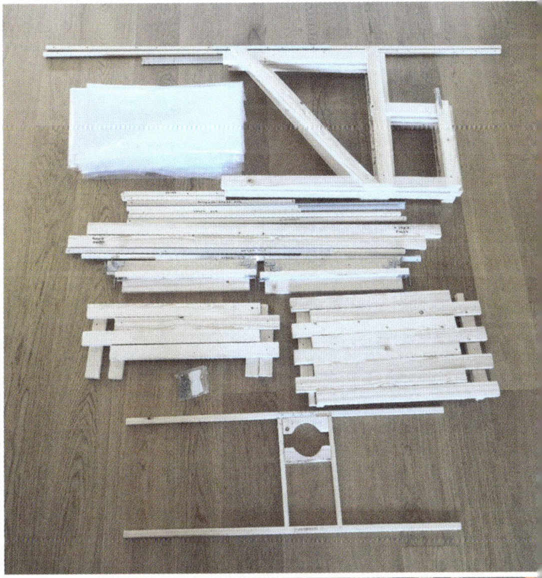

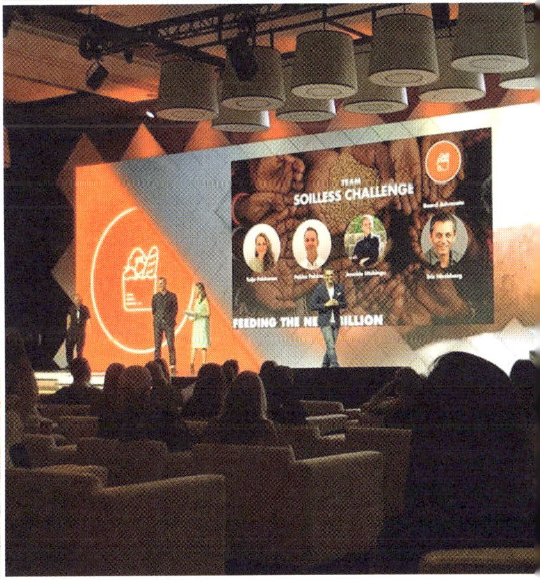
SOILLESS CHALLENGE

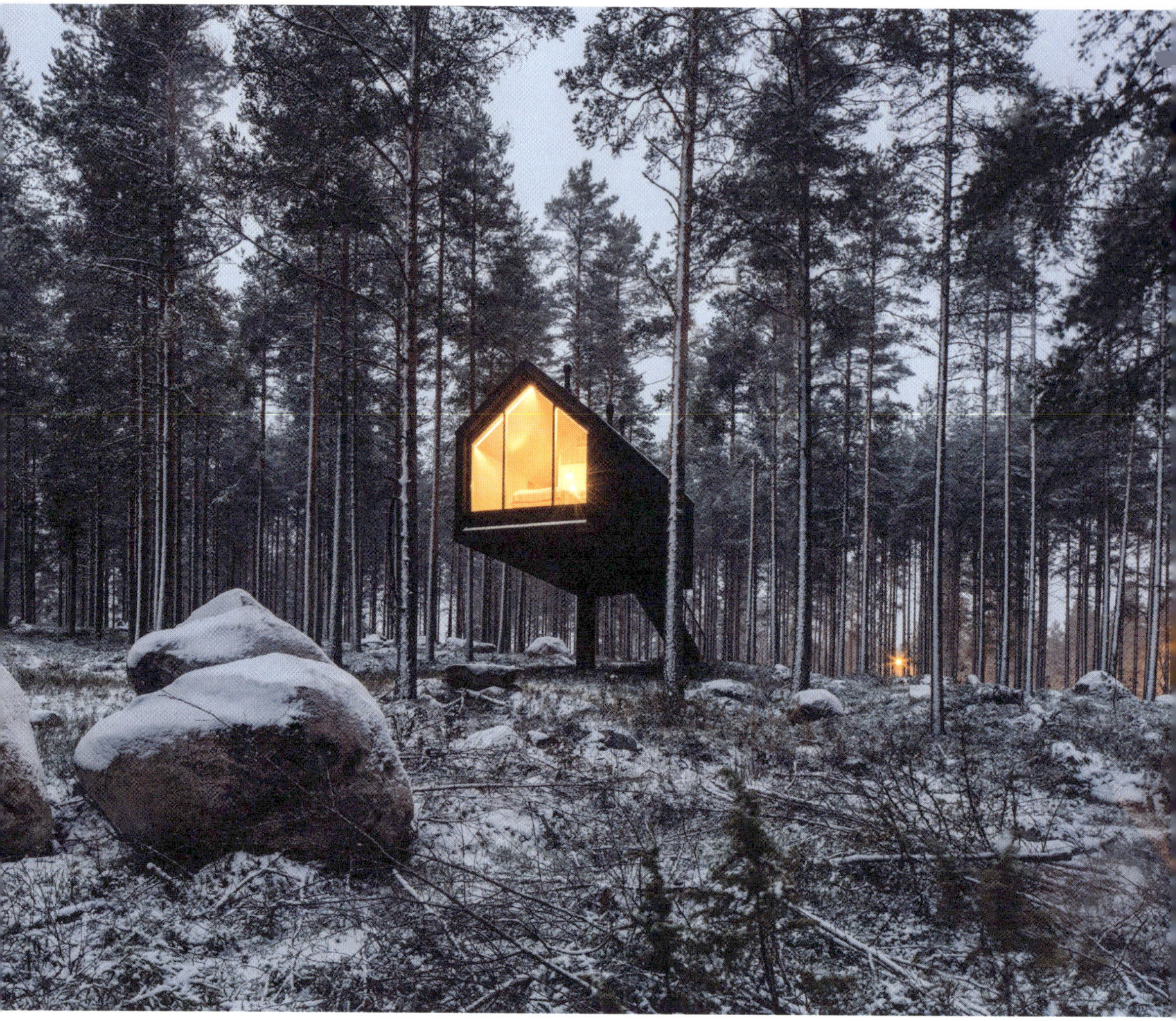

Studio Puisto

Despite its global reach, Studio Puisto – based in Helsinki – is rooted in Nordic design, with a special focus on sustainable construction. They also devote time to urban planning matters and readily involve themselves economically in their design projects. As well as private clients, the studio has designed several hotels, including the highly acclaimed Arctic TreeHouse Hotel. Each project strives to combine ecological, economic and social ambitions, without compromising aesthetics or function. The partners include Mikko Jakonen, Emma Johansson, Sampsa Palva, Heikki Riitahuht and Willem van Bolderen who took part in our interview. Notably, the firm also has a Director of Global Hospitality Development, Sam-Erik Ruttmann, emphasising the importance of hospitality projects to the firm.

studiopuisto.fi

Previous page: Niliaitta, Kivijärvi, Finland

This page: Arctic TreeHouse Hotel, Kivijärvi, Finland

TODD SAUNDERS: You're not actually Finnish, is that right?

WILLEM VAN BOLDEREN: I'm Dutch. I grew up close to Arnhem. I moved to Finland in 2005. I studied at Delft University of Technology and then did my Master's in Finland, worked for a few offices and started our own studio six years ago.

TS: I've done some teaching in Finland, at Oulu. It's a very good school. We did a design and build project for a piece of public sculpture with a group of international students.

WvB: It's small, but the thinking is a little more experimental.

TS: How long have you been at the Aalto School?

WvB: I studied there from 2005 to 2009 and I've been teaching there since 2015. I'm teaching the wood programme – we build one building every year.

TS: Do you get sponsored by Finnforest or other Finnish wood companies?

WvB: It depends. It's on a project-by-project basis, and typically the clients help out by paying something for the construction. So there might be some budget every year and it's a one-year course. There are more design builds where you can build something really nice and sculptural but we're trying to get deeper into the wood issues, to understand the material and how to work it. We've also done structures where we actually deal with the installation process.

TS: A few years ago, when I gave a lecture about how to be a successful architect, I described my top ten mistakes and what I learned from them. That was a lecture that gets the most comments back.

WvB: The relationship with nature is quite strong in general in Scandinavia. The smaller projects are the most fun – you can build on the experience and the building is just part of the process or experience and you kind of add on what was already there. But it's also hard to run a business. We are still always searching for how to find that balance. When we converted the office building into a hotel in Oslo, that was interesting, money wise, and profitable for the office in a way. The client was the country's biggest apartment hotel operator. To only do projects like that would make a very profitable office, but I don't think we'd all be so interested.

We have a lot of requests. Clients who think that you've designed a single-family house and you can just copy it every time. But the initial design work is always much more intensive. We do maybe four or five single family houses every year because it's fun to do. But we are selective on the location and it has to be a client who wants to pay for it and understands what it means – and we still have a hard time turning profits. But they're good for marketing. And you really get satisfaction.

TS: Is there one house you're working on now that you really like?

WvB: We are currently doing one in Montana in the US. It consists of 12 houses as it is a private retreat for family and friends. There will be a restaurant and stuff as well. That project has been going for a long time and it's been really nice to work with US contractors.

Opposite: Rest Area Niemenharju, Pihtipudas, Finland

TS: What is the biggest difference?

WvB: I think the quality is good, like in Finland but they rarely ask, just keep on going and figure it out for themselves. Whereas in the US they're more used to dealing with demanding customers, so they're much more communicative, asking how we should do this. That also means it is harder to keep on top of costs.

TS: What do you miss about the Netherlands and what are you glad to leave behind?

WvB: When I left the Netherlands, the architecture of the era was, let's say, proudly arrogant. In Finland it's much humbler, and humble towards nature as well. Perhaps that's why building in the urban context is somehow harder here. I also think that kind of boldness and arrogance in Holland results in a lot of bad projects. Where we're at now is a more humanistic architecture, which suits Finland better than the Netherlands. You don't realise it until you step out of it.

TS: As an outsider in Norway, I've seen things the architects here maybe overlooked, perhaps because they were so close to it. How do you feel as an outsider in the architecture environment? That's why I love talking to Dutch people – they'll talk about money and creativity at the same time. Norwegians won't do that. I don't know if it's the same in Finland.

WvB: Maybe it's not the same but I think money is important in architecture – not so much the money we make – because you get the client on your side. It's a very strong tool to get your ideas through. You need to use it as a tool for the better, to convince clients or the city. Of course, it's not charity. A private house is the biggest investment in people's lives, so I like to understand their fears and their stress.

TS: There's a lot of money involved in architecture. We can't come in as artists just saying we don't care. In the tourism projects we argue that our architecture can attract those tourists and help generate a sustainable income for rural communities. Architecture can be a tool to give these small communities an extra level of support.

WvB: It's a harder case to make in a private house.

TS: We don't work by percentage because if the cost goes up that means we're not on your side so we work with a fixed price and say this is what we can do. We always deliver on time, the fee is fixed and it has created a lot of safety between ourselves and the client.

WvB: That's an interesting model. In Finland it's a very small scene – we have a hard time criticising each other. There's only one magazine, and what you can charge is set by the only architecture guild. The bigger you get, the more corporate you get as well. But they're at the top of what you can charge. The ways to circumvent that are to work abroad – in the US or in Norway or the Netherlands. In Finland, many private houses are just catalogue designs. Many of them are quite good and done by architects but they're not custom made for a site – they could be anywhere basically. In the Netherlands everyone understands that you can have more expensive architects or cheaper ones.

TS: In Norway, you don't have to be an architect to design a house and there are a lot of really poorly designed projects: quite well

FINLAND | STUDIO PUISTO

> The relationship with nature is quite strong in general in Scandinavia. The smaller projects are the most fun – you can build on the experience and the building is just part of the process or experience and you kind of add on what was already there.
>
> — Willem van Bolderen

built but not functionally solved. Many clients don't see that using an architect could save money and lead to a better, more practical house. After we started doing houses here people could visit them, walk in them, hear the stories, and then you'd hear, "Okay – it's very valuable and beneficial to use an architect and it's actually worth it."

WvB: I think that's why we made that shift maybe three or four years ago to hospitality. The projects have the quality of a private house because you get to the design in the interior as well. At the same time, the added value of design is very measurable in monetary terms.

TS: Which one of these projects met that creativity and monetary balance for the client?

WvB: The tree house was maybe the most extreme and clear case. Two years' exposure because the architecture was worth €23m in marketing. They didn't pay us €23m for the design! Better design costs a bit more at the beginning but you're going to get it back. Of course, we don't take all the credit for it. It has what you might call "Instagrammability" – things that are shared, like the food and the architecture. That's what visitors end up showing people.

TS: We have this thick book of all the articles written about Fogo Island in the first year, in about 30 countries. I think they worked out that if they'd had to buy that press it would have been $9m over the course of one year.

WvB: We focus on hospitality projects because it's a clearer case where we can make a difference, and explain why we're expensive. With private houses it's a bit harder because there's no added value, and there's a limit at least in Finland as to what you can do. We're actually making a new hotel in Lapland. We are doing a masterplan and strategy for regions in Finland, with suggestions of how to take the maximum out of the surroundings and look for entrepreneurs who can take that forwards. And because of how hospitality projects are funded they are typically owner-operators. We own a part of one of the businesses, so our head is on the line in a way. If we had added value how can we capitalise on that? The longer you spend on something, the better the architecture. The main problem is you don't have total control – you're just one part of things. If there's a bad operator or terrible food, that's beyond our control.

We've also done a small cabin. It's about 30,000 euros per unit. We have another design because people contact us for smaller rooms. With the tree house you need about 40 to 50 rooms to make it worthwhile. We've made it easy for you to start your own small resort if you have a nice site – it's a package where we just offer everything. It's another experiment.

TS: In Norway we have the Juvet Landscape Hotel, designed by Jensen & Skodvin, and run by Knut Slinning, an acquaintance. I go up there skiing and mountain biking. That model is the one you're talking about. How can it be written down by architects? Might you be interested in working together on something like that in Norway or Canada with us?

WvB: Definitely. But what we have noticed is that hospitality is too small a market for Finland only. It might work better in the US and in central Europe. Because the Nordic experience would translate into something that works well.

TS: How do you make hybrids of architecture culture in small buildings? At the Aurland Lookout for example, the bent wood couldn't be done in Norway even though it was local timber. It had to be sent to the Netherlands for processing and then sent back to be installed.

WvB: Norway, Finland and Sweden do not have much competition there. But in the Netherlands, there are so many architects as well as outside influences, with builders working there from Germany, Belgium, even the UK.

TS: I think it's healthy to have these different cultures pushing their strengths.

Previous page: Rest Area
Niemenharju, Pihtipudas,
Finland

Right: Studio Puisto,
Helsinki, Finland

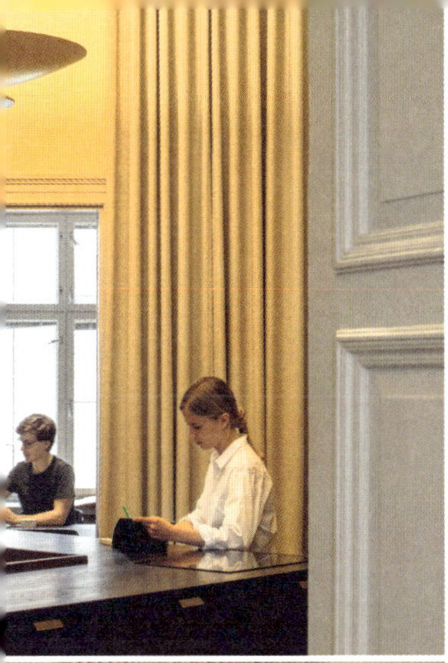
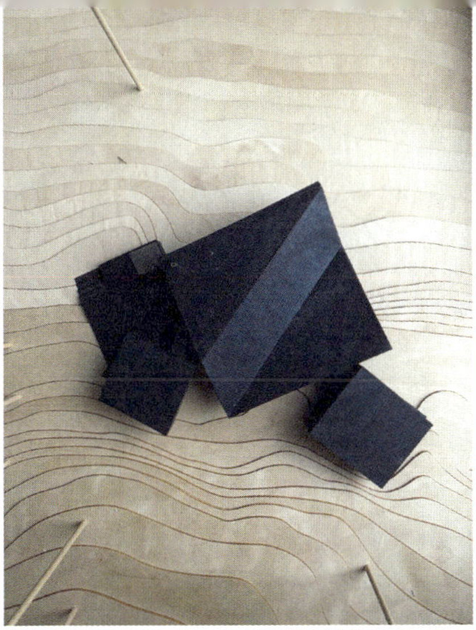
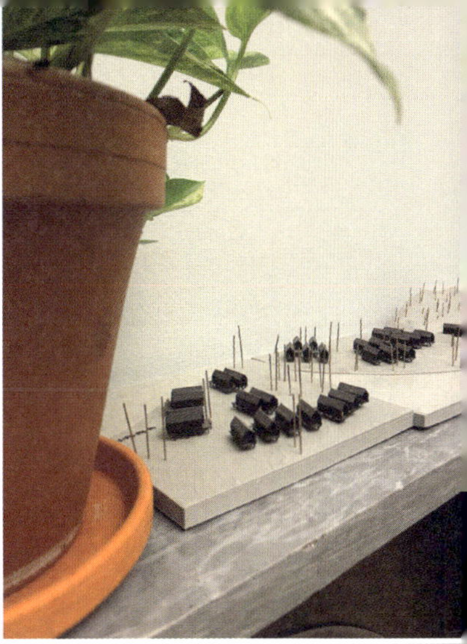
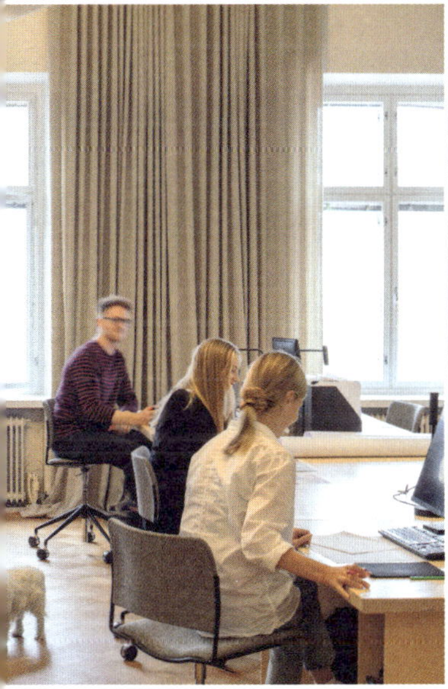
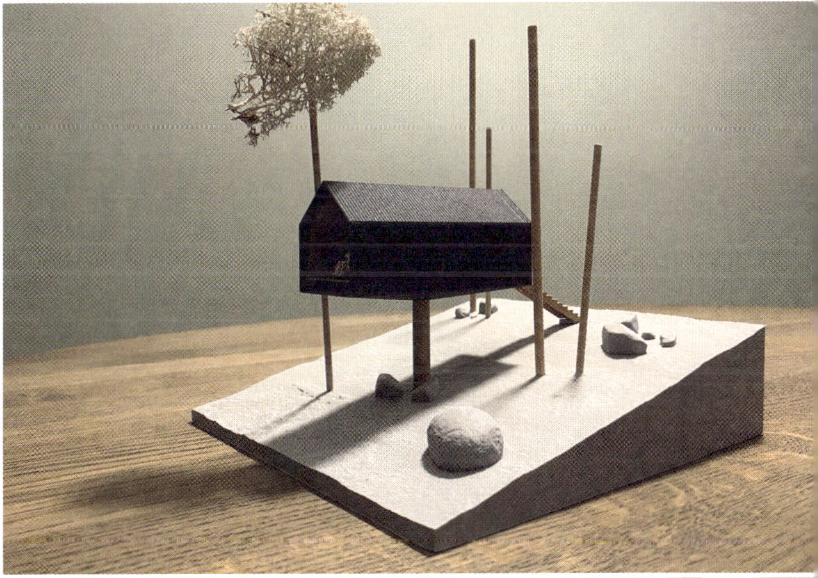
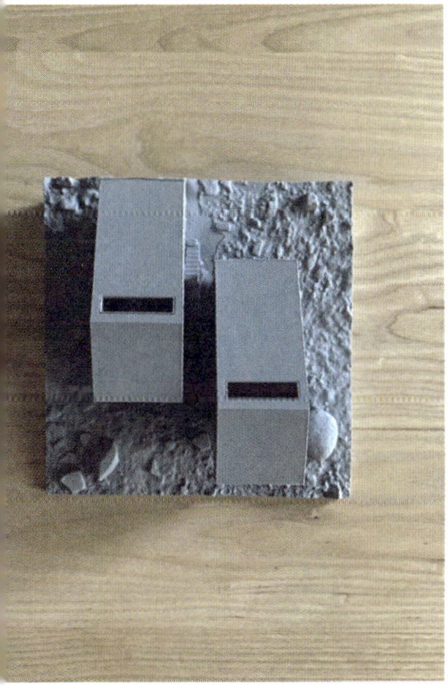
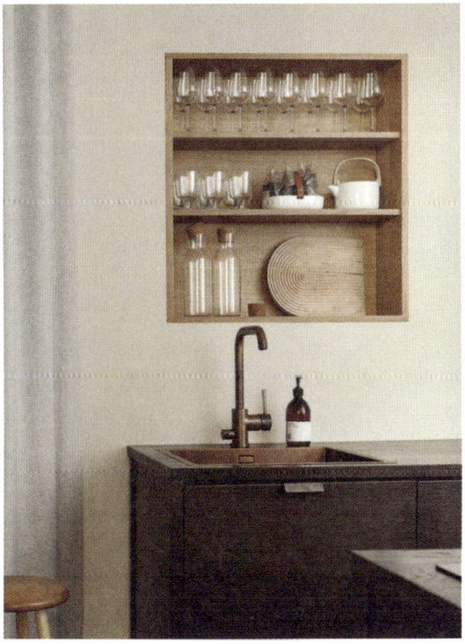
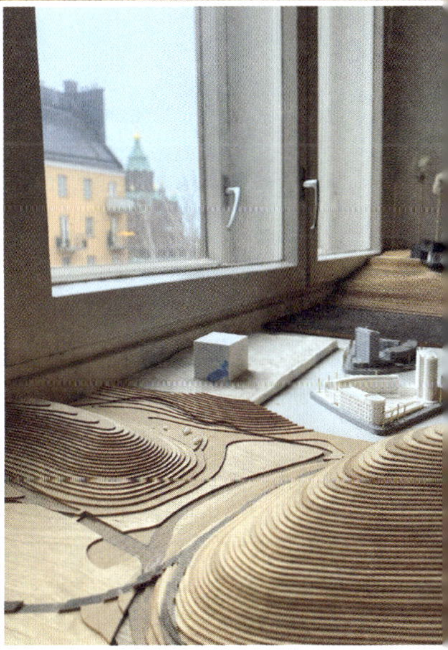

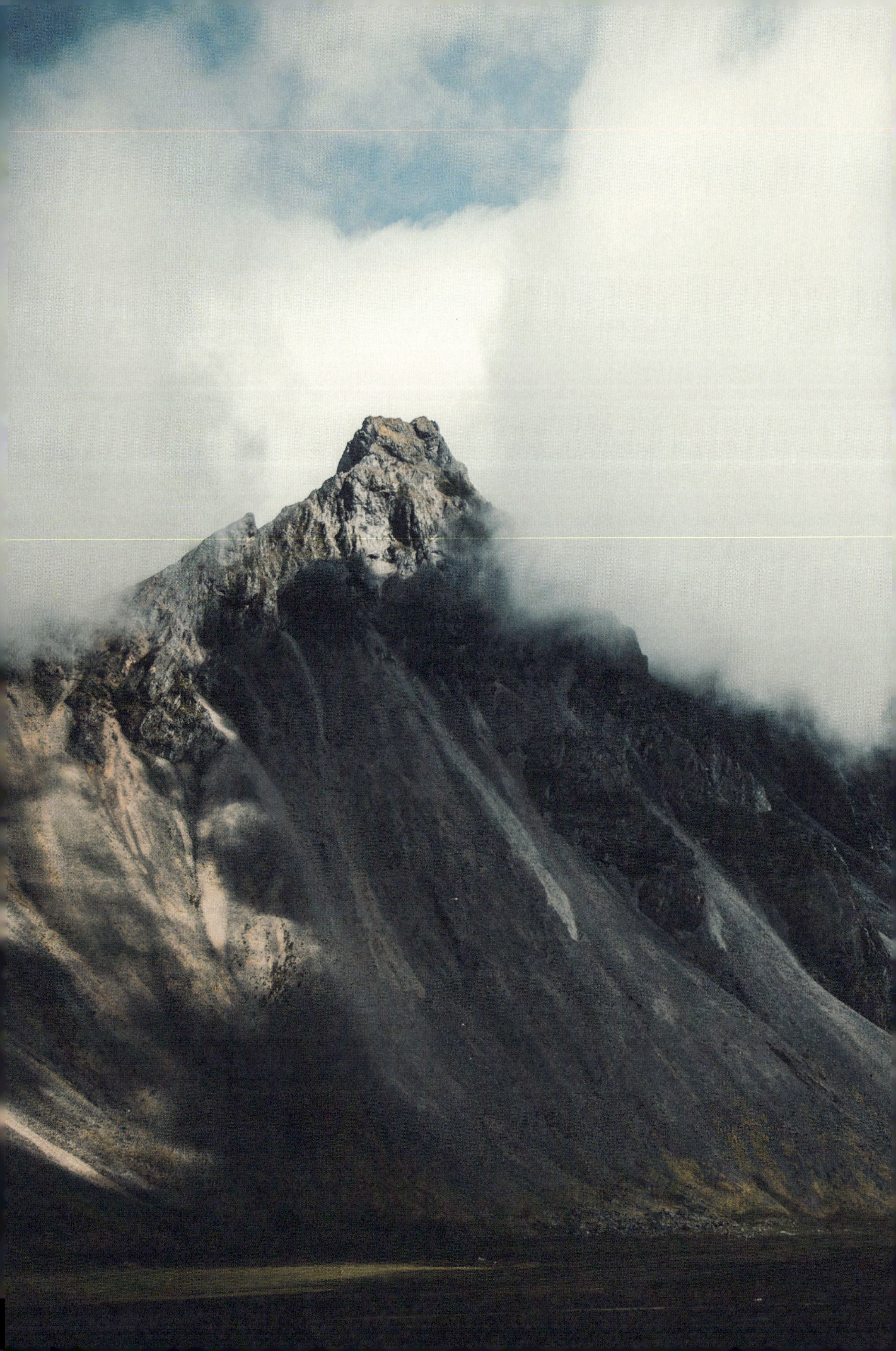

ICELAND

{ ESSAY }

DIALOGUE WITH NATURE

{ BY }

HILDIGUNNUR SVERRISDÓTTIR

Head of Department of Architecture, Icelandic University of the Arts

Icelandic architecture has always been in deep correspondence with nature. This might not be so surprising, as the presence of all architecture and the man-made environment is dependent on natural resources, and the man-made environment is shaped within the framing that nature presents. But in the Icelandic context it stretches further, into a realm stranger and more overwhelming than most of our neighbouring countries must deal with. A realm ruled by a violent land, under endless stretching horizons, opening and closing in whatever context the chameleon weather decides to offer; sometimes with a field of vision spanning merely to your hands, sometimes reaching tens or hundreds of kilometres into the quiet sandy highland plateaus and glaciers far, far away. Earthquakes, eruptions, avalanches, tempests are what this beast has offered its inhabitants for centuries.

The country offers minimal natural resources for construction, almost no trees that can be of use and mostly minerals of porous lava and basalt. Although stone could, in principle, have been used through the ages, the know-how simply wasn't there. Even the calories needed to accomplish the task were not available – too much expenditure of bodily energy was required to send people to the mountains to work the stone and bring it home. Summertime was too precious for gathering hay for the deep dark winter and masonry during wintertime was challenging. Hence, the early inhabitants of this remote island learned that living with the fiend was preferable to fighting it. Making the most of whatever structural material was at hand – driftwood, stranded ships, sometimes imported timber or valuable stone – refined ways to build bearing structures were developed, while the flesh of the earth, the turf, was used to envelop and shelter the structure in and from nature. This way of building carried the modest number of some tens of thousands of inhabitants, growing or declining depending on conditions, through the centuries.

For such a small, sparse population in a challenging country, collaboration was vital – specifically building together and sharing knowledge. The architect Hjörleifur Stefánsson has researched the Icelandic authorities' attempts to build a library of construction information. The documents date back to the year 1900, and cover building technique fundamentals and their respective faults and strengths, as well as the methods farmers and builders used to improve the construction of the turf house. People inherently understood that no chain is stronger than its weakest link. Well into the twentieth century, this focus on collaboration, sharing and optimising continued, not out of romantic idealism, but out of deep and dire need. After the Icelandic Commonwealth era, dating back to the establishment of the Althing in 930, Iceland came under Norwegian authority in 1262, and later Danish rule. It was not until 1918 that Iceland became independent for most parts, and fully so in 1944. During the early twentieth century, the first Icelandic architects were returning home after being educated abroad, along with kindred spirits of other professions such as engineers and doctors. These professionals helped usher the country into a new era, where the Icelandic population took its seat as a nation among nations. In this context, the turf heritage was seen as shameful – a vestige of a humiliating history of poverty and struggle.

Thus started a new chapter, that of modernity in Icelandic architecture. Not only did this revolve around proving one's ability to stand up to others – becoming a sovereign nation with a capital city with high-rise concrete buildings and new institutions and infrastructures established in the first half of the twentieth century – but also, as time has moved on, a phase of trying to understand what local architecture was about. After the Icelandic people had proven that they could build like others, the question of who they were became more pressing. Simultaneously, while design and planning were taking precedence over a direct response to nature, buildings still had to endure the local natural conditions, often very different from conditions in the countries where architects and engineers were educated. It must be emphasised that until the architecture programme at the Iceland University of the Arts was founded in 2002, architects in Iceland were educated abroad. Until 2021, the programme only offered a BA-level degree. Consequently, architects in Iceland have thus far had to finalise their professional education abroad (the first MA-level architects graduate in Iceland in 2023). The highly varied background of architects working in Iceland, educated everywhere from Denmark to Japan, understandably exerts an influence on the local architectural discourse – and the design outcomes. It also complicates the question of what true Icelandic architecture is.

This is, in many ways, the discourse found in the architectural works on the coming pages. An open-minded, open-hearted question to the beast of a land we live on, how to work together, how to serve and be served? What qualities does the country offer and what do they mean economically? How can nature, water, the past and its structures be transformed to serve new purposes and aesthetics? With a new age comes new challenges. Again, we find ourselves small in a daunting situation. It is not only the untamed land that calls for caution and genius. Now it is the whole planet that is in dire need for our thought, for new answers and responsible ways to build on it. In Iceland, we must ask what centuries of sustainable living has taught, what knowledge of living with and in nature has brought, and how this can inform new decisions regarding the man-made environment. In many ways, the country serves as a Petri dish for ideas and solutions that can be tested in local context but applied in the global sphere.

It is my hope that we have the collective stamina and power to look towards the future and to a better world – together. To care. To ask the right questions – and strive with responsibility towards finding healing answers.

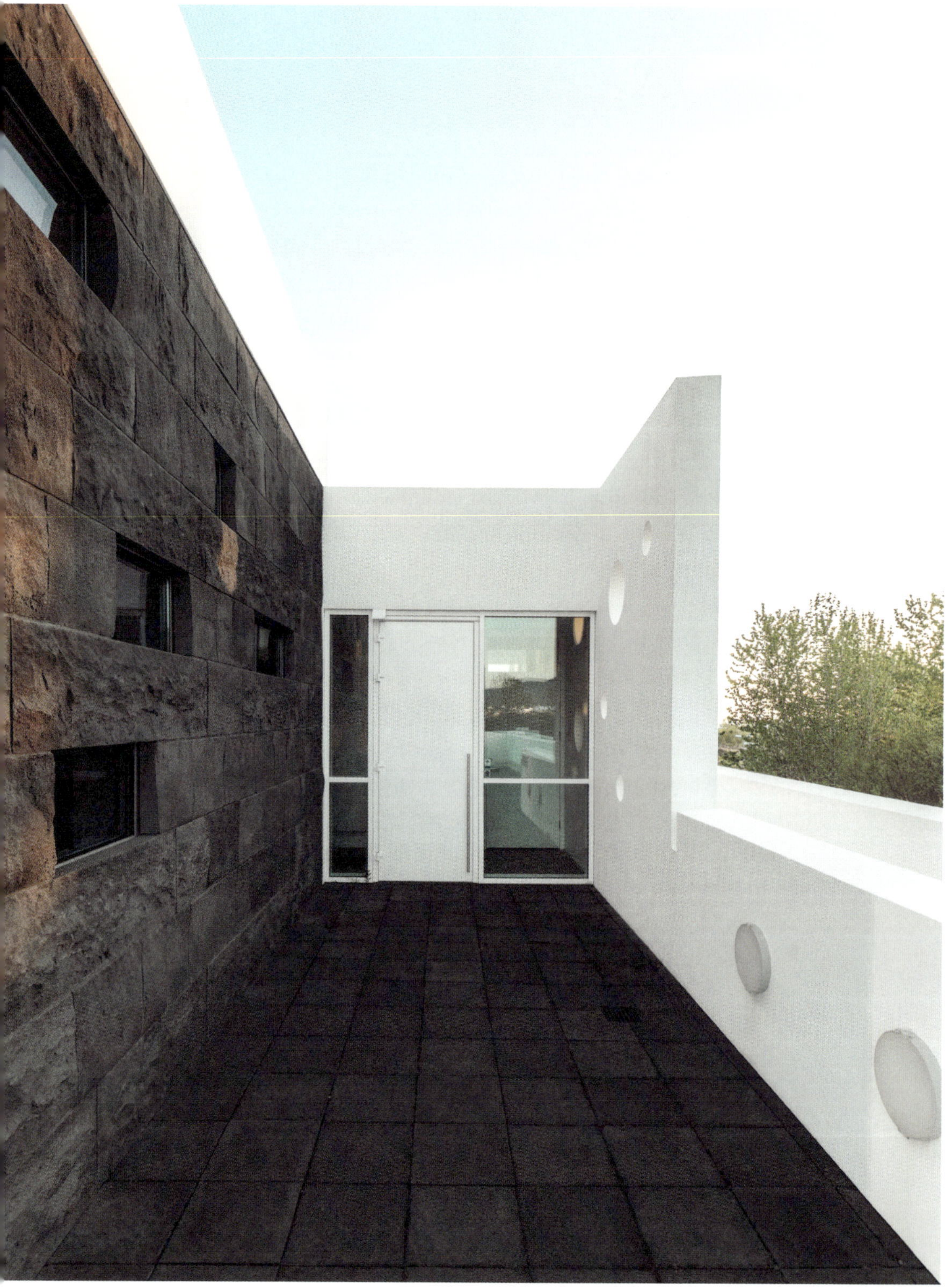

A arkitektar

Architects Hólmfríður Ósmann Jónsdóttir and Hrefna Björg Þorsteinsdóttir have been working together since 1994, setting up Arkibúllan in 1999 with Heba Hertevig. In 2014, architect Margrét Leifsdóttir joined the studio, which recently changed its name to A arkitektar. As well as receiving nominations for the Mies van der Rohe Prize, the European Architecture Prize and the DV Culture Prize, A arkitektar have exhibited widely and been published in a number of books, including *The Phaidon Atlas of Contemporary World Architecture*. The three architects cite the influence of nature and the environment as a major factor behind their work. "Each project begins with a search for clues in as many places as possible: in the landscape, in human life and in one's own mind," they say, "These indicators then become the driving force that leads the work from the first sketch to a fully formed structure." Their work includes renovating existing historic buildings as well as new building structures, creating a hard-wearing aesthetic that suits Iceland's fast-changing climate and rugged topography.

aarkitektar.is

In the old days, inhabitants of this island had to be very imaginative to survive. I guess we have inherited that.

— Margrét Leifsdóttir

Previous page, above and left:
Churchyard offices and staff housing in Gufunes Cemetery, Reykjavik, Iceland

TODD SAUNDERS: This project is about finding out why architects do what they do, and I'm discovering we all do it for very different reasons. Architects are not always very direct. They make out how romantic this profession is when it's all about hard work and stress with no sleep. A few years ago, I started giving lectures about how I make decisions and then I did one about my top ten mistakes. I don't think people were used to architects being open.

MARGRÉT LEIFSDÓTTIR: We regularly discuss how we're feeling in the office. We are all in our fifties now. Hrefna and Hólmfríður are both professors at the Iceland University of the arts. They have this way of communicating that I am totally in love with. In Norway, where Hrefna and Hólmfríður studied, everyone knows each other and it's like a family thing. But in Berlin, where I studied, if you didn't do the work it was your problem. I also thought many of the professors were there to show how great they were, rather than give something to the students.

TS: Emotion is still seen as a negative thing in discussions here in Norway. In Finland and Iceland, it feels that emotions are a bigger part of the architecture culture.

ML: That's interesting – Finns and Icelanders are normally known for being quite closed.

TS: In Norway, very little of the architecture is emotional – like 95 per cent is more technical. What different roles do you each play in the office?

ML: Hrefna and Hólmfríður are the project architects, while I'm more involved in managing the work. We've worked for many municipalities, urban planning and housing. We currently have two projects, involving the remodelling of ten kindergartens in Reykjavik. The original architects are both in their eighties and retired, but they're friends of ours, so they asked us to help them.

TS: What would be the last building you'd like to do in your career?

ML: One of our favourite buildings is Alvar Aalto's Nordic House in Reykjavik from 1968. We would love to design a building that would serve the public.

TS: Do you work mostly in the public realm or is it a mix?

ML: It's a mix. One of the studio's key projects was a sea bathing facility. Then we did a cemetery building, still unfinished. Also some cottages which are for members in the trade union, Icelandic confederation of University graduates.

TS: The bath project in Nauthólsvík was nominated for the Mies van der Rohe Prize, early in the studio's career. Was it one of the first modern public baths in Iceland?

ML: It was the first sea bathing facility in Iceland, built for swimmers in the summer and intended to be closed in the winter. But ocean swimming is becoming very popular so it is open all year round and many more people use the building than we expected. The architect Heba Hertervig worked with us on this project.

TS: Pools in your country are almost an Icelandic typology now, like a community living room for these small villages. The equivalent of the piazza in Italian cities.

ML: That is a beautiful way of describing it. Icelandic pools are very important "get together" places in Iceland. We have great access to hot water and it is an important and very much used way to deal with the cold weather.

TS: It seems to be something you only find in Iceland. The problem we have in Canada is how we define something as being particularly Canadian. Almost all Finnish architects have done a really nice sauna. In Norway, every architect designs a summer house and a winter house. Which project taught you the most?

ML: Two years ago, we did a renovation of a Second World War barracks near the sea bathing facility. We were assigned the project by the Municipality of Reykjavik. It taught us more about attitude than architecture. Everything started well and we were proud to be part of this project and happy that the city was renovating the barracks. They were built by the British and the Americans and left over after the war. At that time there was a housing deficit in Reykjavik because people were moving from the countryside to the city. So many people moved into them – even though they were just temporary buildings and very unhealthy to live in. The kids who lived there would have been teased at school because their clothes smelt from the humidity. There are still people today, in their eighties, who have very bad memories of these barracks.

TS: How big are the buildings?

ML: The barracks itself are just 100 square metres, on a superb plot in Nauthólsvík, close to the bath house. The original idea was for the University to have a café and start-up offices on the site. We did the work and were very happy with it but when it was almost finished, it got political. The media was criticising the budget in particular, not the architecture. This was such a valuable lesson for us. We wanted to preserve the history, but we would have welcomed a discussion about whether these buildings were sufficiently important, or valuable.

TS: What would you have done differently?

ML: Architecturally we would have done it the same. But we would have found out what the extent of our responsibilities to the community were. You have to work from your heart and conscience to weather the kind of storm we experienced for a whole year.

TS: Media storms can really take over. You need to have the strength of your convictions. What is like to have an all-women office? Does it ever come up for discussion?

ML: We're not saying that we want to be an all-female office, but it just happened that way.

TS: Do you think there are different values or angles that come up in how you run the studio?

ML: Yes. Before Covid, we would regularly all work from home. Very often we found we were more effective. I have a personal problem with the idea that you are only a real architect if you drink ten coffees a day, smoke 20 cigarettes and only sleep for two hours.

TS: It's an old model. I notice that a lot of people who come to Scandinavia want to bring their own work culture, and it doesn't work. Another studio I talked to in Finland has an open office every Friday, where anyone can come into their studio and ask questions. It raised some good ideas.

Right and below: Nauthólsvegur 100, Reykjavik, Iceland

ICELAND | A ARKITEKTAR

Left and below: Nauthólsvegur 100, Reykjavik, Iceland

ML: We had this idea, which we've only done once so far, to ask other architects to show us around one of their projects that interests us. Before Covid, we were planning to do it monthly, as an exchange. In Iceland there's a lot of competition between architects and fewer projects, so everyone tends to stay in their lanes.

TS: Practices in Iceland seem to be quite secretive about future projects. I tend to talk most about work with architects in Oslo, rather than Bergen, so we're not really in each other's nests.

ML: It is harder in small areas – Iceland only has 360,000 people – but men and women generally have a shared awareness about working less and having more free time. It used to be cool to say you worked 10 to 12 hours a day, but this is slowly changing. In our office, we've often said that six hours is maximum effective creative time.

TS: Some writers say even less – if you get two to three hours of intense creativity then that's great. It's an interesting theme because a lot of architects have given up a lot in their lives to become architects. I don't think that's always necessary. When you reach 40, perhaps you can choose how important architecture is versus your life. What advice would you give your 30-year-old self or another person in the profession?

ML: When we were 30 years old we were driven by our egos. If we were criticised, we got angry. Looking back now, we see that's because we were afraid and unsure of our competence, of not being good enough. This didn't lead to constructive conversations, nor did it lead to a happy architectural life, let alone a happy life at all.

TS: What do you do now if you get frustrated?

ML: We talk together and find out what is it exactly that is bothering us. We look closely into it, and we ask us these questions: what can we learn from this? Why did it happen? And then we have a treatment which always works. We have what we call "good enough pills". So if we don't feel good enough we take this imaginary pill. A placebo, if you like. If we respond with fiery feelings, that is because we think we are not good enough, and that we need to defend ourselves. If we feel that we are good enough, we can respond in a calm way.

TS: I like the mysticism you have in Iceland.

ML: Yes. In the old days, inhabitants of this island had to be very imaginative to survive. I guess we have inherited that. As soon as you take the pill, you go from your head to your heart, and you know that everything is okay and you're safe. You can contact us if you want some…

TS: Architecture can be a hard, frustrating process. There are still no rules about creativity and emotions. Buddhism talks about healthy anger – do you understand that concept?

ML: The "pills" are about being a grown-up – learning to take criticism and use it for your own good. Architecture is about service, and the ability to give your best in that service. So it is important to know yourself, to understand and meet people's needs and serve the general public and the environment.

TS: What process do you use to understand all this?

Right and opposite:
Brekkuskógur Cottages,
Brekkuskógur, Iceland

ML: We always ask questions instead of jumping to conclusions, and that's equally important in your personal life. If you feel judged by someone and you get afraid, then take a few "good enough pills" and then you can communicate from your heart instead of your head.

TS: Some of the happier architects I've been interviewing have so much energy and passion that they can do anything. One of my clients told me that journalists often ask how we do things, but the more interesting question is "why?".

ML: One way to have meaning is to have something important to give to others. What is your super skill, what is your passion? Is it urban planning, architecture, environmental issues, or cultural aspects? Architecture is an interdisciplinary profession – this makes it easier to find your passion.

TS: There's definitely an empathetic way of designing: to accept other people know more about things than you do, so your role as an architect becomes about translating their ideas to make a much better building.

ML: We had this with one of the kindergarten projects. We were talking to one of the cooks. She was on top of everything and so unbelievably fun to work with. She knew exactly how she wanted to have things.

TS: It's important to never forget the human aspects of architecture. Architecture is most rewarding when the users are engaged, challenged and satisfied.

ML: Thank you for doing this project. I think everyone will learn more from this journey you're taking into the soul of architects.

ICELAND | A ARKITEKTAR

Right: A arkitektar, Reykjavik, Iceland

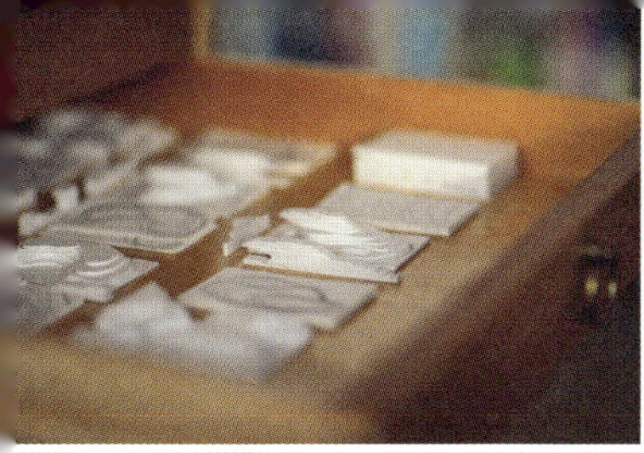
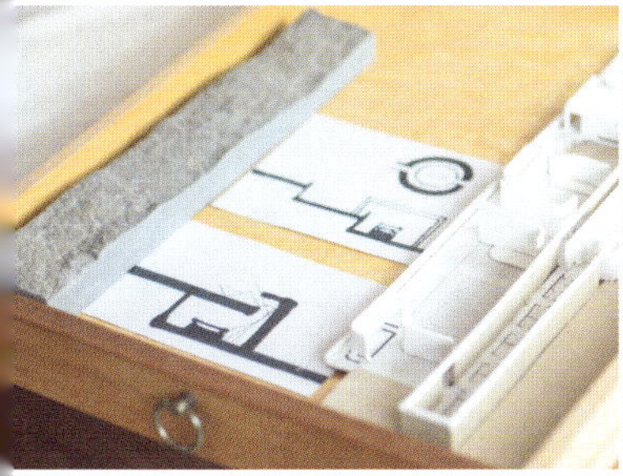
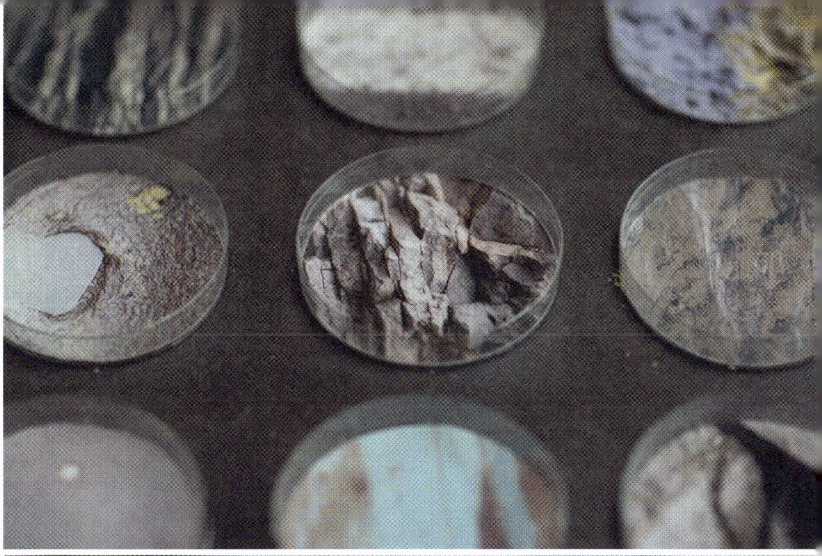
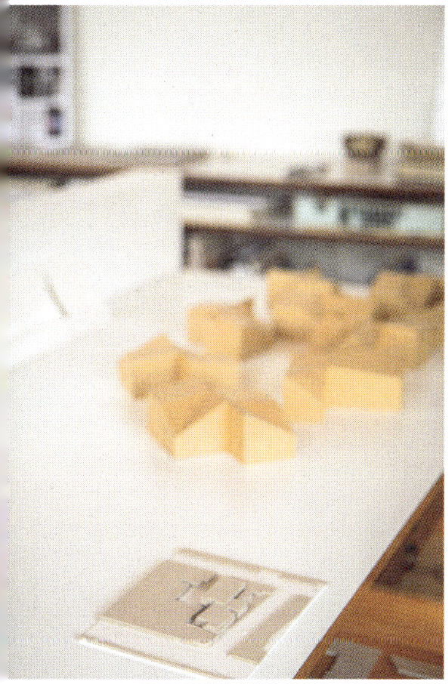
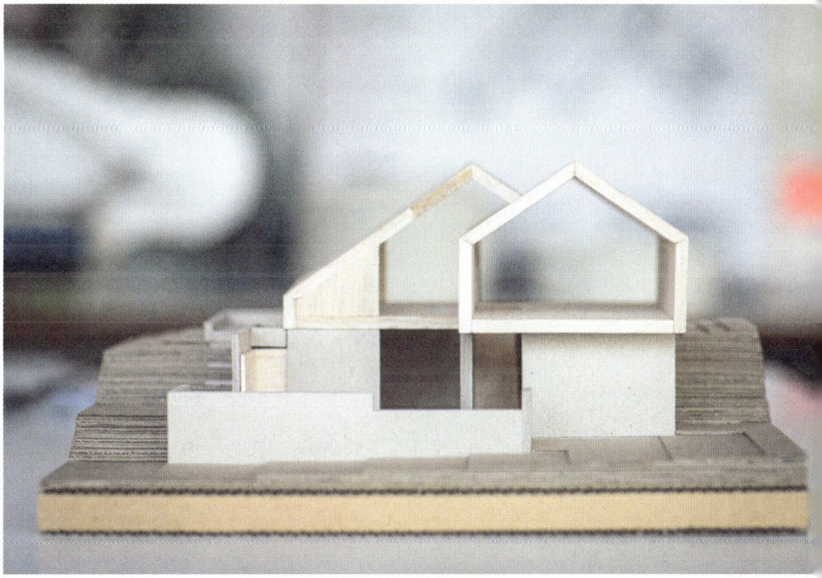
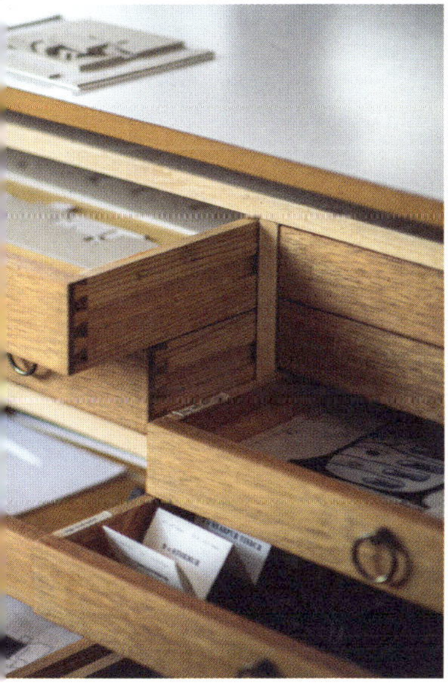
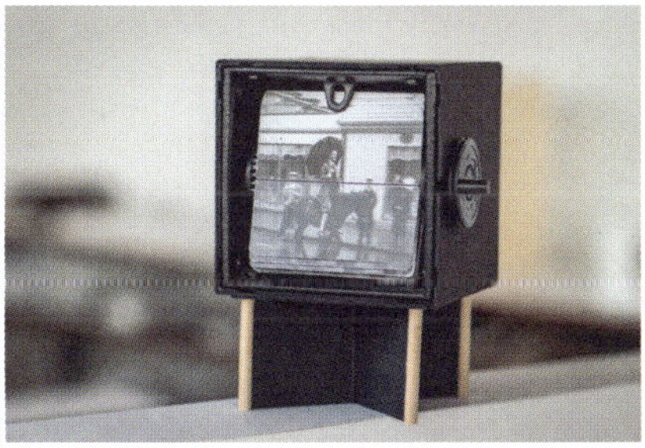
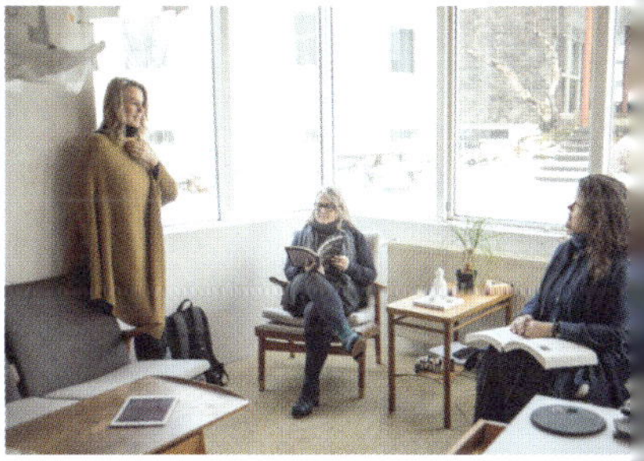
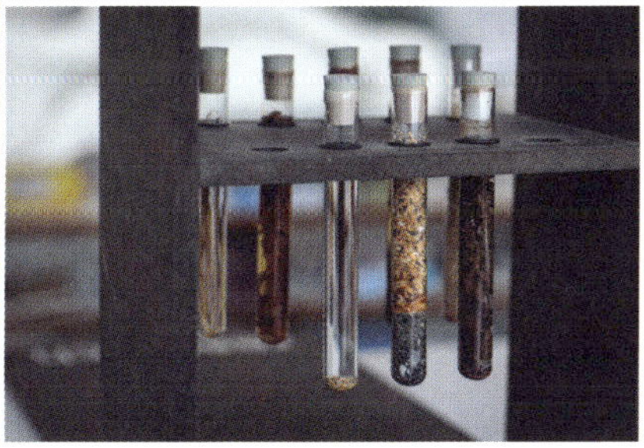
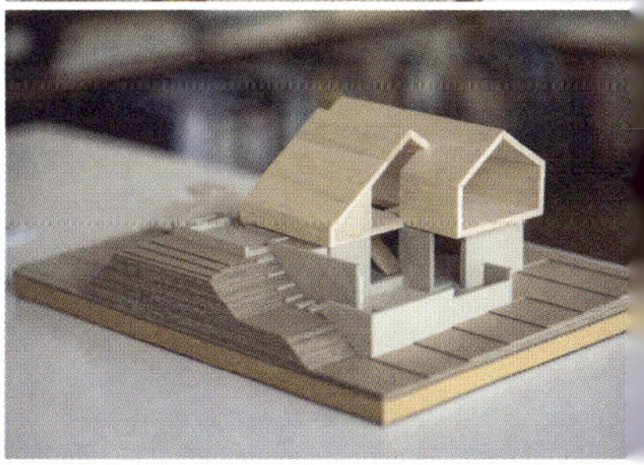

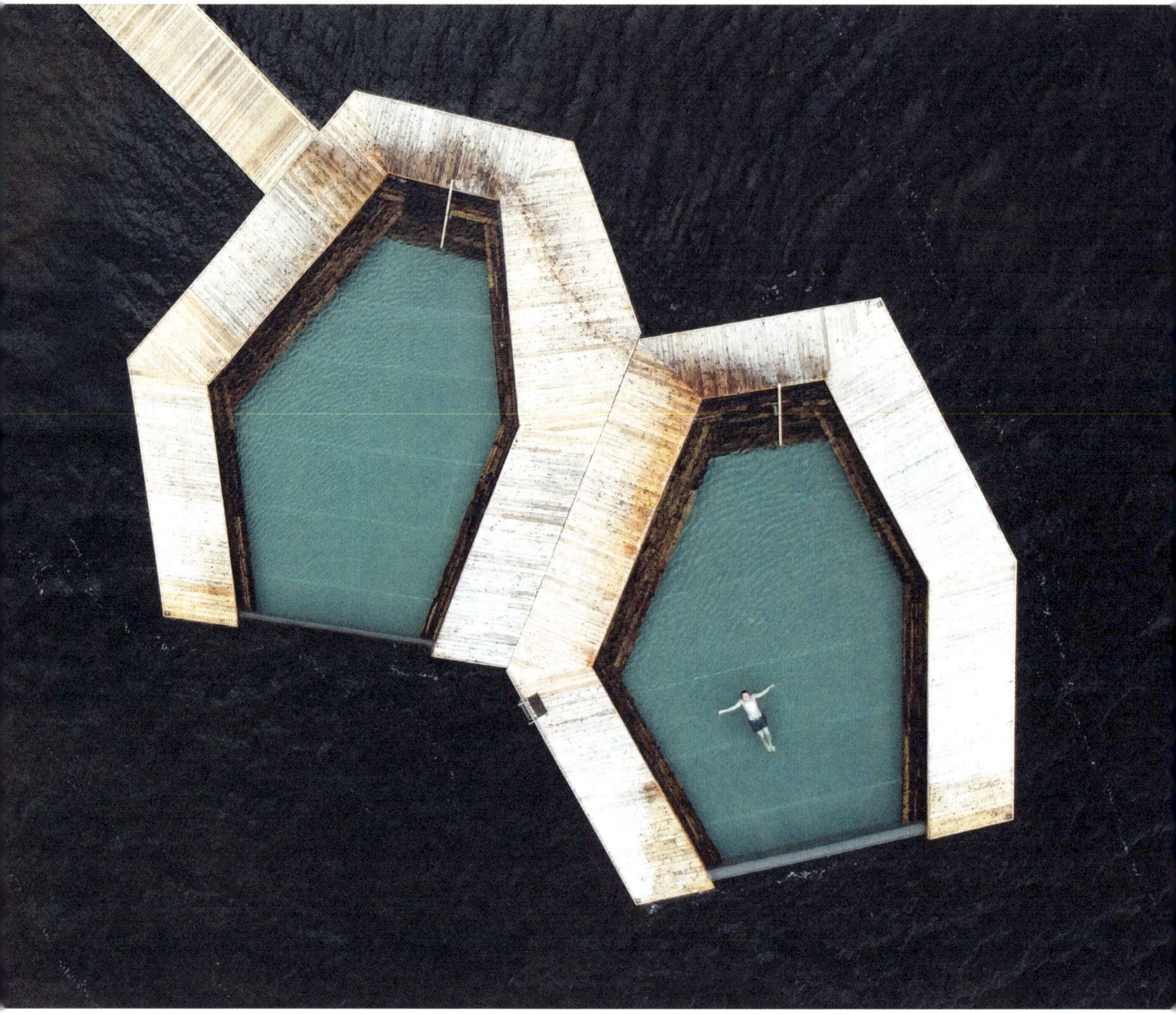

Basalt Architects

Basalt Architects was founded in 2009 by Sigríður Sigþórsdóttir. Led by Sigþórsdóttir, along with Hrólfur Karl Cela and Marcos Zotes, Basalt is best known for its work on the country's burgeoning tourist infrastructure, starting with the internationally acclaimed projects at the Blue Lagoon. Together with hotels like the one at Mývatn (2017) and spas and baths that take full advantage of Iceland's volcanic interior, Basalt has always worked with the raw materials of the landscape. The sheer diversity of their work is united by an approach that seeks to create a unique experience for users, while also acknowledging the environmental, cultural and historic context of the site. The studio won the Icelandic Design Award's Grand Prize for their contribution to the development of the country's bathing culture. Basalt Architects is also a founding member of the Icelandic Green Building Council and Nordic Built.

basalt.is

Previous page, top and above:
Vök Baths, Urriðavatn, Iceland

Todd Saunders: One of the audiences for this book is younger architects, helping them demystify the changing role of the architect. Can you tell us a bit about your early background?

Hrólfur Karl Cela: I went to the Icelandic Academy of the Arts to get my bachelor's degree – the first year they taught architecture in Iceland. So I'm part of this first graduating class. At the moment, Iceland doesn't have a master's degree in architecture – everyone who graduates here needs to go abroad to finish their studies. Because all the older generation of architects here in Iceland have studied entirely abroad, there are all kinds of different influences and styles.

I then went to Parsons School of Design in New York, and graduated into the great year of 2009, after the collapse of everything. So I studied for a teaching degree. Then I studied philosophy and environmental ethics for one year. It was a helpful process.

Marcos Zotes: I was taught architectural draughtsmanship in Spain and started working at an architectural studio in Iceland in 2001. Then I went to London Metropolitan University and graduated with a master's degree in architecture in 2008. I did some work in Rotterdam and Reykjavik before going on to study at Columbia in New York, which is where I gained my post-professional master's degree in 2012.

TS: Is there an architectural identity in Iceland, given that people study all over the world?

HKC: We should probably start with the Icelandic vernacular architecture – the turf houses. Basically, there were no building materials in Iceland, so people made houses from stone, turf and driftwood, for the most part. Our built heritage reflects this. First, you would use stone for the perimeter of the buildings, then you would cut turf using a special kind of technique, developed in Norway of course. We had Vikings as settlers. And then you would use driftwood as the structure of the roof.

All these buildings were essentially made from whatever materials were at hand – they were of the earth on which they stood. From the late 1700s and early 1800s, Icelandic architecture was increasingly built out of imported timber – there was a heavy Danish influence. But they were still simple buildings. Later, in the 20th century, corrugated metal cladding was introduced. There are often strong colours, which reflect our individuality and independent character. But since the middle of the last century it's more or less been about concrete.

TS. Is there an effort to create a modern Icelandic identity, now you have an architecture school and international recognition of architects?

HKC: Sigríður Sigþórsdóttir, our partner here, used to say that you could almost tell where someone had studied, Germany or the UK for example, because it was very apparent in their buildings.

MZ: When people studied abroad there was a clear break from our past, the way of dealing with the landscape and working with vernacular construction methods. That was completely left behind. Contemporary architecture is trying to bring back some of those elements and incorporate them in new ways, making a stronger link with our past. All our projects do this in different ways, depending on the context.

HKC: The right way to create an identity is to be very contextual but that doesn't even mean the same thing everywhere in Iceland. In practice, it means different things on different sites.

TS: Some of your projects feel like three different projects by three different architects. That's a good thing – they're very particular to the site. When you talk about stone, turf, driftwood, presumably that's always different as well in different locations. It's the same in Norway and Canada – there are regional differentiations. This is architecture that is still modern and contemporary, but it is driven by location, culture and even climate.

One of the defining characteristics of Iceland is the weather – many people seem to think that going to Iceland means extreme weather. Is this the case?

HKC: The thing people say about Iceland: if you don't like the weather, wait five minutes. People only really live on the coast here. Inland, there's nothing, and that's where you get the extreme cold and weather conditions.

TS: I've been going to Iceland since 1998, en route to Halifax from Bergen. When I first visited there were no hotels and I had to stay at the Salvation Army hostel. But every year I go the airport gets busier. Many of your projects are focused on leisure and tourism. Is there a sense of architectural tourism in Icelandic terms?

HKC: Since 2000, and then again after the economic collapse, the tourism industry in Iceland has blossomed. The first phase of the Blue Lagoon was opened in 1999 and Sigríður, our partner, was the main architect. That was really the first real tourist project in Iceland, that really looked into the future. People said it was crazy to build this, way too big, it'll never work. Of course, after the first decade the hotel was already too small. Now people are building many tourist hotels for different activities and realising the added value that architecture can bring to their locations.

TS: The blend of architecture with landscape and tourism must be an amazing opportunity.

HKC: But also a dangerous one. Many projects happen without anyone taking the time to make a project last or endure, with no regard for quality.

TS: I think the Norwegian Tourist Routes projects are well paced. In contrast, the Banff National Park in Canada is like Disney World. And you have little towns that are overwhelmed by their ski areas. It can be a double-edged sword.

HKC: There are many wonderful places in Iceland. Twenty years ago you could visit them and it would just be you and your family enjoying this incredible landscape. Today you'll find coaches and a hundred people. You have to find ways of accommodating these numbers and cope with the flow of guests within the landscape.

MZ: There is a conscious effort to spread the tourist traffic around a larger area of the country and across a wider timeframe, so there's no longer a huge peak during the summer. There

Below: The Retreat at Blue Lagoon, Svartsengi, Grindavík, Iceland

ICELAND | BASALT ARCHITECTS

Below and opposite: Guðlaug baths, Akranes, Iceland

used to be an endless number of places that people never visited. But the government is promoting them more and more.

TS: On Fogo Island the population fell from 5,000 to 2,500 people when the fishing industry collapsed. At the Fogo Island Inn there are only 29 rooms and four artist studios. If we made more, it would be too much. We were very careful with that. We're also trying to make the winter season as interesting as the summer.

HKC: Right now, tourism is obviously struggling all over the world. Maybe one positive thing that can come out of the pandemic is that short-term thinking is more likely to get you left behind. This is also a moment of reflection. There are positive signs. Iceland is a big country with a lot of open space, and it's expected that is what people will want when they're able to travel again. The tourist operators here are getting prepared for this.

TS: What makes you different to other Icelandic architects?

HKC: It's a good question. It has to do with our very clear contextual approach to every site. As well as to the community, to history. Our architecture is essentially a platform to enjoy what is already there.

MZ: It's important to say that we come to every project with a clear mindset, with no preconceptions from other projects. It's a very positive thing that the projects are different.

HKC: And of course the client's goal has to be woven into all these contextual thoughts.

> It has to do with our very clear contextual approach to every site. As well as to the community, to history. Our architecture is essentially a platform to enjoy what is already there.
>
> — Hrólfur Karl Cela

TS: For myself, some of the things I brought from Canada into Norwegian architecture made a big difference. Was there anything you brought from Spain, perhaps?

MZ: I'm always influenced by everything, whether it's Spain, New York, London, Morocco. This open-minded approach is also a good way to approach a site.

TS: What changes have you made in the past five years to make you better architects?

HKC: You always have to be looking for better approaches. We just have to be aware of not becoming stagnant. We're moving offices soon and we're using it as an opportunity to look at ways of how we work and re-evaluate our processes. Our new office is by the sea in Reykjavik, which is an improvement.

MZ: In this business you need flexibility so you cannot really be fixed to one particular location.

TS: What is the life/work balance like in Iceland, particularly in architecture?

MZ: It's very well regulated. I worked in the Netherlands for one year and the culture there was 10–12 hours a day, for an 8-hour day salary. It didn't really work at all – it's just impossible to have any free time.

TS: I think Scandinavia's working culture works very well.

HKC: Well, we both came from the New York working environment, which is ridiculous – terrible, really. I wouldn't wish that on anybody. I think it's very healthy here in comparison.

Right: Basalt Architects, Reykjavik, Iceland

ÞETTA ER BESTI DAGUR LÍFS MÍNS!
ÞETTER BESTI DAGUR LÍFS MÍNS!
ÞETTA ER BESSTI DAGUR NÍFS MÍNS!
ÞETTER BLESTI DRAGUR MÍFS LÍNS!
FETTE BLESSTI DRAGUR LÍFS MÍNS!
SETTER GLESTI DAGUR LÍFS MÍNS!
FRETTE GRESTE DRANUL FÍSS BÍNS!
SNETTE BLESSSI GNAGUF DRÍS KÍS!
SPETT NESSTI GANDUÐ BRÍNS FÍT!
SKETTE FLESTIR ANDUR FÍLS KÍR!
PENTI LESTI SPLAGUR SPLÍS SPLÍS!
SKREFTI BRENTSF GRANDF BLE!
SELEN BRONST FRAMT BNÍS!
SELESKR FROMTAS KMMSK FFT!

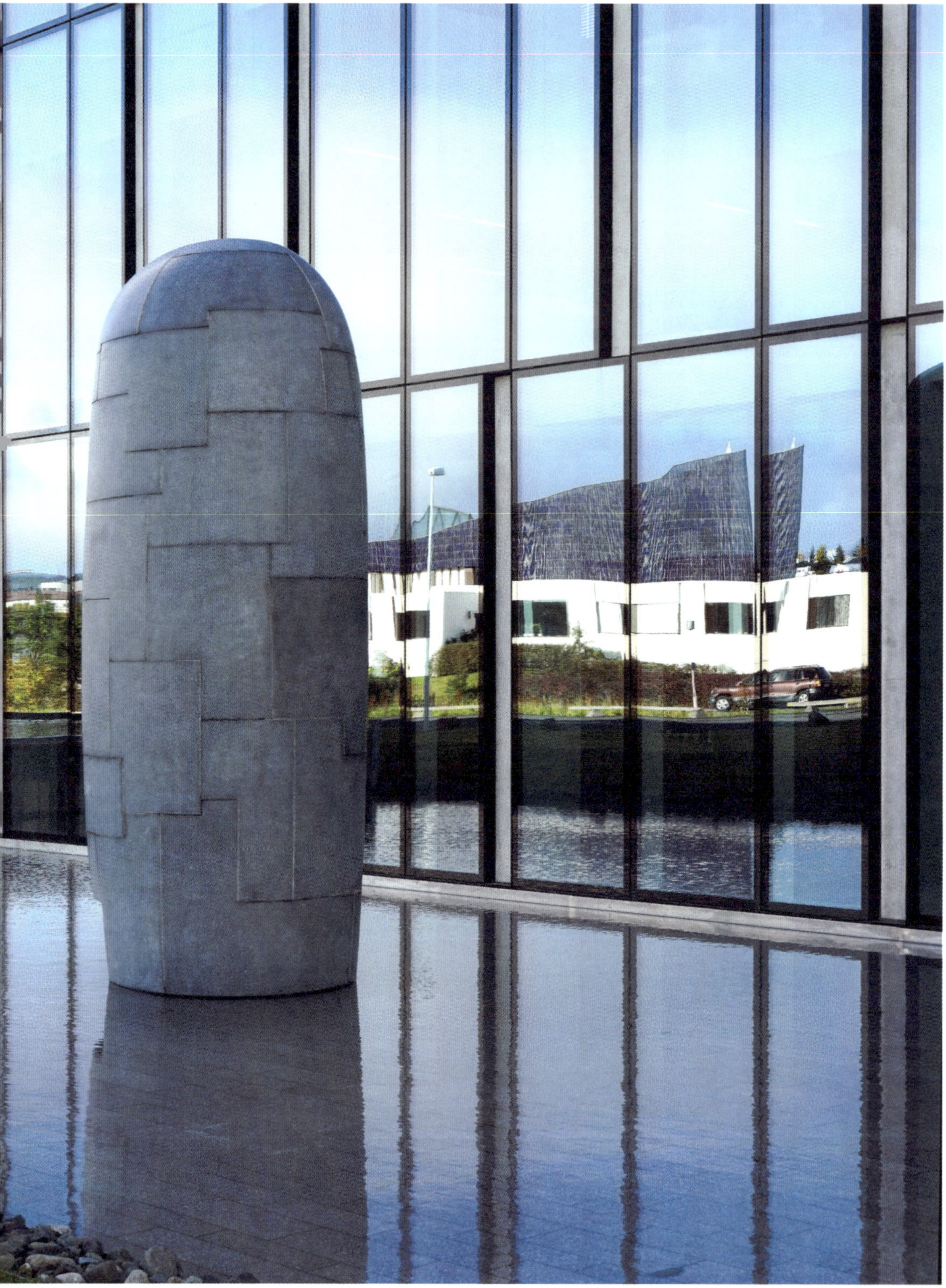

PK Arkitektar

Palmar Kristmundsson set up PK Arkitektar in Reykjavik in 1991. Over the last 30 years, Kristmundsson has shaped a contemporary vernacular that reflects Iceland's dramatic topography, combined with influences drawn from his personal experience of Japanese architecture.

PK's work ranges from public buildings to private houses, including a number of dramatic modern villas nestling in the Icelandic landscape. Other projects include corporate headquarters and radical conversions like the transformation of the Steypustoðin (Concrete Factory), a long-abandoned facility close to the Dýrafjörður fjord that is a dramatic vacation home and occasional extension of the studio space.

The design team creates complementary furniture and lighting design for many of PK's projects, emphasising the very hands-on, craft-based nature of the design and construction process. The studio has been twice nominated for the Mies van der Rohe architecture awards and prides itself on its high quality and environmental performance. The choice of materials, from weathered Corten steel to fair faced concrete, reflects the harsh Icelandic climate and the need for architecture to survive and endure in any environment.

pk.is

Previous page, above and right: Alvogen Iceland Headquarters, Kopavogur, Iceland

> I have more courage to say, "Okay, time is not the limit here, the bigger picture is the quality, and purpose."
>
> — Pálmar Kristmundsson

Todd Saunders: If you had to experience your career all over again, would you do it?

Pálmar Kristmundsson: You think, "Well, would it be nicer to be an artist and not have to deal with clients all the time?" But there are pros and cons because even the most demanding clients make you realise that "I'm not alone in the world, I'm not doing this only for myself." I do still sometimes wonder: "What if I was just an artist and I could just stay in my studio with nobody interfering with anything?"

TS: What parts of the job do you look forward to?

PK: What really attracts me is the desire to see some progress, some change. I admit that sometimes I am a bit scared of the day ahead, but ultimately, it's just this – a day – and it passes. I find satisfaction in seeing something evolve or become re-framed so you can look at it differently from the norm.

TS: On Fogo Island, it was exciting to see the change effected on the community by the architecture project I was involved in. Have you experienced that in the village you work in?

PK: I observe how the economy works, being very much involved in this little community. You have to think of its basic needs, things you don't notice in bigger cities because there's so much happening.

TS: That's a good point. As part of a teaching project with Cornell University, we did a series of "small-scale interventions" along Norway's longest fjord, Sognefjord Fjord. Each project concept was designed to have a big impact or instigate change. What small project might do that in that village?

PK: After staying there and building my retreat in this old concrete factory, I have had a few ideas. From the building, you see the sun setting over the mouth of the fjord. For maybe 5 or 10 years, I've been wondering how to "grab" this moment with a higher purpose. So I came up with an idea called The Sunset Gallery. I drew up a viewing platform for the sunset, which was made from three elements. One is a platform that gives you a panoramic view of the fjord and the magnificent sunset. The second gives a vertical view of the ocean and the sky. And the third building is a black box where you can watch the sunset from 24 places in the world, in real time at the same time you are visiting. The community board liked the idea, so we're trying to raise money to build it. Even if we don't raise enough money, there are other general planning projects for the village.

TS: It can take me a long time to get to know a place in Norway. When I did the architecture on Fogo Island, although I felt like I knew the place really well, I still didn't know people's needs. The answers seemed to come quicker because I was one of them. Do you feel that you can make better architecture in that community because you understand their needs?

PK: Yes. I know the place and the older generation are my friends. What I learned is that there are also creative younger people who have moved there, a guy from Belgium and his Danish wife, Icelanders, young people that live and work in Brussels and move there, stay part of the year and so on. There are always new perspectives to take account for.

TS: I think coming to Norway made me see things differently. It then took me 20 years to appreciate Newfoundland and Fogo Island.

As a foreigner and as a visitor you can bring new light to a place, and then as a local working in your own community, there's something in you that helps you really understand it. Did going to Japan or living and working in Reykjavik give you a new perspective on living and working in the village?

PK: Just buying the old abandoned concrete factory and changing it into a place to live was very unusual. It's a nice experience to come to a community and want to join it, but it can still be difficult. I remember I was sitting with the two brothers who were helping me out at the factory. One of them was asking how they should do this and that, and I was explaining, and finally the other brother – who had just sat quietly, said, "Yeah, you come up with all that nonsense, we will do it for you." For them, the idea of turning an old abandoned concrete factory in a "hopeless" place into a summer retreat house, was very odd to them. In that sense one can also challenge the perspective.

TS: It's like you're like an artist within the community and they really love that you're strange and that you feel like you belong there. I have similar feelings in Fogo – they really appreciate my "weirdness" and it feels good to be allowed to be myself there.

PK: Exactly the same feeling I have. Many of these people are good friends of my late father who was a fisherman here. They have become close friends and they sometimes talk to me like I was my father. I was the son of the captain in the village, and my father tried to make a sailor out of me. He once took me out and we had not even left the fjord before I started vomiting all over his cabin. He turned the boat around, sailed back to the harbour, threw me on the pier and said, "You will never be a sailor." I was the community loser for a while. In such a small community, all these positions are very visible. One journalist described me as "the architect that the sea rejected".

TS: I grew up in a small town and you couldn't really lie, because five minutes later everyone would know and you would get a reputation. But in the international architecture scene, in larger cities, people seem to be able to lie and get away with it. It's a good feeling when you feel you become part of a community in your role as an architect and build trust. Can you talk about the summer house and what it did for you and the office?

PK: The idea started as a studio for my office, actually. For a while we were just using it as part of our office. If there was a competition or we were starting up a project, we could say, "Okay, let's take a long weekend and be somewhere out of the grid where we can figure it out." It is a place where I can do something without having a specific a plan. You're completely free – I never have to finish anything "on time". I don't know if it helps the architecture, but it helps me concentrate . It is good to be more relaxed because the time schedules that we face are ridiculous sometimes and not beneficial to the projects. I have more courage to say, "Okay, time is not the limit here, the bigger picture is the quality, and purpose."

TS: How do you know if a client has a good balance between money and time?

PK: I don't think I ever know before I get into the project. We sometime say that "people with money don't wait". Also, the people with money don't always want to spend the money on what you prefer to use the money for.

Above and right: BHM, vacation rental cottage, Brekkuskógur, Iceland

Left and below: Steypustöðin, Pálmar's personal vacation house and creative station, Dýrafjörður, Iceland

Opposite: B25, private residence, Reykjavik, Iceland

TS: Do some clients really appreciate good quality architecture that takes time to make?

PK: Many appreciate quality but very few understand that quality takes time. And perhaps 95 per cent of our clients have become really close friends, so I'm lucky in that sense. Basically, you're just two parts talking about a certain task.

TS: Do you have any reflections on your relationships with time in architecture?

PK: When you have a lot of time, is the quality always better? I don't know. When I was studying in Denmark, I really learned from the short one-day, two-day projects. I couldn't cope with the slow working ethic of students at the time, so I became a professional cyclist instead, making good use of the spare time.

TS: In Norway, how I work can be very informal. I make a sketch and print it to my 3D printer and then I work directly with my carpenter with no drawings. When we did the twisted artist studio on Fogo Island it was just impossible to do construction details – we had about 100 pages of drawings. The carpenter built a couple of models and that was what they ended up using; no-one looked at the drawings at all. These guys were all boat builders and they've never used drawings. That really changed my whole process. How do you work in Iceland?

PK: For the Steypustödin project I also worked with a boat builder from the village. He did a big deal of the carpentry. In Iceland, you can really talk directly to everybody who is involved in building a project. My experience in places like Germany showed me that this isn't always the case, where it was actually forbidden.

TS: A lot of foreigners come to Scandinavia and find a real difference in working culture compared to the US or Canada. How do you ensure that work doesn't dominate your life?

PK: As you get older everything – life and architecture – gets more and more mingled together. But I don't think we think about these things nearly enough. Personally, outdoor sports help – you can get away and do a completely different thing. However, life in general seems to always be about being the fucking architect, wherever you go and whatever you do.

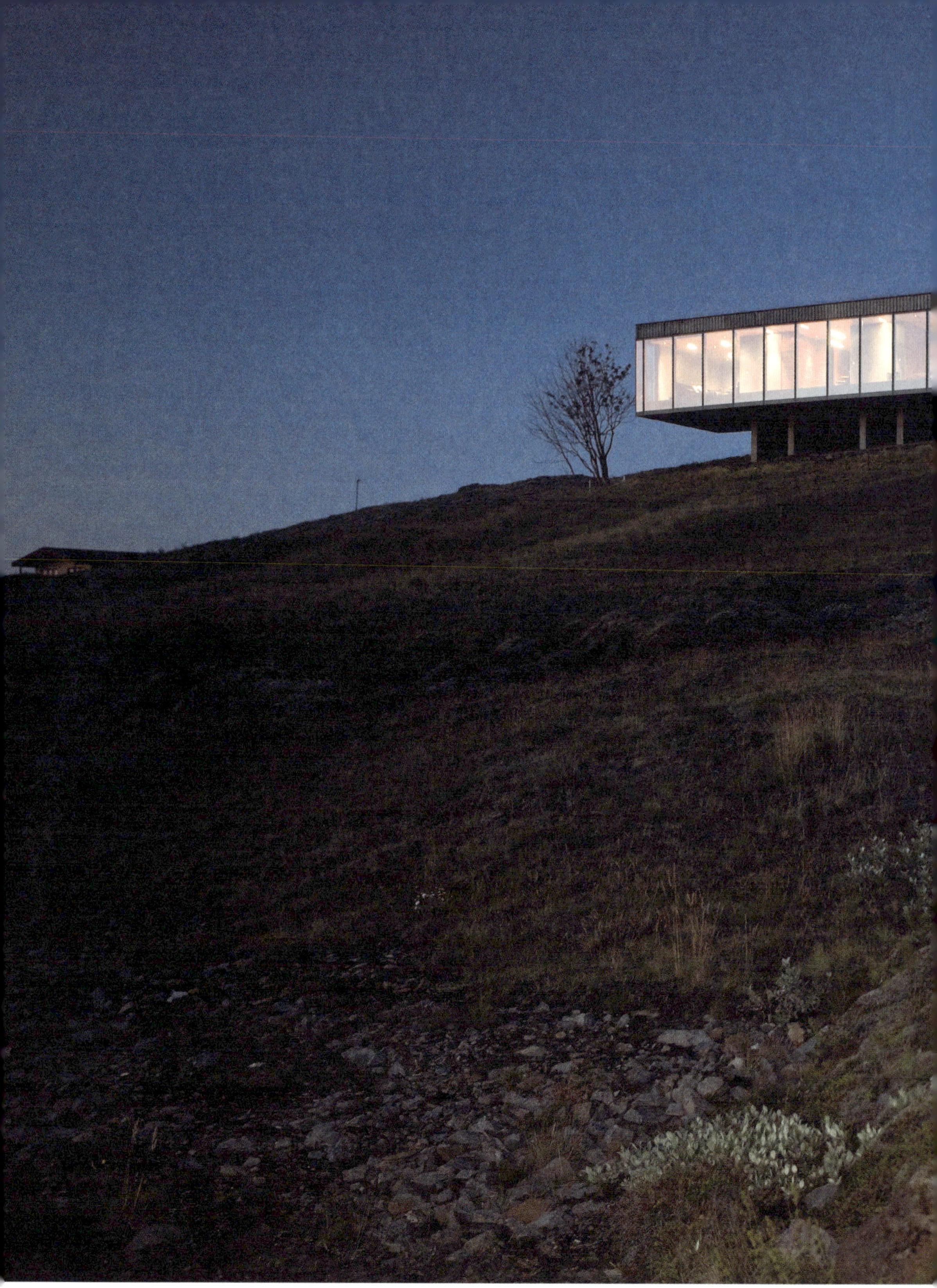

ICELAND | PK ARKITEKTAR

Previous pages: Árborg, vacation house, Sveitarfélagið Árborg, Iceland

Right: PK Arkitektar, Reykjavik, Iceland

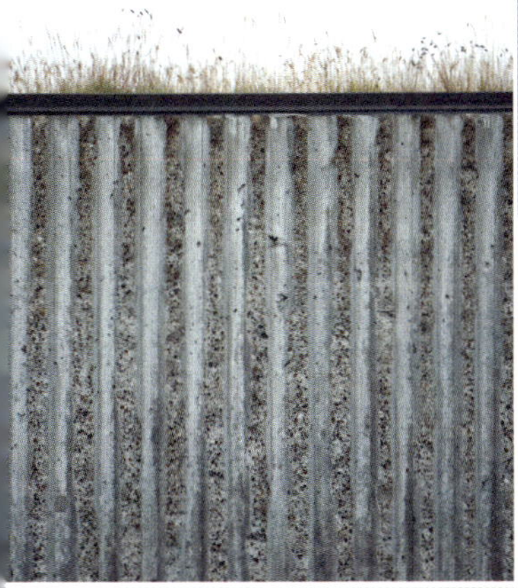
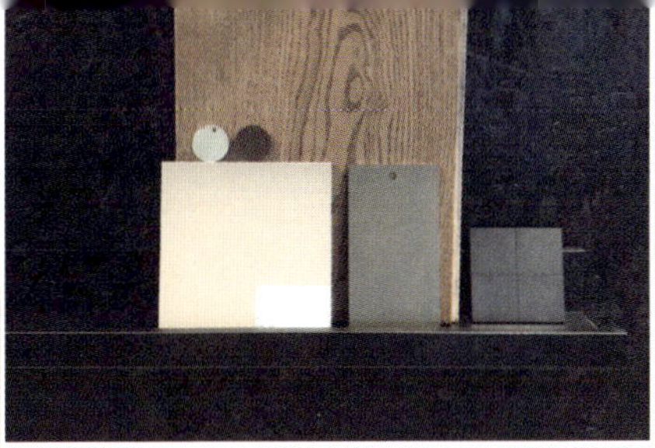
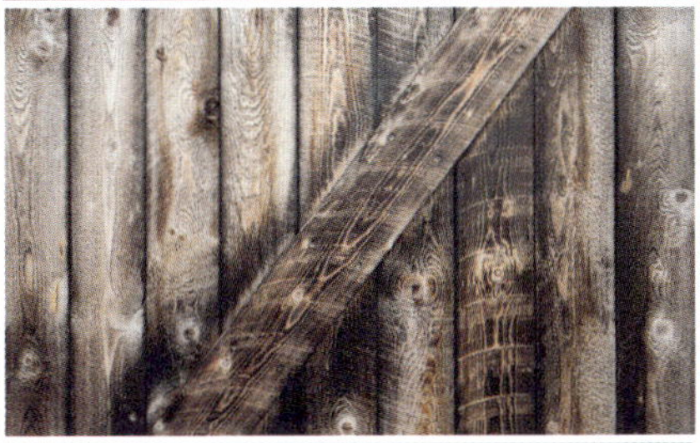
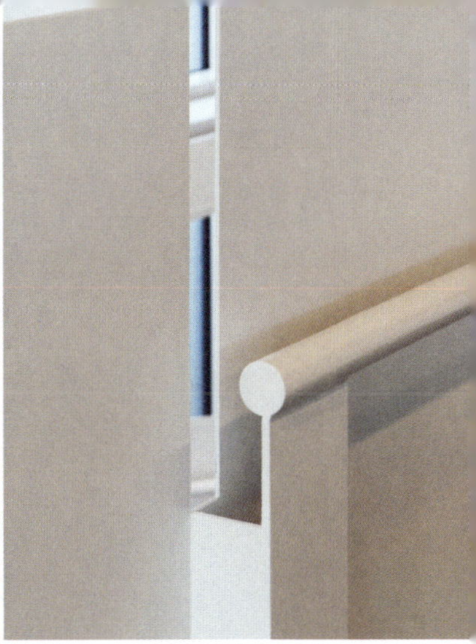
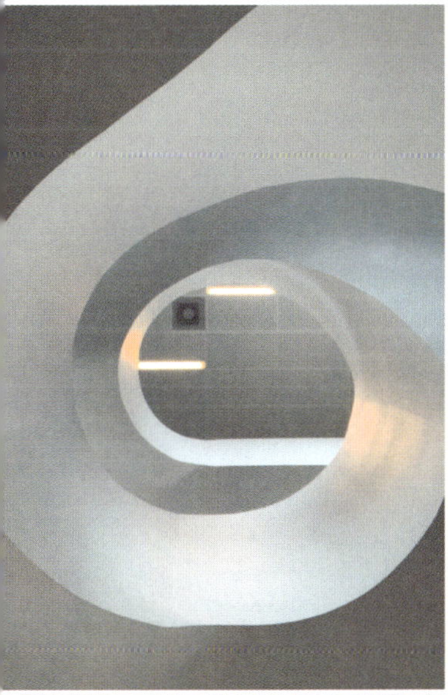
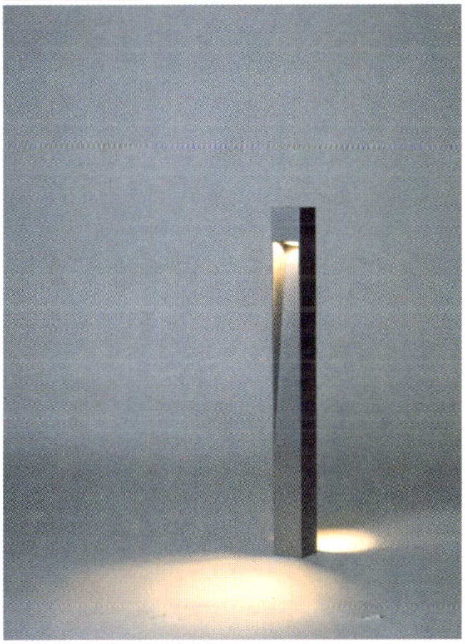
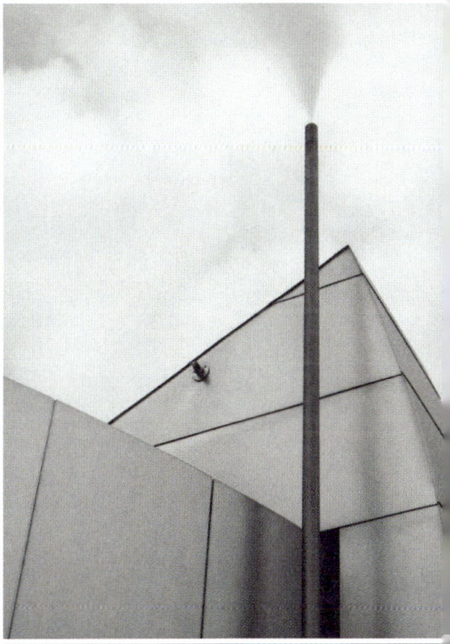
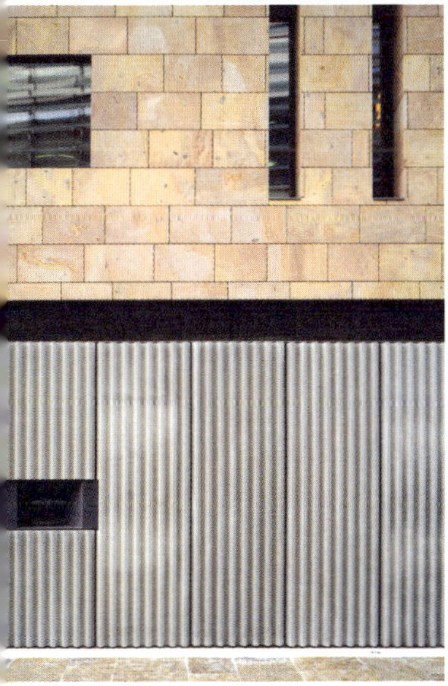
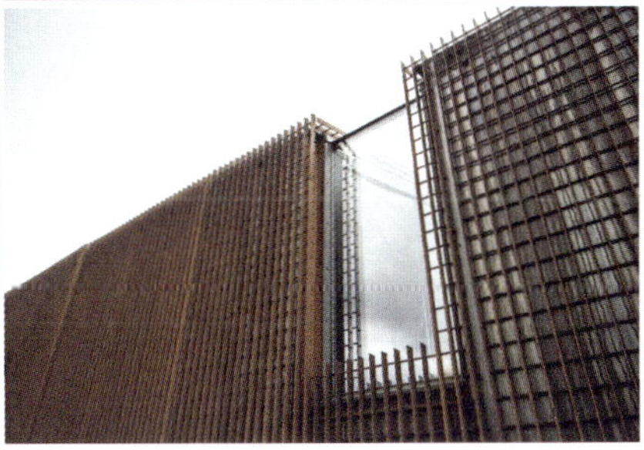
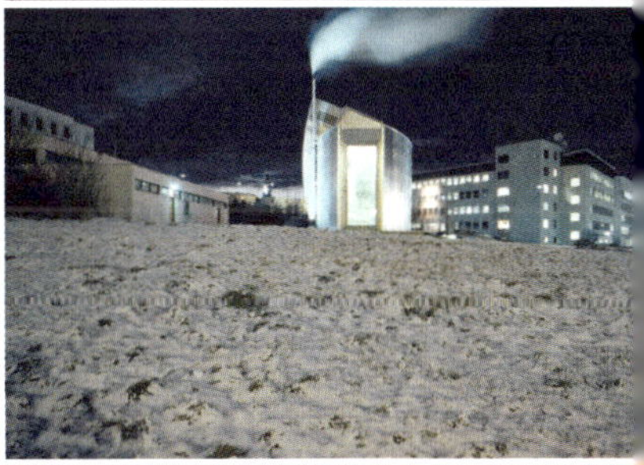
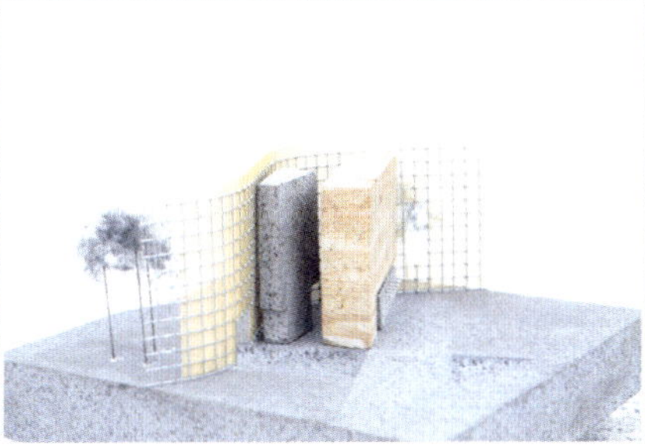
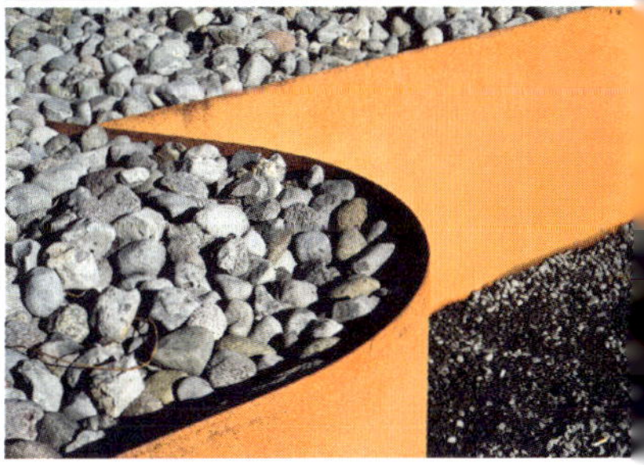

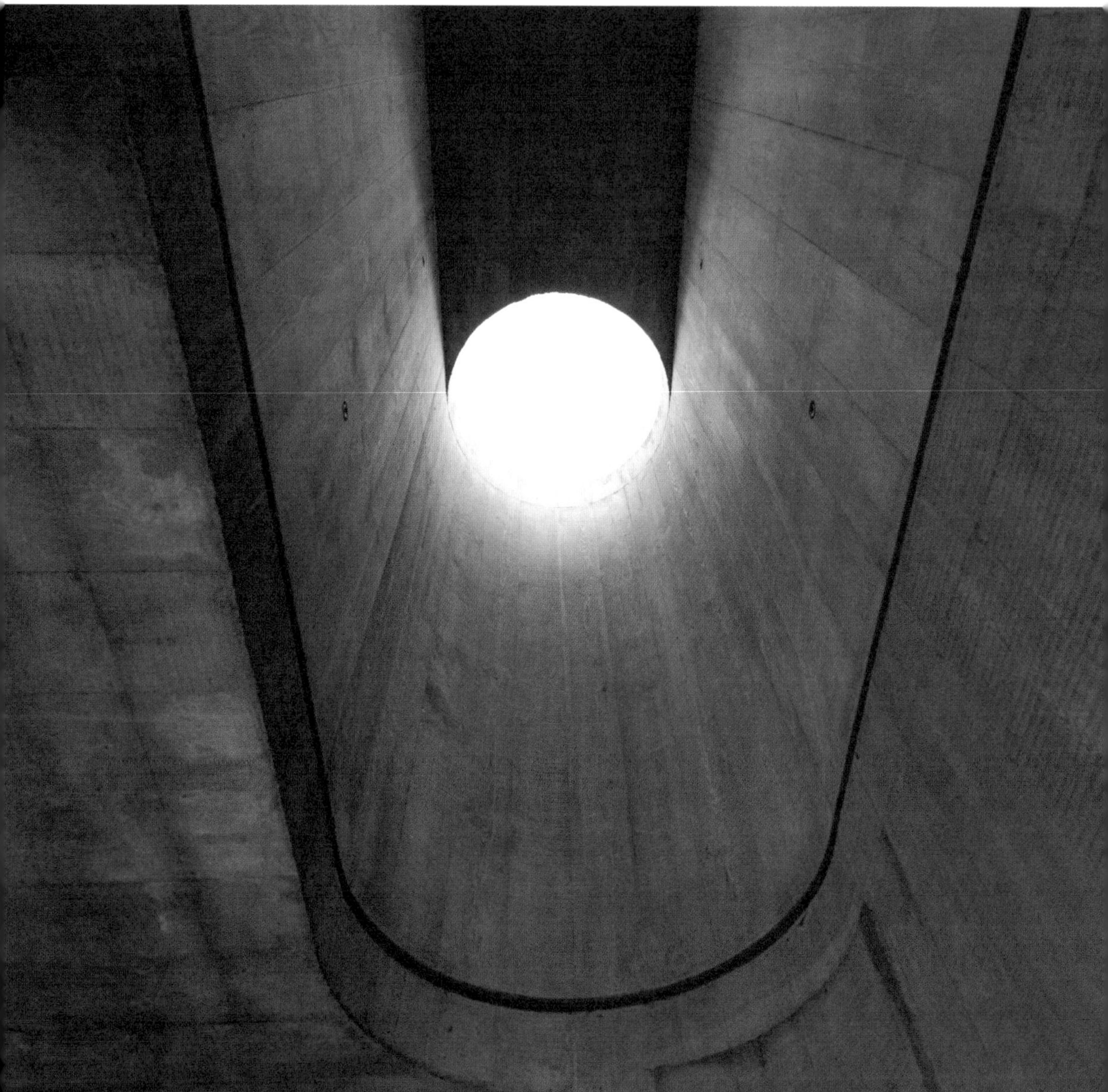

Studio Granda

Studio Granda was established in Reykjavik by Margret Harðardóttir and Steve Christer in 1987. Its first major project was the controversial design for Reykjavik's new City Hall, which opened in 1992. Studio Granda has stayed small and closely engaged with the local architectural scene, building hundreds of projects over the past three decades, from private houses to hotels, apartments and road and pedestrian bridges. Their work directly addresses the stark nature of the Icelandic landscape, incorporating materials and forms that will withstand time and the ravages of the weather. "During the creation of an object the forces of nature, culture, function and time are to be challenged, ordered and re-ordered by the emerging architectural identity," Harðardóttir and Christer write, stressing that the physical requirements of a structure, "unlike thinking or technology", have been unchanged for millennia. For Studio Granda, the craft of construction is essential, not just in terms of the physical quality of materials and workmanship, but in the details, right down to the concrete mix. In 2020, the studio won the Icelandic Design Award 2020 for the Drangar project. "In the final analysis architecture is judged as a complete entity."

studiogranda.is

Previous page, right and below: B14, Iceland

We enjoy it when a project doesn't have to go too fast, when you can sleep on ideas and have conversations with clients, consultants and contractors. It makes a project richer.

— Steve Christer

Todd Saunders: How long have you been in Iceland?

Steve Christer: I've been living here since 1987. Margrét, my partner is Icelandic. I first came here in 1983 and really hated it. It was not the place for me. Back then, Iceland was just Reykjavik and nothing else.

TS: How long did it take you to understand the place and the culture?

SC: That didn't happen until we won a competition here, so I had an important reason to learn the language, in order to talk to the contractor and discuss our aims. Now when I go back to England, people compliment me on my English.

TS: I never worked as an architect in Canada, so I can't always remember the English word for a lot of things I use in everyday architecture.

SC: All the technical knowledge is in your adopted language.

TS: It's strange because then you have to revert and because of my relationship to that technical language I don't sound that knowledgeable in meetings back in Canada and the US.

SC: Also, I speak a very '80s English – it can just get embarrassing.

TS: When you're discussing projects with Margrét is it on a practical level or are you dreaming about things?

SC: It's seeing how the different things add up, conceptually, financially, structurally. We tackle it from all different angles. There's a common ego, I think. We've been together for nearly 40 years, so it works, I think. The discussions end when we are both happy.

TS: I've never heard of the idea of common ego. It's almost like you have a shared value system that's higher than your personalities.

SC: We tend to know when we've achieved something we're both satisfied with. That's why we are Studio Granda – we wanted it to be a name, not our names. That's a very difficult concept to get into the mindset of journalists.

TS: They want design heroes. I challenge that all the time. I always want them to talk more about the project.

SC: We are not the main issue. A project is the product of the office, which is whoever happens to be around at any given time. If we have a bunch of friends here, they will almost certainly affect the way that we think, so the product will change as a result. Even if we haven't been discussing the project, we might be talking about red wine or volcanoes or something. It affects your mindset.

TS: It creates room for more collective thinking. I try to step aside a lot. So what about you, where did you study architecture?

SC: We spent two years at the Architectural Association in London. It was like stepping into another reality. Our year was set up with the unit system, which has now become the de facto standard of how you learn architecture. And it was a complete dog-eat-dog environment, both among the students and the lecturers. Zaha was there, teaching, so was Will Alsop. Peter Cook. Everybody was there. The lecture series was extraordinary. It was like, "Shall we go to Frank Gehry, or see Richard Meier?" So you got the sense that whatever reality threw at you, you were going to have to be hard and ready. It didn't teach you anything about waterproofing, or running an office, all those bigger issues we have to deal with every day, in addition to trying to design.

TS: When you look back at the attitude and energy created by the AA at that time, it basically permeated the whole profession of architecture.

SC: We were just lucky. I had previously studied at Newcastle and considered myself an architect and wanted to know where to go next. I didn't actually understand a word of the AA prospectus – but it turned out that it was everything that wasn't architecture. Everything I learnt at Newcastle just went. It was a complete cut-off. It didn't exist any more. Just like when I came to Iceland, I had to do the same thing again.

TS: To reinvent how you saw architecture?

SC: In England you make a building and you put trees around it, so it might as well not exist. In Iceland, a building is for everybody to see, forever.

TS: It is a beautiful country, don't you think?

SC: Yes, but it's a bit weird that every single site our clients bring to us is always "the most beautiful in Iceland"! All we know for sure is that there is no ready-made solution for that site. Whatever happens will have to come out of a conversation with the client. The more you talk, the more personal a client can be, the better it is. It's as if you are making clothes for these people, and the more they tell you about themselves, the better they will fit. So there are all kinds of discussions. Very often the best ideas come from the clients. We added the bridge at Drangar when the project was under construction. It happened because the client was on site and realised that as their apartment was on the upper floor they had to go all the way downstairs before going up again to reach the adjacent bank. They suggested the idea of a bridge, I sketched a proposal in 20 minutes, sent it to them, and that was it.

TS: My best clients are those people who are confident enough to share their ideas with you. Iceland is a small place, even smaller than Norway. Do you wait for these clients or do you go after them?

SC: They normally just knock on the door when we've got nothing to do. It happens again and again. A good example was maybe five years after the crash. We'd had a family with whom we'd done many projects, which had kept us going. However, they had all finished and we were down to just the two of us in the office. Then someone approached us about a project on a farm. It didn't really sound very convincing – like one of those projects where all they want you to do is come and wave your arms round and choose a paint colour. But when we visited the site with them, we realised that they knew the place very well, they showed their real colours and explained their ideas. It started a five-year conversation. It was just beautiful.

TS: That's almost a checklist for good clients: they know a site well and have a strong, emotional connection to it.

SC: It's also not just about working with the architect. When you talk about the understanding and respect for a place and

This page: Drangar, Renovation, Snæfellsnes, Iceland

ICELAND | STUDIO GRANDA

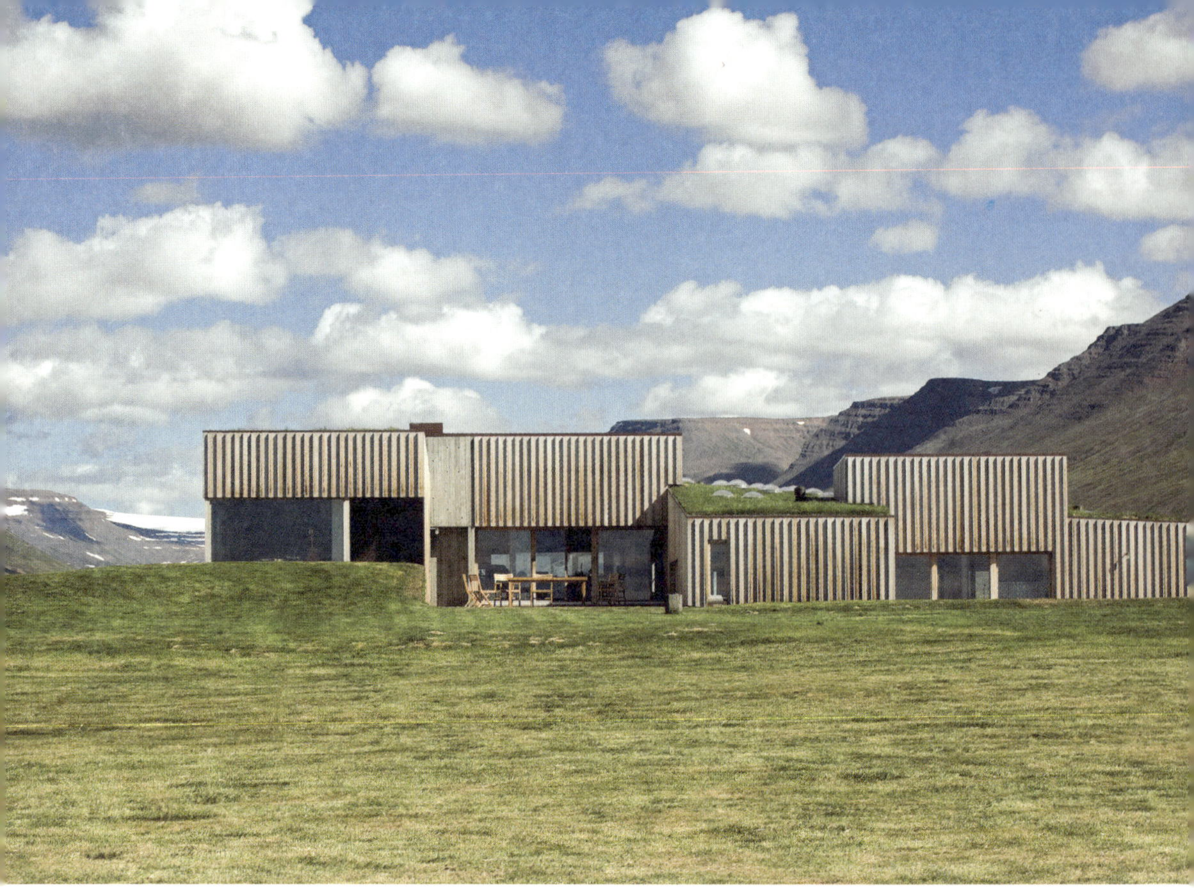

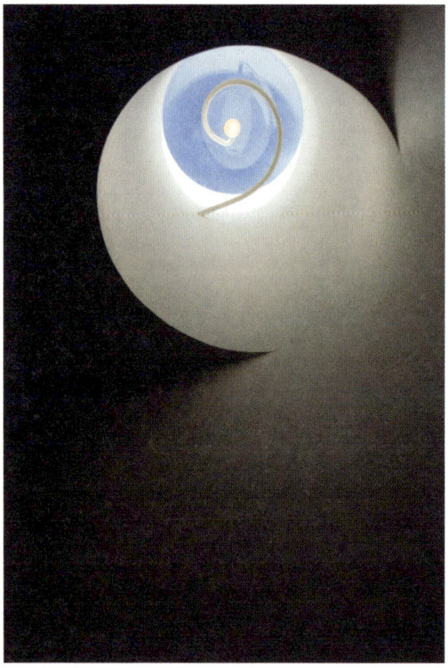

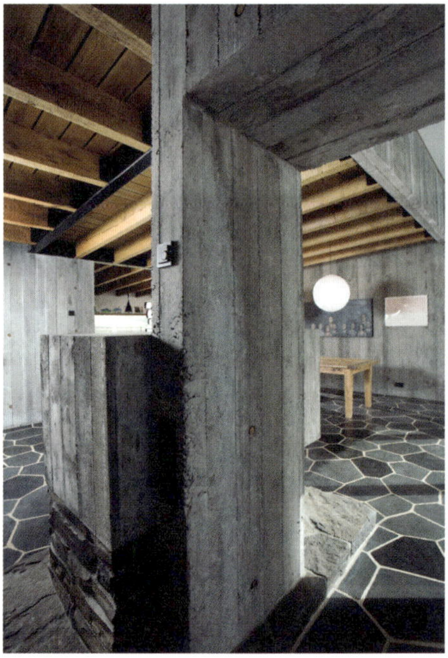

Opposite: Hof Residence, Skagafjörður, Iceland

its values, you're talking about all the other people who are actually needed to make a building. If you have a good client, they often know the names of the contractor. We call that the "love triangle". When that works, something magical happens. There's another house we did some years ago in north Iceland, Hof. Again, an extended family. It took us four years just to refine the concept of the house. We had this great relationship with this contractor up in the north. In wintertime, it's a bit touch and go to drive over four hours so you fly and although it should be under an hour that way, half the flights are cancelled because of the weather. Because of this the drawings are very important and an engaged contractor even more so. When we went on site, I could see within ten minutes that he had followed the drawings precisely. It was brilliant.

TS: How do you build up trust and respect in such a small community?

SC: Relationships are very sensitive. You have to be extremely careful about who and what you say about people to other people.

TS: Can you talk about the importance of time in your design work?

SC: I think you can make design decisions quickly, and you'll get an okay result, because you're using whatever knowledge base you have gained over the years. Some things work and some things don't. It's going to be okay, but it might not have any layers or depth. We enjoy it when a project doesn't have to go too fast, when you can sleep on ideas and have conversations with clients, consultants and contractors. It makes a project richer. Generally, our designs also incorporate materials that have a sense of time built into them, like oak or stone. It's very different to, say, aluminium. But if you put that stone next to aluminium, then you have another conversation about time. We used the idea of geological strata for the façade of the new building for the Icelandic Parliament.

TS: I would ask what you want to do next, but it seems like your attitude is ready for anything.

SC: My answer would probably be to have more fun. Instead of being too concerned about proving yourself all the time, you can allow yourself to work more with ideas and concepts that are more open.

TS: You've been in Iceland longer than I've been in Norway. For a lot of foreigners in Norway, it's a very different culture, but I've reached the point where I can see the value of my kids growing up here. What do you love about being in Iceland as a foreigner?

ICELAND | STUDIO GRANDA

SC: We're especially privileged to be here. We never forget that. We came here trusted with a significant project, the Reykjavik City Hall. It was really humbling, and we still have massive gratitude for that. It was a very close-knit society then, but you could penetrate it by learning to work together. Since then, as just two people, we've done over 300 projects. At its biggest, our office was nine people, with an average of three or four. We've only had five written contracts, two of which were written after the project was completed. But we're only in this position because of the City Hall. We were responsible for the most expensive – and the most hated! – building in the country. At the start there was even an anti-City Hall terrorist organisation, which slashed the mayor's tyres and planted bombs. Seriously. But once the building opened, it went the other way. In three days, more than a third of the population of the country visited the building. That is why we feel so privileged to work in Iceland.

Opposite and below: Hringbraut bridge, Reykjavik, Iceland

ICELAND | STUDIO GRANDA

Right: Studio Granda, Reykjavik, Iceland

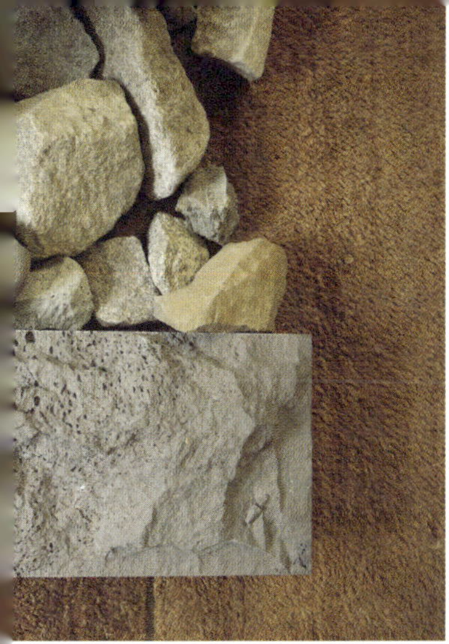
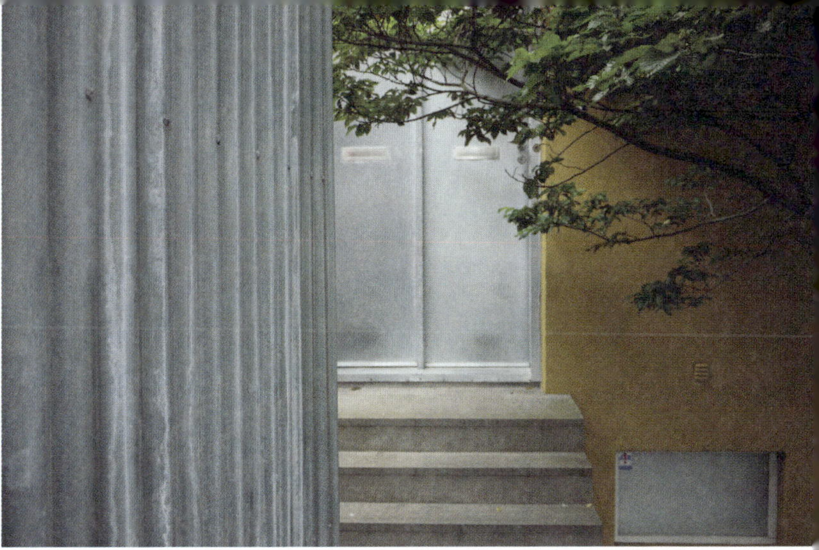
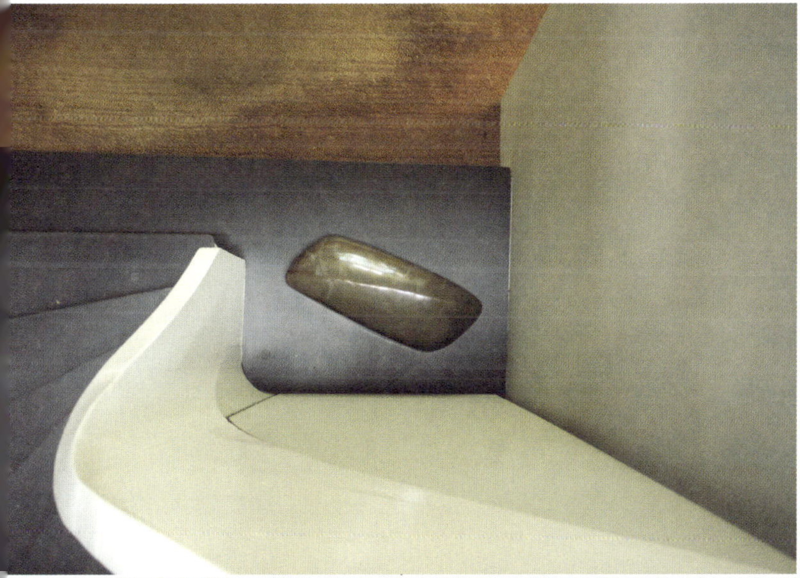
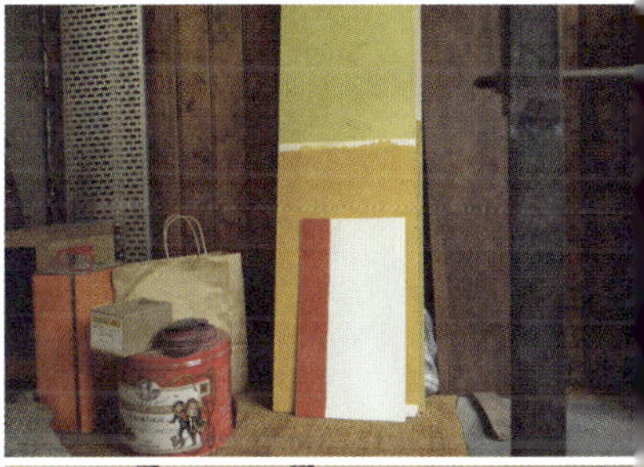
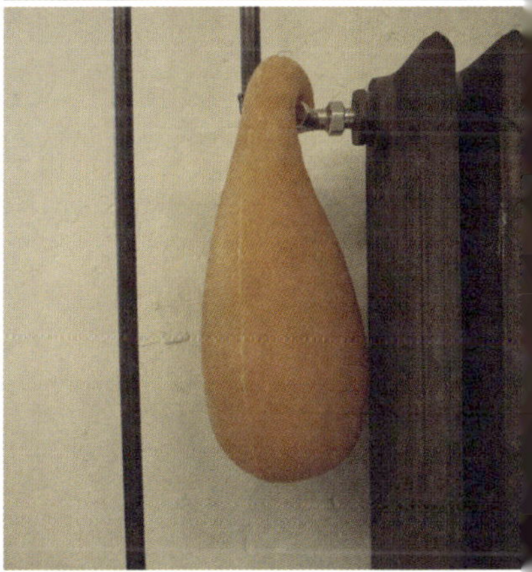
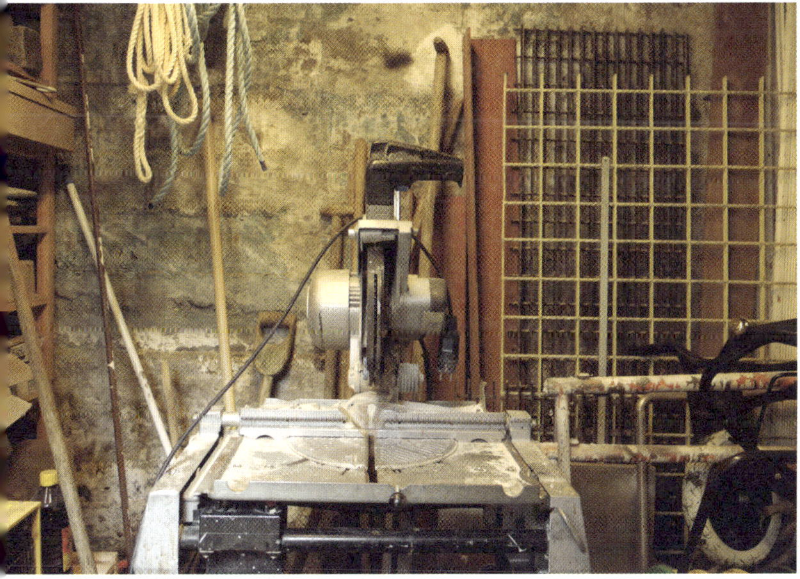
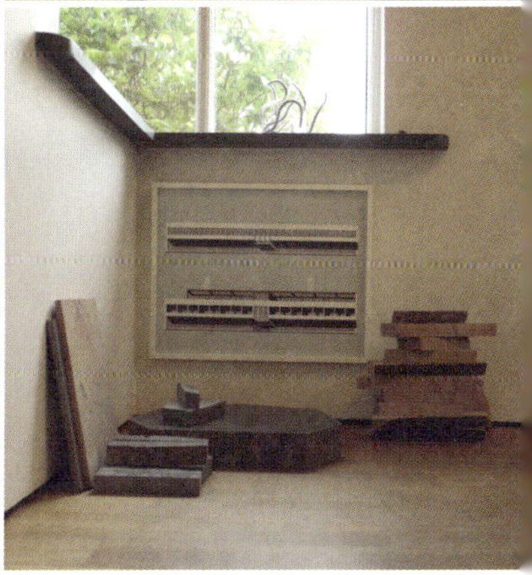

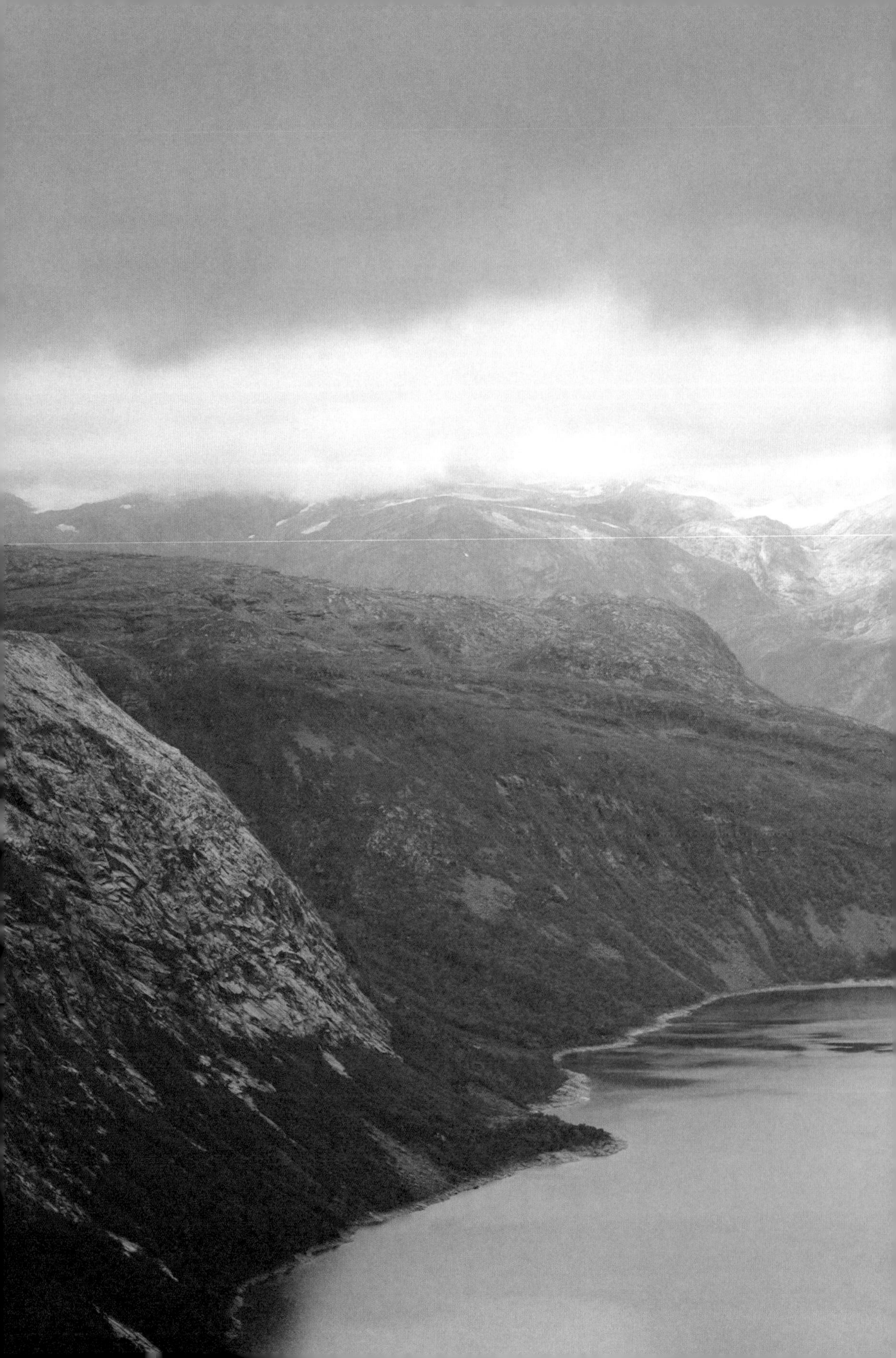

NORWAY

{ ESSAY }

A SHARED PROCESS

{ BY }

JOAKIM SKAJAA

*Architecture curator at the National Museum
of Art, Architecture and Design in Norway*

What is the process of drawing and building architecture? Questions around process seem to have been especially important in the field of architecture recently, from processed materials to computer processing, to open, shared and inclusive ways of working.

For the first few decades after the Second World War, we might speculate that the building industry and architecture still was rooted in pre-modern technologies. Architects, while producing modern buildings, were still drawing by hand on sheets of paper. To a large extent, they were confined to quite narrow set of materials and methods. It was, perhaps, possible to realise buildings with far fewer drawings and documentation than today.

In the final decades of the last century, architecture culture and the building industry becomes increasingly influenced by technology. Everything gets more complicated, from materials to drawings and documentation. Materials are no longer simple monotone things, but hybrid objects made from conglomerates of substances with complicated methods of assembly. The drawings and documentation that architects need to produce to describe these buildings become denser and more numerous. The architect's drawing is no longer a physical object, but a set of vectors on a screen, lines of code, numbers in a database.

On top of these technological developments, the bureaucracy around each building has also escalated. The involvement of developers, financiers, municipalities, external consultants, users and interest groups etc., places the process of producing architecture within an uncertain landscape of technology and politics. I believe that the complexity of process and culture are intertwined.

In the conversations in this book, with a diverse group of Norwegian practitioners, it is clear that process is important. The idea that to master architecture is to master the process shines through. Håkon Matre Aasarød from Vardehaugen talks about staying in control of the process as more and more people get involved, while Sami Rintala and Dagur Eggertsson talk about architecture being a process with many heads. In their workshop model for creating architecture everyone is included.

Dan Zohar from Haugen Zohar describes the design of a "good process", echoing a shift of focus in the architect's role from end result to facilitation. In the constant dialogue about the architect's role within the profession, the idea that an architect is a facilitator of dialogues is increasingly acknowledged. It is a role that works well in response to the complex process of contemporary building , putting the architect in a leadership role, albeit with a softer power than in the idealised past.

Other architects, such as Helen & Hard, strive to invest power with the future users and residents of their projects. Siv Helene Stangeland describes the creation of an open process that includes other voices than their own, a process that spans from hand drawing to participation. It is an idea that resonates with Snøhetta founder Ketil Trædal, who explains how the firm builds a community of knowledge and a collective ownership of ideas and concepts through their design process.

But process can also be a way to shift the focus back to the actual building and the physical manifestation of ideas through architecture. Reiulf Ramstad warns that the focus on inclusive processes sometimes clouds honest discussions about the quality of the actual results. Børre Skodvin talks about how their process is extended into the building phase, asking for clients who are willing to take on the uncertainty of not knowing exactly how the building will turn out. It is a sentiment that is shared by Gartnerfuglen, who liken the process of designing buildings to natural evolution. They let their projects develop, more or less randomly, reacting to new ideas and influences, into "perfectly adapted monsters".

The shift of focus towards the processes of architecture is a natural response to the complex and technologically driven construction industry. An open process is more inclusive and democratic. The challenge is for that inclusivity to extend past the process and encompass the anxiety and ambition that these practitioners demonstrate.

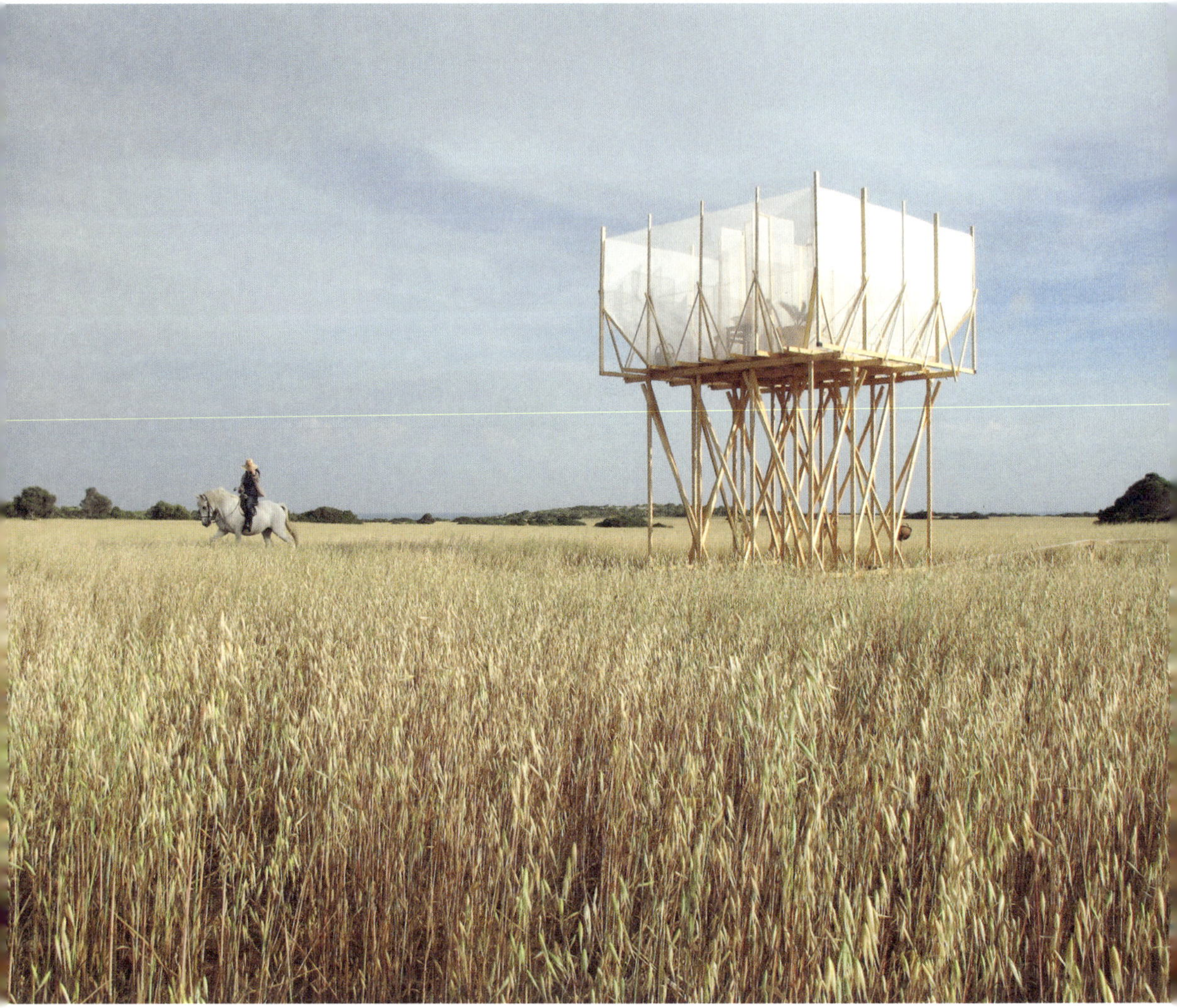

Gartnerfuglen Arkitekter

Gartnerfuglen Arkitekter was founded in 2013 by Astrid Rohde Wang, Ole Larsen and Olav Lunde Arneberg. Based in Oslo, the office works on projects on a variety of scales, with a special focus on housing and cabins. Every project is taken from initial idea through to final detailing on site, often working closely with craftspeople and traditional techniques. The office's international assignments have included projects in India, South Sudan, Bulgaria, Thailand, Spain, Belgium and France. The original *gartnerfugl*, or bowerbird, lives in the forests of Papua New Guinea. "The male collects seemingly useless objects and puts them together in new and beautiful arrangements, only to impress a mate," the architects say.

gartnerfuglen.com

When developing a project, you should always go with ideas so far from the reality that you will get "stretched ligaments". And after they're stretched, they will never return to their original position.

— Ole Larsen

Previous page, above and left: Grooming retreat, Santanyí, Spain

TODD SAUNDERS: I've been talking to other architects about the concept of "shared emotions" from their life and career based on architecture. Has that ever happened with the three of you?

OLE LARSEN: I think we have a shared understanding of architecture.

OLAV LUNDE ARNEBERG: Are we talking about concrete experiences?

TS: For example, when I did the Fogo Island project, it seemed there hadn't been a nice building in Newfoundland for 60 years. I remember walking into the construction site and still not knowing if the builders were any good. I was about 500 metres away and I first saw the Long Studio and I just knew the project was going to be amazing. I'd never had the experience where all that work just came together in one moment.

OLA: With some of our projects, there is no specific building site before we start. Perhaps that's the closest we've got to this feeling – when we've found something about a place or specific site that triggers something in all of us.

ASTRID ROHDE WANG: I trust the others' emotions even if I don't necessarily understand them all. Sometimes that's how we make decisions – the one with the strongest emotion wins. It doesn't make sense – but I really believe in it.

TS: You follow your inner intuition.

ARW: Compromise is what we avoid more than anything.

TS: Isn't the whole of life a compromise?

ARW: I know. It's poison.

TS: How important is surprise and freedom for each of you in terms of thinking and bringing something new?

ARW: Courage is a very important characteristic for an architect. You should be super nervous, at every stage, whether it's presenting your project to the client because it might be too edgy, or when you plan the building and ask for prices, it should feel risky. And then the next stage – I'm someone who is really comfortable with asking for the right price, you know. We have a very ambitious cabin project at the moment. We never lowered the client's expectations, and because we had the courage of our convictions, we have got it in under budget. Had we told the client their budget was too low, we would also have had to lower their expectations.

OL: When developing a project, you should always go with ideas so far from the reality that you will get "stretched ligaments". And after they're stretched, they will never return to their original position.

TS: So how do you start stretching slowly?

OL: Not slowly. We just rip them off. Sometimes we use this as a tactic for "training" the client.

OLA: We usually start off with one concept or one solution to the task but then we also figure out different solutions and put the same care into every one of them. However, one of them will always be super crazy.

ARW: Two crazy ideas and one insanely crazy. That's stretched ligaments.

TS: With three or four ideas, are there tactics you use? Do you all agree between yourselves which one is the best?

ARW: Usually, I like all of them.

OL: We would never present a concept that we wouldn't love to work with. We believe in keeping the passion in every project.

ARW: When we don't have to do the elimination ourselves it saves time. And we also gain from it, because if the client gets to choose, they will be more engaged with the project. They usually realise that they can't have everything.

TS: With clients, I don't tend to draw much until I've met them four or five times. When I understand what they need, then I jump into it. I try to get in a situation where they make the choice. It's almost like when you pick out a puppy from a litter – you should just wait for a puppy to come to you, and that's the one. It is also important to make clients realise that although it is just my project, there's a common understanding that we're on the same team. I try to find out why they want to work with us, and why I should work with them. Usually the budget is not an issue. I had a recent client who was able to build his house by himself on a limited budget – but that's very rare.

OL: I think most clients have an assumption of what it's like to build a house. We try not to give the client what they think they want. There are often weird questions that aren't really related to house building. These help us open up the project. However, money is always a very important part of the business.

TS: The town planner Patrick Geddes once said something like "there's a lot of money in the world and very few good ideas", which is how we drive our projects. We present good ideas, and some are cheap, some more complicated. Many times we've had a client say, "This is exactly what we wanted, but not at all what we expected."

OL: It's also a matter of surprising yourself. You have to trust the process to take you away from first impressions, so you don't go straight to an answer. So be nervous. Struggle. Then at the end you can ask yourself, "Wow, how did we get here?" That's the perfect process, I think.

TS: Is there any relationship between academia and your practice?

ARW: Not really. What I teach is not directly connected to the practice. I'm also doing an engineering course, actually, which helps to develop myself as an architect. But I rarely take students into the office.

TS: How do you all block off time during the day, or be alone, to draw?

ARW: We answer phones in the daytime and then we draw at night. We can do that now, but not for ever.

TS: At one point I had 35 projects in 15 countries. I ended up spending a year saying "no" to everything, save for a visitor centre in Maine. These days I try and divide the office into a design team and a management team. I don't really want to be part of management, although of course I support them and am available. These people are really, really important. They free the creative people up to do what they get energy from.

NORWAY | GARTNERFUGLEN ARKITEKTER

Previous page and this page: Thordentopp, Hardangervidda, Norway

ARW: We do small projects, for people we know, friends and family. And this makes me a control freak as I can't trust anyone else to do it for me. I need to make sure that when I do take risks, I have to know everything about the application. Our manager is also an architect – one of my students – and we give her full responsibility, because ultimately it gives the office more capacity.

TS: We don't do detail drawings any more, but some people, especially in Norway, don't see any separation between the concept and the details. In order to take some risks, you have to let go of the wheel a bit. And that's scary.

ARW: I can imagine.

TS: Have any projects been really hard?

ARW: Not really. Thunder Top cabin is an extension of an old log construction near Møsvatn lake. The contractor is the son-in-law of the man who originally built it and he had never worked with architects before. It was a great experience – he had no prejudices about the process. The people who build cabins in this area have a sort of pride in their work which is missing elsewhere, especially in Oslo, where everything is about time and money. They would add carved details to our minimalist wooden benches, but I just embraced it. We're using the builder again for other projects, even though he doesn't even use email.

OL: It was a very pragmatic process.

OLA: The design process is continuous. The projects have all mutated in a way, like a creature with its own personality.

ARW: I think we embrace these challenges. Like when we're told to get a different kind of wood to what we've specified, and if that means doubling the number of columns we need, then that's what we have to do. In the end, it makes a better project, since it eliminates options and forces us to make better choices. With less choice, you fight to make them good.

OLA: With these three cabin projects, you might think that we tried to make them really unique and special, and very different. But they sort of became this way, because of the process.

ARW: And the lack of options.

OL: We like to compare it to natural evolution. Like when you leave a species in a cave and they end up completely strange, with pale skin and no eyes. They become monsters, but they're perfectly adapted to their habitat. We try to find these architectural mutants to see where evolution takes the project.

OLA: It is about using natural materials, adapting to the terrain and the materials.

TS: I'm interested in how you will keep your attitude as you move into larger buildings. I'm looking forward to seeing these creatures emerging.

NORWAY | GARTNERFUGLEN ARKITEKTER

Right: Gartnerfuglen Arkitekter, Oslo, Norway

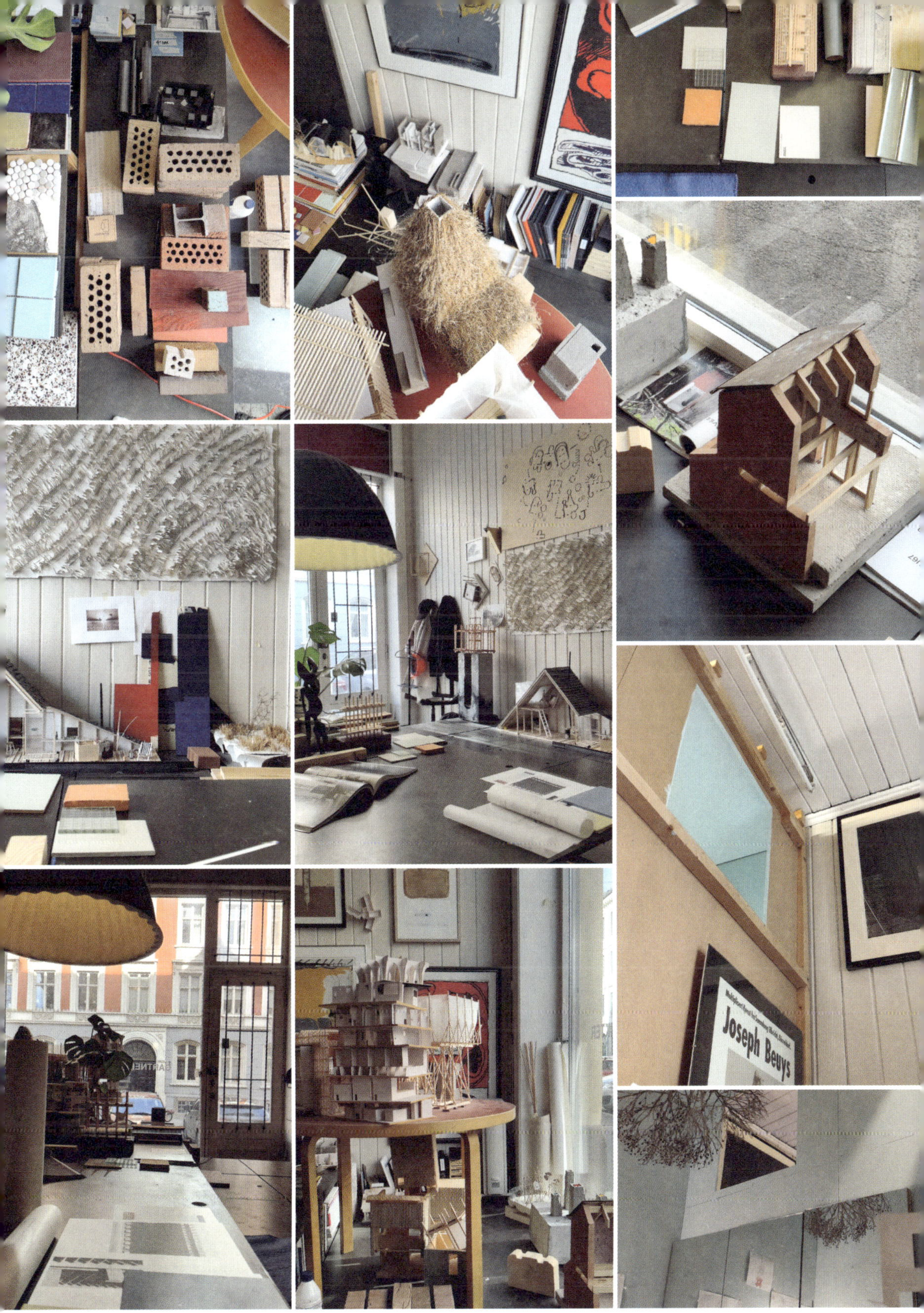
Joseph Beuys

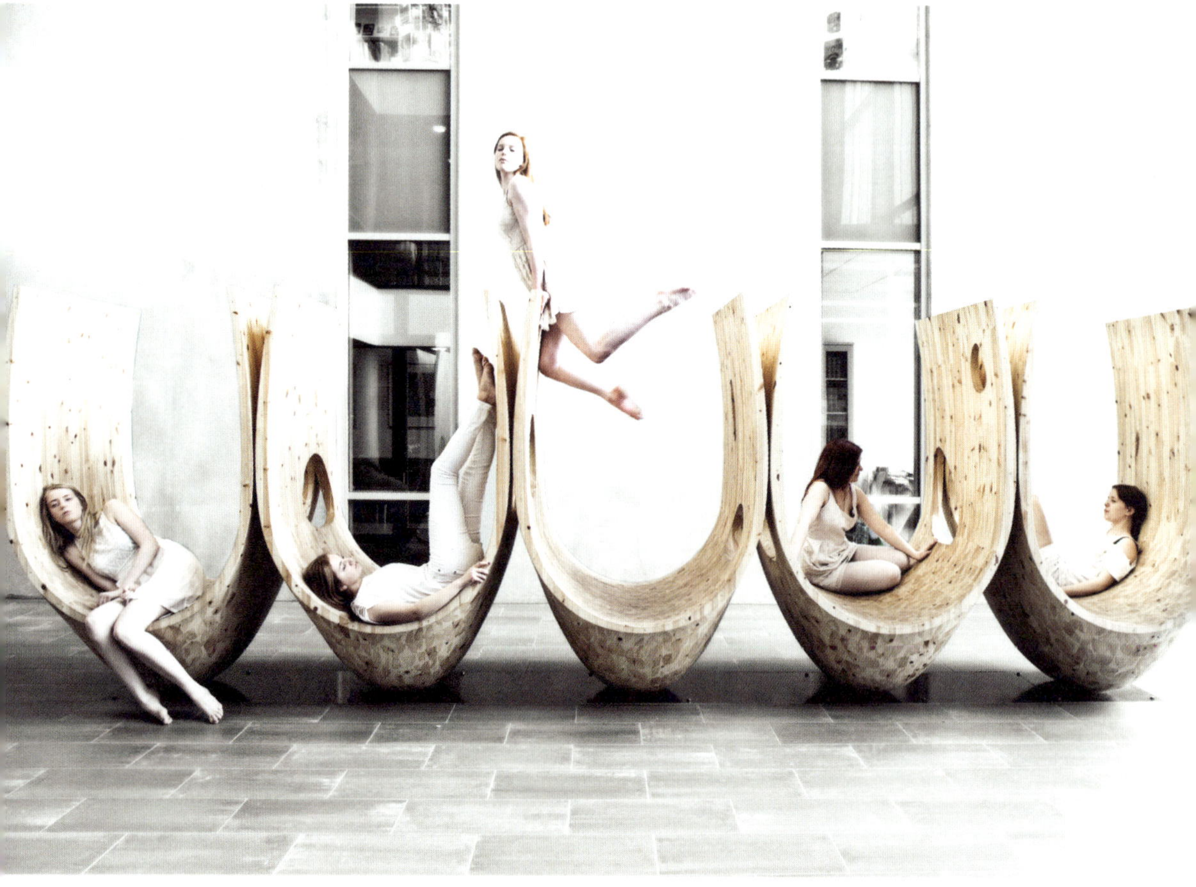

Haugen/Zohar Arkitekter

Haugen/Zohar Arkitekter (HZA) was established in 2007 by the Norwegian architect and artist Marit Justine Haugen and Israeli-born Dan Zohar. The Oslo-based studio has carved itself a niche within the intersection of architecture and art, working on buildings and masterplans as well as installations. The duo began their career by building their own space, by hand, followed by a self-initiated community project for their Oslo neighbourhood, turning an electricity substation into a shared public resource. Their third project, an installation of 750 tents, cemented the practice's main objectives: "creating versatile structures, enhancing social sustainability and building affordable architecture." HZA has won numerous awards for its approach, including The Norwegian Form Award for young architects in 2007 and the Norwegian Architecture Prize in 2017. Their practice is defiantly political, tackling issues of public and private space, as well as the inescapable issue of climate change: "Our work is concerned with social engagement and participation. The studio was initiated on the common perception that architecture is, by its nature, earthbound, drawn by and for people."

hza.no

Previous page: Wooden Hammocks, Charlottenlund high school, Trondheim, Norway

Right: Transformer, Oslo, Norway

TODD SAUNDERS: How long have you lived in Norway now?

DAN ZOHAR: Exactly 50 per cent of my life. So, 24 years.

TS: I'm 51 and this is also the year I have spent more than half my life in Norway.

DZ: It's strange – I've become more Norwegian than Israeli. I really liked being an outsider.

TS: I used to have this eternal homesickness but now I can feel at home in Norway, in Canada, in other countries. Perhaps it's acceptance of being a bit nomadic.

DZ: Yes, being nomadic becomes your comfort zone. For me, Norway feels very safe, stable and predictable, you can normally anticipate what is going to happen. It gives you a sense of calmness and the possibility for continuous focus.

TS: What about the positive aspects of being a foreigner in Norway? Norway is hugely different from Israel. Canada and Norway have very similar aspects, but ultimately, they're also quite different. It's like having two twins, each with a different character. What are the advantages of living in Norway for you?

DZ: For me, Norway is a second home. Being a foreigner gives you the advantage of always having another point of view. The possibility to observe from the side, to compare and reflect, is valuable. You don't take anything for granted, you are grateful for what you are given, at the same time, you can be critical and question local axioms. In many senses, Norway is the opposite of Israel: it is more than ten times the size of Israel, but its population is less than a half, so, the perception of space and density is very different. Norway has a relatively homogenous society with a common vision for the future while Israeli society is very fragmented, with many sectors and minorities, each with its own vision and aspirations, each pulling in its own direction. It makes it very hard to get things going. A lot of energy is being wasted and decision-making can be unpredictable and often counterproductive. In contrast, Norway's circumstances enable long term thinking, which is so crucial for tackling local and global challenges. The Israeli reality is very much about the here and now. These differences affect the way we practice our profession.

TS: Do you want to retain the old role of master builder?

DZ: No – I don't believe the old master builder role is so suitable for our current reality and the challenges we face. At least not in bigger-scale projects. The multicultural society is so vibrant and diverse, at the same time, our current challenges are so complex and interdisciplinary that there is no "one right answer". Collective challenges must be handled collectively. I am a true believer in well-orchestrated teamwork. The integrated design process (IDP) concept is a good example.

On the small-scale tasks, however, I think it is crucial that we, as architects, beyond having the vision, also can manage every aspect of the construction. Having this holistic knowledge helps us fulfil our concepts and defend our design decisions when challenged by the entrepreneurs, the consultants, or the clients. An example of this is the role of the Building Information Modelling (BIM) coordinator. I think that taking this role is an opportunity for the architect to regain control and to easily prioritise architecture rather than other technical constraints (installations) while coordinating the different disciplines.

TS: That coordination has improved recently. I have a client that calls these services the "acne" of the building, these things that just pop out everywhere.

DZ: Yes, it might be too much and must be proportioned in accordance with the scale or complexity of the project. Another issue that demands good teamwork and coordination and that we increasingly need to consider is the issue of material scarcity and fluctuations in material prices. We always strive to make more with less. We used to think all things had to last – not necessarily the case, we find ourselves increasingly thinking about design for disassembly, facilitating concepts such as reuse, recycle, upcycle where the circular economy is the focus.

TS: I've spoken to other architects facing similar issues. We're doing a small house that can be taken apart and can be moved up to 20 times. Instead of a building that lasts forever, we're also having to accommodate the need to move and reconfigure structures for new uses. It becomes about building a kit of parts. What components would make up HZA's architectural kit?

DZ: Movable structures are not necessarily environmentally friendly. Most important for us is to create good, meaningful spaces, houses, neighbourhoods and cities that people identify with. This will prolong the tenant's stay, thus, preventing unnecessary alternations, refurbs, etc. Having that said, we are currently working on a project where circularity is the primary theme. Together with BoligPartner AS, we develop a climate-friendly, demountable, fully circular system house for the residential area of the future. The prefabricated house industry needs to be challenged on social and climate sustainability. For that project, we are establishing a design manual, an architectural kit that can also be upscaled.

TS: What other projects have been very fulfilling for you?

DZ: Most fulfilling for me is not a specific project but rather following a thread that I feel is running through our work. However, I find something special with self-initiated projects. In these, we are not only the architects but also facilitators of the process. These projects aren't just about the design, but very much about how to engage with a community to make their life better. This was for example the electrical supplier project, where we used our architectural palette as a communication tool for gathering the neighbourhood around a common vision. Another project that I value a lot is the "No Comment" project in Oslo (2007). The installation of 750 tents in The Vigeland Park showed the cheapest type of shelter on the most expensive piece of land in Norway. It has introduced a well-known but very far-away scenario right in the heart of the capital. The tents stood for two months before being donated to the Red Cross, who used them to package first aid equipment being sent to the ongoing war in Lebanon.

Ambitious environmental projects are always very fulfilling. We have just finished a zero-emission (ZEB) villa outside Oslo. This project strives to show that building a ZEB is within the economical reach of a young middle-class couple with children. Working to find the

Below: Uredd rest area, Ureddplassen, Gildeskål, Norway

It took time for me to understand that there's no right answer. It's about asking the right questions. I am happy with the direction our questions at the office have taken.

— Dan Zohar

NORWAY | HAUGEN/ZOHAR ARKITEKTER

This page: Nitja Centre for Contemporary Art, Lillestrøm, Norway

combination of environmentally friendly yet economically reasonable solutions is very rewarding.

TS: Was that conscious?

DZ: Yes – in these self-initiated projects, the design was not our main concern but rather the social aspects. Our approach is that, just like teachers, doctors, football coaches, civil workers, etc., we are trying to contribute to our society with the tools that we control, to make a difference.

TS: How did you meet Marit – did you study together in Oslo?

DZ: No, we met before we were architects. We knew each other as children, then, when I was 21, doing my military service, Marit came on a visit to Israel. We split and met again when I followed her up to Trondheim. Originally, I thought I'd be a blacksmith in Norway, but I visited Marit at the architecture school and ended up staying for six years.

TS: Did you have preconceived notions of architectural education?

DZ: I didn't consider an architectural career when I was young. However, I was working with my hands since I was a child. I had a motorcycle garage as a teenager and worked in timber houses and blacksmithing thereafter. During our studies at Trondheim, we took an exchange year at the Bezalel Academy of Art and Design in Jerusalem, which was an interesting experience. The difference between these two realities is very evident in the way they teach architecture. In Jerusalem, politics is always present, there are more hidden layers, for example upon approaching a project you always ask yourself, who owns the site, who owned it 50 years ago, who is going to own it in the future and finally, what do I think about that? In Norway, you usually don't meet these types of hidden layers. Studying in Jerusalem makes you very aware that architecture is beyond merely a profession, it is a way of being, inseparable from who you are and what you believe in.

TS: What are you most happy with at this point in your life?

DZ: It took time for me to understand that there's no right answer. It's about asking the right questions. I am happy with the direction our questions at the office have taken. Looking at our portfolio I see a clear red line from the first self-built installation to the 30,000 square metre office building we recently won. This red line is about understanding the complexity of our profession and finding a place in architecture where we can make a difference. It makes me happy to look back at this journey and see that we manage to navigate our future.

TS: Did any of your teachers resonate with you?

DZ: We had an exceptionally charismatic teacher in Jerusalem. The school was on the eastern side of the city, and we were not allowed to stay at school after sunset, but, when this teacher was on stage, the students would forget the time and stayed just to listen to his words, then had to climb out of the windows because the doors were already locked. He was originally from the Soviet Union, it was this multi-cultural reference that made it so enriching, the use of scattered references, different languages, multiple perspectives, and personal experience across cultures was a real eye-opener for me.

TS: Which Norwegian architects, past or present, do you feel you a kinship with?

DZ: There are many architects to be inspired by in Norway. While teaching abroad, I notice that many of my architectural references go back to Scandinavia, which is fantastic. I am inspired by the respect for handcraft, the love for details, tactility, sincerity and modesty that I think we still have in Norway today. I am also intrigued by the intricate relationship with nature. Among the present architects, I feel a kinship to Helen & Hard's approach to architecture, from their social thoughts and strive for sharing to the love for timber the formal playfulness, the experimental attitude, and the quest for innovation.

TS: Is there somewhere else you'd like to work, taking your experience of both Norway and Israel?

DZ. I am a true believer in the Scandinavian model. Good projects are the result of good processes, and generally, in Norway, we design good processes. Otherwise, I would like to work with projects and initiatives that in my mind push the world a step forward in the right direction, regardless of where there are.

TS: Do you have an ideal project for your local community or even an ideal architecture project?

DZ: Our first project "The transformer" in our backyard in Oslo was such an ideal project. In the classic garden-town-inspired apartment building, a transformer building was converted into a meeting place for 180 families. The project has been referred to as "The transformer that became a parish house" and today houses everything from birthday parties and confirmations to company meetings, exhibitions and opera evenings. The self-initiated project was done entirely using voluntary work, by us and our neighbours. The project took three years. It took some time to understand that the process is the project. During those years we often discussed the essence of this project, a small-scale architecture project or a long-lasting social experiment. Nowadays, the building is occupied 90 per cent of the time every day, 24/7. Most of the time it is an "open house, all invited". It is so simple yet important, as the more densely we live, the lonelier we become. Since then, social sustainability has followed us on several scales. Humans are the driving force behind architecture whether we like it or not. Even though we have all become fully digital, our social mechanisms are the same as in Roman times: We still need belonging, friction and identity, we need to be a part of something, together with others.

TS: Can you remember what the real pure motivation was?

DZ: Yes, I was raised on the concept of the Israeli kibbutz, where all we had was shared, the thought was that everybody contributed as they could and got what they needed. Especially the shared community life and spaces are still a source of inspiration for us at the office. The motivation was to try to introduce something from that in our community in Oslo. A sort of kibbutz – the Norwegian way.

TS: Do you think temporary architecture has more potential for creating free space and showing people its possibilities?

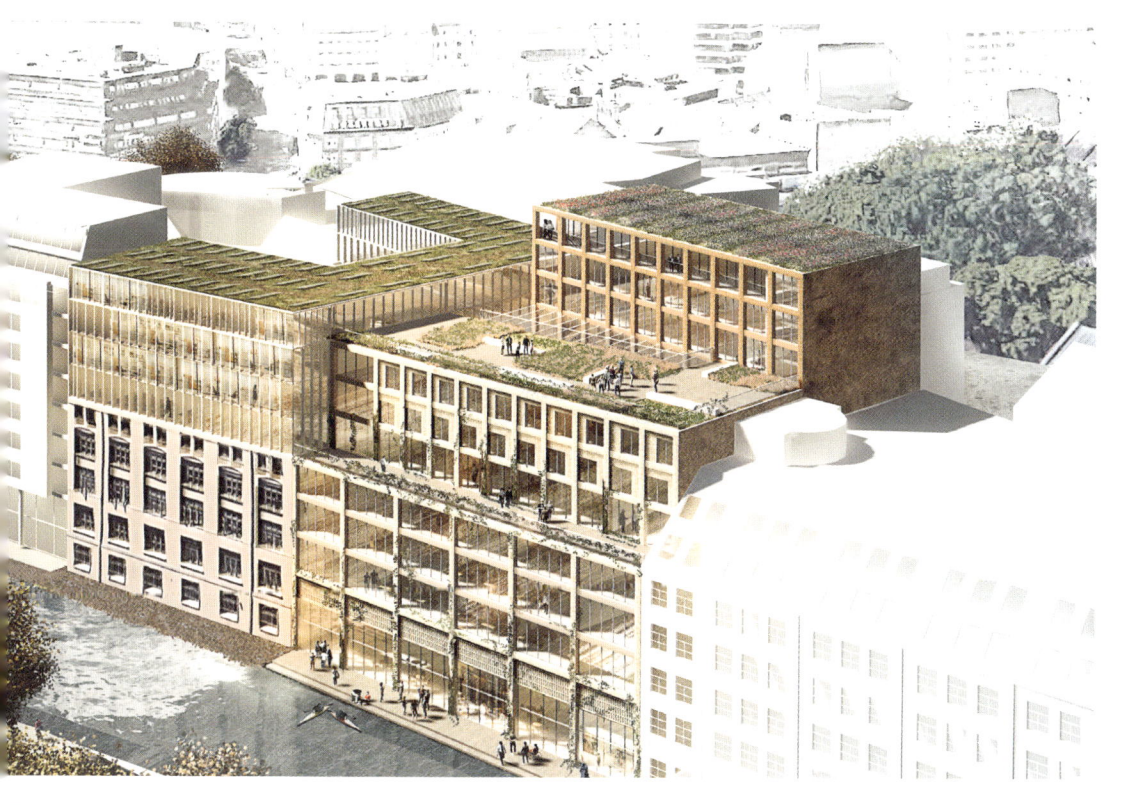

Above: Christian Krohgs gate 2, Oslo, Norway

Left: Fireplace for Children, Trondheim, Norway

NORWAY | HAUGEN/ZOHAR ARKITEKTER

DZ: Yes, I think temporary architecture has much more access to powerful tools and platforms for mapping, collecting, auditing and systemising a huge amount of information from the users of our public spaces. It gives a better understanding of the needs and potentials for the specific site and helps us to develop our concepts, define our design strategies and respond more precisely to every given task.

TS: There seems to be a lack of free spaces in Norway – everything is planned, overplanned perhaps. Do you need surprise and chaos in life to bring beauty?

DZ: I agree with you about this. There is little place for improvisations and surprises. It feels like we are always in control. John Lennon once said that "Life is what happens to you while you're busy making other plans." I think this is very correct – we need a bit of chaos and surprises, we need to laugh, shout, sweat and maybe sometimes lose control to feel that we are alive. We are in shortage of informal public spaces that invite surprises and spontaneity, which stimulate new relationships, sharing, and caring.

This theme was in focus in our project at Ulsholtveien 31 (2018), an affordable, environmentally friendly rental housing project in Oslo. The project was also inspired by the typical design of the Israeli kibbutz with public buildings at the centre and private rooms encircling a common backyard. From the kibbutz, we have learned that sharing is important and sympathetic. We shared bikes and cars, which were otherwise unused. We ate together in a large dining room, a hall that in the evening was used for other purposes. Also, outdoor spaces were shared and in constant use. Many of these qualities were introduced in Ulsholtveien 31. The programme was arranged like an onion: public spaces in the middle, and more private as you get to the outskirts of the project. A variety of meeting places both in plan

Opposite: Housing for Youth, Furuset, Norway

Right: No Comment, Oslo, Norway

and section, in and outdoors offer interaction and stimulate contact between the tenants in order to form a community, despite that the tenants live there only for a limited period of time.

TS: Speaking of which, my life was chaotic for a few years, I was travelling for a third of the year and working so much so I just started saying no to things. I needed the space to think, to get to the core. Are there any projects that you would say no to?

DZ: Of course. We are careful to choose projects that stick to our common thread. We often face the classic choice for a small architectural office; should we say yes to bigger projects, which requires larger staff, or should we remain small? We remain small because it gives us greater freedom to select projects we can vouch for and which are true to what we believe in: social sustainability, sharing, climate-friendly construction and innovation. It is a good feeling to say no to a project, you feel that you keep your integrity, you are in control.

TS: I've had situations where I had a great process, but I wasn't so happy with the result.

DZ: We've actually had the opposite – a difficult process, but happy with the results. With some of the rest areas on the Norwegian Scenic Routes, for example. The best bits of these projects are visiting the site afterwards, meeting the locals, and seeing how happy and proud they are to see their small, remote village gets global attention in the international press.

TS: You've made them feel important and realise that they live in a really beautiful place. The beauty of this profession is the diversity of approach and thinking. There are a million ways to be an architect.

DZ: Exactly. Maybe that's why architects never retire and stay young forever.

Right: Haugen/Zohar Arkitekter, Oslo, Norway

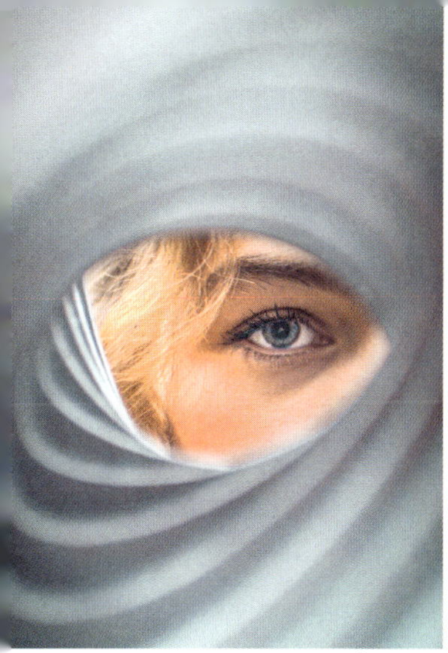
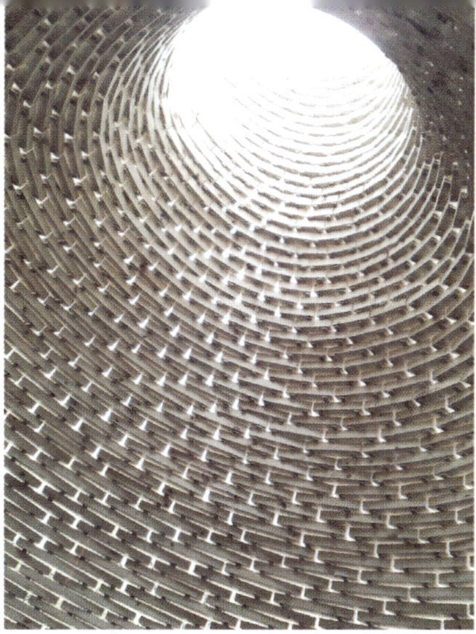
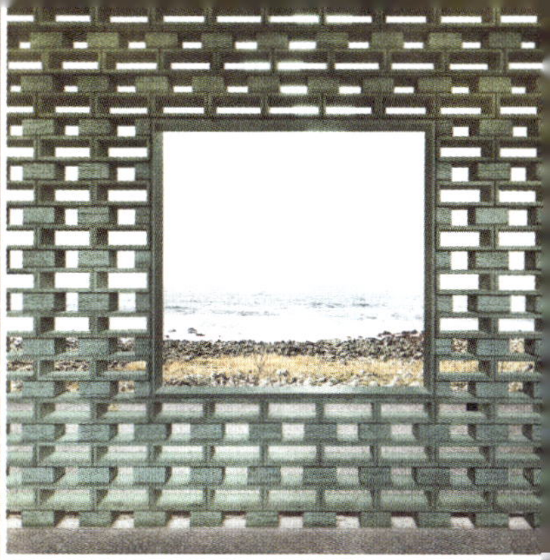
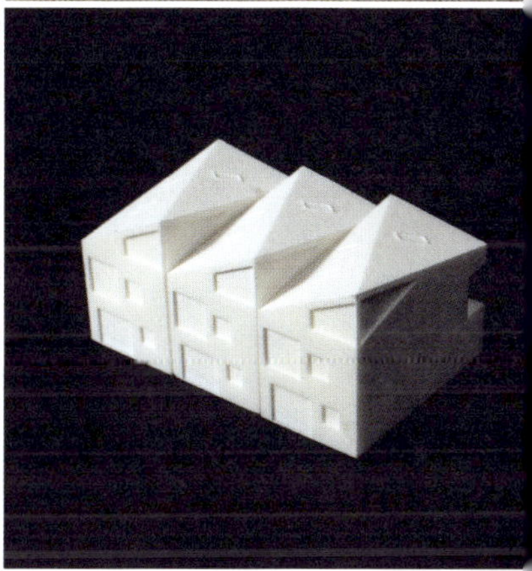
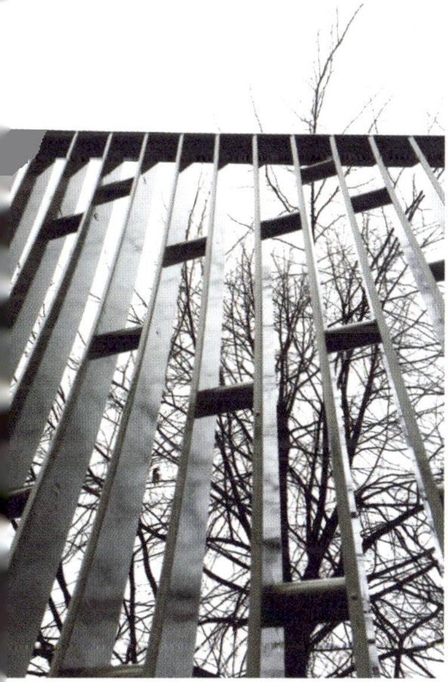
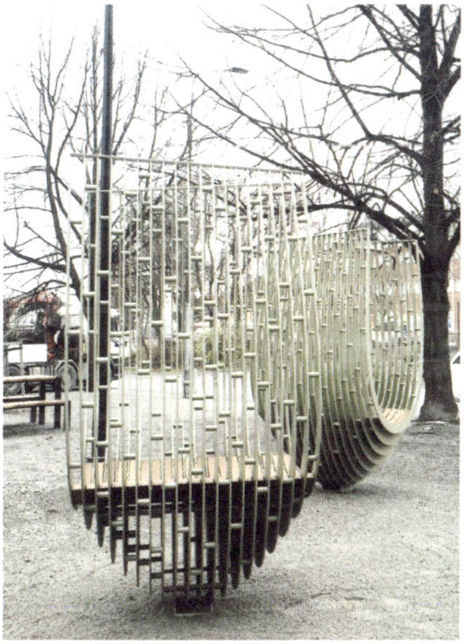
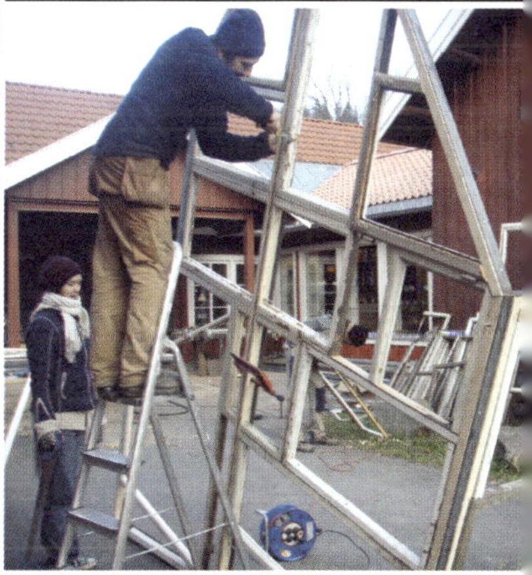
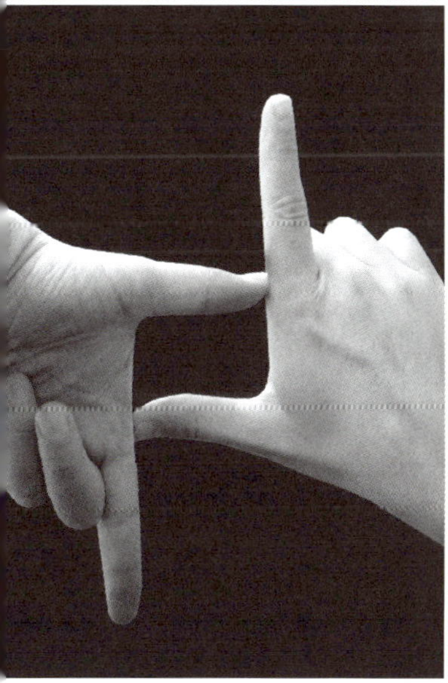
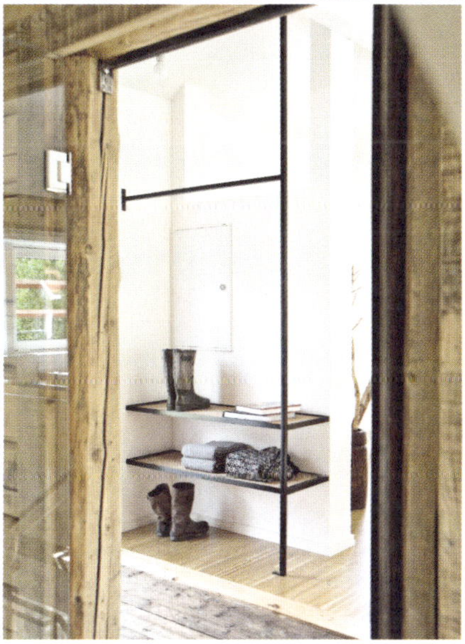
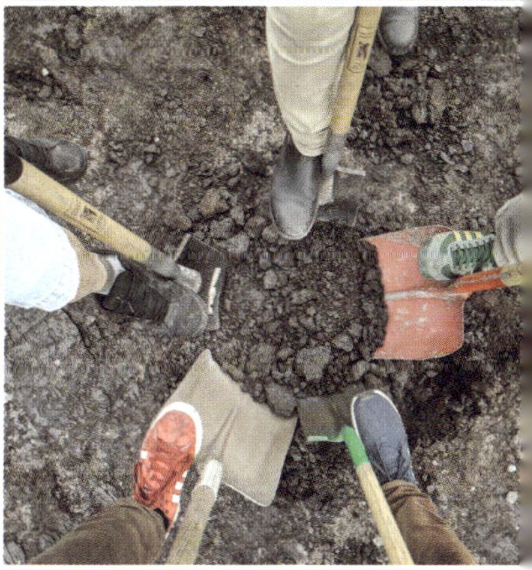

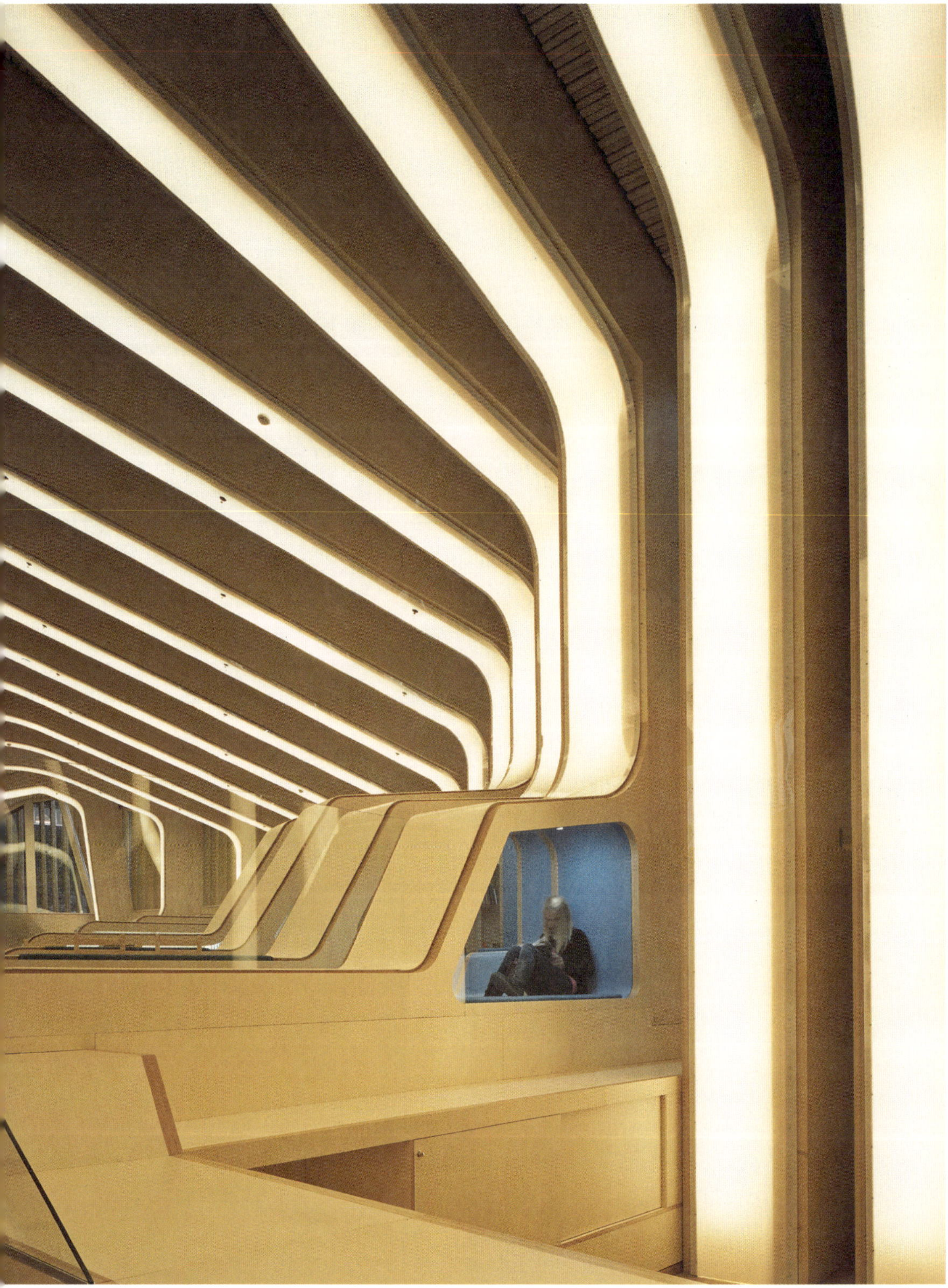

Helen & Hard

Founded in Stavanger, Norway in 1996, by Norwegian architect Siv Helene Stangeland and Austrian architect Reinhard Kropf, Helen & Hard now employs around 30 people and has offices in both Stavanger and Oslo. Stangeland studied at AHO in Oslo and in ETSAB Barcelona. Kropf also studied in TU Graz and at AHO and continues to teach alongside the architectural practice. In the last decade, the firm has undertaken a major focus on timber construction technology, conducting research into new structural and production methods. The firm has won many awards for design and innovation, including the Timber Award from the National Association of Norwegian Architects. Key works include the Vennesla Library and Culture House, the Pulpit Rock Mountain Lodge in Strand, the SR Bank office building and the extension to the Navet Museum on the island of Odderøya. Helen & Hard is also exploring the potential of collective living, starting with the successful co-housing community at Vindmøllebakken. These principles are being developed further by a company, Gaining by Sharing, established by the architects together with Indigo Vekst and Gaia Trondheim.

helenhard.no

Previous page and above: Vennesla Library, Vennesla, Norway

Right: Samling, Sand, Norway

Todd Saunders: Like our studio, yours doesn't predominantly operate out of Oslo. How does that work for you?

Siv Helene Stangeland: I think working in the periphery has given us more freedom to explore and investigate our own approach. The Stavanger region has a very different economy and entrepreneurial culture which gives other opportunities as well as challenges. Being here has given us a different career from working in Oslo or another big city.

TS: You can really concentrate here in Stavanger. You couldn't have a cabin like where you are sitting now near Oslo, but you're only 20 minutes from your office. So have you turned the location into a positive thing for the practice?

SHS: Definitely. We have an Oslo office and a flat there, so sometimes we've been commuting, especially Reinhard. But since the pandemic we've been pretty much here in the cabin.

TS: Has it been good, staying in one place?

Reinhard Kropf: Super nice. You can concentrate more but still work internationally. There are advantages, but sometimes one can get a bit tired of Stavanger and therefore it has been an advantage to also have an office in Oslo and to work internationally.

TS: How long have you been in Norway, Reinhard?

RK: Twenty-six years in fact.

TS: What kinds of opportunities and constraints is the practice facing now?

SHS: All architects relate to the bigger challenges – questions about sustainability and how architecture can contribute to solving them. We ask ourselves that all the time. Then there are different values within these challenges. Do we deal with social issues? Sustainability? Pollution? Segregation? What interests us most is what architecture can do, especially in the commercial housing industry, where we have struggled for 20 years. This is not the easiest place to be an architect, because of limited budgets and an entrepreneurial approach that rules the game. But we have stayed there – consciously because we think how people live is where we can make the biggest difference. The housing industry creates so many challenges, from loneliness and health issues to segregation in society. Even our problematic environmental footprint all comes down to how we live.

TS: So is housing one of your main focuses as a practice?

SHS: There is a lot to be done and that's why we have chosen to stay in the sector. Can we find alternative ways of building housing, as well as planning? Our latest focus is on social and collective forms of living. We started this 10 years ago, when we met a green investor who was very interested in the topic. We are investigating co-living and trying to define a completely new model for it called Gaining by Sharing. We have built one project, in Vindmøllebakken in 2019, and we're now working on five more projects. Vindmøllebakken is a scheme that you can see working in practice and it's something that people want. It combines our interests and skills.

TS: And your values.

SHS: Yes – which makes these projects very fulfilling and meaningful to work on.

RK: It's about turning a problem into an opportunity. We will show this research in the Nordic Pavilion at the 2021 Venice Biennale and continue to develop it. For example, how the inhabitants could also become shareholders and how that can influence the architecture. It's a different model to regular ownership. It's also important that we understand the value chain of construction, working on timber elements to build housing in a different way.

TS: You went into an area of constraints and you created opportunity. Is housing at a tipping point now and moving in the right direction?

SHS: There's a new maturity in the market. People have got to know more about shared spaces. The new generation doesn't have any memories of the '70s or connections to the old clichés of collective living. They think of it more like a practical arrangement; of course, we have to share. We can also control the participatory approach so there's no risk for the developer. Our model is safe and works well – take the pilot scheme at Vindmøllebakken, so you can always go and see how it works. We have learned a lot, especially on user participation. The first question people ask is how do you deal with difficult people [in a collective house]? We also have to care about how you actually live in a community and solve everyday life challenges with 69 people sharing 500 square metres of space.

TS: When I first came to Norway there was no interest in communal living outside of more spiritual communities. Now it seems like it could become a mainstream thing.

SHS: What unifies people is the shared consciousness of reducing our individual footprints. How can we live together in a more sustainable way? We provide this not only in environmental terms, but also in social terms, because you get to be in a community. You need a certain density of people for a self-contained social life.

TS: Did other countries and projects inspire your economic model or was it a completely new platform?

SHS: We looked at co-living models in Germany and Austria, but they worked differently, because they had political systems that supported them to some degree. Here it had to work in the commercial market because there is no state support in Norway. The key difference is the reorganisation of the private unit and the collective, shared space. The idea is that we can make the private unit more efficient and compact, so what you save there you can put into the common areas. People end up buying a lesser amount of space in total.

TS: What are the shared common features?

SHS: There is a central living room and big kitchen, a separate party room, a workshop, two guest rooms you can book, a loft with a library and space for yoga, a roof terrace with a greenhouse where you can grow vegetables. And also flexible space for co-working, lounge and playgrounds. There are only five car spaces for the whole development. The shared spaces are integrated into the centre of the building, with all the flats around it.

Below and bottom: Vindmøllebakken, Stavanger, Norway

> We are more like midwives, bringing out the architecture which is already part of the environment. That is what is so fantastic about architecture; we can explore, become immersed and escape the purely rational mode.
>
> — Reinhard Kropf

Right and below: Vindmøllebakken, Stavanger, Norway

It creates a very important relationship – you feel like you're participating in the activities there, and it feels like an addition to your home.

TS: Are the other collective housing schemes you're working on a similar size to this, Reinhard?

RK: They're maybe a bit smaller. When we started the company Gaining by Sharing, Siv and I discussed how involved we would have to get with things like management, economy, processes, etc. Interesting stuff, but not the typical work of an architect. We always try to find a balance between management and design work, which is hard. But just accepting the typical developer model will not take you anywhere.

SHS: Ultimately, we have provided a platform which makes it possible to investigate and create a completely different housing architecture.

TS: How does this compete with regular developers? In Bergen, many developers used to be contractors specialising in concrete. They have a monopoly.

SHS: The oil industry also provided us with an entrepreneurial culture based on concrete and steel.

TS: We lost many good engineers to the oil industry.

RK: And we also lost almost all the knowledge about timber craftsmanship and engineering. For centuries, it was the most common building material in Norway.

TS: I want to ask about your design process. At our studio, we've integrated more workshops into the way we work. Are there things in your process that apply to all your projects or are they all different?

SHS: One of our procedures is called "Walk the Land". We simply encourage our team to start every project by spending a day alone on the site, and experience the bigger context and the physical surroundings and resources. It's about sensing the space's and environment's qualities and potential. It also encourages people to draw and talk and stay away from digital tools for a day. Then back at the office you show the team something you created. We want to encourage a more direct, intuitive way of working and not get into analysis too early.

TS: Where did this approach come from?

SHS: I did my whole PhD on freehand drawing, and all that happens when you draw. We are keen to keep that as a practice. It opens up other ways of exploring. How does this help create unique architecture? I think it is about getting into an open-ended conversation with context, wondering, trying things out and not fixing things too early.

TS: Is this why Vindmøllebakken is such a good project, because you spent 10 years on the site, first when it was your office? I do my best projects in Canada, because I know places so well.

SHS: Yes, we knew Vindmøllebakken well. This approach also takes in feedback. It's not all our own thoughts – it's about sensing and listening and taking in other voices.

RK: As relational designers, we try to cherish and cultivate that. There are other elements

Below, right and far right:
The Financial Park, Stavanger, Norway

in the design process – other people, other resources or environments. They should all have a say and become more active in the design, as if they were design partners. We are more like midwives, bringing out the architecture which is already part of the environment. That is what is so fantastic about architecture; we can explore, become immersed and escape the purely rational mode.

SHS: Everyone has a way of participating and giving a unique contribution. We must appreciate our team's different personalities. To make us work together as an orchestra is part of our design approach.

TS: These things take a long time. You don't learn them in architecture school. Perhaps the proximity created by your collective housing also helps its occupants increase their understanding of each other. Architecture can play a role in that relationship.

SHS: Architecture's role is physical but it also enhances how we collectively act together,

RK: Around 2005 we changed our focus and got much more into timber architecture and the background of the value chain and the industry. We are lucky to have a really good network of engineers and producers in Switzerland. In Austria, my home country, there's also huge interest in timber. We're trying to explore the architectural and tectonic potential of the material. Wood is an incredible material, and has a resonance with our design approach. Digital tools open a completely new world. Building systems, different ways to build, but also model details, the value chain, local production. Timber design can be connected to new digital processes in many ways. Our generation has an advantage because we were educated in the analogue world and then we switched to digital. In the modern timber world, you have all this crazy parametric design, which often doesn't have much knowledge about the craft

272 | 273

NORWAY | HELEN & HARD

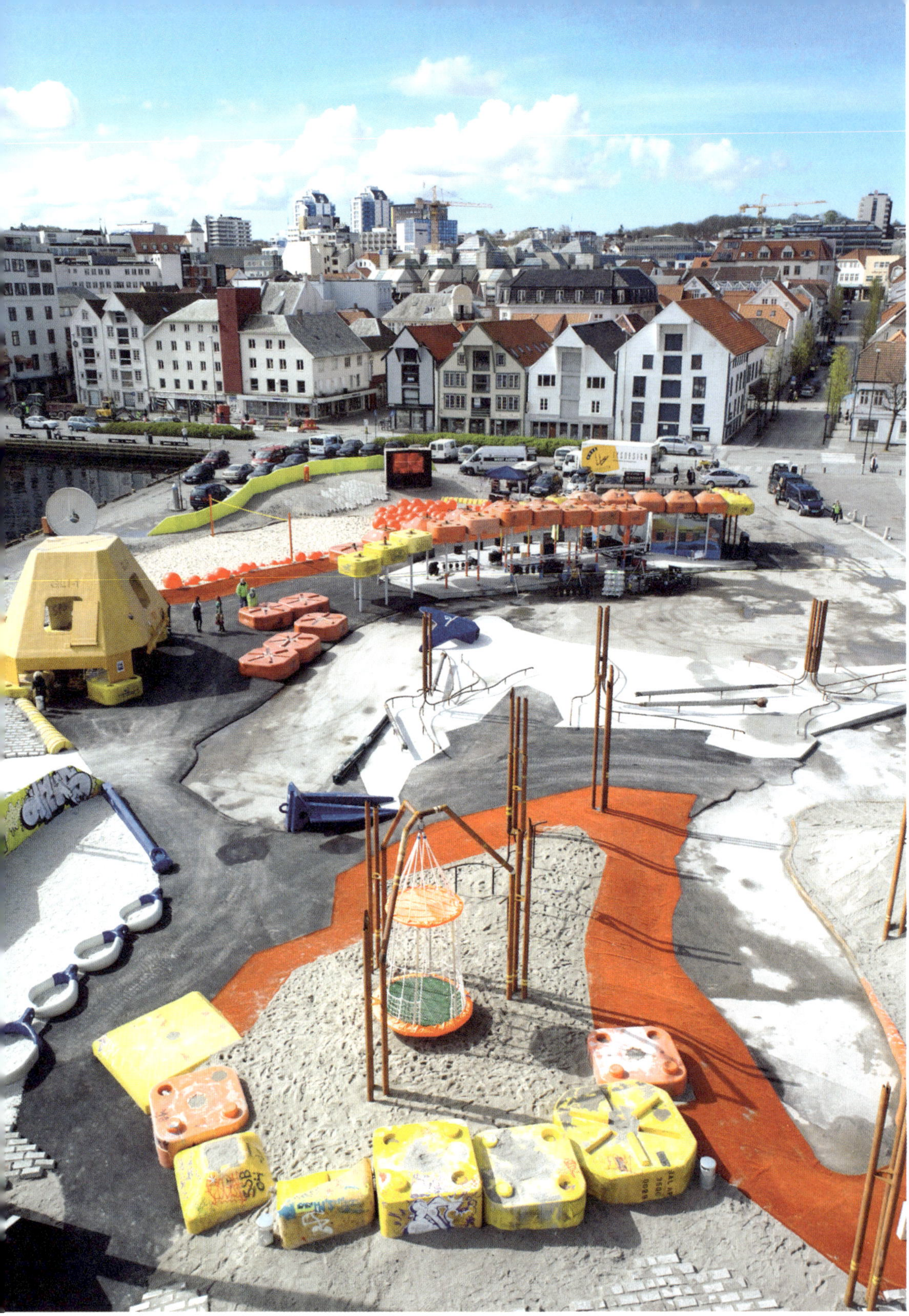

Opposite and right:
Geopark, Stavanger, Norway

of the material. But that kind of a marriage is interesting.

TS: You have a group of people who you work well with. Is this Austrian and Swiss knowledge of wood construction coming to Norway?

RK: It's happening, together with more and more timber projects coming. And more architects are jumping on this train. It's a very interesting time.

TS: I spoke to a Finnish architect who had made a commitment not to use concrete ever again in his practice.

SHS: We did as well. I think 95 per cent of what we do is timber.

RK: All the increased use of CNC machines and robotics is really happening too. And like you said with housing – that general contractors come from the world of concrete – so we have to find a way around this and build up new value chains.

TS: It doesn't seem that there is an incentive for them to change. I think you just have to come in with a better model, and it sounds like this co-housing model is better for the people buying, for the market, and for materials. Can you take this different approach because of where you're based?

SHS: The oil industry is a very important part of both the culture and landscape of Stavanger. We're fascinated by it, but also irritated and challenged. It means we are surrounded by engineering and technology of a very high specification, so it has given us possibilities.

TS: Is Stavanger quite an industrial, construction-focused city?

SHS: Exactly. It feels like everything is possible.

RK: We feel a freedom to do things differently. When we started, it wasn't just about doing competitions but finding different ways to do architecture. We hope we can still explore things. We have bought this factory space for ourselves to do that.

SHS: It was a self-initiated project. We have a carpenter and wood engineer on our staff. They help build prototypes for us.

RK: Maybe we'll be able to directly control the production of timber buildings. These things are all exciting to us.

Right: Helen & Hard,
Stavanger and Oslo, Norway

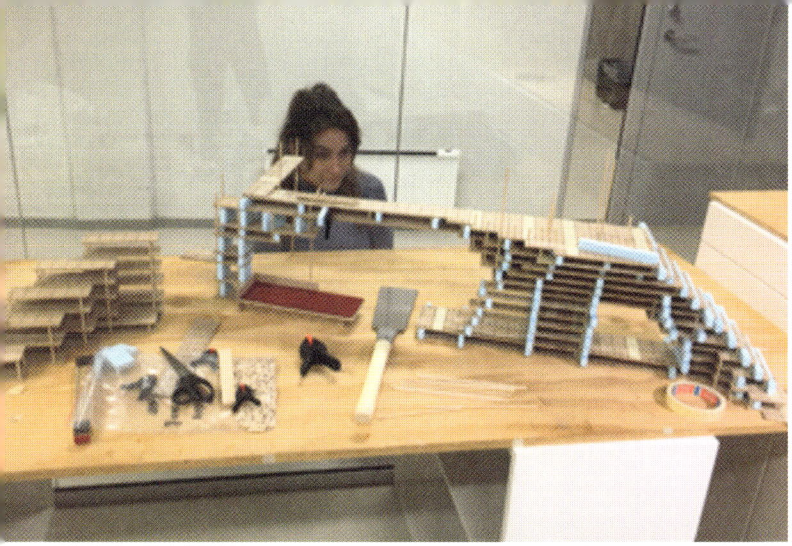

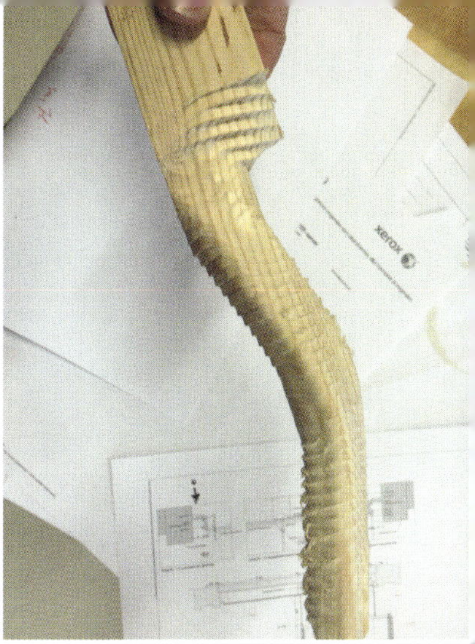

xerox

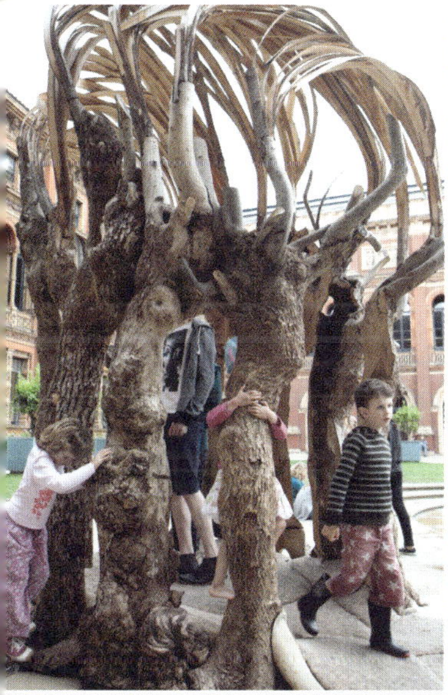

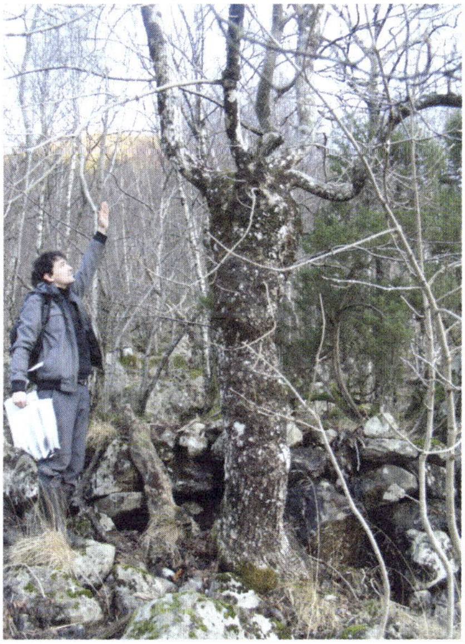

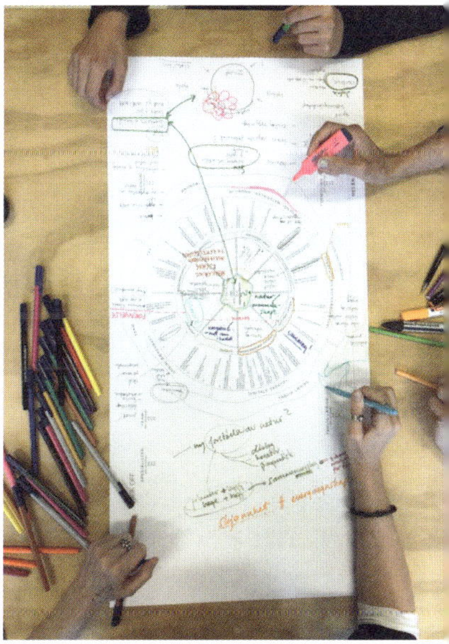

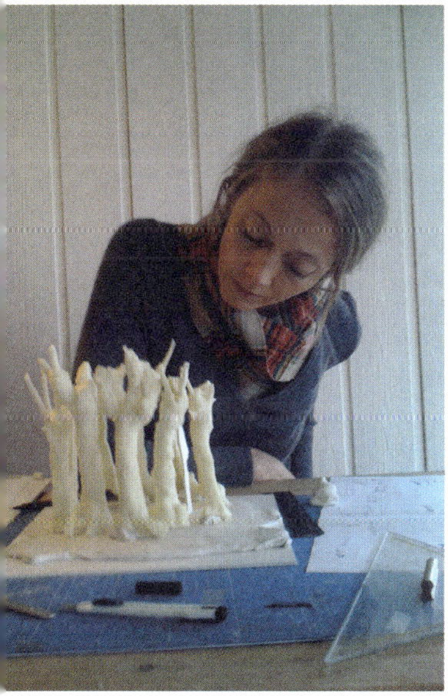

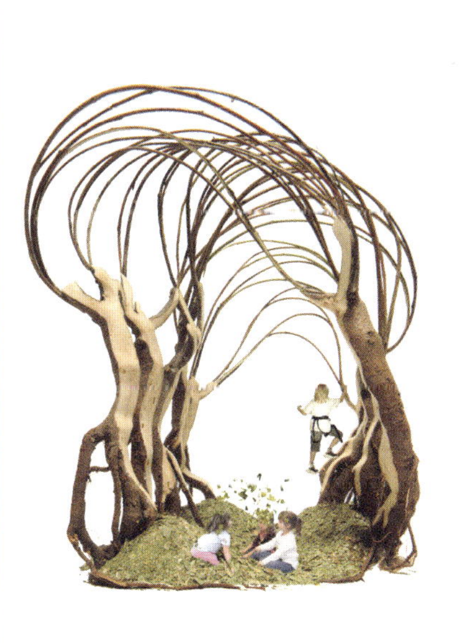

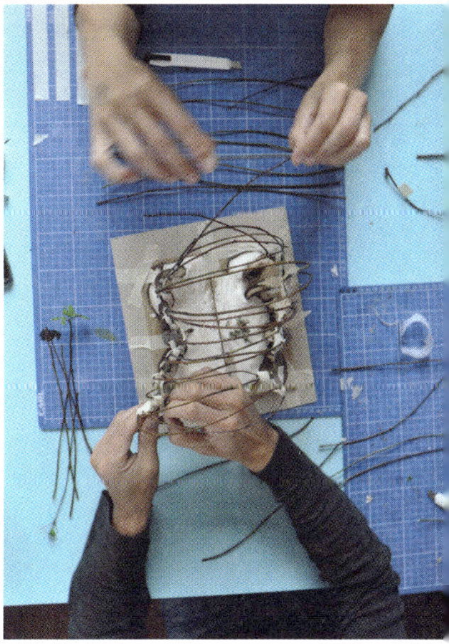

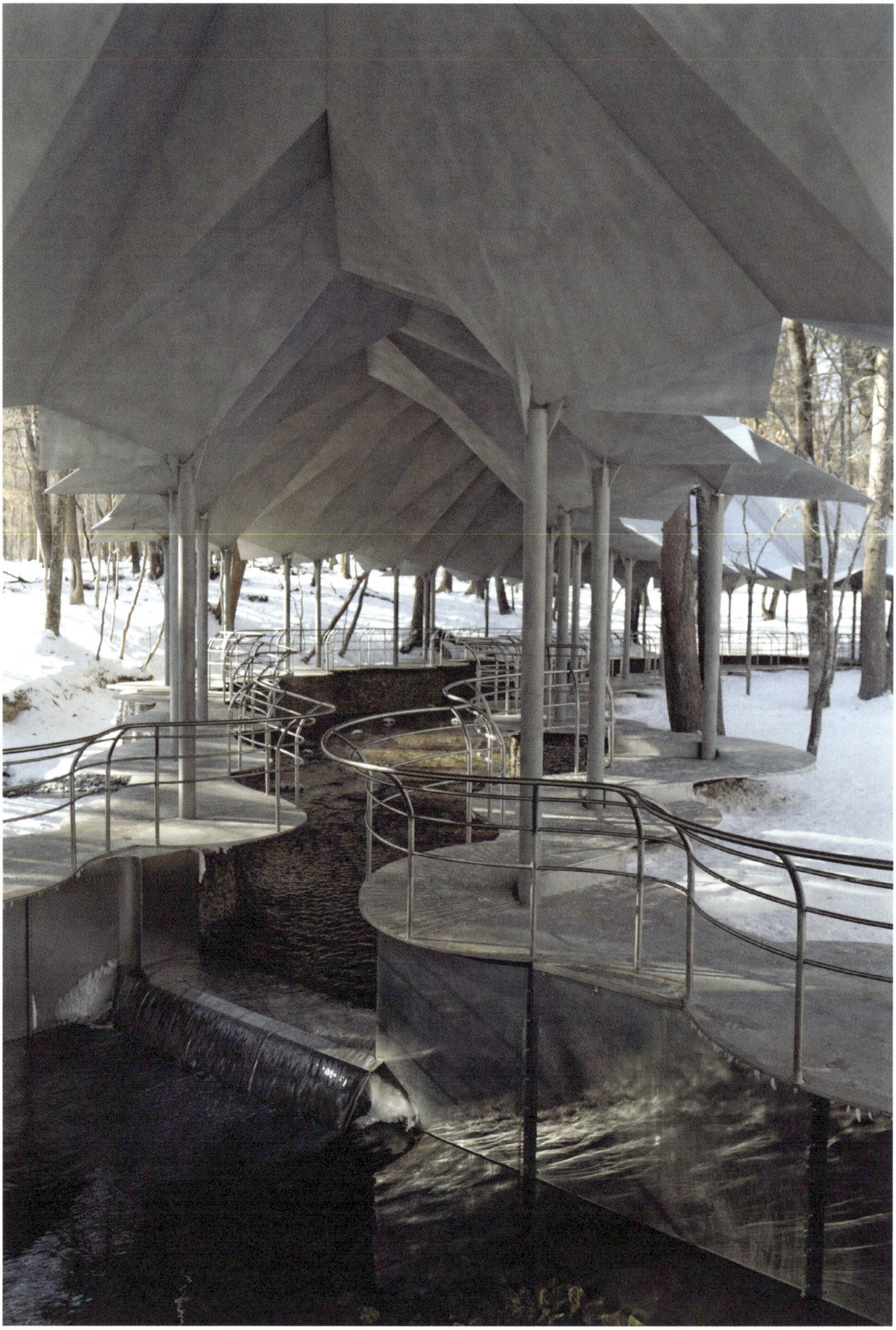

Jensen & Skodvin

Jan Olav Jensen and Børre Skodvin established Jensen & Skodvin Architects in 1995. The office began with an invited competition for the pilot project that initiated the acclaimed Norwegian Scenic Routes. From just four architects in the autumn of 1995 the staff grew to 13 architects by 2019. In 2011 Torunn Golberg became the third partner.

In addition to their work throughout Norway, including the acclaimed Gudbrandsjuvet viewing platform and café for the Tourist Road project, the Oslo-based studio has also worked in China, India and Austria. The award-winning Juvet Landscape Hotel, completed in 2010, encapsulates the studio's holistic approach to site, topography, materials and programme, as well as a close working relationship with the client. JSA's output is hugely diverse, ranging from sculptural landscape interventions through to private villas, public housing and a monastery.

Jensen & Skodvin still believe in engaging with academic activity, including lecturing and publishing. The pair were the founding editors of the "asBUILT" series, an ongoing monograph project that focuses on one or two buildings in forensic detail. "Our main objective is to realise ideas in the form of built work while contributing to the development of the tectonic culture of our profession," they write.

jsa.no

Previous page: Water Source, Changbai, China

Above: Therme and hotel, Bad Gleichenberg, Austria

Regulations are usually just written to ensure nothing goes wrong and nobody does anything wrong. In the office we talk about how every desirable city in the world would be illegal in Norway.

— Børre Skodvin

Todd Saunders: What are you currently working on?

Børre Skodvin: We have some projects in China, bigger and more complicated than some of our projects in Europe. We have a demanding client there, who is really interested in architecture and believes in spending money on high quality materials and planning. They are very particular and are not content to settle for just "good enough".

TS: What about the situation in Norway? Are smaller firms like ours going to become extinct?

BS: Sadly, everything is pointing in that direction. It's not just about the architects, but also production, because many smaller workshops are also closing. There's less and less chance of getting well-crafted, hand-built solutions for doors, windows, furniture.

TS: I'm always amazed at the amount of detail in your work. Has it always been like that?

BS: I think so. We like to delve right down into the smallest constituent parts of a project. We also enjoy working with different materials – how do you cut it, join it, make it into something interesting? The satisfaction we get from a project really depends on how many opportunities there are to do these things.

TS: Do you use CNC machining? Even though these small wood shops and craft specialists are closing, technology might offer even more possibilities.

BS: We love CNC. You can do things now that were unimaginable just a few years ago. Suddenly, you realise some of these long-established materials can do something quite different. For example, the toilets at the Design and Architecture Centre in Oslo used CNC sheet metal rolling, completed by a workshop that was working for the Norwegian ship industry. Traditionally, it would be difficult to shape a piece of sheet metal using a gradually changing curvature. Now you can just programme it and the machine does it for you.

TS: I think both Herzog and Zumthor would build rough physical models and then scan them, because the shapes were so complicated. My workflow has been revolutionised by technology. I sit and draw on my iPad and then I export the results to a 3D printer. At the end of each day I send the best ideas to the printer and look at the models the next morning.

BS: It's difficult to get those kinds of commission. All along, it's been a case of grabbing opportunities that come along. Most of the opportunities reflect that we've been doing fringe events, so we get strange requests. Just this week, I got a telephone call from this guy who runs a little second-hand record shop in Oslo, next door to our last office. He found all the stuff that we threw out, like old models. Now he's been offered the nextdoor space as well, which used to be a bar. He wants it to become a place where people have coffee, meet other people and hear new music. He called me because he remembered us. If we did this project as a conventional commission, we would probably ruin him totally. Instead, I find pleasure in it, helping people out. If you can beat these really rich buyers and developers in the gentrification game, that's good. Nobody there is going to make a huge profit. They're only doing it because they think this is a good idea for this neighbourhood.

TS: If we lived in a world where we just did good things, can you imagine the opportunities? A project like that would probably kill the city if you weren't able to do it.

BS: Exactly. Now everybody is discussing architecture. Even the politicians are saying, "Well, we have to do something." But they just organise committees rather than consider that it's not how things look that matters, but what's actually there and who uses it. And who has the right to use it and for how long would they have that right? When I went to school near that area, there were still factories. Of course, they closed. And everybody is apparently happy with everything getting gentrified and expensive and hip, but sooner or later, the city becomes like a monoculture. It lacks the structural variety that it needs to live. All the professional and commercial activities that go on in Oslo are about food and recreation. There is no space for the unexpected. It's always about paying to receive something.

TS: Do you get involved in community projects like the landscape hotels where people have taken them to a different level of engagement?

BS: We are working on one now, up on the coast. It's difficult, it takes a long time, there are zoning and political issues. I told the client, you have to get an operator, because they're going to be so important for the project. We have an interested client, trying to connect the project to the region in a more committed way than simply organising overnight beds for visitors.

TS: That's where the opportunities are. You said projects will get smaller and smaller, but you could also say that projects are getting better and better. For example, the tourism industry and its relationship to architecture in Norway offers such a great opportunity to do it right.

BS: That's been a big success, and very good for us as a practice.

TS: Can you describe your process?

BS: It's not very systematic. It's about finding the initial idea, usually relating to the topography of the site based on our first visit, or when we look at it on a map. Often there is an early idea that sticks. When we did the Bad Gleichenberg spa and hotel in Austria, we went down there and there had just been half a metre of snow. When we got back home, we did this tiny little sketch for an idea. Then the project underwent a huge transformation, changing into two hotels, going from 3 star to 5 star and moving sites. I forgot all about the original sketch and eventually I found it at the bottom of a drawer. And it was stunning because that was exactly how it turned out.

TS: How do you move on from that area of uncertainty between an initial concept sketch and a finished scheme?

BS: Usually a deadline is a blessing. It cures doubt, because you have to decide. However, we often find that we start building before we know exactly what we're going to build. Things will change during the process, sometimes because you only realise things as they become physical.

TS: Most of my construction details are drawn on the walls of the buildings during construction.

BS: It is possible to change quite a lot, quite late, although it depends on the client. Most

Left and below:
New entrance building to Sognefjellshytta mountain hotel, Sognefjellshytta, Sognefjellet, Norway

NORWAY | JENSEN & SKODVIN

Above: Juvet Landscape Hotel, Gudbrandsjuvet, Valldal, Norway

Left: Sognefjellshytta mountain hotel, Sognefjellshytta, Sognefjellet, Norway

Opposite: Juvet Landscape Hotel – river sauna, Gudbrandsjuvet, Valldal, Norway

public clients will insist that the project is "finished" before you start on site and after that, you can't change anything. You need clients that are comfortable and tolerant of risk and uncertainty and who trust you.

TS: Do you discuss any of these issues with clients in early meetings?

BS: It's good to be flexible. We might not figure out exactly right away, but usually the initial conversations will be about needs, wishes, preferences and ideas. That leads to an idea which can be visualised, and that's when it all starts. Things then happen according to the deadlines. If there's no deadline, very little can happen for a long, long time.

TS: I've found that asking questions and listening before you make decisions also helps things fall into place.

BS: If we have an end result on the horizon, that's the only motivation that's necessary.

Sometimes that can take years. I've recently been sinking into this deep marsh of zoning plans. It's a nice opportunity in many ways, because you can define ground rules that specify the minimum architecture quality. For a housing project we did at Årvoll in Oslo, we were able to work certain basic qualities into the plan, like making the apartments dual aspect. This ruled out a central corridor and removed the division into "good flats" with sunlight, and "bad flats", without. The zoning plan required every flat to have windows to both sides.

TS: Alison Brooks, a Canadian architect who works in London, has this "circle of dignity". She'll do housing projects but she will only work within certain key parameters. It makes a huge difference.

BS: It is interesting to do zoning plans. But they take forever, and they are very tedious with a lot of writing.

Right and opposite:
Competition for a new high-rise hotel in Vals, Switzerland

TS: There are rarely creative people making regulations.

BS: Regulations are usually just written to ensure nothing goes wrong and nobody does anything wrong. In the office we talk about how every desirable city in the world would be illegal in Norway.

TS: What about the monastery on Tautra? How did you create a place where a person could be both social and private?

BS: We tried to make a small village, so that there would be several ways to get from one place to another. You didn't always have to cross the same path, so if you want to avoid someone you could. Rather than having one major courtyard with the buildings all organised around it there are a lot of courtyards. Instead of corridors, you pass through different rooms. Many of the rooms have particular functions and are used only sometimes, so there's a lot of space that is not in use at any time. It's a bit like going from house to house. The island itself is quite small and flat and the monastery is on one of the higher parts of the island, so from the upper chambers you can see the view and the constantly changing weather.

TS: Could anything from that project be transferred to a housing project?

BS: What was interesting about a programme for a religious space was the total absence of any consideration for value for money. It's almost the only abstract programme that's left. It was all about creating a space for contemplation. Everywhere else, you have to allocate every square metre to something. In the monastery we were trying to solve an abstract programme – nobody knows how many square metres they need.

TS: Were they open about their motivations?

BS: They were open in discussing what this building should be like. They had done an initial process with another architect, who withdrew from the commission.

TS: Do you personally think you had to give up anything for architecture?

BS: Not really. It was toughest for me when my kids were small – they were both born just before we started the office. But I hope they have appreciated it. I think for children, it's good to see that grown-ups can be engaged and happy with their life and work.

NORWAY | JENSEN & SKODVIN

Right: Jensen & Skodvin, Oslo, Norway

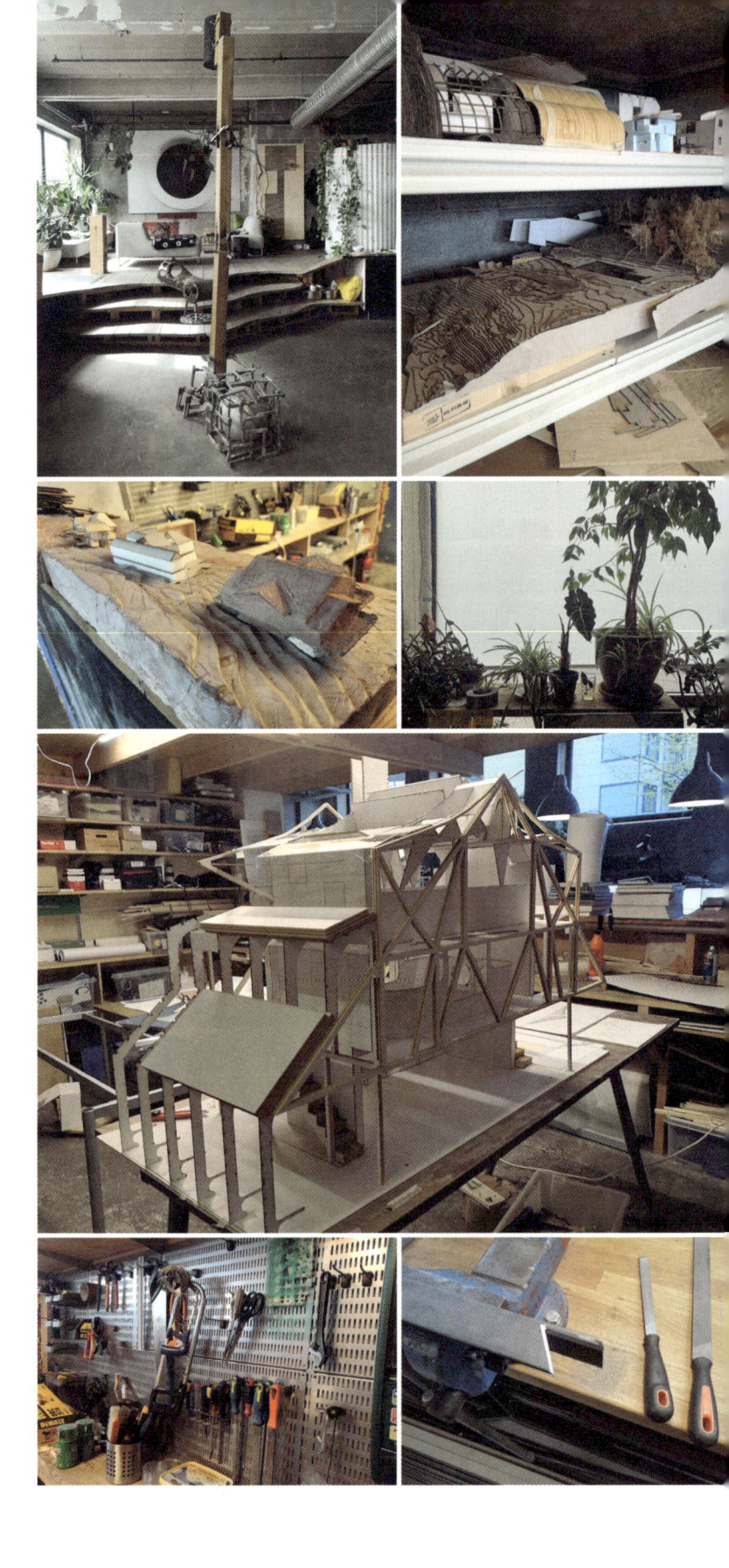

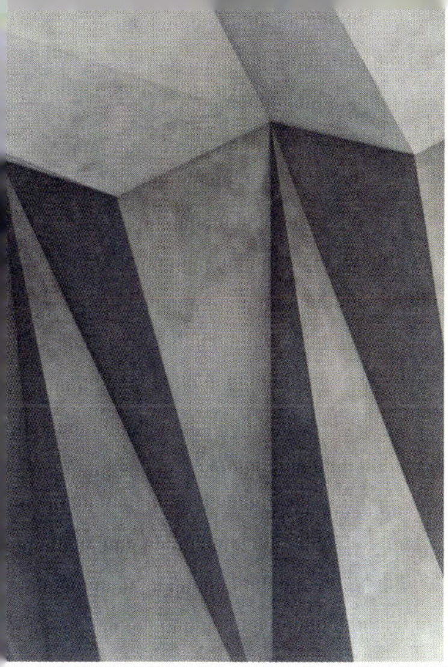
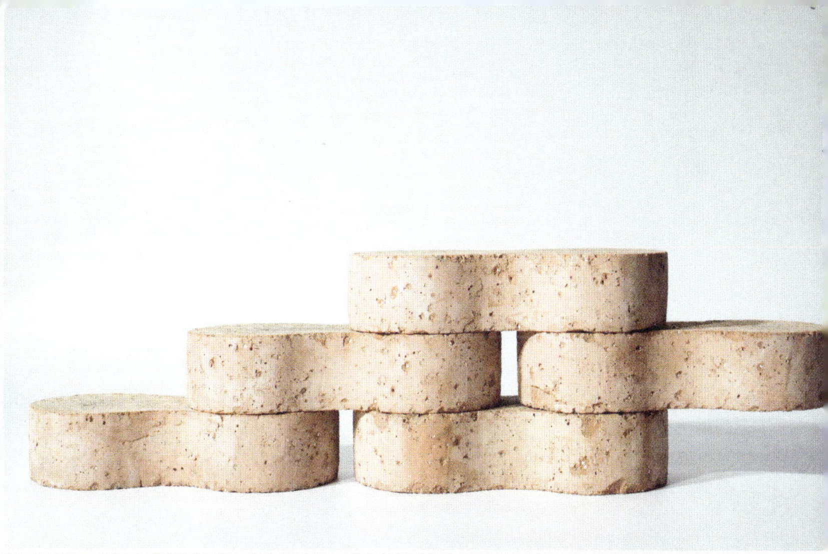
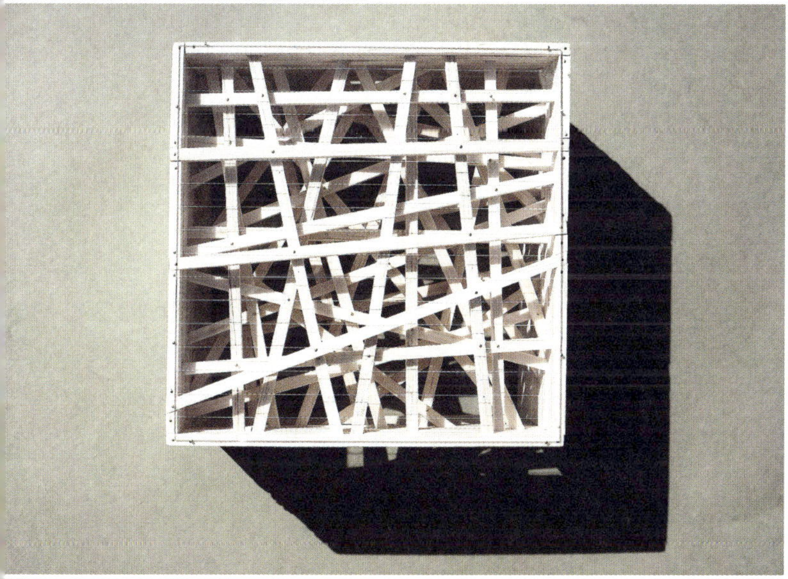
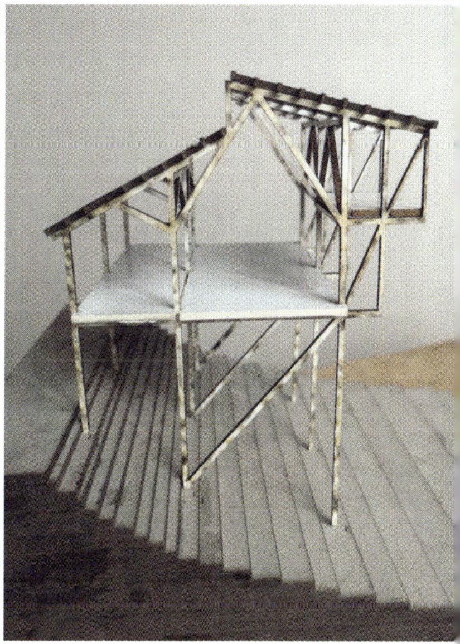
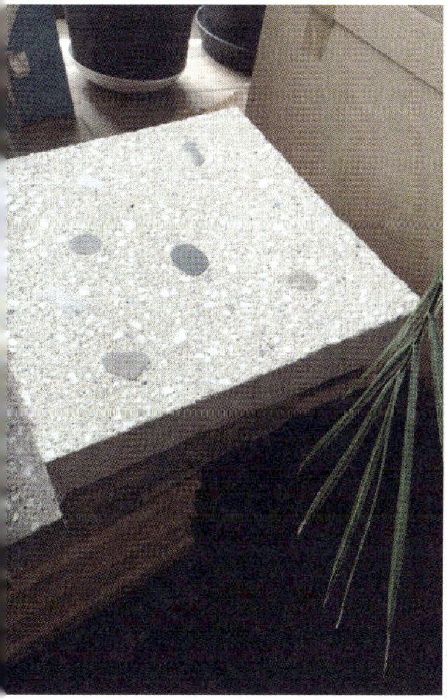
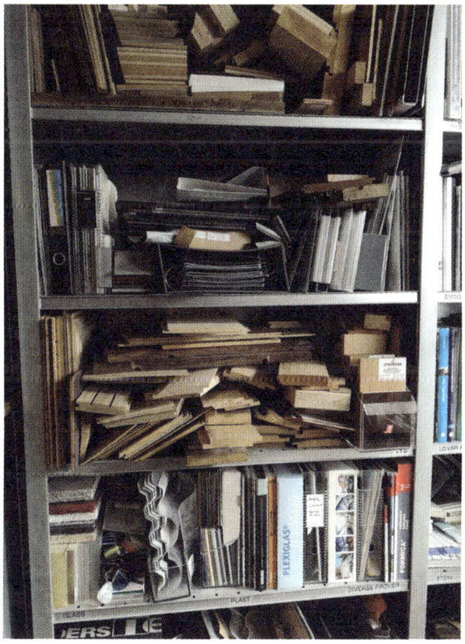
PLEXIGLAS®
PLAST
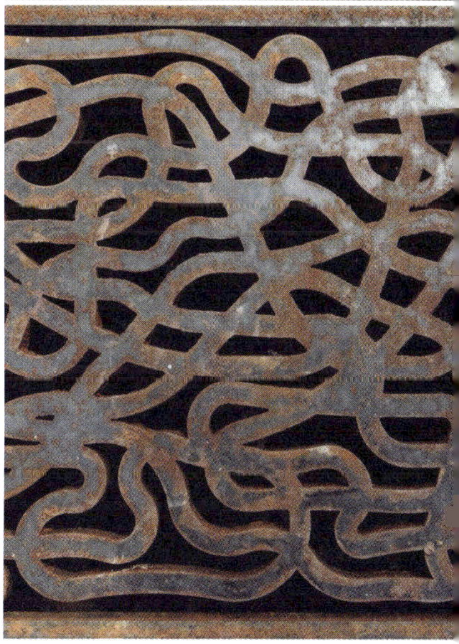

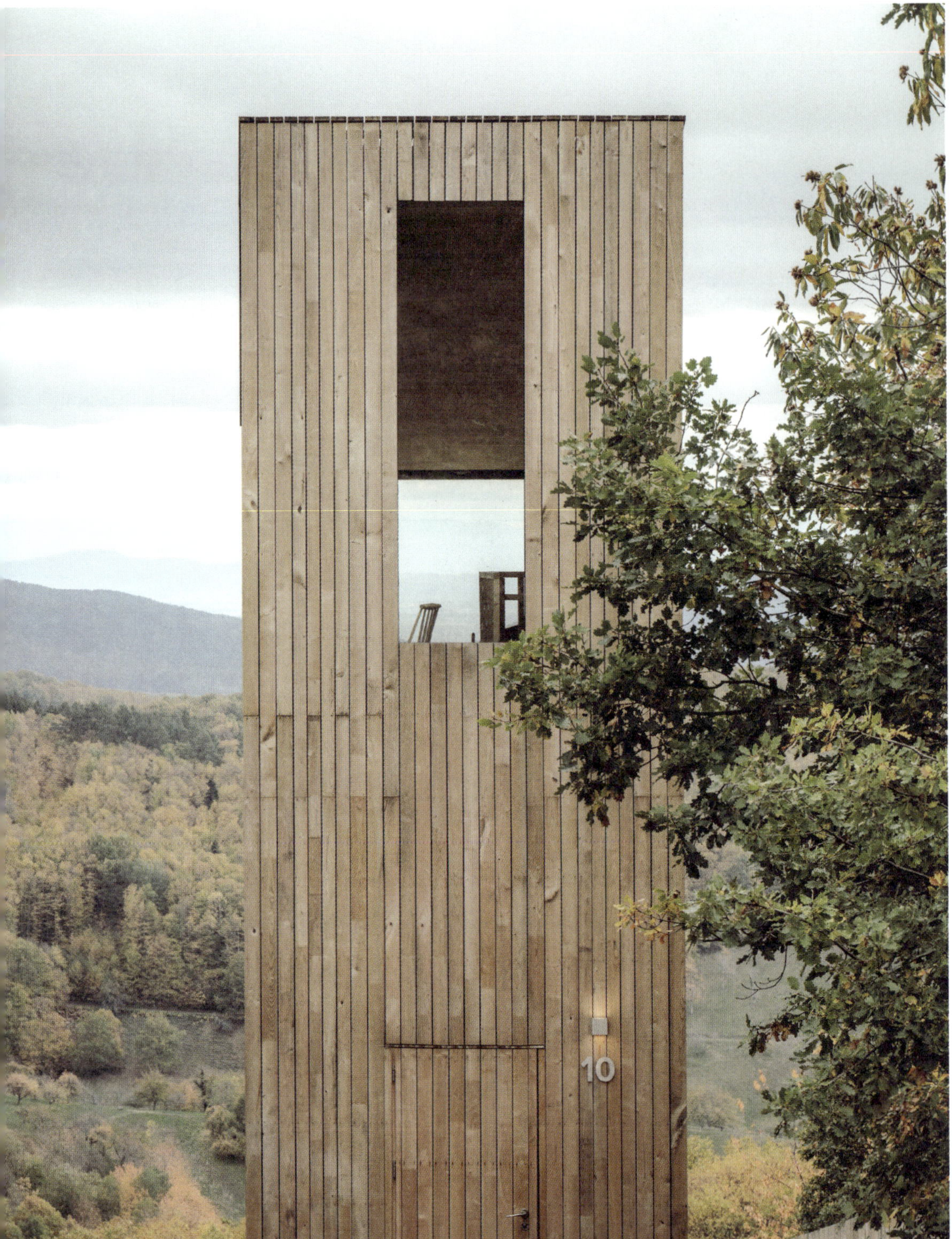
10

Reiulf Ramstad Arkitekter

The Norwegian architect Reiulf Ramstad started his design studio 27 years ago in Oslo, after living and studying abroad, particularly in Venice and the US. Reiulf Ramstad Arkitekter (RRA) now has offices in Oslo and Aarhus, Denmark. It prides itself on a diverse design approach, creating a strong conceptual basis for each project that it strives to see through the entire process, from initial sketch to completion. Landscape is one of the firm's major concerns, with Ramstad making an explicit connection between architecture, the built environment and landscape and man-made landscape. Major works include the Trollstigen National Tourist Route Development, Romsdal Folk Museum and the Community Church in Knarvik, all in Norway, and the House of Grain in Hjørring, Denmark. Drawing and model-making are also integral to the process of creating architecture, as well as the establishment of a close working relationship with clients and contractors. As well as Denmark and Norway, the practice has worked in France and the US. The studio has won numerous awards, including several nominations for the Mies van der Rohe Award.

reiulframstadarkitekter.com

It's an interesting path that I've been on – living your life, meeting other people, travelling to places, and having a dynamic element to your life evolution. I believe that my passion for architecture equals my passion for life.

— Reiulf Ramstad

Previous page, left and below: Breitenbach Landscape Hotel 48° Nord, Alsace, France

Todd Saunders: When I first came to Norway your work appeared very different. You were Norwegian, but you seemed like the first architect on the scene who was educated outside of Norway, you gave these great lectures, and your work was always fresh and diverse. You had one foot in Norway as well as this international overview. I saw a recent film of you where you're sitting up in this little place by yourself, just drawing. How do you protect your time, so you can sit down and draw?

Reiulf Ramstad: I think my work is linked to the pure passion and the curiosity of building. I actually wanted to be a dancer, but I guess I was better at architecture. Now that I've had the office for some years I've met engineers, lawyers, doctors, artists – and I can really relate to those who have the same passion for their work. That is also why I decided to go abroad to live, not just to study. Instead of taking five years, my studies took almost ten years because I was just living as well.

TS: How has your attitude to work changed since you started your practice?

RR: I used to feel disappointed when projects were not realised. Now I'm more relaxed. I think our track record is that maybe only one project out of 11 is built. It's an interesting path that I've been on – living your life, meeting other people, travelling to places, and having a dynamic element to your life evolution. I believe that my passion for architecture equals my passion for life.

TS: Is the scale of your office right for you?

RR: In terms of our evolution, it's not just about volume growth. Unlike many offices in Oslo, we decided not to grow more than we are now, approximately 30 people. That size offers a certain scale and engine of production, but not so huge that you don't know the names of the people you're working with. And there's a practical issue – I live and work in the same building and we physically cannot have any more people there.

TS: What is unique about your architectural process?

RR: We are more focused on the final product than the wrapping or the process. In Norway now, we have these dialogue-based processes, where the end result is less important. The engineering firms have become especially good at having professionalised processes. Maybe it's unfashionable to make quality work, I don't know. The politics of architecture means you can't be honest. If you express concerns about quality, then you get endlessly involved with meetings, not deciding anything. It's very much the opposite of what I believe. We need less wrapping and more content.

TS: How much does the impact of time weigh upon your design approach?

RR: I think we use too much of our time for other things. When you are involved in big projects today, drawings are of secondary importance. The meetings are more important. I personally think that the language of architecture is drawing.

TS: When I arrived here in Bergen, I didn't know these "rules" and went my own way. The houses that I designed – sort of "hybrid Bergen houses" – became popular because they were so different. And the idea of quality in the drawing process is also interesting. We run workshops in the early design stage, about

Right: Brädgården Art Works, Noormarkku, Finland

the site, the materiality and the interior spaces. How do you do ensure quality in your process?

RR: We have around 40 projects running, in eight countries. They range from finding new work to modifying old projects. Some projects are furniture, some are a piece of the city. It's very diverse. But sometimes you start a project, you think the client is really good, and then you realise they are not so interested in quality. You can run into conflict. Sometimes I have conflicts, especially when big clients have chosen to change paths that we don't believe in.

TS: Does that cost you mental energy or are you getting better at managing it?

RR: The most important thing in a project is the client and their values. I have an idea for a really big book, the size of the Bible, just titled "The Client". You can educate a client. You can develop a good relationship; you can learn a lot or you sometimes can run into problems.

TS: A turning point in my career was when I decided to seek clients to work with because I admired them. Have you been making those sorts of changes?

RR: Maybe I should. We originally never had any specific strategy for public relations. We just won competitions all the time, lived off that for many years and then all the good competitions disappeared. In came this garbage process – the lowest price competition, or competitions with juries that don't really understand architecture. I sometimes don't think that open competitions with vague conditions are a quality way of getting projects any more, at least in the Nordic market. Now people contact us. We either get invited to carry out a direct commission or take part in limited competitions. The market has changed.

TS: You've mentioned speed and slowness. Is architecture too fast now for you – do you wish it was slower?

RR: Everybody uses the term sustainable. A lot of stakeholders in the building sector say "we are focused on sustainability and you have to do a project with as little time as possible, so we don't use a lot of resources." For me, for something to be truly sustainable, you have to work through it and understand every element. Too many buildings should never have been built because they are so bad, uninspiring and brutal. It's a huge waste for society. So I believe that architecture should be slower. You can't make good wine at super speed; you have to be patient from the day you start growing the grapes until you drink it.

TS: You once mentioned that the building season at Trollstigen was only four months long, which gave you eight months to think about things, and that seemed to work well for you. Have there been other projects where the timescale has unfolded at just the right pace?

RR: If time were used in a more conscious way, it could be a beautiful part of the process. In our profession you meet a lot of economically successful people, but some do not realise that the only currency that cannot be changed is time, which is valuable.

TS: Is your work related to teaching these days?

RR: We want to connect the missing link between the intellectual side of architecture and the practical reality that surrounds us. For years, we've always had between four and six young interns in the office. They bring with

NORWAY | REIULF RAMSTAD ARKITEKTER

Left and below:
Brädgården Art Works,
Noormarkku, Finland

them a passion for new thoughts and a kind of naïve energy. I guess I'm growing into an old teenager, not just a mature man. I am more curious and playful when compared to the start of my career.

TS: How does it feel to have your studio run as a place of learning?

RR: We've had these interns for more than 20 years now, so I have seen these micro generations evolve. It also keeps my feet on the ground. Now the students in the office are younger than my children.

TS: We have a picture of one of the guys from our office beside me when I'm drawing the first sketches of the studios on Fogo Island. My daughter is sitting on my lap. And she's 15 now. It's also great when we see interns go on to do great things.

RR: In our last book, Contours & Horizons, I defined my fields of research and my beliefs in architecture. We also did an exhibition at The Utzon Centre in Denmark in 2018/19, which focused on our way of working. We even had some one-to-one scale tectonic structures as part of this exhibition. It was a real turning point – it made us conscious of where we are and where we want to go.

TS: Where do you want to go now?

RR: In terms of projects, we must consider the global conditions of architecture and how they are changing our lives. How will the Covid pandemic create a new direction in architecture, from the home office to the way we socialise and so forth? It has changed our mindset. Back in history, plagues, wars and political revolutions changed the conditions of life, but also changed architecture and developed new typologies and made people aware of their needs in a different way.

TS: How does your architecture make the world a better place?

RR: I have to visit the places where we make architecture, not only to see the topography and understand the people and local communities, but also to feel the atmosphere so that it can become a part of me. It's an important way of making connections.

TS: Are there any unconventional professions or people you collaborate with?

RR: The best way of developing architecture is with different talents and different people. Just as the best music is made from different cultures. And even if a lot of elements are prefabricated off-site, I also believe in talking to the people who physically build your project. For me, everything is landscape, whether you're in France or Norway. They could be natural or man-made.

TS: I was recently working with the photographer Ivar Kvaal who really admires your work. He said you're very open about how you feel about your architecture. I think my architecture is very intuitive, and there are many times I can't explain why I do what I do. Can you talk a little about the invisible things?

RR: When I wanted to study abroad, I moved to Venice. It's such a unique place because of the absence of the car. The car is probably the most conditional object that has surrounded humanity for the last century now. I discovered walking and slow speeds. It was a time when slow things became popular – slow cooking, for example. "Slow" had a deeper sense. It goes back to the idea of wanting high quality and having to work hard for it. Venice also showed me all these physical conditions and spaces which would not pass Norwegian building laws. You see streets that are just 1.5m wide. If there are not a lot of people, why does it need to be wider? And if you live surrounded by lots of people and you have limited daylight in some places, in other places you could see the reflection of water off the canals. You realise that modern building codes are very general and don't take context into account at all. Architecture should be carefully developed for each specific case. Most of the buildings that are built today are within the building code and they often look horrible. We're surrounded by too many rules now.

TS: Once the car was introduced, it made a new separation in how people connected in a relaxed way in a city. The car took up more space and humans got put in second place. Now the digital world seems to be putting humans in third place. There's more and more separation.

RR: The car is in the centre of the street and the people are on the side. We ought to think differently. But if you air these thoughts with clients, they sometimes don't understand what you're saying.

TS: You're doing a lot of work outside of Norway. Has that made a positive difference on your practice?

RR: Norway is such a long, thin and irrational country. There's a lot of difference here. But we've also had some good experiences in Alsace in France. We have realised two projects there and are working on a third. Travelling between small villages and collaborating with the mayors, sitting with them, eating their food, drinking their wine, has all become a significant part of our current project, making it stronger and simpler. The scheme is more of a landscape project than a building, a path through a region in Alsace to link five villages together. It's very different from making and designing a building.

TS: When I go to Fogo Island sometimes and meet clients, we'll start at the Inn and walk to the four studios. It takes all day, about 10,000 steps. It's great to go on a walk with people to get to know them and experience the architecture.

RR: In our office, architecture is not just related to buildings, but it's a way of conceiving space. It can be everything from making a chair to a house or even an 11km walk through landscape. These things all belong to the different bands of architecture, like an old radio with FM and medium wave and long wave. You find architecture in all these kinds of places.

Opposite and above:
Pilestredet 77–79, Oslo, Norway

Right: Reiulf Ramstad
Arkitekter, Oslo, Norway

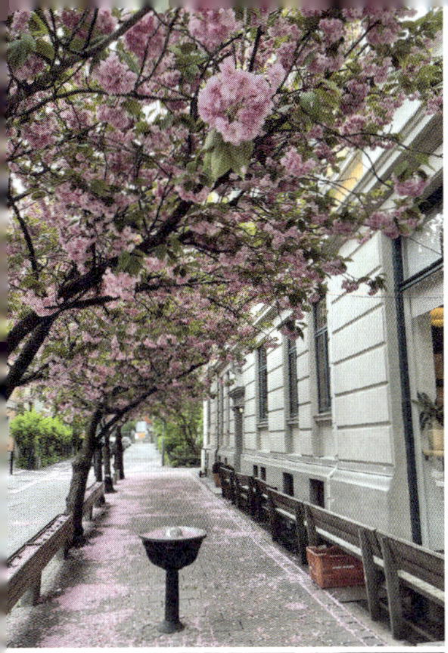
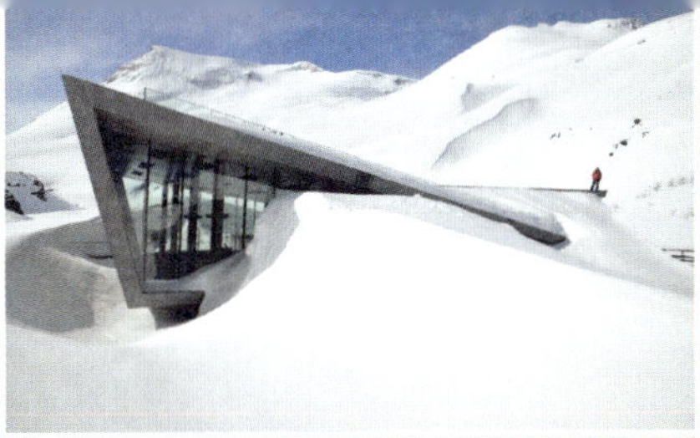
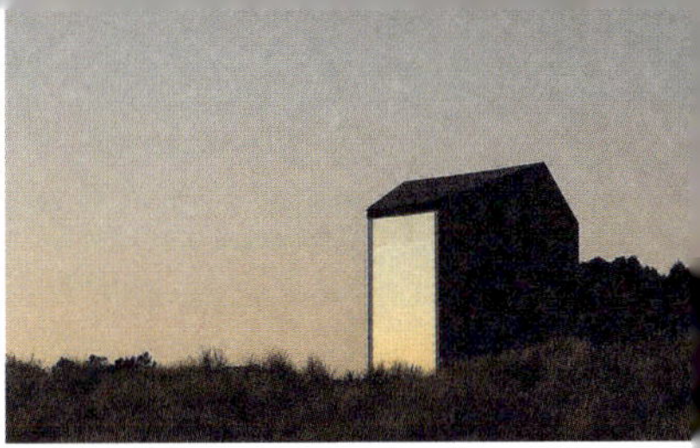
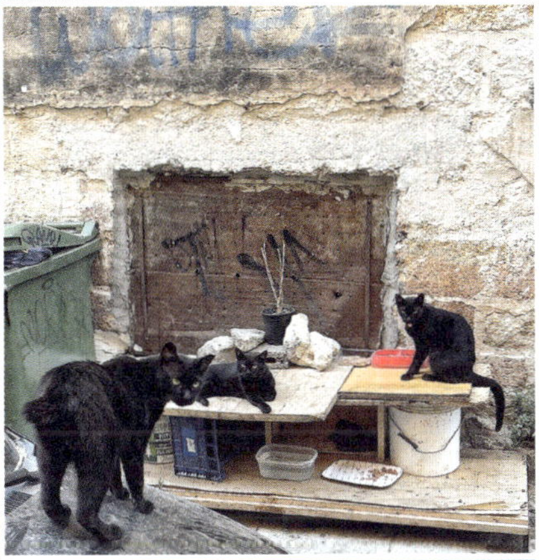
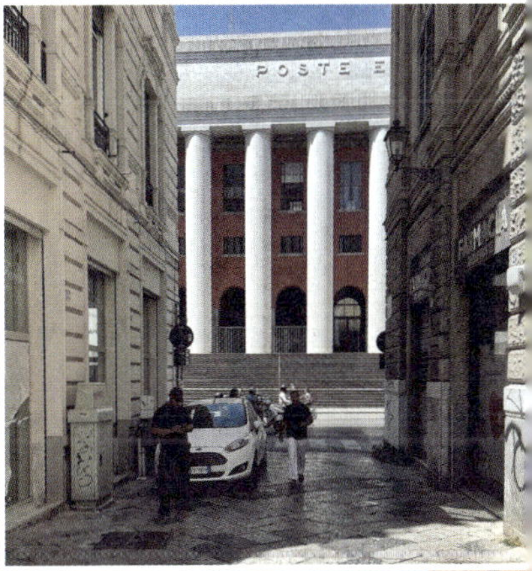
POSTE
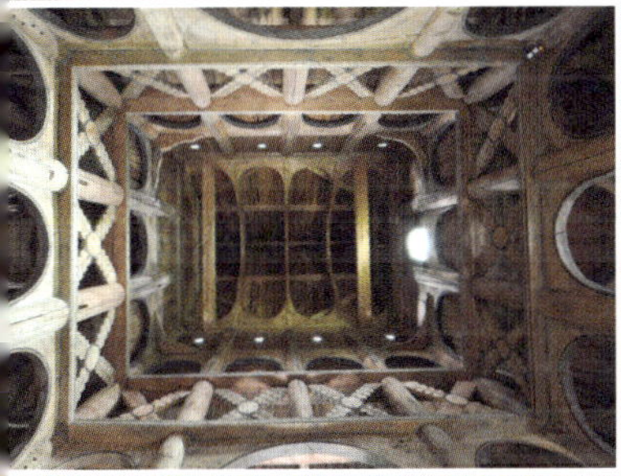
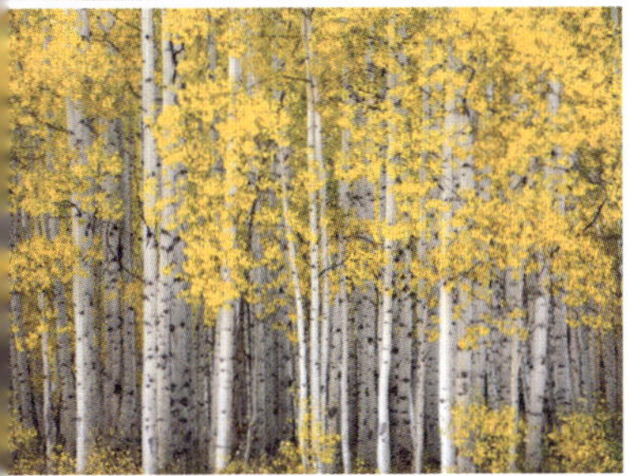
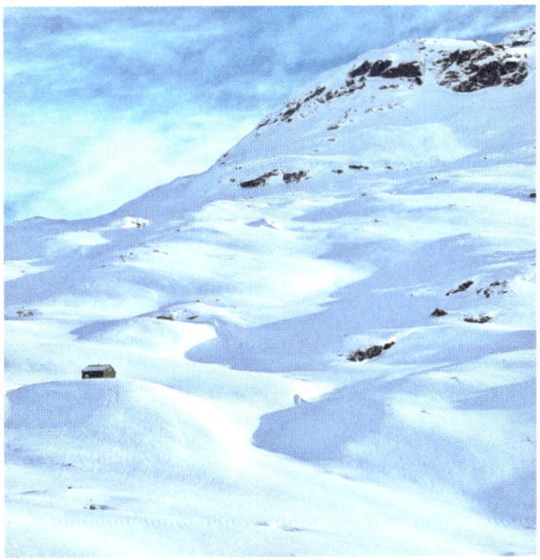
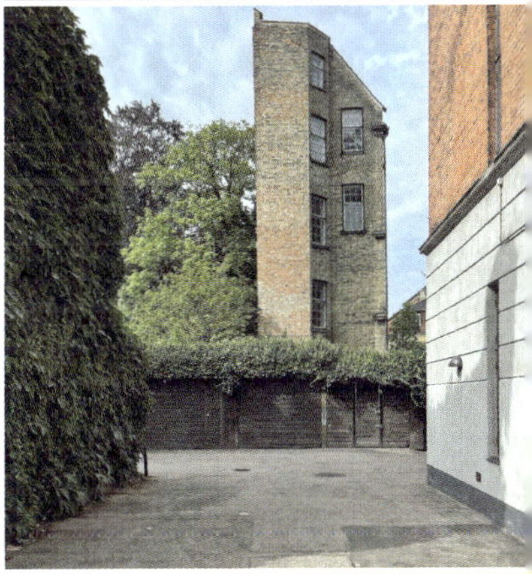
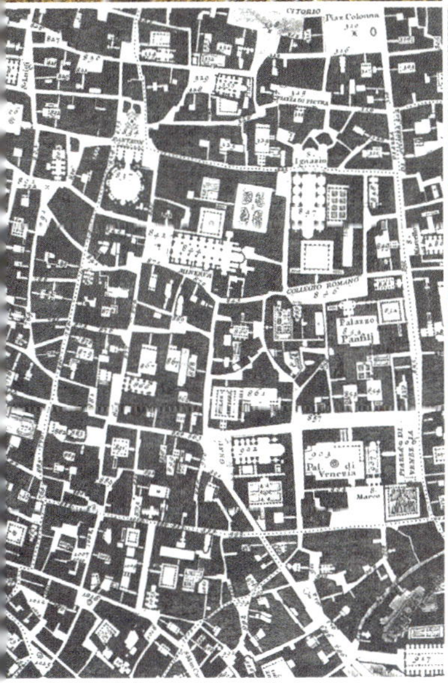
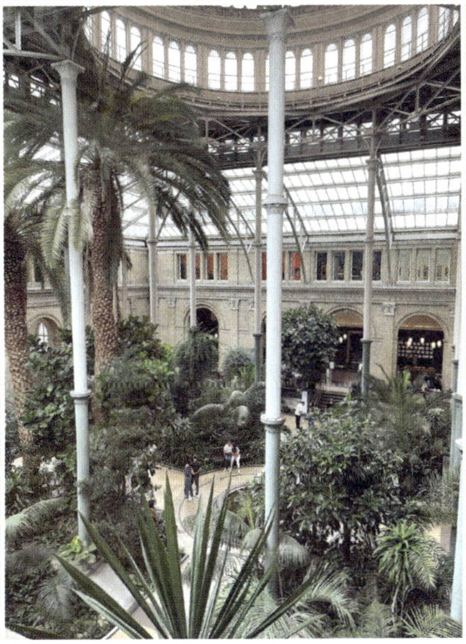
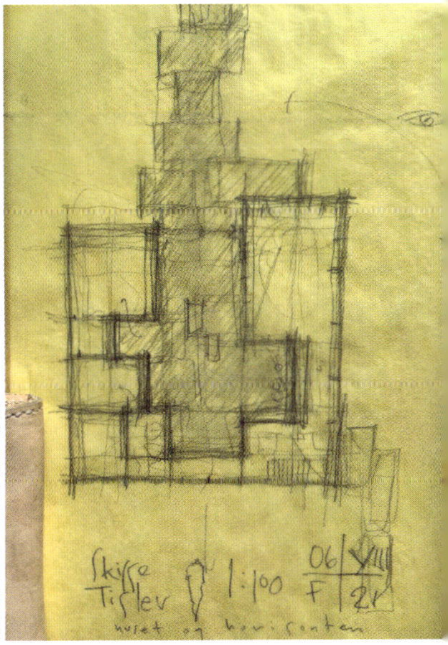

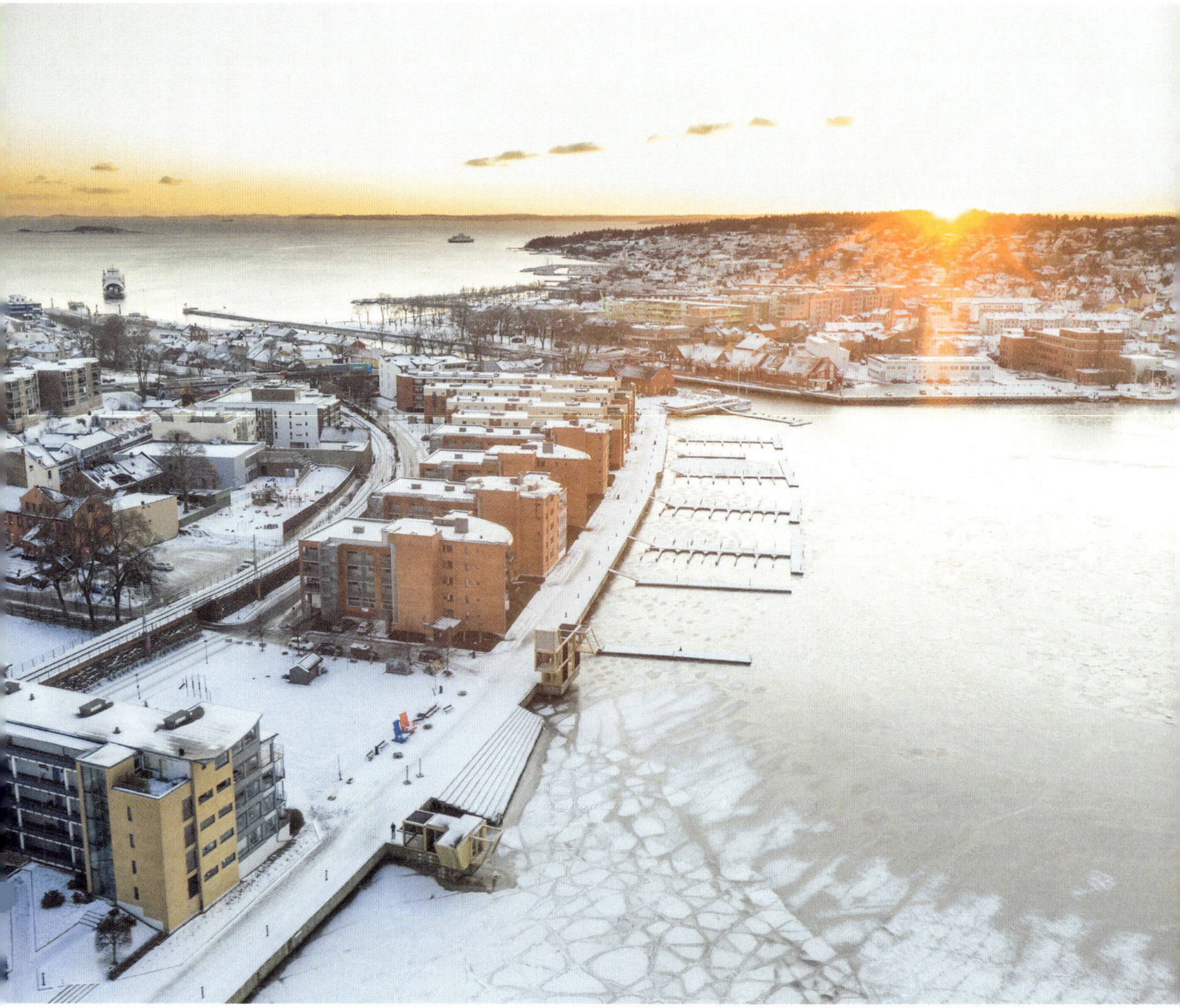

Rintala Eggertsson

In 2007, the Finnish architect and artist Sami Rintala and the Icelandic architect Dagur Eggertsson created a studio that developed the type of work they had started first as fellow students and later as educators. Rintala Eggertsson has studios in Oslo, and Bodø in northern Norway, and has designed and built projects around the world. Combining architecture with art, along with teaching, furniture design and planning, projects have included installations in London, Venice, Rome, Cuba, Japan and Alaska, along with a series of teaching workshops. Built works include the Høse pedestrian bridge in Suldal, and the Tintra Footbridge in Vossevangen, both in Norway, along with the Boxhome and Cabinet Home concepts and the Seljord Watchtower. Working closely with local communities, as well as builders and craftspeople, each Rintala Eggertsson project is a poetic response to site that is designed to be accessible, achievable and practical.

ri-eg.com

Previous page, above and right: FLYT bathing installations, Moss, Norway

Todd Saunders: Is being in an office more challenging, now that you've moved away from academia and into practice?

Sami Rintala: When we started the office, we gave ourselves three months, then six, and then, we started thinking about it seriously. You don't want to let go of the professional part of what you're doing, or the architectonic possibilities that lie within each and every project. We have always tried to be loyal to the task itself. Now, with a few years of experience, we're looking ahead.

TS: Are you going after the right work and creating projects you want or are you in a situation where you're just providing a service? How much control are you trying to take in your future?

SR: That's difficult to answer. I think things are calmer now somehow. We are slowly getting contacts for culture- and education-related projects that have a certain scale. But some things change, like when we lost the last phase of a museum project and all the details were done by another office. It was unnecessary because we'd been working for six or seven years, saving the project for our clients by reducing the scheme in a way that they were still really happy with.

Dagur Eggertsson: What happens is that procurement rules for these projects are actually defining the quality of architecture. If the dynamics were better understood then architecture would be 1,000 times better, because there is a relationship between quality and having to break a project into phases and then procure new offices for each phase. As a result, you lose some of the magic that existed at the beginning of the process. We're extremely critical of the procurement system and we're trying to break through this ceiling and get slightly bigger projects so we can focus on the communication of ideas and narrative.

TS: I call that ceiling the institutional barrier. How do you think we can remove that?

SR: You see better things happening in the art world, where we've also been working. With one foot in the art world, you see much more quality when a great curator decides what's best for the client. They will support the artist until the end. In the architecture world, the architecture-client relationship is full of scepticism and distrust.

DE: When you got a really good client, Todd, you had the chance to show what you can do. Without endurance, you will follow the surroundings too much and end up producing something that you can't stand fully behind.

TS: I've decided not to do open competitions any more, just invited competitions. There's too much work involved. Where do you put your energy to avoid these situations?

DE: I agree with Sami that the focus has to be on endurance. But there is a systemic problem: we teach and send people off into the professional world knowing that they would have to survive for a couple of decades to do something big and juicy. And nobody's saying anything about it.

TS: There's an elephant in the room.

DE: I mean, are we obliged to say something? I think we have been extremely honest to our students. Not trying to paint things black – just to make them more resilient.

Opposite and below: Høse Bridge, Suldal, Norway

We have already survived the world of smaller projects and now go for slightly larger projects. But all these talented architecture school graduates are entering a world they don't know anything about.

TS: We've already interviewed a few foreigners working in Norway. You're Icelandic and Finnish. What are some of the benefits of working in Norway?

SR: I think Norwegian architects are seen as more interesting than the Finnish ones in the last 15 years or so. We're lucky in that sense to be here because it's more significant internationally what happens in Norway. It's an easier base to travel from – and we are a bit closer to the world than Finland. Of course, Finland is not really a bad country and Helsinki is already quite international and cultural in many ways.

DE: I have nothing to compare it with because I've never practised in Iceland. However, I think that many things are very similar in Scandinavian countries, maybe all of Europe, basically. But the relationship with nature is quite different here in Norway compared to Iceland. We were discussing this back in Helsinki, when we were studying together. The relationship with surroundings is different and that often defines possibilities in the projects and tasks that you're doing.

TS: How does the Icelandic relation to nature compare with Norwegian?

DE: The wind and the rain and that ever-changing climate in Iceland, as well as the distances and the smaller population, means it is more about survival than simply enjoying nature. Here in Norway, people enjoy nature more – the climate is friendlier and more predictable, and you can wander off into the woods for days without being in any danger. That defines the relationship with nature in a very different way.

SR: I think Norwegians go out to look around, so it's a very visual thing. In Finland, we go into nature to hide; you are trying to merge in, and dress in green and black so that nobody sees you. In Norway, they put on red so you can be seen from many kilometres away. And Norwegians often talk in nature while in Finland you're silent. That's the biggest difference for me. But these things change – often when I say this sort of thing I realise it's more that times are changing and I'm just old-fashioned.

TS: Is nature a place to recharge for Norwegians and Finns?

SR: That's a Nordic thing in general, for sure. You go there to tap your roots somehow.

TS: Going back to your architectural process – is there anything in the early stages of a project that you've changed over the last few years?

DE: They're not changes, but we've been going back and forth between workshops to find out the defining factor in a project. I can understand there's a wish to put some of the discussion behind you, so you move on because these things are eating up time and money for the clients.

SR: Sometimes clients don't share the same goals. So it becomes about constant communication, learning each other's values, because they are such long-term projects. It can take time to get to know each other. I've learned not to be too sceptical.

If you solve a problem too early without knowing what the question is, it's almost even more dangerous than giving a wrong answer. You need to learn the questions at first. That's what you learn in a good team.

— Sami Rintala

Above and right: Corte del Forte, Venice, Italy

DE: Sparring with the client became a rule because pushing them for answers was important. Right from the very start, we encouraged clients to participate in a visual approach through sketches. We're pushing the boundaries, even creating caricatures of the projects in a way to boil things down to the essential elements. This has been a very efficient way of breaking the ice and establishing mutual trust.

TS: Can you describe a really enjoyable process in relation to a project?

SR: When we did the Høse Bridge over Sandefjord in Suldal, we spent a week on site, drawing concepts and perspectives. Then at the end of the week we presented them directly to the locals. It's a great method, smooth and low risk for both of us. You usually realise if it is going to work or not.

TS: Fantastic idea. Just to see what comes out of working together for a week.

SR: The client pays for those days and the travel. If they don't want to cover the travel you know that it's a bad sign. When we started practising I realised there was this enormous distrust towards academics who were coming from Oslo and suggesting transformations for a small community. There was a distrust in whatever we came up with. I would be sceptical or annoyed as well – it's a natural thing. So living in a place is like breaking the ice, especially when people have seen you for a few days, going to the supermarket or whatever. They realise you're genuinely interested in their culture and community.

TS: Is there now some pre-existing trust from the people who reach out to you now, based on your portfolio?

SR: Some curious people contact us but it doesn't always lead to a project. We need to test the ground with them, especially if it's a private project – there's some psychology mixed in as well. You need to be extremely patient with people while they're organising finances and planning. There are lives on the other side that we need to relate to.

DE: I surprise myself by saying that I think we still have fun when we work. I don't want to do things any other way. There's a lot of trust.

TS: What is your take on the juxtaposition of vernacular and contemporary architecture, and how they relate to each other?

DE: I think it's a very culturally related issue. Coming into the profession in postmodern times taught us to think in broader terms about defining modernism and vernacular architecture as being two aspects of the same thing. A good idea can fit into either category. When we're talking to our students, we're looking for the idea that frames the architecture over the technique of producing the architecture. Some talented architects can barely draw, but their ideas are brilliant – and some people are amazing at drawing but have a very limited number of ideas.

SR: The spatial quality of architecture is something that surpasses time and price and technology, so it's the idea level which is most important. When I was a student, I was really interested in old buildings, because they not only told a story of the space but also about the era they were built. There's another kind of authorship in it.

Right and opposite: Seljord tower, Seljord, Norway

TS: I see this fresh take on old Norwegian architecture in your projects all the time. How do you use intuition to create architecture? Do you ever have shared intuition about a site?

DE: I think this connects with our workshop method, if you can call it that. No idea is a bad idea. There was a project we did in Virginia, at UVA in Charleston. It was just a few weeks after the shootings and the white supremacy rallies. People were in shock in many ways, the students were shocked, they wanted to address the issue. But it was tough to get them to communicate about the common ground in the project, because people were internalising so much. I've never experienced architecture being used as a form of psychotherapy in this way. It eventually became a very good process, but thinking is so related to our experiences and people were just trapped in their own bubbles.

SR: That's a good way of putting it. There was also a different perception of what an architect is – some people thought it similar to being a lawyer, that you were simply there to develop land into a more valuable asset. They felt strongly about their ideas because of the political situation. Sometimes it's best to ignore intuitions because normality isn't always about wanting to push things forward.

TS: You must know each other's strengths so well.

DE: Yes, you need to think in terms of being a team. You need to allow people time and possibility to come up with ideas, even the silliest ideas. If you start censoring or pre-defining things, you ruin the flow of intuition into a project. We started off playing football together in university many years ago, and architecture is a bit like that. We were good at different things so when we're playing together, we use each other's way of working. Sometimes you are paving the way for others and sometimes you take the lead. We're always using intuition as a guiding force.

TS: What did you like most about the process of working together as a small team?

SR: It was quite complicated, to be honest. We had to use local workers and the restrictions in Venice are pretty tough, with local cultural heritage rules and Italian bureaucracy, as well as workers who hadn't really worked with wood before and who didn't always agree with us. But they pulled it off and we could actually include everybody's ideas, which is why it became such a rich yet small project.

TS: Do you both know your own speeds, like when one person needs more time to decide?

DE: I'm not very keen on comparing it to a marriage, but you have to refrain from pre-defining everything.

SR: Sometimes, when you're working alone, you can move a bit too fast. You answer the wrong questions, or you make a good argument but it's in the wrong place. If you solve a problem too early without knowing what the question is, it's almost even more dangerous than giving a wrong answer. You need to learn the questions at first. That's what you learn in a good team.

NORWAY | RINTALA EGGERTSSON

Right: Rintala Eggertsson, Oslo and Bodø, Norway

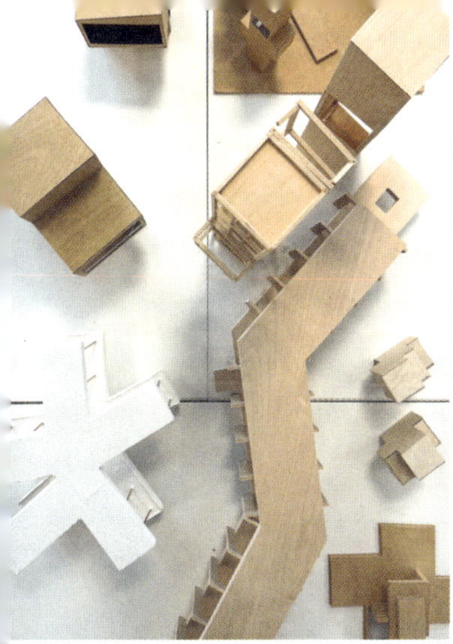
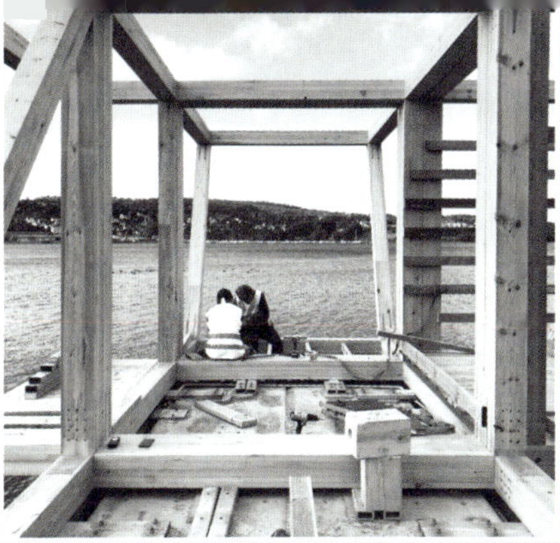
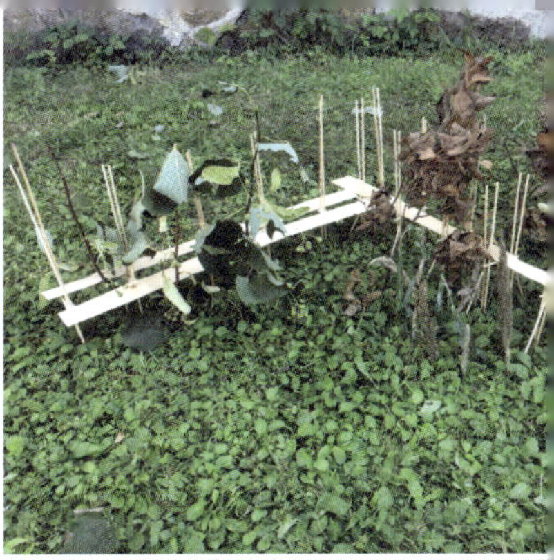
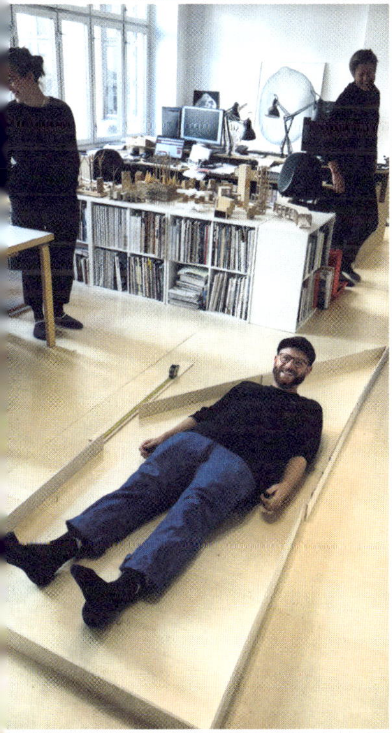
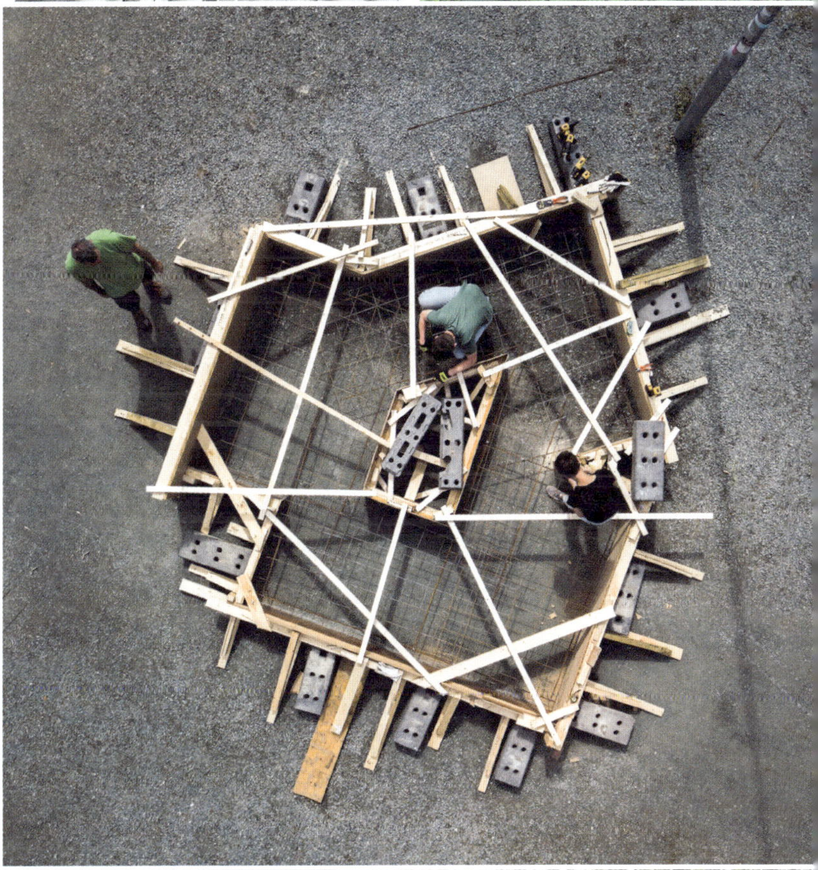
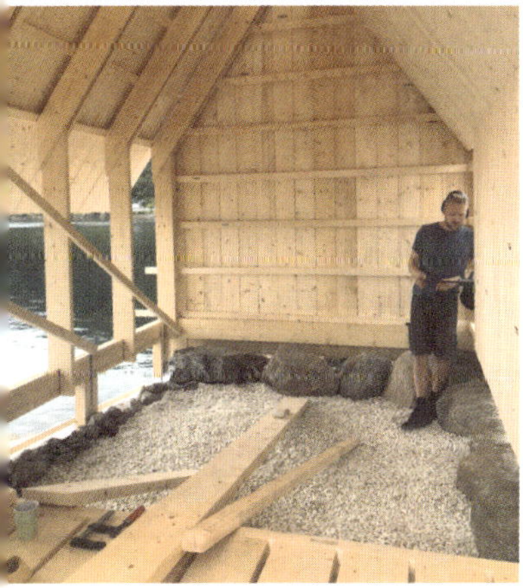
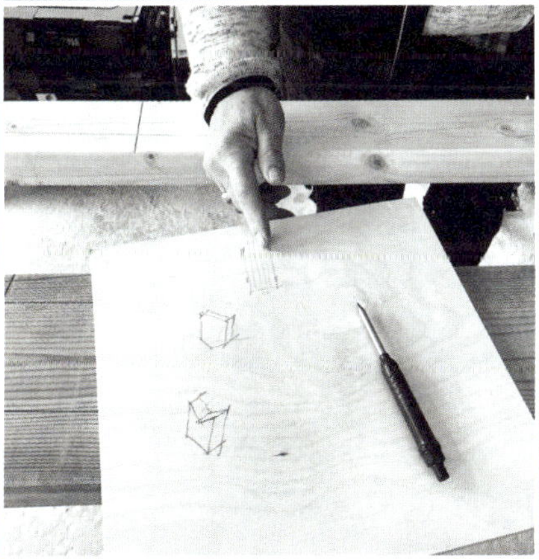
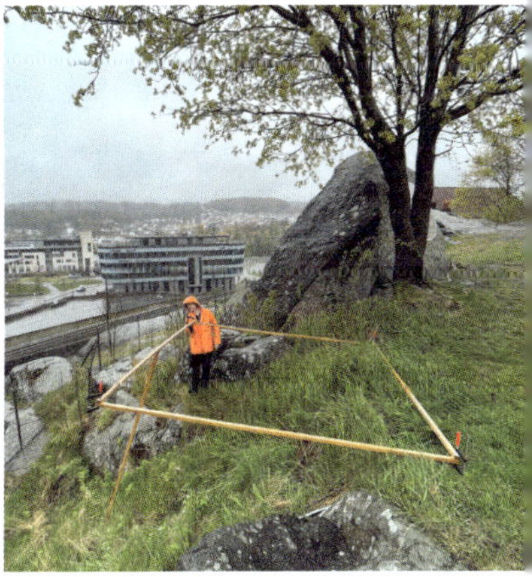

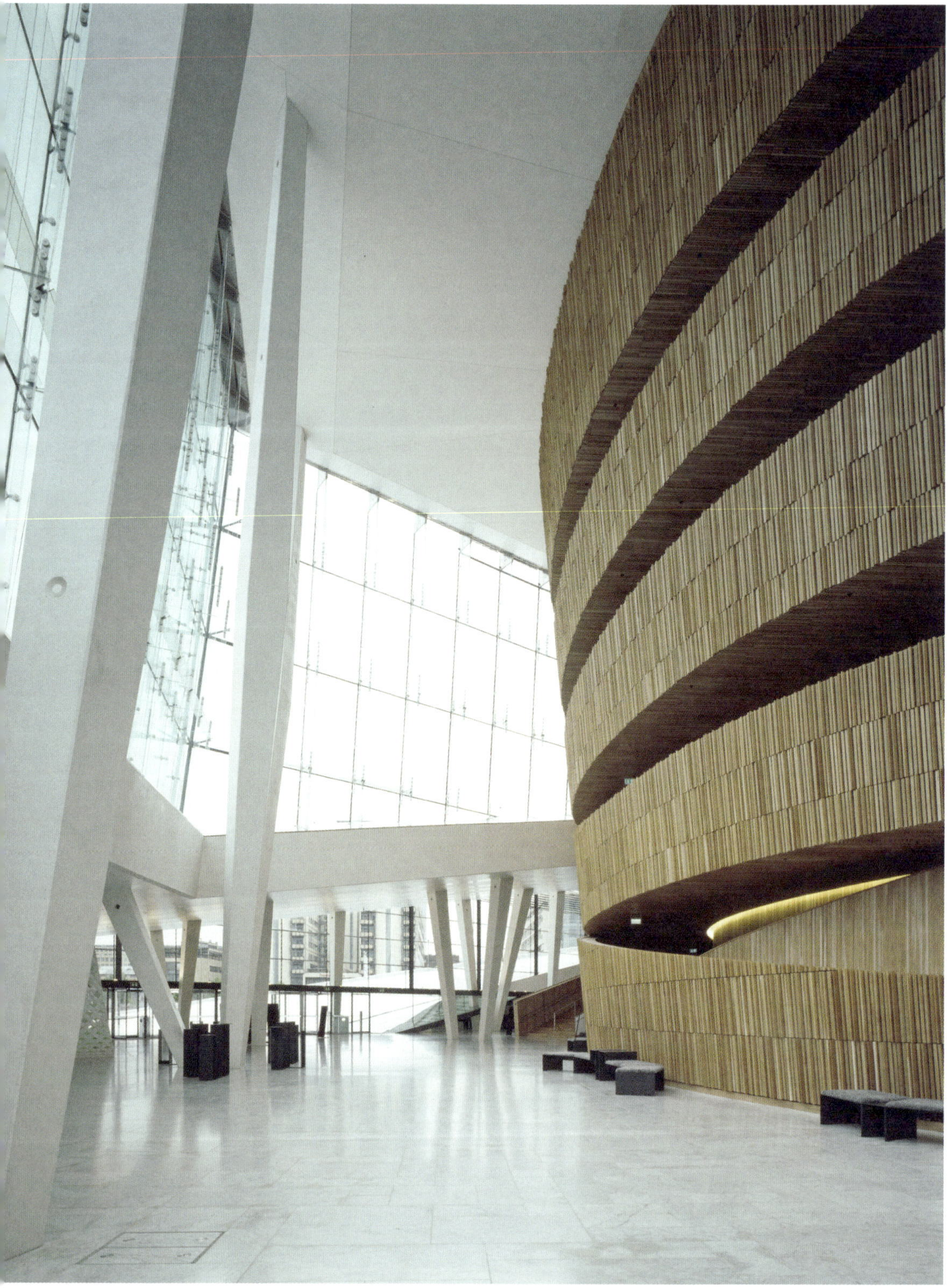

Snøhetta

Named after the highest mountain in Norway's Dovrefjell range, Snøhetta is one of the world's pre-eminent collaborative architectural and landscape firms. Founded in 1989 by Kjetil Trædal Thorsen and Craig Edward Dykers, it grew out of a workshop-based and transdisciplinary approach from the outset. When its competition entry for the Bibliotheca Alexandrina in Alexandria, Egypt beat over 1,400 rivals, the firm had not completed a single building. Construction of the library began in 1995 and took seven years, but the ethos at the heart of the scheme has gone on to inform all its subsequent projects. "Our work strives to enhance our sense of surroundings, identity and relationship to others and the physical spaces we inhabit, whether feral or human-made," they write. Snøhetta now has offices in Oslo, Paris, Innsbruck, New York, Hong Kong, Adelaide and San Francisco, with over 300 employees representing around 40 nationalities. There is also equal gender distribution among staff. Major projects include the new Library in Alexandria, Egypt, Norwegian National Opera and Ballet in Oslo, the National September 11 Memorial Museum Pavilion in New York, the Lascaux IV International Centre for Cave Art in France, Le Monde Group Headquarters in Paris, Europe's first underwater restaurant, Under, in Lindesnes, as well as Powerhouse Brattørkaia in Trondheim. The firm combines architecture with landscape design, interior architecture, graphic design, digital design, product design and art. Collaboration is an essential component of every project.

snohetta.com

Saying when enough is enough? I always ask the question, "Do we really need this or that?"

— Kjetil Trædal Thorsen

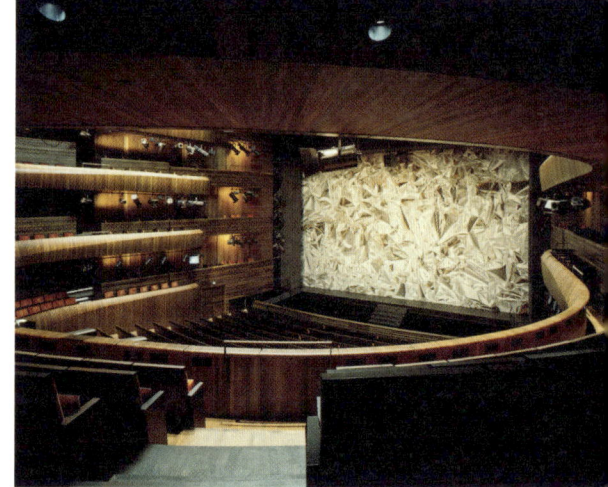

Previous page, opposite top and opposite bottom:
Norwegian National Opera and Ballet, Oslo, Norway

Todd Saunders: Where are you speaking from?

Kjetil Trædal Thorsen: Paris. In the Marais, just two minutes from our office here.

TS: This book project would have been useful to us when we were starting out.

KTT: I like its shared and inclusive aspect. In Norway we don't see other architects as competitors, but we're trying to establish a better foundation for the future of the profession.

TS: You've mentioned the idea of giving more than you take. Does that approach give you energy?

KTT: Absolutely. We recently curated an issue of Baumeister Magazine. Rather than just promote yourself, it's interesting to share knowledge of invited guests. We think the profession should have a solid base to make a difference, not necessarily focus on the production of one office.

TS: We first met in the days before email. No connections – I don't even know how you and I got in touch. But now with Zoom, things like location and even age have been completely erased.

KTT: It's given us opportunities. The outreach we have is so much wider. We did work for Wikipedia and I was fascinated by how they built up their community and knowledge base. Suddenly, you're meeting people who are specialists in growing potatoes in Siberia.

TS: The experts are suddenly attainable.

KTT: Yes – the complete deep level experts, who you would normally never have met or talked to or seen. I've always thought of architecture as about building a specialist community, where things are shared. On the negative side, you're drawn into the computer all the time for far too long. There is no real life. The light sensitivity thing makes it harder to sleep sometimes.

TS: How has the design process changed for you?

KTT: At first, as a landscape and architecture practice, we wanted the level of architecture and landscape architecture to be equal. We included these two professions – architect and landscape architect – at the very beginning and since then it's expanded: digital design, graphic design, product design, interiors, landscape, urbanism. We have a wide range of different people, and we've also developed our processes more scientifically.

TS: You seem to be quantifying a lot of your analysis of buildings these days.

KTT: We have a workshop-based set-up, which comes out of our book Idea Work. This was the result of a PhD programme and research programme by two of my colleagues, looking at creative and collaborative practices in companies in Norway. We wanted to know what the drivers would be to generate cross-collaboration early on in a project. We developed these intuitive workshops that include working with pictograms. We call it

NORWAY | SNØHETTA

a "springboard session" – you choose three photos from a selection that represent what you want and three that represent what you don't want, and begin working from these. We change the photos slightly year by year – you have about 80 pictures.

TS: Are the clients involved in that phase or is this just internal?

KTT: Oh yes. Everyone. Right down to the cleaners at the client's company. We try to spread out the user group and include a wide variety of positions and personalities and professions. Normally, the workshops consist of 25 to 30 people. They take about a day, without designing anything.

TS: Is there no pen to paper at all?

KTT: The last session of the workshop continues the springboard sessions in the model workshop. We build a 3D model – they are more like sculptures, randomly assembled representations of possible concepts, which will normally be one word, or a sentence maximum. We started the process about ten years ago, and it's developed into a self-defined kit of words and terminologies like "transposition".

TS: Are there any absolutes that come out of these workshops – things you absolutely would never do?

KTT: We keep it more open-minded – so we might have three or four different proposals. Then we examine how these things might perform in relationship to the actual programme, the site, to climactic conditions or whatever the performance of the object in the landscape or the design should be.

TS: For how long do you allow things to be open-ended?

KTT: We try to keep to a certain time limit. Sometimes it comes fast. Sometimes it goes slow. It's all about catching the moment and making sure that everyone's focus and concentration is working together.

TS: Did you notice that the workshops created a lot of energy for people to feed off?

KTT: That's most important. We try not to influence the thinking until we've generated similar associations in the heads of everyone involved. We want to end up with a diagrammatic approach, not just a physical shape or form.

TS: Do you agree anything with the clients at this stage?

KTT: We don't really formalise it. But we often film the workshop. We wanted to put a GoPro on every participant's head so you get something that shows the position of every individual in the group and you have a grid of 25 different films. It turned out to be too much work but it's something I still want to do.

TS: Are you good at finishing projects – landing them and getting them down on the ground?

Below: Norwegian National Opera and Ballet, Oslo, Norway

NORWAY | SNØHETTA

Left and below: Bibliotheca Alexandrina, Alexandria, Egypt

KTT: Saying when enough is enough? I always ask the question, "Do we really need this or that?"

TS: That takes a long time. The idea must be strong enough at the beginning.

KTT: And people have to catch on and it has to generate pictures in your mind. In these workshops – the "transpositioning process" – people leave their professions behind. The engineer does not represent engineering as a cross-collaborative element. He represents himself as a person. We're getting the hobbies and interests of the people to the table, not just their professional specialisations.

TS: Do you consider yourself to be autodidactic as a person?

KTT: Yes, yes.

TS: Do you value the emotional component of this first phase?

KTT: For me it's when we go from sitting around the table doing the prepping and the analysis, to moving into the workshop. That's the hands-on stage; where you get a company director to build a model, for example.

TS: From day one, you had this oasis of international culture in your studio, which was really inspiring. It reminds me of Toronto, where you hear 20 languages walking down one street.

KTT: We knew we needed to have people educated in different cultures with a different focus, and a diverse team although maybe diversity hasn't expanded to the extent I was hoping yet. Maybe right now, we have around 40 nationalities – but the architectural profession still seemingly has a very bourgeois, Western focus. We're seeing how we can increase our social responsibility into even wider diversity. We're still challenging ourselves to break our own mould or habits.

TS: How about teaching? Is that influential?

KTT: I was a professor for some time at the University of Innsbruck, which has a policy of openness; everyone can get in. You finish your secondary education and you get a place. I was there for over five years, teaching with Patrik Schumacher. We split our professorship 50/50.

TS: You're also such an international firm. I'm doing some projects near Banff National Park. I was in Calgary and went into your library – I was there for five hours. It really works and the town owned it. It was a game changer for Canadian architecture.

KTT: My favourite project in Canada is the Ryerson University Student Learning Centre in Toronto. It not only changed how a community could relate to something but also how function could be appropriated by students. It's basically just outdoor spaces stacked on top of each other and then given a skin to maintain the right temperature and keep out the rain. The building is self-programmed with students spaced over many floors. All we did was give the areas different names so they could get attached to different ways of using the building. It's open 24 hours. It was about breaking out – not so much about shape, but about programme. The structure itself is top down, but the programming is bottom-up. It felt like a plaza that you just leave for the public to do whatever they want in the space.

Right: Le Monde Group Headquarters, Paris, France

TS: Do you have recollections of seeing an unexpected happening there?

KTT: There are performative activities happening all the time, dancing and skating or just hanging out. You basically change your behaviour when you have the possibility of recreating the spaces given to you. I agree that Calgary was one of these big urban living room situations where the library took on a different position in society.

TS: It was powerful. That's a pretty conservative part of Canada too, so to get that type of building there is really impressive.

KTT: This international approach probably came about because we struggled in Norway initially. Snøhetta didn't really become an organised company until 1989. We couldn't win any competitions, but slowly we started getting invited to them. Then we won the competition for the Alexandria Library and we set up a temporary office there.

TS: How did it feel, winning the Alexandria competition and the Norwegian National Opera in Oslo?

KTT: Sometimes, anything you do with a project just makes it better. Whatever you do, you're in the flow. The Library was this type of project. There are sometimes these intuitive parts when you feel it's all going right. I remember we were in the office working on the competition for the new Oslo Airport and the telephone call came from Egypt. It was such a bad line that we couldn't tell whether they had said first or third prize. I thought it was a joke initially. We started celebrating almost immediately.

TS: Gert Windgardh talked about slowly building up his practice but he also referred to you guys having a big bang type start. That learning curve must have been extreme.

KTT: I was extremely happy we didn't have to start doing the project the day after. We negotiated contracts for almost four years. We got the Norwegian government involved early on and they helped us set up a preliminary design review. It all helped build a solidity that would support the project.

TS: Let's go back to emotions. Although I work alone, I have considered changing the name of my company because I like the idea of collective ownership. I've had other practices talk about their experiences of shared emotions within their company. Do you experience that?

KTT: Yes. The last book we produced was Collective Intuition, which seems like a contradictory term but it's basically the same thing. Individuals have different positions which push them forward, but there's also a shared emotion of something everyone wants to achieve. It's important to find the overriding principles of right or wrong that guide a project and become the lead protagonist.

TS: It takes an enormous amount of energy but it's really good when you can align all these people.

KTT: I think this is part of our success because we are deeply embedded in the collaborative notion of communal associative thinking. It gives us the advantage once we start drawing. Although it doesn't always work, I have to tell you.

NORWAY | SNØHETTA

Above: Le Monde Group Headquarters, Paris, France

TS: You're always growing, editing and evolving. I also wanted to talk about the value of architecture to communities. Back when I did Fogo, the client, Zita Cobb, said that I should "Look back 400 years. Look ahead 4,000 years. Respect your ancestors but whatever you make, your descendants should be proud of it." One of your lectures raised one particular question: Can architects be challenged to ensure that every building we make gives back?

KTT: For us, the breakthrough came very early. In 1987, Gro Harlem Brundtland came out with the report, Our Common Future for the UN. That inspired nearly all subsequent thinking about environmental, social and economic sustainability, and we focused on social sustainability at first. In Alexandria it was not just about creating accessibility to a library in a city where only 50 per cent of the population was literate, but about ensuring the construction site provided workers with a stable salary, toilets, clean water, boots and hard hats, and set out a procurement system that wouldn't kill anyone on the building site. The worst possible starting point for a construction site in a place like that is to have ten people dead when the building opens. That was almost the standard in Egypt at that time. We also wanted to emphasise the education of craftsmen and a mix of workers who were 50 per cent Egyptian, 50 per cent foreign. A lot of these things were driven by this common future thinking.

TS: We studied Our Common Future at school. It was one of the reasons I moved to Norway. It's been really nice watching how Snøhetta has stuck to its principles for the whole 25 years I've been here. It's really paying off.

KTT: Our basic ideology is still the same, though you change with time and new possibilities. We started with social responsibility and expanded into environmental sustainability nearly 20 years ago and now these things are being combined. Hopefully at some point we can move into economical sustainability. We can see how we can use our brand and our standing to have an influence there.

TS: What opportunities are coming your way now?

KTT: We're doing some social housing in Paris – interesting as we don't do any housing in Norway. There is a much more obvious diversification of income in Paris and a lot of challenges that we would like to try to solve.

TS: Have you worked with any philanthropists?

KTT: These things happen once you start getting deeper into systems. It's why we decided to establish studios around the world: Hong Kong and Adelaide, Paris and Innsbruck, New York, San Francisco. It gave us a deeper insight into local possibilities. You have to connect to the local way of thinking and operating. You also need this deep core of communal understanding of where we're going and why we're doing it.

TS: Do you think those values are innately Norwegian?

KTT: No, I think they're human. I think they've been established throughout thousands of years.

TS: Have your values and process worked particularly well in certain countries?

KTT: Sometimes I feel like an explorer. In Saudi Arabia we opened up the idea of the larger public looking into pre-Islamic culture and there is now a museum showing exhibits of pre-Islamic art, as well as a public cinema. To me, it's opening up possibilities for people without the accessibility. We're not trying to impose Western egalitarian thinking, but we're simply highlighting certain aspects of what is humanly understood as shared culture.

TS: Opening up possibilities like a library, creating a building for people to explore their own minds.

KTT: Exactly. These things then came as part of our social thinking.

TS: Which countries are commissioning interesting work now, in terms of social, collective ownership?

KTT: We're involved in some projects that are a hybrid of urban or landscape elements. Like the Under restaurant, which is also a marine biological research platform. I keep reminding people that some of the fish shops in Bergen also sell flowers. While China is problematic in many ways, they're also experimenting with these hybrid combinations because they talk to their public in a very different way.

TS: I remember when NL Architects started doing basketball courts on top of bars and the like. Are there countries that are cultivating a new architecture culture now?

KTT: We're seeing now, after Brexit, all those firms that established themselves in London now trying to get into Paris. France is a complex European country. There are very different attitudes here – quite idiosyncratic. Like a French car where all the buttons are in a different place. But what drew us to Paris over London was that culture is an everyday business, not just a weekend activity. Combining this attitude with projects that pair seemingly unrelated things are the elements that we can contribute to.

Opposite and below: Le Monde Group Headquarters, Paris, France

NORWAY | SNØHETTA

Right: Snøhetta, Oslo, Norway

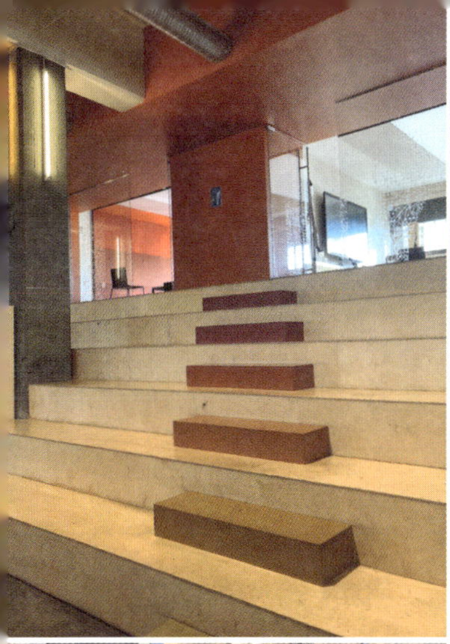
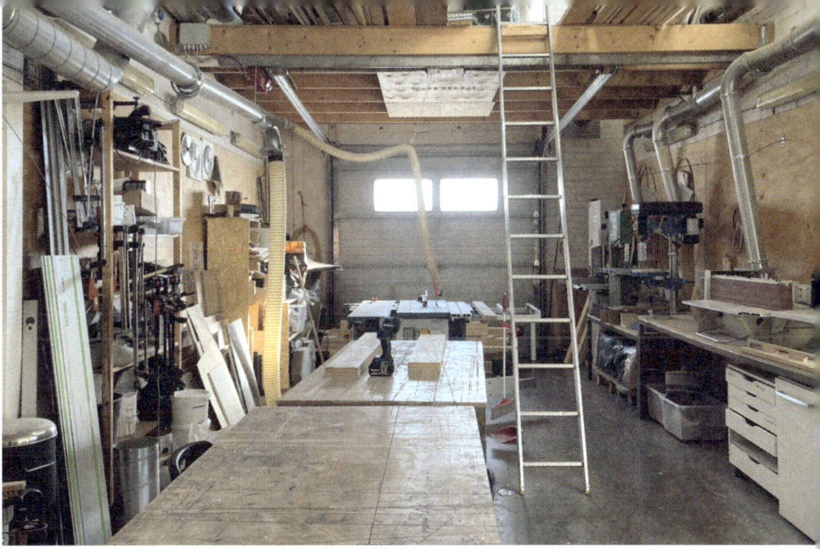
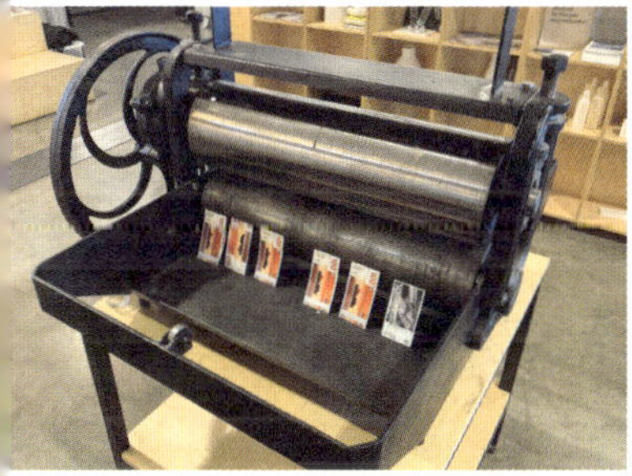
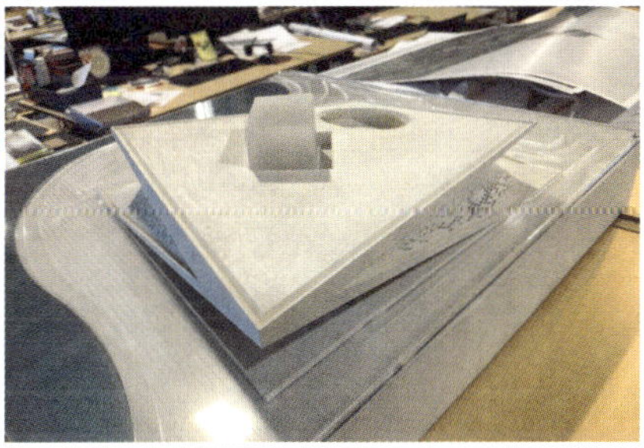
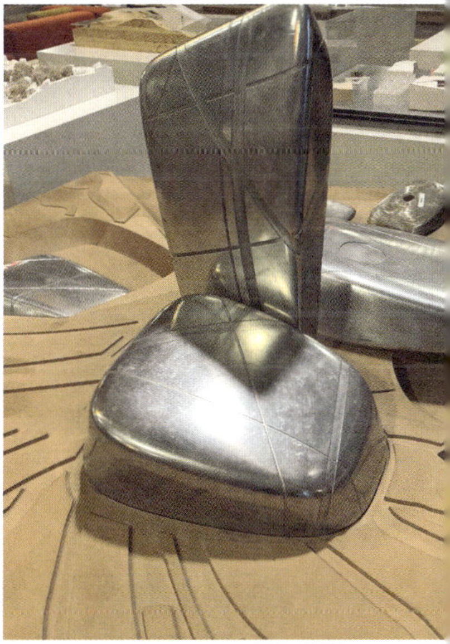
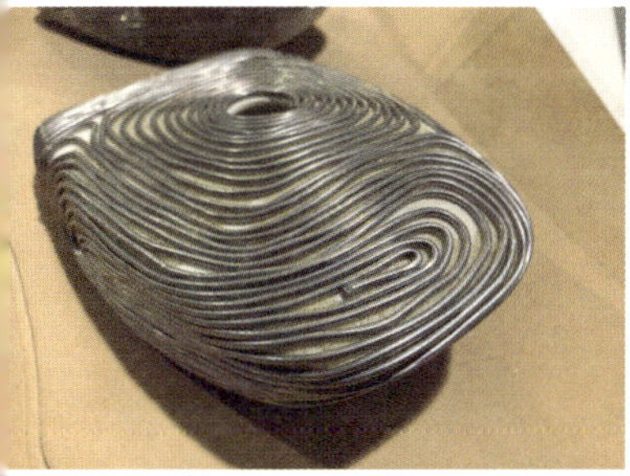
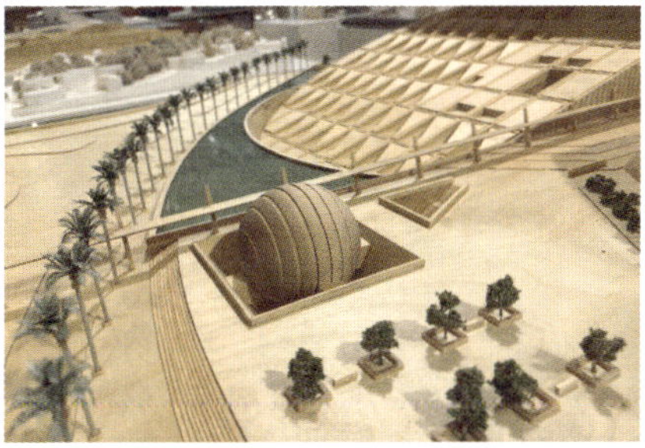
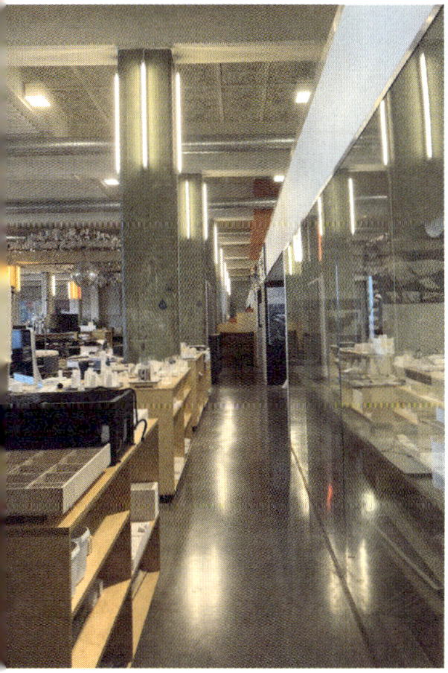
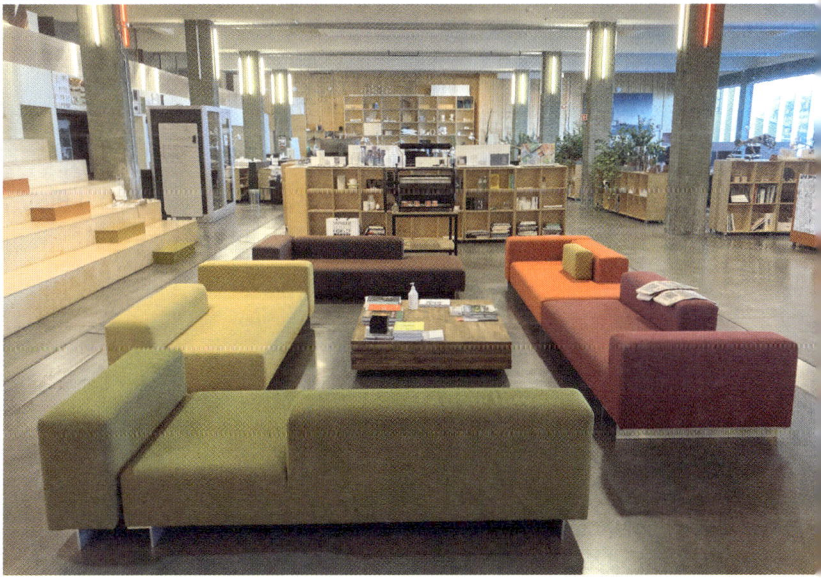

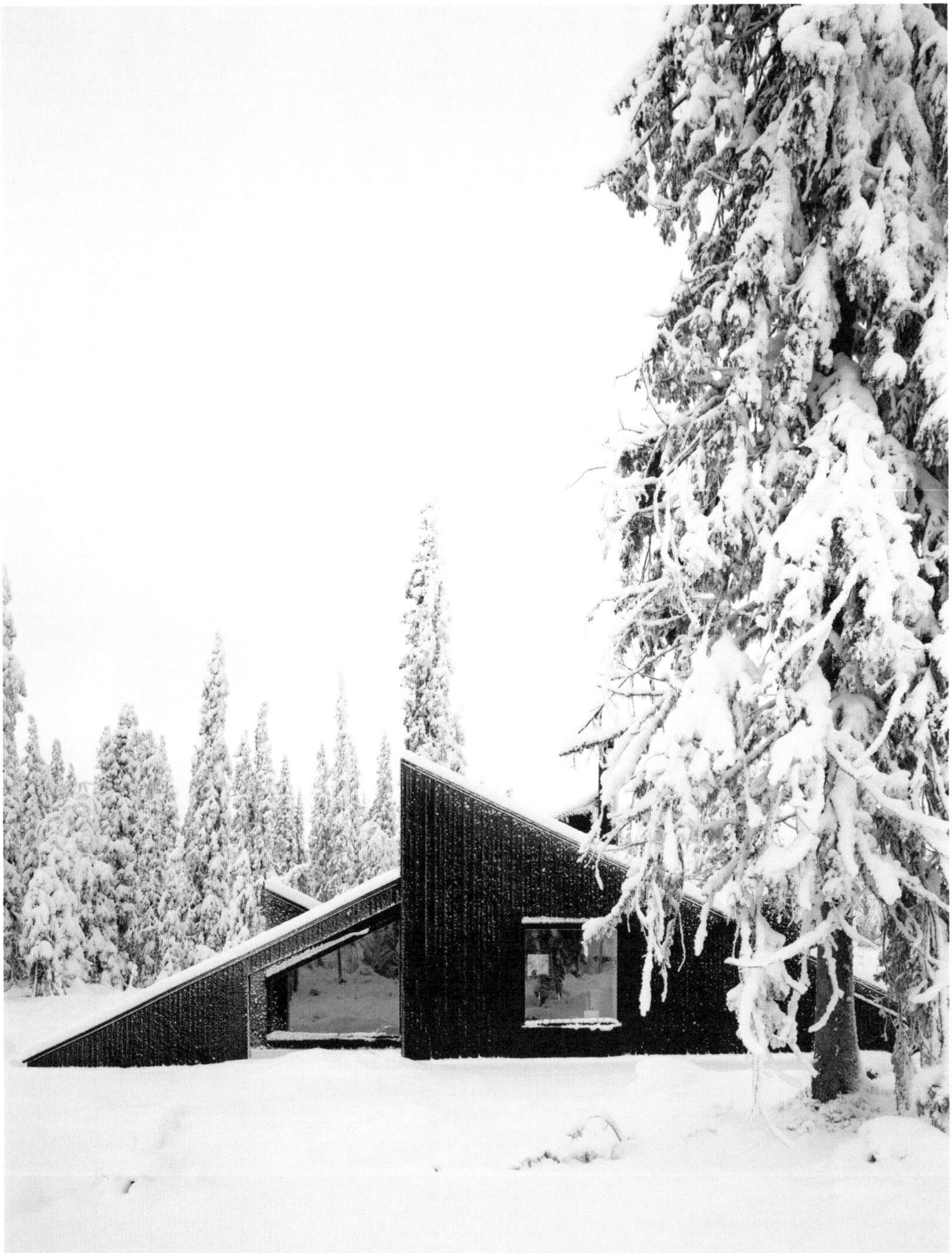

Vardehaugen

Vardehaugen is a Norwegian architecture studio set up in 2015 by Håkon Matre Aasarød, who previously co-founded and ran Fantastic Norway from 2003 to 2013 with Erlend Blakstad Haffner. Based in Oslo, Vardehaugen has a broad and diverse project portfolio, united by Aasarød's esoteric approach and desire to explore the role of architecture as a toolbox for problem solving. Projects range from modest cabins and pavilions through to private houses, community projects and urban planning, and are located in both Norway and abroad. A talented draughtsman, Aasarød's presentation is often bold and unconventional, using graphic art as a way of creating new narratives for architecture. An emphasis on collaboration, whether it is with a single client or a whole community, underpins the studio's approach. "Every client is different; every place is in some way peculiar and unique. We aim to embrace this in all of our projects."

vardehaugen.no

Previous page: Cabin Sjoga, Lillehammer, Norway

Right: Helgeland Museum, Træna, Norway

Below: Villa Tiller, Trondheim, Norway

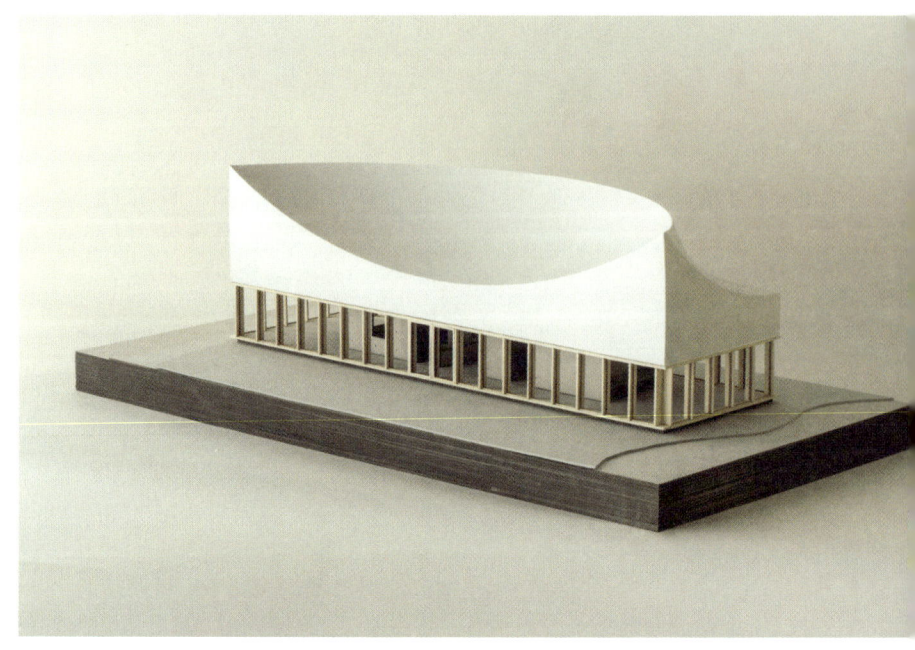

The client is really the community, a small island of just 350 people and you quickly get to know almost everyone there just by going out drinking, swimming and whatever.

— Håkon Matre Aasarød

Todd Saunders: Hi, Håkon. You're the only person in this book who has been one of my students.

Håkon Matre Aasarød: I really enjoyed that course at the Bergen Architecture School. I remember that you and Tommie Wilhelmsen opened the door to the rest of the world. I really enjoyed BAS, but it was also a little bit like North Korea. I enjoyed its philosophy, but everyone outside the school was seen to be "doing it wrong". Looking back, us students were almost brainwashed, but you and Tommie had another vibe, which was really appreciated.

TS: I had forgotten all about that. We really respected the school, but we also saw there was potential in the world beyond it.

HMA: The course was very useful for me. I was there for three years, and then we started the Fantastic Norway project. When I went back to school, I went to Oslo, which was very different and had space for a lot of different directions. Bergen was more political and had a strong, ethical idea. It was interesting to see how those two approaches contrasted. At BAS, you were the underdog – people thought that if you went there, you probably were a crazy artist. We practically lived in the school and even slept there.

TS: Why did you choose to study architecture?

HMA: Growing up, I had never met an architect, but I enjoyed doing projects and drawing. I knew I was probably heading in a creative direction, thinking about film, art, everything. I felt I had to move away from the town I had lived in.

TS: Did you feel like you had landed in the right place when you got to Bergen?

HMA: Very, very quickly it felt right. I was 19, and I didn't know much about architecture. BAS divides the three-year course into "I", "you" and "we". In the first year you start with design for shelters as you know. In the second year, you have that "you" where you get a client to work with. And the third year is about "we" – the urban scale. The first year is inevitably very personal, which worked well for me and has stuck with me. When I started that first office with my friend Erlend Blakstad Haffner, I had no real idea what an architectural office was. In some ways, I think I still don't. But it was an important way in, because I saw it as a tool to investigate things of interest. I had no idea how a classical architectural office was run, so it stopped things being predetermined. These first ten years have been a struggle in a way, as I've spent a lot of energy figuring out things that were quite obvious. As a result, I made different career choices, although I wished I had more experience

TS: A lot of my clients are autodidactic, as are many architects in this book. Do you see that as one of your strengths?

HMA: For sure. With the Fantastic Norway project, we drove around Norway with a red caravan, and we initiated projects or dialogues with different communities. It was a business idea but also an ethical project. We knew most architects were working in the big towns and hardly anyone was in these smaller places. In one project, we were trying to save this wonderful old fire station from being torn down and turned into a parking lot by developers. We thought no one would listen to us. When we talked to some politicians,

Right: The Wolfhorse, Oslo, Norway

Opposite bottom: Blue pavilion, Moskenes, Norway

I remember thinking, "This is just words. They're not going to listen to it," but they did, and we managed to save that space. From that point on, I had some trust in our knowledge, even though we still had no experience. We were probably naive, but that also gave us self-confidence.

TS: I remember the sketch of that fire station, the red one with a tower.

HMA: It never got built, but we weren't really ready. We still had to figure out how to use our knowledge, run our office. For the first ten years, it was all about learning from other people.

TS: These days, is the pace of your office fast or slow?

HMA: Early on, I guess we had that romanticised idea of the architect's 24/7 lifestyle. When we had kids, I was forced to make some changes. For instance, the projects you build from a first idea or sketch tend to get less interesting the longer you work with them. They lack something or don't have that level of detail or quality. We are trying to be consistent with ideas that can run for longer periods.

TS: Do you feel you have enough time to work things through now? How do you control your time?

HMA: Time estimation is a very big issue. Architecture can be both a hobby and a passion as well as work. I think about our projects every night when I go to bed. I'm happy it's that way, but I have worries as well. Several of my employees have smaller kids now as well, so we have discussed it.

TS: When I first met you, I saw how good you were at drawing. How is your process today and the way you use drawing?

HMA: For the first ten years, it was all about communication, dialogue, stunts, and initiating projects. Now I'd like to just let the work speak. I grew up reading and creating a lot of cartoons. My drawing is strongly linked with the narratives you find in cartoons, and I have always been interested in how presentation can shape the work. For example, architectural illustrations always show happy people. What if you angled it differently? Drawing is both a way of presenting architecture and a way of investigating it. I want my projects to be stories, or characters from a story.

TS: What does it feel like when you draw?

HMA: It's like meditation. I get into a space and feel a direct connection with what I'm creating and who I am. I can easily sit for hours. Fantastic Norway was very much a dual project with me and Erlend as two different personalities, but I needed to draw because it was just me, and it makes me happy as an architect. Right now, we're on the brink of a couple of large projects and I hate it somehow – not because we're making bigger projects, that's great, but because I'm scared of losing control or losing my role as a creative person in the office and suddenly just becoming an employer.

TS: That transition can be beneficial, but the current system is a challenge, especially here in Norway. The big clients want you to draw and manage everything, and that's not human.

NORWAY | VARDEHAUGEN

Right: Villa Trekrona, Ugedal, Norway

HMA: I've been thinking about alliances and finding partners I trust with the machinery or volume to help with big projects.

TS: Which of your recent projects best expresses how you want to work?

HMA: We've been working on this landscape hotel for the past few years, which is like reaching back to my roots and the Fantastic Norway period, where there wasn't an established project. An inspiration in all projects is the "prime mover", who brings the energy. You can have it as an architect, but if the client doesn't share that enthusiasm, then you have to carry that all by yourself. The idea was to build a sustainable hotel that could work for the community as well. The work involved design but also figuring out who could be a part of this project, finding partners and funding. It would never have become a project if I hadn't started that dialogue, and created this team, so I'm proud of that. We don't do competitions – we believe that energy is better used to initiate things that you find enjoyable or significant. So now we've got an investor for the main hotel, we'll start with the small cabins, then we'll build a museum. It'll look great, but the process was about initiating a dialogue with that place and what was special about it. The Fogo Island project was one of the inspirations.

TS: Thank you! What is special about your client and what are they doing?

HMA: The client is really the community, a small island of just 350 people and you quickly get to know almost everyone there just by going out drinking, swimming and whatever. But there's one fantastically interesting woman who is very talented at city planning. She chose working on the island over a job offer in New York and she is the perfect example of a "prime mover" to see the project through. That kind of relationship is super important, whereas in the early days of Fantastic Norway, we could throw out idea after idea but, as soon as we left, they would just fall to the ground. These days I always look for that "prime mover" person, especially in self-initiated projects – the best idea in the world doesn't work if nobody can run it.

TS: You have to have people you can believe in.

HMA: Every place, and every person, is slightly different. In my early days at architecture school, everyone was focusing on the complex urbanism of the Dutch architects – they all wanted to draw opera houses and big towns, while small towns and places were dismissed. I want my architecture to somehow reflect the unique aspect of every place, no matter how large or small.

TS: Norway is like a playground of beautiful sights and we have some phenomenal opportunities here for small community-led projects.

HMA: You have to figure out the structures in society to make things happen. There are finances involved, there are legal permissions. It is difficult. I'm sure you're familiar with that.

TS: Which project taught you the most in the last few years now that you're getting larger projects?

HMA: I'm growing in confidence. I probably learned the most from the first house I built, but other projects didn't go as planned. There was a cabin that went straight to hell. There wasn't

NORWAY | VARDEHAUGEN

Right: Villa Trekrona, Ugedal, Norway

really a budget limit, so I thought I could do whatever I wanted, but I forgot that I get the best energy out of places and people. The client treated me like I was one of his consultants, and I felt humiliated by the end.

TS: I learned that if clients start talking about money in the first meeting, then the project will be all about money. How do you vet clients?

HMA: We don't work for developers where it's obviously a commercial transaction, or those people who you sense have just Googled "architects". We try to make a careful selection based on the motivation of the client and the chemistry. Our best clients are private persons who want to work with us, and then maybe 40 per cent are public works.

TS: What type of projects do you want to pursue now?

HMA: I have projects that I daydream about, without knowing where they'd be built. We self-initiated the project in Årdal, the Vertical Boathouse. It's a service building, but also a museum. The community didn't have a tourist strategy, even though it's at the end of Norway's largest fjord, the Sognefjord, and at the foothills of the Jotunheimen range. We invited friends of ours who develop tourist destinations to help establish a strategy and then we illustrated the possibilities with architecture. I like creating architecture, but I especially like the early stage of a project when it is pregnant with possibilities. I can't think of anything better than taking something from imagination to reality.

TS: I call those "zero projects". There's nothing there, but the architectural mind can see the possibilities.

HMA: It's all about getting to where we can do our thing and design or create stuff. When you're running an office, it's easy to just put those things on a shelf, but it's so rewarding when you manage to do these projects because you're not just responding to a design task, your DNA is also in the whole idea of why we build.

TS: I had forgotten all about the "I, you, we" at BAS. There's a lot of "we" in my projects now. Over time I had forgotten the "I" in my own company, which led to my change of focus. How does the relationship between "I, you, we" work for you now?

HMA: When we started focusing on "we", we remembered that architecture isn't just about houses. That thinking was very fresh in my mind when I left BAS. I don't want to lose the feeling that I can use architecture to explore and test things out. I might end up doing cartoons and stop building buildings.

I like to refresh things, rather than just do this for the rest of my life. Maybe in 5–10 years I'll get fascinated with something else I can use architecture for. Ultimately, my office is my project and it needs to reflect what I want to do.

TS: Being a sole practitioner is like being in a cage with the door wide open. If you realise that, then it's fine. You're only as free as you want to be.

HMA: We ended Fantastic Norway because it had run its course. At the end of my career, I would love to look back on a series of projects, not just houses.

TS: Are you involved in academia?

HMA: Not on a permanent basis right now, but I've done some teaching. I've been running two-week workshops at the Oslo School of Architecture on cartoons in architecture, attached to the urbanism course. A lot of students have a problem translating project data into a narrative. When you analyse and analyse it's just like dissecting the frog; suddenly it's not a frog. It's just a lot of parts. And it doesn't jump any more. In the workshops, the students find a story in their material that they can make a statement from, and I've been able to revisit my fascination with both drawing and cartoons. I think architects often use complex language and words to justify that what they're doing is academic. It's a cliché of how an architect should be – creating a mystical art. But if you make architecture more accessible, more people can respond to it. I have a few older architectural mentors, architects who have retired that I meet every now and again. One told me that "architects are like our dogs. But there are two kinds of dogs. One is the kind that when the owner throws the stick, he retrieves it for him, but the other is like a hunting dog that runs out in the bush and scares up the birds so the owner can shoot them." I want to be that hunting dog.

Right: Vardehaugen, Oslo, Norway

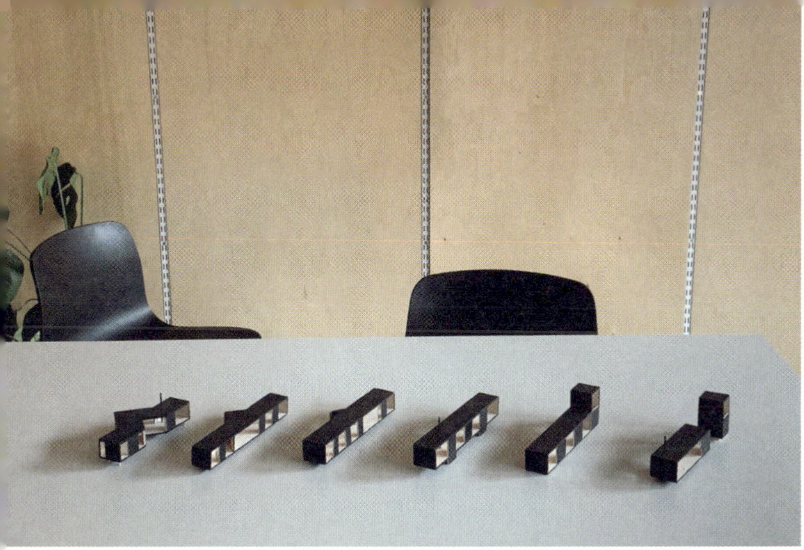
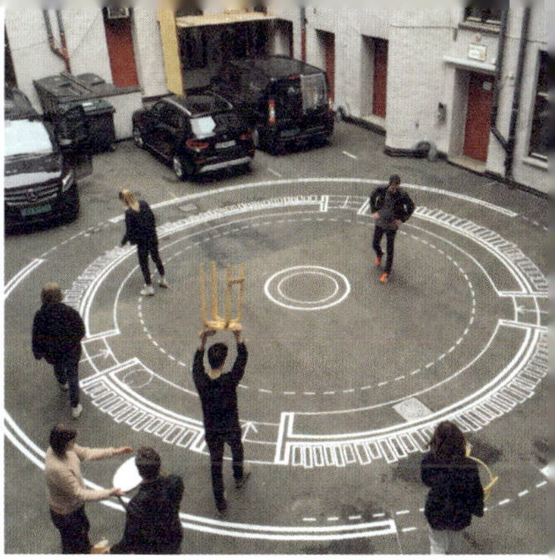
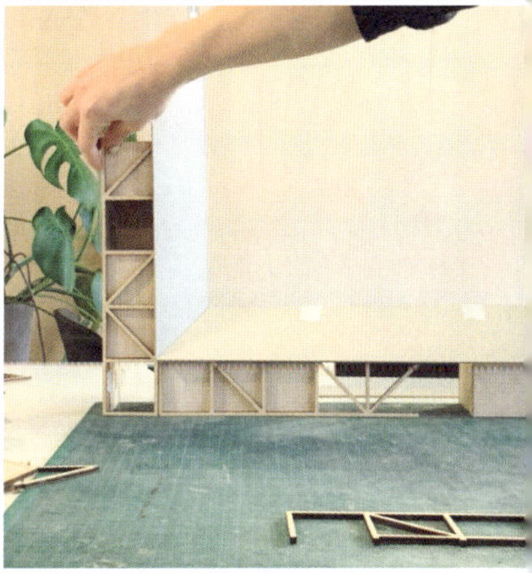
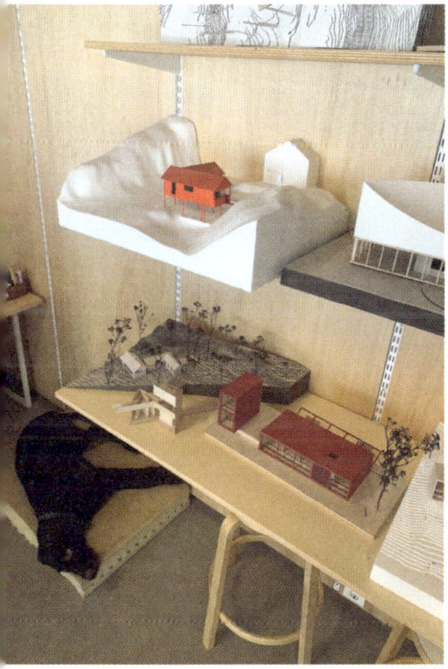
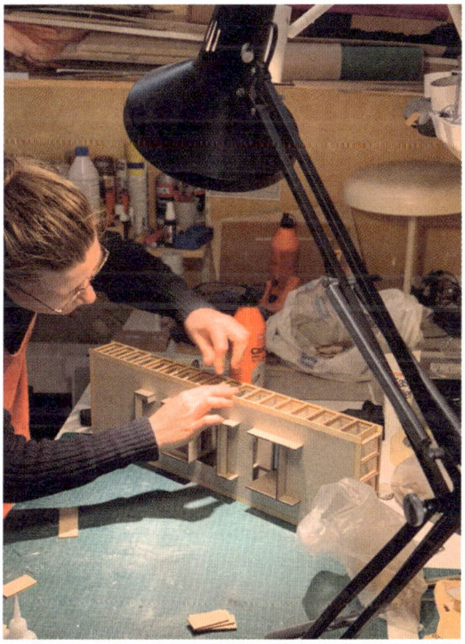
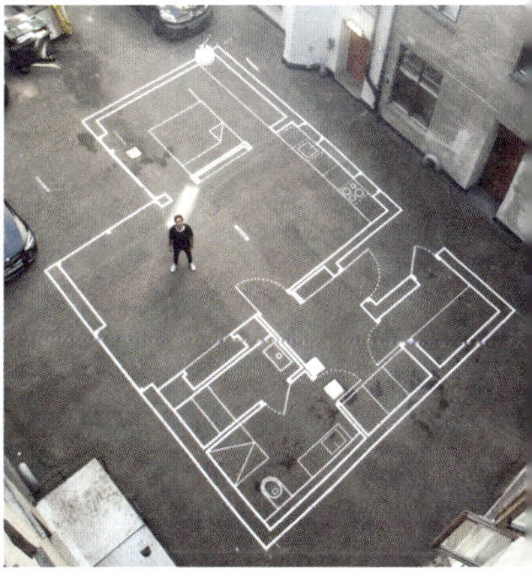
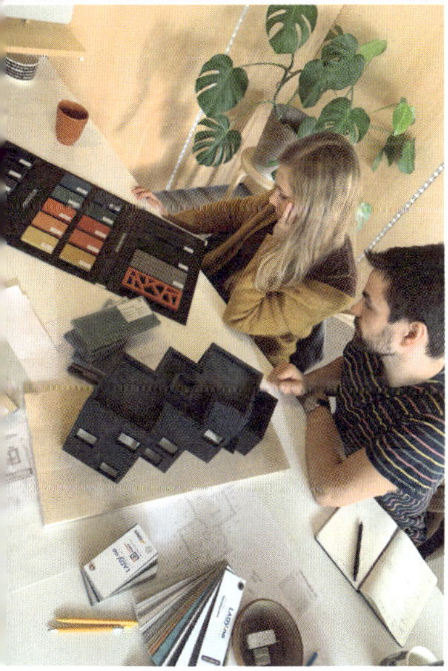
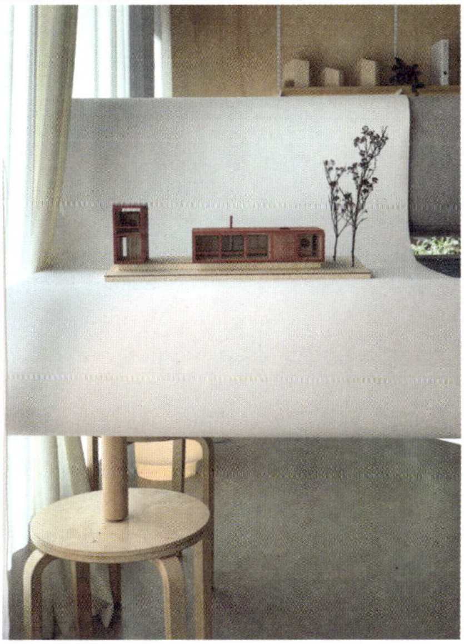
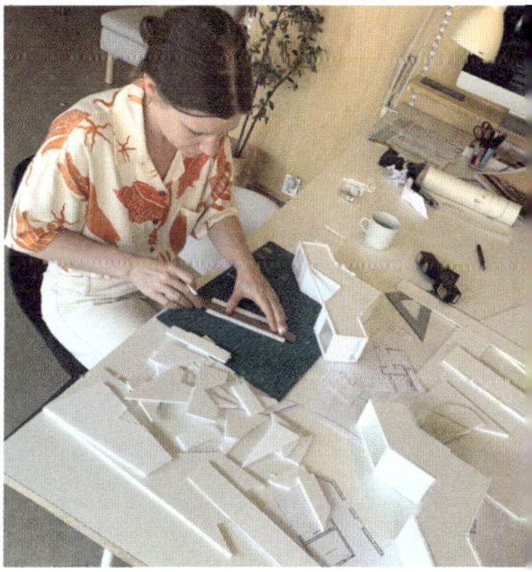

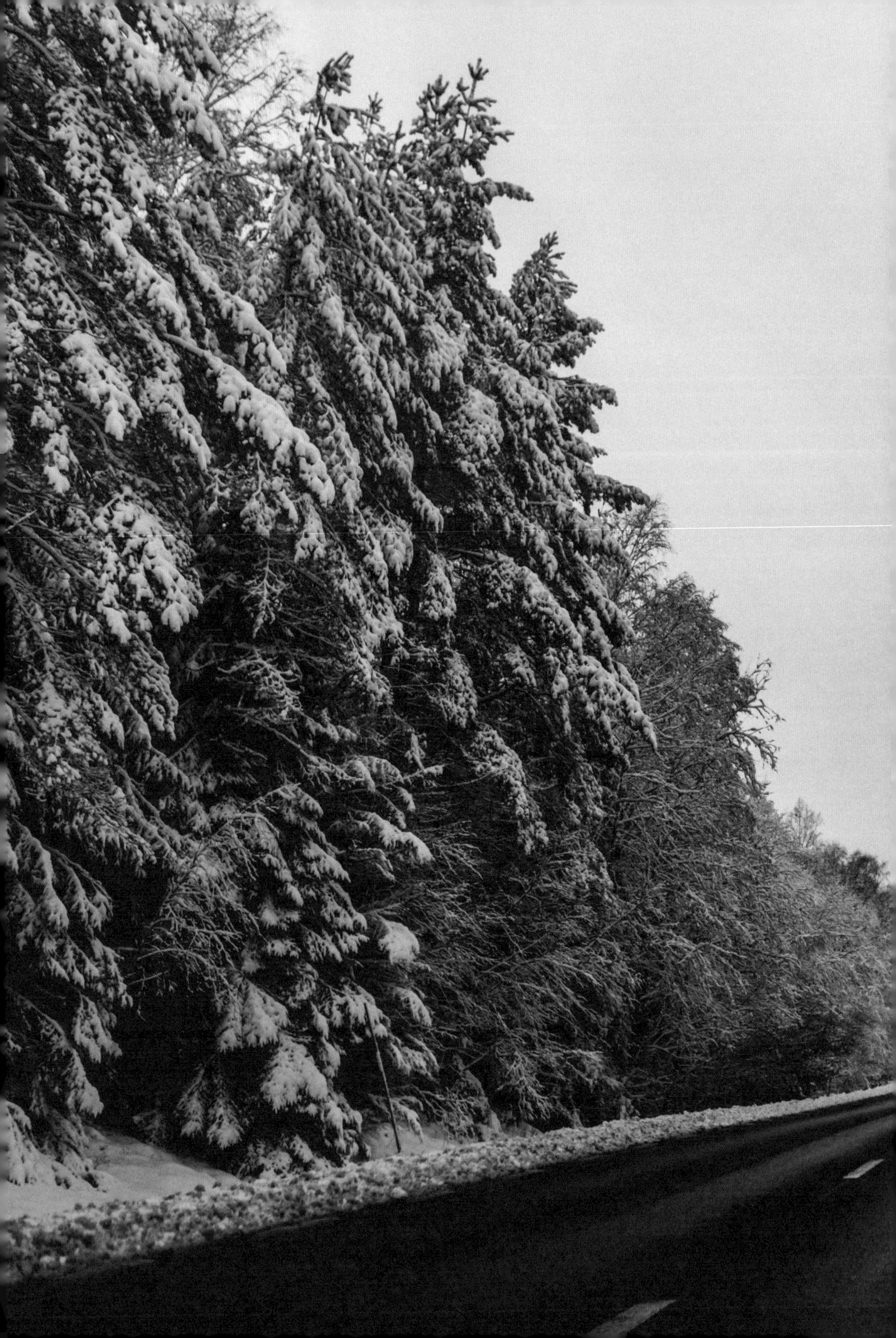

SWEDEN

{ ESSAY }

IN A STATE OF BECOMING

{ BY }

MALIN ZIMM

Editor-in-Chief of Arkitektur

2021 was the 100th anniversary of democratic Sweden. In the year 1921, men and women alike could cast their votes in the parliamentary election. Nobody knew then that Sweden, a century later, would be called "the most extreme country in the world". In the World Values Survey presented in 2015, surrounded by our closest neighbours in Scandinavia, Sweden occupied a position in the top right corner, at the summit of the self-expression axis and at the peak of secular-rational values.

The architectural state of the nation is formed between the departure point of modern democracy and the peculiar twin peaks of individualism and rationalism. While Swedish democracy celebrated its century, the Swedish architecture journal *Arkitektur* celebrated 120 years, making it the perfect mirror image of the emerging welfare state. To illustrate the parallel lines of architecture and state building, we selected one significant project per publication year, to form a timeline of the development of *Folkhemmet* – the People's Home.

The first tier of the timeline starts in 1901 with the neo-renaissance Malmö museum, and only to mention a few stops, takes us to the completion 1906 of the Government building in Stockholm that already at the time of its completion appeared hopelessly dated. In 1912 the national romantic Stadion is the main arena for the Olympic Games. Official buildings grow higher over the 1910s, manifesting public institutions in the growing cities, still rivalled only by churches, while cultural institutions like Liljevalchs (1917) embody the identification process of a young nation. The ideas of architecture as "civic art" grows stronger in the 1920s, culminating in the functionalist triumph of Stockholmsutställningen 1930, the influential Stockholm Exhibition.

The standardisation committees, the race from rural filth to urban hygiene, the carefully studied measurements of kitchens and bathrooms made the home an architectural task to defeat health problems and poverty. Sports facilities, industrial complexes, hospitals and cemeteries were designed in that perfect balance between serenity and triviality that is functionalism. 1935 is represented by Folkparken, an outdoor fun palace for a population beginning to learn the ropes of a life divided into labour and leisure. The latter should be spent with an ambition for education and participation in the political life. Asplund's and Lewerentz's Skogskyrkogården is the monumental project of 1940, unfortunately also the year of the publication of Asplund's obituary.

Housing reaches its prime in the 1940s, establishing the Swedish standard that is still viable today, executed in impeccable plans signed Backström & Reinius. The influential KF office of architecture was framing everyday life in the Konsum retail architecture and many industrial complexes covering the entire country. In the 1950s, public buildings become more approachable, public space becomes more important, and the satellite city centre Vällingby is the talk of the global town in 1956. The closest Sweden comes to Le Corbusier is through Léonie Geisendorf, whose contributions were scarce but indisputable, most notably St Görans Gymnasium, published in 1960.

High on the spirit of renewal, large parts of big- and mid-sized city centres were demolished for the sake of centralised parking and shopping. Yet the global interest in the Swedish way of manifesting political progress in the built environment did not slow down until the far end of the Million Homes Project that ran from 1965 to 1974, first celebrated, then debated. The 1970s saw the genius of Peter Celsing come and go, too soon, leaving cultural landmarks that are indisputable in their urban presence.

As we approach the 1980s, two thirds down the timeline, the selected practices in this book enter the scene. They coincide with a slight shift in favour of capitalism in the Swedish middle way combination of socialism and capitalism. When the radical 1970s fade in the glare of economic growth of the 1980s, Gert Wingårdh starts his practice, marrying the radicalism and the opportunities created by new clients with new money. His golf club house in Öjared is a powerful metaphor. Under a blanket of turf, it is a sleeping beauty waking up in an era of new confidence, yet humble enough to obey the rules of the first church of Sweden: nature.

Even though firmly planted in northernmost Protestant Europe, Swedish souls are saved in and by the natural environment, rather than in church. People in need of a spiritual boost take a walk in the woods. Facing the sun with closed eyes is a national all-purpose remedy. The ability to emphasise the experience of nature while achieving architecture that makes it accessible is a key feature of Swedish architecture.

The next generation of architects in this last tier of the timeline, Claesson Koivisto Rune, is a practice that embodies the shift between the post-modern and minimalist materialism. At the time of forming their practice, Sweden was attracting interest in the architectural global community which would result in the new Modern Museum in Stockholm by Rafael Moneo and Turning Torso by Santiago Calatrava in Malmö, among others around the turn of the century. CKR met in the University College of Arts, Konstfack, a design school, and later completed their architectural studies in international schools. The design profile of their practice is equally strong today, but at the time, it gave the young office an international profile.

CKR were still studying as the financial crisis raged in the early 1990s, as were Bolle Tham and Martin Videgård, who studied at the Royal Institute of Architecture in Stockholm. As the crisis hit the building industry, many renowned architects migrated temporarily from practice to academy to teach and lecture. This was a great time to study architecture in Sweden. The result of the influx of skilled practitioners to the architecture schools would become apparent at the turn of the millennium, when many young practices were formed directly after their final exams, Tham & Videgård being a prominent example. These practices were successful in architectural competitions and careful not to outgrow themselves as a tight design team.

At the end of a century of parallel development of welfare and architecture, investments in the public sector have lost some of their momentum. Architecture is still shaping the interface between citizen and society, but more importantly, it is aspiring to reconstitute the balance between people and planet. The huge interest in wood and timber constructions is an alignment of the need for carbon-neutral building material, the technical advances in wood building techniques, a strong timber tradition and native identification with the material and the architects' desire to expose the beauty and healthy aspects of wood. Swedish welfare was, at its roots, built upon the wood and steel industry. Local knowledge and tradition are more important than ever to appreciate, and the development of new products and techniques is promising.

Förstberg Ling and Dehlin Architects are contemporary practices who share a sense of precision, directly related to the respect of material, craft and scale. The most prominent projects are often private houses, where the consistency and discipline of the architects is clearly visible. The home has always been a manifestation of status, but the perception of the contemporary house is reinforced by a more equal investment of time in the household. The increased status of the institution of the family is in turn reinforced by social media, making the home a central task for the younger practices to make a statement of sustainable solutions and attention to detail. Small-scale projects are often a dense concentrate of ideas, of tendencies, where the relation to the context and the "insertion" on a site is the real test for the architect in relation to the builder. The art of the small footprint is an endless pursuit which young architects are taking seriously.

The architects on the following pages represent a strong design branch along the general trajectory of Swedish architecture as it develops in parallel to the welfare society. It is true that there are also more experimental, research-based, relational and diversified practices who are providing new perspectives on both the profession and performance of architecture. Then again, Sweden would not occupy that extreme position of individualism and rationalism on the World Values Survey chart, if we did not sustain several lines of development of architecture at the same time.

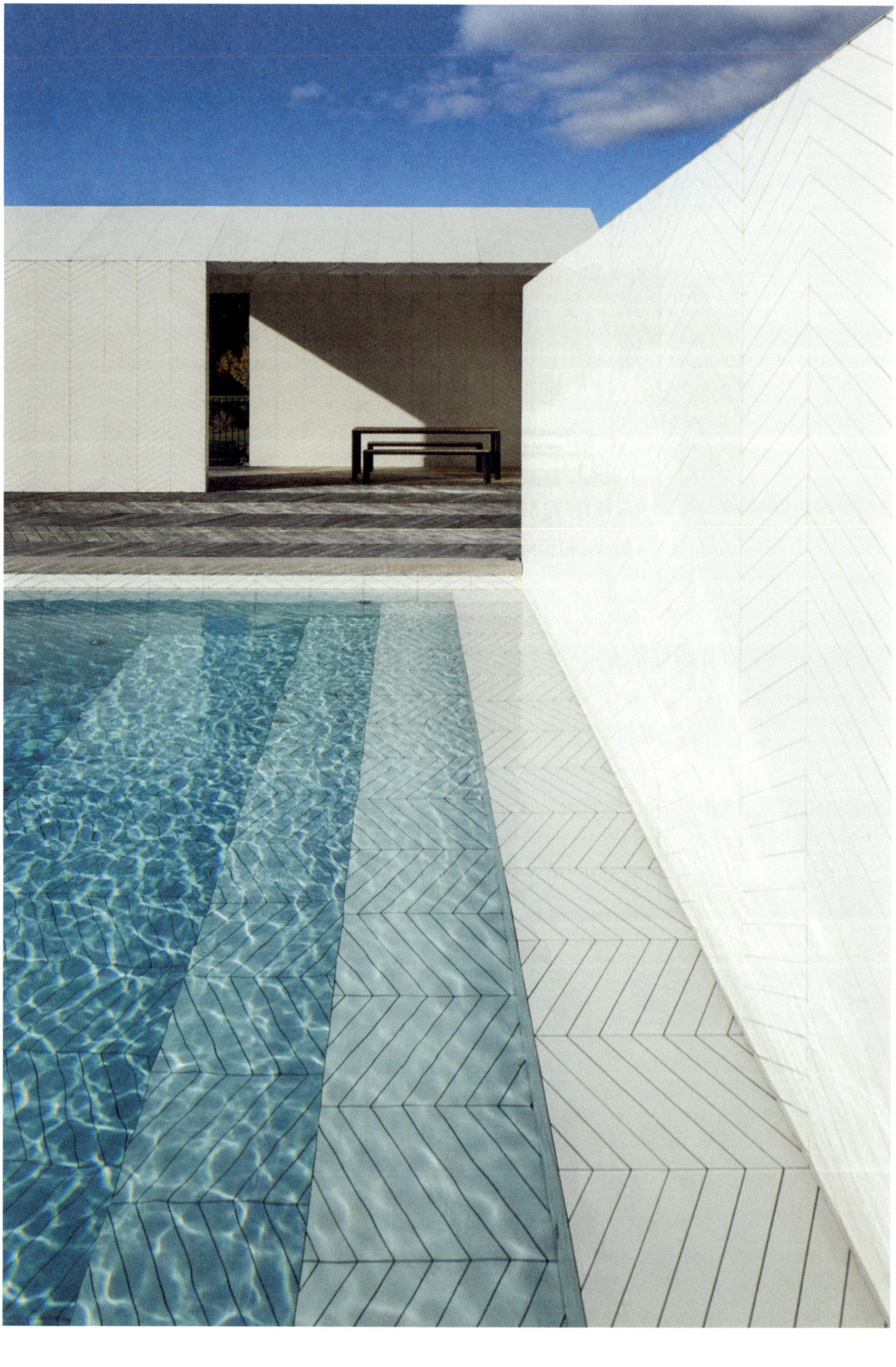

Claesson Koivisto Rune

Claesson Koivisto Rune is a Swedish architectural partnership, founded in Stockholm in 1995 by Mårten Claesson, Eero Koivisto and Ola Rune. Originally an architectural firm, it is now an internationally acclaimed, multi-disciplinary office with an equal emphasis on both architecture and design.

Claesson Koivisto Rune is the first Swedish office to have exhibited in the international section at the Venice Architecture Biennale, in 2004. The office has received an array of awards and recognitions, among them the prestigious Red Dot in five different categories and Designer of the Year by *Elle Decor Italia*, 2011 and 2014. In 2020, they were awarded Interior Designer of the Year by *Elle Deco Japan* and also received The Prince Eugen Medal for outstanding artistic achievement in architecture from the King of Sweden, Carl XVI Gustaf.

Designs by Claesson Koivisto Rune are found in the collections of international brands including Arflex, Boffi, Cappellini, Design Within Reach, Fontana Arte, Living Divani, Muuto, Paola Lenti, Time & Style, and Wästberg. A recent example of their architecture is the K5 Hotel in Tokyo. A 400-page architectural monography was published by Birkhäuser, Basel, in 2020.

claessonkoivistorune.se

Computers are good, but to me, they are a very unsharpened, clumsy tool. With physical models, you are forced to think about everything spatial at the same time.

— Eero Koivisto

Previous page: Parquet Patterned Pool and Spa, south Sweden

Above right: Susanne af Stockholm

Right: Galleri Örsta, Kumla, Sweden

TODD SAUNDERS: Let's start with your favourite project at the moment.

EERO KOIVISTO: I would say our Espina de Cruz house, an ongoing project situated on top of its own hill northwest of Punta del Este, Uruguay. It's maybe a few months away from being ready.

TS: When were you last there?

EK: Maybe two years ago? It has been very complicated. With the first scheme they found the hillside was not strong enough to support it. So we had to place the house on some flat ground and ended up redesigning the whole thing. We lost two, three years. Then they had to build a new road to the site, and that took another year. Finally, the house is done, but we're doing the interior now. One of the client's oldest friends bought some land – a whole mountain, about 250–300 metres high, set in this beautiful Tuscan-style landscape in Uruguay. The client knew our work, had our books, and visited a lot of architects, but chose us.

TS: You work all over the world now. What do you enjoy about that?

EK: We're a very small office and we've worked abroad a lot, especially with design. But we're seen as more international than we actually are, perhaps because we did a lot of furniture for Italian and Japanese companies. The reality is that in 25 years we've only built maybe 20 projects in other countries.

TS: Which Scandinavian or Nordic country's architecture do you get excited about?

EK: I don't know about you, but after a certain amount of time, I don't really look so much at other architecture any more. There are really good architects in all the Nordic countries, but the work which excites me most is by people like Valerio Olgiati or [Jacques] Herzog & [Pierre] de Meuron.

TS: I also get a good feeling from Herzog & de Meuron's buildings, and Koolhaas's Educatorium in Utrecht. I visited Snøhetta's Calgary City Library – like a big sitting room for the city. It gives you fresh energy for another 20 years.

EK: About two or three years ago I was pretty worn out. We were doing three hotels at the same time. I was responsible for the projects – not the design, which we all work on – and I worked every single day for 60 days in a row. I was starting to think, "Is this really my life?" And then by some funny set of circumstances, we got to stay for a week in Pezo von Ellrichshausen's Solo House in Spain – the house with the swimming pool in the middle. I think it's maybe the best piece of contemporary residential architecture I've experienced. Everything is very minimal in a good way, just solving problems. It was beautiful. Go and stay there for a week.

TS: What did you learn about yourself after working on those hotel projects for so long?

EK: I told my client if they ever wanted to do more than one hotel at a time with me again, then it wouldn't happen.

TS: The hotels turned out really well.

EK: I like doing hotels because it's incredibly difficult to do them well, to create atmosphere and the feeling of space. You can also carry over the knowledge from designing a hotel

Opposite: K5 Tokyo, Tokyo, Japan

into a house project. I don't think you do better hotels because you do houses, but I think you do better houses because you do hotels. One hotel is like five houses, maybe, if you compare the amount of thinking you have to do. I don't want to stop that, but I also want to do other things. For example we just finished our first watch for a high level Swiss manufacturer. I like doing different things. It's more intellectually rewarding I believe.

TS: When you look at a hotel and a house, they're about celebrating the good parts of life. How does your process change when you're going from buildings to objects? Is there any similarity?

EK: My sketchbooks combine everything – thoughts about houses and furniture. I can start a furniture project and start considering an architecture project at the same time. If you look at our furniture output in the last 8 to 10 years, at least half comes from hotel projects. Because you get this thought in your head, "Oh, I need a chair like that." Rather than trying to find precisely the right chair, it is much faster to just draw it. It's also a pleasure to make furniture. It's a little bit like solving the crosswords over breakfast. Keeping a bit of your brain alive, because the problem is not as big as solving a house.

TS: What's the practice's ratio between architecture and products now?

EK: It is maybe 70 per cent architecture.

TS: How do you get projects? Do clients just call?

EK: Yes. I never chase projects and we never pitch. Mostly people contact us. Of course, a lot of projects never happen, for various reasons.

TS: Reiulf Ramstad told me that only one in 11 projects gets built. For me it has almost been the opposite. I could never relax, because as soon as I picked up my pencil and put a line on the paper, I was setting off on five years of work that was to be built.

EK: For us, maybe one in four projects get built.

TS: Have you done anything with an existing building?

EK: The "K5 Tokyo" hotel we just finished in Japan incorporates a lot of saved elements. Architecture is not necessarily about making new things. For example the Pritzker Award winners, Lacaton & Vassal, do a lot of renovations. One of their projects was the Palais de Tokyo in Paris, which I think is a fantastic project.

TS: This approach is getting easier now – we're working with these 3D scans of a building which are 100 per cent correct, so your decision-making is never off. How does the studio approach the business side of architecture?

EK: One person in the studio handles the economics – maybe the best decision we ever took. Through our design work we have hundreds of royalty contracts, a lot of work to administer. We also have a lawyer friend to help with our building contracts. We try not to discuss money with clients. I don't even know how much I cost an hour.

TS: How much difference has that separation made on your life?

EK: It's really good. We all need money to be able to live and it sounds such a cliché, but

SWEDEN | CLAESSON KOIVISTO RUNE

Above: Hillside House, Mataojo, Uruguay

Right: Inde/Jacobs Gallery, Marfa, Texas, USA

I'm not really interested in money. But I think every architect should charge by the hour, because it's a clean way of doing it, like going to the dentist. Instead, a lot of people try to make a deal, and somebody always ends up losing out. Either you do too much work, or the client thinks you have overcharged them, and they're getting too little in return. It doesn't create a good feeling for the project process.

TS: We never charge by the hour. In the end, though, it's always about building up trust with the client. How much have you changed the way you work over the lifetime of the studio? Are you always trying new things, or are you completely comfortable with your processes?

EK: We have very passionate people who have worked for 20+ years in the studio. We believe that everything should be in constant evolution. Once we've used a certain solution to do something, we get bored by it. Sometimes the studio gets a little mad about this and ask why can't we do it as before. And we're like, "No, no, we want to do it in another way." It's important to develop, because that's what makes us humans.

TS: Are there any architects you admire in that respect?

EK: A couple of years ago, right before the pandemic, I drove around in Finland for almost two weeks. I visited a lot of architecture, and obviously because it was Finland, a lot of Aalto buildings. And no two Aalto buildings had the same handrail detail. I think Aalto did 800 lamp designs in his career. He was always discovering himself afresh. I really like that idea, that you try to develop. Personally, like most architects, I think I am much better than when I started. What really improves over time is your feeling of spatiality. At first, we could spend enormous amounts of time trying to find the nicest, most minimal light switch, or trying to find ways of not having wall skirtings and all those things. I don't care so much about it any more. The architecture I liked before – and still like and which got me going – had no styling in it, no adding something just for the effect. It's all about space, space, space.

TS: With Aalto, he was growing and learning through those 800 light designs.

EK: He just had a joy of drawing. He always had a new solution for every building.

TS: When I look at your sketchbook, there's a lot of time invested in there. When does drawing come into your day?

EK: Five minutes here, one hour there, half an hour there, six minutes there. To me, drawing is an extension of your brain and thinking. I can't speak for Marten and Ola on this, but when I draw, I'm also thinking about a problem. And while I draw, it's like I see something, so then I do a new drawing, and then another, and the second drawing forms a new step, and so does the third, and so on. I'm always solving problems and drawing is so much faster than computers. We also make a lot of sketch models. They don't necessarily look good as we take whatever we find in the studio and just put it together quickly, to bring an idea into the physical world. Computers are good, but to me, they are a very unsharpened, clumsy tool. With physical models, you are forced to think about everything spatial at the same time.

TS: I'm not presenting drawings any more. The computer has finally caught up with my process; it acknowledges that the analogue world is where intuition and architecture can truly relate to one another.

EK: We never show our early sketches to the client. Likewise with the quick sketch models. We prefer better physical models so that the client can understand the space.

TS: I show clients everything, from the first line I draw sometimes. They come into my world, and they see the joy and difficulties all in one. Of course, I edit them and present the sketches I love best. Do you use drawing to settle your mind?

EK: Drawing is like playing an instrument, like picking up my guitar, like following a line of thought. I can have an idea when I wake up, have my first coffee, and start thinking, "That would be an interesting way of doing a plan." So I get out the sketchbook, and then I draw. After 30 minutes, I'm still trying to think, "Well, if you move that wall there and we raise the roof, then you could see from that room to the next room." And another 30 minutes go by.

TS: I've been finding really good ideas in old sketches.

EK: I go through old sketchbooks on a regular basis. But I don't really recycle ideas, rather I see something I did before, and something new comes to mind. Because you develop as an architect, and get better over time.

TS: Sometimes you might touch on an original idea, but you were too young to bring it to fruition. If you go back into your sketchbooks you might realise you're ready to take it further.

EK: The brain inside your head now is not the same as 10 years ago. When I was younger, I was more concerned what other people thought about the studio. Now, I don't really care. It's too late to change other people's opinions about myself. I'm more interested in understanding the artistic side of architecture. In fact, today I'm more interested in what artists do, rather than architects.

Opposite: Widlund House, Öland, Sweden

Above: Stiller Studios, Lidingö, Sweden

Left: Sfera Building, Kyoto, Japan

Right: Claesson Koivisto Rune, Stockholm, Sweden

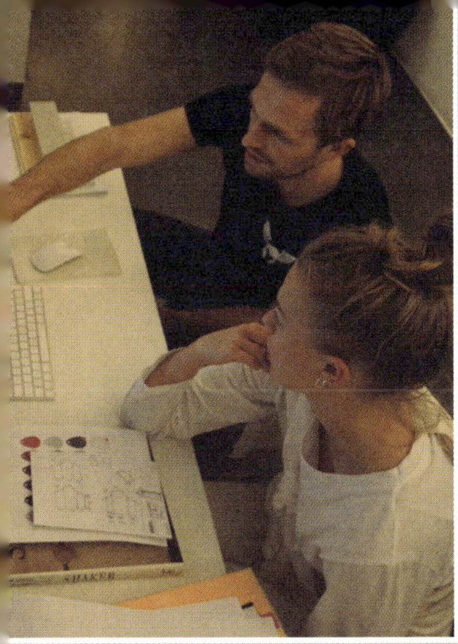

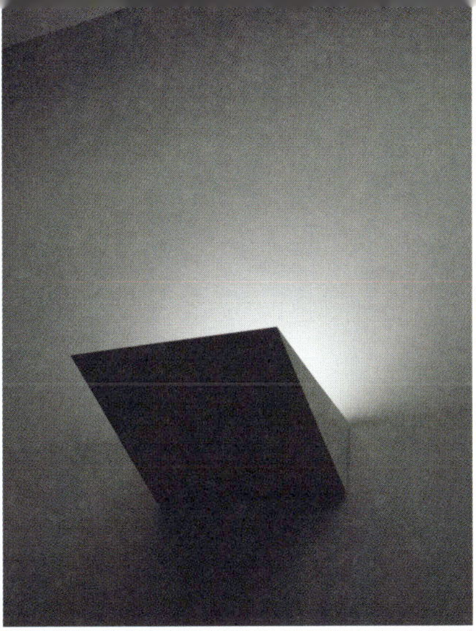

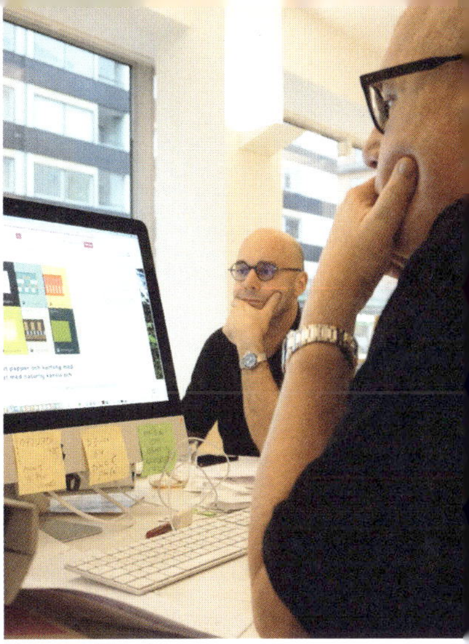

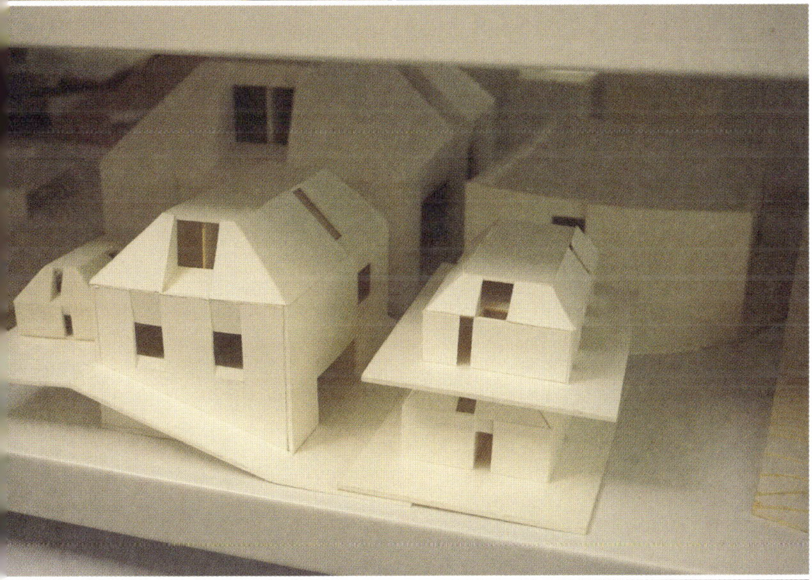

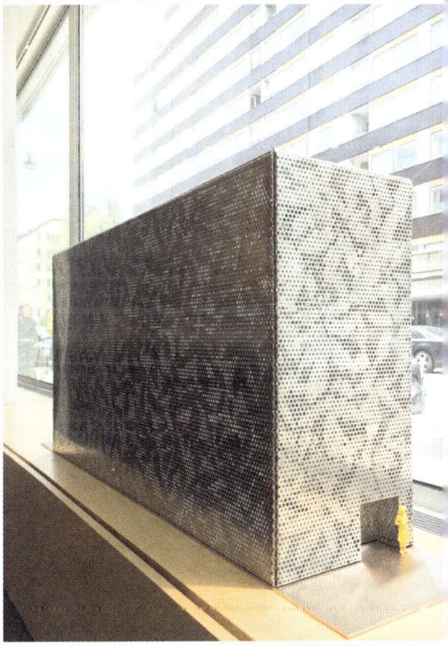

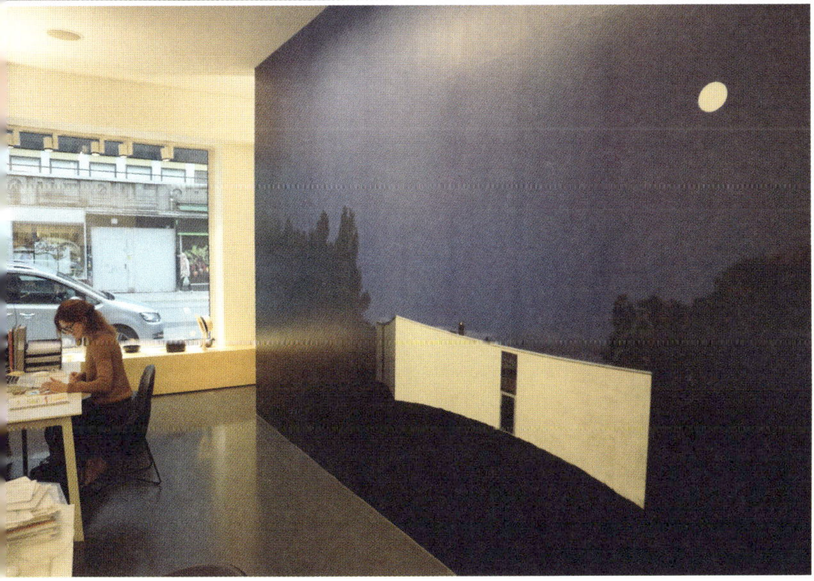

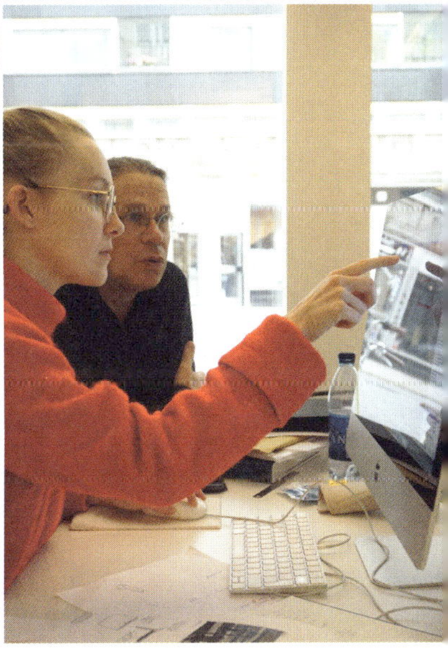

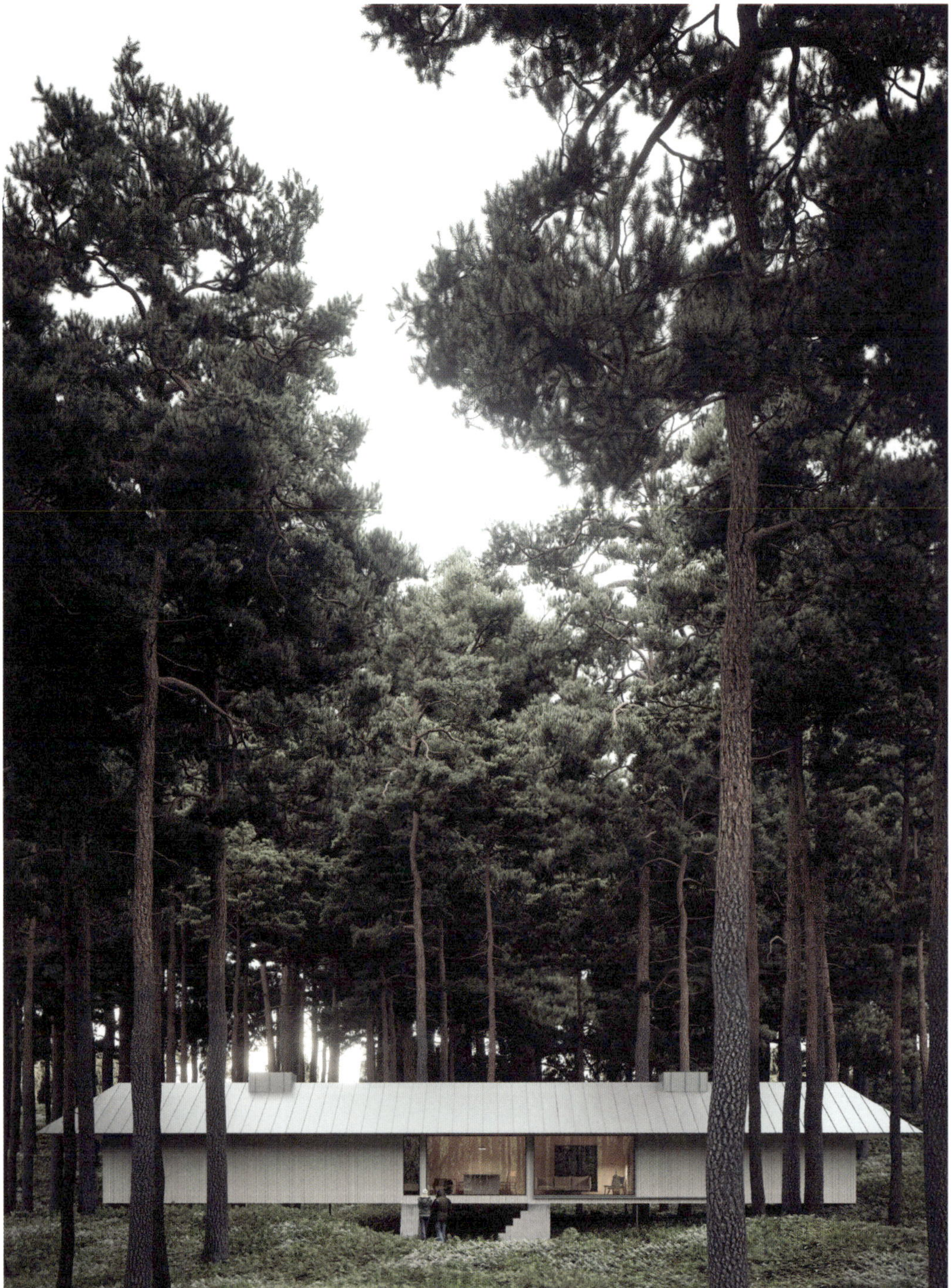

Förstberg Ling

Förstberg Ling was founded in Malmö in 2015 by Björn Förstberg and Mikael Ling, whose first major project, House for Mother, was shortlisted for the 2016 Private House Award by Architects Sweden and won the Plåtpriset Award in 2017. Since then, Förstberg Ling have acquired a reputation for designing for longevity and with integrity, starting with a hands-on approach to their projects and ensuring concepts and materials are always deeply considered and consciously chosen. Process is vital, as are the practicalities of construction and the delivery of details. Each project, from residences to interiors to furniture and objects, is designed with a strong technical approach just as much as an aesthetic sensibility. They describe their work as "falling into the realm between the obvious and the surprising". They are currently working on a collection of twelve row houses in Malmö and recently completed the House for Two Artists in Röstånga.

forstbergling.com

Previous page, above and right:
House on two stairs, Yngsjö, Sweden

Todd Saunders: How are you different from the generation before you?

Mikael Ling: All architects are different. I don't think we're wrong to paint ourselves as being unique in any way. Broadly speaking, in Sweden at least – and this applies to many smaller offices – we are quite involved in our projects and we visit our building sites regularly. Of course, a lot of architects do that. But we're especially hands on in that respect.

TS: I find Sweden very proper, composed and well organised. It's no criticism of Swedish culture but I feel there's this strive for perfectionism in its architecture. It has parallels with the architecture scene in Berlin and Vienna, where I used to work. Your work seems to resonate more with Norway and Canada, a combination of precision and roughness. The materials you use are honest and simple – plywood, simple white paint, concrete. It's very similar to where I grew up in Newfoundland. It's a pure form of beauty.

Björn Förstberg: We try and bluntly convey a few concrete ideas in every project. Sometimes the idea is a refined detail. Sometimes it is more brutal. We recently finished a project that has taken a few years to build, an extension for some artists in Röstånga, Sweden. We wanted to maximise the space, light and use of materials, so we had three crucial things to say, from the black tar paper on the outside façade to the rough wooden walls inside. These were the important points and we tried to make them as clear as possible.

ML: We already work closely with skilled carpenters. It would be great to build a whole house with handcrafted furniture throughout – if super expensive, of course. But that would be getting out of our comfort zone.

TS: What project excites you most at the moment?

ML: The Twelve Houses project. It's our own project, so we're the builders as well as the owners. Although we don't have a client, we still enjoy the budget, the economics of it, as well as the architecture. We're having to actually balance everything ourselves. Eventually we're going to sell the houses although Björn is going to live in one.

BF: There's so much to learn – all the legal and economical stuff. We liked the whole idea of owning your project yourself and not having a project manager who comes in and cuts something that you really care about without realising the impact on the whole scheme.

TS: What were some of the constraints you put into this project? Where was the line between architect and client?

ML: I think we go through this process in other projects as well. For example, I'm not able to critically examine how I would use a particular room myself.

TS: It sounds like you have a list of core values.

ML: I don't know if it works like that. It's nothing we really put down on paper as core values. Of course, you can discuss things. But most people have of course lived in buildings and houses, so they have a lot of experience.

BF: There were some limitations from the council as to what they wanted from the project. Do they really need to have a garage?

This is a major design decision. For the sake of the permits, the plans show the space as a garage but who knows if it will be used for cars. Then there's the whole CO_2 impact of the construction. Of course, we try and simplify the construction while also keeping the spaces interesting.

TS: What have you learned during this process that you might continue in the next project?

ML: We've been working on another project where we're also using Cross Laminated Timber and a brick façade. A lot of the solutions are being refined in the larger row house project. We're doing three houses in Brunnshög, each with its own character but sharing a lot of details, so it's become quite complicated. We recently spent a lot of time working on an intricate, small summer house just outside of Copenhagen, that should start construction in the fall. It is a small space, but designed as if it was a big piece of furniture. After a couple of months of that, we then started the House for Two Artists. In response, we reduced that project to only a couple of key details. So it's back and forth all the time.

TS: Did you study together?

ML: We went to Edinburgh as exchange students. I remember seeing you lecture about the process of architecture – I liked it when you talked about failures and things that go wrong.

TS: On your webpage it said the way you learn is from experience.

BF: Everyone does. You don't make a mistake and then keep on repeating it.

TS: I've made gigantic mistakes. When I built my own house, it turned out the land was terrible. It was hugely expensive to dig it out because it was a bog. It's one of the mistakes that I'll never forget.

ML: But you wouldn't do that again!

TS: Had you done a project like the Twelve Houses before with no clients?

BF: In some ways. Our first built project was the House for Mother. She of course was the client, but she also had a bit of a backseat approach. She was very open to adopting ideas. We've been working like that ever since, doing as much management of the site as possible.

TS: Were any mistakes made there? I never work with friends or family as I'd rather still have them at the end of it. It's too risky – things can go wrong. Certain things in my process now have become like facts on a checklist – I always use a 10cm contour map for the survey, for example. Is there something from five years ago you do completely differently now?

BF: We're not as nervous when we don't have enough work. We have more responsibility now – putting together builders, getting quotes from different contractors, putting it all together. And we try and get things more simple and very clear on paper so there are no questions as to what you want when you start to build.

ML: It's also good practice to build part of the project yourself, I think.

TS: You use physical models as well. It's the same here, we have models everywhere, the 3D printer is going constantly. How else do you communicate other than through drawings?

This page: House for two artists, Röstånga, Sweden

SWEDEN | FÖRSTBERG LING

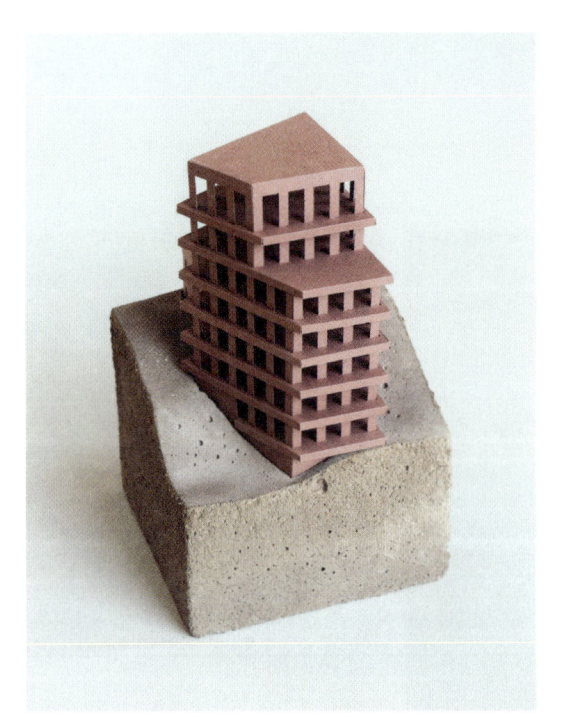

We like simple forms, forms at the intersection of the fine grain of the texture itself and the kind of larger-scale geometry of the project. It's a clear shape but it's still full of life in terms of material.

— Mikael Ling

Above and right:
No. 7, Stockholm, Sweden

ML: The drawing is like a language and sometimes you assume that the people working in the product will be able to read them correctly. We use a lot of 3D imagery, perspective visuals. Not just for presentation for clients, but also to communicate with builders so they don't come out with something different. It's also part of working with CLT now. The material is routed in the Stora Enso factory from our drawings so there's no need for translation. You get exactly what you design. This leads to minimising measurements and decisions on site.

TS: The word "translation" is interesting. Our ideas tend to lead somewhere but there's always a filter in between, whether it's the builder or the carpenter. With CLT you're saying there's no translation – it's direct with no-one in the middle. I think your architecture is very human. But do you think your architecture will stay this way if you use machines instead of craftspeople?

ML: Hopefully that'll be in the design! There are still relationships with material – there will always be parts that are more detailed, involving hands-on carpentry for example, that just can't be done with CLT.

BF: Early on in the Row House project we introduced other materials and elements that had to be built on site, so combining them with the CLT will add a certain something.

ML: It's very important to us that our projects feel natural. They're not cold and dead spaces. In House for Mother, the white rooms are still painted plywood – they have a texture and a roughness to them. It still has something that's a bit gentler and warmer to it.

TS: How do you design in warmth and a human aspect when you change scales? I think we managed to do this at Fogo Island.

BF: It's a question for us to answer in ten years, definitely. The Row House project will all be finished in brick. We are currently discussing how the bricks will work. They have a very strict, simple and repetitive geometry. Of course, we'd like to use the most skilful bricklayer possible. The bricks' natural finish gives this façade life, despite the strict pattern.

TS: We were asked to do a surf centre in Bali and the client had just finished a project with Rem Koolhaas and another with Sou Fujimoto. He did this hotel, the Katamama Suites at Desa Potato Head, with one million handmade bricks sourced from a village in Bali. All the furniture and the bricks were handmade, so it was one of the nicest pieces of architecture I've ever been in. Are there buildings that you've visited that convey this feeling to you?

ML: Sure, although it's easier with older buildings. We like simple forms that intersect with the fine grain of the texture itself and the kind of larger-scale geometry of the project. It's a clear shape but it's still full of life in terms of material.

TS: Have you ever seen any of Sverre Fehn's work? His Ivar Aasen Centre is very strict: all the windows, doors, bookshelves are in oak while the structure is exposed concrete. It's only 25 years old but there's this feeling that it's only going to get more and more beautiful.

BF: That's an important aspect. So many new products are "perfect" from the start but then they only really get worse with age. Like white painted walls. But wood and brick patinate and persist.

Right: Förstberg Ling, Malmö, Sweden

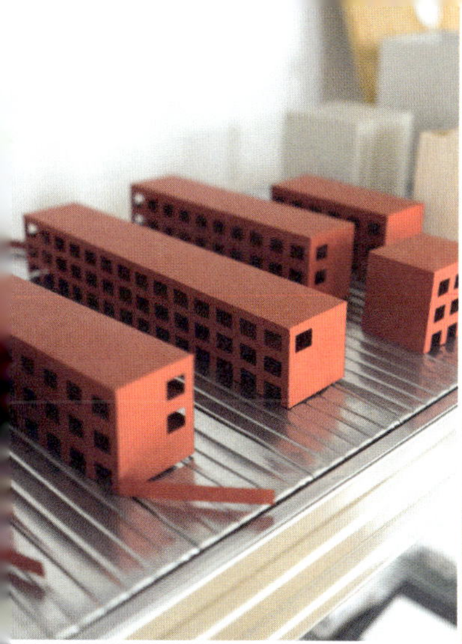
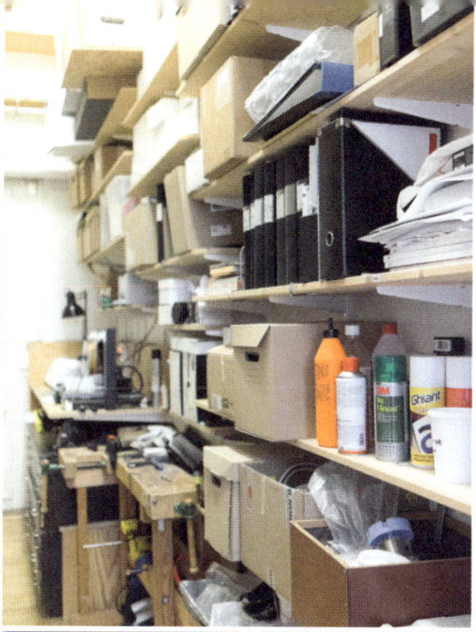
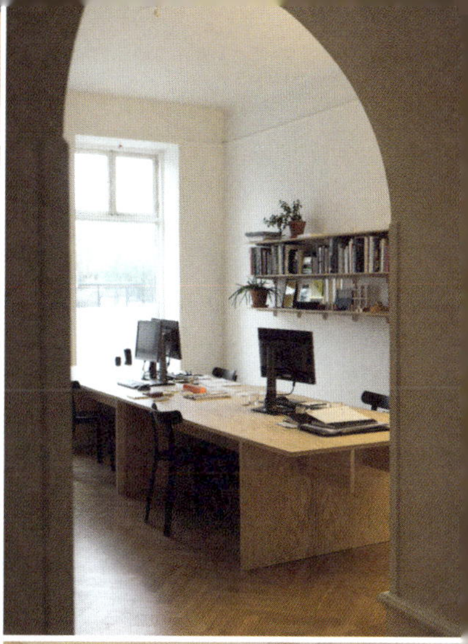
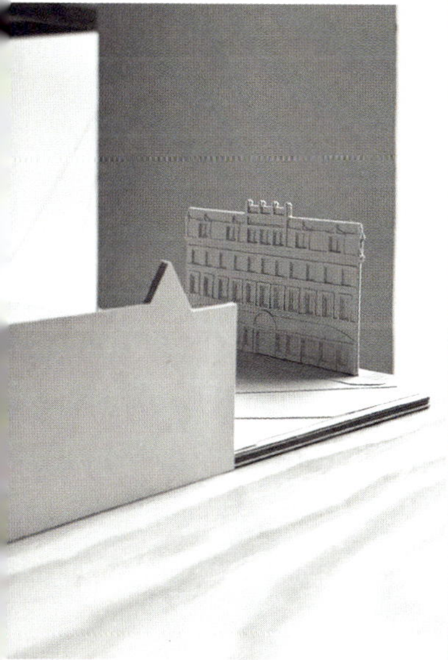
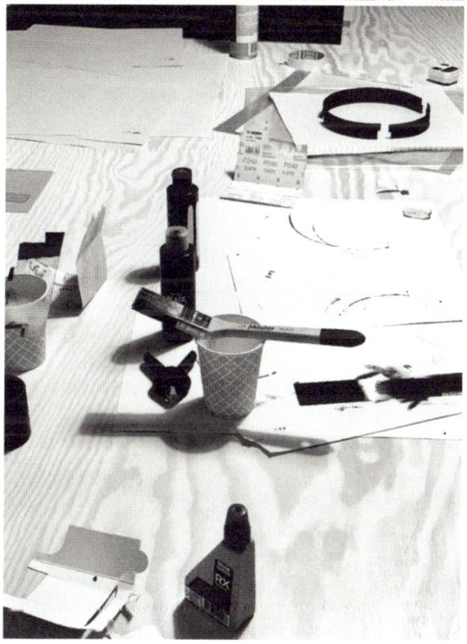
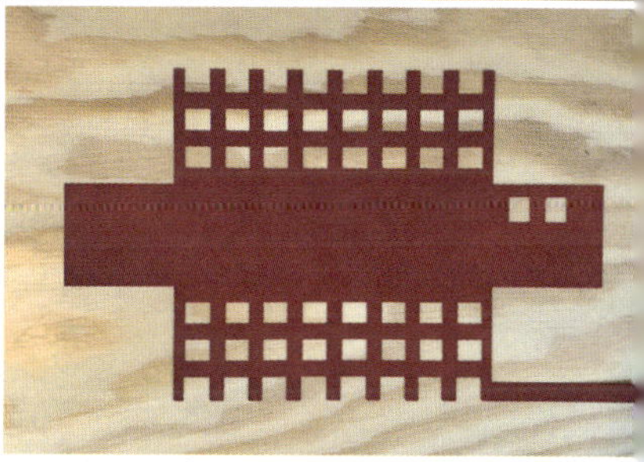
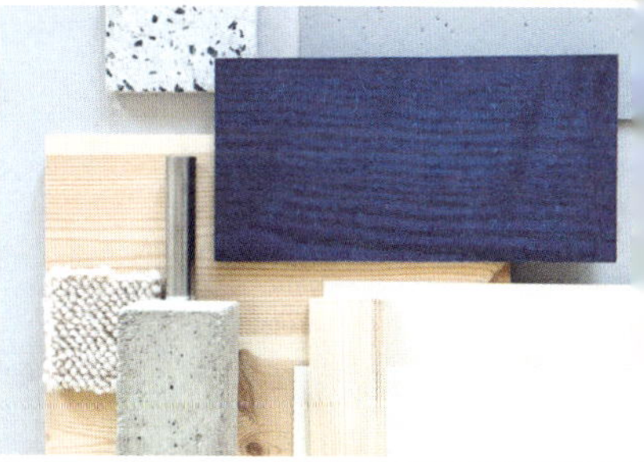
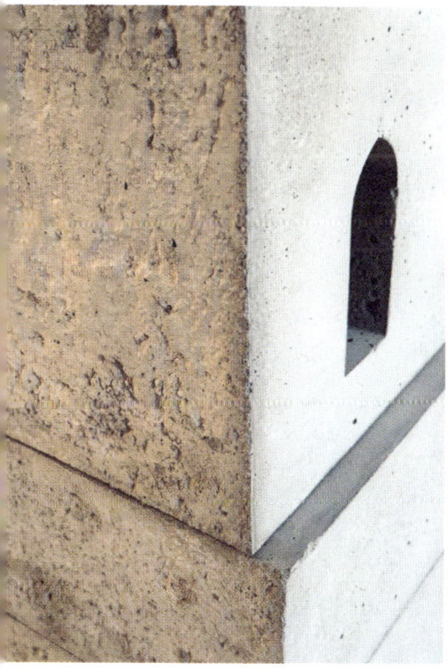
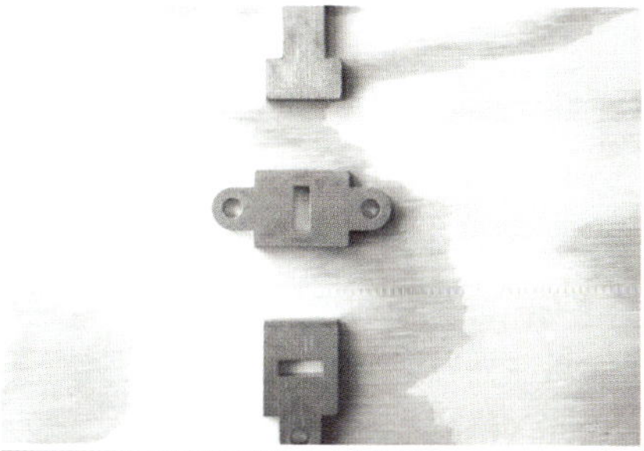
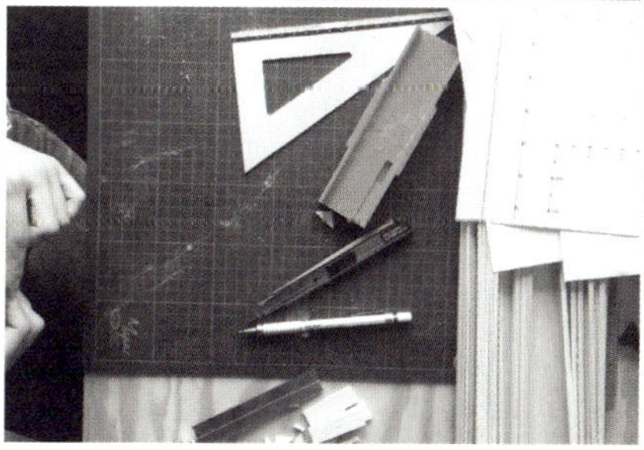
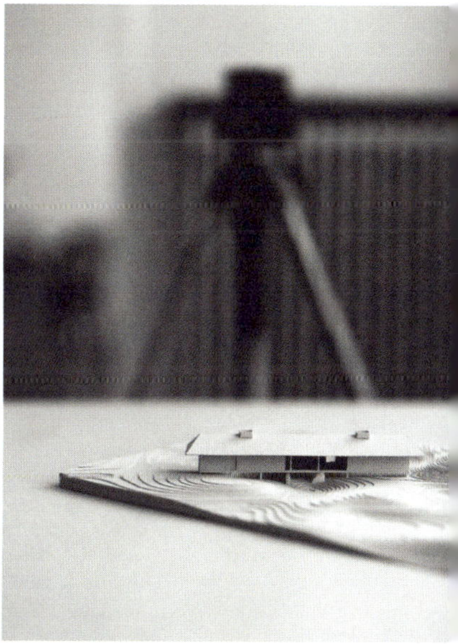

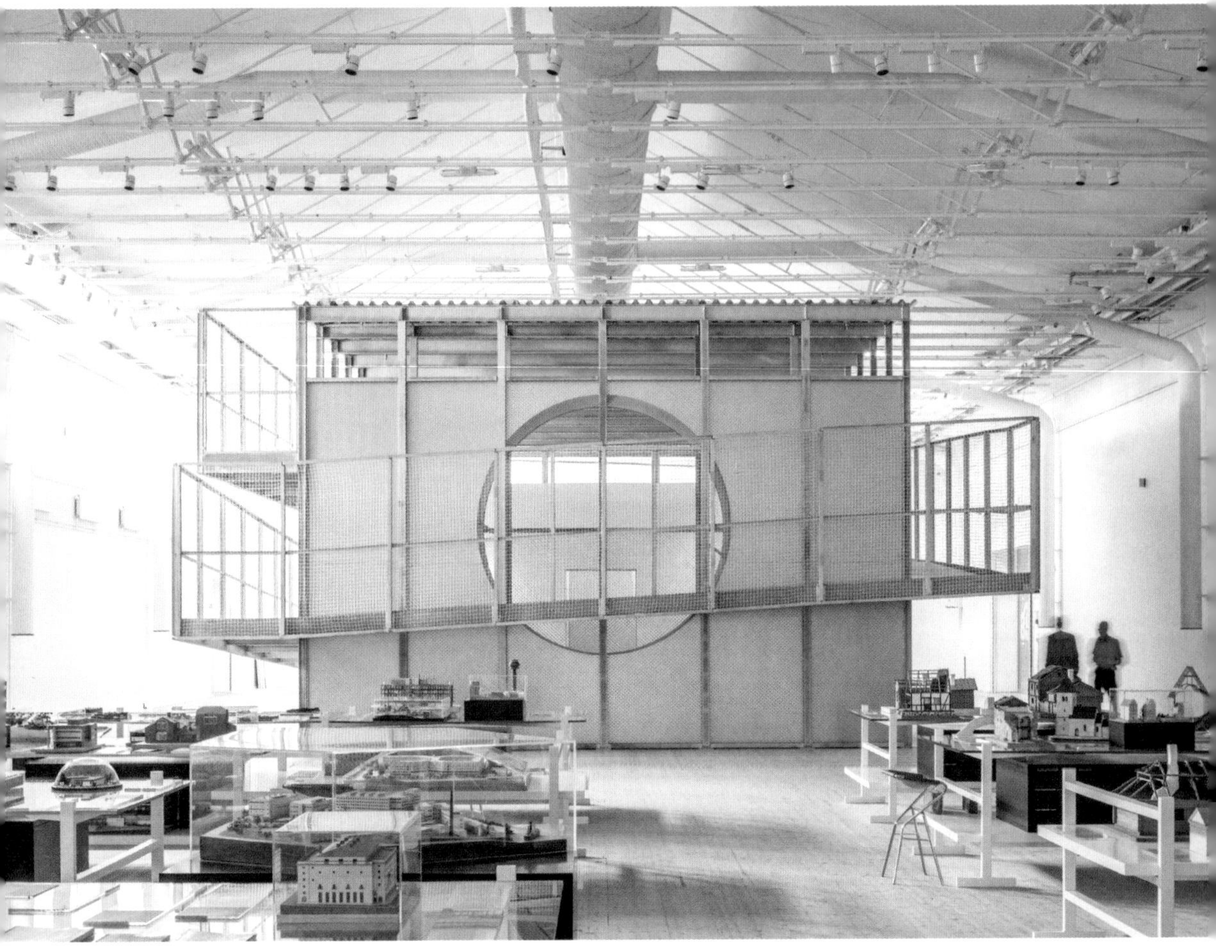

Johan Dehlin

Johan Dehlin grew up in Sundsvall, on the east coast of Sweden. After studying engineering and technical design he went to the Chalmers School of Architecture in Gothenburg, then spent a year in OMA, Rotterdam, before continuing his architecture studies at the London Metropolitan University. Here, he developed an interest in architectural photography and he continues to practise as both architect and photographer. He studied under lecturer David Grandorge and was introduced to Tom Emerson, who co-founded the award-winning London firm 6a architects with Stephanie Macdonald, and in 2010, Dehlin went to work for the firm. He was involved in designing major projects like the studio complex for Juergen Teller and also photographed many of the practice's works. He subsequently founded Dehlin Brattgård Arkitekter in Stockholm with Johannes Brattgård. In 2021, he left to start his own practice.

johandehlinarchitects.com | johandehlin.com

Previous page and this page: Boxen Studio Gallery, Stockholm, Sweden

Todd Saunders: Are you excited to have started your own practice?

Johan Dehlin: I am free to make my own strategic decisions. I also want to find a balance with my architectural photography, although I consider myself an architect doing photography, not a photographer.

TS: How did you get into photography?

JD: It was a long-time interest which I was able to evolve while studying in London under architect and photographer, David Grandorge, who has a similar set-up. He taught me architecture photography – the course blended both together.

TS: Do you shoot your own work?

JD: Yes. Models, finished projects, sites, materials and so on. It's a way of being on both ends of the building process. Images have different purposes and as most architects I use different tools to create them – cameras but also renderings and other computer programs. Maybe it's about control but I like to know many different tools to not limit myself.

TS: You know you'll have control over the image. In contrast, we can work for five years on a project. When it's finished, the photographer might visit the building for just one or two days and the shots they take might condense all that work into two or three images, which become the public representation of the building.

JD: It can be exciting to come in as a photographer when the dust has settled and everyone is happy, hopefully. The quick results are a nice contrast to doing architecture work. It's a very condensed experience, with some responsibility as you're the one who creates the final image of the project.

TS: It's quite powerful, even dangerous, how one or two images can make such an impact on a project. As an architect, you find yourself going towards the image, not the building. Where did you work first?

JD: I spent a year at OMA, around 2007. Beforehand I'd been very uncertain about my career, but OMA gave me confidence – I worked on a lot of competitions in the Middle East and Russia. You really have to find your place in that office – and connect with the right people. Even as an intern I had a lot of responsibility. We did the competition for the Design Museum in London, which we won, and I worked on that for the last six months of my time there. It was the conversion of the Commonwealth Institute in Holland Park and three residential blocks next to it. It was a steep learning curve.

TS: Was the office run in a way that influenced you?

JD: The open design process inspired multiple ideas – you were not limited at the start of projects. There was a freedom for everyone to interpret the co-founder Rem's agenda and direction. Then the team could evolve that idea together. Looking back, I find it astonishing that interns could be in the meetings with Rem and propose ideas to him. There was a flat structure.

TS: One thing we adopted from other practices was to not let the client set the first deadline for ideas. That means you're free to deliver when it's ready.

Right and below right: Row Houses / Town houses in Köping, Sweden

JD: There were deadlines of course, especially for competitions. You would have run to the taxi and fly to Saudi Arabia and Rem would be editing the presentations in the back of the cab.

TS: Tell me about London Metropolitan. What happened there?

JD: At the Met, I studied under David Grandorge. I met Tom Emerson in a crit and finally came back to work for him at 6a architects after graduating in Sweden. It was my dream workplace – it was also my main learning experience. 6a work quite intensely with the art community in London. At the time, they were getting a lot of attention for a small gallery project on Raven Row in Spitalfields. The main project I worked on was a studio building for photographer Juergen Teller. It's where everything came together – a fantastic client, interesting site in West London, and a great team of engineers. I worked on it from 2011 to 2013 as a project architect and then left for Sweden with my girlfriend. But I came back to photograph it a number of times during construction. A client is everything to a project. Creative people in particular can relate and might be more open to us as professionals being able to do our work.

TS: How do you think you will keep an ideas-driven culture in your own practice?

JD: I am lucky because I can support myself with photography and then choose smaller projects to work on and go from there. This gives me the freedom not to compromise too much in order to make a living. I'd be interested in doing bigger projects at some point but I'm not in a hurry. I'm still interested in working outside of Sweden so I'm trying to keep that alive in different ways.

TS: How has your experience in other studios shaped your process?

JD: Although very different on the surface, there were similarities between 6a and OMA – the freedom of creativity, proposing ideas and working closely with the directors. There is an investigative process where the shape and materiality would be very open in the beginning and evolve as we learned more about the project. It would also mean that the design would keep changing close to deadlines which could be frustrating as well. I'm bringing this with me, as well as the importance of being on site. In London we worked on a lot of construction sites, including an artist's studio in Hampstead that belonged to the 18th-century painter George Romney. It was unusual as we were doing the design work while being on site.

TS: Some of the other architects in this book have always been based in Scandinavia. But you studied there, worked abroad and then came back. Was there anything about English architectural culture that doesn't exist here in Sweden?

JD: There's a stronger connection between academia and practice and there's a more active debate about architecture in general. Also, the clients are different. It's hard, if not impossible, in Sweden to find the kinds of projects we were doing with 6a – there isn't that art world client base here. On the other hand, a young practice in the UK would rarely get to build large housing projects, which happens in Sweden.

TS: 75 per cent of what I work on is outside of Norway – because I'm actually not Scandinavian or Norwegian. In London I find the industry

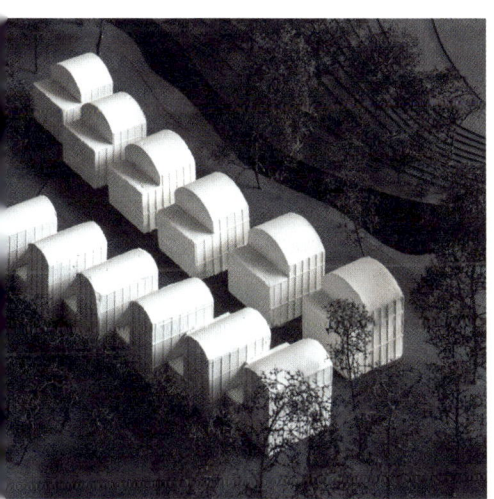

I am lucky because I can support myself with photography and then choose smaller projects to work on and go from there. This gives me the freedom not to compromise too much in order to make a living.

— Johan Dehlin

SWEDEN | JOHAN DEHLIN

Above left and left: IJ Guest House, Stockholm, Sweden

is very professional, with project managers, lawyers, etc.

JD: Yes, it's very structured. You have these clear phases of work to be signed off. In Sweden there's not such a clear guide to follow.

TS: There are professional organisations in Scandinavia, but they seem very passive.

JD: In Sweden, the organisations are more focused on employees, not facilitating architectural projects. "Architect" is not a protected title in Sweden. It seems that architects are more respected in the UK, perhaps because they take on more responsibility. You also have to go through a more demanding education before getting your license.

TS: What always interested me is going out for myself, not just becoming an employee. Are there particular strengths you can bring to your business after being an employee?

JD: When I started my own company, I was 35. It's not like starting fresh out of school with all the naivety and ambition that that brings. Perhaps it was more strategic but when I came back to Sweden, I was already doing photography, which is difficult to combine with being employed, so the freedom to plan my own time was an important reason for going out on my own. And of course, the joy of developing my own ideas and projects instead of, ultimately, somebody else's. I couldn't see any other option, so I decided to go for it. I think you still need a necessary naïvety to start out without a client base, and not worry about financing a big expensive apartment and a big family, although I now have two young kids. There is an excitement in being able to combine previous, quite different, experiences and create something of my own.

TS: Sometimes we don't work with clients if they have a brief. We prefer it if they put it to one side and we restart and the do the brief together. It's made my life easier and it's why we don't like to enter competitions as the brief is already decided.

JD: Developing a brief with a client is such a big part of a project. It removes a conflict of ambitions. Setting up limitations with a client can be much more generative, rather than an obstacle. The Boxen Studio Gallery at ArkDes, the Architecture and Design Museum here in Stockholm is a good example where we worked with a supportive client who understood what we were trying to do. There were accessibility and fire regs that almost killed the project at one point, but we found solutions together with the client and pushed through. In the end it became a much better project after working with those limitations.

TS: Why did you decide to move on from Dehlin Brattgård Arkitekter?

JD: I guess you have a strong sense when it is time to take the next step. I am still very much about conversation and collaboration and evolving ideas together with other people. That worked really nicely in the beginning of our partnership, but ultimately, I found it frustrating, especially with the separate photography business. I had to take time off from my practice which I didn't feel was fair towards my partner.

TS: Perhaps it's not the big decisions in your life that make a difference, but the small decisions – every day you make a thousand decisions. If you don't know why you're doing what you're doing, four years down the road you end up way off track. I am sure you did the right thing.

JD: I hope so. The joy of doing architecture and running your own practice is the freedom. It's a slippery slope – suddenly you find you really aren't happy. My new practice is an experiment. I have good faith in it.

TS: So it's progression not perfection?

JD: I'm for taking risks, but I realise that I take risks in sensible steps somehow. You can strengthen your own position by collaborating with other people. I'm doing this to expand my practice, not to contract it to just me.

TS: I think it's a very good time not to have a big office, but a larger group of people that you connect with.

JD: More people are collaborating within individual companies on projects, but not being co-dependent on people.

TS: What are you working on now?

JD: A couple of summer houses in the archipelago and a restaurant in an old slaughterhouse are about to go on site. And I'm working with a group of semi-established artists in Sweden who want to move on from the idea of renting a studio forever. They're interested in a collective, joint space. I'm open to the idea of moving in myself, but haven't decided yet. I got the job through a friend who knew my history of working with artists and art institutions. We are currently developing a brief and a programme and seeing if there's an interest for a building like this. It might also be a launching pad for my practice in Sweden as it would be an unusual project for Stockholm and a semi-public building that everyone can see.

Opposite and this page:
Kallbadhus Riddarfjärden,
Stockholm, Sweden

SWEDEN | JOHAN DEHLIN

Right: Johan Dehlin, Stockholm, Sweden

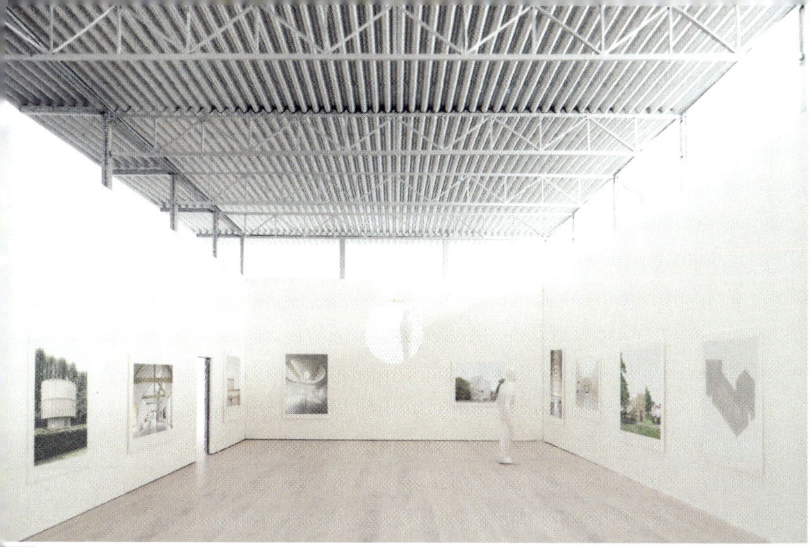
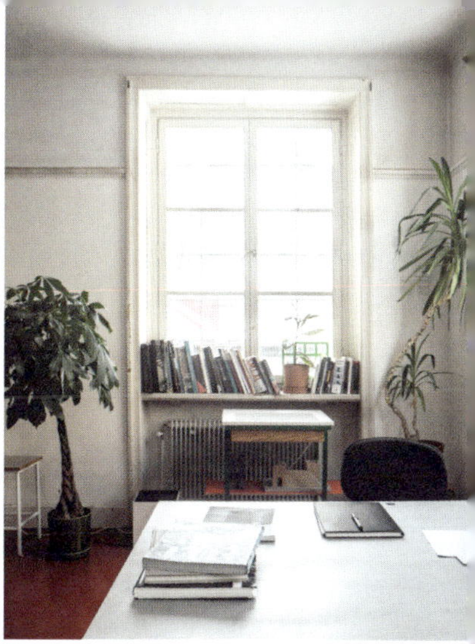
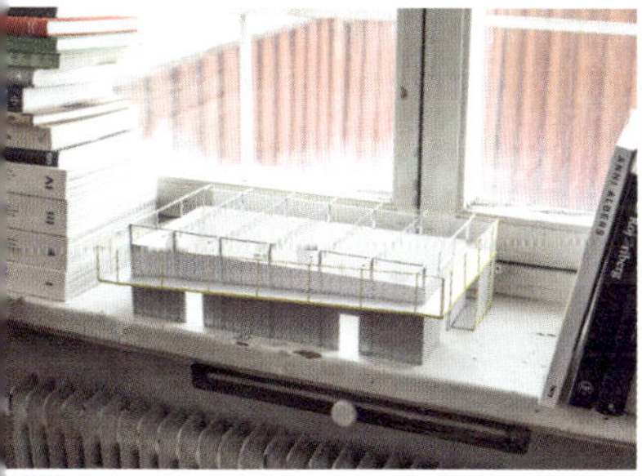
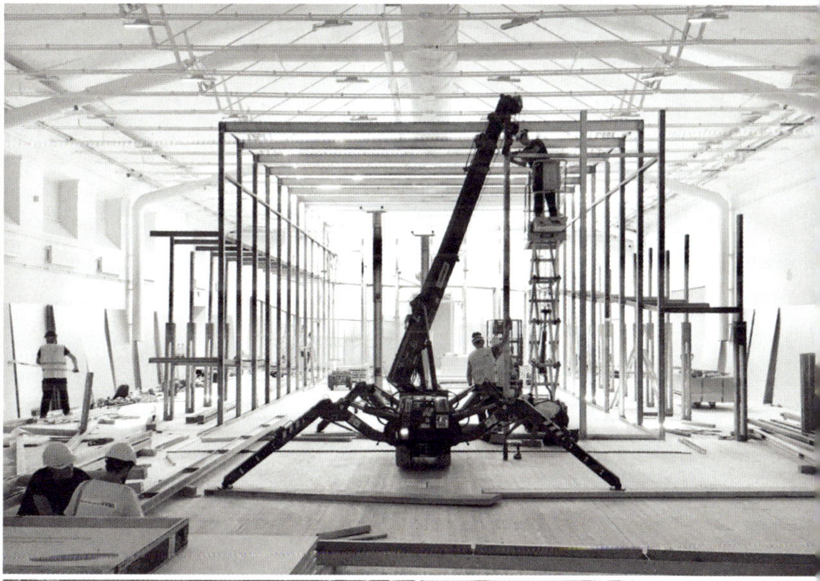
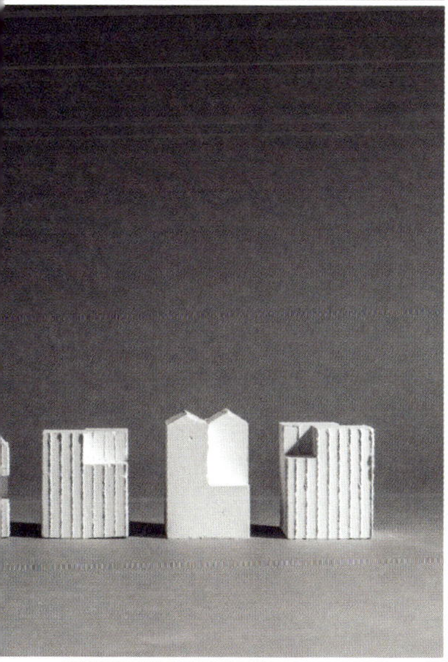
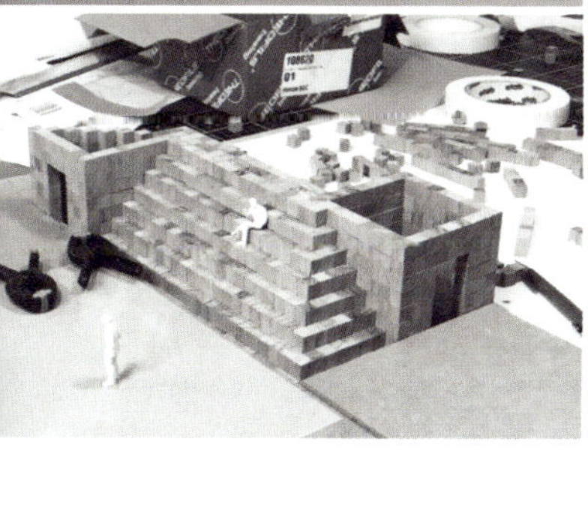
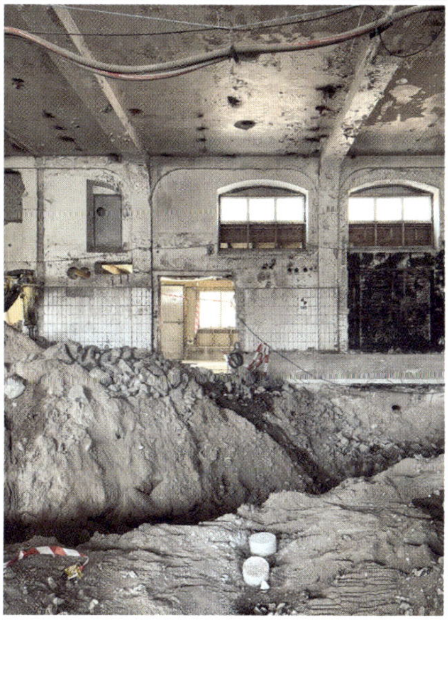
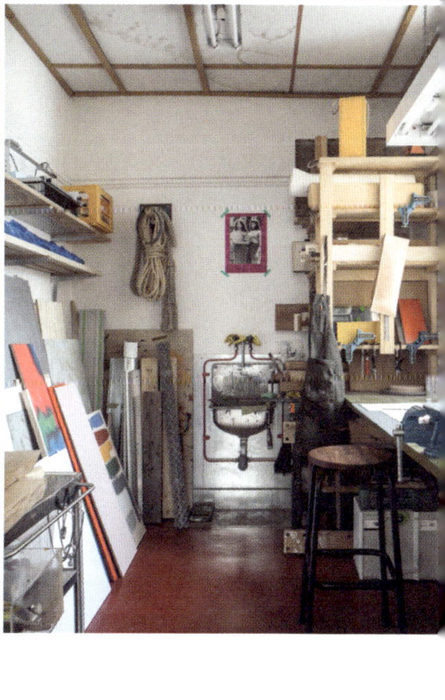

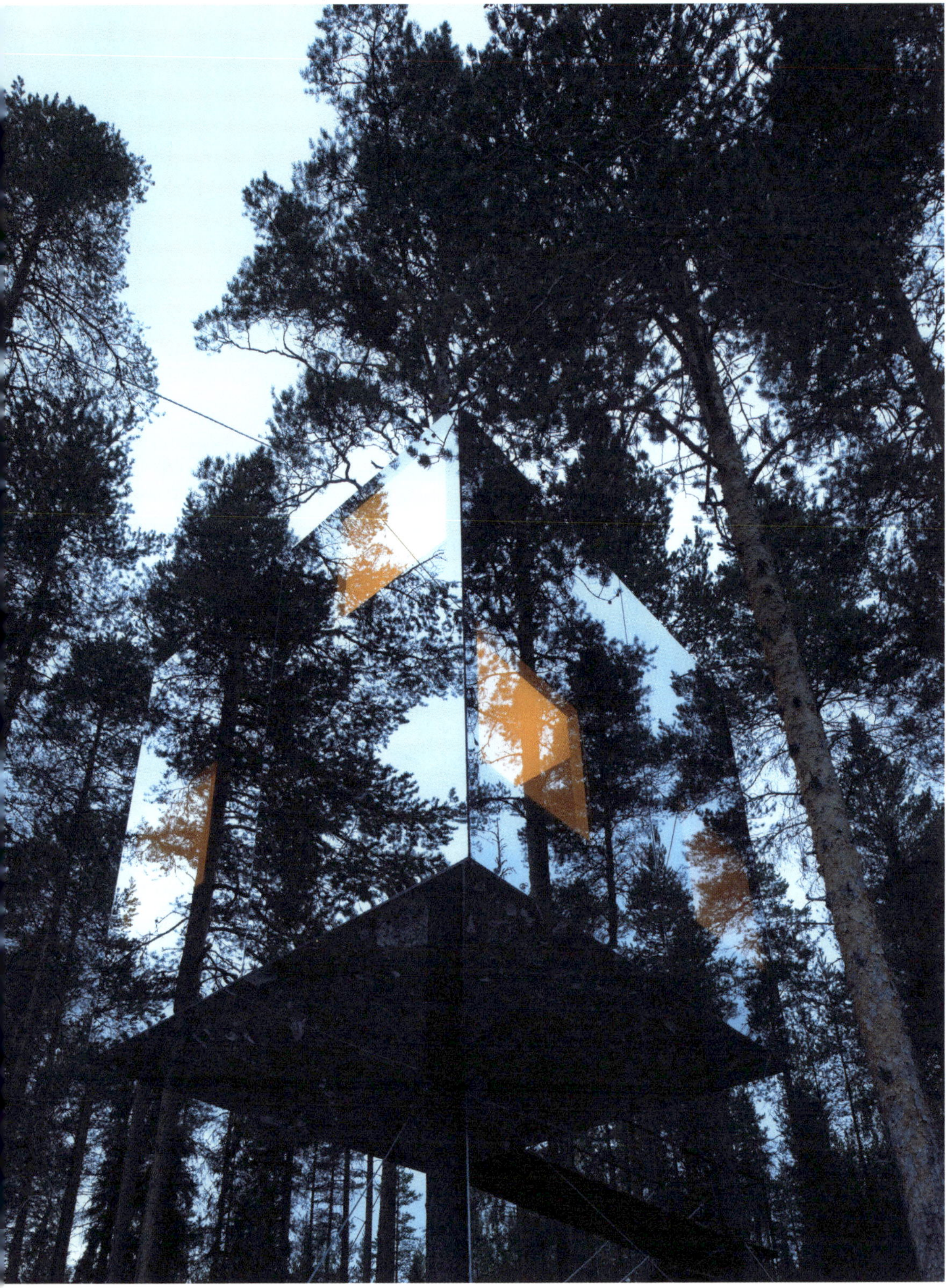

Tham & Videgård

Bolle Tham and Martin Videgård founded their studio in Stockholm in 1999, and since then Tham & Videgård has evolved with an experimental approach into a substantial practice with global reach. The studio has won several national and international awards, including two of Sweden's most prestigious titles, Sveriges Arkitekter's Kasper Salin Prize, for the Kalmar Museum of Art and the KTH School of Architecture in Stockholm. These projects join a diverse portfolio that runs from education buildings to modern art museums, housing, exhibition design and the hugely influential Tree Hotel in Harads. The firm has exhibited around the world, including at the Venice Architecture Biennale and London's Victoria & Albert Museum, and to date has published five monographs. Tham and Videgård are members of the Royal Swedish Academy of Fine Arts and have taught and lectured around the world. "Architecture is about the future," they explain. "A building stands for hundreds of years, so inevitably it is not only contemporary but also a form of continued history projected into the future." This strong sense of permanence and the desire to maximise quality and architectural integrity inform Tham and Videgård's work. "The end result is the only thing that matters."

thamvidegard.se

Regarding architecture and its relationship with time, we feel that we are part of something that is flowing, so what we do now will eventually become the past.

— Bolle Tham

Previous page, above and right: Tree Hotel, Harads, Sweden

Todd Saunders: I heard a lecture you gave where you said that Tham & Videgård is about finding the right answer to complex questions. That's probably why people come to you – they know you will answer their questions in a good and different way.

Martin Videgård: We've found you can bring new inspiration to any project by carefully looking at each specific situation, whether it's high tech in a city or a country lodge. And beauty isn't always subliminal – sometimes it is something you can grasp, like craftsmanship.

TS: In Norway it sometimes feels that if you talk about beauty and architecture then they dismiss you as pretentious. I disagree with that, but we still have a hard time explaining it. Perhaps it is because beauty is more of a feeling, something you experience when you walk into a building. When we did the projects on Fogo Island, there was a special feeling in the houses there and I kept asking myself what it was. It touched on what you just said – that they were made by hand, at a different speed and scale to what we're used to, based purely on needs. I call it "ugly beauty" – a bit like the French term *jolie laide* – but it was still hard for me to put words to beauty.

Bolle Tham: In vernacular architecture, which is often not "fancy" or unnecessary, there is a directness and humbleness. Maybe this is about ethics – that you should do as much as possible with less, rather than waste all your resources.

TS: When I was younger, I travelled around Scandinavia, up to Stockholm, then Helsinki. I heard a guy interviewed on the radio after he won nine million kronor. He was asked what he was going to buy. He thought for a second, and then said, "I think I'd like a new tent." It really encapsulated values and needs in one sentence. I see that as well in your architecture.

BT: The ethics behind those values are quite important when we define what is or isn't beautiful.

MV: Or quality, or joy – what you feel when you arrive in a special space and there is this shared feeling of elevation. Perhaps the difference between an architect and everyone else is that we have trained ourselves to predict when this will happen, so that we can create those spaces again.

TS: Was there a point in your career where you no longer had to convince people that you could do this? Only when I built a tiny cabin that people could actually experience did my career take off. Even today, my best clients often go somewhere like Fogo and experience the architecture before even contacting me.

BT: In terms of attracting new business, from the start, we didn't promote ourselves. Instead, we wanted to produce real buildings so that people could come and see them. The hard thing is to get the first building built, of course.

MV: The client comes to us because they are interested in our work, so the power balance in the collaboration is therefore different. That goes hand in hand with not looking for media or press; they have to come to us as well. We often say yes, but sometimes we say no – especially to TV programmes that we didn't find serious enough. Being quite passive has been good for us – in the long run it has given us a certain kind of integrity. Not only for ourselves but also in the eyes of our colleagues and in the industry. It was a tough decision to make when we started out, but it was just me and Bolle for a couple of years. After five years we were still only four or five people. Then we were happy to win an open international competition which got built. After that we won a couple of prizes and new assignments and professional clients came in. We were both fortunate in our decision to just sit still. It might not be the best recommendation for everybody but that's how we did it.

BT: We also live in a small country. If you include all the architects, landscape architects and physical planners, I think the architectural community in Sweden is only about 10,000 people, of whom perhaps 5,000 are in Stockholm. Whenever someone asked us if we would come and talk about architecture, we would say yes. We didn't feel obliged, but if you have a small community then everyone needs to contribute or else you can't have a living culture. That's also why we were invited abroad to collaborate or talk quite early on.

TS: What's your track record with competitions?

MV: We win every third competition we enter, I think. We won a competition in Prague recently, and in Paris. Invited competitions have been very important for us. And sometimes there are direct assignments, but you can always reject them if you don't find it interesting.

BT: From the start, we were interested in doing public work. Before we even had an office, we did an open international competition for a city library in Finland. We thought we had no hope but we got down to the last ten finalists, which was fantastic for us. If you just do small projects like private houses, it's very good for your mind to work on a different scale sometimes. We used competitions as inspiration. After a few years we ended up just being two people in the office again, so we did two competitions. One of them was the Kalmar Museum of Art, which opened in 2008. Which turned out to be an important moment.

MV: Sometimes we were happy afterwards that we didn't win a big competition, because it is important to start on a small scale and learn the craft. Like I said, we hope all our products are built, so we wanted to learn from the process – the ideas are not finished until they're built.

TS: I remember Håkon Vigsnæs from Jarmund/Vigsnæs giving a lecture at the Bergen architecture school. He said, "Focus on building". So we decided to build this little cabin, which made all the difference. But some studios in this book started by practically jumping off a cliff – Snøhetta won the Alexandria Library, ALA won their concert hall, for example. What if you'd won a big competition very early on?

MV: We were fortunate to win at the right time. But we also don't think of ourselves as representatives of typical Swedish architecture. It's up to others to label it as Swedish or perhaps Scandinavian architecture. We're autonomous in that sense. On the other hand, we teach here, we have Scandinavian values, and all these affect our architecture in the long run.

BT: On day one, we decided on our life/work balance attitude – the best workers were not the ones who stayed in the office the longest.

This page: Creek House, southwestern Sweden

SWEDEN | THAM & VIDEGÅRD

Top left and top right:
KTH School of Architecture,
Stockholm, Sweden

Right: House on Krokholmen,
Krokholmen, Sweden

My son was born the same year we started and now I have two children and Martin has three. So we knew we needed a balance. And it has worked out – it's a mindset. We've trained ourselves to be quite efficient in the office. It's a lot of work, but it's fun – our rule is to not work more than eight hours a day. If you work late one night then you have to take time off to compensate for that.

Regarding architecture and its relationship with time, we feel that we are part of something that is flowing, so what we do now will eventually become the past. It would be stupid not to consider the past – it doesn't necessarily mean that we should reference it directly – but the past is one of the many different layers of context that informs a project. I think architecture is about bringing the past into the future. This gives us a freedom – you're not just designing for the people across the table, but those who will turn up in 20 or 50 years. And our goal is that the building should still be useful to them.

MV: This way of looking at time is contrary to Modernism's approach a hundred years ago – the attitude that older architecture reflected an unequal society so therefore new architecture had to look different and not reference what came before. But we've been brought up in a very equal society, a welfare state where nobody is left behind, and we can allow ourselves to look at history in a different way. We can appreciate the good craftsmanship of an architect that lived 500 years ago or a thousand years ago. The progression of a society always influences how you look at the history of architecture.

BT: In that context, you have to look at the situation with fresh eyes. That is something we enjoy – exploring and adapting the opportunities of every context. Parallel to this is the sustainability aspect. The oldest building that's still being used is the most sustainable one. If it is important to you then you can't really work with materials or tectonic solutions that don't stand the test of time. Sustainability has shifted our way of looking at decision-making during construction.

MV: The Swedish building industry is very wary of risk. A lot of solutions are possible if the person or organisation using the building is willing to maintain the building. But what happens in Sweden – and elsewhere – is the clients and users don't even want to spend money cleaning the windows.

TS: Which one of your buildings do you think would last a thousand years?

BT: I don't know if any of them could, certainly not without a lot of maintenance. In the office, we've had a discussion on solid construction – masonry, wood, concrete – perhaps not completely applicable in our climate. But look at the centre of Stockholm – it's all solid brick walls, no insulation. They're still functional buildings and very attractive.

TS: What average lifespan do you hope for something like the Kalmar Museum of Art?

MV: The structure will probably be there for ever. The façades are made out of wood so will have to be maintained. But it'll stay there as long as you wish.

TS: A building can be a generator of income for a society. Our hotel in Fogo gives back 15–20 per cent of its profits to the community

Opposite: Kalmar Museum of Art, Kalmar, Sweden

every year. Should this be a requirement baked into each building?

MV: Over time people will appreciate and care for a beautiful building. If the structure is generic enough to hold different functions, then it will also last a long time.

TS: Time is such a big factor in designing and building things. How do you approach the speed of architecture in your office?

BT: The scale of our projects varies hugely. Large-scale projects always come with a long schedule. You can work on those projects for years and refine them, taking into account new information and requirements that arrive along the way. The smaller projects are much more sensitive to speed – sometimes the clients are more restless. But we always try to create as much time as possible. We're getting better – and if someone turns us down it's not the end of the world.

MV: If you can only pick two from fast, cheap or good, most people pick "good" and "cheap", so the project is going to take some time.

TS: Is there a place for imperfection in your work?

MV: I remember reading an article by Peter Eisenman called "Mies-Reading", about how to appreciate something with the knowledge that you will somehow misunderstand a part of it, and that this misunderstanding could be the seed of a new idea. To be 100 per cent in someone else's mind is impossible. If you can get to 70 per cent then you must put the extra 30 per cent in by yourself. Perhaps you could call these mistakes, but it's also a way of allowing an idea to go in a different direction.

TS: Do you have higher ambition for your work than your clients have?

MV: Always, I think [laughter]. If you make architecture that is clear enough you can not only understand it easily but also misunderstand it in many different ways. We strive to make architecture that is not making a stand or being neutral. If it is too neutral, it is not engaging you to have your own feelings. That's the most important quality.

BT: Jasper Morrison's furniture designs are considered exceptionally "normal", very close to being boring. His work also references vernacular forms – they are functional in a good way, but also versatile.

MV: That connects to fashion. Uniqlo is "normal" clothing for "normal" money, whereas haute couture could be normal clothing for a lot of money, so it becomes exclusive. Sometimes we find it is almost more expensive to make something look simple and relaxed; exposed concrete can be more expensive than having plaster on top of it.

TS: I feel that your work respects the past but also looks to the future, without jumping too far ahead. It operates at a very healthy speed, with a beautiful transition from the Swedish vernacular.

SWEDEN | THAM & VIDEGÅRD

Above and opposite:
Kalmar Museum of Art,
Kalmar, Sweden

SWEDEN | THAM & VIDEGÅRD

Right: Tham & Videgård, Stockholm, Sweden

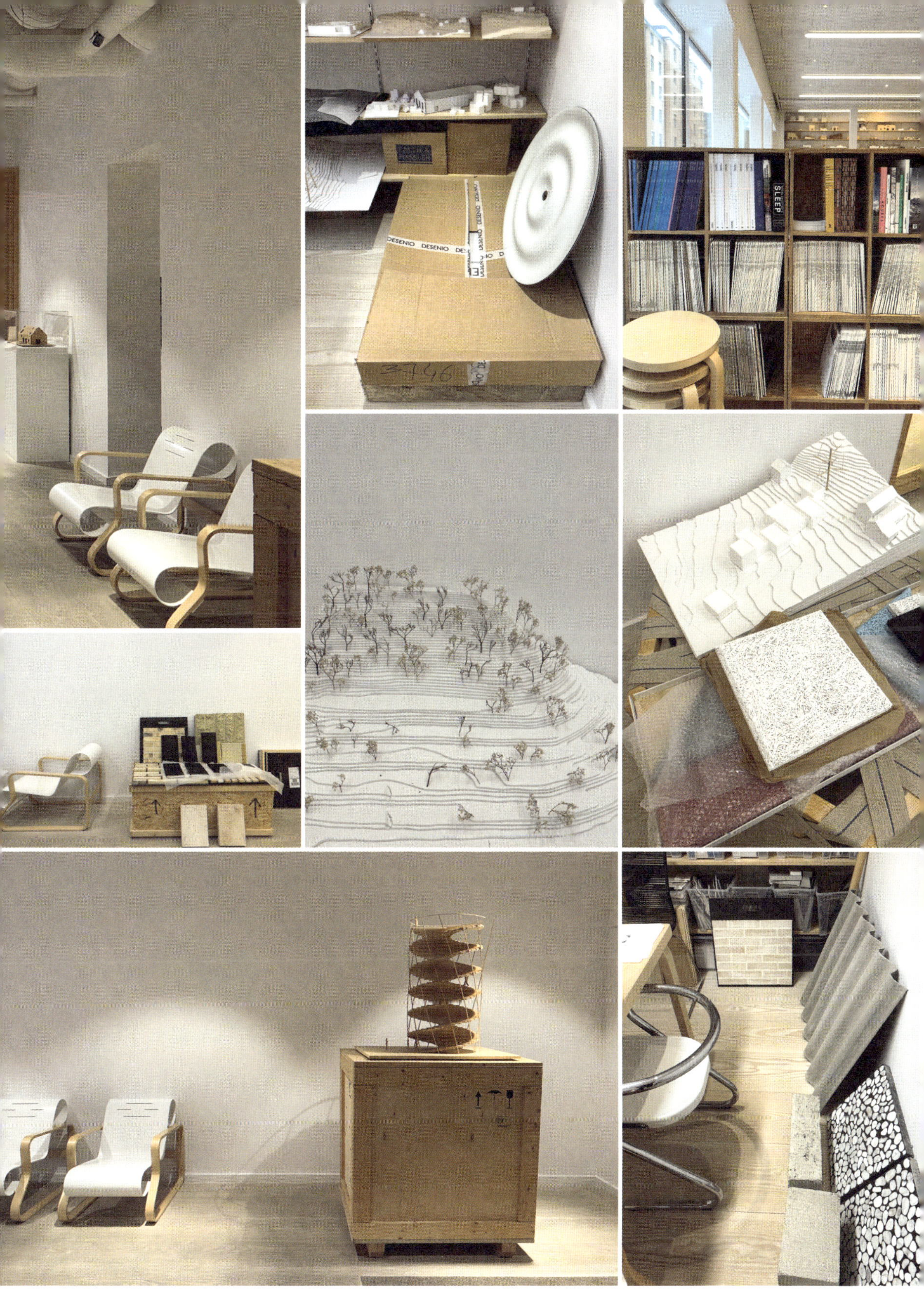
DESENIO
SLEEP

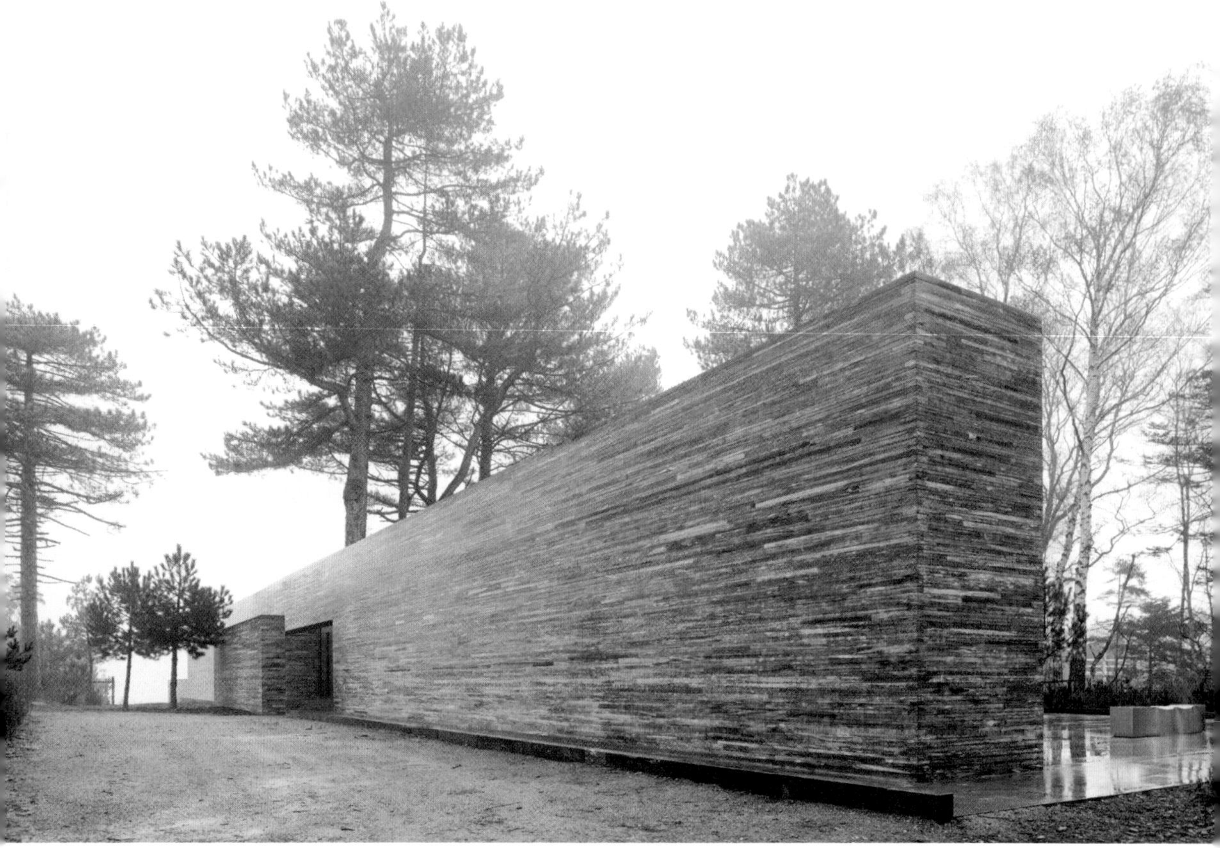

Wingårdhs

The Swedish architect Gert Wingårdh established his practice in Gothenburg in 1977. Beginning with commercial interiors like stores and restaurants, Wingårdh grew the studio gradually. Wingårdhs' first major architectural commission was the award-winning Öijared Executive Country Club near Gothenburg, completed in 1988. The practice subsequently expanded hugely, and now has over 200 employees spread across three offices. Wingårdhs has undertaken projects around the world and is acclaimed for its work in stone, concrete and particularly wood. The studio continues to work on a variety of scales, from furniture design and private houses, to hotels and urban masterplans. The studio's plans for Gothenburg's Fiskhamn, or Fish Harbour, proposes a modernisation that preserves and enhances the local economy while also increasing the housing density of the site. Gert Wingårdh is also a familiar face on Swedish television, and perhaps the most identifiable architect in the country as a result.

wingardhs.se

Previous page: Villa F,
Græsted, Sjælland, Denmark

Above: Liljevalchs+,
Stockholm, Sweden

Todd Saunders: Were you interested in architecture from a young age?

Gert Wingårdh: I'm an only child, that's important, and my father always pointed me towards becoming the artist that he hadn't been. I was always given brushes, pencils, crayons. In secondary school, I started to understand art a bit more, and realised it was tricky to be successful in, so I decided to be an art gallerist. I was very influenced by French New Wave cinema, and the bourgeois life they portrayed. You'd go to the artist, buy a piece of art for €1,000, have a very nice lunch, with your mistress, then sell the painting for ten times more in the evening. This was the kind of life I envisioned for myself!

TS: A gallerist and a patron?

GW: Exactly. That image has had a strong influence on me throughout my life. My family was not at all into it though, so I had to learn the business side by going to business school. I also went to art school to study art history, where I realised that architecture was also considered an art. It was a revelation to me because architecture appeared to stem from positive experiences, whereas art often seemed to come out of trauma of some kind. I travelled to Italy as part of the course, and that also made a big impression on me. I was intrigued by the idea that you had this flat floor, and then everything happened above that in, say, Francesco Borromini's work. It wasn't just about the function, but the section, the complications.

TS: So how did you make the transition from studying art history to architecture?

GW: I was fairly ambitious, and I thought I could just apply for architecture school as well. Unfortunately, I couldn't do three different things at once. But at the end of the first year I had to do a piece of work that imagined all the objects you should have in a house. I made them for real, and as a result I got a very good pass. In a way it got me a very early following – I was labelled the "architect of the class", and ever since I have identified myself with architecture and architects.

TS: How did you find architecture as an art?

GW: In many ways, I found it effortless to come up with solutions. I had to make an effort to make the business add up, but architecture was almost the most lazy way of doing things. I would later discover that laziness is perhaps not the architect's greatest trait, but I definitely started with a laid-back approach.

TS: How old were you at this point?

GW: Twenty-one or something. In those days we had the draft in Sweden. I was born in '51 and there were a lot of kids born that year, and the army couldn't take us all, so I didn't get in the first wave of doing my draft. It hovered over me and I was supposed to do it when I turned 24, but you're a very different person from when you're 19. I had also met my first wife, and our first son was on the way. I had an urge to escape that by leaving the country. So I did a compressed architectural education and went to London, and visited Foster, Rogers, Stirling, and Powell and Moya and a few other offices. However, there was a late recession because of the oil crisis in '74. Our first son was born premature, so I decided to go back to Sweden. My wife worked in advertising, and made much more money, and eventually I started by designing my own office in 1977,

Opposite: Water tower, Helsingborg, Sweden

Below right: Laponia, Vietasjåkk, Gällivare, Sweden

when I was 26. It was of course very tricky to get any commissions, but eventually I was successful in getting restaurants and shops.

TS: When did you get your first employee?

GW: 1982. I spent five years on my own. I got the opportunity to do a lot of shops, which involved a lot of hustling, and getting very streetwise.

TS: You have to be quick too, with short delivery times and deadlines.

GW: In architecture school you don't really learn anything and become sort of arrogant. I quickly learned that you can get whatever you want if you put your mind to it. You must learn to work with people and there is never just one price, just negotiations and relationships and whatever you have. In hindsight, it was good experience, but at the time I was very frustrated.

TS: What was your biggest strength in those five years of working alone?

GW: I kept doing competitions. I was very dedicated, and very sure about what was right and wrong. At architecture school you had the post-1968 radicalism, but also these small islands of "old knowledge" based around professors that they could not get rid of. So I sort of jumped between these islands, and made my alliances there. We had an American perspective drawing teacher who pointed us towards Denise Scott Brown, Robert Venturi and Steven Izenour's Learning from Las Vegas, mainly because of how the renderings were done, with scalpels and different coloured layers and stuff. Then I turned to learning from Venturi's Complexity and Contradiction in Architecture, and all these arguments that Venturi had for Mannerism and Baroque and pointing towards Corbusier and undiluted Modernism. It attracted me because the radical Swedish system at that time was focused on cost and making things simple. The functionalist movement was very rational.

TS: It seems like you were born at a perfect time to create your own architecture in Sweden, because as you said, it was all very functionalist and practical. But you introduced a level of both art and economics. When did you find your own personality in your buildings?

GW: I'm still searching for it. Then, we thought we were out of tune with the times and the judges and the jurists for all the competitions. But then, in the '90s, we were suddenly in tune with common opinion, so we had a lot of success. I got a commission out of the blue in 1986 for the Öijared Executive Country Club, which was highly influenced by merging architecture with landscape and then doing Fontana-like cuts into that. Over two years I put a lot of detail and effort into that one building.

TS: When I moved to Norway, that building was just being finished. I followed your career from that point. There was nothing else in Sweden that was that different, whereas in Norway, Sverre Fehn had just arrived. Compared to a firm like Snøhetta, who arrived with one big competition, you learned the slow, step-by-step way. Are you happy your practice evolved like this?

GW: I'm extremely lucky with how things have proceeded in my professional life. Also, in my 60s, starting a career on Swedish television with Husdrömmar (Dream Houses).

SWEDEN | WINGÅRDHS

The joy is always in finding the solution, that eureka moment.

— Gert Wingårdh

Opposite top: Nationalmuseum, Blasieholmen, Stockholm, Sweden

Opposite bottom: Malmö Market Hall, Malmö, Sweden

We have 1.6 million people just watching that programme, the fifth most popular in Sweden. When I walk down a street, everybody acknowledges my presence, and wishes to talk. That level of recognition at a late stage in your life career is amazing. For me, everything has been a slow, but developing climb, without any real downturn.

TS: What type of people came in your studio that helped you move to a higher level?

GW: During the '80s I developed a different approach to luxury design. I was alone in this market for a while, which allowed me to design the most interesting shops and restaurants possible, as well as hotels and then the golf club we mentioned. That project was an instant success – it was very detailed and put the architecture in control, because I was not so afraid of costs and knew to get the right people to do it. I had developed a sort of street smartness doing the shops that could be applied to a larger scale. We won a competition for AstraZeneca's research facility in Gothenburg, and that grew into the biggest building site in western Sweden, at the very same time as the property crisis.

TS: Did you move to computers at this point?

GW: Many other offices had to lay off their young staff, many of whom had been the computer operators just as CAD was taking off. When we were finished with that job in '94/'95, we had perhaps 40 people in the office and we were very, very knowledgeable. We were computerised, a well-trained company of soldiers. From a design point of view, there was a lot of repetition in the R&D facility. My main input into that project was in the first year or second year, then it could easily be finished by my employees. After this we did a secondary school, and we took things in an entirely different direction. We were the name on everybody's lips, so we got invited to quite a few competitions. We had some success with them, like at the Nordic Embassy in Berlin, and the control tower at Arlanda Airport. Suddenly we were the architects to go to in the mid '90s.

TS: What are the positive things about being based in Gothenburg and not Stockholm, although I know you have an office there?

GW: There are probably more disadvantages than advantages. We opened the Stockholm office in 1985, so I came up once or twice a week and I developed a very close affinity with Stockholm, although I didn't really take part in the life of the city. One advantage was that you got to be a bit mythical – nobody really sees you and you're leaving all the time.

TS: You mentioned ambition earlier. How has your ambition changed throughout your career?

GW: I'm single-minded but curious and open. I never shy away from making a decision because I'm quite certain about what I like. Of course, I can change my mind. And I think I've been very ambitious, up until now. I will turn 70 in a few weeks' time, and I am thinking what goals I will lay out for the next ten years.

TS: Do you think you're still learning things?

GW: Absolutely. For the past four or five years, I've been trying to find out what will happen to the factory that I now solely own. I'm thinking of making it into a foundation and try to get it to live on its own, but I realise that then, it would be of no more interest to me.

TS: Were there any particularly hard projects during your career which taught you a lot?

GW: Most projects are hard. The research facilities that we did were, and I learned a lot of negotiation skills. Interrogation techniques, almost! Since it was a research facility, they had an open mind, so if you had an argument for something, then anything was possible. It was a tough school for all of us.

TS: Are there things you can say no to?

GW: No! Of course, now we're better positioned to understand if a client will be worth our while.

TS: The Laponia Visitor Centre is one of my favourite projects. How did that come about?

GW: There was to be a parliament for the Sami people, and I was on the judging panel for an invited competition. That meant that I had to get to know them. We went through quite a few proposals, and it became apparent that the Sami feel as if a lot of Swedish architecture is from an occupying force. Their culture is focused on circular structures. On receiving the commission for the visitor centre, I visited the site. You could put the building in the woods, or outside which is what we proposed. But this site was also the furthest from the parking lot. I remember walking through the forest and getting all these mosquitoes at my feet and realizing it would be of great benefit to be out in the wind. The Sami also stressed that the site is effectively lent to us for a short period of time, like 100 years, rather than being a permanent part of the site. I thought

it would be very interesting to do a very lightweight structure. Do you remember the Serpentine Pavilion by Álvaro Siza? I think it was made of glulam beams, with pieces that could be moved by one or two people, with slight variations on the geometry. I had the idea that the building should be a very lightweight framework, kind of rounded, kind of tilted, covered with fabric, with woven wool on the inside. There are also herds of reindeer moving past the building, so we thought it would be good to protect it from their horns.

TS: I always loved that building, with the fireplace at its heart. Are you still doing a lot of houses?

GW: I've actually designed a house every weekend now, for a while.

TS: Do you get a sense of joy out of creating a house?

GW: The joy is always in finding the solution, that eureka moment. The last house we did was extremely constrained. There was space for only 150 square metres. I realised that we could proportion the building so it could look different to the other buildings alongside it, but also somehow effortless. Before that I was designing a log house. The result looks like it could've been done in the 14th century, yet it still has these big panes of glass, which makes it extremely contemporary. I've always been very intrigued by collage methods.

TS: Your work is a patchwork of very different things, at very high quality.

GW: Exactly. And sometimes those elements can appear to be quite alien.

Above: Örebro Kulturkvarter, Fabriksgatan, Örebro, Sweden

Right: Wingårdhs, Gothenburg, Sweden

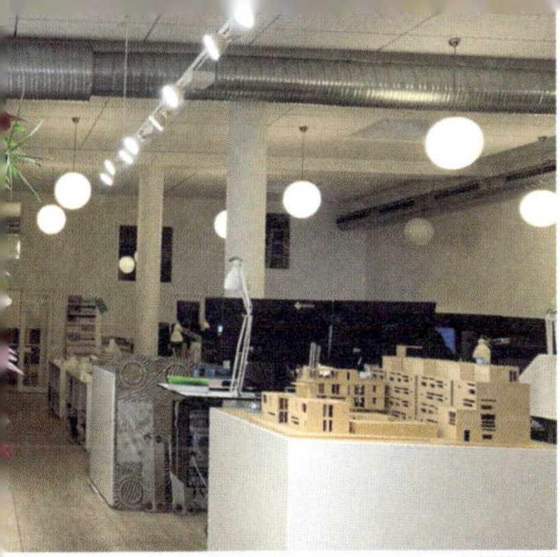
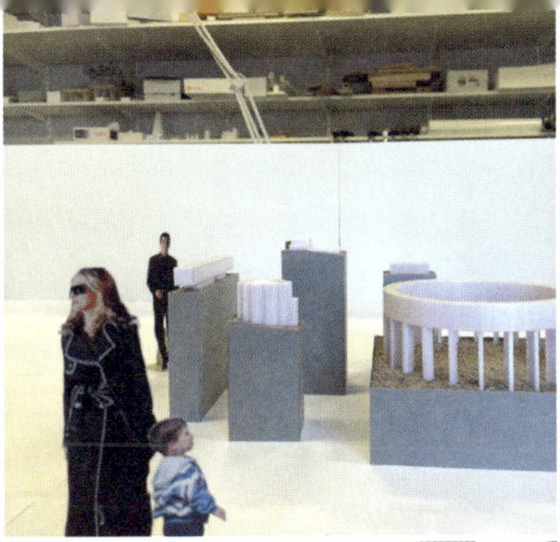
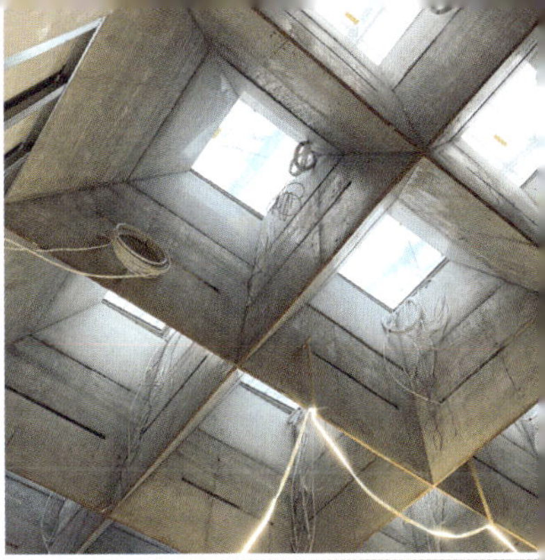
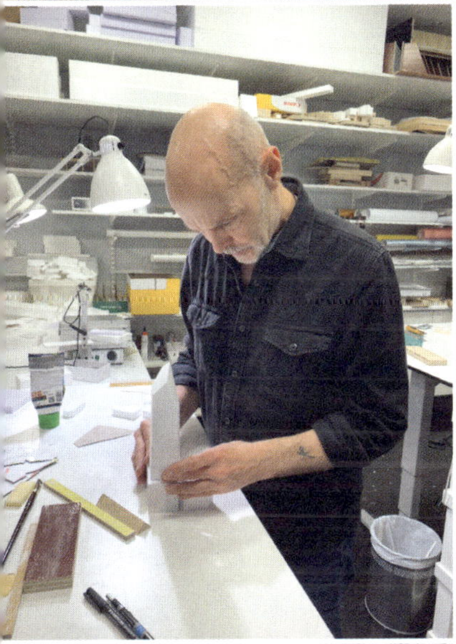
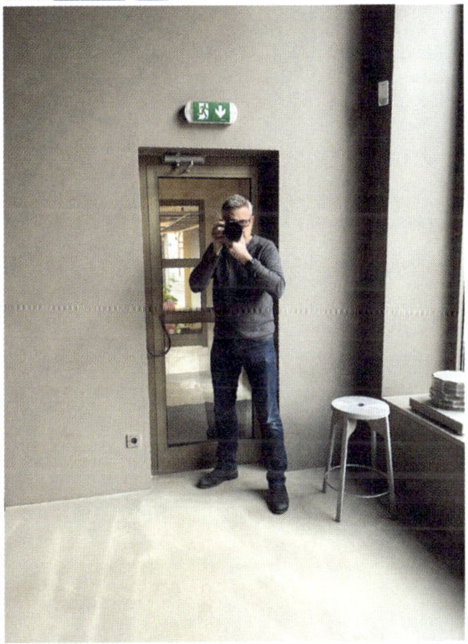
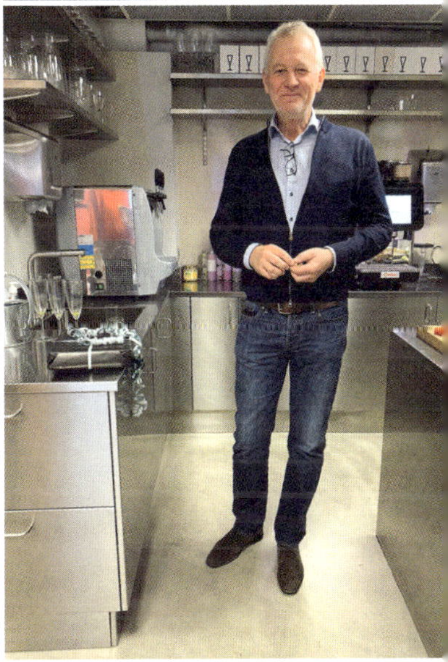
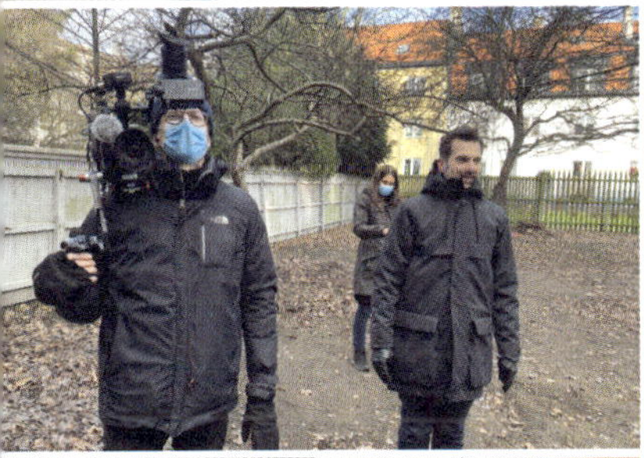
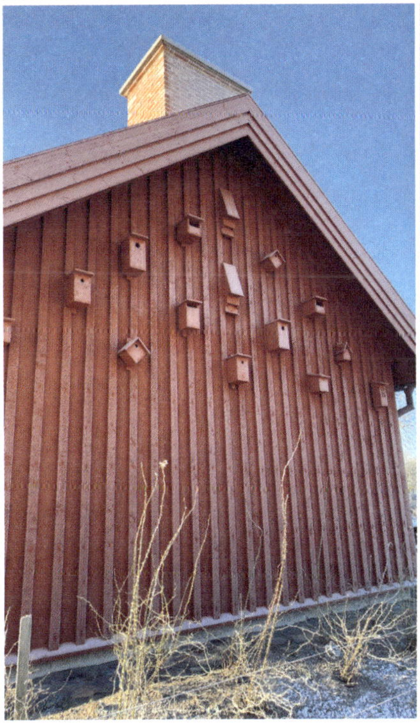
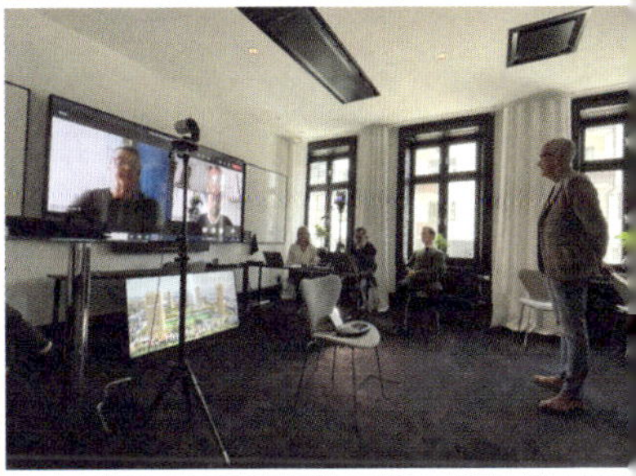
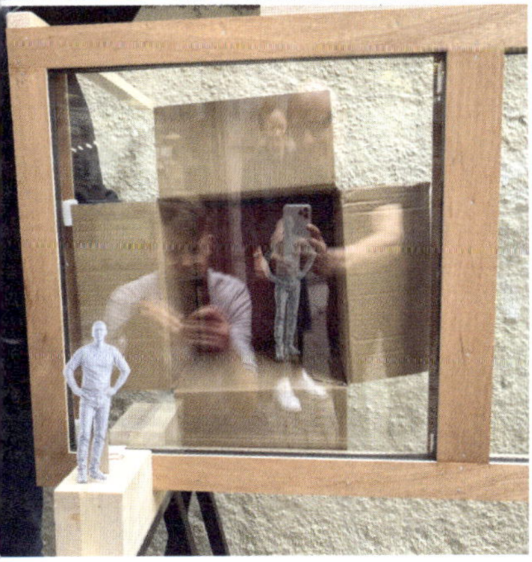
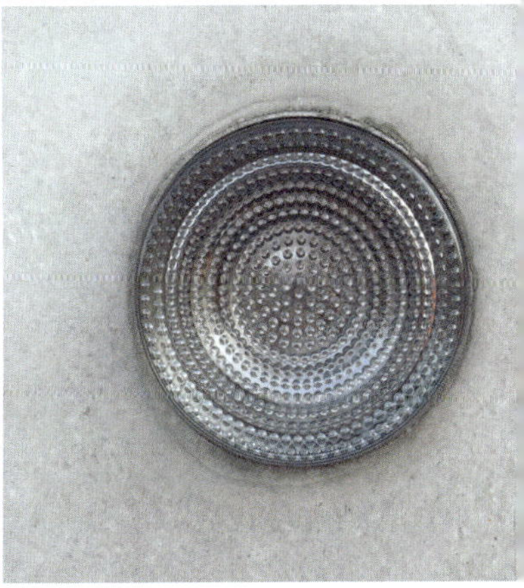

ACKNOWLEDGEMENTS

A book and a piece of architecture are rarely made by one person. This book was an enjoyable process that involved some very hard-working, smart and enthusiastic people. Thank you to Jonathan Bell for over 15 years of collaborating, starting with our practice's first monograph. I would like to thank you for your clarity and for always believing in the ideas and explorations that I have presented to your over the years. Ian Holcroft and I have worked together over 20 years, and this is also our second book together. Thank you, Ian for always being so decisive, open and never buckling to adversity. You have a strength and tenacity that creates a calmness and safety that adds a confidence to a team. Thank you both.

Camilla Vassdal is the office manager at Saunders Architecture. Camilla has kept this book on track and on time with the rigour of a Swiss railway timetable. Thank you, Camilla for your constant diligence and for accepting my unorthodox processes. Thank you to my design assistant Éva Baráth who has been a joyful addition in joining the interviews and sorting out technical issues along the way. Your enthusiasm for the project helped convince me that the younger generation of architects will enjoy these intimate insights into practice. I would also like to thank Tone Fondevik and Celine Falck for their help in the early phases of this book.

We invited one architectural critic from each of the Nordic countries to analyse, comment and offer insights into their respective countries. Thank you to Hildigunnur Sverrisdóttir in Iceland, Malin Zimm in Sweden, Joakim Skajaa in Norway, Katrine Lotz in Denmark and Kristo Vesikansa in Finland.

This book has been partly funded by our work at Saunders Architecture. I would like to thank my staff for running the studio when my focus is on another project that's also important to me. My thanks also go to the City of Bergen for their financial support of this book.

Artifice Press in London took this book on immediately after a short conversation with Jonathan Bell. Thank you to Ludovica Bellomaria (project manager), Stephen Mitchell (Editor-in-Chief) and Anna Danby (Publishing Director) for taking this book across the finish line. We look forward to working together in the future.

Thank you to the 30 architects that I had conversations with. I know that you are all extremely busy and I cannot thank you enough for taking the time to share your insights, being supportive and in helping the profession evolve. Thank you for being extremely open, honest and thought-provoking. I hope that this book is a gift back to you and that you enjoy the other twenty-nine conversations. I am convinced that everyone will find some shared experiences, emotions and ambitions within these pages, bringing architects closer together and creating a sharing environment, rather than a competitive one. Giving information away is a gift, and I am constantly experiencing that giving and sharing is the path to creating a better world in which to practice architecture.

This book is a first of a series of books. In the coming years, we will make other books interviewing influential and change-making architects in the US, Canada, Europe and Asia. We encourage your feedback and suggestions and hope you follow us on this ongoing journey. Thank you for taking the time to read this book.

Todd Saunders.

BIOGRAPHIES

Todd Saunders is a Norway-based Canadian architect with a unique understanding of Nordic landscapes. His architecture, set in some of the most remote locations on Earth, splices modern sculptural forms with a deep-rooted respect for nature. Rather than imposing themselves upon the environment and coast, Saunders's buildings seek a sensitive accommodation within the topography, among the icy flora, fauna and treescapes of the landscapes they inhabit. In addition to practice, Saunders is a visiting professor at Yale University, Connecticut, USA.

Jonathan Bell is a London-based writer who specialises in architecture and transport design. He co-wrote Todd Saunders's first monograph in 2012, and his recent books include *21st Century House* and *The New Modern House*. He is a regular contributor to many international lifestyle and design magazines, including *Wallpaper** magazine.

Ian Holcroft is a Bergen-based designer with over 20 years' practice within visual communication, exhibition design and book design. He recently designed Todd Saunders's monograph *New Northern Houses* (2021) and has designed the art and poetry journal *Kraftverk* for Bergen City Council for the past decade.

Kristo Vesikansa is an architect and architectural historian based in Helsinki and the editor-in-chief of the *Finnish Architectural Review*. His research topics include post-war architecture, in particular the works of Raili and Reima Pietilä. In 2021, Vesikansa co-curated the *New Standards* exhibition in the Finnish Pavilion at the Venice Architecture Biennale.

Malin Zimm is Editor-in-Chief of Sweden's architecture magazine *Arkitektur* since 2019. Zimm is an architect, trained at KTH, Stockholm and UCL, London, and holds a PhD in Architecture. Her dissertation was presented in the field of Critical Theory at KTH School of Architecture 2005, Zimm has been a freelance writer and architecture critic since 2000, while working as Chief Editor of the architecture magazine *Rum*, Senior Adviser in Architecture at ArkDes, followed by the role of Research Director and Analyst at White Arkitekter. Together with Mattias Bäcklin she is running the mobile art and architecture gallery Zimm Hall since 2015.

Hildigunnur Sverrisdóttir is an architect and educator located in Iceland. She has a background in architectural practice, critique and theory and has been a guest professor and critic at various schools of architecture. She has taught at the Icelandic University of the Arts since 2006, where she now holds the position of Head of Department of Architecture.

Joakim Skajaa is an architect educated at Bergen School of Architecture. He is the founder of SKAJAA architecture office and a curator at the National Museum of Art, Architecture and Design in Oslo.

Katrine Lotz is an architect and researcher at the Royal Danish Academy, School of Architecture, where she heads the Institute of Architecture, Urbanism & Landscape. Her main research interest is the relationships between the Nordic welfare states, their architecture and spatial planning, both in a historical perspective and in relation to the current changes. Among her recent publications are contributions to the anthology *Architectures of Dismantling and Restructuring – Danish Welfare Spaces 1970–present*, Lars Müller Publishers 2022.

IMAGE CREDITS

Cover; Eberhard Grossgasteiger, pexels.com. Denmark; p. 18 TheGenner, pexels.com. BIG – Bjarke Ingels Group; p. 24 Rasmus Hjortshoj; p. 26 (both) Iwan Baan; p. 29 Laurian Ghinitoiu; p. 30 (top) Tomasz Majewski, (bottom) Laurian Ghinitoiu; p. 33 (top) Laurian Ghinitoiu, (bottom) Hufton+Crow; p. 35–37 BIG – Bjarke Ingels Group. Henning Larsen Architects; p. 38–40 Nic Lehoux; p. 43 (all) Javier Callejas Sevilla; p. 44–47 Philippe Ruault; p. 60–61 Henning Larsen Architects. Marianne Levinsen Landskab; p. 50 Marianne Levinsen Landskab; p. 52 Adam Mørk p. 55 (top) Lars Just, (bottom, both) Torben Petersen; p. 56 Adam Mørk; p. 58–59 black & white studio portraits by John Ehbrecht, landscape photos by Adam Mørk, all other images Marianne Levinsen Landskab. Norrøn; p. 60–69 Torben Eskerod; p. 70–71 Norrøn. Studio dominique + serena; p. 72 Morten Pihl; p. 74 Ruben Slot; all other images p. 77–83 Studio dominique + serena. Vandkunsten; p. 84 May Line Knutsen; p. 86 (top left) Astrid Marie Busse Rasmussen, (top right) Lasse Bech Martinussen, (bottom) Astrid Marie Busse Rasmussen; p. 89 Andreas Omvik: p. 90 (left) Rasmus Hjortshoj, (right) Katrine Lunke; p. 91 Rasmus Hjortshoj; p. 92–93 Vandkunsten. 3XN; p. 94 3XN; p. 96 (top) 3XN, (bottom) MIR; p. 99 (all) Rasmus Hjortshoj; p. 100 (both) Adam Mørk; p. 102–103 3XN. Finland; p. 104 Jamo Images, pexels.com. ALA; p. 110 MIR; p. 112–119 (all) Tuomas Uusheimo; p. 120–121 ALA. Avanto; p. 122–126 Kuvio.com; p. 129 (all) Archmospheres.com; p. 122–123 Avanto. K2S Architects; p. 132–134 Tuomas Uusheimo; p. 137 Mika Huisman; p. 138–143 Tuomas Uusheimo; p.144–145 K2S Architects. OOPEAA; p. 146 Hannu Rytky; p. 148 (top) Sakari Majantie, (middle) Angel Gil, (bottom) Sakari Majantie; p. 151–152 Mikko Auerniitty; p. 143–159 Jussi Tiainen; p. 156–157 Anssi Lassila (childhood photos from the family album courtesy of Anssi Lassila). Planetary Architecture; p. 158–160 Planetary Architecture; p. 163 Mika Merikanto, p. 168 (bottom) Tuija Pakkanen, p. 170–171 (Studio portrait) Pihla Meskanen, (Top left) Arttu Muukkonen, (Ski portrait) Mika Merikanto, (Bottom right) Xprize Foundation, (all other images) Pekka Pakkanen. Studio Puisto; p. 172 Archmospheres, Marc Goodwin, p. 147 (top and left) Archmospheres, Marc Goodwin, (bottom right) Riikka Kantinkoski; p. 177–178 Archmospheres, Marc Goodwin; p. 180–181 Riikka Kantinkoski, Marc Goodwin, Studio Puisto. Iceland; p. 182 Pixabay, pexels.com. A Arkitektar; p. 188–190 A Arkitektar; p. 193–194 A Arkitektar; p. 196–197 Hannu Rytky; p. 198–199 Ragngeidur Arngrimsdottir. Basalt; p. 200 Vök Baths; p. 202 (top) Martijn Veenman, (bottom) Vök Baths; p. 205 Ragnar Th Sigurðsson; p. 206–207 Guðlaug baths; p. 208–209 Basalt. PK Arkitektar; p. 210 PK Arkitektar; p. 212 Ake Lindman; p. 215 Rafael Pinho; p. 216–221 PK Arkitektar. Studio Granda; p. 222–224 Sigurgeir Sigurjónsson; p. 227 Pancho Gallardo; p. 228–231 Sigurgeir Sigurjónsson; p. 232–233 Studio Granda. Norway; p. 234 Alleksana, pexels.com. Gartnerfuglen Arkitekter; p. 240–242 Gartnerfuglen Arkitekter; p. 245–246 Ivar Kvaal; p. 248–249 Gartnerfuglen Arkitekter. Haugen/Zohar Arkitekter; p. 250–252 Haugen/Zohar Arkitekter; p. 255 Stainar Skaar; p. 256–263 Haugen/Zohar Arkitekter. Helen & Hard; p. 264 Erieta Attali; p. 266 (top) Erieta Attali, (bottom) Sindre Ellingsen; p. 268 (top) Sindre Ellingsen, (bottom) Jiri Havran; p. 270 Sindre Ellingsen; p. 272–273 Sindre Ellingsen; p. 274–275 Emile Ashley; p. 276–277 Helen & Hard. Jensen & Skodvin; p. 278–285 Jensen & Skodin; p. 287 MIR, p. 288–289 Jensen & Skodvin. Reiulf Ramstad Arkitekter; p. 290–292 11h45; p. 295–296 Reiulf Ramstad Arkitekter; p. 298–299 Ivar Kvaal; p. 300–301 Reiulf Ramstad Arkitekter. Rintala Eggertsson Architects; p. 302 Dag Jenssen; p. 304 Nick Coates; p. 308–311 Dag Jenssen, p. 312–313 Rintala Eggertsson Architects. Snøhetta; p. 314 Gerald Zugmann/Vienna; p. 316 (top) Jens Passoth, (bottom) Gerald Zugmann/Vienna; p. 319 Helene Binet; p. 320 (both) Gerald Zugmann/Vienna; p. 323 Jared Chulski; p. 324 (top) Ludwig Favre, (bottom) Jared Chulski; p. 326 Ludwig Favre; p. 327 Jared Chulski; p. 328–329 Snøhetta. Vardehaugen; p. 330 Rasmus Norlander; p. 332–339 Vardehaugen; p. 340–341 (collage) Vardehaugen, (portrait) Thomas Ekström. Sweden; p. 342 Karolina Kot, pexels.com. Claesson Koivisto Rune; p. 350 Åke E:son Lindman; p. 352 Claesson Koivisto Rune; p. 355 Yıkın Hyo; p. 356 (top) Claesson Koivisto Rune, (bottom) Åke E:son Lindman; p. 358 Åke E:son Lindman; p. 359 Claesson Koivisto Rune; p. 360–361 Claesson Koivisto Rune. Förstberg Ling; p. 362–364 Förstberg Ling; p. 367 Markus Linderoth; p. 368–371 Förstberg Ling. Johan Dehlin; p. 372–381 Dehlin Brattgård Arkitekter; p. 382–383 Johan Dehlin, (top left) Anna Nilsson, (below top left) Joakim Nyström. Tham & Videgård; p. 384–395 Åke E:son Lindman; p. 396–397 Tham & Videgård, (portrait) Jonas Lindström. Wingårdhs; p. 398 Åke E:son Lindman; p. 400 Christoffer Grimshorn; p. 403 (top) Werner Nystrand, (bottom) Åke E:son Lindman; p. 404 André Pihl; p. 407 William Gustafsson; p. 408–409 Wingårdhs.

COLOPHON

© 2022 SJH Group, the authors and the photographers. All rights reserved.

This book is published by Artifice Press Limited, a company registered in England and Wales with company number 11182108. Artifice Press Limited is an imprint within the SJH Group. Copyright is owned by the SJH Group.
All rights reserved.

Artifice Press Limited
The Maple Building
39–51 Highgate Road
London NW5 1RT
United Kingdom

+44 (0)20 8371 4047
office@artificeonline.com
www.artificeonline.com

Designed by Ian Holcroft
Edited by Jonathan Bell
Printed in Latvia by Amber Book Print

ISBN 978-1-911339-49-6

British Library in Cataloguing Data. A CIP record for this book is available from the British Library.

Neither this publication nor any part of it may be reproduced, stored in a retrieval system or transmitted in any form or by any means, electronic, mechanical, photocopying, recording or otherwise, without the prior permission of the SJH Group or the appropriately accredited copyright holder.

All information in this publication is verified to the best of the author's and publisher's ability. However, Artifice Press Limited and the SJH Group do not accept responsibility for any loss arising from reliance on it. Where opinion is expressed, it is that of the author and does not necessarily coincide with the editorial views of the publisher. The publishers have made all reasonable efforts to trace the copyright owners of the images reproduced herein, and to provide an appropriate acknowledgement in the book.

ADAPTABLE LIVELIHOODS

Adaptable Livelihoods

Coping with Food Insecurity in the Malian Sahel

Susanna Davies
*Deputy Director, Institute of Development Studies
at the University of Sussex
Brighton*

First published in Great Britain 1996 by
MACMILLAN PRESS LTD
Houndmills, Basingstoke, Hampshire RG21 6XS
and London
Companies and representatives
throughout the world

A catalogue record for this book is available
from the British Library.

ISBN 0–333–63386–5

First published in the United States of America 1996 by
ST. MARTIN'S PRESS, INC.,
Scholarly and Reference Division,
175 Fifth Avenue,
New York, N.Y. 10010

ISBN 0–312–12682–4

Library of Congress Cataloging-in-Publication Data
Davies, Susanna.
Adaptable livelihoods : coping with food insecurity in
the Malian Sahel / Susanna Davies.
p. cm.
Includes bibliographical references and index.
ISBN 0–312–12682–4
1. Food supply—Mali. 2. Mali—Economic conditions. I. Title.
HD9017.M282D39   1995
363.8'096623—dc20   95-8216
                                                                CIP

© Susanna Davies 1996

All rights reserved. No reproduction, copy or transmission of
this publication may be made without written permission.

No paragraph of this publication may be reproduced, copied or
transmitted save with written permission or in accordance with
the provisions of the Copyright, Designs and Patents Act 1988,
or under the terms of any licence permitting limited copying
issued by the Copyright Licensing Agency, 90 Tottenham Court
Road, London W1P 9HE.

Any person who does any unauthorised act in relation to this
publication may be liable to criminal prosecution and civil
claims for damages.

10   9   8   7   6   5   4   3   2   1
05   04 03 02 01 00 99 98 97 96

Printed and bound in Great Britain by
Antony Rowe Ltd, Chippenham, Wiltshire

For Richard

Contents

List of Diagrams	xi
List of Graphs	xii
List of Maps	xv
List of Tables	xvi
Acknowledgements	xviii
List of Abbreviations	xix
Glossary of Foreign Terms	xxi

1 Introduction — 1

Introduction	1
Objectives	2
Challenging Conventional Famine Early Warning	5
Famine and Food Insecurity	7
Location and Scope	9
Defining Normality, Monitoring Change	10
Responsibility and Utility	11
Conclusions	13

2 Security and Vulnerability in Livelihood Systems — 15

Introduction	15
Food Security	15
Livelihood Security	18
Entitlements	20
Vulnerability	21
Past Security, Current Vulnerability	24
Livelihood-System Diversity	33
Framework of Analysis	35
Conclusions	44

3 Coping and Adapting — 45

Introduction	45
Coping Strategies and Early Warning	46
Indicator Development Using Coping Strategies	48

	Unpacking Coping Strategies	51
	How Useful are Coping Strategies?	52
	Coping with Security, Adapting to Vulnerability	55
	Conclusions	59
4	**Monitoring How People Feed Themselves**	**60**
	Introduction	60
	Classifying Livelihood Systems	61
	Listening Posts, Coverage and Counting	63
	Personnel, Training and Existing Information	65
	Livelihood-System Surveys	66
	Monitoring Season and Livelihood-System Specific Indicators	70
	Market Surveys	71
	Household Surveys	72
	Conclusions	77
5	**Drought, Food Insecurity and Early Warning in Mali**	**79**
	Introduction	79
	The National Food Balance	81
	Patterns of Food Insecurity in the 1980s	87
	Food-Security Planning	89
	Implementing Food-Security Policy	92
	Long-Term Planning Tools: Macroeconomic Adjustment and the PRMC	93
	Short-Term Planning Tools: Famine Early Warning and Response	95
	Conclusions: Progress in National Food-Security Planning in the 1980s	105
6	**Livelihood Safety Nets: The Inner Niger Delta in the Sahel**	**109**
	Introduction	109
	Population	110
	The Bases of Livelihood Systems	111
	Regional Food-Security Planning	117
	Listening Posts	121
	Overview of Food Security, 1987–8 to 1990–1	124
	Indicators of Food Security, 1987–8 to 1990–1	131
	Conclusions	135

Contents ix

7 Livelihood Systems — 137

Introduction — 137
The Past: Food Security in Traditional Livelihood Systems — 138
Characteristics of Secure Livelihood Systems in the Past — 148
The Transition from Security to Vulnerability — 152
The Present: Food Insecurity in Livelihood Systems Today — 152
Characteristics of Present-Day Vulnerable Livelihood Systems — 166
Conclusions: Information Needs for Indicators of Food Stress — 172

8 Production Entitlements — 176

Introduction — 176
Regional Production — 176
Household Food Availability — 183
Filling the Food Gap — 185
Conclusions: Indicators of Production Entitlements — 195

9 Exchange Entitlements — 198

Introduction — 198
Market Dependence in Vulnerable Livelihood Systems — 198
The Sample of Markets — 204
Analysis of Data — 206
Prices — 209
Terms of Trade — 216
Condiments — 226
Other Products — 227
Levels of Market Activity — 231
Conclusions: Indicators of Exchange Entitlements — 234

10 Coping and Adaptive Entitlements — 238

Introduction — 238
The Changing Use and Mix of Strategies — 238
The Seasonality of Coping Strategies — 246
Coping and Adaptive Strategies in the Inner Niger Delta and Sahel — 246
Allocation of Household Time as an Indicator of Coping Strategy Use — 253
Coping or Adapting? — 260
Conclusions: Indicators of Coping and Adaptive Entitlements — 266

11	**Tracking and Tackling Food Vulnerability**	**280**
	Introduction	280
	Summary of Findings	280
	A Simplified Methodology for Monitoring Livelihoods	287
	Policy Implications: Saving Lives, Saving Livelihoods	305
	Conclusions: So What?	308

Notes	311
References	317
Index	324

List of Diagrams

2.1	Sensitivity and resilience of environments and food-supply systems	27
2.2	The transition from high resilience/low sensitivity to low resilience/high sensitivity in Sahelian livelihood systems	28
4.1	Classification of food-insecure populations according to multiple vulnerability criteria	62
4.2	Components and outputs of livelihood-system surveys	67
5.1	Structure of Malian food-security planning at national level, 1990	92
6.1	Structure of Malian sub-national administration, 1990	118
7.1	Impact of three-year drought cycle on cultivators in secure livelihood system	150
10.1	The vicious circle of low primary production	250

List of Graphs

5.1	Mali: cereal production, 1971–2 to 1990–1	83
5.2	Mali: total cereal imports as a proportion of domestic production, 1971–2 to 1990–1	86
5.3	Mali: food aid as a proportion of total imports, 1971–2 to 1990–1	86
5.4	Mali: crude national food balance, 1971–2 to 1990–1	87
6.1	Comparison of flood levels in the Inner Niger Delta, 1957–9 and 1983–5	116
7.1	Drought/recovery curve in secure livelihood systems	151
7.2	Annual cycle of subsistence in vulnerable cultivating livelihood system	168
8.1	Cereal production by crop in Mali's 5th Region, 1975–6 to 1990–1	178
8.2	*Per capita* net cereal production in Mali's 5th Region, 1975–6 to 1990–1	179
8.3	Number of livestock in Mali's 5th Region, 1980s, various years	181
8.4	Fish production in the Inner Niger Delta, 1971 to 1990	182
8.5	Annual household cereal availability, by livelihood system, 1989–90	184
8.6	Expenditure on food and non-food items, by livelihood system, 1989–90	187
8.7	Cultivators: proportion of expenditure on food and non-food items, 1989–90	187
8.8	Agro-pastoralists: proportion of expenditure on food and non-food items, 1989–90	188
8.9	Agro-fishers: proportion of expenditure on food and non-food items, 1989–90	188
8.10	Cash income from different sources, by livelihood system, 1989–90	191
8.11	Cultivators: proportion of cash income from different sources of entitlement, 1989–90	192
8.12	Agro-pastoralists: proportion of cash income from different sources of entitlement, 1989–90	192
8.13	Agro-fishers: proportion of cash income from different sources of entitlement, 1989–90	193

List of Graphs

8.14	Cultivators: seasonality of income and expenditure balance, 1989–90	194
8.15	Agro-pastoralists: seasonality of income and expenditure balance, 1989–90	195
8.16	Agro-fishers: seasonality of income and expenditure balance, 1989–90	196
9.1	Comparison of hungry season wetland millet prices in 1984–5 and 1987–8	208
9.2	Comparison of millet prices in good and bad years	211
9.3	Comparison of goat prices in good and bad years	213
9.4	Comparison of cattle prices in good and bad years	214
9.5	Comparison of milk prices in good and bad years	215
9.6	Comparison of fish prices in good and bad years	216
9.7	Goats for millet terms of trade, 1987–8 to 1990–1	217
9.8	Cattle for millet terms of trade, 1987–8 to 1990–1	218
9.9	Milk for millet terms of trade, 1987–8 to 1990–1	219
9.10	Fish for millet terms of trade, 1987–8 to 1990–1	221
9.11	Comparison of goats for millet terms of trade in good and bad years	222
9.12	Comparison of cattle for millet terms of trade in good and bad years	223
9.13	Comparison of milk for millet terms of trade in good and bad years	224
9.14	Comparison of fish for millet terms of trade in good and bad years	225
9.15	Comparison of condiment prices in good and bad years	227
9.16	Mats for millet terms of trade, 1987–8 to 1990–1	230
9.17	Comparison of mats for millet terms of trade in good and bad years	230
9.18	Comparison of number of traders in good and bad years	232
10.1	Number of hours per week spent on primary, secondary and coping/adaptive activities, by livelihood system, 1989–90	255
10.2	Cultivators: proportion of time spent on primary, secondary and coping/adaptive activities, 1989–90	255
10.3	Agro-pastoralists: proportion of time spent on primary, secondary and coping/adaptive activities, 1989–90	256
10.4	Agro-fishers: proportion of time spent on primary, secondary and coping/adaptive activities, 1989–90	256
10.5	Cultivators: seasonal allocation of time between activities, 1989–90	257

10.6	Agro-pastoralists, seasonal allocation of time between activities, 1989–90	258
10.7	Agro-fishers: seasonal allocation of time between activities, 1989–90	259
10.8	Number of hours worked per week by gender, type of activity and livelihood system, 1989–90	260
10.9	Cultivators: proportional allocation of labour by gender, 1989–90	260
10.10	Agro-pastoralists: proportional allocation of labour by gender, 1989–90	261
10.11	Agro-fishers: proportional allocation of labour by gender, 1989–90	261

List of Maps

1	Mali, showing rainfall isohyets	80
2	Mali, showing administrative Regions and the Inner Niger Delta	97
3	The Inner Niger Delta	112
4	The Inner Niger Delta and surrounding drylands	113
5	The flood and rainfall regime of the Inner Niger Delta	115

List of Tables

1.1	Typology of early warning systems	6
1.2	Principal droughts in the Sahel since 1740	8
2.1	Differences between a 'food-first' and a 'sustainable-livelihood' approach to household food security	19
2.2	Level and nature of vulnerability	30
2.3	Characteristics of resilient and sensitive livelihood systems	31
2.4	Livelihood entitlements matrix	35
2.5	Common early warning indicators within the livelihood entitlements matrix	39
2.6	Critical gaps in early warning indicators within the livelihood entitlements matrix	41
2.7	Livelihood entitlements matrix for indicators of the transition from security to vulnerability	43
3.1	The sequential use of coping strategies	47
3.2	Role of coping strategies in vulnerable and secure livelihood systems	57
5.1	Mali: summary of food production, 1960–5 to 1980–2	82
5.2	Mali: estimated population and cereal needs, 1976 and 1987	85
5.3	Stages of SAP early warning and response	100
6.1	Population of Mali's 5th Region, 1976 and 1987	110
6.2	Cycles of livelihood vulnerability in Mali's 5th Region, 1982–3 to 1990–1	125
6.3	Summary of indicators of food security in the Inner Niger Delta and Sahel, 1987–8 to 1990–1	132
7.1	Dryland cultivators: traditional seasonal activity calendar	140
7.2	Wetland cultivators: traditional seasonal activity calendar	141
7.3	Agro-pastoralists: traditional seasonal activity calendar	142
7.4	Agro-fishers: traditional seasonal activity calendar	144
7.5	Transhumant fishers: traditional seasonal activity calendar	146
7.6	Transhumant pastoralists: traditional seasonal activity calendar	147
7.7	Characteristics of secure livelihood systems	149
7.8	Dryland cultivators: present-day seasonal activity calendar	156
7.9	Wetland cultivators: present-day seasonal activity calendar	157

List of Tables

7.10	Agro-pastoralists: present-day seasonal activity calendar	159
7.11	Agro-fishers: present-day seasonal activity calendar	162
7.12	Transhumant fishers: present-day seasonal activity calendar	164
7.13	Transhumant pastoralists: present-day seasonal activity calendar	167
7.14	Characteristics of vulnerable livelihood systems	171
7.15	Barriers to re-entry in vulnerable livelihood systems	172
8.1	Sources of production entitlements by livelihood system	177
9.1	Key seasonal terms of trade in secure and vulnerable livelihood systems	199
9.2	Differences in market relationships between secure and vulnerable livelihood systems	203
9.3	Frequency with which wild foods appear on markets	228
9.4	Summary of indicators of exchange entitlements	236
10.1	Classification of coping/adaptive strategies by entitlement base and type of strategy	240
10.2	Seasonality of coping/adaptive strategies	247
10.3	The cost of acquiring paddy in good and bad years	249
10.4	Coping strategies used in a good and bad year	263
10.5	Classification of coping/adaptive strategies according to livelihood criteria	269
10.6	Grading of coping/adaptive strategies according to use	275
10.7	Examples of indicators to monitor the use of coping/adaptive strategies	277
11.1	Summary of indicators in the livelihood entitlements matrix	288
11.2	Methodology for livelihood vulnerability monitoring and entitlement enhancement	292
11.3	Indicators of the transition from security to vulnerability	295
11.4	Examples of sources of information for livelihood monitoring	303

Acknowledgements

I should like to thank the Save the Children Fund (UK) for the opportunity to participate in the early years of their experimental local food monitoring system, the *Suivi Alimentaire Delta Seno,* on which the findings in this book are based.

I am also grateful to the *Ministères de l'Administration Territoriale et du Développement à la Base* and *de la Santé* of the Government of the Republic of Mali for collaborating with the project. Research on the basis of the project's work was made possible by a grant from the Overseas Development Administration's ESCOR.

The staff of the SADS project, especially Adam Thiam, Mamadou Karambé, Abdoulaye Ag Hatalaya and Mamadou Coulibaly, made this work possible. Julius Holt's assistance was also very useful. I hope that the story told rings true to them and reflects what we found out, as well as what is still to be learned.

The SADS project owes much to its early collaboration with the International Union for the Conservation of Nature's 'Project for the Conservation of the Environment in the Inner Niger Delta', the staff of which unselfishly shared their deep understanding of the Delta with us. Particular thanks are due to Mamadou Bangaly, Arsiké Coulibaly, Amadou Touré and the late Nouhoun Baalo. Our collaborators in OXFAM are also to be thanked.

Especial thanks are due to the people of the Inner Niger Delta and surrounding drylands for their generosity in working with us and for their unfailing good humour in responding to our incessant questions.

I should like to thank members of the IDS Food Security Unit for their collegiality in helping me to develop the ideas in the study. Ana Marr, Trudy Owens and Mark Adams provided essential research assistance. Both Margaret Cornell's and Jane Kennan's editorial skills were invaluable.

Finally, I should like to thank Richard Moorehead for introducing me to the Delta and its mysteries, and for explaining so tirelessly and comprehensively how it all worked. Were it not for his eternal support I would have lost my way much more often than I did.

SUSANNA DAVIES

List of Abbreviations

CILSS	*Comité Permanent Inter-états de Lutte contre la Sécheresse dans le Sahel*
CIPEA	*Centre International pour l'Elevage en Afrique*
CNAUR	*Comité National d'Aide d'Urgence et de Réhabilitation* (formerly CNAVS)
CNAVS	*Comité National d'Aide aux Victimes de la Sécheresse*
COC	*Comité d'Orientation et de Coordination*
CPR	common property resource(s)
CRD	*Comité Régional de Développement*
DNA	*Direction Nationale de l'Agriculture*
DNSI	*Direction Nationale de la Statistique et de l'Informatique*
EC	European Community (now European Union)
ENDA	*Environnement et Développement du Tiers Monde*
EW	early warning
EWS	early warning system(s)
FAO	Food and Agriculture Organisation (of the UN)
FCFA	*Franc(s) Communauté Financière Africaine*
FEWS	Famine Early Warning System (USAID)
GIEWS	Global Information and Early Warning System (FAO)
GRM	*Gouvernement de la République du Mali*
GTZ	*(Deutsche) Gesellschaft für Technische Zusammenarbeit GmbH*
IDS	Institute of Development Studies, Sussex
IER	*Institut d'Economie Rurale*, Bamako
IFAD	International Fund for Agricultural Development
IFAN	*Institut Fondamental d'Afrique Noir*, Dakar (formerly *Institut Français d'Afrique Noir*)
IIED	International Institute for Environment and Development, London
IMF	International Monetary Fund
IRRT	*Institut Royal des Régions Tropicales*
IUCN	International Union for the Conservation of Nature and Natural Resources
MATDB	*Ministère de l'Administration Territoriale et du Développement à la Base*
MRNE	*Ministère des Ressources Naturelles et de l'Elevage*

List of Abbreviations

NFS	National Food Strategy
NGO	non-governmental organisation(s)
NORAD	Norwegian Agency for International Development
OCDE	*Organisation de Coopération et de Développement Economique*
ODEM	*Opération de Développement de l'Elevage dans la Région de Mopti*
ODI	Overseas Development Institute, London
ODR	*Opération de Développement Rurale*
OECD	Organisation for Economic Cooperation and Development
OICMA	*Organisation Internationale contre les Criquets Migratoires en Afrique*
OPM	*Opération de Développement de la Pêche dans la Région de Mopti (Opération Pêche)*
OPAM	*Office des Produits Agricoles du Mali*
ORM	*Opération de Développement du Riz dans la Région de Mopti (Opération Riz)*
PEM	protein energy malnutrition
PIA	*Projet Information Alimentaire*, SCF, Mali
PRA	participatory rural appraisal
PRMC	*Programme de Restructuration du Marché Céréalier*
RDI	Relief and Development Institute, London
RIM	Resource Inventory and Management Limited, St Helier
RRA	rapid rural appraisal
SADS	*Suivi Alimentaire Delta Seno*
SAP	*Système d'Alerte Précoce*
SCF	Save the Children Fund (UK)
SIM	*Système d'Information sur le Marché de Céréales*
SNS	*Stock National de Sécurité*
UDPM	*Union Démocratique du Peuple Malien*
UNICEF	United Nations Children's Fund
USAID	United States Agency for International Development
WFP	World Food Programme

Glossary of Foreign Terms

Fulfulde

Bella	Former slave class of the Tuareg
Benti	Milk herd during cold and dry seasons
Bourgou	*Echinochloa stagnina*
Cram-cram	*Cenchrus biflorus*
Dina	Fulani theocratic state in the nineteenth century
Dioro	Head of Fulani pasturing clan
Dounti	Milk herd which stays in village during rainy season
Fonio	*Digitaria exilis*
Garti	Bulk of a herd, including non-lactating animals, which departs on transhumance in rainy season
Guigile	*Boscia senegalensis*
Kalsireri	Local floodplain wild grain
Kolaki	Fulani season
Kossam	Milk
Leydi, Leyde	Traditional natural-resource management unit(s) or pasturing territory
Rimaïbe	Former cultivating slave class of the Fulani
Soumbala	Local seasoning made of onions and leaves
Ton	Bambara association

French

Arrondissement	(Administrative) sub-district (sub-division of *Cercle*)
Associations Villageoises	Village Associations
Campement	(Fishing, herding) camp
Cellule d'Appui au Développement à la Base	Unit to support grass-roots development

Glossary of Foreign Terms

Cercle	(Administrative) district
Chef lieu d'arrondissement	Administrative Head of Sub-district
Comité de Gestion des Donateurs du PRMC	Donor Management Committee of the Cereal Market Restructuring Programme
Comité Technique CNAUR/Donateurs	Technical Committee of the National Committee of Emergency Aid and Rehabilitation and of Donors
Commandant de Cercle	Administrative Head of District
Diagnostics Régionales	Regional Planning Documents
Directeur du Plan	Director of Planning
Direction Régionale du Plan	Regional Planning Directorate
Marmite	Patrilocal consumption and production group, usually a household (lit. a cooking pot)
Office du Niger	Irrigated rice scheme to the south-west of the Delta
Opération de Développement Rurale	Rural Development Operation
Projet d'Appui Villageois	Village Support Project
Saison morte	dead season

1 Introduction

INTRODUCTION

Poor rural people in marginal environments have a remarkable capacity to cope with food shortages. Because famines have traditionally been understood by outsiders as abnormal, time-bounded events, survivors' capacities to cope have been viewed as short-term responses. If policymakers can recognise how people cope, and reinforce this capacity, famines can be predicted and mitigated. Thereafter, it will be business as usual. In contrast, this book endorses the view that famines are part of a downward spiral of impoverishment and increasing vulnerability towards destitution and sometimes death. As a result of the two Sahelian droughts of the early 1970s and the mid-1980s, fundamental changes are taking place in livelihoods, as people adapt to confront declining food security. This book explores the nature of this process of adaptation, which can be envisaged as a transition from highly resilient and insensitive livelihood systems to vulnerable ones. It examines how these changes can be tracked over time to predict periods of unusual food stress and to indicate appropriate ways of improving household food security in sustainable ways. Understanding adaptation is the bed-rock on which successful famine prediction is based; identifying the limits to and potential of adaptation is the basis on which famines can be prevented.

The story is based on information collected by a local food monitoring system – the *Suivi Alimentaire Delta Seno* (SADS)[1] – in the Malian Sahel and in the Inner Niger Delta, a wetland in these drylands and, as such, a traditional safety net in drought years. The diversity of natural-resource availability in the Delta (and to a lesser, but significant, extent in the surrounding drylands), both between seasons and between years, is central to the adaptive strategies pursued by its poor inhabitants. The area is characterised by a great variety of livelihood systems, each of which relies on a different mix of activities to achieve food security. Equally, the process of adaptation of each system is distinct. This variation in livelihood systems is the basis on which adaptation has been analysed and changes in food security monitored.

Like a great sponge, the Delta's capacity to absorb people in search of food and livelihood security has traditionally expanded and contracted according to the year in question. But, as livelihood systems both within the Delta and in the drylands become less resilient, outsiders' reliance on the Delta in certain seasons of every year is increasing, whilst at the same time indigenous Delta inhabitants are themselves becoming ever more dependent on its key resources. These changes in how people get access to food fundamentally alter their livelihoods. To monitor changes in food security from one year to the next, these evolving livelihoods must also be tackled. Consequently, the SADS did not set out to be a conventional famine early warning system (EWS) based on standard indicators of food stress, but sought instead to develop indicators of food insecurity derived from changing livelihoods. Whereas most EWS focus on the breakdown of food systems and the failure to acquire food, SADS sought to find out *how people feed themselves*. It tried, therefore, to go slow on traditional famine EWS, focusing attention on what people do to gain a livelihood of which food security is a part, in contrast to the approach preferred by most EWS, which concentrates on what people *cannot* do. In so doing, the system aimed to fill a critical gap in food-security planning: namely, what can be done by governments, donors and non-governmental organisations (NGOs) once the drought and food aid stop, but the hunger and insecurity continue? And what can be done to help people prepare for and increase their resilience to subsequent droughts? This focus does not preclude the use of indicators for short-term prediction in crisis years, but this is not its *raison d'être*.

Information systems providing indicators of famine tend to approach the problem after the horse has bolted, and merely to define how food aid should be distributed. There is an obvious need for (and lack of information on) upstream knowledge of *anterior* events leading to disaster, in order to give the tried and tested coping strategies of local people a better chance of working. SADS was based on the assumption that, whereas free information about access to food of a sufficiently high quality is not readily available to decision-makers, it can be reasonably and cost-effectively collected by well-trained local field researchers who tap indigenous sources of information. It challenged the much-vaunted argument that detailed local information, whilst theoretically useful to national-level planners, is in fact too difficult, costly and time-consuming to collect and sensibly interpret, or to exploit in food-security planning and famine mitigation.

OBJECTIVES

This book tells the story of an experiment to find out how people feed themselves in marginal areas, and shows how this approach can be made relevant to decision-makers. Its objectives are as follows:

Introduction 3

- to develop a livelihood entitlements framework for analysing the ways in which people achieve food security, and for monitoring changes in the intensity of food insecurity (Chapter 2);
- to re-examine the recent burst of interest in the coping strategies of chronically food-insecure rural producers, in order to determine the implications of coping for monitoring food and livelihood security (Chapter 3);
- to describe the SADS monitoring system and, in so doing, to examine the logic and feasibility of turning conventional EWS on their head, by monitoring adaptation rather than the collapse of food availability and/or entitlements alone (Chapter 4);
- to examine the development of EWS within national-level food-security policy and planning in Mali in the 1980s and the constraints it has encountered in tracking the livelihoods of rural populations and in triggering timely response (Chapter 5);
- to analyse data collected by the monitoring system, in order to: (a) define the livelihood systems practised by different producers; (b) determine how these have become more vulnerable in successive years of drought, by analysing changes in the mixes of entitlements bundles; (c) distinguish between permanent adaptation and the residual seasonal coping strategies available to rural producers and hence their security or vulnerability to shocks and trends leading to food insecurity; (d) identify a set of indicators which can be used to track livelihood vulnerability and identify appropriate interventions to promote household food security, which build on indigenous adaptive practices (Chapters 6 to 10);
- to explore how the approach and the data it gives rise to can be used by planners, and the policy implications for national and sub-national food-security planning as an alternative to conventional top-down famine EWS and food aid-based response (Chapter 11).

Approaching vulnerability to food insecurity from the perspective of livelihood adaptation necessitated a monitoring system which was experimental in its approach. In its initial phases, the SADS sought to answer a number of strategic questions. Are livelihood systems the single most important determinants of food security for poor rural producers? How did people achieve food security in the past in different livelihood systems and what changes have occurred since the droughts of the early 1970s and mid-1980s to prevent them from doing so now? What strategies are used to confront these changing conditions and do they amount to fundamental changes in livelihoods, rather than short-term coping? What kinds of indicators are best suited to predict worsening food insecurity under such conditions, and to indicate appropriate responses?

Very little was known about how livelihood systems operated in the area in the post-drought period: early warning (EW) attention had focused almost exclusively on system failure – not system adaptation – up to this point. Information was required on a far broader range of issues than is conventionally the case for EWS, before a relevant set of indicators could be developed. This included: how the mix of producers' activities has changed since the droughts for each livelihood system in the area; what determines vulnerability to food insecurity between and within livelihood systems; how effective the strategies pursued by producers to cope with increasing food insecurity are, and whether these are used only in bad years; and how the role of the market has changed in the acquisition of food security in the post-drought period. The working hypotheses on which the SADS system was based, and which this book explores in analysing its results, are as follows:

- Local livelihood systems have become less resilient and more sensitive (more vulnerable) to food stress with successive periods of drought, and the nature and intensity of vulnerability vary according to the livelihood system in question.
- Insecurity of and fluctuations in food availability and access are principally determined by the primary and secondary activities of producers and the particular mix of livelihood entitlements derived from them. Differences in food security within communities need to be tracked according to different livelihood systems.
- The ability to cope – or take up tertiary activities – is endemic to Sahelian livelihood systems. The coping strategies of producers must also be tracked to monitor changes in levels, and the intensity, of food insecurity.
- A distinction must be made between *coping* strategies as short-term, temporary responses to declining food entitlements, and *adaptive* strategies which are long-term permanent changes in the mix of activities, necessary to reduce the vulnerability of livelihood systems to collapse.
- Although structural individual or household vulnerability (e.g. being a female-headed household) contributes to food insecurity, it is not the optimum focus for monitoring *changes* in vulnerability from one season or year to another. To monitor such changes, the focus must be proximate livelihood-system vulnerability.
- By developing a set of indicators capable of monitoring both proximate livelihood-system vulnerability and the ability to cope and adapt, not only can the collapse of food security be predicted for particular

productive groups, but also means of reinforcing livelihoods to make them sustainably less food-insecure can be identified.

CHALLENGING CONVENTIONAL FAMINE EARLY WARNING

Most famine EWS are concerned with the failure of food systems; more precisely, with predicting such failure, in order to intervene in a timely manner to mitigate the effects of system failure on immediate consumption. The thrust of the development of EWS since the mid-1970s has been towards standardisation of methodological approaches (if not of the methodologies themselves), implicit in which is the assumption that there are certain key truths about food systems which are vulnerable to failure, defined as their inability to guarantee adequate consumption for participants. Concern focuses on the food system itself, rather than on the food-insecure people who strive to subsist within it, and the system is limited to food, not wider livelihood considerations. Broadly speaking, such truths do exist, and for resource-poor and information-poor countries setting up EWS, minimalist approaches are seductive. By monitoring a handful of key indicators of pending system failure (typically staple food production, national stocks, import availability), a rough and ready national balance can be calculated using population estimates and *per capita* needs (FAO, 1990: Annex 9). Many EWS have evolved beyond this to monitor upstream input determinants of production (e.g. rainfall) and downstream outcome indicators of the effects of the national (im)balance on sub-national supply and demand (e.g. market prices for food, nutritional status of under-fives). But the focus remains food-systemic and collapse-driven.

This model of EWS can be characterised as top-down, famine-oriented, concerned with production rather than access to food as the key determinant of food security; operating at the macro-level in a highly centralised manner; focusing on geographic entities as the units of analysis; being data- not people-centred; and geared towards food aid responses to unusual system failure which threatens famine (Davies *et al.*, 1991). It has been modified to a greater or lesser degree in many countries in the Sahel and Horn of Africa, but most EWS in these regions retain a conventional *famine* EW approach.[2]

Although, theoretically, conventional EWS – and the predictions derived from them – are based on knowledge of the food systems in question, all too often they are managed by technicians with little knowledge of those systems, or of the people who depend on them. This is not necessarily a problem particularly if, as is the case with many EWS, the objective is to determine quantities of food aid required at national level, solely in crisis years. Targeting, in such situations, tends to be a fairly crude exercise using blunt instruments, often carried out on the basis of broad administrative boundaries, irrespective of socio-economic or agro-ecological variations within such areas, not requiring detailed knowledge of who is hungry, when, where or why.

At a conceptual level, however, EWS are increasingly concerned with distributional aspects of food insecurity, now coming under the rubric of 'vulnerability mapping' (see Borton and Shoham, 1991). In practice, most EWS cannot identify vulnerable groups within food-insecure areas with any precision. This book tells the story of an EWS or, more accurately, food monitoring system which sought to answer the who, when, where and why questions. It started not with questions about where food aid was most needed and when, or with predetermined methodologies and indicators to detect collapse of the food system, but sought instead to focus on the success of people within the system and what factors were compromising that success. The ways in which such a system differs from the conventional model described above, is summarised in Table 1.1. Although this table presents extremes at either end of the spectrum of EWS, most fall closer to the conventional model, whereas the SADS comprises all the characteristics of the alternative food information system model.

Table 1.1 Typology of early warning systems

	Conventional famine early warning system	*Alternative food information system*
Scope	Famine-oriented	Food security-oriented
Determinants of food security	Food production	Access to food
Level of operation	Macro-centralised	Micro-decentralised
Unit of analysis	Geographic e.g. nation/districts	Socio-economic e.g. vulnerable groups
Approach	Top-down Data-centred	Bottom-up People-centred
Response	Food aid-oriented	Sustainable improvement in access to food

Source: Davies *et al.* (1991).

Introduction 7

Conventional EWS are typically preoccupied with standardisation of methods and data; with short time-frames (a maximum of a year); with symmetry, between supply and demand, deficits and food aid; and with the data they have, rather than with what they do not know, however pertinent the gaps in their knowledge may be. In contrast, the food monitoring system in this study used a deductive and process approach, based on the demands of the livelihoods being monitored. Key characteristics of the system are:

- a concern with what *people do* rather than with how food systems influence abstract notions of production, exchange and consumption;
- medium- to *longer-term* time-frames, with attention paid to how livelihood systems change over time as people adapt to changing socio-economic and climatic conditions;
- an emphasis on *diversity* not standardisation, between livelihood systems, seasons and years;
- *flexibility*, both in the monitoring methods and in interpretation of data;
- *mobility*, between livelihood systems and geographically.

In order to incorporate these characteristics into the monitoring system, a number of conventional EW assumptions and approaches which were found to be inappropriate to the Malian case (and indeed more generally) were questioned. The methods used to collect information were also very different from standard EW monitoring, discussed in Chapter 4. Conventional approaches to EW were challenged in the Malian Sahel, given: the nature of food insecurity in the region; the location and scope of the system; the demands of monitoring food insecurity in an area undergoing a transition from secure livelihood systems to vulnerable ones; responsibility for the system; and finally, use of the information produced for response. These issues are discussed in turn.

FAMINE AND FOOD INSECURITY

The Malian Sahel and the Inner Niger Delta in its midst are characterised not by frequent periods of acute food shortage leading to famine, but rather by chronic seasonal food insecurity in most years, which can sometimes degenerate into acute shortages for some groups. Famine, although by no means absent, is not a common occurrence in the Sahel, as Table 1.2 shows. In this sense, the study area is far more typical of much of the Sahelian zone than those parts of the Horn of Africa which have

Table 1.2 Principal droughts in the Sahel since 1740

1740	Drought, famine
1750	Drought, famine
1790	Drought
1855	Drought
1900–3	Drought
1911–14	Drought, famine
1931–4	Drought, famine
1942	Drought
1950	Drought
1968–73	Drought, famine
1983–5	Drought, famine
1987	Drought
1990	Drought

Source: Adapted from ENDA (1985), cited in Moorehead (1991).

suffered repeated episodes of famine in recent years, due to political – as much as agro-ecological and economic – factors. Periods of drought have been more frequent since the late 1960s, although there is little consensus as to the origin of these changes (IUCN, 1989b) or as to whether it is a permanent trend.

As with much of the Sahel and Horn of Africa, the Inner Niger Delta and surrounding drylands is an area which habitually guaranteed secure livelihoods for its population, but which has become increasingly incapable of doing so in the last twenty years, due not only to periods of drought (in 1968–73, 1983–5, 1987 and again in 1990) and the inability to recover from its effects, but also to rural impoverishment, both of the economy and the natural-resource base upon which people depend for their livelihoods. Nowadays, people are not simply suffering from periods of food insecurity, but from livelihood insecurity, as the basis of their subsistence is progressively eroded.

Whereas some of the natural contributory elements to this impoverishment cannot be changed (e.g. rainfall cannot be increased), much of it is due to factors which can be controlled or mitigated, implying that the inability of people to achieve food security is not an irreversible trend, if their attempts to adapt are supported. By focusing on how people feed themselves, or on the potential for security which can be derived from the livelihood systems in the area, the policy implications of the monitoring system are very different from one which seeks simply to treat the outcomes of system failure in a short-term, curative manner.

Finally, the area in question is one which, until the 1990s, had not been subjected to armed conflict, increasingly recognised as a major contributory factor to both famine and chronic food insecurity in Africa (Duffield, 1990b). Again, this distinguishes it from the more headline-gripping countries in the Horn of Africa where famine has repeatedly struck since the 1980s, invariably hand in hand with prolonged conflict, but not from much of the rest of the Sahelian belt, although in Mali and elsewhere, such conflict is increasingly prevalent in the 1990s. In conditions of conflict, systematic EW monitoring becomes difficult, if not impossible. The biggest drawback is data collection which often needs to be reduced to a bare minimum (Hall, 1991), whilst at the same time the range of issues about which information is required grows (e.g. military and political intelligence). Moreover, in the case of civil war, EW information carries an even higher political premium than usual. The system under discussion here presupposes the absence of armed conflict, although the framework of analysis and indicators developed are not necessarily irrelevant to highly unstable political situations.

LOCATION AND SCOPE

SADS is a local-level system, initially designed to complement rather than replace the national EWS. It covers four districts (*cercles*) in the 5th Region of Mali, as well as the regional capital of Mopti. About 750 000 people, who either live in the area (c.500 000) or who migrate into it seasonally, are monitored by the system. This represents about 10 per cent of the population of Mali, and about 38 per cent of those most prone to food insecurity (Chapter 6).

Typically, EWS are concerned with administratively defined areas which are seen to be most vulnerable to drought. Rarely are they based there, and the focus of their analysis is to identify such *areas* and recommendations for action seek to target them. In the case of SADS, monitoring is based not in those most drought-prone areas which marginal producers typically leave once the rains fail, but rather in the traditional agro-ecological safety net of the Inner Niger Delta, to which *people* migrate early on in the cycle of a failed harvest. This should not be confused with migration to urban areas or emergency feeding centres, which tends to be a last-ditch attempt to survive, and as such a late indicator of food stress. Data analysis also focuses on *people* who are most vulnerable, irrespective of where they are at a given moment in the agricultural or pastoral cycle. This is particularly important, given that mobility increases with food stress and effective interventions need to promote this strategy, necessary for the maximum exploitation of seasonally-specific resources.

A further reason for concentrating monitoring activities in the traditional safety net was to maximise efficiency of data collection about extremely sparsely distributed populations. By focusing on four key listening posts, the system is able to cover not only residents, but also seasonal migrants from the northern Regions of Tombouctou (6th) and Gao (7th), as well as the drier parts of the Mopti (5th) Region. These migrants increase in number in bad years, and the timings of their arrivals and departures change, but the pattern of migration does not fundamentally alter. By monitoring where people move to, rather than areas they leave, a far better idea can be ascertained of who is vulnerable and what their food entitlements are. The notion of traditional safety nets as appropriate listening posts to monitor widely dispersed but highly mobile populations is not restricted to this part of Mali. Right across Sahelian Africa there are safety nets fulfilling similar functions.

DEFINING NORMALITY, MONITORING CHANGE

As with many drought-prone parts of the Sahel, little good baseline information existed for Mali's 5th Region. Reliable collection of data on conventional indicators is difficult using standard survey techniques: local variations are complex and extreme; access to key areas is difficult for much of the year; infrastructure is weak and local bureaucracies are often unable to provide even rudimentary information. Even when conventional indicators can be reliably monitored, their sensible interpretation is impossible without a fairly detailed understanding of the area in question. Existing approaches to interpretation of food monitoring indicators have not been found relevant to the Malian case, for two reasons. First, such an approach assumes some knowledge of what happens in a normal year and this is very little understood in Mali, exacerbated by the fact that such fundamental changes have occurred in the recent cycles of drought that 'normality' needs to be redefined on a regular basis. Second, the extreme mobility of the population (habitually during certain seasons, and most intensively and perhaps unusually in dry years), necessitates a monitoring system that is as mobile as the people themselves. This is much more complex than following arrivals and departures of migrants into urban areas. People move between livelihood systems, as well as to different places, and this often constitutes the key to their survival (or destitution if the strategy fails) in a bad year.

Four sets of concepts underlie the approach used to define normality and monitor change: livelihood systems and diversity between them;

Introduction 11

sources of and calls on entitlements; security and vulnerability; and coping and adaptation. Taken together, they can be used to construct a framework for analysing how people feed themselves. This framework is developed in Chapters 2 and 3.

RESPONSIBILITY AND UTILITY

The monitoring project was principally concerned with development interventions, not emergency relief. This is due in part to criticism of NGOs which were primarily responsible for executing relief operations during the 1984–5 famines, that they should be more involved in prevention than relief. It is also consistent with the development activities of the NGOs concerned and increasing recognition of the need to link relief and development activities. Many NGOs have become unwitting 'experts' in the logistics of emergency food aid distribution which, while undoubtedly fulfilling an important and justifiable role, can make them little more than the foot soldiers of governments and donors, wedded (by accident or design) to supporting emergency relief at the expense of sustainable improvements in the food security of the poor.

The SADS system operates outside government structures and its utility has been frequently questioned. Yet, it began from a different premise from government-run EWS (invariably) financed by donors. The motivation was to inform decisions about project identification and developmental interventions to reduce vulnerability to famine, not simply to predict famine so as to trigger emergency responses. As such, the information system has none of the constraints of needing to plan import requirements or make requests to donors, or of wider national resource allocation issues. NGO-operated EWS are criticised for creating parallel structures and their relative freedom of operation can, at worst, make their information systems irrelevant to government planning and decision-making. Alternatively, this independence can create the conditions under which innovation occurs. Whereas government EWS are inevitably driven by the priorities of famine prediction and crisis management, not to mention the concerns of donors, NGO systems have freedom to manoeuvre beyond this famine orientation towards a multi-purpose information system, useful for annual and longer-term planning, yet capable of predicting famine in crisis years. Their apparent irrelevance can, therefore, be turned around: they can be essential if they are experimental systems, and succeed in demonstrating the utility of the information they generate in a range of planning exercises. Their methodologies can then be incorporated into government food-security planning capacities.

This is an important issue, given the increasing doubt surrounding the capacity of conventional EWS to *prevent* famine, despite their recent progress in *predicting* it (Davies *et al.*, 1991). One explanation for the inability to translate prediction into prevention is that the information provided by conventional EWS cannot be used by decision-makers in preventive exercises, but only to justify emergency relief retrospectively (Buchanan-Smith *et al.*, 1994). Indicators which solely predict system *failure* appear to be ill-suited to identifying ways of sustaining system *success*. Those responsible for EWS within government are caught in the trap of trying to use information for prevention which is inappropriate for this purpose. Responsibility for the failure to prevent famine is frequently placed at the door of the EWS, and of governments which fail to use the information it provides, whereas the real problem may be that the nature of the information collected feeds the conditions under which crises develop.

On an institutional level, Mali has a more conventional national-level EWS – the Système d'Alerte Précoce (SAP) – whose brief is to monitor for food aid requirements. In contrast to critics of the proliferation of EWS in the Sahel and Horn of Africa in the 1980s, it is argued here that both systems can be complementary rather than conflicting or duplicating. Most countries in the Sahel and Horn of Africa now have national EWS, but examples of local-level monitoring systems are rare, with the result that there is little systematic data collection in famine-prone areas of the type outlined here.[3] Structuring data collection to meet emergency needs means that countries desperately in need of long-term food-security planning are, in fact, led towards short-term crisis-driven and food aid-based solutions by the very systems set up to improve the data available to planners trying to prevent emergencies. Ultimately, top-down and bottom-up systems need to be integrated into a single information system, but local systems need to be tested and found useful in the planning process before they will be given priority by governments and donors. In order to identify who is hungry, when and where, it is necessary to find out what people do to help themselves to overcome chronic and transitory food shortages. This, in turn, makes it possible to identify ways to reinforce existing coping strategies to help people to help themselves. Whereas food aid invariably assists producers only when they have lost the means to feed themselves, this approach seeks to protect and reinforce these production strategies *before* they collapse, thereby protecting livelihood security rather than curing transitory insecurity.

Introduction

At the end of its first phase, SADS produced a series of recommendations for action based on the results of the information system, designed to improve the food security of particular groups by supporting indigenous responses to food stress and reducing some of the constraints encountered in coping (SADS, 1989). These were classified according to livelihood system and addressed specific food-security problems encountered in the first years of monitoring. The proposed interventions sought to reinforce household food security on the basis of indigenous adaptive strategies, to see what could be done before it is too late. The system not only identifies interventions but also, crucially, has the potential to monitor their impact on local food security, as well as fulfilling its predictive function. Since 1991, a new arm of activities has been initiated – the *Projet d'Appui Villageois* – which consists of small-scale village interventions to promote food security (SADS, 1992). Although at an embryonic stage, this is the next step in the process of developing an integrated system of monitoring, response and impact assessment. The links between generating information and using it to inform planning and decision-making and to assess impact require further work. But, unlike system failure-driven EWS, one which focuses on system success does have the potential to be useful in a far wider range of planning tasks. This orientation of the monitoring system makes SADS particularly relevant to NGOs and other donor agencies operational in the field, because it suggests more permanent means of intervening to raise people's food entitlements than emergency food aid distributions.

CONCLUSIONS

To what extent are these challenges to conventional approaches to famine EW justified? What are the methodological implications and data needs, and is it possible to develop an operationally feasible and sustainable monitoring system which provides such information? Can the information be reliable and accurate, and can it be sensibly interpreted? Does the system produce a set of indicators which can really show how people feed themselves and predict when they are no longer able to do so? What does the information indicate about how Sahelians gain access to food, how they cope and how they adapt? What does it suggest in the way of response options and can it be used by planners and policy-makers? These are the questions which this book addresses, based on the results of the monitoring system from 1987 to 1990, the first four years of its operation. The experiment had mixed success. After the first two years, it was clear that, whereas a preliminary research exercise to understand changes in post-drought livelihood systems was essential to define the parameters within which any subsequent monitoring could occur, there remained a number of factors central to household food security which could not be tracked over time by a small-scale system. Furthermore, the use to which information of this nature is put – both by the NGOs collecting it and by government and other donors – encountered a number of problems, not least because the information did not provide a handful of key indicators which implied the need for standard food aid-based responses to food stress. These two key issues of feasibility and use of information are addressed in the conclusions of the book. But there are important lessons to be learned from the experiment, and the methodology developed and results obtained. Although based on one part of Mali, the results of the SADS experiment have implications for famine EW, food and livelihood-security monitoring methods and food-security planning throughout the Sahel and Horn of Africa.

2 Security and Vulnerability in Livelihood Systems

INTRODUCTION

This chapter sets out the conceptual framework for the analysis of the data presented in this book. Five concepts are used in its construction:

1. *livelihood systems and security* within them, encompassing a broader range of factors than household food systems and security to explain how and why producers pursue particular mixes of strategies to confront food insecurity;
2. *entitlements* to explain different sources of food and the range of calls on them within households and livelihood systems;
3. *vulnerability* to explain the nature and intensity of food and livelihood insecurity;
4. *resilience and sensitivity*, useful in analysing changes in levels and intensity of vulnerability to food insecurity within different Sahelian livelihood systems;
5. *livelihood-system diversity* to account for variation in the nature and intensity of vulnerability, depending on the different ways in which people acquire access to food.

FOOD SECURITY

Food security is generally defined as 'access to enough food at all times for an active, healthy life' (World Bank, 1986: 1). This working definition has been modified to emphasise different aspects of having enough to eat: thirty-two such variations have been identified by Maxwell and Smith (1992: 68–70). Differing units of analysis (the nation state, the household or individual) reflect a paradigm shift in the 1980s away from preoccupation with national food security towards household food security, which is primarily concerned with how available food is distributed between groups within the population, and secondarily with filling aggregate shortfalls in supply, in order to improve the access to food of vulnerable groups. The idea of food security has thus moved from a uni-dimensional concept to a multi-faceted one, which ideally should be people-driven and encompass elements of livelihood rather than just food security (*ibid*). The advantage of a multi-dimensional approach is that it is a far closer reflection of how people fail to feed themselves than previous models. The drawback is its complexity, not least in respect of information needs.

If *household* food security becomes the focus of food policy in general and of famine EW in particular, the volume and complexity of information required tends to increase exponentially. Most obviously, this arises from the need to understand whether people can get access to the food which is available, typically monitored for in EWS using food price data. The second additional requirement is to distinguish between those who succeed in getting access to enough food under prevailing conditions and those who do not (the identification of vulnerable groups). A third dimension is to see why some of those who appear to be vulnerable in fact manage to survive periods of famine (how they cope).

These superficially simple issues mask huge information needs, which have been confronted in a number of ways. First, although rarely admitted to, the quest for a single right indicator which will track the complexity of household food security is the Mantra underlying much methodological development. The reasons for this are not hard to discern. Cumbersome information systems rarely deliver what policy-makers require and can rapidly become costly and unsustainable. A tension thus exists between what is operationally feasible and useful and what the conceptual understanding of household food security indicates is required.

Second, an ahistorical approach is generally adopted. The dimension of time in household food security is typically limited to the World Bank's (1986) distinction between chronic insecurity (a household continually at risk of an inability to meet its food needs) and transitory insecurity (a temporary decline of short – but perhaps intense – duration). In practice, the two are intimately linked, especially because chronically food-insecure households will usually be most vulnerable to those shocks which create transitory insecurity. But whereas time is central to definitions of household food security – and predicting future insecurity is the *raison d'être* of EWS – both are concerned only with current and future states. The past is covered only in so far as (recent) baselines exist against which current indicators can be measured. If the objective is to improve future security, does this matter? Yes, it does matter because the reasons for the failure of households to achieve food security are rooted in the ways their livelihood systems have evolved over time and how they have responded to these changes. Under the current ahistorical regime, policy implications are forced to tackle system failure, not the reinforcement of system success, and must do so without knowing why the current system no longer delivers household security.

Critics will argue that this is not the case, and that the causality of declining household food security is well-documented at a sectoral and aggregate level: national indices show that *per capita* food production is falling in much of the Sahel, due to declining productivity of land, population growth and successive periods of drought, all exacerbated by inappropriate state policies. What does this mean for different types of households? The logic of the paradigm shift towards household food security suggests that just as outcomes of system changes must be tackled at household level, so must their causes, and critically, the household responses to them. The causality of household food insecurity is conventionally divided between short-term shocks (which may be general, e.g. drought, or specific, e.g. illness) and long-term trends (e.g. declining production). Most EWS are understandably concerned with general short-term shocks which will shift household insecurity from a chronic to a transitory state, likely to be widespread and intense if a background of chronic insecurity exists, as in much of the Sahel. Little attention is paid to the details of how long-term trends affect the impact of shocks on household security, or how household responses make their capacity to withstand shocks more or less effective. For example, one of the consequences of a declining trend in *per capita* food production is to make households more market-dependent, with a shock leading to sharp rises in food prices rendering them more vulnerable than before. But what if they have adapted to increased market dependence by diversifying sources of off-farm income, including activities which provide income that is resilient to food price inflation? In this case, the impact of the shock would be less than for habitually non-market-dependent households which were ill-equipped to cope with only a transitory drop in household production leading to temporary reliance on the market.

It is precisely these kinds of causal links which explain the nature and intensity of present and future vulnerability. Yet they are rarely incorporated into indicator development for EW and food-security monitoring purposes. Leaving their consideration to a level of abstract generality makes the likelihood of finding out how people feed themselves and how they can be assisted to do so in the future remote. It is not surprising that the policy options for EWS are short-term palliatives which answer immediate consumption requirements. How can this need to understand the anterior events leading to food insecurity and famine be addressed? The answer lies in understanding not simply how household food security has changed, but how livelihoods have adapted to meet changing conditions.

LIVELIHOOD SECURITY[1]

The premise of a livelihood-security approach is that food security is a sub-system of needs, neither independent of nor necessarily more important than other aspects of subsistence and survival within poor households. Contrary to the often-cited 'hierarchy of basic needs'[2] in which food needs must be satisfied in preference to all others, food-insecure households in fact juggle between a range of requirements, including immediate consumption and future capacity to produce. Thus the food-security strategies of the poor need to be understood in the context of their complex and dynamic livelihood strategies, and, in the process, the presumed preeminence of food security must be re-evaluated.

A starting point for discussing the differences between a food-security and a livelihood-security approach is Chambers's (1988: 1)[3] definition of sustainable livelihood securities:

> Livelihood is defined as adequate stocks and flows of food and cash to meet basic needs. Security refers to secure ownership of, or access to, resource and income-earning activities, including reserves and assets to offset risk, ease shocks and meet contingencies. Sustainable refers to the maintenance or enhancement of resource productivity on a long-term basis.

In this framework, the achievement of food security is but one sub-set of objectives and the need for food one of a range of variables which determine why the poor take decisions and spread risk, and how they balance competing interests in order to subsist both in the short and longer term. Frankenberger and Goldstein (1990: 22) have thus argued that 'the dilemma facing small-farm households ... involves a trade-off between immediate subsistence and long-term sustainability'. But, as yet, there is little evidence to show how this trade-off has been made in the past or how it will function in the future. Central to this balancing act is the use of coping and adaptive strategies (Chapter 3).

Table 2.1 summarises the differences between the two approaches. Most *conceptual* work on household food security is moving in the direction of a wider livelihood view. However, on a *practical* level and especially at the level of policy implementation, the shift from national to household food security is still under way. The change from a food-first to a livelihood approach remains largely on the drawing board. In so far as EWS are concerned, movement away from aggregate indicators is still in its infancy and, indeed, argued against by critics who favour minimalist

Table 2.1 Differences between a 'food-first' and a 'sustainable-livelihood' approach to household food security

	Food-first approach	Sustainable-livelihood approach
Objective	Access to food	Secure and sustainable livelihood
Point of departure	Failure to subsist	Success in feeding, living
Priorities	Food at the top of a hierarchy of needs	Food one part of a jigsaw of livelihood needs
Time preferences	Food needs met before and in preference to all others	Food needs met to the extent possible given immediate and future livelihood needs
Entitlements	Narrow entitlement base (current and past consumption; household defined)	Broad entitlement base (includes future claims, access to common property resources (CPRs), etc.); defined at household and community level
Vulnerability	Lack or want of food	Defencelessness, insecurity, exposure to risk, shocks and stress
Security	Opposite of vulnerability is enough food, irrespective of the terms or conditions on which it is acquired	Opposite of vulnerability is security
Vulnerable groups	Based on social, medical criteria	Also based on economic and cultural criteria
Coping strategies	Designed to maximise immediate consumption	Designed to preserve livelihoods
Measuring and monitoring	Present and past consumption	Livelihood security and sustainability
Relationship between food security and natural-resource base	Degrade environment to meet immediate food needs	Preserve environment to secure future

EWS which seek exclusively to inform about food aid and commercial import requirements.

20   *Adaptable Livelihoods*

In contrast, the SADS system embraced the broad livelihood-security approach and monitored household security as a sub-system. It did not cover *all* aspects of livelihood security, but nevertheless encompassed much more than a narrow food-first approach. In so doing, many of the operational pitfalls of a livelihood-security approach were stumbled upon, as subsequent chapters will show. The premise of a livelihood-security approach remains valid, however, if household responses to changing chronic and transitory insecurity are to be understood. Indicators to monitor these changes must be derived from a spectrum of entitlements which cover both food and other livelihood needs. It is to these that we now turn.

ENTITLEMENTS

Entitlement to food is gained via a combination of production, exchange (of cash, goods, services), sale of labour, transfers and assets (including investments, stores and claims). Entitlements derived from coping and adaptive strategies are a sub-set. Although their sources may be production-, exchange- or asset-based, it is useful to distinguish them from primary sources of entitlement, if the exploitation of coping and adaptation-derived entitlements is used as an indicator of food stress (Chapter 3).

Monitoring cereal production is the basis of most EW indicators and few have the capacity to monitor other food entitlements, despite widespread acceptance of Sen's (1981) thesis that famines are caused not only, nor indeed primarily, by food availability decline, but rather by food entitlement decline. EWS tend to focus on production entitlements because, in subsistence rural economies, they remain the cornerstone of inter-annual variations in food entitlement as well as availability. Production is the variable which fluctuates most in national food balance sheets and is relatively easy to measure (although aggregate national estimates can mask huge errors). Furthermore, if crop forecast techniques are used (e.g. rainfall levels correlated with expected output), food production can provide a potentially *early* indicator of food stress.

The development of indicators to monitor other entitlements, whilst given a great deal of attention in the literature[4] and accepted as a crucial complement to production data, has been pursued with much less vigour on the ground. Market prices are the most frequent indicator of exchange entitlements, used to monitor not only food prices, but also terms of trade between goods that the food-insecure may be selling (e.g. livestock) to buy food. Such data are comparatively easy to collect, at least on major

Security and Vulnerability in Livelihood Systems

markets, and are attractive because they are quantifiable and objective. Monitoring migratory movements, particularly from rural to urban areas, and the demand for and price of labour in recipient zones is an indicator of coping strategy-based entitlements used by some EWS. Yet this has justifiably been criticised as a late indicator (migration in towns often being a last resort) and finer monitoring of migration – within rural areas – is held to be too difficult for a national EWS.

Further forays into monitoring entitlements tend to meet with opposition, on the grounds of time, cost and representativity. The particular bundles of entitlements which determine the food availability of vulnerable groups can be highly location- and livelihood system-specific. Drawing generalisations from, say, evidence of inter-household transfers or unusual sales of assets can be a dangerous business. Such data tend to be qualitative and hence less credible than 'hard' quantitative data about prices or production, and are difficult to interpret, let alone translate into policy options. As a result, although entitlements are held to be at the core of much EW rationale, in practice their inclusion into EWS tends to be marginal and incomplete.

The premise of the SADS system, whilst recognising these constraints, was that entitlement bundles *could* be relatively easily mapped out for particular groups, by enlisting their participation in the process. By drawing up, for example, seasonal calendars of activities and sources of food, a baseline of entitlements can be developed, deviations from which can, in turn, be followed. This process, although by no means problem-free, placed entitlement rather than food availability alone squarely at the centre of the information system – essential for a genuinely early response to protect livelihoods or, indeed, for longer-term planning to increase resilience to food insecurity by non-emergency interventions. If these are the aims of policy, there is no way around the difficulties inherent in developing indicators to monitor entitlements. Unless information about them is available, sensible planning will be impossible. On this basis, a livelihood entitlements matrix has been developed to show the range of possible relationships for which indicators could be developed to monitor household food security as a sub-system of livelihood security. But, before turning to this, the concept of vulnerability needs to be considered.

VULNERABILITY

Recurring vulnerability, defined as 'not lack or want, but defencelessness, insecurity, and exposure to risks, shocks and stress' (Chambers, 1989: 1), as distinct from poverty, has become an increasingly important consideration in rural development in recent years. Security is the opposite of vulnerability: food vulnerability is thus synonymous with food insecurity. National EWS, whilst recognising the need to differentiate between populations within a given geographical area, rarely have the capacity to monitor the food situation at such a level of disaggregation. In contrast, identifying those groups which are particularly food-insecure is a feature of most sub-national EWS. Adopting a livelihood-security approach to monitoring how people feed themselves has direct implications for how these vulnerable groups are defined (according to which criteria) and how changes in vulnerability are tracked (based on which entitlements).

Farming systems research places production system-based classification, which Maxwell (1986: 66) describes as 'the identification of homogenous groups of farmers with similar natural and socio-economic characteristics', high on its list of priorities, and indeed as an essential prerequisite for subsequent phases of systematic research.[5] EWS, in contrast, have been rather lax in differentiating between groups of rural producers according to what they do, preferring instead to classify vulnerability according to their level of need, or what they do not do (the landless, the unemployed). Recent developments in vulnerability mapping have sought to redress this. Downing (1990: 9), reviewing the utility of vulnerability in the context of famine EW monitoring, has argued that: 'Vulnerability typically refers to underlying processes and causes of hunger, rather than the consequences of immediate events.' He distinguishes between indicators for measuring vulnerability ('an underlying condition, distinguished from the current events that may trigger a famine') and those for monitoring famine risk. Similarly, Cannon (1991: 3) distinguishes between vulnerability (a predisposition to famine before the impact of any trigger event) and the ultimate causes of famine. This division contrasts with Chambers's (1989: 1) idea of vulnerability as having two sides:

> an external side of risks, shocks, and stress to which an individual or household is subject; and an internal side which is defencelessness, meaning a lack of means to cope without damaging loss.

Chambers thus encapsulates both the *process* and the *state of being* within the term vulnerability. Keeping the two sides together supports the livelihood-security approach that immediate shocks are coped with in the context of past adaptations and future needs and priorities.

In EWS, however, the concept of vulnerability is generally limited to describing underlying factors. Thus, food-insecure vulnerable groups are typically defined according to structural criteria which do not change much from one year to the next. Most either describe an individual's physical characteristics (e.g. children under five, the old and the infirm) or a type of household (e.g. female-headed, with high dependency ratios). Such vulnerability can be termed *differential* (Swift, 1989a), and describes a potential for being at risk. Yet, if famines are to be predicted, those at risk of destitution and death by starvation cannot be identified solely on the basis of generalised categories of structural differential vulnerability, that is characteristics which are *independent of the productive capacity of their livelihoods in a given season or year*. When proximate causes of famine are added to these structurally differentially vulnerable groups, it is assumed that they will be the most at risk. But this two-step approach jumps from social and physical characteristics of vulnerability to production and exchange entitlement-based vulnerability, without making the connection between the two explicit.

This link is explicit in a second, much less used, set of criteria which relate to *structural livelihood-system vulnerability*, encompassing not simply productive elements but the range of entitlements derived from a given livelihood system. Thus, the landless, those displaced by natural disasters, famine or war, recent migrants to urban areas and the unemployed also figure on lists of those habitually vulnerable to food insecurity. Most of these describe negative states: the lack of a productive base. Pastoralists are one of the few productive groups habitually defined as vulnerable to food insecurity on the basis of their productive capacity (what they have), rather than their productive incapacity (what they lack). Yet, despite the recognition that pastoralists are not always vulnerable – indeed, when agro-climatic conditions are favourable, they can be amongst the most secure Sahelian producers of all – their vulnerability is invariably described in a structural sense, independently of the year in question.

In order to interpret changes in the livelihood-security status of particular vulnerable groups, a clear idea is needed of the nature of their bundle of entitlements rather than simply of their structural vulnerability, and crucially, *how these change from one year to the next*. Thus a further dimension to the concept of vulnerability is required: *proximate vulnerability*, i.e. that which changes from one year to the next, as opposed to the more or less permanent state of structural vulnerability. Proximate vulnerability, unlike proximate causes of famine, describes people, not events, reflecting the idea of vulnerability having an internal and an external side. Most proximate vulnerability is of the livelihood-system variety, although there are differential examples (e.g. short-term illness).

24 Adaptable Livelihoods

Whereas structural vulnerability can go a long way towards explaining why certain categories of people fail to feed themselves, it cannot say much about what happens when habitual 'winners' start losing. This is important, because acute food crises are distinguished from chronic underlying food insecurity by the fact that those who are only proximately vulnerable join the ranks of those who are structurally so, making everyone worse off. Again, pastoralists offer a good illustration: they experience structural vulnerability in that when things go wrong (e.g. drought), both their source of immediate consumption (milk) and their asset base (livestock) can rapidly evaporate; but they are proximately vulnerable only in certain seasons or years (e.g. when it does not rain or when the terms of trade swing against them).

Structural vulnerability – whether of the differential or livelihood-system kind – increases the likelihood of proximate vulnerability, or reduces the ability of people to weather transitory disturbances in their livelihoods. There is thus an iterative process between the two. People subsisting under such conditions are vulnerable because of what they do (or can no longer do), not because of one-off disturbances to an otherwise secure livelihood. As the following chapters will show, more and more Sahelian producers fall into this category. For those who are doubly structurally vulnerable – i.e. both differentially and in terms of their livelihood system – proximate vulnerability will hit even harder. The relationship between the two is central to understanding the process of change which eventually leads to famine, via a series of stages of intensification of vulnerability. To understand this relationship at the level of analysis of livelihood systems, vulnerability needs to be unpacked, to take account of its two dimensions of resilience and sensitivity.

PAST SECURITY, CURRENT VULNERABILITY

To monitor changes in proximate vulnerability to food insecurity, the transition from structural livelihood-system security to vulnerability (or the changing degree of sustainability of a livelihood system) must be understood. Otherwise, short-term household responses to food stress will be confused with underlying transformations of livelihood systems. To see whether present-day livelihood systems were structurally vulnerable and, if so, in what way, an historical approach was adopted: how had livelihood systems changed since the time when those dependent on them felt secure in their livelihoods? The broad periodicity used was before the 1973 drought ('the past') and after the mid-1980s drought ('the present') – an intentionally imprecise division, with a decade of transition, to distinguish between broad categories of livelihood system evolving in a continuous process of change. Neither households nor livelihood systems become structurally vulnerable overnight, nor do all become so at the same rate.

As livelihood systems become more vulnerable over time, resilience and sensitivity are useful concepts to explain what happens. They originate from analyses of the sustainability of land use and management systems. Blaikie and Brookfield (1987: 10–11) thus define resilience (based on Holling, 1978: 11) as a property that:

> allows a system to absorb and *utilise* (or even benefit from) change. Where resilience is high, it requires a major disturbance to overcome the limits to qualitative change in a system and allow it to be transformed rapidly into another condition

and sensitivity as:

> the degree to which a given land system undergoes changes due to natural forces, following human interference.

In applying these concepts to environments and food supply systems, Bayliss-Smith (1991: 7-8) has argued that:

> the first can be assessed by the magnitude of a system's response to an external event, or its *sensitivity* ... the second ... is the ease and rapidity of a system's recovery from stress, or its *resilience*.

This distinction is shown in Diagram 2.1, which also shows that least vulnerable (hazardous) systems are those with properties of high resilience/low sensitivity, and most vulnerable ones are those with low resilience/high sensitivity properties. Taken together, these two dimensions show how systems change over time. Length of time is not specified in the diagram, but it is reasonable to assume that each event or 'shock' and its aftermath is less than a decade long (e.g. a single cycle of drought and recovery).

Sahelian livelihood systems would thus be classified as being highly sensitive because of their susceptibility to change. From the recent attention to the use of coping strategies in periods of drought, it can be inferred that they are also highly resilient, given the ability of human populations to adapt to variable resources with great flexibility, exploiting a wide range of environments and economic processes, as Maxwell and Smith

(1992: 37) characterise resilient livelihood systems. Yet, as will be shown, the capacity to recover (or bounce back) has been systematically eroded, such that Sahelian livelihood systems are no longer highly resilient.

The question here, however, is rather how Sahelian livelihood systems have moved from a prior state of high resilience/low sensitivity to a current one of low resilience/high sensitivity. This distinction cannot be picked up from the matrix in Diagram 2.1 unless a given system moves between boxes. It is precisely this transition that is central to understanding how access to food within livelihood systems has evolved over time-frames that are longer than a single cycle of drought and recovery.

The starting point for the analysis is that time in the past (say the 1960s) when, *according to local people's own perceptions*, their livelihood systems were highly resilient (able to bounce back) and of low sensitivity (not subject to intense change as a result of shocks). This latter categorisation belies conventional wisdom about Sahelian livelihood systems – that they are always highly sensitive to shocks such as drought. But, in terms of people's own perceptions, their sensitivity has greatly increased over time. In other words, the intensity or severity of shocks has increased and recovery, when it does occur, takes a long time or the system never reverts to its pre-shock state (a movement from the top left-hand box to the bottom right-hand one in Diagram 2.1). Over the longer term, the system follows the pattern of Diagram 2.2, which illustrates schematically the major periods of drought and famine in the Sahel in the twentieth century. This transition is the process of increasing structural livelihood-system vulnerability to food insecurity, which in turn increases the impact of proximate vulnerability, both by intensifying the impact and reducing the ability to bounce back.

Whereas the conceptual distinction between resilience and sensitivity can be usefully transferred from systems based on natural resources to those based on human livelihoods, carrying over the relationship between the two is more problematic. When resilience and sensitivity are used to describe two dimensions of sustainability or vulnerability of natural-resource systems, there is an implicit assumption that the fundamental properties of these resources exist in a state of natural equilibrium prior to interference. Degrees of resilience and sensitivity describe how the system responds to change in order to return to this natural state. The concept of resilience, it will be recalled, originates from Holling who contrasts it with stability, that is 'the ability of a system to return to an equilibrium state after a temporary disturbance' (Holling, 1973: 17, cited in Mortimore, 1989: 214). Even though 'sensitivity' focuses on the degree of deviation from the norm, it nevertheless implicitly adopts this presumption of

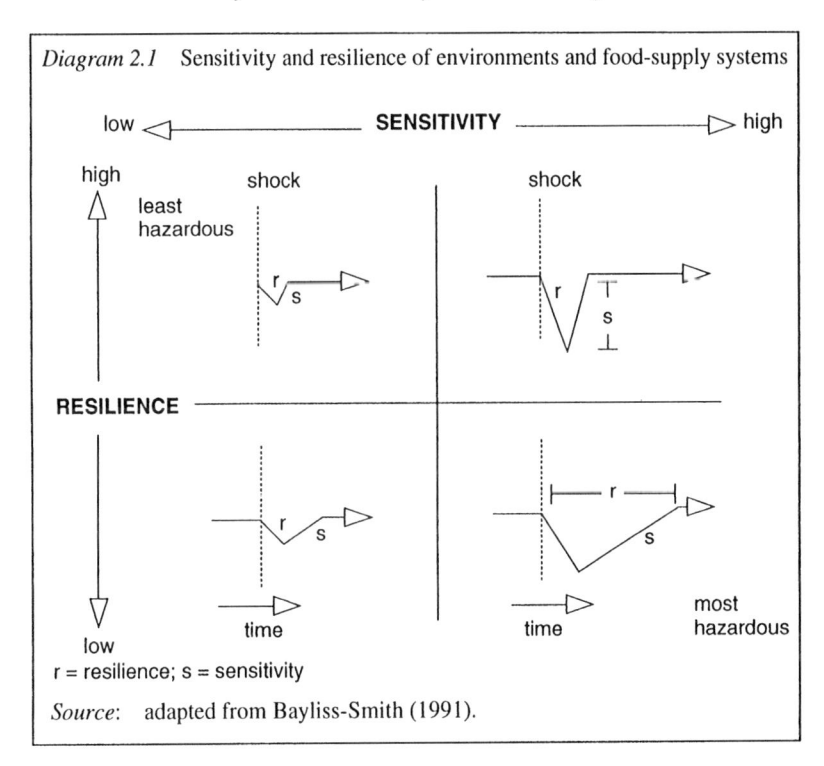

Diagram 2.1 Sensitivity and resilience of environments and food-supply systems

r = resilience; s = sensitivity
Source: adapted from Bayliss-Smith (1991).

returning to the norm, as Diagram 2.1 shows. Diagram 2.2, in contrast, indicates that there is no such automatic return following a shock. In his analysis of the adaptation of human systems to environmental uncertainty, Mortimore (1989) explicitly separates resilience from stability, arguing that, although most proposals for the conservation of arid and semi-arid areas assume that stability, in the sense of equilibrium, is possible, in fact this is at variance with empirical evidence and the perceptions of the people subsisting within these systems. He further argues (*ibid.*: 217):

> the extension of the idea of resilience from ecosystems to human systems directs emphasis away from a futile search for equilibrium to the strengthening of social adaptive behaviour.

Because resilience and sensitivity are independently rooted relative to a normal state of equilibrium in natural-resource systems, it is perfectly possible for external shocks to have different consequences for each of them: hence, the four possible combinations shown in Diagram 2.1. In contrast, livelihood systems are not based on some natural equilibrium, but

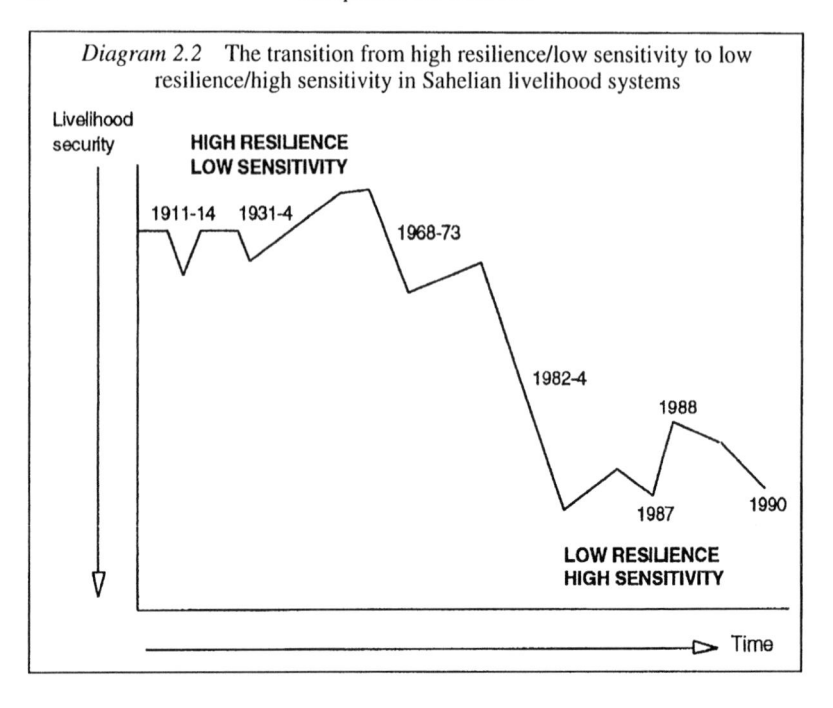

Diagram 2.2 The transition from high resilience/low sensitivity to low resilience/high sensitivity in Sahelian livelihood systems

```
Livelihood
security    HIGH RESILIENCE
            LOW SENSITIVITY
            1911-14  1931-4
                              1968-73


                                        1982-4
                                                1988
                                                        1990
                                           1987
                                        LOW RESILIENCE
                                        HIGH SENSITIVITY
                                                  ▷ Time
```

are a function of how humans interact with environmental, socio-economic and political factors in order to subsist. Diagram 2.2 shows that this gives rise to fundamental changes in the nature of such systems over time. How likely is it that the sum of these processes will give rise to resilience and sensitivity moving in the same direction? Is it not the case that precisely those same characteristics which result in *increasing* sensitivity (e.g. fewer buffers against sharp reductions in production) are causally related to *decreasing* resilience (the absence of those buffers which facilitate recovery)?

If both resilience and sensitivity are understood in terms of what people do to sustain their livelihood systems – whether or not they succeed – their decisions will seek to enhance resilience whilst minimising sensitivity. The decisions taken and the strategies pursued to achieve this objective are based on a continual trade-off. This is why people – such as those in the Sahel – in systems characterised by what Mortimore (1989: 214) has called 'uncertainty-as-norm' (as opposed to 'uncertainty-as-aberration') have developed complex methods of adapting to that uncertainty. In the very short term, it is possible that increasing resilience will be given priority over minimising sensitivity. In empirical studies of how people survive famines, it has been shown that they will seek to protect future livelihoods (increase resilience) even at the cost of current consumption (greater sensitivity) (e.g. De Waal, 1989; Corbett, 1988; see Chapter 3). Studies of a single cycle of famine and recovery, however, whilst indicating a temporary trade-off between greater resilience and greater sensitivity, can tell us nothing about the longer-term costs of that choice. People cannot go on protecting livelihoods forever at the cost of greater sensitivity, because greater sensitivity will itself put increased strains on resilience: as the troughs in Diagram 2.1 deepen, so does resilience have to grow to return to the norm. Thresholds beyond which there is no return (no resilience) are commonly ascribed to those who die from starvation, followed by those who are destitute (having lost their means of livelihood but survived) and then by those who have changed their livelihood systems (e.g. from rural to urban, or from pastoralism to cultivation).

But there is a further group, commonly left out of this typology, of those who have ostensibly 'succeeded' – survived and retained their previous livelihood – but who in fact subsist under very different conditions from those of their former livelihoods. Successive 'shocks' mean that an increasing number of 'survivors' fall into this category, and these new livelihoods are both more sensitive and less resilient than those pursued in the past. Short-term trade-offs to protect resilience at the cost of higher sensitivity are therefore not sustainable: either an intense shock or repeated shocks will mean that stable or even increased resilience is inadequate to achieve full recovery. By implicitly assuming that livelihood systems stay in the same box in Diagram 2.1, this issue is rarely addressed. Instead, it is presumed that people in highly resilient systems *do* cope. The sustainability of the systems to which their coping gives rise is not explored. Our concern therefore centres on changes in resilience and the sustainability of coping, which is in fact a much more fundamental process of adaptation. It implies a clear distinction between coping with shocks and adapting to more permanent changes, the subject of Chapter 3.

Coping with shocks brings us to the issue of how resilience and sensitivity affect the ability to confront proximate vulnerability. For people subsisting in *structurally vulnerable* livelihood systems, decisions and strategies to confront *proximate vulnerability* are primarily conditioned by low resilience and high sensitivity. They aim to minimise sensitivity and to increase resilience, but the more structurally vulnerable it is, the fewer options a livelihood system offers. Structurally secure systems, in contrast, which benefit from high resilience and low sensitivity, are also proximately secure in so far as they have buffers or strategies to minimise the shock and to facilitate recovery. Proximate security is the ability to cope, whereas proximate vulnerability is the necessity for constant adaptation.

The threshold between coping and adapting occurs when the pattern in Diagram 2.1 shifts to that in Diagram 2.2. This shows the relationship at system level, but what happens at household level? Households are typically regarded as being differentially vulnerable, but they can also be structurally so. Table 2.2 expresses the combinations of vulnerability at individual/household and system level schematically. Within each, there is a further dimension of resilience and sensitivity. Furthermore, differential vulnerability can be unpacked to reveal intra-household differences. The intensity of vulnerability may thus be assessed in terms of how many of the four categories a household or individual falls into: the greater the number of categories, the more intense the vulnerability.

Thus, people in categories A (e.g. children under five) and B (most Sahelian producers in the post-drought period) are always potentially vulnerable to food insecurity and are doubly so if they are in both categories. It is people who fall into category A who are the usual targets of EWS: structurally vulnerable individuals or households who then encounter proximate vulnerability (typically drought). Proximate differential vulnerability (category C) is almost impossible to monitor systematically; an exception would be outbreaks of disease. The concern of this study is primarily with categories B and D. Category D is critical because, when filled, both the extent and intensity of food crisis are likely to increase sharply and, to predict this, EWS must know what is happening in category B. People in category B are most likely to be able to respond to interventions which increase their capacity to feed themselves.

In order to capture this important gap, vulnerability is best approached via the unit of analysis of livelihood systems. The SADS analysis sought to identify those people who are in category B, by virtue of their membership of a structurally vulnerable livelihood system (high sensitivity/low resilience), irrespective of proximate conditions. Identifying which types of producers are particularly vulnerable in a given season or year is not intended to replace categories of differential vulnerability, but the working hypothesis of the SADS system was that in a bad year, extreme food insecur-

Table 2.2 Level and nature of vulnerability

Vulnerability	Level	
Nature	Differential	Livelihood system
Structural	A	B
Proximate	C	D

ity is likely to be found amongst producers in livelihood systems in category B. What will make a difference to whether they mitigate this vulnerability is how they adapt their livelihood systems to 'being in category B'. Being in categories A and C will further intensify vulnerability to food insecurity, but will not be the principal cause of *widespread* food insecurity in a given year.

The ability to adapt to being in category B is the subject of Chapter 3. It is, however, important to note that being in category B is conditioned by positive as well as the negative shocks presumed thus far in the discussion. What are the consequences in resilience and sensitivity for positive shocks as opposed to negative ones? In livelihood systems, positive shocks originate from one of three sources: from natural factors (e.g. increased rainfall – as in the case of the peak between the drought cycles of 1931–4 and 1968–73 in Diagram 2.2); as a result of internal management (what people do within livelihood systems to alter levels of resilience or sensitivity); or, finally, as a consequence of external policy-induced intervention. The second is the most important group.

Sources of shocks – particularly (but not exclusively) positive ones – are thus far more diverse in livelihood systems than in natural-resource ones. Adapting Blaikie and Brookfield's descriptions of the four possible combinations of land-management systems to livelihood systems, Table 2.3 shows the implications of each for food security and its management, defined as the options open to the people in the system without recourse to external assistance. In Blaikie and Brookfield's original typology, the

Table 2.3 Characteristics of resilient and sensitive livelihood systems

Livelihood system	Characteristics
1. Low sensitivity/high resilience	Food insecurity only occurs under conditions of poor management and persistent practices which erode entitlement
2. High sensitivity/high resilience	Suffers food insecurity easily but responds well to management designed to raise entitlements
3. Low sensitivity/low resilience	Initially resistant to food insecurity but once thresholds are passed it is very difficult for management to restore entitlements
4. High sensitivity/low resilience	Suffers food insecurity easily, does not respond to management

Source: Based on Blaikie and Brookfield (1987: 11).

fourth type of system (high sensitivity/low resilience) is characterised as one that 'easily degrades, does not respond to land management, and *should not be interfered with in any major way by human agency*' (Blaikie and Brookfield, 1987: 11, emphasis added), the implication being that for the most vulnerable systems interventions or internal management cannot work and should not be attempted. But it is here that the limits of this conceptualisation are reached for livelihood systems. Let us consider what happens to a high sensitivity/low resilience livelihood system when faced first with a natural positive shock and then with policy-driven positive shocks.

A natural positive shock – e.g. unusually high rainfall – is potentially beneficial to a highly sensitive system, *if* it is also highly resilient. A typical example is a pastoral livelihood system, highly sensitive to a loss of animals in a drought year but also able to capitalise rapidly on abundant pasture in a good one. However, in highly sensitive systems in which resilience has been eroded over time, this is no longer the case. In a year of abundant rainfall, the ability to be highly sensitive to a positive shock presupposes that the system has bounced back (that there are sufficient herds to exploit the good conditions) or, in the case of cultivators, that there is sufficient seed and labour to yield a good harvest. Inevitably, in livelihood systems as opposed to natural-resource ones, high sensitivity to natural negative shocks goes hand in hand with low resilience, which in turn means that such systems are insensitive to positive shocks, or are unable to exploit them beneficially. In the case of livelihood systems, therefore, it is inappropriate to ascribe a constant characteristic to the degree of impact on the system of both a positive and a negative shock. Resilience and sensitivity to natural negative shocks move in opposite directions (the greater the sensitivity, the lower the resilience), whereas with positive natural shocks they move together (the greater the sensitivity, the greater the resilience to being able to respond to the opportunities they afford).

There is an even more striking problem when considering policy-driven positive shocks, either of the developmental (e.g. improved inputs or irrigation) or the emergency (e.g. free food distributions) kind. If negative shocks to highly sensitive livelihood systems are associated with greater food insecurity, it follows that positive policy-induced shocks should enhance food security. But given that the preoccupation of people in highly sensitive systems is to make trade-offs between the intensity of sensitivity (positive or negative) and the preservation or enhancement of resilience, their response to positive policy-induced interventions will be determined not by the innate high sensitivity of the system but rather by

Security and Vulnerability in Livelihood Systems

the extent to which a given intervention can facilitate an optimum trade-off. The speed of response to an intervention is thus determined by the intervention in question. People will opt for food-for-work projects rather than the collection of wild foods, if the former is more likely to facilitate the trade-off. Equally, they will incur debt to acquire productivity-enhancing (or risk-reducing) inputs only if the overall risk of so doing (in terms of both sensitivity and resilience) is judged to be less than not responding rapidly. Conversely, highly resilient systems which help to provide food security are not necessarily incapable of absorbing change: positive shocks which reinforce their ability to bounce back will increase resilience further. There is, therefore, a major operational drawback to the conceptualisation of livelihood systems in terms of resilience and sensitivity: neither the degree of sensitivity nor of resilience can indicate how appropriate a particular intervention will be in reducing food insecurity, either in terms of mitigating the intensity of a shock or of improving the ability to bounce back.

This dilemma cannot be resolved in the abstract. Characteristics of resilience and sensitivity – and critically the ways in which these change over time – must be mapped before any sense can be made of either the sustainability of a given system or the ways in which interventions could enhance or reduce food and livelihood security within it. To identify these characteristics, the entitlement bundles which people operating within a given system depend on for their livelihoods must be understood. Furthermore, the precise characteristics of a given household will determine how it responds to particular shocks and interventions.

LIVELIHOOD-SYSTEM DIVERSITY

Changes in the vulnerability of large numbers of people from season to season or year to year come about not because of structural or proximate differential vulnerability, but because of variation in the mix of entitlements a particular livelihood system has access to at a given point in time; in other words, because of proximate livelihood-system vulnerability. As livelihood systems become increasingly structurally vulnerable, the likelihood of proximate vulnerability increases; but equally these systems adapt to the threat of being doubly vulnerable.

There are five principal livelihood systems in the study area: cultivation; agro-pastoralism; agro-fishing; transhumant fishing; and transhumant pastoralism. They are structurally vulnerable in distinct ways. The diversity of livelihood systems, and of the natural resources from which they are derived and on which they depend (which vary between dry and wetlands), enables producers to engage in a number of activities to optimise the trade-off between reducing sensitivity and increasing resilience, depending on the season and the year. Consequently, each system has very different ways of acquiring food and responding to food shortages.

Membership of a given livelihood system and the ability to move temporarily into a neighbouring one are the key determinants of how a household sustains its livelihood and feeds itself. Classifying food-insecure populations in this way provides information about: relative poverty (e.g. diversified producers tend to be richer than specialist cultivators); reliance on particular resources (pasture, rainfed land, etc.); and vulnerability to a given set of declining food entitlements (e.g. collapse of small-stock prices will be disastrous for dryland agro-pastoralists, but will have little impact on the food security of transhumant fishers). Above all, it focuses on those elements of livelihood-system vulnerability which will *change* from year to year. Understanding how each livelihood system normally feeds itself permits a sensible interpretation of seasonal information, and identification of what kinds of people are vulnerable to food insecurity in a particular season or year and why, and suggests what could be done to reduce vulnerability within the context of existing livelihoods.

Diversification is at the root of food and livelihood-security strategies in the Sahel. Risk avoidance or reduction by diversifying on- and off-farm activities is a common household strategy throughout the Sahelian zone. Livelihood-system diversity constantly evolves in response to changing agro-ecological and socio-economic conditions. One of the most obvious patterns of change is the incorporation of activities which were reserved in the past for periods of food stress into normal strategies for poorer households. Consequently, when the next cycle of drought hits, resort can no longer be had to traditional fall-back strategies to increase food entitlements. What are perceived to be coping strategies have thus become the livelihood strategies of certain groups.

Multiple livelihood systems and the extreme seasonal mobility of producers in the Malian Sahel mean that conventional indicators used to predict food shortages are often inadequate and indecipherable. These livelihood systems (sometimes complementary, sometimes in conflict) are the key to food security in the area. The diversity and flexibility which they provide cannot be adequately monitored by, for example, following pasture as well as crop conditions in isolation from the way in which different types of producers depend on and exploit these in particular seasons and years. Similarly, interactions between livelihood systems are rarely taken into account by general indicators.

But the diversity and constant adaptation of livelihood systems also pose a dilemma for local monitoring systems based on coping strategies, illustrated clearly by the data collected by the SADS system. At what point does a coping strategy become an adaptive strategy or a permanent change in how people acquire food? And how does a monitoring system recognise such a shift? Further, at any moment, one person's coping strategy may be another's source of livelihood, given that households encounter differing degrees of food insecurity at different times. Do these problems mean that data about coping strategies are impossible to interpret sensibly? We return to these questions in Chapter 3.

FRAMEWORK OF ANALYSIS

How can changes in these complex elements of food and livelihood vulnerability be captured by a set of predictive indicators? Table 2.4 shows a matrix for identifying indicators of food insecurity on the basis of: (a) sources of and calls on entitlement and (b) mediators of those entitlements. Sources of entitlement are based on production (both primary and secondary); exchange (including market and non-market transfers); assets (stores and claims); coping (short-term responses to unusual food stress); and adaptation (coping strategies which have become permanently incorporated into the normal cycle of activities). Taken together, these sources

Table 2.4 Livelihood entitlements matrix

Sources of and calls on entitlements	Mediators of entitlement					
	Natural	Individual/ household	Livelihood system	Moral economy	Market	State
Sources: Production Exchange Assets Coping Adaptation						
Calls: Consumption Claims Livelihood protection						

are the 'income' side of the household's food entitlement. Calls on entitlement are the 'expenditure' side. They include: consumption (of food and other goods to meet short-term needs); claims (the obverse of 'assets', including debt to traders, the state [taxes and fines] and payments in kind or cash to neighbours and kin); and livelihood protection (investments in the future, distinguished from claims because they represent future stores and claims which need to be paid now, rather than past ones which can now be realised). Taken together, these sources of and calls on entitlement represent what Sen (1983) and Drèze and Sen (1989) have called 'an extended entitlements approach'.

In vulnerable livelihood systems, it is the balance between them which determines food security at a given point in time, because such systems have little or no capacity for accumulation. Consequently, in monitoring food security, it is not enough simply to look at sources of entitlement. They may be at their height precisely when calls are also greatest (as in the case of post-harvest tax and debt collection). Households are not sponges, merely absorbing entitlements, but more like a bath in which entitlements can be both poured in and drawn out. Indicators must be able to track calls as well as sources. This two-directional supply of and demand for food and other entitlements is well recognised in nutritional literature, for example (Lipton, 1983), but is less frequently taken into account when estimating household food entitlements.

Both sources of and calls on entitlements are mediated by a number of factors, all of which have structural and proximate dimensions. Thus, a proximate natural mediator would be drought, a structural one soil degradation. Individual and household mediators are significant in terms of how the process of acquiring or liquidating entitlements changes according to different kinds of household, and how this is unequally shared within households. Structural individual or household mediators would include gender mix or household size and dependency ratios; proximate ones include pregnancy, illness or temporary increases in dependency ratios (e.g. if impoverished kin come to stay).

Livelihood systems mediate entitlements in a structural sense by determining the options available on the 'sources' side, but also in a proximate sense in that a particular season or year will influence the level of entitlement (e.g. for pastoralists, a lack of pasture will undermine production, exchange and possibly assets, whereas cultivators may be unaffected).

Moral economy, following Swift's (1989a) definition, refers to a range of redistributive processes which occur within communities: from households to extended families, through shallow kinship groupings to major lineages and upwards to political structures. Membership of these moral economies involves implicit mutual recognition of both an obligation to share resources and a claim on resources in times of need. There is nothing intrinsically 'welfarist' about the moral economy: indeed, it often engenders relations of subservience and dependence, which are indicators of structural vulnerability for the dependant, or of a source of entitlement for the 'asset' holder. Proximate indicators of the moral economy are principally concerned with the 'assets' that can be called on in times of stress (e.g. the loan of food or animals by kin) or their liquidation (e.g. the sale of jewellery). But a second critical dimension needs also to be tracked: the breakdown of structural reciprocal ties or the calling in of claims when people can least afford them.

Markets equally have proximate and structural effects on household food entitlements. In the short term, prices and (in a drought year) availability are the most important mediators, whereas structural mediators include how efficiently the markets operate, whether they are liberalised or controlled and the degree of market dependence of the household in question.

Finally, the state mediates entitlement through its long- and short-term policies. Whereas, on the sources side, state intervention in production and exchange entitlements is well recognised, state policies towards coping and adaptation may be less apparent. Does the state reinforce or undermine such strategies, for example by restricting migration, by fining travellers without identity cards, by impounding goods on the way to market, and by generally pursuing policies to encourage sedentarisation of rural producers? Or does it by-pass coping strategies by distributing free food aid? Equally, the impact of state policies on the calls side is less well-documented. Most obvious under the claims category is the extraction of taxes and fines.

When monitoring household vulnerability to food insecurity, each of the cells in the matrix can be filled with an indicator. These fall into two categories: baseline indicators to identify structural mediators of entitlement, and proximate indicators to track changes in them. Taken together, these will give a composite picture of the level of vulnerability to food insecurity in a given season or year.

Most famine EWS rely on proximate indicators in only some of the cells, the most common of which are shown in Table 2.5. Thus, under natural mediators rainfall trends (structural) and actual rainfall (proximate) will be monitored for effects on production, possibly supplemented with information on pest attacks. Under individual/household mediators structural characteristics of vulnerability (children under five, female-headed households, the landless, etc.) are used as a proxy for proximate vulnerability: these may be monitored by proximate indicators, usually of nutritional status. Livelihood-system mediators are rarely disaggregated by type of system, cereal production standing as the proximate indicator for all livelihood systems, sometimes supplemented by pasture conditions. Market data are amongst the most common sources of proximate indicators: particularly cereal prices (and occasionally livestock, used to calculate terms of trade). Sometimes indicators of asset depletion and coping (demand for casual labour) are tracked by local EWS. Monitoring of state activity is usually restricted to how the state responds – food aid distributions or levels of imports – against a background 'policy climate' that is generally strangely absent from analyses of EW data.

The indicators in Table 2.5 thus focus on very specific parts of the entitlement matrix. Differentiating between vulnerable groups is decided either on geographic/administrative criteria or on structural characteristics. Rarely are attempts made to monitor *how* people are vulnerable, *how* they are responding, and hence what the most appropriate form of intervention might be. Monitoring the sale of assets or the price of daily labour is a step in this direction, but one that is only infrequently taken.

By focusing on production and exchange sources of and consumption calls on entitlements, EWS implicitly assume that the principal preoccupation of vulnerable people is to meet current consumption requirements, and that the ways in which they do this are either through subsistence production or exchange, or some combination of the two. This ignores the other critical parts of the matrix, which present a whole new set of problems for famine prediction:

- The most frequently ignored *sources of entitlement* are those derived from *coping and adaptation*. Current debates about the development of EWS indicators advocate monitoring the sequential uptake of coping strategies as sensitive indicators of proximate vulnerability but, as Chapter 3 will show, this approach has a number of drawbacks, not least the difficulties associated with distinguishing between coping and adaptation. As livelihood systems become structurally vulnerable, many coping strategies are incorporated into the normal cycle of activities and thus become part of the process of adaptation.
- On the *calls* side, *livelihood protection* has until recently been excluded from analyses of how poor people confront food insecurity. Evidence from Darfur (De Waal, 1989) and Ethiopia (Turton, 1977) and elsewhere shows that people will subsume immediate food needs

Table 2.5 Common early warning indicators within the livelihood entitlements matrix

Sources of and calls on entitlement	Mediators of entitlement					
	Natural	Individual/ household	Livelihood system	Moral economy	Market	State
Sources:						
Production	Rainfall		Cereal production			
Exchange		Typical vulnerable groups			Cereal prices	Import levels
Assets						
Coping						Food aid distribution
Adaptation						
Calls:						
Consumption		Nutritional status of under-5s				
Claims						
Livelihood protection						

40   Adaptable Livelihoods

under the quest to preserve future livelihoods (e.g. by reducing current consumption in order not to sell productive assets, or by returning home from remunerative migration in order to cultivate). Yet, again, indicators to track such behaviour are very hard to use in practice, as Chapter 3 will show.

- Equally, *claims as calls on entitlements* are very difficult to track and have received less attention in EW than livelihood protection or other assets as sources of entitlements. This is due in part to the erroneous assumption that the moral economy is an informal insurance system which provides a community safety net in times of stress, whereas in fact such relationships can be both extractive and exploitative and can become more so in periods of acute stress (Gore, 1992). Further, such relationships change both in periods of transitory stress and when structural changes occur in the ways in which people get access to food. Like coping strategies, there is no guarantee that investments, stores or claims will follow the same pattern of accumulation or depletion in repeated episodes of food stress.

Moving now to mediators of entitlement, it is clear from Table 2.5 that some of these are conventionally accounted for in EWS (natural, market), whilst others are sometimes included in more finely-tuned systems (e.g. some aspects of individual and household mediators). A further category is either ignored (moral economy), or covered (usually very incompletely) in only one or two cells in the matrix (livelihood system and state). Obviously, there would be little sense in trying to fill every cell. Natural mediators (e.g. drought) will directly affect production and have ripple effects on other entitlements, but these will be picked up by indicators in other cells (e.g. cereal prices in the market/exchange cell). Nevertheless, to monitor vulnerability between different groups, how people confront or fail to reduce this and what interventions might successfully mitigate it, some of the empty cells need to be filled. Distinction must be made however between indicators of what it would be nice to know and those of what is necessary and feasible to find out. Table 2.6 shows these missing indicators which fall into the latter category. Some of them, it will be noted, appear to be already filled in Table 2.5, but the limitations of these existing indicators are such that the cell is effectively empty or inadequately filled.

The central gap concerns *livelihood-system mediators,* which are rarely explicitly addressed by EW indicators other than for cereal production, with all other productive activities (and combinations thereof, e.g. agro-

Security and Vulnerability in Livelihood Systems

Table 2.6 Critical gaps in early warning indicators within the livelihood entitlements matrix

Sources of and calls on entitlement	Mediators of entitlement					
	Natural	Individual/ household	Livelihood system	Moral economy	Market	State
Sources:						
Production	▓		▓			
Exchange					▓	
Assets						
Coping		▓		▓		▓
Adaptation						
Calls:						
Consumption						
Claims			▓	▓		▓
Livelihood protection	▓					

pastoralism) subsumed under this proxy umbrella. Exchange entitlements, which refer to non-market transfers within and between different systems (e.g. bartering) also tend to be left out, but the levels of such exchanges and the terms of trade under which they are carried out compared with those of formal market exchanges can be critical indicators of vulnerability. Coping and adaptation (and the important distinction between the two) have, as argued above, only recently been incorporated into models of famine prediction, but almost always without reference to the livelihood system in question. On the calls side, livelihood protection – although also now recognised as a valid component of household response to food stress – is rarely incorporated, and, again, the crucial differences *between* different livelihood systems are not accounted for. Finally, both assets and claims are generally not accounted for, and claims are especially significant as 'hidden' calls on entitlement.

Market mediators, whilst perhaps the most monitored for what they can indicate about distribution of food between vulnerable groups, are neglected in two key respects: first, in relation to the key terms of trade between different goods for each livelihood system; and second, in so far as coping and adaptive activities are market-based. Critically, as livelihood systems become more market-dependent, market mediation affects more and more sources of and calls on entitlement.

Those *individual and household mediators* which are most critically ignored relate to how the capacity for and burden of coping and adapting are differentially distributed between households of different sizes and by gender within households. These issues are most critical in determining both proximate and structural vulnerability in the two cells indicated.

Moral economy mediators are rarely taken into account in developing indicators of food and livelihood stress. In terms of changing vulnerability, they are most important in respect of assets and claims, and intimately bound up with coping, adapting and livelihood protection.

Indicators of *state mediators* of entitlement are, as has been mentioned, generally excluded from EWS, on the grounds that EWS should inform the overall policy climate rather than report on it. There are, nevertheless, two critical aspects of state mediation which need to be addressed: first, indicators of whether the state facilitates or inhibits coping and adaptation, and second, whether it makes damaging and untimely claims on entitlements.

Finally, *natural mediators*, whilst quite well covered by most EWS in a proximate sense, are nevertheless restricted to proximate indicators. Rarely are the cumulative effects of natural-resource degradation on production and livelihood protection monitored for, even though these will have major impacts on future vulnerability.

These indicator gaps have major implications for the ways in which vulnerability is monitored. Having identified them, the SADS system sought to address them in the following ways:

- to define and monitor entitlements according to the extended list shown in the matrix, paying especial attention to coping and adapting sources of entitlement as the critical determinants of proximate and structural vulnerability respectively;
- to use livelihood systems as the unit of analysis, subsequently complemented by household-level monitoring to address household mediators of entitlement also;[6]
- to monitor both market and non-market exchanges, on the basis of the critical terms of trade for each livelihood system.

This approach did not encompass all the gaps identified: declining natural resources and the state as a mediator of entitlement were not centrally included in the design of the monitoring system, although effects of their impact were looked for when interpreting other indicators.

Entitlement bundles operate within systems exhibiting characteristics of high or low resilience and sensitivity. As resilience and sensitivity change, so these changes are mirrored in sources of and calls on entitlements. Before current and future entitlement bundles can be mapped, it is necessary to know how resilient and sensitive the system is. In a highly resilient/low sensitivity system, food security may be guaranteed by production entitlements alone, whereas in a low resilience/highly sensitive one, a more complex bundle of entitlements is required. In the first system non-production entitlements would be used to meet other livelihood needs, whereas in the second they would also be required for subsistence. This distinction has direct implications for the indicators used to monitor changes in proximate vulnerability: the more resilience declines and sensitivity increases, the more food security depends on factors other than primary production.

Table 2.7, using the livelihood entitlements framework, shows a simple matrix for identifying indicators of the transition between the two systems. Taking production entitlements as an example, high resilience could be indicated by annual food production to meet more than one year's requirements, and low sensitivity derived from this because, in the event of a bad year, there would be at least some months' buffer. Conversely, low resilience would be indicated by a structural food gap from primary production, which would also mean high sensitivity (the absence of a buffer). This model is developed empirically in Chapter 7.

Table 2.7 Livelihood entitlements matrix for indicators of the transition from security to vulnerability

Sources of and calls on entitlements	*Sustainability of entitlements*			
	Security		Vulnerability	
	High resilience	*Low sensitivity*	*Low resilience*	*High sensitivity*
Sources: Production Exchange Assets Coping Adaptation				
Calls: Consumption Claims Livelihood protection				

Most applications of an extended entitlements model to monitor food insecurity implicitly assume highly resilient systems: coping strategies, assets and claims are all equated with the capacity to raise entitlements and hence to bounce back. There is, however, no automatic correlation between the existence of extended entitlements and resilience and the use of coping strategies is frequently confused with longer-term adaptation to conditions of low resilience/high sensitivity.

In addition to identification of indicators, distinguishing between levels of resilience and sensitivity within livelihood systems (and food subsystems) enables a second critical step in famine prevention to be taken: to consider the sustainability of entitlement bundles in the long term and hence which sources of entitlement should be promoted and which calls reduced by policies and interventions. The first question to pose therefore is whether a system is resilient, followed by whether it is sensitive – to enable us to look at the future reproducibility of particular entitlements and mixtures of them, or their unsustainability. This is in stark contrast to advocating that all coping strategies should be reinforced (because they imply resilience). In fact, it is only those entitlements with the capacity to be highly resilient (and to reduce sensitivity) in the future which policies and interventions should seek to reinforce.

CONCLUSIONS

The framework of analysis presented in this chapter has none of the elegance or simplicity of the handful of key indicators used by most EWS. Further, as subsequent chapters will demonstrate, the pitfalls – both methodological and operational – are legion. But if the objective of a monitoring system is to find out how people feed themselves, not how they fail to do so, and if, in turn, this is decided within a wider livelihood system, short cuts can only be taken once the whole journey is known. The data presented in Chapters 7 to 10 plot the whole journey and conclude by showing the short cuts. If policy options are to be arrived at which address vulnerability to food and livelihood security in terms of how they actually affect people's lives and how people in turn respond to them, there is no way around this long route.

3 Coping and Adapting

INTRODUCTION

This chapter explores the nature of coping and adaptation in vulnerable livelihood systems, in order to see whether monitoring coping strategies can be useful in predicting food stress. Much conceptual confusion between coping and adapting characterises current debates about the utility of coping strategies both as indicators of stress and of appropriate interventions. People in marginal environments have always lived with a portfolio of options, and are well aware of the pathways that follow if their efforts to mitigate proximate stress are unsuccessful. They are fairly clear about how their livelihoods have changed over a two to three generation time-frame. To some extent, the confusion arising from Northern practitioners' and academics' failure to grasp the complexities of adaptation is of their own making. It implies that the immense amount of thinking about these issues in the developed world needs to be supported by much more information about how poor rural people themselves see them.

Coping strategies are the bundle of producer responses to declining food availability and entitlements in abnormal seasons or years. Households do not respond arbitrarily to variability in food supply; people whose main sources of income (and food) are at recurrent risk develop strategies to minimise that risk (Frankenberger and Goldstein, 1990: 1). Although the importance and proliferation of coping strategies have long been recognised by anthropologists (Campbell, 1990; D'Souza, 1985), it is only recently that their significance for food security monitoring has been acknowledged with any consistency. Interest arose particularly in the aftermath of the famines of the mid-1980s (and, to a lesser extent, the early 1970s), as a means of understanding why it was that some people survived periods of dearth, whilst others did not. To this extent, coping strategies are concerned with food-system success rather than failure. This success was explained in part by the re-interpretation of food entitlements, to include a wider range of sources of and calls on entitlements than was habitually associated with food-insecure households, as used in the entitlements framework in Chapter 2. Corbett (1988), Longhurst (1986) and Watts (1983, 1988), amongst others, have identified successful patterns of coping behaviour based on a widely defined entitlement base. In addition, the ability of the rural poor to manage risk and to adapt to longer-term changes in their food systems has been accorded greater importance than in the past (Mortimore, 1989). It has been shown that populations in more marginal environments are probably much better equipped to cope with periods of food stress than those accustomed to more secure conditions (Reardon and Matlon, 1989). The enthusiasm for coping strategies has been further fuelled by redefinitions of household food security in the light of the sustainable livelihood-security approach to understanding rural communities, discussed in Chapter 2.

COPING STRATEGIES AND EARLY WARNING

In line with the recognition of coping strategies as a means of explaining how poor households deal with food stress, there has been a call for their incorporation into famine EWS, particularly local-level food monitoring systems. Finding out what producers do to help themselves to overcome chronic and transitory food shortages is increasingly seen as essential to interpret standard indicators of stress (e.g. does a particular pattern of migration signify a normal or abnormal activity?); to assess the degree of insecurity (e.g. if the harvest fails, are there sufficient fall-back options to meet needs?); and to identify appropriate responses (e.g. do people need food to eat or help in retaining their productive assets?). Implicit in much (but by no means all) of this call for coping strategy-based monitoring, is a belief that not only will it assist in predicting food crises, but also that it will indicate what appropriate and sustainable interventions would mitigate that crisis. As Frankenberger and Hutchinson (1991: 2) have argued:

> Rather than focusing on the outcome of farmer responses to production constraints and food crises, ... methodologies [can be developed] that monitor the processes by which households cope with food insecurity. Monitoring these processes will improve famine early warning systems as well as guide interventions for increasing farm productivity.

Indigenous coping strategies can therefore be reinforced, in preference to imposing external, often late, inappropriate and, above all, unsustainable solutions, epitomised by emergency food aid distributions. Whereas food aid invariably assists producers only when they have lost the means to feed themselves, monitoring coping strategies has the potential to identify ways of protecting and reinforcing system success and adaptation before it collapses. If successful, such interventions would warn earlier of the destitution implicit in drought and possibly even prevent it. The long-term effects of structural livelihood-system vulnerability to food shortages which persist once the crisis is over could thus be reduced. There is therefore an appealing symmetry in a coping strategy-based approach to EW: it can simultaneously predict famine and inform its prevention.

For these reasons, identification and monitoring of coping strategies were a central part of the SADS system. The ability to monitor coping strategies to predict food crises is predicated upon the assumption that they follow a discernible and repeatable sequence, reflecting the pattern which characterises most food crises. Evidence from Africa and Asia supports the view that common patterns of the uptake of groups of coping strategies can indeed be identified from very different food systems (Longhurst, 1986; Downing, 1988). Watts (1983) drawing on evidence from northern Nigeria in 1973–4 identified the ten most commonly observed responses to food crisis as follows: collect famine foods; borrow grain from kin; sell labour power; engage in dry season farming; sell small livestock; borrow grain or money from merchants/moneylenders; sell domestic assets; pledge farmland; sell farmland; and migrate out permanently.

Corbett (1988), reviewing this and other empirical evidence[1] for the sequential uptake of coping strategies, identifies the sequence in Table 3.1. The idea of sequential uptake has been refined to distinguish between insurance strategies and coping strategies. *Insurance strategies* are those

Table 3.1 The sequential use of coping strategies

Stage one – insurance mechanisms	changes in cropping and planting practices sale of small-stock reduction of current consumption levels collection of wild foods use of inter-household transfers and loans increased petty commodity production migration in search of employment sale of possessions (e.g. jewellery)
Stage two – disposal of productive assets	sale of livestock (e.g. oxen) sale of agricultural tools sale or mortgaging of land credit from merchants and moneylenders reduction of current consumption levels
Stage three – destitution	distress migration

Source: Corbett (1988).

activities undertaken to reduce the likelihood of failure of primary production. *Coping strategies* are employed once the principal source of production has failed to meet expected levels and producers have literally to 'cope' until the next harvest. Thus, Frankenberger and Goldstein (1990) distinguish between various types of risk management and patterns of coping behaviour (e.g. asset depletion, breakdown of community reciprocity, non-farm coping strategies), as well as between types of household assets which will play different roles in the process of coping. Equally, the World Food Programme (WFP) (1989: 3) differentiates between *accumulation* and *diversification* (or insurance) *strategies*. The former aim to increase a household's resource base, and the latter to promote a variety of sources of income with different patterns of risk, to avoid the exposure associated with a single income source. A further distinction is made between hungry season strategies used for part of most years and strategies to survive particularly bad years.

INDICATOR DEVELOPMENT USING COPING STRATEGIES

Although increasingly advocated, examples of the use of coping strategies to monitor food security are rare. Buchanan-Smith *et al.* (1991) identify a handful of local-level systems in the Sahel and Horn of Africa which incorporate them to some degree. Eele (1987), amongst others, has demonstrated how possible sources of information about coping strategies could be grafted on to existing EWS. Broadly speaking, there are three phases in the evolution of indicator development based on coping strategies: the 1970s, when coping strategies were ignored by most famine EWS, reflecting the preoccupation with supply of food and with aggregate indices of supply and demand; the 1980s, when models of sequential uptake predominated especially in the aftermath of the famines in the Sahel and Horn of Africa; and the 1990s, when a new realism now comes into play, based on the realisation that earlier models were over-simplified and often operationally impractical. Whether or not the new realism at a conceptual level can be translated into functioning EWS remains to be seen.

Within the framework of models of sequential uptake, three sets of indicators have been developed to monitor changing coping responses. Building on the work of the WFP, Frankenberger and Hutchinson (1991) summarise these as follows: *early (or leading) indicators*, that is, changes in conditions and responses prior to the onset of reduced food access; *stress (or concurrent) indicators*, i.e. those which occur simultaneously

Coping and Adapting 49

with reduced access to food; and *late outcome (or trailing) indicators*, which occur once food access has declined.

Refinements in the categorisation of coping strategies are informed by a desire to simplify complex patterns of decision-making and response. As models have been refined, much justified caution in their application been cast aside, including Corbett's (1988: 1109) point that 'variations in observed strategies also suggest that there are few universal indicators of impending famine and famine warning systems need to be locally specific', and Frankenberger's (1992: 84) argument that 'models that ignore the locational specificity of ecological and economic aspects are likely to select proxy indicators which are inappropriate or misinterpreted'. If coping strategies are to be employed as predictive indicators of food stress, it is essential that their use by food-insecure groups follows discernible patterns capable of being monitored. Otherwise, they are little more than random responses. It is at this point that their use to monitor changing levels in food security runs into difficulties. Despite the apparent simplicity of models of sequential uptake, operationally they pose a number of difficulties.

The major drawback is that households juggle between different activities simultaneously and in response to the seasonal options available to them. In the case of sales of assets, for example, rural people are highly conversant with the seasonal terms of trade between goods and will seek to maximise revenue by playing the market. Although the literature identifies the grey area between strategies as responses to unusual changes in access to food and as more permanent reactions to fundamentally altered conditions, once coping strategy uptake becomes an indicator of transitory food stress, this grey area must of necessity be ignored. Either use of a particular strategy signals stress or it does not. Attempts to differentiate between *why* different people pursue a particular strategy at a given moment make for highly complex monitoring requirements.

Second, a coping strategy-based approach to monitoring access to food is criticised, and rejected by most EWS, because its information needs are too complex, expensive and time-consuming. In recent years, the thrust of much EW thinking, and views about information needs for rural development more generally, has been to opt for what advocates of rapid rural appraisal (RRA) term 'optimal ignorance' (McCracken *et al.*, 1988). A coping strategy-based approach contradicts this trend, although methodologies can be developed which simplify information collection (Chapter 11). Further, the raw data used as indicators can be misleading, necessitating the validation of data quality which can further add to the burden of the information system (Frankenberger, 1992).

The third obstacle is the capacity to analyse data and to interpret them quickly enough to permit timely response. Almost all concurrent indicators, for example, are prefaced by the word 'unusual', which implies some baseline by which deviations from the norm can be measured. Without such a baseline, indicators are hard to interpret sensibly; further, what is normal in one context, may be very different from another area (*ibid.*). Unusual migration is a frequent casualty in this respect: empty villages after the harvest are used to indicate migration driven by poor harvests, whereas in fact they can be due to habitual reciprocal labour exchanges between neighbouring agro-ecological zones with differing harvest times (part of the moral economy, not of a collapsing food economy), and are a function of the usual variability of production in the same or neighbouring agro-ecological zones.

Fourth, such models can easily disguise intra-community variation, by failing to take account of the fact that one person's coping strategy is another's livelihood. Mortimore (1989), for example, shows how adaptive behaviour to drought over a thirteen-year period in northern Nigeria varies between households in the same village. Differences in options and choices occur at individual, household, community and livelihood-system levels. If a particular activity is identified as being a coping strategy for the purposes of food security monitoring, the assumption is that all people who take up that activity do so in order to cope with food stress. Yet, there is no easy way, for example, of distinguishing between someone who is choosing to go hungry to preserve assets and someone who is hungry and who has no choice, having previously liquidated all assets. Thus, whereas the stress indicator of increased dependence on wild foods appears to be a robust indication of local food entitlements, in fact in many marginal Sahelian communities there are groups who now habitually depend on wild foods for subsistence in part of every year. If early response is at the heart of monitoring coping strategies, it would be necessary to disaggregate food-security profiles for all groups in a given area in a normal year.

Finally, the models fail to account for changes over time. Coping strategies are not cast in stone and with each cycle of drought and partial rehabilitation, the range of options will change and the rate of take-up of particular strategies will vary. Riely (1991), for example, found that in Kordofan, Sudan, asset redistribution and changes in markets meant that the experience of drought itself changes the scope for coping with the next food crisis. So, even if one cycle has been successfully monitored and understood, there is no guarantee that, next time around, the same pattern will repeat itself for the same groups of people, in roughly the same proportions.

UNPACKING COPING STRATEGIES

To illustrate the difficulties inherent in developing indicators which are predicated upon standardised sequences of coping strategies, and thence to identify who is food-insecure, the starting point must be the range of factors which affect the options open to different livelihood systems (and communities and households within them) in periods of food stress. Choice of the mix of entitlements used – including coping strategies – depends on a combination of structural and proximate factors, as explained in Chapter 2. The menu of available options is further differentiated by livelihood system and by differential (household or individual) criteria. Structural livelihood-system factors can either be specific to that system or generalised, but, in the latter case, may have different implications for the system in question. Such factors include: the variety of production options available in a given agro-ecological zone; the robustness of the local marketing system for food, non-food, credit and labour, and the nature of dependence on that market of livelihood systems; the status of the moral economy of the community; and the level of provision of safety nets and other state-induced insurance mechanisms, and conversely the burden of taxation and other forms of extraction by the state on the community.

Household-specific structural factors are firstly determined by membership of a given livelihood system. Additional household-level factors determining choice of options include: [2]

- the available production options, determined by agro-ecological zone and the household's capacity to exploit them;
- the resource endowment at the onset of the crisis, which can be subdivided into: (a) household size and composition; (b) the amount and mix of productive assets, stores and claims, including access to communal resources;[3] (c) the status in the community (e.g. whether from a founding lineage or a stranger community; whether from a former slave class or a noble one);
- the mobility profile.

At a livelihood-system level, proximate factors which determine choice of strategies include: the nature of production failure; the exact sequence of events resulting in food insecurity; and commercial private sector and state responses to those events.

At a household level, proximate factors include: the range of 'chance' factors affecting output in a given year; access to information about local conditions and employment and other opportunities elsewhere; and the health status and nutritional needs of household members, including numbers of pregnant and lactating women and the infirm. The reasons why households pursue a particular mix of coping strategies and their timing for so doing thus depend on a complex range of criteria which are intimately linked to the different dimensions of vulnerability explored in Chapter 2. Clearly, it is not possible to monitor all these different criteria. Structural factors which determine coping choices are insensitive to short-term changes in the overall food situation, and tracking proximate factors at *household* level is beyond the scope of even local food monitoring, let alone those operating over larger areas. Theoretically, there is a two-step approach to resolving this problem: first, identifying groups which are 'doubly structurally vulnerable', in both an individual/household and a livelihood-system sense; and second, developing indicators for those groups which will detect proximate vulnerability whether individually/household or livelihood-system determined. Practically, however, the information requirements of this approach remain untenable for local food monitoring systems. The SADS system sought a compromise by focusing initially on the nature of structural livelihood-system vulnerability and then developing indicators to track proximate livelihood-system vulnerability. Livelihood systems provided the only criteria on which groups of producers were differentiated for the sake of simplicity, and no data were collected which enabled them to be classified according to more standard criteria of individual/household vulnerability. The results only tell part of the story as a consequence, but as Chapters 7 and 10 demonstrate, even this level of disaggregation creates problems of data collection and interpretation that are not obviously manageable by monitoring systems. Nevertheless, the indicators advocated to monitor coping strategies need to take account of differences within communities if they are to detect who is vulnerable to food insecurity and when this is likely to occur.

HOW USEFUL ARE COPING STRATEGIES?

More fundamental than these operational constraints are reservations about the validity of coping as a concept. Increasingly, coping strategies are regarded as being an inherently good thing, with little dynamic in their analysis. The following issues are important. First, 'coping strategies' is often used as a catch-all term to describe everything that rural people do over and above their primary activity. Whilst it is perhaps justifiable to argue that, for food-poor households, all decisions are influenced by and have some bearing on food poverty, it is not analytically very helpful to think of everything as a coping strategy. Hence, to include such factors as education and training under the rubric of accumulation strategies (WFP, 1989) says no more than that everything is a trade-off and all household decisions have a bearing on each other.

Second, and related to this, focusing on coping strategies in situations of food stress implies that people *do* cope and thus that food insecurity is a transitory phenomenon. This is in contrast to the World Bank (1986) distinction between transitory and chronic insecurity. If people also 'cope' with chronic insecurity, then the distinction between their normal and their coping behaviour is far from clear. At the extreme, all behaviour becomes a coping strategy when, for example, pastoralists have lost their animals and hence their means of primary production. Such groups who have fallen out of the bottom of livelihood systems are uniquely vulnerable and indeed have to cope to survive. But it is conceptually confusing to lump the means of subsistence eked out by the ultra-poor and destitute with pre-planned strategies used by producers within a livelihood system to overcome an exceptionally bad period. Searching for and monitoring coping strategies can mask the collapse of livelihood systems by presupposing that people cope even in subsistence economies which are no longer viable from the point of view of either food or livelihood security. Duffield (1990a), drawing on evidence from Sudan, argues that there are parts of the country where the combination of agro-climatic conditions, civil war and impoverishment from repeated famine has rendered some groups incapable of surviving, irrespective of proximate conditions. These are precisely the circumstances in which famine risks becoming endemic and where rural producers will need to alter their livelihood strategies radically to survive.

Third, while coping strategies may be useful in the short term (and, indeed, those who employ them have little option), they may be bad for development in the longer term. Implicit in them is that the entire working life of subsistence producers is taken up in acquiring some stock of food – enabling people to stand still, but preventing them from moving ahead. A focus on coping strategies also hides the (increasing) need of rural producers to develop livelihood strategies that will provide for greater numbers of people in the future. Growth linkages are thus central to the process of adaptation, but rarely included in analyses of coping behaviour. This assertion is, to some extent, contradicted by the sustainable livelihood-security approach, in so far as meeting food needs may be pushed into second place behind securing future livelihoods. But this holds only to the point where such choices make those livelihoods *more* secure in the future than in the present. All too often, this is not so. These choices may be good indicators of food stress, but they imply that there is no saving in the household, and that livelihoods are taken up which avoid risk, including the risk of investing in production. In a study of the famine in Darfur, Sudan in 1985, De Waal (1989) distinguishes between 'non-erosive' and 'erosive' coping, in order to differentiate between those strategies which use extra sources of income and do not erode the subsistence base of the household, and those which do, thereby compromising future livelihood security. There is as yet little evidence to show how the trade-off between subsistence and sustainability works. To find out about this, the reasons for and timing of the use of coping strategies, as well as their success or failure in meeting perceived needs, would need to be tracked over much longer periods than a single cycle of famine and rehabilitation. In other words, the ability of these strategies to maintain or increase resilience and to minimise sensitivity over time would need to be determined.

This criticism has implications for the often advocated (albeit rarely implemented) reinforcement of indigenous coping strategies as a more appropriate and effective method of famine prevention (and livelihood sustainability) than distributing emergency food aid, once livelihoods have been eroded. Echoing many proponents of a coping strategy-based approach to famine mitigation, the WFP (1989: 4) therefore argued:

> Well-meaning external assistance provided with insufficient knowledge and appreciation of anti-hunger strategies that are constantly adapted ... can ... undermine poor households' own attempts to manage periods of scarcity. On the other hand, with forethought, assistance can be delivered in such a way that coping strategies are reinforced.

Yet, if coping strategies simply allow people to stand still, or fall back more slowly, reinforcing these strategies may lock them into a vicious circle of subsistence and coping. If, on the other hand, food insurance for the very poor is provided, it enables them to be economically active (to take risks, to save). Thus, whereas there is an economic efficiency argument for guaranteeing food security over and above the purely humanitarian one, reinforcing coping strategies may be economically inefficient because it will reinforce the risk-averse survival-orientation of poor people.

Any monitoring system, to be sustainable, has to derive indicators which can be monitored over time and sensibly interpreted without too much difficulty. It is by no means clear that coping strategy indicators of food stress can do this, certainly they cannot by implicitly assuming

Coping and Adapting

homogeneity of motive and livelihood status. Even when livelihoods are differentiated (e.g. by livelihood system), differences between communities and households within the same broad system can be as great as those between systems. Further differentiation by individual or household determinants of vulnerability could assist the process, but in practice the spread of sequences of uptake would be so great as to make monitoring (let alone interpretation) fantastically complex.

COPING WITH SECURITY, ADAPTING TO VULNERABILITY

Underlying most of these caveats are two sources of confusion. First, there is the concern that coping strategies simply become a way of disguising change in rural economies by mixing up short-term coping with longer-term adaptation. Second, there is the confusion between coping strategies as fall-back mechanisms during periods when habitual food entitlements are disrupted, and as outcomes of fundamental and irreversible changes in local livelihood systems. If coping strategies are to remain a useful conceptual tool, both for monitoring declining food availability and for identifying appropriate interventions, clarification of these issues is required. *Coping* is therefore defined as a short-term response to an immediate and inhabitual decline in access to food. *Adapting*, in contrast, means a permanent change in the mix of ways in which food is acquired, irrespective of the year in question. As Gore (1992: 16) has correctly argued, '"coping" essentially means acting to survive *within the prevailing rule systems*'. When adaptation occurs, the rule system (or the moral economy) itself changes. Indicators have to be able to differentiate between coping within the existing rules and adapting the rules to meet livelihood needs; in other words, to detect when transitory food insecurity becomes chronic.

How to deal with change within production systems is a problem familiar to farming systems research. Thus, Maxwell (1986: 69) has identified the need to move away from a general awareness that conditions in farming systems are constantly changing, towards incorporating a notion of change into analyses of the determinants of farming systems. He distinguishes between four types of change: normal variations, shocks, cycles and trends. The idea of shocks and trends is now familiar within analyses of the causes of food insecurity (Maxwell, 1991). Equally, the idea of cycles of food insecurity and recovery is central to understanding change within food-security systems. But, within these cycles, distinctions need to be made between habitual seasonal variations and unusual, unseasonal disruptions. There is a danger, as coping strategies increasingly become the focus of attention for understanding producer responses to declining food entitlements, that they merely become a synonym for change within livelihood systems or, more seriously, a means of disguising changes which lead to increasingly low resilience/high sensitivity systems eventually losing their capacity to support livelihoods altogether. Even though analyses of coping strategies as explanations of how food-insecure households adapt to changes over time recognise the transition from coping to adaptation, when coping strategies are used as EW indicators, this process is not adequately accounted for. Coping strategies on their own cannot explain system change.

It will be recalled from Chapter 2 that whether livelihood systems have properties of high or low resilience and high or low sensitivity leads to very different options for producer responses to periods of food stress or uncertainty. Table 3.2 shows the different roles which (what are called) coping strategies occupy in each system. In highly resilient and insensitive systems, these strategies are reserved for abnormal years. In low resilience/highly sensitive ones, they are used in difficult seasons of every year: in the case of coping strategies to manage seasons of dearth; and in the case of insurance mechanisms, in every productive cycle. Eventually, both types of strategy become incorporated into the normal cycle of annual activities, if no alternative forms of adaptation exist. So, although the activities themselves may remain the same, the *reasons* for doing them, the *timing* of their use and their effectiveness or *capacity to increase entitlements* to a system under stress are very different in the two types of system.

This distinction has direct implications for the use of coping strategies in famine EWS, because monitoring their sequential uptake implicitly assumes that the livelihood systems are highly resilient. Coping strategies are the means by which resilient systems weather the bottom of the drought/recovery curve (see Graph 7.1 in Chapter 7); if they are to be good indicators of unusual food stress, they are used *only* at this point in the curve and are abandoned once recovery is under way. If, on the other hand, such strategies are part of a low resilience/highly sensitive livelihood system, they will be used *every* year in some seasons to bridge the food gap; in this case, they can only indicate an anticipated hungry season and not deviations from the norm. Furthermore if, as argued in Chapter 2, low resilience systems are characterised by fundamental adaptations after each period of severe drought, then any sequence of coping in subsequent periods of drought will be very different from what went before.

Many people in the Sahel and the Horn of Africa, who have been identified as potential beneficiaries of monitoring systems based on coping

Table 3.2 Role of coping strategies in vulnerable and secure livelihood systems

	Secure system (high resilience/low sensitivity)	Vulnerable system (low resilience/ high sensitivity)
Normal years		
1. Production	Food supply guaranteed in most years by primary activity(ies)	Food supply not guaranteed by primary activity(ies) hence food gap every year
2. Claims	Reciprocal links can fill food gap in unusual circumstances	Reciprocal links under increasing strain
3. Accumulation	Secondary activities permit savings and investment (1st buffer when primary production fails)	Secondary activities essential to meet food gap (no buffer)
		Coping strategies used when (1) and (2) fail to meet food needs, in part of every year (no 1st or 2nd buffer)
		Over time, coping strategies become part of secondary activities (3), i.e. *adaptive* strategies
Abnormal years		
4. Coping	Coping strategies used only in abnormal years (2nd buffer)	Genuine coping strategies reserved for famine become fewer and fewer

strategies, subsist in low resilience/high sensitivity food and livelihood systems.[4] The difficulties in using these strategies as indicators of food stress under such circumstances may add grist to the mill of those early warners who argue that systems should remain minimalist and deal only at a high level of aggregation, because they can never collect sufficient information or make sense of it at a local level – despite the fact that local people already have and make use of such information. Broad indicators of output and estimates of projected consumption, perhaps with some proxy indicators of demand such as market prices, must suffice. Yet, as argued in Chapter 1, these systems too have real drawbacks, not least their inability to understand how people feed themselves and what kind of interventions would reinforce this process early on in the cycle of drought and destitution, and before livelihood systems become unsustainable. The challenge is to retain the element of coping strategy-based monitoring which can fulfil these functions, whilst recognising that existing models are too sweeping in their definitions and too simplistic in their assumptions about when and why different people use them, and advocate remedies that are unsustainable.

The problem is where to draw the line between behaviour that is principally driven by food stress, and that which is peripherally influenced by it. Convention dictates that food is the most basic human need, within a hierarchy of concerns (Chapter 2). This has been challenged by the sustainable livelihood-security approach, which shifts food security to a piece in a jigsaw of immediate and longer-term needs, and blurs even more the boundaries between food stress-driven and livelihood needs. One way to resolve the problem is to use quite rigid temporal cut-off points to differentiate coping strategies from other household behaviour. What were once coping strategies increasingly determine the level of food availability within households, irrespective of the year in question, and hence become part of a process of adaptation. The key question for the purposes of monitoring changes in levels of food insecurity is where the threshold between coping and adapting lies. Given that, in terms of activities, coping and adaptive behaviour can be indistinguishable, the only way to identify this threshold is to ascertain the reasons for particular activities being pursued and the timing and effectiveness of their use in livelihood systems. This is a far more complex set of issues than simply monitoring whether or not particular activities are being undertaken.

Secure livelihood systems bounce back and restrict the use of coping strategies to periods of shock. In vulnerable systems, in contrast, coping strategies move up the hierarchy of activities after each shock to become simply an intensification of normal behaviour. This clarification goes some of the way towards differentiating between their roles in secure and vulnerable livelihood systems. It is not, however, sufficient to answer the question of whether – and if so how – distinctions can be made on the ground in monitoring systems between coping and adaptive strategies, bearing in mind that (a) the activity itself has not changed, but only its motivation and frequency of use, (b) at any given moment in a community, one person's coping strategy may be another's adaptive strategy, and (c) the shift between coping and adaptation is occurring all the time. Furthermore, coping strategies are always pursued inquisitively, so that if they demonstrate that a better option than current behaviour exists, they are taken up as permanent activities.

CONCLUSIONS

The SADS system set about monitoring coping strategies, for each livelihood system in the area, based on the assumption that they would be robust and sensitive indicators of food stress, and would facilitate the identification of appropriate and timely responses. The shortcomings of this approach described in this chapter are derived from the results of this process. The concept of coping strategies needs to be treated with caution. To summarise. First, they can be defined so broadly as to be indistinguishable from general patterns of individual, household and community-level decision-making. Second, they can be based on the false assumption that people do cope and thus that food insecurity is a transitory phenomenon. Third, if coping strategies and their reinforcement were to become the centre-piece of household food security monitoring and interventions, there is a risk of people remaining locked into a vicious circle of subsistence and coping, reinforced by interventions designed to support coping strategies. Fourth, the idea of coping strategies being cast in stone and of people following an identifiable and repeatable pattern of uptake ignores the fact that one person's coping strategy is another's livelihood, making the identification and monitoring of repeated patterns of coping behaviour more or less impossible for representative groups. Finally, the very complexity of coping strategies makes for potentially huge difficulties in data collection and interpretation. To address these issues, a distinction has been made between coping and adaptation: whereas coping is a characteristic of structurally secure livelihood systems, vulnerable ones are characterised by adaptation. The results of trying to monitor coping strategies as indicators of food stress in what were found to be low resilience systems are analysed in Chapter 10, and on this basis the policy implications of monitoring coping and adaptive behaviour in vulnerable livelihood systems are considered in Chapter 11.

4 Monitoring How People Feed Themselves

INTRODUCTION

This chapter explains the methodology developed by the SADS system, which had the following objectives:

- to establish a baseline of habitual food entitlements (based on the livelihood-entitlements framework presented in Chapter 2), against which temporary deviations or permanent changes could be measured. This baseline was defined in terms of when people last felt habitually secure in both their access to food and in their livelihoods;
- to develop a set of indicators which would predict whether or not people would achieve food security relative to this baseline, in a given season or year as well as over the longer term. Such indicators needed to address three dimensions to the success or failure of meeting food needs: (a) whether primary and secondary activities would guarantee food security;[1] (b) if not, how people would cope with food insecurity; (c) how and whether they would recover from episodes of food insecurity or adapt to permanent changes in their food-security status.

In contrast to most EWS, which focus on the first dimension alone, the methodology sought to monitor the continuum of successful access to food, entitlement failure, coping and recovery – a process defined as much by the different livelihood systems whereby people acquire food, and their status within them at the outset of a period of insecurity, as by independent variables such as rainfall or aggregate production in a given year. It also sought to differentiate between the success or failure of maximising the different sources of entitlement and meeting calls on entitlement identified in Chapter 2. It therefore had to be capable of differentiating between a failure of productive entitlements and, for example, exchange entitlements, and hence to identify which parts of the entitlement bundles of producers were robust in situations of scarcity and could be reinforced by interventions to protect the food security of particular groups. It also sought to identify circumstances in which dryland cultivators, for

Monitoring How People Feed Themselves

example, were at risk of entitlement failure as opposed to, say, pastoralists. To do this, it was necessary to understand the degree and nature of structural livelihood-system vulnerability, in order to identify appropriate indicators of proximate vulnerability, which vary from one livelihood system to another. The aim was not simply to monitor a single cycle of food insecurity and coping, but to track over time the ability of different livelihood systems – and people within them – to minimise sensitivity to food insecurity and to recover after periods of food stress. Further, it sought to identify the constraints preventing some groups from achieving this and the extent to which these could be mitigated by preventive – rather than curative – interventions.

In order to meet these requirements, the information system had to monitor livelihood security rather than simply food security (see Chapter 2). The former is distinct in a number of ways:

- the unit of analysis is the different livelihood systems in a given area;
- within such systems, access to food is arrived at by a complex combination of sources of and calls on entitlement. This is in stark contrast to 'minimalist' EWS which seek to reduce information needs to a handful of key indicators which can serve as proxies for the overall pattern of availability and, to a much lesser degree, entitlement to food;
- both sources of and calls on entitlement are determined not simply by immediate circumstances and needs, but by the nature and intensity of livelihood vulnerability at the outset of a period of food insecurity, as well as by the need to preserve livelihoods for the future, perhaps at the cost of immediate food-security needs;
- the objectives of monitoring are to predict collapse of livelihoods, not simply of food access, and thereby to identify ways of intervening to secure livelihoods in the future which in turn will help to guarantee future food security.

CLASSIFYING LIVELIHOOD SYSTEMS

Livelihood systems were used as the basis on which to differentiate between sources of and calls on entitlement for different groups. There are, of course, differences *within* livelihood systems including rich and poor households and a range of other criteria of structural individual vulnerability (including intra-household differences). There is also movement *between* livelihood systems when, for example, pastoralists are forced to

62   Adaptable Livelihoods

Diagram 4.1   Classification of food-insecure populations according to
              multiple vulnerability criteria

```
                                            HOUSEHOLD/INDIVIDUAL
                                            VULNERABILITY

                                                              Children
                                                             / under 5
                                            Poor
                                           / households  ←— Women
                            Cultivators  ←
                          /                 \ Rich        \ Elderly,
              Rural people ←                  households    infirm
            /             \ Agro-
  LIVELIHOOD               pastoralists
  SYSTEM     ←— Displaced people
  VULNERABILITY
            \ Urban people
```

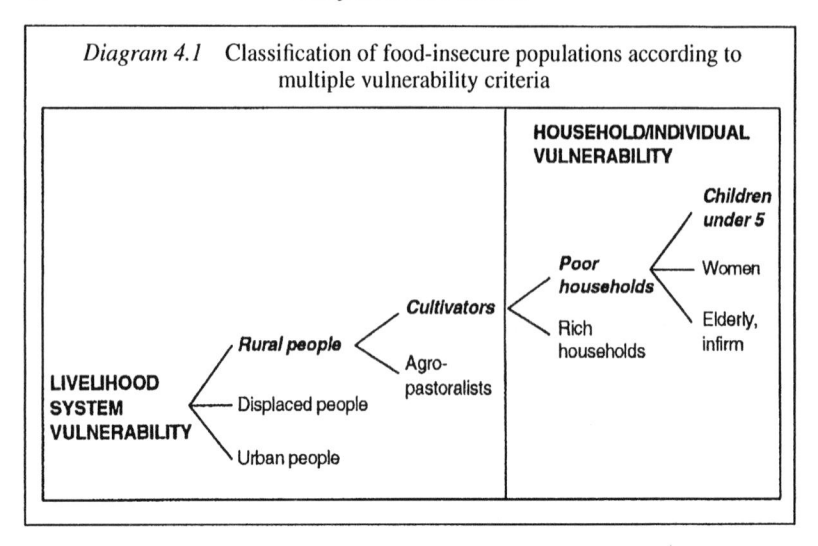

take up cultivation or when agro-pastoralists sell their last animals and become undiversified cultivators. In methodological terms, a livelihood-system classification was used to strike a balance between numerous highly differentiated groups within rural communities on the one hand, and a classification which takes no account of the basis of subsistence on the other. Diagram 4.1 shows how such different levels of classification might operate.

The methodology drew on the extensive research of the IUCN 'Project for the Conservation of the Environment in the Inner Niger Delta', which had spent two years identifying livelihood systems in the area, based on an initial survey of all communities in the *cercle* of Youvarou (IUCN, 1987a, 1987b). For the *cercle* of Douentza, a survey of communities carried out by OXFAM in 1986 was used (Hesse and Thera, 1987). The classification used was as follows:

● *Cultivators*, who are defined as sedentary farmers dependent on undiversified rain- and flood-fed cultivation for their subsistence with a distinction made between dryland cultivators of millet and wetland cultivators of rice. Revenue from livestock accounts for much less than 50 per cent of income and livestock are regarded primarily as a store of assets.
● *Agro-pastoralists*, who depend on a mixture of cultivation and livestock for subsistence, including black Fulani (as opposed to red Fulani, who traditionally only herded animals) who have shifted

from cattle to goats (and are thus no longer transhumant) and dryland former cultivators who have switched from entrusting their cattle to the Fulani to herding their own goats.
- *Agro-fishers* – sedentary wetland rice cultivators who also fish individually and collectively at the end of the season on the Delta floodplains near their villages and in the lake zone of Douentza.
- *Transhumant fishers* originating from the riverine area to the south of the Delta, outside the SADS zone, who are also millet and rice cultivators, but leave their villages in the high water season and transhume downstream through the Delta following the flood retreat. These are specialist fishers, employing capital-intensive techniques, including the construction of dams along the main branches of the Bani and Niger rivers. From the point of view of the SADS system, only their fishing activities were monitored.
- *Transhumant pastoralists* – 'pure' pastoralists who depend on livestock for subsistence and acquire grain only through barter or purchase. Within the SADS zone, different groupings habitually follow distinct circuits of transhumance based on the seasonal availability of pasture and traditional access rights.

This classification was not intended to be an exact reflection of all mixes of productive activities pursued in the area. Monitoring five livelihood systems on a seasonal basis, in particularly complex and diverse agro-ecological zones, was difficult enough; further precision of productive groups was judged to be cost-ineffective. The classification does not include certain important groups, notably those who subsist by constantly moving between livelihood systems and those who have fallen out of the bottom of one of the five systems and have failed to join another. To monitor this group in particular, tracking of displaced persons congregating around semi-urban centres would also be necessary.[2] The groups not included are nevertheless dependent on the absorptive capacity of each system in times of food stress; it was therefore possible to monitor indirectly the opportunities for access to food for those outside the main livelihood systems.

LISTENING POSTS, COVERAGE AND COUNTING

Data collection was organised around four permanent listening posts, or strategic monitoring points, where food-insecure populations pass through or seek refuge in at times of most acute food insecurity. This system was successful in decentralising data collection and concentrating monitoring in strategic places, with the proviso that although local livelihood systems do not respect administrative boundaries, planners' decisions about interventions do. For this reason, data were increasingly presented according to administrative boundaries – as well as by livelihood system – even though these were somewhat artificial from the point of view of the information itself. Two listening posts were based in district capitals, one in the regional capital and the fourth in a *chef lieu d'arrondissement* (the lowest administrative unit, below *cercles*).[3]

Maximising coverage of different people was much more problematic. The first stumbling block was an underestimation of personnel requirements, both of field agents and supervisors. The original idea was to have one (and subsequently two) people covering all livelihood systems in each listening post, to enable them to compare information across systems. In fact, it would have been better to have had one agent per livelihood system, covering a somewhat larger area but specialising in a particular system, with an overall supervisor to co-ordinate the various information flows. Supervision was originally conducted by the same people moving between all listening posts, but eventually supervisors were based in listening posts. Coverage was, consequently, sporadic at times, particularly for transhumant livelihood systems, which required long journeys to monitor them.

In contrast, the failure to quantify numbers of food-insecure people was a fault in the design of the methodology, which deliberately set out to avoid the error of so many EWS of estimating the number of food-insecure people in a given area by means of highly inaccurate quantification. Very early on SADS data showed that the distribution of food insecurity was much more varied and complex than the calculation of the total population of an area identified as at risk. Frequently, people would have moved to a more secure area, which as a result was where the concentrations of food-insecure people were really found. Thus, although the monitoring system was able to identify relative food insecurity, it could not put an absolute figure on the numbers affected and was frequently criticised on this score. A fairly rough and ready demographic survey, collecting data on the membership of livelihood systems, should have been undertaken, both to add credence to the monitoring results in the eyes of planners and to facilitate numerical estimates of the numbers of vulnerable groups in each season.

This leads on to the question of relative versus absolute values. As argued in Chapter 1, the objective was not to inform about tonnages of food aid required, but to ascertain and then track the types of livelihood system on which people depend and the extent to which these fulfil food and livelihood-security needs. The monitoring could, therefore, show the sorts of people facing particular problems, where they came from and where they were at a given time and how their situation compared with other producers. But whereas it was possible to reveal a hierarchy of insecurity, the system could not say precisely how many people were at each level. As the intended outcome was small-scale local-level interventions, relative ranking sufficed. But much of the reason for the third phase of quantitative household surveys, discussed below, was to respond to the issue of absolute values of food insecurity, again in response to planners' requests for numbers.

PERSONNEL, TRAINING AND EXISTING INFORMATION

Project field agents educated up to Standard 5 in secondary school were selected, where possible, from the areas in which they were to work; supervisors were usually educated to university level within the Malian system.[4] Crucially, on-the-job training for field agents involved not only methods of data collection, but also of analysis and presentation. This enabled them not only to interpret their own data (which they were often much better qualified to do than the project co-ordinators), but also to suggest where the methodology was not working, and how it might be improved. This was essential as the methodological approach centred on using local people's own perceptions. The integration of field staff is in stark contrast to the practice of many EWS, and much of the success of SADS' information collection is due to this iterative process.

The first six months or so of the project, whilst the methodology was being developed, was taken up with exploiting existing information both on the area and on food security at regional and national levels. The principal source of local information was the IUCN research project (see IUCN, 1986, 1987a, 1987b, 1989a, 1989c, 1989d) and the OXFAM survey in Douentza (Hesse and Thera, 1987). In addition, government records and reports were consulted, including the *Diagnostic de la Région de Mopti* (République du Mali, 1985), census data (République du Mali, 1987b), SAP reports and unpublished material available at the *arrondissement* and *cercle* level. Standard historical texts for the region (e.g. Gallais, 1957, 1958, 1967, 1984; Bâ and Daget, 1962) were also consulted to assist in the identification of traditional patterns of access to food and more recent research reports used to update this (e.g. CIPEA and ODEM, 1983; Hesse *et al.*, 1984; Hesse, 1987). Regional and national-level information was collected from official government sources and interviews with key personnel (see Chapters 5 and 6). Baseline monographs were produced as working documents for each listening post, to determine gaps as well as to distil existing information. This was also the first step in the training of field staff, to familiarise them with available material about their listening post. Results of this work were presented at the first quarterly meeting of the monitoring system, when the methodology described below was formulated.

LIVELIHOOD-SYSTEM SURVEYS

The objective of the first phase of monitoring was to test the working hypotheses described in Chapter 1. These, it will be recalled, focus on finding out about whether and how local livelihood systems had become less resilient and more sensitive to stress over time; levels of food security derived from primary activities and the range of other sources of and calls on entitlements that were available to producers; changes in vulnerability from one season to the next; coping strategies employed; and longer-term adaptive strategies to increase resilience. On this basis, Phase 1 sought to identify a set of season- and livelihood system-specific indicators, to 'unpack' the total bundle of entitlements, and to monitor these on a seasonal basis. Diagram 4.2 summarises the components and outputs of Phase 1.

For each of the three rural listening posts (Toguéré Koumbé, Youvarou and Douentza), data collection was organised on a seasonal basis (the harvest season, October–December; the cold season, January–March; the hot dry season, April–June; and the rainy season, July–September) for each livelihood system. The level of collection was the village (or *campement* in the case of transhumant livelihood systems) and data from a number of sample villages were aggregated to form community profiles. Livelihood systems were identified in groups of villages (in productively homogenous areas), or as specific productive groups within a sample of comparable villages (where more than one livelihood system co-existed side by side).

In those listening posts where collaborating organisations had already conducted village surveys (IUCN in Youvarou; OXFAM in Douentza), survey data were used to identify key villages for sedentary populations and strategic places for transhumant populations in particular seasons. In Toguéré Koumbé, chosen for its strategic position in one of the most productive parts of the central Delta, all villages were visited during the first

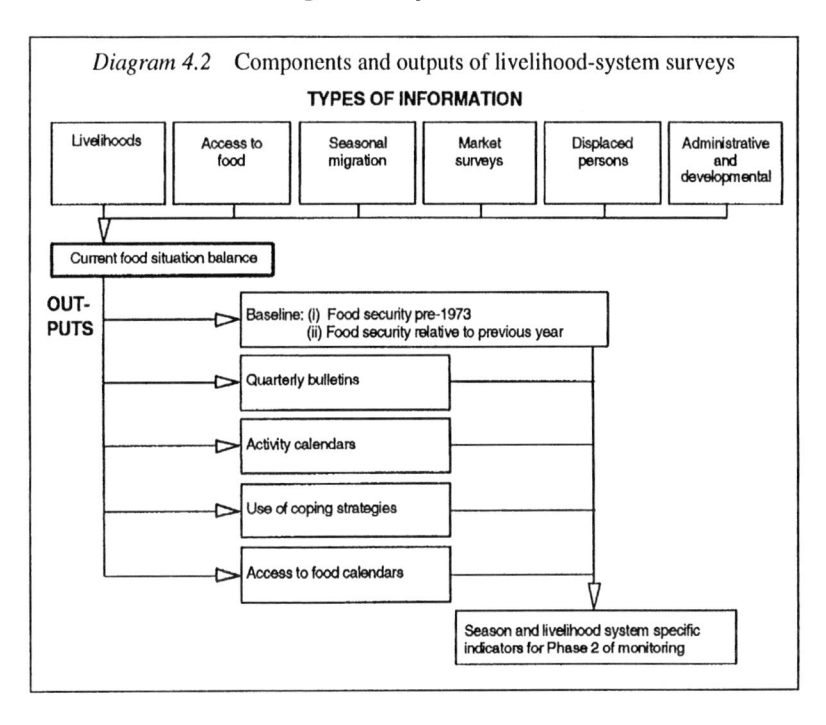

Diagram 4.2 Components and outputs of livelihood-system surveys

TYPES OF INFORMATION

Livelihoods	Access to food	Seasonal migration	Market surveys	Displaced persons	Administrative and developmental

Current food situation balance

OUTPUTS
- Baseline: (i) Food security pre-1973 (ii) Food security relative to previous year
- Quarterly bulletins
- Activity calendars
- Use of coping strategies
- Access to food calendars

Season and livelihood system specific indicators for Phase 2 of monitoring

year to classify their populations. In the neighbouring *arrondissements* of Diondiori and Tenenkou Central,[5] this classification was carried out in consultation with the Local Development Committee. Villages were classified according to: livelihood systems; diversity of productive and exchange activities; agro-ecological zone; number of households; relative 'wealth' compared with neighbours; and willingness to participate in the monitoring exercise.

Data collection was based on check-lists rather than on formal questionnaires, completed on the basis of discussions with meetings of villagers (male and female, sometimes together, sometimes separately) as well as directed interviews with key informants, such as village chiefs, old men and women, village traders, representatives of stranger families. Further key informants were identified in local markets (see Chapter 9); also representatives of state *Opérations de Développement Rurale* (ODRs); *arrondissement* and *cercle*-level functionaries (including local MPs and representatives of the political party); and, where appropriate, representatives of local and foreign NGOs and other development initiatives. These more formal informants met regularly in meetings of the Local

Development Committees, at both *arrondissement* and *cercle* level, of which listening post staff were members. At regional and national level, project staff also attended relevant working groups.

Sources of information in Phase 1 were thus divided into three principal groups, which served distinct functions within the process of data collection: *villagers*, whom the monitoring system sought to tap as the most reliable 'indigenous information system'; *market traders and people attending markets* to buy or sell, again to tap local knowledge in order to monitor how exchange entitlements were working; and *government officials and local representatives of organisations*, both to assimilate information collected by the SADS system with that collected by the local administration,[6] and to acquire information about the administrative and developmental context in which people were making decisions about their food security.

Data collection in the fourth listening post of Mopti-ville was organised somewhat differently. The second and third groups of informants were more numerous and important than in the rural posts, because of Mopti's position as commercial centre of the 5th Region and regional capital. Further, displaced persons congregating around the town and seasonal migrants were also monitored. Information on employment opportunities, wage rates and labour supply and demand was also collected.

The check-lists for information gathering in Phase 1 had to serve three functions: to establish how livelihood systems operated in the past, to show how things were in the present, and to identify ways of predicting what would happen in the future. The following types of information were therefore collected by season and by livelihood system:

- *Activities*. Men and women were asked separately about their main and secondary activities, activities not linked to primary production, activities not previously undertaken, and the reasons for the particular mix.
- *Production*. Depending on the season, villagers were asked about: the constraints they were facing, their current production and how they rated it according to a reasonable year, and where they were fishing or pasturing animals and their assessment of conditions, relative to a reasonable year.
- *Levels of stocks*.
- *Labour*. Whether they were employing any casual labour or had any kin staying and, if so, on what basis they were remunerated; equally, whether they were seeking work within the village or elsewhere.
- *Exchange*. What they were selling, buying and/or bartering; who they traded with; why and whether these were habitual or unusual exchanges or, for example, investments in productive assets.

Monitoring How People Feed Themselves 69

In addition, in the first year of monitoring villagers were asked how their current situation compared with the past, i.e. before the 1973 drought; the inter-drought years; the 1982–5 drought; and the post-drought years.

Access to food information. These indicators were cross-checked using a further check-list relating directly to sources of and calls on entitlement to food, rather than to more general livelihoods. In the first year of monitoring, people were also asked how they defined food security and the ways in which their own perceptions of food (in)security had changed over time. Throughout there were discussions about where food habitually came from in this season, compared with actual sources; where the cash came from if food was being bought; where wild foods were gathered; how long the current source of food was expected to last; how many meals were eaten a day and what they consisted of; whether additional kin were arriving for meals; whether any gifts of food were being received or given, plus discussion of the particular food-security problems encountered at the time, and villagers' estimates of the proportion of their total food supply coming from different sources.

Seasonal migration. A further check-list was concerned with habitual and inhabitual movements into, out of and around the zone, and the reasons for these movements. In seasons where large concentrations of strangers were identified by villagers, interviews were held with them. Similarly, habitual and unusually high (or low) numbers of kin arriving in villages were noted.

Administrative and developmental information. Both secondary data from local administrative offices and regular meetings with government personnel were part of the monitoring process. Questions included the technical services' own estimates of production levels, information on reports from village chiefs and details of movements (particularly of displaced people) in and out of the *cercle*. This information was mainly relevant in the context of the administration's own longer-term planning objectives and how SADS information fitted in with this. More information was available at regional and national levels, particularly in respect of aggregate production estimates, decision-making regarding movements of livestock through the Delta, requests for food aid and deliveries, and development initiatives in the region.

Mopti-ville. In addition to the administrative information collected in Mopti, and monitoring markets and commercial activity, enquiries focused on demand and supply of casual labour and daily wage rates, and seasonal migration to and from the town (as above), particularly to cross-check information about migration from rural areas, much of which would pass through Mopti, and returning migrants from the south of the country.

Displaced persons. The congregations of displaced people in and around Mopti were also monitored, first via a census to see the extent to which they were people who had fallen out of the bottom of livelihood systems, and subsequently how they subsisted, what the seasonal migration to and from the camps was and whether numbers increased as food insecurity intensified in the surrounding rural areas. A similar exercise was conducted in Douentza. Elsewhere, where displaced populations were smaller and less permanent (i.e. they frequently dispersed at certain moments of the year), the monitoring came under the rubric of seasonal migration.

Analysis, outputs and techniques

On the basis of these various check-lists (and the market surveys discussed below), a qualitative balance of the food situation for all livelihood systems was compiled to assess the relative security or vulnerability of different groups. Additional outputs included: seasonal SADS quarterly Bulletins; activity calendars; coping strategy use; and access to food calendars (Davies *et al.*, 1990d, 1990c, 1990b).

The basic approach to data collection via check-lists of issues to be covered in discussion with groups of villagers and key informants was being developed whilst comparable RRA and subsequently participatory rural appraisal (PRA) techniques were becoming increasingly popular. This was not an explicit objective at the outset; rather, techniques evolved in line with the monitoring system. One important caveat to this loose association with RRA is that the premise of the methodology was based on field agents being stationed *permanently* in or near the communities they monitored; there was none of the rapid flying visit associated with RRA. Familiarity with local people was central to the approach of data collection but it was not realistic to repeat time-consuming PRA exercises in the same communities over and over again. The SADS system was based on people's own perceptions of what food security meant and their own views of which indicators were critical at certain times of the year. We return to this issue in Chapter 11.

MONITORING SEASON AND LIVELIHOOD-SYSTEM SPECIFIC INDICATORS

Results from the check-lists used in all seasons and for all livelihood systems gradually made it possible to develop more precise indicators for each livelihood system by season, and at the end of the first year, general check-lists were replaced with much simpler lists of indicators (Chapter 7). These reflected to a far greater degree the real decisions being taken and the bundles of entitlements producers were actually relying on, and enabled the monitoring system to adapt to the circumstances in a particular season and to concentrate its endeavours on unusual activities which appeared to be associated with food stress. By the end of the first year, although by no means complete, information collected on livelihood systems in the past was judged to be sufficient and this component was dropped.

MARKET SURVEYS

Monthly market surveys were maintained throughout the different phases of monitoring, with the aim of monitoring the exchange entitlements of rural people and providing information on the overall commercial and economic climate in which they made decisions. Further, they gave the opportunity for some reliable quantification at the outset of the monitoring exercise.

Twelve markets were monitored on a monthly basis, including the regional market of Mopti/Fatoma, the district markets of Youvarou, Douentza and Tenenkou, and eight local markets. A more conventional questionnaire format was used for the market surveys, to allow comparisons between months and markets. Cereal and livestock prices are the backbone of most EWS which seek to monitor access to food as well as availability. Prices for cereals and other staples were collected, for fresh, smoked and dried fish, for goats, sheep and heifers, for fresh and soured milk, for gathered products (including wild foods), wood and mats made from doum palms, for non-essential (but often purchased) foods such as tea and sugar, and for a representative selection of condiments. In addition, levels of commercial activity were monitored by recording the number of buyers and sellers of particular goods.

A range of qualitative information was also collected, including: where buyers and traders came from, the presence of very small-scale traders (i.e. producers turning to commerce as a coping strategy), the sale of unusual assets, the availability of cereals and other essential products and, if wild foods were available, where they had been gathered, and so on. This type of information enabled the surveys to provide a great deal of information about people's coping strategies in general, as well as about their exchange entitlements and the coping strategies related to exchange in particular.

HOUSEHOLD SURVEYS

The household is central to understanding how different people achieve food security, and particularly so in vulnerable livelihood systems, where the means by which security is achieved (e.g. via market dependence and reallocation of household labour) are based on household-level decisions. But households are conventionally excluded from EWS because this level of disaggregation is regarded as too complex and costly (in time and other resources), and thus unsustainable. Yet, by focusing exclusively on higher levels of aggregation, most EWS monitor for the end-product of destitution, rather than for how some households get into that situation whilst others manage to escape it. As a result, the *early* detection of the threat of food insecurity for certain groups within communities is very difficult. Instead, EWS must wait for system-wide collapse. This, in turn, makes interventions almost inevitably reactive to a widespread crisis that is already under way, rather than aimed at the mitigation of destitution of vulnerable groups. In failing to elicit timely response, one of the principal objectives of EWS is defeated.

For food information systems which have a broader remit than simply *famine* prediction and prevention, the role of the household is even more critical to guiding effective and targeted policy-making. As Kabeer and Joekes (1991: 1) have argued:

> The household is the link between macro- and meso-economic changes and changes in personal welfare, and between price or incentive policy reforms and individuals' resource allocative behaviour.

Consequently, any changes in macro- or sub-national level policy-making which are to be appropriate to individual food-security requirements must take into account how those needs are met – or not – at the household level. To respond to these issues, a third more detailed and quantified phase of monitoring was launched at household level, based on the indicators established in Phases 1 and 2. Regarded as a pilot exercise, it consisted of monthly household surveys for 15 months, which aimed to assess in a purely indicative way, given the small size of the sample, the relative vulnerability of different livelihood systems and to quantify these differences, in respect of: the size of the structural household food gap in a normal year; the importance of exchange entitlements in filling this gap; and the allocation of time between main and secondary activities and coping/adaptive strategies.

Phase 3 was also informed by the need to clarify the extent to which monitoring food access within households denies or confirms the utility of conventional EW indicators; to see what components of household food availability and entitlements could be measured at household level, not as a one-off research exercise, but as a sustainable monitoring process, thereby assessing the viability of the methodology and how it could be refined; and to tackle the problem of whether the sequential uptake of coping strategies can be used as indicators of unusual food stress, if they are in fact adaptive strategies pursued every year at least by certain households. In addition, there was a need to assess the personnel requirements of such a monitoring system. Finally, Phase 3 sought to disaggregate data collection to cover such critical issues as levels of indebtedness, access to credit, size of household stocks, use and division of family labour, about which accurate information could only be obtained at household level. It was also designed to test the feasibility of establishing sentinel villages, within which data could be collected over time, and to identify pilot villages for small-scale interventions arising out of the findings of Phases 1 and 2.

The intention was to collect data simultaneously in five dryland villages in Douentza and five wetland ones in the Delta. For personnel reasons, the dryland sample never got off the ground. This weakened one of the principal objectives of Phase 3: to compare the relative food insecurity of similar livelihood systems in different agro-ecological zones. Consequently, the results of the surveys of 50 households (ten in each of five villages) offer a picture of food security available to those inhabiting the traditional wetland safety net, and not of Sahelian producers more generally. Even though dryland producers migrate seasonally into the Delta, particularly in dry years, in order to increase their range of natural-resource base entitlements, they do not exploit these resources under the same terms and conditions as residents of the Delta.

For the purposes of the survey, the household was defined by people in the sample on the basis of the numbers of people who shared food resources (both in terms of production and consumption) and who took collective decisions about acquiring such resources. The idea of a 'marmite' (literally cooking pot) is well established as a patrilocal consumption and production group, which may be a nuclear family (albeit unusually so) or an extended one, some of which are polygamous, and often including adopted kin as well as more or less permanent 'migrant' kin.

Households within the villages were selected by the chiefs somewhat artificially to include three small (six people or fewer), four medium (7–11 people) and three large (twelve or more people), and to represent two of each of the five livelihood systems. No reliable household data were

74 Adaptable Livelihoods

collected for transhumant livelihood systems,[7] and data were analysed for the three sedentary systems only. All but one household in the sample were founding families, giving a bias towards those with more secure access to resources.

Data were collected on the basis of two 'questionnaires' which incorporated some of the techniques familiar to PRA (e.g. diagramming, mapping). The first solicited information on: ethnic group; whether or not the household belonged to a founding lineage or was a stranger one; household size and composition; and amount and value of productive and other assets, including livestock and food stocks. Each household also provided a history of the basis of its livelihood, particularly the changes since the 1973 and 1984 droughts. The second included questions on expenditure and income, gifts and credit, and time budgets, all of which yielded data that could be interpreted, plus questions on consumption of food over the previous 24 hours, migration to and from the household, bartering, and acquisition and disposal of assets, which were not answered in any consistent fashion. Cereal production was estimated and details of disposal of harvests other than through sale (e.g. repayment of loans, gifts to kin, etc.) were also recorded.

A number of problems arose with the data collection for specific indicators. These are discussed in turn, since they are instructive in the context of the development of indicators which are feasible and sustainable. It is worth noting at the outset that, for all the weaknesses elaborated, the key point about these data is the relationships between different variables, and their changes from season to season, rather than absolute values. Furthermore, it should be reiterated that the household surveys were intended to provide indicative not statistically representative results.

Consumption. Certain elements included in the monthly questionnaires proved impossible to complete with any degree of accuracy; 24-hour consumption recalls met with overwhelming resistance from respondents, and were abandoned after six months. Even a much simplified approach requesting information on the number of meals consumed in a day yielded no reliable results.

Credits, gifts and other transfers. Data on gifts and other transfers were generally unreliable. In particular, the sensitive issue of credit, whether from traders or from kin, was also virtually impossible to track and went largely unrecorded despite continued mention of the need to repay debts.

Assets and stores. At the outset of the survey data were very incomplete. Livestock numbers are notoriously hard to collect and information on them was almost certainly consistently underestimated, not least because they are taxable. Data on other assets (e.g. productive equipment,

conventional EW indicators; to see what components of household food availability and entitlements could be measured at household level, not as a one-off research exercise, but as a sustainable monitoring process, thereby assessing the viability of the methodology and how it could be refined; and to tackle the problem of whether the sequential uptake of coping strategies can be used as indicators of unusual food stress, if they are in fact adaptive strategies pursued every year at least by certain households. In addition, there was a need to assess the personnel requirements of such a monitoring system. Finally, Phase 3 sought to disaggregate data collection to cover such critical issues as levels of indebtedness, access to credit, size of household stocks, use and division of family labour, about which accurate information could only be obtained at household level. It was also designed to test the feasibility of establishing sentinel villages, within which data could be collected over time, and to identify pilot villages for small-scale interventions arising out of the findings of Phases 1 and 2.

The intention was to collect data simultaneously in five dryland villages in Douentza and five wetland ones in the Delta. For personnel reasons, the dryland sample never got off the ground. This weakened one of the principal objectives of Phase 3: to compare the relative food insecurity of similar livelihood systems in different agro-ecological zones. Consequently, the results of the surveys of 50 households (ten in each of five villages) offer a picture of food security available to those inhabiting the traditional wetland safety net, and not of Sahelian producers more generally. Even though dryland producers migrate seasonally into the Delta, particularly in dry years, in order to increase their range of natural-resource base entitlements, they do not exploit these resources under the same terms and conditions as residents of the Delta.

For the purposes of the survey, the household was defined by people in the sample on the basis of the numbers of people who shared food resources (both in terms of production and consumption) and who took collective decisions about acquiring such resources. The idea of a *'marmite'* (literally cooking pot) is well established as a patrilocal consumption and production group, which may be a nuclear family (albeit unusually so) or an extended one, some of which are polygamous, and often including adopted kin as well as more or less permanent 'migrant' kin.

Households within the villages were selected by the chiefs somewhat artificially to include three small (six people or fewer), four medium (7–11 people) and three large (twelve or more people), and to represent two of each of the five livelihood systems. No reliable household data were

74 Adaptable Livelihoods

collected for transhumant livelihood systems,[7] and data were analysed for the three sedentary systems only. All but one household in the sample were founding families, giving a bias towards those with more secure access to resources.

Data were collected on the basis of two 'questionnaires' which incorporated some of the techniques familiar to PRA (e.g. diagramming, mapping). The first solicited information on: ethnic group; whether or not the household belonged to a founding lineage or was a stranger one; household size and composition; and amount and value of productive and other assets, including livestock and food stocks. Each household also provided a history of the basis of its livelihood, particularly the changes since the 1973 and 1984 droughts. The second included questions on expenditure and income, gifts and credit, and time budgets, all of which yielded data that could be interpreted, plus questions on consumption of food over the previous 24 hours, migration to and from the household, bartering, and acquisition and disposal of assets, which were not answered in any consistent fashion. Cereal production was estimated and details of disposal of harvests other than through sale (e.g. repayment of loans, gifts to kin, etc.) were also recorded.

A number of problems arose with the data collection for specific indicators. These are discussed in turn, since they are instructive in the context of the development of indicators which are feasible and sustainable. It is worth noting at the outset that, for all the weaknesses elaborated, the key point about these data is the relationships between different variables, and their changes from season to season, rather than absolute values. Furthermore, it should be reiterated that the household surveys were intended to provide indicative not statistically representative results.

Consumption. Certain elements included in the monthly questionnaires proved impossible to complete with any degree of accuracy; 24-hour consumption recalls met with overwhelming resistance from respondents, and were abandoned after six months. Even a much simplified approach requesting information on the number of meals consumed in a day yielded no reliable results.

Credits, gifts and other transfers. Data on gifts and other transfers were generally unreliable. In particular, the sensitive issue of credit, whether from traders or from kin, was also virtually impossible to track and went largely unrecorded despite continued mention of the need to repay debts.

Assets and stores. At the outset of the survey data were very incomplete. Livestock numbers are notoriously hard to collect and information on them was almost certainly consistently underestimated, not least because they are taxable. Data on other assets (e.g. productive equipment, gold, domestic stores of value) yielded no reliable information, probably because of people's perceptions that investment assistance would be more likely to be forthcoming if asset levels were seen to be minimal or non-existent. No households reported cereal stocks of any significance at the outset of the survey (prior to the 1989 harvest). Given the bumper harvest of 1988, explanations included the need to sell large quantities of cereals to meet debt repayments and other cash needs.

Migration and remittances. The overwhelming impression from migration data was that in contrast to the idea of decisions being made at key moments of the year (e.g. after the harvest, returning before the next agricultural campaign), household migration in vulnerable livelihood systems is a much more fluid affair in response to diverse opportunities ranging from long-term reciprocal arrangements to news of employment opportunities in particular areas or to individual whims. There was little evidence of these decisions being driven primarily by the need to leave in order to reduce household consumption, although this was cited as an important contributory justification. Perceptions of the reasons for migration varied between household members: older men, for example, invariably argued that younger sons left for essentially selfish reasons, whereas those migrating reasoned that it was to find work to be able to send money home. Above all, older members of households consistently argued that the decision to migrate was no longer a collective decision, implying that reciprocal links (certainly in terms of migrating to send back remittances) are under strain and that further research is needed if migration is to be a reliable indicator of food stress.

Household food supply. Cereal production was surveyed at the time of harvest. Data on fish and milk production were far less reliable. Information on quantities of barter was highly inaccurate, or often not forthcoming at all. The key issue here seemed to be whether or not it was taking place; barter tends to be abandoned in times of scarcity in favour of the market. Data on cereals acquired by participating in other people's harvests and being paid in kind (i.e. off-farm harvests) could have been collected, but were not, leaving an important gap in the overall assessment of household food availability after the harvest. Estimates of collection of wild foods also proved elusive, which is in itself interesting, given the popularity of wild food collection as an indicator of food stress. Post-harvest disposals of stocks (repayment in kind of loans of seed and food, sales to meet cash needs, payment in kind of casual labour helping with the harvest) were also generally unreliable. Household budget data on the quantities of cereals bought have been used to complete food supply estimates.

Household budgets. Overall, the most reliable data were collected for expenditure and, to a lesser extent, cash income.[8] Expenditure consistently exceeded cash income, and attempts to cross-check this with respondents met with little success. It can be explained by a number of factors: households may be running credit lines with merchants that they do not register as income; the fact of an NGO collecting information about food security was undoubtedly associated with the promise of food aid or other transfers in respondents' minds, however much this was repudiated by those conducting the survey; particular sources of household income were regularly under-reported (e.g. women's income from small-scale commerce, often for fear that revelation would render it liable to taxation and to appropriation by their husbands).

Household labour allocation. Some field agents felt the data accurately reflected labour allocation in line with their own observations, whereas others considered it unreliable, largely because of their surprise at how long women worked and how the length of the working day varied from one month to the next. This latter variation is consistent with the need to intensify certain activities at difficult times of the year. The time budget data in fact present a remarkably consistent picture.

Analysis of household data. Phases 1 and 2 demonstrated that producers in vulnerable livelihood systems have a structural food gap which they seek to fill by a combination of exchange entitlements to meet subsistence needs (leading to high market dependence) and the reallocation of household labour towards secondary activities and adaptive strategies, to generate the revenue to fund these market exchanges. Vulnerable systems are characterised as being insecure, unstable and risky (Chapter 7). Outcomes of these characteristics include: forced diversification, including imperative mobility between livelihood systems and geographical areas; the inability to save or accumulate; and a lack of safety nets or fall-back mechanisms in bad years.

Analysis of the household data collected by Phase 3 is divided into two parts: first, household food production data, in conjunction with household budget data, are used to estimate annual food supply, and hence the size of the annual food gap. Second, household budget data and time allocation data are used to show what strategies households pursued to fill that gap. Income and expenditure data are used to indicate where and in which seasons households acquired the cash to buy food in the event of a deficit in cereal production, or whether and how they were able to accumulate in the event of a surplus (Chapter 8). Labour allocation data are used as an indicator of the relative importance of main and secondary activities on the one hand, and coping and adaptive strategies on the other. The differences between main and secondary activities relate to their relative importance in each livelihood system (explained in Chapter 7). As shown in Chapter 3, coping strategies effectively become secondary activities (i.e. part of normal activity patterns in every year) in vulnerable livelihood systems and, as such, become adaptive activities over time (Chapter 10).

The first determinant of a vulnerable livelihood system is an annual food gap, mitigated by production strategies. Vulnerability is indicated when a low proportion of needs are met by own production and a low proportion of the remaining gap is met by purchases.

The second determinant is market dependence, mitigated by exchange strategies. Vulnerability is indicated by a high proportion of total expenditure going to food, by a high proportion of cash income being derived from adaptive activities, and by a high cash income deficit in the hungry season. It should be noted, however, that a high proportion of cash income from secondary and adaptive activities is only a signal of high vulnerability if a high proportion of total food availability comes from cereals bought. Dependence on cash income from adaptive strategies is more sensitive than income from secondary ones, which presuppose prior investment in either animals, which can be sold, or in fishing equipment, which can bring in some income.

The third determinant is diversification for subsistence, mitigated by labour strategies. Vulnerability is signalled when a low proportion of time is spent on own food production, although this indicator presupposes subsistence production; clearly, in wealthy households which do not depend on subsistence production, a low proportion of time spent on own food production is not an indicator of high vulnerability. Second, a high proportion of time spent on adaptive activities signals vulnerability, although, as in the case of a high proportion of cash income from secondary activities, this is only an indicator of vulnerability if the household's food gap from subsistence production is large. Third, a high proportion of time spent on adaptive strategies in those seasons when own food production should be the main activity also signals vulnerability. Finally, a high proportion of women's time spent on atypical activities indicates vulnerability. This includes both switching female labour to activities traditionally carried out by men, and increases in overall female working hours, as 'non-productive' activities (domestic duties, child care) remain constant even when productive activities increase.

CONCLUSIONS

Analysis and outputs from Phase 3 did not achieve all the original objectives, the principal reason being the sheer volume of data collected which was by no means systematically exploited by the monitoring system. To some extent, this could have been overcome by additional personnel, but the costs in terms of time and training requirements were beyond the scope of the project. The alternative, which is what happened by default rather than design, was that the quantitative data collected in Phase 3 were, for the most part, a distinct data set, analysed retrospectively more as a research exercise than as an integral part of a sustainable monitoring system. Consequently, the methodological justification for Phase 3 – to identify sentinel villages and households and to plot and measure their progress over time, both before and after interventions – never materialised.

Overall, Phase 3 was dogged by operational difficulties arising from the failure to recognise at the outset the demands in terms of staff time and technical input. This is in itself an important lesson for local-level monitoring systems: there is a clear trade-off to be made between *accurate* quantification of data and sustainability in the sense of a system which is neither too complicated nor too demanding.

Although Phase 3 was implemented, albeit partially, it remained more or less hermetically sealed from the overall monitoring process. In this sense, Phase 3 overloaded the system. Further, there were undoubted opportunity costs to Phase 2 (running concurrently with Phase 3), as personnel were spending time collecting information much of which was not exploited. Although village-level interventions were implemented in 1991, these were not directly linked to the findings of Phase 3, which raises the critical issue of linking information to response. Although the monitoring system has given rise to a set of village-level interventions (the *Projet d'Appui Villageois*), the idea of using Phase 3 data as a baseline from which to monitor the impact of interventions has not been implemented. The results of Phases 1 to 3 are the subject of the following chapters, while Chapter 11 proposes a revised methodology, taking account of the strengths and weaknesses of the SADS system, and seeks specifically to identify ways of improving the ability of a local food monitoring system to inform, trigger and evaluate flexible response options.

5 Drought, Food Insecurity and Early Warning in Mali

INTRODUCTION

The principal causes of Mali's food problem are low resource endowment and low standards of living, exacerbated by inter-annual climatic fluctuations, the long-term effects of successive dry years and macroeconomic stagnation. The country covers an area of 1 240 142 square kilometres, between latitudes 11° and 25°N, divided into five broad agro-ecological zones, defined according to annual rainfall levels. Rainfall is highest in the Sudanic-Guinean south of the country, averaging more than 800 mm a year. In the Sudanic zone, it averages 600–800 mm; in the Sahelian-Sudanic zone, 350–600 mm; in the Sahelian zone 200–350 mm; and above latitude 16°N in the Sahelian-Saharan zone, less than 200 mm (Map 1). The highly fluctuating rainfall (the uncertainty of which increases as one moves north), and in the Sahelian zone the flood levels of the River Niger and its tributaries, are the main determinants of food production.

Between 80 and 90 per cent of Malians depend on the rural sector for their livelihoods, and agriculture accounted for 49 per cent of GDP in 1988. The fourteenth poorest country in the world, and the tenth poorest in sub-Saharan Africa, Mali had a GNP *per capita* of US $210 in 1987, compared to an average for sub-Saharan Africa of US $330 (excluding Nigeria) and US $240 in the low-income economies (World Bank, 1989, 1990). This overall figure disguises differences between the relatively productive south (sometimes called the bread basket of the region) and the Sahelian north, where the average *per capita* income of a rural producer is less than US $100 a year.

At Independence in 1960, Mali was the leading exporter of cattle and cereals in the Sahel,[1] and had a small trade surplus in the agricultural sector. Despite the low productivity, lack of modern equipment or inputs and neglect of much cultivable land, the output of the seven principal crops rose in volume terms by 40 per cent between 1945 and 1959 (Amin, 1965), due to increases in land under cultivation rather than better yields (Lecaillon and Morrisson, 1986). Cattle raising and fish exports also grew in the period between the Second World War and Independence.[2] Colonial investment was concentrated on irrigated rice in the *Office du Niger*

Map 1   Mali, showing rainfall isohyets

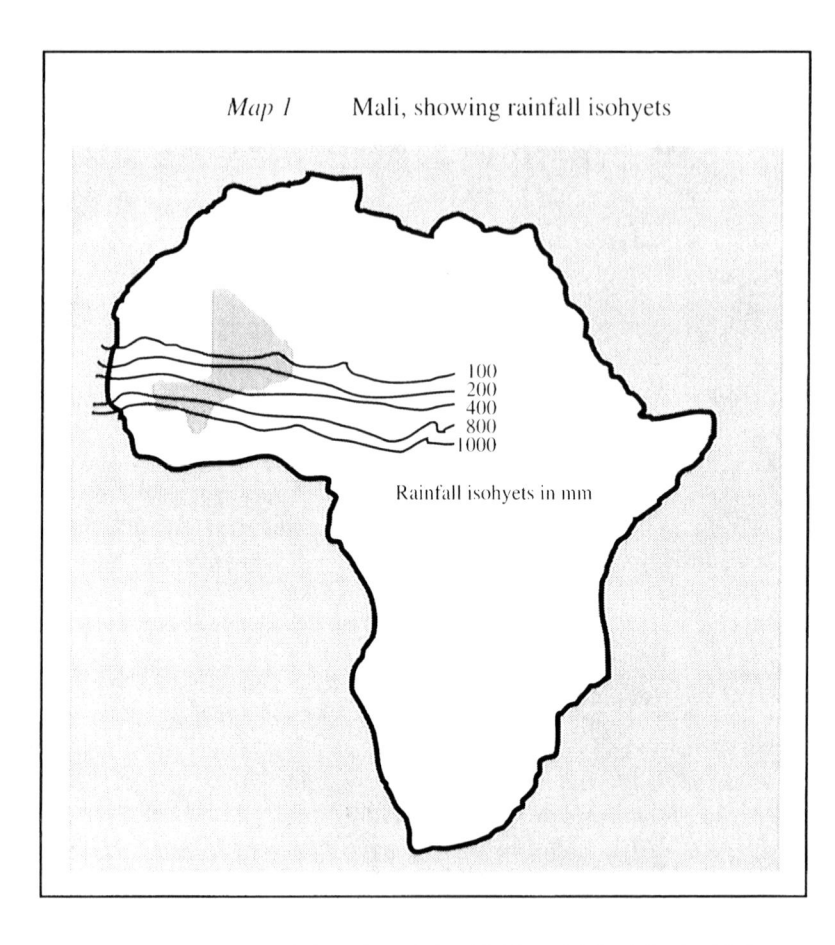

100
200
400
800
1000

Rainfall isohyets in mm

(established in 1932) which, although justifiably criticised for its high cost per hectare approach, nevertheless represented substantial investment in food production, on a scale rarely seen since in Mali. Lecaillon and Morrisson (1986: 22) argue that: 'In 1960, Mali's agriculture was no doubt underdeveloped, but it was by no means stagnant ... [and] the agricultural trade balance was in clear surplus.'

The post-Independence socialist regime of Modibo Keita (1960–8) fixed low producer prices for food crops to subsidise urban consumption and promote exports of cash crops (cotton and groundnuts). Collectivisation was pursued via the establishment of co-operatives. The lack of support for these policies amongst rural people contributed to a shift from Mali being the only net grain exporter in West Africa at Independence, to being

Drought, Food Insecurity and Early Warning in Mali 81

a net importer by the second half of the 1960s, with an increasing preference for rice rather than millet in urban areas fuelling demand for imported rice.

With the military coup in 1968, policy moved from Keitist central planning towards a more open economy, although until the early 1980s, state intervention favouring exports continued to dominate food sector policies. The state monopoly over food crop marketing and production was not completely abolished until 1987.

Since Independence, agricultural production has fallen by about 1 per cent a year (Speirs, 1986), affecting all crops except cotton. Table 5.1 summarises the story of food production from Independence until 1982. The ability of domestic production to meet cereal consumption requirements fell from an average of about 95 per cent in the early 1960s to 86 per cent in 1970, collapsed to 40 per cent in 1974 due to drought, and recovered to 86 per cent in 1976. Declining *per capita* food availability was due to population rising faster than agricultural output, which itself increased but not fast enough to maintain self-sufficiency at the national level (*ibid.*: 31–2). Nevertheless, Mali has not suffered from a permanent structural food deficit. Increasingly in the 1980s, however, household food entitlements have declined to critical levels for certain groups, particularly on a seasonal basis, leading to the classic illusion of national food balance sheets: apparent surplus at national level when, in fact, many people no longer have sufficient entitlements to gain access to food, even in good years.

IRRT (1984) identified the following problems facing Mali's food sector in the early 1980s: growing urbanisation due to migration from rural areas, with few opportunities for urban employment; institutional rigidity, particularly in respect of inefficient parastatals; price disincentives to producers and inadequate food marketing policies; the absence of improved input packages to boost small farm production; and expensive, inaccessible and inappropriate agricultural credit facilities.

THE NATIONAL FOOD BALANCE

Production. Mali is one of the few Sahelian countries with a good potential for cereal production, mainly of sorghum and millet. Ninety-nine per cent of cultivation is rainfed and most cereals are produced on a subsistence basis. Significant quantities of cash crops (particularly cotton, groundnuts) are also grown in addition to sorghum and millet, the principal food crops. Whilst responsible for the overall food balance in good

Table 5.1 Mali: summary of food production, 1960–5 to 1980–2

Period	Producer price deflated by:		Area sown	Output	Yields (output/area)	Total value of output at 1970 prices	Farmers' real monetary net incomes (MF m deflated by the cost of living)
	Input	Cost of living					
	(MF[a]/kg)		(000 ha)	(000 t)	(kg)	(MF m)	
Millet-sorghum-maize							
1960–3	15.0	18.0	1 460	847	577	15 250	1 012
1964–7	20.5	15.0	1 422	867	610	15 600	1 997
1968–71	18.2	16.7	1 410	780	685	14 050	1 052
1972–5	20.5	18.7	1 285	720	560	12 975	1 827
1976–9	15.0	16.2	1 375	910	662	16 375	3 762
1980–2	25.0	21.0	1 403	770	547	13 867	1 557
Rice							
1960–3	11.0	16.2	165	173	1 062	4 335	542
1964–7	19.5	16.7	173	162	942	4 062	567
1968–71	22.7	22.2	155	164	1 065	4 105	842
1972–5	18.0	20.7	148	166	1 070	4 162	1 092
1976–9	16.5	19.7	182	209	1 152	5 217	1 520
1980–2	23.7	25.0	148	156	1 076	3 897	1 177

Note: [a] MF = Malian Francs. Mali did not join the *Franc Communauté Financière Africaine* (FCFA) zone until 1984.

Source: Lecaillon and Morrisson (1986). © OECD, Paris, 1986, *Economic Policies and Agricultural Performance: The Case of Mali, 1960–1983*. Reproduced by permission of the OECD.

years, the south does not automatically provide for the Sahelian north, where rainfed millet is the main crop, production is usually in structural deficit and, increasingly, poverty is endemic. In some years, wild grains, such as *fonio*, can account for up to a third of consumption in poorer households. In the midst of the Sahel, the annual flood of the Niger and Bani rivers combines to form a distinct ecosystem, enabling the growth of wetland crops (especially rice), and providing substantial fishing and pasture reserves. To the north of the River Niger, in the Sahelian-Saharan zone, cultivation is impossible, but extensive livestock rearing is the backbone of subsistence for its seasonal transhumant pastoralists.

Graph 5.1 shows total cereal production over the 1970s and 1980s. Inter-annual fluctuations are large. At worst, Mali is hit periodically by successive years of drought. The most recent, from 1982–3 to 1984–5, resulted in an annual production deficit of over 500 000 tons in 1984–5. In every year, aggregate figures disguise regional variations, including the contributions in many regions of livestock products to diet.[3] This variability makes national strategic planning very difficult.

Consumption. Although the decline in *per capita* output is not in question, there is much current debate as to whether Mali suffers from a structural food deficit,[4] fuelled by unreliable (but improving) statistics for

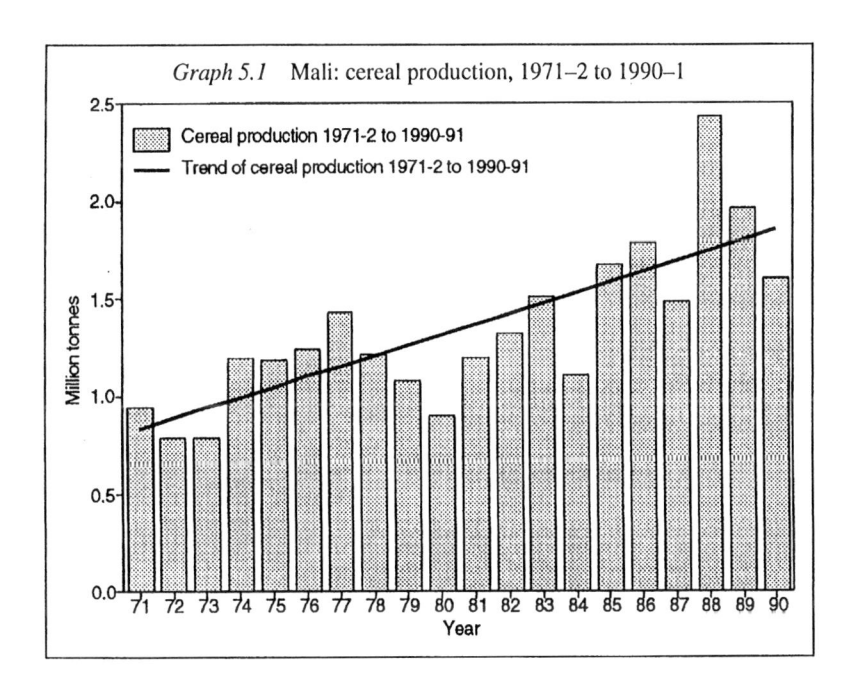

Graph 5.1 Mali: cereal production, 1971–2 to 1990–1

output and further complicated in recent years by controversy over the figure used to calculate consumption needs. Problematic population estimates contribute further to the uncertainty. Population density ranges from 14–16 people per square kilometre in the south and the Delta, to one person per square kilometre in the north and east of the country. Population distribution is difficult to estimate because of the extreme seasonal mobility of much of the population in the north, and the wariness of local people about being counted in censuses and included on the fiscal list. Out-migration towards the south and to neighbouring countries increases substantially in drought years. Table 5.2 gives an indication of the population–cereal needs situation at the time of the 1987 census, in which the annual rate of population growth was found to be much lower (1.7 per cent) than previously estimated (2.5–3.0 per cent). This, in turn, led to substantial over-estimates of cereal needs.

Since 1984, there have been approximately 50 studies of the prevalence (7–20 per cent) of acute protein energy malnutrition (PEM) among children under six. Far fewer data are available for the incidence of chronic PEM, but prevalence rates of 13–36 per cent, peaking in children aged two to four are given (Sundberg, 1988: vii). Vitamin and mineral deficiencies are also widespread, particularly in the north of the country.

Imports and food aid. Mali ceased to be an exporter of cereals in 1964 and in 1966 commercial imports of sorghum, maize and rice were required for the first time. Graph 5.2 shows cereal imports as a proportion of domestic production. Commercial imports averaged 58 000 tons a year in the 1970s, and 93 000 tons in the 1980s. The cereal deficit rose dramatically during the mid-1980s drought, but was met substantially by food aid. A programme of food aid had been initiated in 1971.[5] Food aid as a proportion of imports averaged about 40 per cent throughout the period 1971–90, only rising above 50 per cent in drought years (see Graph 5.3). In terms of composition, emergency food aid was unknown in Mali until the 1973 drought and then arrived too late to have much impact.

With the establishment of the *Programme de Restructuration du Marché Céréalier* (PRMC) in 1980–1, food aid policy changed substantially. Indeed, part of the initiative behind this programme – and specifically the use of counterpart funds in the process of cereal market restructuring – was a desire to 'introduce some order in food aid management' (Pirzio-Biroli, 1988: 11). Since then, over 70 per cent of food aid is provided by a group of regular donors;[6] as a result, the proportions have shifted in favour of programme aid during the 1980s.

Summary. Widely fluctuating production and continuing uncertainty in the estimates of both production levels and consumption requirements, not

Table 5.2 Mali: estimated population and cereal needs, 1976 and 1987

Region	Population 1976	Estimated population 1987 [1]	Estimated cereal needs [a] (000 t) 1987	Actual population 1987 [2]	Rate of population growth (%)	Actual cereal needs 1987 (000 t)	Over-estimation [1]-[2] (000 t)
1st	872 750	1 145 124	191.2	1 058 575	1.87	176.8	14.4
2nd	932 237	1 223 176	204.3	1 180 260	2.28	197.1	7.2
3rd	1 090 068	1 440 760	240.6	1 308 828	1.70	218.6	22.0
4th	1 082 224	1 419 972	237.1	1 328 250	1.98	221.8	15.3
5th	1 129 041	1 481 400	247.4	1 261 383	1.07	210.7	36.7
6th	490 456	643 521	107.5	453 032	-0.77	75.7	31.8
7th	370 903	486 657	81.3	383 734	0.33	64.1	17.2*
Bamako	419 239	550 078	91.9	646 163	4.19	107.9	-16.0
Mali	6 394 918	8 390 588	1 401.3	7 620 225	1.70	1 272.6	128.7

Note: [a] Calculated as population × 167 kg.

86   *Adaptable Livelihoods*

Graph 5.2   Mali: total cereal imports as a proportion of domestic production, 1971–2 to 1990–1

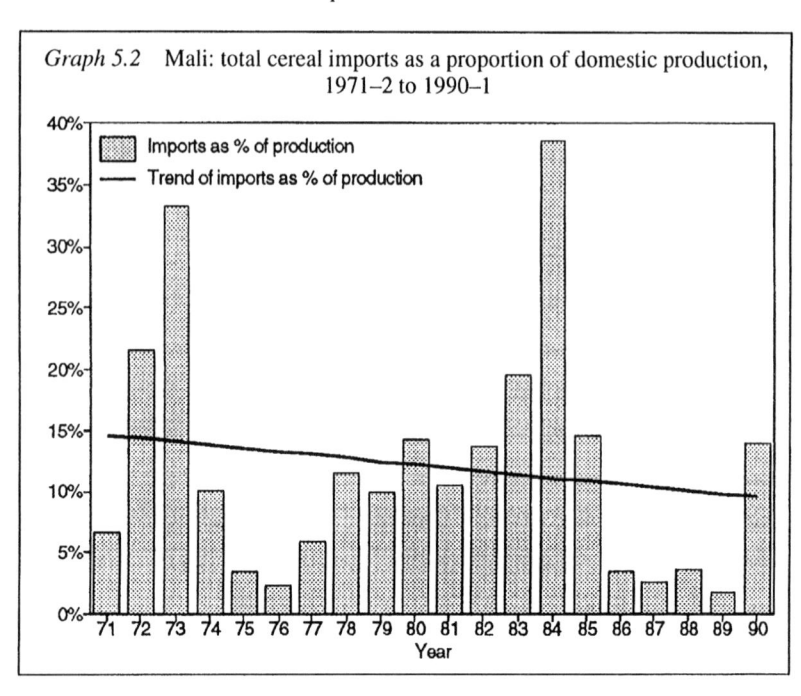

Graph 5.3   Mali: food aid as a proportion of total imports, 1971–2 to 1990–1

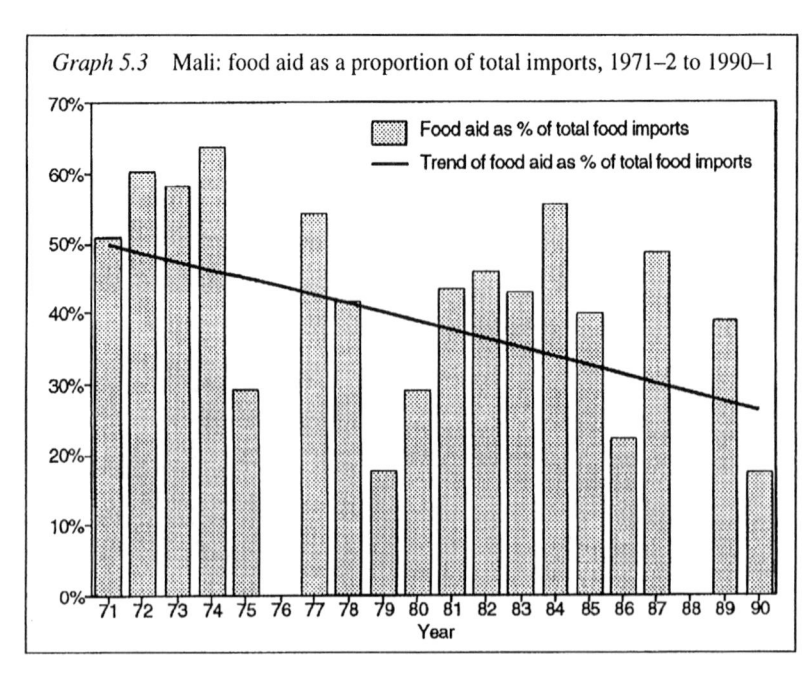

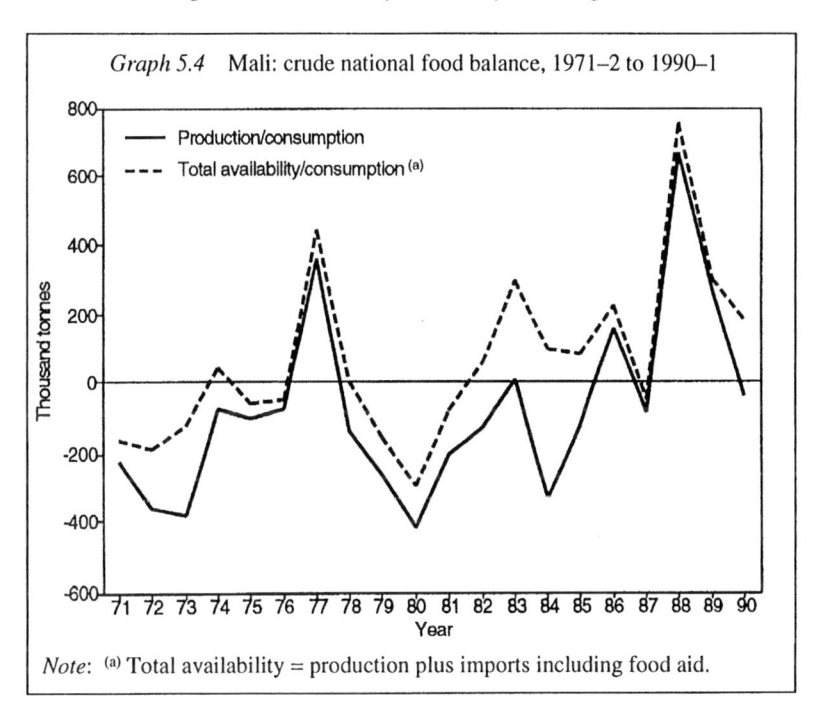

Graph 5.4 Mali: crude national food balance, 1971–2 to 1990–1

— Production/consumption
--- Total availability/consumption [a]

Note: [a] Total availability = production plus imports including food aid.

to mention little or no available data on household stocks or other sources of food, make the calculation of a national food balance for Mali more an art than a science. Given that quite small variations can make the difference between a national food surplus and deficit, these data constraints are especially important. Graph 5.4 summarises the crude national food balance for the 1970s and 1980s, using only production, consumption and import data, as information on levels of carry-over and household stocks are not available for the whole period.[7] The pattern shows that, in the 1970s, Mali suffered a structural deficit in all but one year, and in 60 per cent of the 1980s, implying some improvement in food security at the national level, particularly associated with better rainfall conditions towards the end of the period.

PATTERNS OF FOOD INSECURITY IN THE 1980s

The food insecurity problems facing Mali, over and above climatic vulnerability, are thus more complex than a permanent, structural food deficit. They can be summarised as follows:

- high annual variations in output;
- in the northern parts of the country, increasingly vulnerable livelihood systems, resulting in seasonal shortages in most years during the 'hungry season' from May to September;
- significant groups of rural people who, having lost their means of production and/or most of their capital in the last two periods of drought, are now too poor to be able to purchase sufficient quantities of food at almost any price;
- growing urbanisation as a consequence of the impoverishment of rural areas, and few opportunities for urban employment;
- logistical difficulties in distributing food from the productive south to the dry north, in a huge country with few roads, many of which are impassable during the wet season;
- until the progressive liberalisation of the cereal market in the 1980s, a pricing policy which led to low producer prices, discouraging production and stimulating unofficial cross-border trade, whilst at the same time failing to subsidise consumption for most of the population.

Mali has suffered only two widespread famines in the last fifty years (in 1972–3 and again in 1984–5). The impact of the failure of the 1984 rains on food security was due as much to the cumulative effects of three dry years as to one particularly poor rainy season. The Sahelian zone, and to a lesser but significant extent the northern part of the Sahelian-Sudanian zone, are always on the margin for cultivation. The local food shortages in late 1984 and 1985 gave rise to what the government and food aid donors called a 'food emergency'. The extent and degree of this emergency have since been questioned. Undoubtedly many people were hungry, but there is little evidence of mass starvation or of what De Waal (1989) has called 'famine that kills' or, indeed, of emergency relief arriving soon enough in the right places to have prevented this.

Whereas famine is a relatively rare event in Mali, chronic seasonal food insecurity for certain groups, which becomes acute for some of them in deficit years, is endemic in the north of the country. The reasons why Mali avoided widespread famine in the 1970s and 1980s are less to do with astute policies of famine prevention than with the nature of the country's food insecurity and the absence of contributory factors, which elsewhere have been closely identified with tipping the balance from serious food shortages to famine resulting in widespread death.

First amongst such factors is that, until 1990, there had been little armed conflict and none on a sustained and widespread scale. Since 1990, conflict between Tuareg in the north and the Malian army, as well as banditry between rival groups, has continued sporadically. Second, Mali has a relatively small population of less than 8 million, with growth rates found to be considerably lower in the 1987 census than was previously imagined, particularly in the north. Third, the population is highly mobile, and has been able to migrate (on a seasonal or longer-term basis) to the south of the country and further afield, to the coastal West African states in particular, where opportunities for employment were sufficient to guarantee some accumulation in the 1970s and at least enough in the 1980s to enable migrants not to become a drain on already low household stocks back home. Fourth, producers have been able until now to cope in the short term with seasonal fluctuations in food availability, and have developed an array of coping strategies to raise food entitlements and a capacity to adapt, principally by diversifying productive activities and increasing market dependence, in line with changing agro-ecological and economic conditions.

FOOD-SECURITY PLANNING

Mali has been recognised by government and donors alike as being in need of a coherent national food-security policy since the crisis of 1973. But a long-standing commitment at national planning level to promoting food self-sufficiency, most clearly elaborated in the 1982 National Food Strategy (NFS) (République du Mali, 1982), has tended to be at variance with much policy implementation. Pricing and institutional policies have favoured the urban consumer over the rural producer (who is, of course, increasingly a consumer as well) and extracted surplus more generally from the agricultural sector to finance other parts of the faltering economy, much of it to finance public consumption rather than development expenditure or other forms of investment.

Those incentives which were offered to producers sought to increase cash crop output, with the exception of some ODRs and the *Office du Niger*, to the west of the present 'living' (i.e. flooded) Delta. Many of these ODRs ran at a loss, with heavy and costly bureaucratic structures, and have been a target for reform.[8] Benefits available from ODR-supported programmes were enjoyed by the better-off – notably civil servants and traders. Poor rural producers in ODR zones received little, and those producers who did not come under an ODR received almost no state encouragement in the form of agricultural extension, preferential credit access and/or improved inputs.

Since the 1980s, policy reform has been driven by macroeconomic structural adjustment rather than by prioritising household food security. The rising food import bill, as well as costly and inefficient state marketing mechanisms, were targeted early on as requiring policy reform, within the overall context of chronic economic decline. The need for a structural adjustment package arose from the worsening balance of trade and foreign reserves in the period 1980–2. A first International Monetary Fund (IMF) standby credit arrangement of US $30.375 m. was announced in May 1982. A second credit line at the end of 1983 (US $38.6 m. for the period December 1983–5) acknowledged substantial progress in correcting structural imbalances, reducing disequilibria in public finances and the balance of payments, and cutting domestic and external arrears – largely due to increased cotton production in 1982–3, improved world cotton prices, reduced imports in 1983 and the devaluation of the Malian franc (to be followed by rejoining of the FCFA zone in 1984) (Lipton and Heald, 1984).

Mali launched an NFS in 1982, as part of the EC's initiative arising from the Pisani Plan.[9] The key problems identified in the food sector were: an increasing food deficit, with population rising faster than growth in food output; ineffective pricing policies; inefficient and monopolistic grain market management; lack of access of small producers to improved agricultural inputs, agricultural extension services and credit; and an overall decline in the agricultural terms of trade (*ibid.*). The general aims of the NFS proposals (République du Mali, 1982), set in a time-frame extending to the year 2000, contained few surprises and were consistent with almost every other African food strategy document:

- to produce the maximum amount of food, with a view to guaranteeing national food self-sufficiency and possibly exporting food in the future (thereby reducing balance-of-payments problems);
- to diversify food crop production to improve the nutritional balance of the national diet;
- to improve food distribution so as to provide adequate consumption levels for the population at the least cost (assumed to be via the achievement of national self-sufficiency);
- to assure adequate returns on farmer investment, i.e. to increase producer prices;
- to reduce costs at all stages of the production system;
- to increase rural incomes, stimulate rural savings and hence investment in the food-producing sector; and
- to minimise the negative effects of the strategy on state finances, by substantially keeping up cash crop production.

Drought, Food Insecurity and Early Warning in Mali 91

Proposals given priority by the NFS were:

- to liberalise and stabilise the cereals market, thereby providing better price incentives to producers;
- to provide credit for private traders to stimulate their participation in the cereal trade;
- to improve access to extension, inputs and credit, particularly via institutional reform and improved access to subsidy packages;
- to improve agricultural research, in order to promote farm-level technology and better technical conditions of production;
- to research methods of reducing grain storage losses, estimated to be 20–25 per cent;
- to generate a better understanding of the integration of livestock raising into cereal crop production systems.

Mali was one of the four original food strategy countries supported by the EC, initially via food aid pledged to assist in the restructuring of the cereal market. Further donor support came from the World Bank and the IMF, with Mali being given preference in securing development loans. When the NFS was launched, Mali was seen as something of a test case for structural adjustment policy in Africa (Speirs, 1986). The principal forum for donor activity in respect of food-security policy has been the PRMC, discussed below.

Diagram 5.1 shows the structure of food-security planning at the national level in 1990. The bureaucratic arrangements for managing drought relief have undergone numerous changes since the mid-1980s. This is indicative of the high political value of food aid and its management which, certainly until the overthrow of the Traoré regime in 1991, was a political football fought over by competing interest groups. The marginalisation of the *Comité National d'Aide d'Urgence et de Réhabilitation* (CNAUR) within this framework represents the triumph of the co-ordination between donors (the PRMC) and part of the administration, the *Comité d'Orientation et de Coordination* (COC), over the single political party under President Traoré, the *Union Démocratique du Peuple Malien* (UDPM), of which CNAUR was the mouthpiece.[10] The pro-PRMC part of the administration which allied itself with the donors sought to bolster assistance for the economy by supporting structural adjustment initiatives. This shift of power, whilst occurring at a bureaucratic level in 1990, only began to have real operational significance after the overthrow of the UDPM regime in March 1991.

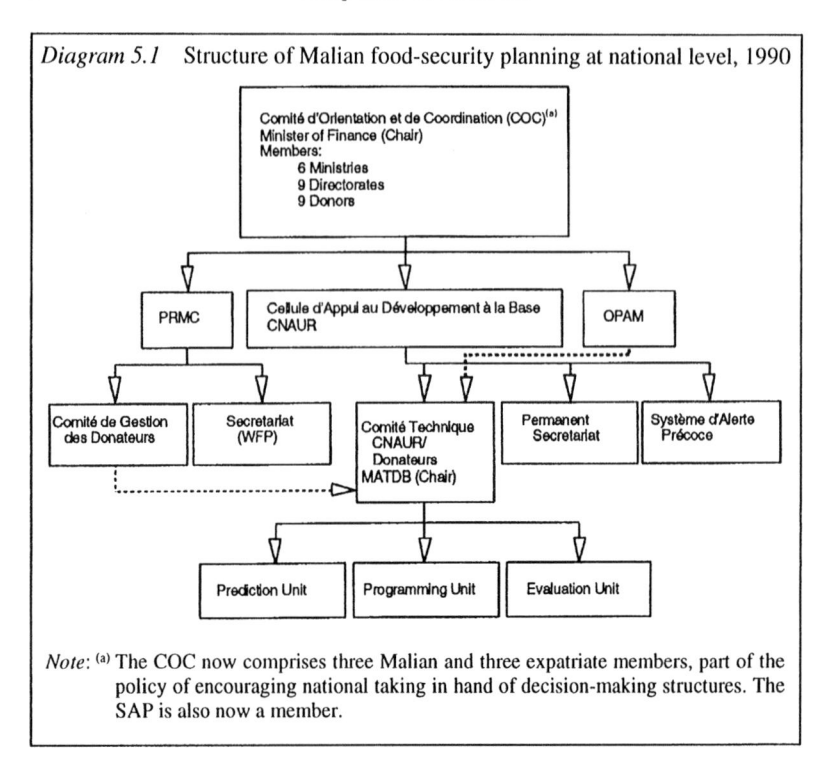

Diagram 5.1 Structure of Malian food-security planning at national level, 1990

```
                    Comité d'Orientation et de Coordination (COC)⁽ᵃ⁾
                    Minister of Finance (Chair)
                    Members:
                         6 Ministries
                         9 Directorates
                         9 Donors

         ┌──────────────────────┼──────────────────────┐
         ▼                      ▼                      ▼
       PRMC          Cellule d'Appui au Développement à la Base        OPAM
                                 CNAUR

   ┌────────┬──────────┬──────────┬──────────┬──────────┐
   ▼        ▼          ▼          ▼          ▼
Comité de  Secretariat  Comité Technique  Permanent    Système d'Alerte
Gestion    (WFP)        CNAUR/            Secretariat  Précoce
des                     Donateurs
Donateurs               MATDB (Chair)

              ┌────────────┼────────────┐
              ▼            ▼            ▼
        Prediction Unit  Programming Unit  Evaluation Unit
```

Note: ⁽ᵃ⁾ The COC now comprises three Malian and three expatriate members, part of the policy of encouraging national taking in hand of decision-making structures. The SAP is also now a member.

Whilst the policy of cereal market liberalisation, although a gradual process, was successfully pursued during the 1980s period of tension, policy regarding EW and timely response was far more constrained. Despite the development of a national EWS – the SAP – the use of this information in response planning fell victim to the conflicting objectives of the CNAUR on the one hand (maximising food aid receipts) and the PRMC on the other (keeping these to a level that would not disrupt the policy of liberalisation). As will be seen below, this conflict was eventually resolved in 1990, by the development of a PRMC-driven programmed response mechanism. Taken together, these dual food-security policy objectives had met with considerable success by 1991.

IMPLEMENTING FOOD-SECURITY POLICY

The NFS was from the outset linked to the IMF-supported programme of structural adjustment and food-security policy in the 1980s was characterised by macroeconomic adjustment of markets. A second strand of policy,

Drought, Food Insecurity and Early Warning in Mali 93

largely in reaction to the food crisis of the mid-1980s, involved persistent attempts to improve the timeliness of emergency food aid response. In between these two policy initiatives there is a gaping hole: the other NFS objectives have remained largely untouched. Consequently, there is an almost complete absence of national policies focusing on how rural people feed themselves and how constraints on them have intensified since the drought of the mid-1980s. In broad terms, the NFS envisaged considerable private investment in small-scale improvements to achieve its objectives at the local level, with the *Gouvernement de la République du Mali* (GRM) undertaking the major investments such as rehabilitation and/or extension of irrigation systems. But there has been little co-ordinated action either within the framework of an NFS or elsewhere in government to regenerate or develop the food production sector and the strategy has not yet resulted in direct policy initiatives to stimulate production. Few aspects of the sector were left untouched by the problems and proposed policies identified in the early years of the NFS, with the notable exception of targeted interventions to help the poorest withstand the exacerbation of their existing problems by the process of adjustment. Whilst macroeconomic adjustment has been an important precondition for improving the resilience of local producers to food insecurity, and famine EW and response have to a limited extent 'stepped in' when food crisis has threatened, the horizons of national food-security planning remain too limited to address the real issue confronting rural producers: declining livelihood security, of which chronic food insecurity is a critical part.

A major casualty as structural adjustment policies took hold was the civil service, which was required to shed some 5000 employees over three years from 1988, as well as ending all new recruitment. As a major employer, the civil service 'streamlining' had a number of direct consequences for food security. A civil service family member had been a traditional insurance for rural people, guaranteeing some cash income even in bad years; some estimate that for every civil service job lost, some twenty livelihoods also vanished. At the same time, the demands of the increasingly bankrupt national exchequer were stepped up with a rising level of tax collection, effectively to pay the salaries of rural administrators.

LONG-TERM PLANNING TOOLS: MACROECONOMIC ADJUSTMENT AND THE PRMC

Reform of the cereal marketing system began in 1981, prior to the drafting of the NFS, and was the major plank of national food-security policy in the 1980s. It was the budgetary cost of the *Office des Produits Agricoles du Mali* (OPAM), the parastatal responsible for cereal marketing, which provided the major stimulus for reform. Like that in much of Africa, cereal marketing in Mali in the 1970s and early 1980s had attracted much justified criticism. The first problem was the inability of OPAM to exercise its legal monopoly over trade, controlling less than 35 per cent of the market in the 1970s owing to its pricing policy. Second, producer prices were set below border prices and generally below those on the parallel 'black' market (by up to 50 per cent). Third, consumer prices were set to protect urban elites, although many of the poorest urban dwellers were forced to buy on the unofficial open market and pay its much higher prices.[11] The GRM's pricing policy led to structural subsidies appearing as deficits on OPAM's accounts (Lipton and Heald, 1984: 72–3).

The principal objective of the liberalisation was to raise producer prices to border levels and adjust consumer prices upwards; this, it was hoped, would stimulate production as well as the private commercial sector, and at the same time reduce the operating deficit of OPAM. The key element of the programme, over a five to six-year period, was to use the revenue from the sale of food aid (i.e. counterpart funds) to support producer prices (initially substantially raising farmer incomes) at levels above consumer prices, which were to increase gradually (via the sale of food aid). 25 000 tons of food aid a year were guaranteed by donors for the programme, administered under a joint account held by OPAM and the WFP. Coupled with the dismantling of OPAM's monopoly was PRMC support for private traders.

The first phase of the PRMC coincided with three years of drought (1982–3 to 1984–5), followed by two surplus years, reflecting the perennial difficulty in Mali of designing a national food-security policy flexible enough to accommodate wide annual variations in output. A mixed marketing system persisted until the late 1980s, with OPAM's role as buyer and seller of last resort ending only in 1988. It remains in charge of physically stocking the *Stock National de Sécurité* (SNS – see below) and managing distributions to traders in receipt of government contracts for the free distribution of food aid.

A major obstacle for the PRMC was the background of the public sector financial crisis, with the risk of using counterpart funds simply to cover various public sector deficits. A further weakness was the lack of support from the private sector; 1986 was the first year that counterpart funds were used to stimulate its participation in cereal marketing. Private traders remain reluctant to take on the costs of medium-term storage and need seasonal and regional price differentiation to stock from one season to the next and to service more remote (invariably deficit) parts of the country.

Producer incentives arising from the liberalisation of the market are harder to assess. The major lesson to be drawn from the first two phases of the PRMC is that cereal market management in Mali is more complex – and requires greater flexibility – than the approach of simply liberalising in order to stimulate production implies. Year-to-year fluctuations are so great, due to the predominant impact of rainfall (not price) on production levels, that a cereal marketing strategy must be able to switch from managing surpluses in one year to managing major deficits in another. It was this dilemma which encouraged the PRMC to become directly involved in food aid management in the latter part of the 1980s, developing the programmed response mechanism described below, and is indicative, to some extent, of a recognition of the limits of the market.

The success of the PRMC in co-ordinating the liberalisation of cereal markets is held up as something of a model within West Africa, particularly the innovative use of counterpart funds in the process. In terms of wider food-security planning objectives, perhaps the most positive achievement has been consistent multi-donor co-ordination and participation; continuous policy analysis and dialogue; and joint government/donor programming of food aid flows, based on joint management of counterpart funds (Simmons, 1987). For the majority of the rural poor, the decade which launched the NFS was characterised by 'business as usual': no greater support for production than previously, and few effective consumer safety nets for the poorest, unless provided by foreign NGOs. Even the liberalisation of the cereal market, whilst favouring surplus producers, has had less effect than intended on the food deficit populations of the north, who have traditionally relied on informal market mechanisms for exchange and who continue to pay high prices for cereals bought on credit (Chapters 7 and 9).

SHORT-TERM PLANNING TOOLS: FAMINE EARLY WARNING AND RESPONSE

In conjunction with the need for structural reform of the food sector, Mali faced a second set of food-security problems arising from the drought and ensuing food emergency of the mid-1980s. In line with many Sahelian countries, planning to address these two sets of issues has tended in the past to operate along parallel tracks: it was not until the end of the 1980s that these two strands of policy were pulled together in any consistent fashion.

After the mid-1980s drought, Mali was perceived as being in urgent need of a famine EWS which would better equip its government to respond to periodic droughts and resulting food shortages in a timely and effective manner. Lack of information was widely identified amongst donor and relief agencies as a critical constraint to planning and executing famine relief in 1984–5 (McLean, 1987), though the Malian state has had effective internal methods of regular reporting for many years, and the amount of information available in 1984–5 has been underestimated. Nevertheless, the links between available information and decision-making were random, leading to long delays in response (WFP, 1986).

The pervasive belief in an absolute lack of information gave rise to something of a boom industry in famine EW systems in 1986. Already part of the Food and Agriculture Organisation's Global Information and Early Warning System (GIEWS) and the *Comité Permanent Inter-états de Lutte contre la Sécheresse dans le Sahel* (CILSS) Diaper/Agrhymet system, a national system – the SAP – was set up, funded initially by the EC and executed by the *Association Européenne pour le Développement et la Santé/Médécins sans Frontières*. The Famine Early Warning System (FEWS) Project also began a programme in Mali, funded by USAID.[12] Thus, in addition to the SADS, there were three main sources of EW information in Mali by 1987, of which the SAP was by far the most important.

The SAP was set up as the information branch of the CNAUR, responsible for co-ordinating food aid distribution, and covers 168 *arrondissements* in the 1st, 4th, 5th, 6th, 7th and 8th Regions (a total of about 4 million people, or half the population of the country – see Map 2).[13] SAP comes under the direction of the *Ministère de l'Administration Territoriale et du Développement à la Base* (MATDB), and is now funded by the PRMC at an annual cost of about 200 million FCFA.[14]

Data collection at the level of the *arrondissement* was originally divided into three phases: Phase One concerned with the agricultural season and qualitative monitoring of crop patterns; Phase Two a monthly socio-economic survey of demographic movements, market prices, food habits and levels of food stocks; and when a food shortage and 'at risk' area was signalled, Phase Three nutrition surveys were selectively conducted for vulnerable populations.

In the late 1980s, much progress was made in improving understanding of areas at risk and in standardising criteria for defining food aid needs (Egg and Teme, 1990: 3). Phases One and Two were merged into a single phase, comprising questionnaires on the agricultural and socio-economic situations, and Phase Three has been redesigned to encompass village sur-

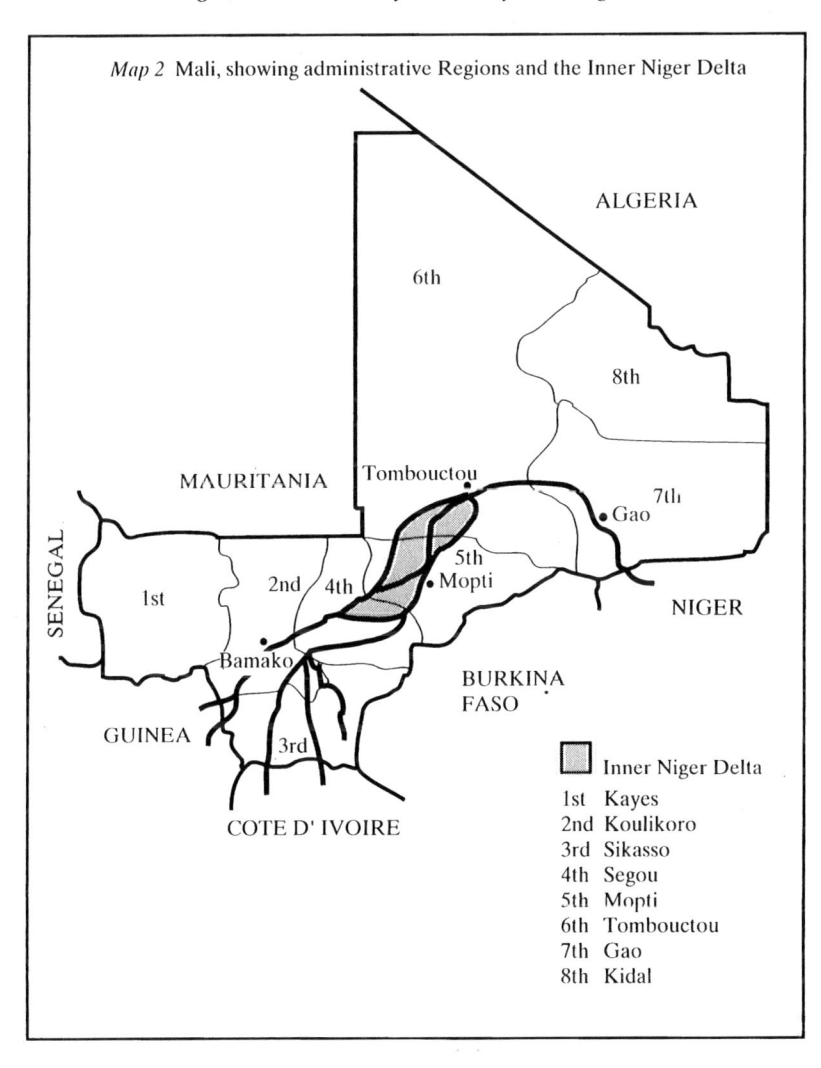

Map 2 Mali, showing administrative Regions and the Inner Niger Delta

Inner Niger Delta
1st Kayes
2nd Koulikoro
3rd Sikasso
4th Segou
5th Mopti
6th Tombouctou
7th Gao
8th Kidal

veys and household-level nutritional and socio-economic surveys. Three criteria are now used to assess the food-security situation: a decline in revenue and asset levels; the nature of unusual responses to stress; and the onset of the hungry season and what people are consuming.

The SAP is closely tied to government, both because it was originally situated within the national drought relief office (CNAUR) and in terms of data collection. Even though it is financially supported by donors, its close co-ordination with the government is regarded as fostering a 'participative information network' (Autier et al., 1989: 19), but not in the sense of participating with local people. The approach remains essentially top-down.

Although SAP information has improved substantially in terms of quality, accuracy and utility to decision-makers, it still has a number of limitations. First, the sources of SAP data are both the system's greatest strength and weakness. With the exception of some nutritional surveys, the SAP relies on local government officials to complete questionnaires with no direct reference to target populations. There is limited systematic quality control, and no explicit incentive to provide accurate data. It fails to incorporate adequately information that is not part of its own system. Further, much of the information collected is not exploited and retrospective and detailed comparative analyses of data over time are rarely undertaken.[15]

Second, whilst the credibility of SAP data has undoubtedly improved, insufficient understanding of the information system makes potential users sceptical about its capacity to target vulnerable areas. SAP has to strike a balance between contradictory objectives – to avoid errors by omission whilst at the same time minimising false alarms (Egg and Teme, 1990). Third, SAP has been criticised for failing to clarify its system and methods, particularly how data are validated, thereby alienating many potential users. Fourth, the methods which are used to classify *arrondissements* remain opaque, notably the critical distinction between those areas at risk which simply require surveillance and those which merit food aid distributions. There is almost certainly a tendency to over-estimate the severity of food insecurity in SAP questionnaires, given that it is so closely associated with the distribution of free food aid. This has been further complicated by the political tensions within the food aid lobby, all seeking to use food aid to serve particular interests.

Fifth, by not covering the south of the country, SAP is entirely dependent on DNSI and *Direction Nationale de l'Agriculture* (DNA) harvest estimates for the overall food situation. Over-dependence on an assessment which reports its final balance in January negates much of the *early* warning of the SAP system, and inevitably limits the credibility of its recommendations (even though preliminary recommendations are made in November – see Table 5.3). Sixth, SAP monthly Bulletins tend to be snapshots of the current situation, rather than predicting what may or may not happen to those groups identified as being at risk. This is principally an analytical problem, and ignores the underlying structural constraints facing producers, particularly those who are not cultivators. Inadequate attention is paid to non-agricultural sectors, especially pastures and, in the 5th Region, fisheries. The

Drought, Food Insecurity and Early Warning in Mali 99

Opération de Développement de l'Elevage dans la Région de Mopti (ODEM), for example, has argued that reports on pasture availability do not take adequate account of the critical relationships which determine pastoralists' access to food: water and pasture availability; the terms of trade between livestock and cereals; the quality of pasture; the significance of changes in transhumance routes, etc.. SAP does not cover transhumant cattle camps. Equally the *Opération de Développement de la Pêche dans la Région de Mopti* (OPM) argues that the fisheries sector always tends to be marginalised in SAP reports and the difficulties facing fishers are not adequately covered. Fish prices, for example, are not published in the SAP Bulletin, and SAP does not cover the fishing camps in the Delta nor the conflicts between transhumant fishers and local agro-fishers.

Seventh, the political role of the SAP is rarely explicitly addressed, especially its difficult relationship with the UDPM until the overthrow of the Traoré regime in 1991. The UDPM frequently by-passed the SAP, allocating food aid according to political not humanitarian objectives. Finally, despite its integration into local government for the purposes of data collection, there is a question mark over the sustainability of the SAP if the donor-funded project is discontinued.

The recommendations of the SAP are restricted to food aid distributions and, as such, are famine-oriented. No explanation is given in the SAP Bulletins as to how recommendations are arrived at, which leads to considerable consternation amongst readers (Egg and Teme, 1990: 17). Table 5.3 summarises the three critical stages in the SAP system: monitoring, reporting and decision-making.

Response. By 1990, the array of EWS, stretching from local to international level, had fundamentally altered both donor and government perceptions of the availability of information for the purposes of planning relief needs. The establishment of the SAP in particular has meant that access to local information from government sources for food relief planning purposes and its credibility amongst donors have increased. This improvement needs to be assessed against a background of the belief that very little information was available prior to the establishment of the SAP, and of limited and highly incomplete (and at times incorrect) information required by donors to justify usually very small quantities of emergency food aid; SAP data are rarely – if ever – used for wider food-security planning purposes. More information has not automatically led to either more effective emergency response to food crises, nor to better longer-term planning, particularly at the local level. Indeed, such has been the concentration on macroeconomic adjustment, that attempts to improve the food and livelihood security of local people have remained almost entirely

Table 5.3 Stages of SAP early warning and response

Stages of EW and response	J	A	S	O	N	D	J	F	M	A	M	J
Monitoring												
Monthly												
Basic physical and socio-economic indicators[a]	■	■	■	■	■	■	■	■	■	■	■	■
Cyclical												
Agricultural campaign[b]		■	■									
Livestock				■	■							
Population movements					■	■	■	■	■	■	■	
Periodic												
Socio-medico-nutritional surveys[c]	▒											▒
Reporting												
Monthly												
SAP Bulletins	■	■	■	■	■	■	■	■	■	■	■	■
Cyclical												
SAP Diagnostic Report		■	■									
SAP Provisional Balance Sheet				■								
SAP Definitive Prognostic Report									■			
Periodic												
Socio-medico-nutritional reports	▒											▒

Table 5.3 Continued

Stages of EW and response	J	A	S	O	N	D	J	F	M	A	M	J
Decision-making												
Cyclical												
Recommendations in Bulletin					■	■			■			
COC meetings												
Response triggered												
PRMC/CNAUR/OPAM					░				■			

Key: ■ Regular monitoring ░ Periodic monitoring

Notes: (a) Depending on the season, these include: rainfall, insect infestation, the agricultural campaign, pasture conditions, fishing conditions, migration, market prices (millet and goats), food stocks and health and nutrition status.
(b) For flooded rice, the period of monitoring is extended to January. For irrigated crops, monitoring takes place from February to June and for counter-season crops the harvest is estimated in February.
(c) This is variable, but the maximum period of monitoring is from January to August.

absent from analyses of the data available. Until 1990, the use of SAP recommendations in planning food aid distributions, let alone wider food security, was marginal (FEWS, 1990; Davies, 1992).

Differences in the objectives of decision-makers are central to the failure to use SAP data. SAP data were effectively by-passed in many decisions that SAP had explicitly been set up to inform. An evaluation in 1988 argued that SAP should not expand its activities beyond using data already collected for decision-making about food aid requirements (Lalau-Keraly and Winter, 1988). More recently, Egg and Teme (1990) recommend that SAP data be used for wider planning purposes, particularly in respect of identifying large population groups at risk of food insecurity and in need of more permanent interventions than emergency aid. A wider related issue is whether alternatives to free food aid distributions could be more appropriate to all vulnerable groups in certain circumstances.

In response to the failure to use EW information even for the narrow purpose of triggering timely and orderly release of food aid stocks up until 1990, the PRMC's programmed response mechanism was developed as the second major component of the SAP/response system. The PRMC's interest in EW has arisen from its preoccupation with market liberalisation. The PRMC has sought to develop a response strategy as a means of offsetting some of the adverse consequences of liberalisation in the event of food deficits and, even more important, reducing the negative impact of free food distributions on the private sector. There are three elements to the strategy: the financing of the SNS via counterpart funds[16] (amounting to c. 37 000 m. FCFA in 1990) and two information projects – the SAP and the *Système d'Information sur le Marché de Céréales* (SIM), which monitors cereal markets. A further branch of PRMC activities involves the funding of credit lines to traders and local *Associations Villageoises* to stimulate the development of cereal marketing by the private sector.[17]

The PRMC presents a co-ordinated donor position to the COC, which meets every 6–8 weeks (more frequently when required) to present its recommendations to the GRM. Since 1990, PRMC recommendations to the COC have almost exclusively been a reflection of SAP recommendations, including the financing of transport of the cereals released from the SNS and its replenishment via the common counterpart fund.

There had been much consternation amongst donors that despite substantial investments in EW, the response process was chaotic. At the end of 1990, an evaluation of the SAP concluded that:

> The impact of the project on decisions and free food aid distribution is weak. The divergence of interests between decision-makers results

either in a reduction of recommended aid, or in long delays in distributing ... (and further) ... Although SAP recommendations are greatly anticipated, the direct impact of the project on food aid decisions is in reality weak and does not show any real progression. (Egg and Teme, 1990: i and 26 – author's translation)

Donors therefore undertook to agree a concerted position and to stick to it throughout the following year. Since then, there is a widespread view, both within government and among donors, that the evolution of EW and response has been a success, not least because the early discrepancies between SAP recommendations and the actual distributions of food aid have largely been ironed out. The 'fit' between them is now very tight, indicating that Mali is a rare example of an EWS that has succeeded in forging the missing link between provision and use of EW data (Buchanan-Smith *et al.*, 1994).

Yet the story is less straightforward than this. The principal criticisms of the ways in which SAP EW data are used to trigger response are as follows:

- over-institutionalisation of the response process, leading to long bureaucratic delays;
- over-dependence on donor resources and technical assistance, and consequent questions about the long-term sustainability of the SAP and its programmed response system;
- the necessity of continued donor co-ordination in the PRMC which, whilst a substantial achievement, nevertheless comes under serious pressure at times, almost inevitably in a bad year;
- an inability to overcome the endemic problems of conflicting interests within the food aid lobby, both between donors and government, and within these groups. Donors are driven by the desire for free food distributions not to disrupt markets, and to target only those who are 'victims of liberalisation' (Egg and Teme, 1990: 32), whilst the GRM regards food aid as an economic resource which can be used to meet a variety of political and social ends. The SAP finds itself caught between its bureaucratic links to the MATDB and its financing by the PRMC (*ibid.*);[18]
- continued delays between the request for food aid and its arrival (9–12 months);
- insufficient targeting (the smallest unit being c. 5000 people) and inadequate monitoring on the ground of what actually happens to the aid that is distributed. Evaluations carried out by CNAUR in 1991 (République du Mali, 1991a, 1991b, 1991c, 1992) concluded that

food aid often failed to reach intended beneficiaries and that the system of programmed response did not extend to monitoring at the level of distribution. Numerous malpractices were identified. As one evaluation summed it up: '*Pour la population, une distribution sans contrôle est un don à l'administration de base*' (République du Mali, 1991a: 10).[19]

In the event of a substantial food deficit (greater than the size of the SNS – a maximum of 58 000 tons of local millet and sorghum), the programmed response mechanism no longer suffices. Since the programme's inception, Mali has not had such a harvest failure, so the ways in which programmed response would assist a large-scale emergency response have yet to be tested. Both the SAP and PRMC argue that the system is sufficiently developed to be geared up to respond. A parallel system also exists, whereby the GRM makes annual requests to bilateral donors, on the basis of its own assessment of the food situation. Both government and donors assert that the PRMC's programmed response mechanism does not preclude bilateral transfers of food aid, but conflicts of interest easily arise.

The PRMC also finances the SIM which collects and broadcasts cereal prices in key markets, as a means of improving the transparency of the newly liberalised cereal marketing sector, in the belief that greater access to information about prices will improve competitiveness for surplus producers, consumers and small-scale traders. This approach is based on the implicit assumption that the private sector is ill-equipped with market intelligence, and that lack of timely price, supply and demand information is a barrier to entry to markets and hence a constraining factor on competitiveness within the private sector.

Prior to liberalisation, there was an active private sector trade in cereals in Mali, accounting for significantly over 50 per cent of all cereals traded. Then, as now, the private sector depended on accurate information for its profitability. Linked to this is the particular nature of Mali's food production, which can fluctuate by 60 per cent from one year to the next, with the result that traders move in and out of cereals, and to do this profitably, they must have accurate and timely indicators of projected demand. Large-scale traders in regional urban centres have long-established and highly developed information systems. Even small-scale traders are highly conversant with local food-security conditions; it is factors such as access to credit and transportation, rather than lack of market intelligence, which inhibit further growth of the small-scale private cereal marketing sector.

Traders do not use official information networks (SIM, SAP, SADS), preferring their own highly developed information systems. Indeed, they argue that it is these official systems which come to them for information, as they always know the prices first.[20] In fact, the establishment of public information systems to broadcast prices as a means of making newly liberalised cereal markets more competitive appears to be based on a misapprehension. Lack of current information about supply and demand – and hence prices – is not identified as a constraint to competitiveness by local and regional traders. The PRMC's initiative to fund credit lines to traders and local *Associations Villageoises* is therefore far more likely to assist in market development than is the provision of information which is already widely available to the private sector. Cheaper credit and transport for traders will, in turn, help to reduce the cost of cereals to food-insecure people.

CONCLUSIONS: PROGRESS IN NATIONAL FOOD-SECURITY PLANNING IN THE 1980s

The PRMC and the programmed response mechanism which it has developed with the GRM are the clearest manifestation of national food-security planning in Mali in the 1980s, and their achievements should not be underestimated. In so far as EW and response is concerned, however, the programmed response mechanism comes into action only once people are already hungry. Little progress has been made in respect of other NFS objectives. Improving producer access to credit and other inputs, more effective co-ordination of rural development planning or effectively reforming rural development programmes have not been tackled in any systematic sense. Food-security planning has not progressed from the general outline of the original NFS document to the development of a specific and coherent set of policy prescriptions. This is particularly disappointing, given that in Mali, in most years, food insecurity is a distributional issue, not one of food deficits of emergency proportions. So far, policy responses to this have polarised around two extremes: leaving it to the market on the one hand, and distributing emergency food aid on the other.

A major reason for neglecting the middle ground between these two extremes was the drought of 1982–4, during which short-term crisis management (the distribution of food aid) replaced the pursuit of longer-term objectives. An emergency mentality developed, which was not appropriate to the nature of food insecurity in the country. The prolonged effects of drought have focused attention on better prediction and management of crisis years: in particular, the setting up of the SAP and the programmed response mechanism. Such activities can, of course, complement wider national food-security aims, especially by improving the collection, quality and analysis of information; but these wider objectives have been largely ignored, with the exception of the PRMC. The clearest lesson from the PRMC is that if general food-security objectives can be unpacked into precise programmes of action, there is potential to implement policy reforms and to monitor their impact. The emergency component of the package has been addressed, just as wider macroeconomic structural adjustment has been tackled; but the central issue of how people's livelihoods can be made more secure has not been on the agenda in the 1980s. The second lesson from the PRMC is that food-security issues in Mali are far more complex than general policy prescriptions suggest, requiring detailed planning and continuous reassessment. Chronic financial difficulties – and the poverty of much of the population which this entails – persist, despite attempts at structural adjustment. Preoccupation with improving food security continues, but if Mali's NFS is to develop beyond the PRMC, a radical shift away from macro-level generalities towards identification of local problems and solutions is required.

There is a serious risk of neglecting the underlying, chronic problems of the food sector, if preoccupation with (rather infrequent) crisis years is too great. In stark contrast to the shopping list of food sector reform requirements, the 1980s were characterised, for rural producers in the north in particular, by the worst cycle of drought in ten years (indeed, some argued it was the worst since the Kitangal famine of 1912–13) and limited emergency relief, organised principally by NGOs. Recovery has been slow and hesitant, few had regained by the end of the decade the level of livelihood security they had at the beginning and many are considerably more food-insecure. Most of the characteristics of livelihood insecurity in Mali, many of which have been exacerbated rather than caused by the drought, have still to be addressed.

Livelihood systems in Mali are highly diversified. This poses a major problem for national planning strategies which, although aware of agro-ecological differences, cannot take into account the extreme diversity and localisation of ways in which people increase their access to food. An NFS is obliged to minimise these differences, by virtue of its global objectives, despite the fact that they provide the key to household food security for most of the people living in areas at risk. Equally, national food-security policies focus too much on the agricultural sector, making only very general references to the need to integrate pastoralism (and, in the riverine zones, fishing) into planning.

Part of the difficulty is the huge variation between Regions in the nature of food insecurity. Appropriate policies need to be both location- and

Drought, Food Insecurity and Early Warning in Mali   107

livelihood system-specific. The remaining chapters of this study explore food insecurity in one part of Mali, with a view to outlining such a decentralised plan. This kind of approach is consistent with recent trends within the GRM towards decentralisation, first tackled by the preparation in 1985 of *Diagnostics Régionales* (regional planning documents) covering, *inter alia*, the food sector,[21] and accelerated since the new democratically elected government came to power in 1992. The development of a Regional planning capacity and, crucially, the ability to introduce policy initiatives at the Regional level are at an embryonic stage. Even at the national level, the cross-sectoral implications of an NFS place phenomenal strains on existing structures and resource levels. Nevertheless, the success of the PRMC in achieving sustained GRM/donor collaboration as well as donor co-ordination suggests that, if individual food-security objectives reach the stage of a specific programme of action, there is scope for improved planning and implementation in other areas. Equally, the process of monitoring and evaluation of the PRMC, both by government and donors, has worked well, resulting in a clear reassessment of PRMC objectives in its third phase. There is, as yet, little evidence of this process extending to other elements of national food-security planning, but this is not surprising given that there has been little action either.

By the end of 1986, when most of the EW projects became operational, it was no longer clear that the major food problem in Mali was the threat of famine. The aftermath of drought left many people chronically food-insecure, seasonally developing into an acute problem, even in a good year. Moreover, the food aid-oriented famine EW stage was somewhat crowded by late 1986. It therefore made sense for SADS to gear its activities towards an information system which sought to monitor access to food and indigenous coping mechanisms, with a view to identifying non-emergency interventions to improve household food security sustainably, thereby addressing part of the gap in national planning.

This shift was consistent with changing government and donor attitudes. Realising that many of the conditions and outcomes of the 1973 drought were being re-enacted a decade later, donor policy in the post-drought period was at last refocusing towards the need for development-oriented and longer-term solutions to food insecurity. This, in turn, encouraged the government to pay more attention to these longer-term considerations, which had been raised in the NFS. Reducing dependence on food aid was a primary objective, yet the ideas in the NFS had received little practical support since 1982, with the notable exception of the PRMC.

A major reason for this lack of progress was a striking shortage of information about and understanding of how Mali's food economy worked. Although there were some data and analyses at the macroeconomic level (particularly with respect to the PRMC), very little was available to planners in government and donor agencies about Regional and micro-level livelihood systems. The diversity of these systems, even within the Malian Sahel, made this gap all the more of an impediment to realistic food-security planning. By way of example, none of the original designs of the various EWS took account of the Inner Niger Delta, despite its key influence on the food security of producers in the Sahelian zone, particularly in dry years.

6 Livelihood Safety Nets: The Inner Niger Delta in the Sahel

INTRODUCTION

This chapter moves from the national picture of food security discussed in Chapter 5 to the regional level. It thus sets the context in which local livelihoods are monitored.

The Inner Niger Delta, a seasonal floodplain in the midst of the Malian Sahel, is a traditional safety net for victims of drought and food shortages in surrounding dryland areas. The diversity and seasonality of its natural resources give rise to the livelihood systems found in the zone: on the drylands, millet cultivators, agro-pastoralists, and transhumant pastoralists, and on the wetlands, rice cultivators, agro-pastoralists, agro-fishers, transhumant fishers and transhumant pastoralists. These systems in turn determine how and whether food security is achieved. Seasonally-specific exploitation of the Delta's key natural resources (land, pasture, fish, forests) and exchanges of labour between different livelihood systems have always characterised the livelihood security of the inhabitants and of strangers from the surrounding drylands who migrate into the area. Since the early 1980s, these livelihood patterns have undergone a number of changes, which call into question the continued ability of the Delta to fulfil its function of safety net in periods of dearth.

Indigenous inhabitants of the Delta are becoming increasingly impoverished. By way of illustration, rice cultivators in Youvarou and Tenenkou would have habitually expected to harvest two years' worth of food supply, and used to define their own food security as always having this amount stored on-farm. Nowadays, they rarely harvest enough food for a single year's consumption. Food security is now seen to mean having enough food or other sources of income to last until the next harvest. At the same time, the ability of livelihood systems in the surrounding dryland zones to sustain inhabitants is declining. In response, both dry and wetland producers have intensified exploitation of those resources on which they habitually relied, and their overall numbers have increased, as more people move in to the Delta every year and stay for longer periods. The traditional safety net is thus becoming central to livelihood security for more and more people every year. Monitoring the food situation in the Delta, as well as the arrivals of strangers seeking sanctuary in the zone, means that a far more diverse population group can be covered than by an information system selectively spreading its network across the sparsely populated areas of the Malian Sahel, which people tend to leave when there is a rainfall deficit. This central importance of the Delta's natural-resource base and its seasonality is the reason for its being at the heart of the SADS monitoring system. Few sensible generalisations could be made about how people feed themselves, and still fewer indicators derived which could uniformly monitor changes in access to food, without embracing the productive and exploitative diversity at the core of local livelihood systems. Rather than beginning with vulnerability as a defining characteristic of food-insecure groups, the SADS system took as its starting point productive choices, created by the natural-resource base.

POPULATION

Table 6.1 shows the population of the 5th, 6th and 7th Regions in 1976 and 1987, as well as its average annual rate of growth, which is con-

Table 6.1 Population of Mali's 5th Region, 1976 and 1987

Region	Population 1976	Population 1987	Average annual rate of growth (%)
Total Mali	6 394 918	7 620 225	1.70
Total 5th, 6th, 7th Regions i.e. most vulnerable to food insecurity	1 990 400 (31.2%)	2 098 149 (27.5%)	
Population of 5th Region	1 129 041	1 261 383	1.07
% 5th Region of total population	17.7%	16.6%	
% 5th Region of most vulnerable	56.7%	60.1%	
Resident population covered by SADS[a]		584 444	
% of most vulnerable population covered by SADS		27.9%	

Note: [a] *Cercles* of Mopti Central, Douentza, Tenenkou, Youvarou.
Source: République du Mali (1987b).

siderably lower than was previously assumed. These Regions are the ones most vulnerable to drought and food insecurity in Mali and 60.1 per cent of this vulnerable population lived in the 5th Region in 1987. Taking the four *cercles* covered by the SADS monitoring system, the table shows that they comprise 27.9 per cent of the populations of the three Regions, or 33.8 per cent if the population of the *cercles* of Koro and Bankass, which are habitually surplus-producing areas, are excluded. This figure does not include seasonal migrants from the surrounding drylands (other than inhabitants of Mopti Central and Douentza): in a bad year, they can amount to c. 200 000 people. In a bad year, therefore, about 38 per cent of those potentially vulnerable are covered by the system.

THE BASES OF LIVELIHOOD SYSTEMS

The Inner Niger Delta is a flat plain covering about 15 000 square kilometres, crossed by the Niger and Bani rivers and numerous small waterways (see Map 3). To the north and east lie the Sahelian drylands of the Seno (east) and Mema (north-west). On the west is the 'dead' Delta, plains which no longer flood, and to the south the highlands of the Bandiagara plateau. Between KéMacina in the south-west and Lake Debo in the northeast, the plain falls in height by 10 metres over 200 km (Gallais, 1967, cited in Moorehead, 1991). The topography consists of sand dunes on the borders with a transition zone which floods seasonally, leading to the floodplain proper containing the principal waterways and their tributaries, with inhabited islands occurring at intervals. Soils range from sand on the borders to clay on the floodplain.

The surrounding drylands are composed of expanses of stabilised sand dunes, interspersed with laterite/clay plains where wet season water-holes are more plentiful, but permanent water points remain scarce. In the *cercle* of Douentza to the east of the Delta, there are two further agro-ecological zones: first, the lake system in the north-west, which has similar characteristics to those of the northern Delta, and second, a chain of sandstone mountains, rising to between 400 and 1000 metres, which are a fragmented continuation of the Bandiagara plateau (Map 4).

Models of food insecurity typically characterise the vulnerability of Sahelian populations by their dependence on a single rainy season which determines the productivity of both cereals and pasture. Recognition of the importance of coping strategies has gone some way to redressing this over-dependence on a single natural resource (rainfed land), for example, by identifying the importance of wood fuel or wild food gathering. The

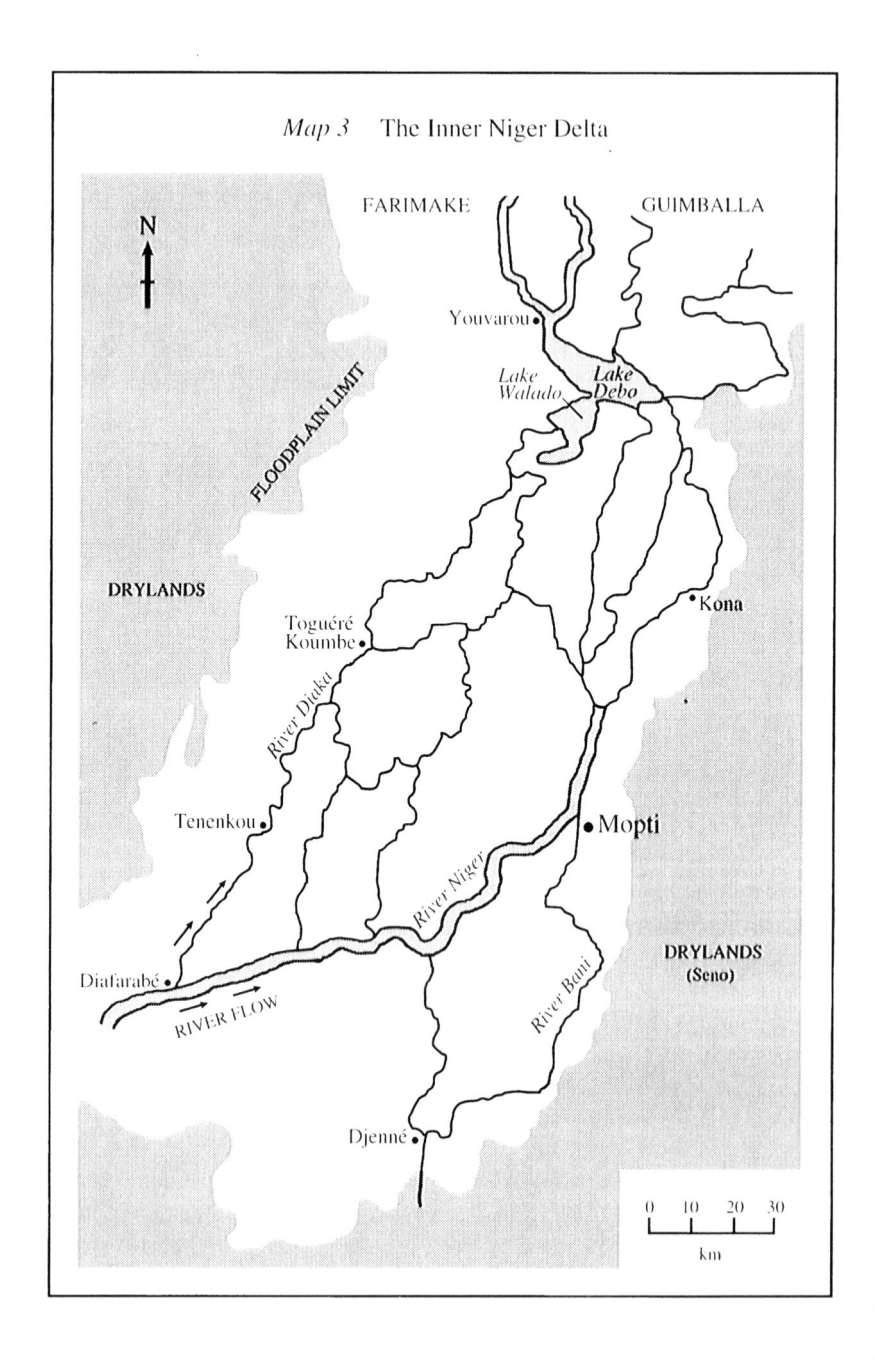

Adaptable Livelihoods

Map 3 The Inner Niger Delta

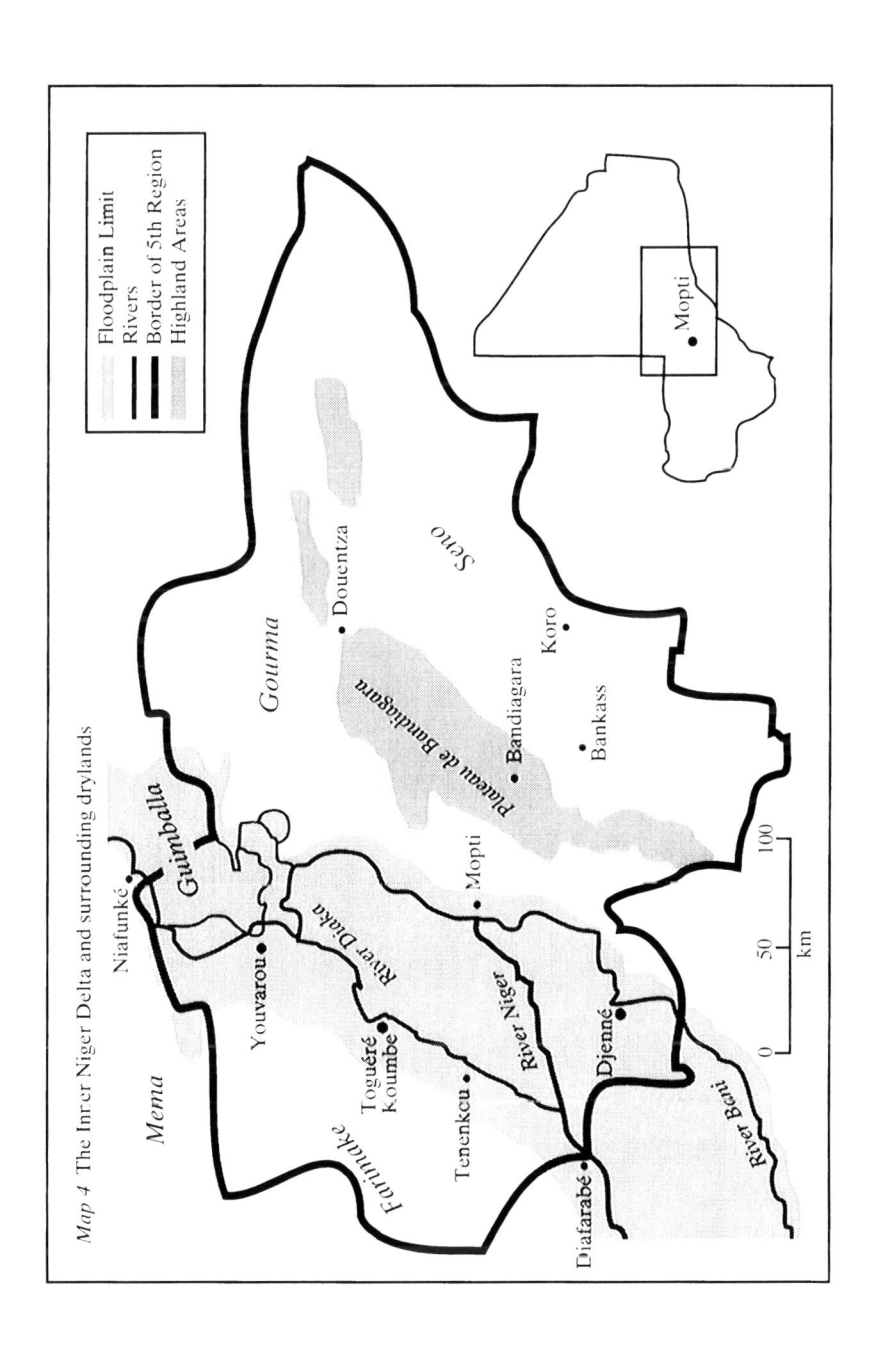

Map 4 The Inner Niger Delta and surrounding drylands

diversity of the natural-resource base in the Inner Niger Delta, derived from the twin regimes of flood and rainfall, represents the antithesis of single resource-based livelihood systems. In addition to rice cultivation on the floodplains and flood-retreat crops and millet cultivation on its borders, prior to the mid-1980s drought 100 000 tons of fish were caught every year and the Delta sustained two million sheep and goats and one million cattle, 20 per cent of the national herd (IUCN, 1989a). Since then, fish production has fallen, sometimes to less than half this figure, and the composition of livestock has changed, with a shift from cattle to goats (Chapter 8). The Seno drylands to the east rely solely on rainfall and, as such, are more representative of typical Sahelian zones; but despite a single rainy season, dryland producers, like their Delta counterparts, have more diversified sources of livelihood than traditional models suggest. Further, the inhabitants of these drylands have the option of migrating to the more diverse area when the rains fail.

Rain falls in a single season from June/July to September/October. The northern part of the Delta has rainfall levels consistent with Sahelian zones (200–300 mm a year), whilst at its southern end rainfall averages 500–600 mm a year. The seasonality of the Delta is determined by the synergism between the rains and the flood. There are four principal seasons: the rainy season (July–September), during which the flood waters rise; the high water season (October–December), also the time of harvests; the falling water season (January–March), when the Delta dries out and the weather is cold; and the dry season (April–June) when the Delta reverts to a dry plain, and temperatures are at their highest. In the surrounding drylands, the seasons follow the same pattern in terms of rainfall, but not flood, with the important exception that from November/December until June/July, the drylands are largely unproductive in natural-resource terms. These categories also broadly determine the seasonality of patterns of access to food.

Rainfall levels in Mopti, the regional capital situated in the Delta, have fallen consistently during this century from a mean of 546 mm in the period 1920–69 to an average of 421 mm in the 1980s. It is worth noting that since the 1972–3 drought, fifteen years have fallen below the average for 1956–90, including nine consecutively, indicating that conditions are both drier and more persistently dry now than in the 1950s and 1960s, when livelihood systems were seen by those dependent on them as secure. The timing and distribution have also altered, reducing the length of the rainy season. Rainfall levels in the drylands of Douentza have also declined in recent years, and, in comparison with the data which are available for the period 1956–90, more steeply than in Mopti.

Livelihood Safety Nets: The Inner Niger Delta in the Sahel 115

The distinguishing feature of the Delta is the annual flood which transforms a dry plain into an inland sea. The progress of the flood is represented diagrammatically in Map 5. An estimated 60 000 million cubic metres of water flow in annually from the catchment area in the Guinea mountains, of which half disappears in evaporation, transpiration or filters into the ground to feed the water table. High water levels reach the upstream (southern) end of the Delta at the beginning of October, the centre (Tenenkou) in December and the downstream (northern) end (Youvarou) in February. At the northern end, the floodplain is stopped by the Erg of Niafunké, stationary sand dunes running from west to east, which back up the floodwaters into Lakes Debo and Walado (Moorehead, 1991: 51).

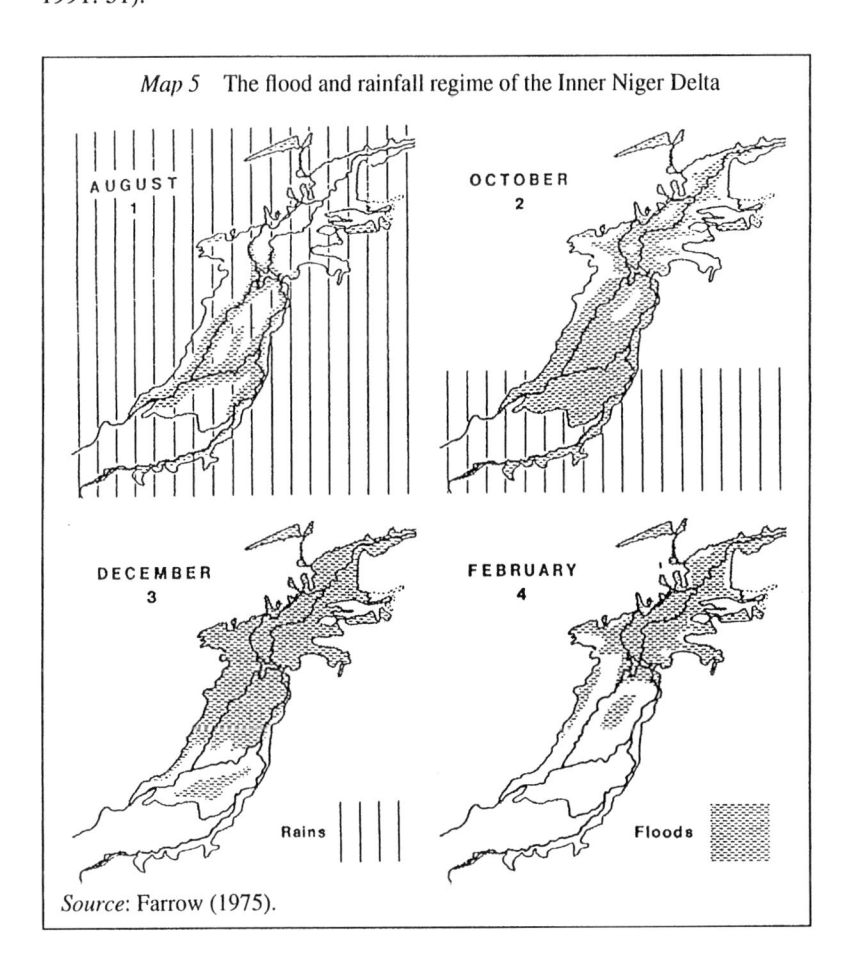

Map 5   The flood and rainfall regime of the Inner Niger Delta

Source: Farrow (1975).

Flood levels have also fallen. Whereas average maximum flood heights were 570 mm from 1956 to 1965, they had fallen to an average of 393 mm in the 1980s. Graph 6.1 compares the timing and level of flood water between 1957–9 (a good year) and 1983–5 (a bad one), showing that both the overall quantity of water and the duration of flooding have diminished. As Moorehead has argued (*ibid.*: 71):

> The effect has been to shorten the time when the floodplains were inundated from a period of five to six months in 1957–59, to two to three months in the early 1980s, thereby doubling the length of the dry season.

On the drylands and the borders of the Delta, the only rainfed cereal which can be grown is millet, with various types of flooded and rainfed rice on the floodplain. Both produce about 500 kg/ha in reasonable years (*ibid.*: 55). A number of flood-retreat crops are traditionally cultivated, including sorghum, groundnuts and cotton, although production of these has declined with the lower flood levels since the 1970s.

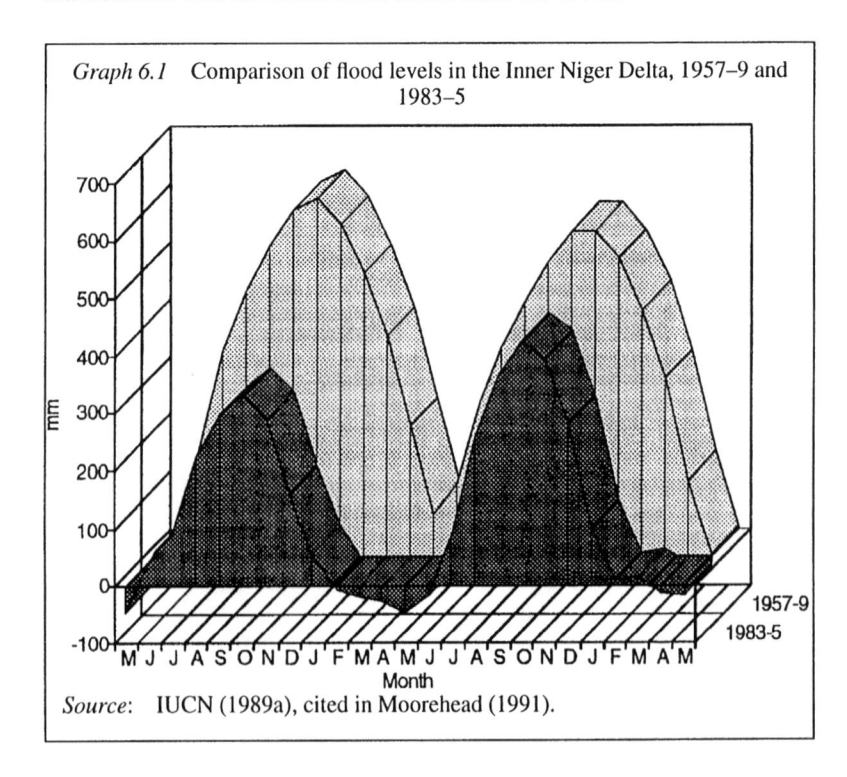

Graph 6.1 Comparison of flood levels in the Inner Niger Delta, 1957–9 and 1983–5

Source: IUCN (1989a), cited in Moorehead (1991).

The stabilised sand dunes of the drylands and the dry borders of the Delta are covered in *cram-cram* grass (*Cenchrus biflorus*), with some tree cover. Numerous dryland grass species, both annuals and perennials, are found on the borders of the Delta and in the drylands proper. The vegetation of the wetlands is unique to the area, dependent on the coincidence of flood and rainfall. The main vegetation is *bourgou* (Fulani term for floodland pasture) or *Echinochloa stagnina* (the *bourgou* proper). This pasture is highly productive, averaging 7000 kg/dm/ha a year, rising to as much as 25 000 kg/dm/ha in particularly productive years (*ibid.*: 55, citing Hiernaux and Diarra in IUCN, 1987a). Forest resources on the floodplains include *Acacia nilotica, Acacia seyal* and *Andira inermis*. Wild foods are a significant source of food for both dry and wetland inhabitants. On the drylands, the main ones are *cram-cram, guigile* (*Boscia senegalensis*) and *fonio* (*Digitaria exilis*); on the floodplains, wild rice, water-lilies (tubers and seeds) and the grains from the *bourgou* grass are gathered.

Daget (1954) cites 130 genera of fish in the Inner Delta, the total estimated annual productive capacity of which is c. 100 000 tons. The rate of fish reproduction is directly related to the area of Delta flooded, as Moorehead (1991: 55-6) explains:

> Delta fish reproduce on the floodplains, and follow the leading edge of the floodwaters to their spawning grounds between July and October. Between November and January they grow on the floodplains ... before returning to the main watercourses and secondary channels as the water falls between January and March.

REGIONAL FOOD-SECURITY PLANNING

The *Comité Régional de Développement* (CRD), comprising the regional heads of government services and (non-executive) representatives of NGOs and other aid agencies working in the region, and chaired by the Regional Governor, is the decision-making body for regional development planning and execution (Diagram 6.1). This structure is repeated at *cercle* and *arrondissement* level. Villagers are represented on Local Development Committees by the head of the village in which *arrondissement*-level administration is based. The central government is responsible for the formulation of development initiatives and their implementation, management of funds and evaluation of projects. On paper, at least, the bare bones of decentralised planning exist, although the ability of the District Development Committees, and their even more disadvantaged counter-

Diagram 6.1 Structure of Malian sub-national administration, 1990

REGION

Regional Development Committee:

Governor (Chair)
Development Adviser
Regional Directors of: Planning and Statistics
Public Health
Social Affairs
Livestock
Water and Forests
Meteorology
Agriculture
Public Works
Representatives of UNTM, UNFM, UNJM[a]
Representatives of donors, NGOs

CERCLE

District Development Committee:

Commandant de Cercle (Chair)
Premier Adjoint du Commandant de Cercle
Head of the Central *Arrondissement*
Heads of Services of: Public Health
Agriculture
Water and Forests
Meteorology
Public Works
Livestock
Police
Territorial Militia
Co-operative Action
Representative of OPAM
Tax Collector
Representatives of UNTM, UNFM, UNJM
Representatives of donors, NGOs

ARRONDISSEMENT

Local Development Committee:

Chef d'Arrondissement (Chair)
Head of Health Centre
Representatives of the Services of: Agriculture
Livestock
Water and Forests
Territorial Militia
Head of the Village of the *Chef Lieu d'Arrondissement*
Representatives of the UNTM, UNFM, UNJM
Representatives of donors, NGOs

Note: [a] UNTM – *Union Nationale des Travailleurs Maliens*; UNFM – *Union Nationale des Femmes Maliennes*; UNJM – *Union Nationale des Jeunes Maliens*. All these ceased to exist when the UDPM government was overthrown in 1991.

parts at *arrondissement* level, are severely constrained by lack of resources.[1]

Food-security planning remains highly centralised in Bamako, the only sub-national planning capacity being with the regional SAP representative, situated in the *Direction Régionale du Plan*. The *Directeur du Plan* presides over the monthly regional SAP working group, which meets to discuss questionnaires (completed by the Local Development Committees at *arrondissement* level) and the summary report of their findings (see Chapter 5). Membership of this working group is essentially the same as that of the CRD. The regional depot of the SNS, managed by OPAM, is based at Sévaré, 13 km from Mopti on the mainland, from where distributions in response to SAP recommendations for free food aid are supplied. Apart from this food aid management, food-security planning as such does not figure in the concerns of the CRD and there is no specific unit charged with such planning at the regional level. In the principal regional planning document, the *Diagnostic de la Région de Mopti* (République du Mali, 1985), food security is discussed under the rubric of health and increased agricultural, livestock and fish production. No co-ordinated regional food-security policy exists.

Wider development initiatives, which are sectorally based and often tend to be 'high-tech' in nature, amount to shopping lists of projects, ranging from irrigating perimeters with motorised pumps, to digging dykes to control floodwaters and wells to improve access to water, to setting up village woodlots and restricting access to forests, with some coverage of fisheries and livestock vaccination. These tend to meet with little success (e.g. parts and fuel are unavailable for technological inputs, and expertise is lacking when they go wrong) and receive even less support from local people (Moorehead, 1991: 232–3). The biggest investment in productive development in the 1970s and 1980s was in the sectorally-based ODRs, for millet, rice, livestock and fisheries,[2] but these tended to concentrate investments on infrastructure and recurrent costs, and many of the benefits of increased production were purloined by urban elites (e.g. in the case of ORM, rice polders around the town of Mopti were largely farmed by traders and civil servants) (*ibid.*: 239). ODRs are now being run down, as donor funds have been withdrawn.

Regional development planning operates, in theory, within the policy framework described in Chapter 5. It is conditioned by four factors. First, information about the area being planned for is patchy and, where it does exist, little attempt is made to exploit it systematically. No direct connection is made, for example, between the identification of projects and SAP data, the use of which is confined to food aid targeting. Lack of local knowledge is exacerbated by the policy of appointing higher-level

120 *Adaptable Livelihoods*

civil servants who are outsiders to the area and moving them every few years.

Second, the attitude of these civil servants has been informed, since Independence, by the guiding principle of making local people and their productive activities more 'progressive' (*ibid.*: 230). Under the Keita regime (1960–8), the centre-piece of this strategy was the establishment of collective fields (*Tons Villageois*), covering about a third of all land under cultivation, production from which was handed over to state marketing bodies. Although pursued well after 1968, this policy has gradually withered away, accelerated by the progressive dismantling of state control of cereal markets. But the determination of the civil service to 'modernise' producers persists, with the result that:

> Both the political party and the administration promote development plans that are based upon sedentary activities, use of high inputs of technology, and involve 'collective' methods of production to all intents and purposes unaffected by the special conditions in the Delta. (Moorehead, 1991: 232)

Third, identification of development needs reflects the different interests of the various technical services shown in Diagram 6.1, on the one hand, and until 1991, those of the single political party on the other. Until the UDPM was ousted from power in 1991 this tension between the civil service and the politicians led to effective ossification of rational planning at local level.

Fourth, most actions of the local administration – including development initiatives – are principally informed by the need to raise cash to fund both civil service salaries and informal payments to the administration, as well as other revenue. Formally, local administrators have the power to levy taxes, issue licences and extract fines, a proportion of which is retained locally. Local forestry agents, responsible for policing natural-resource use including fishing, pasturing, gathering and hunting and household fuel wood collection, are especially prominent in this capacity. Moorehead (1991: 234) argues that the costs of these controls are high (around 50 per cent) relative to *per capita* incomes. Non-payment of taxes can have further knock-on effects on access to food: in a bad year, those who are behind in their payments are often ineligible for free food aid distributions; in a good year, zealous collection of arrears immediately after the harvest forces people to sell cereals when their price is lowest (and when the price of repayment of credit taken out in the dry season is high), in order to meet tax bills. The levying of fines on illegal fishing and graz-

Livelihood Safety Nets: The Inner Niger Delta in the Sahel 121

ing of small-stock inevitably peaks at the end of the dry season (when they are concentrated and hence easy to find) – i.e. the midst of the hungry season – when producers can least afford to spend cash on supporting the local administration (*ibid.*: 243). These are indications of the cost of state calls on entitlement, identified in the entitlements matrix in Chapter 2, and of their disproportionately adverse effect on food security; although such extraction by state officials has declined since the new government came to power.

LISTENING POSTS

Because of the strategic role it plays in providing livelihood security for neighbouring peoples in the dry season and in times of stress, the Inner Niger Delta is an ideal monitoring area for the SADS system. Listening posts were established in places that were the hubs of networks of livelihood systems, from which key indicators of activity could be monitored. Further, they were a mid-point between the regional-level picture and the highly diverse reality on the ground, which regional planning ignores so completely in its rigid adherence to sectoral boundaries. One listening post was set up in each of four administrative districts chosen for different reasons, although they were not necessarily located in the administrative capital, as discussed in Chapter 4. Crucially, by monitoring in these places, project staff were able to track what was happening beyond the boundaries of the Delta, because of movements of people into the zone. This approach was a departure from most EWS which typically choose administrative boundaries as the basis for data collection and analysis. Whilst sensible in terms of bureaucratic decision-making, using administrative boundaries to define food-insecure groups cannot reflect differences in how people get access to food in the structure of information collection. At the same time, to present the results of monitoring solely by livelihood system can make administrative targeting difficult. Results were thus presented both according to livelihood system and *cercle*. This enabled *cercles* to be identified in terms of the systems practised within them, as well as showing livelihood entitlement networks found on a more regional basis.

As regional capital, the town of **Mopti** is the administrative centre of the 5th Region, where the CRD is located and from where administrative activities can be followed. It also serves as a barometer for: local, inter-regional and – in the case of fish and livestock – international commerce; rural–urban migration; and the general economic health of the Region.

Situated where the rivers Niger and Bani converge, on the eastern side the Delta, with the Seno drylands to the east and south, it is not only the transportation hub of the Region, but also the centre through which all trade to the north passes, either by road to Gao, or by river to Tombouctou and Gao when the Niger is navigable.[3] Even though there is only one paved road (running on the Bamako–Mopti–Douentza–Gao axis – see Map 2 in Chapter 5), unpaved roads, servicing the Delta and north to Tombouctou (when the flood is in retreat), the productive *cercles* Koro and Bankass to the south-east of Mopti and the Seno to the south of the arch of the River Niger, all converge, albeit sometimes rather circuitously, on Mopti. Commercially, the town acts as a conduit for imports to and exports from the 5th, 6th, 7th and 8th Regions, the most important imports for subsistence producers being cereals from the south of the country and manufactured household requirements (paraffin, clothing, kitchen wares, fishing equipment, etc.), and the main exports dried and smoked fish (to southern Mali, Burkina Faso and Côte d'Ivoire). Livestock export points are more diffuse: although traded in significant numbers at the terminal market of Fatoma (10 km from Mopti), other livestock markets in the region (e.g. Douentza) are also important. Trade in Mopti is an important indicator: in years of surplus, rural producers look to the merchants of Mopti to supply them with essential productive equipment and consumer goods; in years of deficit, the same merchants provide credit and cereals. Habitual seasonal migrants, moving to take up long-established opportunities for work in other rural areas, may go via Mopti (e.g. those from the Seno drylands in search of work in the Delta, or those from the northern Delta heading south to the *Office du Niger*). More importantly, Mopti is the centre through which migrants in search of urban employment pass. In bad years, few find work in Mopti itself, although since the 1984–5 drought concentrations of displaced people have congregated in the town, some staying on a semi-permanent basis.

Douentza *cercle* lies under the arch of the river Niger, between the Delta to the west and the 7th Region to the east, the 6th Region to the north and the border with Burkina Faso to the south. As one travels north, it is the last area before the Sahara where cultivation is possible. In terms of food monitoring, there are a number of reasons for its importance. First, it is on the frontier between transhumant pastoralism and millet cultivation. Its predominantly agro-pastoral producers are, in agro-ecological terms, some of the most vulnerable to production failure in the country. Second, it is representative of those parts of the Malian Sahel where recurrent periods of drought have recently undermined traditional livelihood security, to the point where the continued viability of these systems may

Livelihood Safety Nets: The Inner Niger Delta in the Sahel 123

be in question, unless climatic conditions improve and considerable investments in the area are made. To this extent, Douentza is a barometer for the future of marginal areas. Third, the main transport artery – the paved road from Bamako to Gao – runs through the *cercle*, and in its wake has brought new trade flows into the area, although Douentza remains a transit zone for such commerce and there is little evidence of its having contributed to local growth. Fourth, Douentza continues to be a traditional transit zone for Sahelian livestock moving to southern markets, despite disruptions caused by currency devaluations and changes in border controls (e.g. the closing of the Nigerian border to Malian livestock during the 1982–5 drought). Fifth, many of the migrants to Mopti, the Delta, Bamako, the coastal states and, recently, the gold mines of Burkina Faso, originate in Douentza: it has become, in this sense, an area which people leave once the harvest fails. But traditionally this was not its role; it has been the first refuge of people from the drier 6th and 7th Regions, predominantly transhumant pastoralists in search first of pasture and water, but eventually of human sustenance. Increasingly, the impoverishment of Douentza makes it impossible for it to fulfil this function.

The *cercle* of **Youvarou** is in some ways a microcosm, in agro-ecological and livelihood security terms, of the Inner Niger Delta and the surrounding drylands. The five livelihood systems on which the SADS system is based (cultivation, agro-pastoralism, agro-fishing, transhumant fishing and transhumant pastoralism) are all practised in the *cercle*. The lake areas of Debo and Walado, which provide greater productive potential than higher ground (see Map 3), constitute refuges within the Delta for all producers in dry years. They are the point of convergence both for fishing and dry season pastoral transhumant routes, and attract many inhabitual migrants in bad years, in addition to the habitual seasonal visitors. From a food-security point of view, the lake area of Youvarou is a barometer for the ability of the most productive rural areas to support both indigenous and stranger populations in bad years. The success or failure of livelihood-system diversity and the ability of livelihood systems to absorb food-insecure people from other groups and areas can be monitored there. The drier parts of the cercle are representative of the livelihood systems of dryland inhabitants.

The *cercle* of **Tenenkou**, to the south of Youvarou and in the middle of the Delta, is the heart of the Delta livelihood systems. The SADS listening post is based not in the central *arrondissement* but in **Toguéré Koumbé**, which is more significant in terms of productive and migratory behaviour than the town of Tenenkou itself. The same livelihood systems are found as in Youvarou, including dryland cultivators on the western border. In terms of cultivation, Toguéré Koumbé is one of the least risky rice-growing areas in the Delta, as well as being one of the most productive fisheries. As a comparatively wealthy zone, it is a magnet for rural–rural migration, attracting dryland cultivators on to the floodplains in search of paid work in the rice harvest and in fishing camps. As such, the area is a useful indicator of the overall health of livelihood systems in a given year. If it is comparatively unscathed, potential exists for surplus labour absorption (albeit often via informal and kinship channels, rather than via the market), whereas if Toguéré itself is facing food insecurity, this is a sure indication that producers from less well-endowed areas will meet with little success in their coping strategies of migration to more productive rural areas. Commercially, Toguéré Koumbé is one of the most important markets in the Delta during the fishing campaign, and levels of activity and prices are a reliable indicator of the strength or failure of the campaign. It is also a cross-roads for cereals coming from the south (via Diafarabé) and the east (via Mopti), for resale within the more remote parts of the Delta (see Map 3). Most transhumant pastoralists who rely on Delta pastures enter through the *cercle* of Tenenkou: Diafarabé in the south is in this sense the gateway to the Delta, as Youvarou is the exit.[4] Similarly, the fishing campaign begins in Tenenkou and progresses downstream with the flood retreat, towards Lakes Walado and Debo in Youvarou. Like Youvarou, Tenenkou is a traditional refuge for food-insecure people from the surrounding drylands, but they arrive earlier in this southern part of the Delta and move northwards to Youvarou as the dry season progresses.

OVERVIEW OF FOOD SECURITY, 1987–8 TO 1990–1

This section sketches the food-security situation in the Inner Niger Delta and the surrounding drylands over a four-year period, from 1987–8 to 1990–1. It is analysed in more detail in subsequent chapters. Data are presented by agricultural year (October to September). Table 6.2 summarises the cycles of good and bad years since the start of the drought cycle of the mid-1980s. Using rainfall averages for the four listening posts and maximum flood heights, as well as producers' own perceptions of the year in question, three cycles of bad to satisfactory years, with a single good year, are identified. The norm in the 1980s has been bad to satisfactory years, interspersed (once every three to four years) with a good year, comparable to those of the inter-drought decade between 1972–3 and 1982–3. To this extent, productive activities and strategies used in bad to satisfactory years

Table 6.2 Cycles of livelihood vulnerability in Mali's 5th Region, 1982–3 to 1990–1

Cycle	Year	Producers' own judgement	Rainfall[a]	Maximum flood height[b]	Livelihood status
1st	1982–3	Bad/satisfactory	Bad – 241 mm	406 mm	Resources left from previous year. No crisis.
	1983–4	Bad	Satisfactory but poor distribution – 324 mm	378 mm	Last assets liquidated. Crisis averted.
	1984–5	Disaster	Drought – 195 mm	331 mm	Third bad year. Reserves and assets depleted. Crisis.
	1985–6	Satisfactory	Satisfactory – 328 mm	425 mm	Partial recovery. Good year for fishing and flooded rice.
2nd	1986–7	Satisfactory to bad	Satisfactory but poor distribution – 373 mm	386 mm	Use of few resources acquired.
	1987–8	Bad	Bad (worst since 1984–5) – 302 mm	354 mm	Last resources depleted. Crisis brewing.
	1988–9	Good	Good – 423 mm	428 mm	Partial recovery. Repayment of debts incurred since 1984–5.
3rd	1989–90	Satisfactory	Good but grasshopper attacks – 440 mm	388 mm	Stocks accumulated in previous year depleted.
	1990–1	Bad/satisfactory	Satisfactory but poor distribution – 385 mm	374 mm	Use of last resources.

Notes: [a] Rainfall data for 1982–7 are the average for the *cercles* of Mopti, Douentza and Tenenkou. From 1988, Youvarou is included.
[b] At Akka.

Source: Adapted from *SADS Bulletin*, no. 14.

may be seen as the habitual pattern. Good years are, however, essential to relieve pressure which builds up over two to three bad ones (e.g. debt, labour shortages due to long-term migration, unpaid fiscal dues, liquidation of assets). Successive good years are unknown and, as will be seen in the following chapters, this would be a necessary precondition for accumulation and the re-establishment of secure livelihood systems.

The reason why the Delta is a safety net is because the productivity of both natural and cultivated resources is not solely dependent on rainfall. Flood heights are determined by rainfall levels in the Guinea mountains, 1000 km to the west and south-west of the Delta, where annual rainfall is between 1300 and 1800 mm (Moorehead, 1991: 51). Maximum flood heights do not tell such a clear-cut story as rainfall. In 1982–3, for example, the flood exceeded 400 mm. This was classified as a bad year by dryland producers and a satisfactory one by wetland ones, but this latter assessment was almost certainly on the basis of previous expectations of flood levels. Similarly, flood levels in 1985–6 were nearly as high as in 1988–9. The critical relationship is when rainfall is bad *and* flood heights do not exceed c. 350 mm (as in 1984–5 and 1987–8). In the two years (1983–4 and 1990–1) when maximum flood heights were around 380 mm, bad conditions were reported in parts of the Delta, particularly the more shallow areas. But maximum flood levels can be misleading: very small changes in the height of the flood can have dramatic consequences for the *area* flooded.

1987–8 (bad year). This was a year of agricultural drought resulting in harvest failure on the drylands (less than three months' stock) and almost equally poor conditions for rice cultivators. In Toguéré Koumbé, only three out of 31 villages reported a good harvest, in Youvarou, it was a complete failure, and in Douentza producers compared conditions with those of 1984–5. Pasture and fishing conditions were comparatively good, however, contradicting the conventional wisdom that pastoralists are always the most vulnerable group in a dry year. Undiversified cultivators moved temporarily into other sectors, either migrating to more productive areas such as the irrigated *Office du Niger* to the south or seeking casual employment in fishing camps, for example. Agro-fishers were dependent on fishing which was reasonable, but credit for equipment was expensive and in short supply. Specialist (transhumant) fishers had better access to credit but overall, pressure on fisheries was intense, though fish maintained a high price relative to cereals. Poor harvests were supplemented with wild foods, indicating labour availability and very low household stocks. Barter was almost non-existent in the post-harvest period due to lack of cereal stores. The whole year was characterised by high market dependence, high cereal prices and declining terms of trade between small-stock and millet.

By the cold season, the knock-on effects were hitting all groups. Pastoralists were feeling the effects of having come into the dry season pastures early and herds from the 6th Region were adding to pressure on wetland pastures. The potentially disastrous effects of a further failure of the rains would find producers with no safety net of resources left to sell and few, if any, other assets or lines of credit. Strategies pursued included migration to the gold mines in Burkina Faso and continued attempts to find casual work in fishing camps. The reserves set up for collective fisheries were not respected, thereby removing the safety net of the fishing communities.

By the time the dry season began, most cultivators had already experienced two months without food stocks. During this season, everything turned on the market. A shortage of rice was announced, and the price of the cheaper staple millet rose above that in 1985, the crisis drought year. Surveys revealed that coping strategies appeared to be keeping those who had not migrated just above the critical hunger line; nevertheless, undiversified cultivators (particularly in the drylands) compared the season with 1985, the difference being that pasture and fish added some flexibility to the overall food situation. Migrants failed to return home at the start of the agricultural campaign in May but, unlike 1985, there were no significant new waves of migrants to Mopti. Transhumant pastoralists fared relatively well; despite pressure on pastures, there was no evidence of distress sales of cattle.

This increasingly serious situation was turned around by good rains for the 1988 agricultural campaign and pastoral conditions in the drylands that were comparable to pre-1973 levels. The good rains released southern producers' and traders' stocks on to the market, before their price collapsed after the harvest. But for most cultivators, it was the wild food harvest in the drylands which broke the hungry season two to three months before the millet harvest, a particularly good one owing to the rains. With the promise of good harvests, trade outside formal markets picked up (wild food, milk), confirming that barter is an indicator of relatively good conditions. Producers were unable to exploit the good rains to the full, however, owing to the lack of seed and equipment, as well as localised shortages of family labour where migrants had not returned. Moreover, credit (for cereals, seed) would have to be reimbursed at pre-harvest prices, and the value of the crop was set to plummet once the harvest was under way. Fishing continued into July, many transhumant fishers never returning to their villages of origin. Yields from the first fish of the new season (*kolaki*) were high.

In summary, what kept people going in 1987–8 and prevented a repetition of 1984–5 were: an agricultural, rather than a generalised, drought provided diversity in the range of resources available for exploitation; despite very high cereal prices, purchasing power did not collapse; the abundance of wild foods with the onset of good rains broke the hungry season; and the promise of a good harvest released stocks in the south of the country on to the market and brought down prices.

1988–9 (good year). The 1988 rains were comparable to those of 1980–1 in the Delta and 1974–5 in the Seno, both very good years. Flood levels were as high as those of the early 1970s. The millet and rice harvests guaranteed a minimum of nine months' stocks for producers and, in some cases, stocks of more than a year, though rice production was not as high as it could have been, owing to seed shortages. Wild food continued to be abundant and was collected up to the harvest. Very low rural–rural migration led to temporary labour constraints during the harvest. Millet prices collapsed after the harvest, owing to excellent harvests in the south of the country. Total national cereal production was estimated at 2.4 million tons (gross), over one million tons more than 1987 and more than 50 per cent over national requirements (Chapter 5). Pasture conditions and dryland water points were the best for more than ten years, with the result that transhumant herds stayed on the drylands until the official crossing dates into the Delta (Chapter 7). Fishing conditions were also good (comparable to 1981) and credit relatively easy to come by with the promise of a good campaign. A rapid flood retreat, however, indicated that it would be short. Barter between all livelihood systems was plentiful, although the terms of trade were set according to prevailing market prices, indicating the degree of monetisation of exchange in the local economy. Both herders and fishers were able to benefit from the low price of millet.

The 1988 cold season (January–March) started with at least six months' guaranteed food stocks for all types of producers in the zone. The good agricultural campaign had reduced dependence on the market, whilst at the same time surplus in the local economy meant that the informal sector was more dynamic than in previous years. The long harvest and increased opportunities for income-generating activities cut into the so-called 'dead season' for cultivators; activities such as construction, barter and transport were pursued with a view to small-scale accumulation. Pasture conditions continued to be good throughout the zone and terms of trade between millet and livestock continued to favour pastoralists throughout the season, enabling them to accumulate stocks without selling animals. Migration continued to be much less than in previous years, particularly as local demand for casual labour was high. As the season progressed, however, it became clear that although a good year could assure short-term food security, it was insufficient to enable investment in future livelihood security. In particular, the fiscal burden on producers, as well as other long-outstanding debts, continued to challenge food access directly.

At the end of the dry season, millet from the south of the country began to appear on Mopti market for the first time, but prices stayed low. Barter continued in some areas throughout the season, confirming that barter, owing to its reciprocal nature, becomes a much more important form of exchange in a good year than in bad ones. Stocks continued to last for some producers throughout the rainy season, although in Youvarou and some parts of Douentza, cultivators were purchasing on the market by July. Overall rainfall levels were good, but the rains started late and stopped early, indicating that the bounty of 1988 would not be sustained. Grasshopper attacks caused serious damage. Conditions were once again returning to the norm of bad to satisfactory years, with the proviso that some debts and fiscal dues had been repaid and new debts for subsistence had not been incurred in 1988–9.

The conditions of this good year did, however, underline the extent to which successive dry years have forced producers to become dependent on the cash economy, in which their cereals are almost worthless in an abundant year. Low prices and the presence of undiversified cultivators on the market showed the extent to which they had to sell much of their crop to repay debts and back-payments of taxes immediately after the harvest. Moreover, cultivators were unable to invest in productive equipment or goats because of these high cash needs. Although one good year can break the downward spiral towards famine, it is insufficient to enable producers to re-invest in their own production; to do this they would require a string of good years or financial support (or both).

1989–90 (satisfactory year). Although rainfall levels in 1989 were good, their distribution coupled with grasshopper attacks meant that harvests were only satisfactory. In contrast to 1987–8, however, most households had a few weeks' carry-over stocks and those that did not avoided incurring debts to buy cereals in the preceding season. The uneven distribution of good and satisfactory harvests re-animated labour exchanges between productive and non-productive zones. In better years, barter and labour exchanges also re-animate social ties between livelihood systems and across ecological zones, which traditionally formed an important part of safety nets in bad years. These are breaking down under conditions of increasing vulnerability, although they can re-establish themselves in good years. For those whose harvests had failed, wild foods were collected in the harvest and cold seasons. Pasture conditions were very varied. The early end to the rains meant that herds congregated in waiting zones around the Delta very early. As the cold season progressed, conditions were generally satisfactory to good, although more strangers arrived in the Delta than in the previous year. Fishing also started early in October, but catches were inferior to those of 1988. A rapid flood retreat meant a short season, but the lower catches led to higher prices than in the previous year.

The dry season was characterised by market dependence for cereals. Migration intensified and cultivators were forced to take out credit for cereals in millet-growing areas. By June, consumption was cut to one meal a day in Douentza and Youvarou. Intensive use of other coping strategies (e.g. gathering of wood, cow dung, straw) was reported in all areas, and during the cultivating season conflict was widespread over the allocation of labour between daily subsistence and future production. This was exacerbated by a shortage of traction animals, identified in the preceding good year as a constraining factor on the ability of cultivators to maximise returns to labour and areas cultivated.

The 1990 rains started well, but overall levels and flood levels were lower than in 1988 or 1989 in the Delta. Cultivators had to re-sow as many as four times; herders left late on transhumance owing to the uncertainty of the rains and animal sales increased; fish production was low. By the end of the season, the limited accumulation was wiped out, and the food situation was in the balance: the pattern of a bad year was starting to re-establish itself with dependence on the market for credit for cereals and high levels of wild food collection.

1990–1 (bad/satisfactory year). Millet harvests around the Delta were very poor in 1990 and only slightly better in Douentza; rice cultivators fared somewhat better, leading to high rural–rural migration from millet to rice-growing areas. Yet, unlike the previous year, cultivators no longer had carry-over stocks; wild food collection continued throughout the harvest season as a result. In keeping with a bad year, migration levels were high and exploitation of CPRs intense (rice cultivators taking up subsistence fishing, cutting and sale of *bourgou* and wood). The flood was lower than in 1989, and the flood retreat faster; fishing was therefore intensified, contractual relations with creditors were not honoured and competition for fisheries was widespread. Pastoralists moved into waiting zones early in October and many stranger herders moved into the Region. Levels of barter were low in keeping with the poor harvests and non-cultivators were, therefore, forced to acquire stocks of cereals via the market.

Daily subsistence characterised the months until the next harvest: reducing consumption; seeking work on richer households' fields, in

Livelihood Safety Nets: The Inner Niger Delta in the Sahel 131

fishing camps, in local urban centres; migrants staying on. But as more people became dependent on these strategies, so their market value declined. The rainy season brought a good wild food harvest, and cereal prices began to fall. Cultivators nevertheless experienced once again the acute shortages of seed and labour of a bad year. By mid-1991, Tuareg uprisings against the GRM exacerbated food insecurity: people were unable to move freely; food stocks were seized by armed bands; and transhumance routes were disrupted. The conflict did, however, result in fewer strangers than usual venturing into the Delta, thereby mitigating the prediction of intense pressure on pasture. All producers were subject to the uncertainties arising from a period of political unrest, wherein long-standing local as well as national conflicts came to the fore.

INDICATORS OF FOOD SECURITY, 1987–8 TO 1990–1

These years represent a more or less typical cycle of the 1980s, with one good year breaking up a pattern of bad to satisfactory years. Table 6.3 uses a variety of indicators, following the livelihood entitlements matrix presented in Chapter 2, to compare the different years: for sources of entitlement, standard indicators of natural conditions, followed by indicators of production entitlements, then exchange entitlements, producers' assessments of the levels of asset accumulation, and the intensity of use of coping strategies; and finally, calls on entitlement, on the basis of producers' own assessments.

Natural conditions. As argued above, crude indices of rainfall and flood cannot, by themselves, indicate what kind of year it will be. Distribution of rainfall, as well as the coincidence of the arrival of the flood and rainfall, are strong determinants of overall productivity in the Delta. Further, rainfall distribution is highly uneven between quite small geographical distances.

Production entitlements. Producers' assessments of cereals and fish broadly confirm regional estimates. Regional as a proportion of national production varies between 10 and 20 per cent. This proportion was highest in the good year, and lowest in the worst one. Systematic official estimates of pasture conditions are not available, but producers' estimates show that pastoralists were the least vulnerable group over the four-year period. Wild food availability, grouped with production entitlements for the sake of simplicity, is one of the more robust sources of entitlement; the critical issue is the timing of the wild foods' appearance and the fact that they are gathered almost every year. Not gathering wild foods is now an indicator

132   Adaptable Livelihoods

Table 6.3 Summary of indicators of food security in the Inner Niger Delta and Sahel, 1987–8 to 1990–1
Note: all producers' assessments are scored according to the following scale:
<---1---2---3---4---5--->
low   high

Indicator	1987–8	1988–9	1989–90	1990–1
Overall producers' assessment	Bad	Good	Satisfactory	Bad/satisfactory
Sources of entitlement				
1. Natural conditions				
Total rainfall (mm)				
Delta[a]	312	443	445	288
Seno[b]	231	360	415	464
Maximum flood height[c] (mm)	354	428	388	374
Grasshopper attacks			severe	
2. Production entitlements				
Cereal production (000 MT)				
Mali	1 482	2 428	1 959	1 599
5th Region	155	495	225	255
5th Region as % of total	10%	20%	11%	16%
Fish production				
Delta (000 MT)	55.7	55.9	71.8	68.7
Producers' assessment (grade)	2–3	2–3	3	3
Pasture				
Producers' assessment (grade)	3	5	4	3–4
Wild food[d]				
Producers' assessment (grade)	5	4	3	3
Post-harvest household food stocks[e]				
Producers' assessment (months)	<3	9>12	3–6	3
3. Exchange entitlements[f]				
Average millet price (FCFA/kg)				
Wetlands	160	78	108	115
Drylands	128	41	85	122

Table 6.3 (continued)

Indicator	1987–8	1988–9	1989–90	1990–1
Average (smoked) fish price (FCFA/kg)[g]				
Wetlands	176	132	126	121
Average cattle (heifer) price (FCFA/head)				
Wetlands	36 000	40 000	33 000	32 000
Drylands	37 000	39 000	27 000	27 000
Average terms of trade goats/millet (kg millet for 1 goat)				
Wetlands	23.5	52.4	27.0	15.6
Drylands	23.2	83.5	28.1	19.4
Average terms of trade fish/millet (kg millet for 1 kg smoked fish)				
Wetlands	1.12	1.74	1.47	0.74
Average terms of trade milk/millet (kg millet for 1 litre milk)				
Wetlands	0.99	2.91	1.37	0.81
Drylands	0.70	3.17	0.97	0.76
Levels of barter[h]	1	4–5	3	1
4. Asset accumulation				
Producers' assessment (grade)	1	2	1	1
5. Intensity of use of coping strategies[i]				
Producers' assessment (grade)	5	2	3–4	4–5
Calls on entitlement				
6. Consumption levels				
Producers' assessment (grade)	1–2	5	3–4	2–3
7. Claims called in				
Producers' assessment (grade)	4	5	3	4

Table 6.3 (continued)

Notes: (a) Tenenkou and Youvarou average. In 1987–8, rainfall in Youvarou was only 157 mm, whereas in Tenenkou it was 468 mm.
(b) Douentza.
(c) At Akka.
(d) The assessment of the wild food harvest refers to the harvest at the end of the agricultural year (i.e. in the rainy season following the harvest). It is this wild food availability that is critical to food access in the year in question, arriving as it does before the millet and rice harvests, thereby breaking the hungry season. A good wild food harvest can be an indicator of a good agricultural campaign to come, as in 1987–8.
(e) Number of months (approximate).
(f) Wetland prices are based on the average seasonal retail price for Youvarou and Toguéré Koumbé; dryland prices are average seasonal retail prices for Douentza; wholesale prices are average seasonal ones for Mopti (see Chapter 9).
(g) Fish prices have been converted into equivalent wet weights (see Chapter 9).
(h) This is a general index of barter, but refers principally to bartering cereals for milk and fish. Different barter exchanges are explained in Chapter 7.
(i) The intensity of use of coping strategies refers to the amount of time spent on and income derived from coping strategies (see Chapters 7 and 10).

of a good year, rather than their consumption indicating a bad one. Producer estimates of post-harvest household food stocks indicate a structural food gap for all but the exceptional year of 1988–9. Even in the good year, not all producers had stocks of 12 months or more (Chapter 8).

Exchange entitlements. Millet prices are clearly robust indicators of local food availability; fish prices show less variation, but over the last twenty years, falling fish production has been more than compensated for by price. Average cattle prices vary less than other products, indicative of the relatively stable pastoral conditions throughout the period. The terms of trade between goats/fish/milk and millet have declined over the period (Chapter 9). Levels of barter clearly increase in good years, and fall to almost nothing in bad ones.

Asset accumulation. In terms of the longer-term decline of livelihoods, low asset accumulation in every year indicates that, even when there is a surplus, producers are unable to save or invest in production (Chapter 7).

Intensity of use of coping strategies. The intensity of use is above average in all but the exceptional year 1988–9. This indicates than such strategies are not purely reserved as fall-back mechanisms in periods of dearth (Chapter 10).

Livelihood Safety Nets: The Inner Niger Delta in the Sahel   135

Consumption levels. These were high only in the good year and even in the satisfactory one of 1989–90 scored only just above average, reflecting seasonal shortages prior to the following harvest.

Claims called in. As with levels of asset accumulation, claims called in were less sensitive to differences in years than expected. Such calls actually increase in good years, when people have the capacity to repay outstanding debts. They are lowest in satisfactory years, when neither the capacity to pay nor the need of the recipient to claim is great.

CONCLUSIONS

The Inner Niger Delta has traditionally served as a safety net, its capacity to do so being derived from the multiple natural resources in this wetland amidst drylands, and their seasonally-specific availability. As livelihoods become increasingly vulnerable both in the Delta itself and in the surrounding drylands, pressure on the safety net increases, and more and more people seek to spend longer in the wetlands and exploit its resources more intensively. The regional administrative structure does not reflect this central role of the Inner Niger Delta in promoting livelihood security, and development initiatives have done little to reinforce its potential to protect vulnerable livelihoods in bad years.

The SADS system sought to exploit this safety-net function, by selecting its strategic monitoring points so as to reflect the ways in which people move between resources and places to maximise their resilience and minimise their sensitivity to bad years. The general conclusion from reviewing the food situation over four years since the drought cycle of the mid-1980s is that bad to satisfactory conditions in at least one sector (usually agriculture) now characterise most years. Periods of dearth are commonplace, yet famine is not. This is primarily because of the relative rarity of all productive sectors experiencing drought conditions in the same year. Whereas in 1984–5 this indeed was the case, in the period 1987–8 to 1990–1 no year saw productive failure in cultivation, pastoral and fishing conditions simultaneously. Secondly, the periodic occurrence of good years, whilst allowing very limited accumulation or investment, serves at least to reduce some debt burdens and avoid incurring new ones for that year. Were it not for 1988–9 (good) and 1989–90 (satisfactory), 1990–1 might well have been worse than 1984–5. But, falling where it did within the cycle, producers were able to keep going despite the failure of primary and secondary productive activities. The extent to which this is because of their ability to exploit coping strategies is considered in Chapter 10. It is worth bearing in mind that from the early 1970s until the mid-1980s, the Delta as a whole produced more than it imported; hence the inability of rural producers to accumulate is tied to commercial and fiscal pressures which export capital from the zone (Moorehead, 1991).

Several indicators show that vulnerability to bad years was less in 1987–8 than in 1990–1, despite the proximity of the former to the great drought of the mid-1980s. Before turning to the ability of producers to cope and adapt to the increasing livelihood insecurity that this implies, we consider this transition of livelihood systems in the Inner Niger Delta and surrounding drylands from security to vulnerability (Chapter 7), followed by a more detailed examination of present-day sources of production entitlements (Chapter 8) and exchange entitlements (Chapter 9).

7 Livelihood Systems

INTRODUCTION

This chapter examines how livelihood systems in the Inner Niger Delta and the surrounding drylands have evolved from being highly resilient and insensitive to food insecurity before the drought of the early 1970s, to their current state of low resilience and high sensitivity. Resilience and sensitivity are, it will be recalled from Chapter 2, two dimensions of vulnerability or its opposite, security. The chapter demonstrates:

- how different livelihood systems achieved food security in the past and the extent to which the resilience of local systems to stress has declined with successive cycles of drought, whilst their sensitivity has increased;
- how these livelihood systems now achieve food security and what the precise bundle of sources of and calls on entitlements is for each system in a 'normal' (but post-drought) year;
- the nature and extent of seasonal vulnerability to food insecurity faced by different livelihood systems.

Most of the data were collected between October 1987 and September 1989. As Chapter 5 has shown, whereas 1987–8 was a poor year, both in terms of flood and rainfall, 1988–9 was a very good year.[1] Results are presented by season for each of the five principal livelihood systems found in the area: cultivators; agro-pastoralists; agro-fishers; transhumant fishers; and transhumant pastoralists, as defined in Chapter 4. The seasonal pattern is as follows: harvest (October–December); cold (January–March); dry (April–June); and rainy (July–September).[2] During given seasons or years when the same types of producers experienced different conditions in various parts of the zone covered by the monitoring system, results are further disaggregated by listening post.

It is important to note that the five principal livelihood systems do not represent the entire population of the area. Unrepresented groups include those people who have 'dropped out' of a given livelihood system, invariably because of the loss of productive assets during periods of drought, and who are now the 'displaced persons' who congregate around larger villages and urban centres. Equally, there are groups – notably the *Bella*, the former slave class of the Tuareg – who have become de-linked (or been excluded) from the pastoral livelihood system (again, often because of reduced labour requirements following the wiping out of herds in drought years). They subsist by a combination of attaching themselves to different livelihood systems in particular seasons when labour requirements are high (e.g. to transhumant pastoralists in the dry season or to cultivating communities in the harvest season); by providing services (often of the most menial tasks) to other livelihood systems; and by gathering wild foods, firewood, pasture, etc. This group have, in a sense, the most evolved adaptive strategies of all: their livelihoods consist in pursuing one adaptive strategy after another.

THE PAST: FOOD SECURITY IN TRADITIONAL LIVELIHOOD SYSTEMS

Until the drought cycle of the early 1970s, and particularly that of the 1980s, the population of the Inner Niger Delta did not experience chronic food insecurity. Even dryland producers in the Seno were not subject to regular seasonal food shortages. Droughts, sometimes leading to famines, were sporadic events, as Table 1.2 in Chapter 1 shows; Kitangal, in 1913, is the only famine which people recall before 1973. For a period of sixty-odd years, despite periods of shortage, all types of producers expected their livelihoods to provide them with food security, defined by cultivators on the floodplains as having at least two years' stock of cereals; even in the less productive drylands at least a year's stock was the norm. The purpose of this section is to describe the main livelihood systems prior to the drought of the early 1970s. In subsequent sections, the changes which have taken place – both long-term trends and short-term shocks – will be plotted against this background of livelihood security.

Cultivators

There are two principal groups of cultivators in the zone. On the floodplains of the Delta, wetland cultivators grow flooded rice as their main staple and some flood-retreat crops after the main rice harvest. The vast majority of cultivators farm on the drylands, producing a single millet crop a year. Although dryland cultivators are habitually the more vulnerable to inadequate and erratic rainfall, wetland cultivators perform a fine balancing act between the first rains and the arrival of the flood, both of which are essential to the success of their crop. Disruptions in the flood/rainfall cycle can be disastrous.

Food security in traditional cultivating livelihoods. Tables 7.1 and 7.2 summarise the seasonal activity calendars of dry and wetland farmers, differentiating between main activities which guaranteed food security and secondary activities which served to secure other aspects of livelihood security. The distinguishing characteristic of these livelihood systems was that the single annual harvest, and subsequent reciprocal arrangements for bartering or selling both labour ('off-farm' harvests) and cereals, guaranteed households at least twelve months' supply of food. Secondary activities were to invest surplus (e.g. sale of millet for purchasing animals); to accumulate savings (migration of the young); or to diversify diets and sources of cash income (counter-seasonal cropping, vegetable gardening). In this sense, cultivators' access to food was highly secure: not only did the livelihood system guarantee current food supply, it also had an in-built safety net for bad years, through capital accumulation (invested in livestock) and savings (stores of cereals and cash from migration). In cycles of bad years there was recourse to coping strategies once reserves had been exhausted: typically this included collection of wild foods and longer-term migration further afield. But these activities did not form part of the normal activity calendars of cultivators.

An incidental, but important, feature of cultivators' investment in livestock was that it guaranteed the herders, to whom they were entrusted for pasturing, a secure source of cereals. In the case of the pastoral Fulani and their former slaves, the cultivating *Rimaïbe*, this system of food security was entrenched in social relations of control. Not only did it guarantee the supply of cereals to the Fulani overlords, but it also provided the *Rimaïbe* with opportunities for diversification and risk spreading of productive investment. Despite the legal abolition of slavery by the French in 1903, these relations continue, although reciprocal exchanges are coming under increasing pressure and linkages are becoming contractual.

Agro-pastoralists

Traditionally these were the black Fulani who cultivated as well as having some cattle. Household labour was divided such that one part looked after the animals (as transhumant pastoralists), and the other cultivated (as dry or wetland cultivators). This livelihood system was particularly practised in the more marginal millet-cultivating areas of the drylands, where mixed production was the most economic use of household labour.

Food security in traditional agro-pastoral livelihoods. Table 7.3 shows a combination of the seasonal activities of agro-pastoralists. For those who divided family labour into cultivating and herding units, their traditional seasonal calendars were the same as in Tables 7.1 and 7.2 on the agri-

140

Table 7.1 Dryland cultivators: traditional seasonal activity calendar

Activities	Seasons											
	Harvest			Cold			Dry			Rainy		
	O	N	D	J	F	M	A	M	J	J	A	S
First purchase of cereal if short											▒	
Return of migrants												■
Millet cultivation							■	■	■	■	■	
Wells dug							▒	▒				
Early maturing varieties sown								■				
Preparation for next agricultural cycle						▒	■					
Repairs to housing, etc.				▒	▒	▒						
Fields manured by pastoral herds			▒	▒	▒	▒						
Departure of young males on migration												
Vegetable gardening			▒	▒	▒	▒						
Sale of millet to meet other cash needs												
Investment of surplus in animals		■	■	■	■	■	■					
Bartering millet for milk/rice												
Off-farm rice harvest		■										
Own millet harvest	■											

Key: ■ Primary activities to guarantee food security   ▒ Secondary activities

141

Table 7.2 Wetland cultivators: traditional seasonal activity calendar

Activities	Seasons											
	Harvest			Cold				Dry		Rainy		
	O	N	D	J	F	M	A	M	J	J	A	S
Rice cultivation	■	■						■	■	■		
Return of migrants		■										
Repairs to housing, etc.								▒	▒			
Manuring of fields by pastoral herds							■					
Early preparation of rice fields					■	■						
Departure of young males on migration				▒	▒	▒	▒	▒				
Cultivation of flood-retreat crops			▒	▒	▒	▒	▒					
Sale of rice to meet other cash needs			▒	▒	▒	▒						
Investment of surplus in animals			■	■	■	■	■					
Bartering rice for millet/fish/milk												
Own rice harvest	■											
Off-farm millet harvest												■

Key: ■ Primary activities to guarantee food security   ▒ Secondary activities

Table 7.3 Agro-pastoralists: traditional seasonal activity calendar

Activities	Seasons											
	Harvest			Cold			Dry			Rainy		
	O	N	D	J	F	M	A	M	J	J	A	S
Animals on transhumance	■	■								■	■	■
Animals depart for rainy reason pastures										■		
Rice/millet cultivation[a]		■								■	■	■
Manuring of fields					▒	▒						
Milk herds recovered and divided				■	■	■	■					
Dry season wells dug				■	■	■	■					
Bourgou cut for animals in dry season			■	■	■							
Purchase of small ruminants								■				
Sales of cattle			■	■	■							
Bartering milk for cereals			■	■	■	■	■					
Rice harvest[a]	■											
Millet harvest[a]												■

Key: ■ Primary activities to guarantee food security   ▒ Secondary activities
Note: (a) One or the other.

cultural side, and on the pastoral side, they followed Table 7.6 below. In contrast to cultivators, almost all their activities fell into the category of primary activities to guarantee food security. This is not, however, to imply that they were less secure than cultivators, but rather that the division of household labour left little time for secondary activities. Their primary activities effectively met both subsistence and accumulation needs.

The security of the agro-pastoral system was founded in this diversification of main productive activities. As such, it was distinct from cultivation where livestock were acquired as an investment against risk. For agro-pastoralists, cereal production was lower than for cultivators, owing to the division of family labour, but livestock accounted for a significant proportion of their habitual food entitlements, either directly through milk or indirectly by bartering milk for grains, or unusually by selling animals to purchase grains. Normally, they would have expected adequate annual cereal supply by a combination of own production and barter.

This duality of primary production also enabled them to spread risk in the event of a bad year. Pastoral droughts (i.e. insufficient rain – and in the Delta, floodwaters – resulting in lack of pasture) by no means always coincide with agricultural droughts (i.e. insufficient rain to cultivate) in the Sahel. As such, agro-pastoralists were uniquely well adapted to guaranteeing success in at least one part of their primary productive activities and could shift resources between the two sectors (e.g. by reallocating household labour, by buying or selling cattle or cereals). They too had coping strategies to fall back on when both parts of their productive activities were under threat, but these were reserved for periods of extreme food stress.

Agro-fishers

Agro-fishers are sedentary fishers living on the floodplains of the Delta, who also cultivate substantial quantities of rice.

Food security in traditional agro-fishing livelihoods. Table 7.4 summarises the traditional seasonal activities of agro-fishers. Like agro-pastoralists, they had few 'secondary' activities because of lack of family labour and the ability of their primary activities to meet both subsistence and accumulation requirements. They also had built-in safety nets to enhance food security within their livelihood system. In a normal year, fishing for sale was largely for surplus generation, whilst cereal needs were met through own production and bartering fish. In the event of harvest failure, they could fall back on fishing. The access of agro-fishers to the floodplains also provided them with a range of coping strategies to fall back on, not available to dryland producers, including gathering water

Table 7.4 Agro-fishers: traditional seasonal activity calendar

Activities	Harvest			Cold				Dry			Rainy	
	O	N	D	J	F	M	A	M	J	J	A	S
Rice cultivation	■	■						■	■	■	■	■
Bartering fish for cereals/milk		▒	▒			▒	▒	▒				
Collecting wood to smoke fish		■	■	■	■	■	■					
End of fishing campaign (collective fishing)[a]								▒	▒			
Main fishing campaign[a]					■	■	■	■				
Start of fishing campaign		■										
Rice harvest			■	■								

Key: ■ Primary activities to guarantee food security   ▒ Secondary activities
Note: [a] Exact timing dependent on location relative to flood.

lilies, cutting and selling *bourgou* and transporting goods in their boats. But, as with other livelihood systems, such activities were genuine coping strategies, employed only when both primary activities failed to provide food security.

Transhumant fishers

These are natives of the riverine area to the south of the Delta (the *cercle* of KéMacina), where they cultivate rice as a secondary activity. Unlike agro-fishers, they are transhumant for the duration of the fishing campaign, literally following the fish downstream from the base of the Delta at Diafarabé to its neck at Lake Debo. Traditionally, the circuits of transhumant fishers were well-established and were based on reciprocal links with indigenous fishers in the areas to which they transhumed. These are the 'professional' fishers of the Delta, specialists in more advanced fishing techniques, fishing principally for sale not subsistence and small-scale barter.

Food security in traditional transhumant fishing livelihoods. Table 7.5 summarises the traditional activities of transhumant fishers. This was habitually the most secure livelihood system of all, enjoying the characteristics of wetland cultivators (a substantial rice harvest, supplying at least one year's supply of food) as well as those of the dual livelihood systems which had in-built insurance against crop failure in the diversification of their primary activities. Furthermore, it was the only system which relied, to a significant extent, on the market for its subsistence: taking out credit with fish merchants for equipment and repaying this with substantial profits from the catch. This market was highly developed, run from Mopti and dependent, to a large extent, on foreign exporters who arrived seasonally to purchase the fish (Chapter 9). Such was the security of the system that coping strategies were rarely required: significant surpluses were accumulated in the event of either poor harvests or poor fishing campaigns.

Transhumant pastoralists

Food security in traditional transhumant pastoral livelihoods. Table 7.6 summarises the main traditional activities of transhumant pastoralists. It is based on the cycle of transhumance for those with traditional access rights into the dry season pastures of the Delta. Although the precise routes and timing of transhumance are different in the Seno, the pattern is broadly similar.

Table 7.5 Transhumant fishers: traditional seasonal activity calendar

Activities	Harvest		Cold				Dry			Rainy		
	O	N	D	J	F	M	A	M	J	J	A	S
Rice cultivation		■									■	■
Repay credit to merchants, invest, return home										■		
Small-scale bartering of fish for cereals/milk				▒	▒		■	■	■			
Sale of fish to merchants			■	■								
End of fishing campaign (collective fisheries)							■	■	■			
Fishing campaign (transhumance)			■	■	■	■	■	■				
Start of fishing campaign		■										
Rice harvest	■											

Key: ■ Primary activities to guarantee food security   ▒ Secondary activities

Table 7.6 Transhumant pastoralists: traditional seasonal activity calendar

Activities	Harvest			Cold			Dry			Rainy		
	O	N	D	J	F	M	A	M	J	J	A	S
Milk herds to remain in villages for barter	■									■	■	■
Transhumance on drylands with rains	■									■	■	■
Preparations for transhumance						■						
Sale of animals if need to buy cereals							░	░	░			
Animals rented to cultivators for manure							░	░	░			
Establishment of fixed camps in the Delta			■	■	■	■						
Progression through the Delta		■	■	■	■	■						
Bartering milk for cereals		■	■	■	■	■						
Return from transhumance	■											

Key: ■ Primary activities to guarantee food security   ░ Secondary activities

148   *Adaptable Livelihoods*

The transhumant pastoralists of this area have traditionally been viewed as being particularly vulnerable to food insecurity in times of drought. Undoubtedly, in years when pasture was scarce and livestock died, they were uniquely vulnerable. Yet, when pasture was abundant, they were probably the wealthiest producers of all. Moreover, their inherent vulnerability to food insecurity was mitigated by a number of factors. First, their continuing links of 'reciprocity' with their cultivating traditional slaves gave them access to cereals in most years on favourable terms of trade, even when milk for barter was scarce. Second, traditional rights of access to the Delta pasturing territories amounted to a safety net against the failure of dry season pasture not traditionally available to pastoralists in the Seno or further north and east. It could not cover all needs, but was certainly able to offset some of the consequences of pastoral drought. Security was derived from movement between two different but complementary areas. In the Delta, both flood and rainfall would have to fail for pastoral livelihood systems to become vulnerable to food insecurity. Traditionally, this almost never happened. In the Kitangal famine of 1913, for example, cultivators who were hardest hit recalled that there was nevertheless milk available.

CHARACTERISTICS OF SECURE LIVELIHOOD SYSTEMS IN THE PAST

All the livelihood systems examined were traditionally food-secure and, to a greater or lesser degree, highly resilient and insensitive to food insecurity. Table 7.7 summarises their characteristics. In drought years they would not all be met (e.g. primary production might fail and stocks would be run down), but taken together, the systems were able to withstand shocks and bounce back to a pre-shock state.

Diagram 7.1 shows schematically how a highly resilient and insensitive cultivating livelihood system was able not only to withstand a three-year drought, but also how it could bounce back within a period of three to four years. It demonstrates how the different characteristics of high resilience/low sensitivity are drawn on: first, to survive periods of drought, but also to recover once conditions return to normal. Crucially, coping strategies are used only as final options, once other dimensions of security (e.g. stocks, investments) have been drawn down, and their use is limited to the critical bottom of the drought/recovery curve shown in Graph 7.1. They are, therefore, genuine coping strategies and not adaptive strategies, the use of which would continue in the post-drought period.

Table 7.7 Characteristics of secure livelihood systems

Sources of/calls on entitlement	High resilience	Low sensitivity
Production	1. Primary activity meets annual subsistence needs plus up to one year's stocks 2. Secondary activities for accumulation/investment	1. One-year buffer against failure of primary activity (1st buffer) 2. Second buffer against failure of primary activity
Exchange	3. Self-sufficiency in basic food means low market dependence 4. Closed supply and demand of local economy but access to multiple internal resources (terms of trade reflect cereal procution relative to other goods)	3. Limited vulnerability to rising cereal prices (3rd buffer) 4. Sensitivity is localised, mitigated by access to multiple internal resources (rare for all to fail in the same year) (4th buffer)
Assets	5. Capacity for accumulation 6. More certain mobility between agro-ecological zones for high return	5. Ability to liquidate assets progressively (5th buffer) 6. Mobility between agro-ecological zones for accumulation, spreads risk (6th buffer)
Coping	7. Coping strategy options reserved for periods of successive drought or other disturbance	7. Coping strategy options are in-built bottom-line safety nets when all buffers exhausted
Claims	8. Extensive reciprocal ties (claims)	8. Calls on claims are for other people's surplus not for their basis of subsistence (7th buffer)
Livelihood protection	9. Investment of surplus capital and labour to diversify production	9. Diversified production spreads risk, insures against sectoral failure (8th buffer)

150 *Adaptable Livelihoods*

Diagram 7.1 Impact of three-year drought cycle on cultivators in secure livelihood system

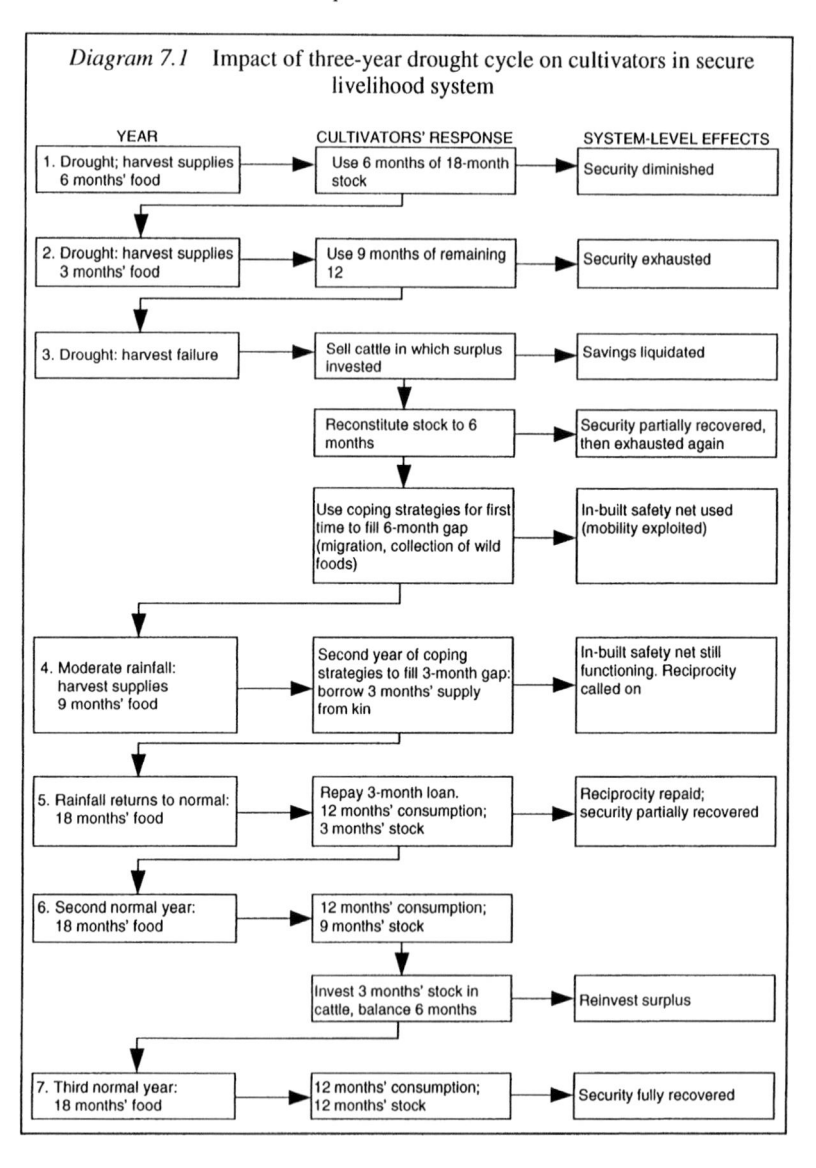

YEAR	CULTIVATORS' RESPONSE	SYSTEM-LEVEL EFFECTS
1. Drought; harvest supplies 6 months' food	Use 6 months of 18-month stock	Security diminished
2. Drought: harvest supplies 3 months' food	Use 9 months of remaining 12	Security exhausted
3. Drought: harvest failure	Sell cattle in which surplus invested	Savings liquidated
	Reconstitute stock to 6 months	Security partially recovered, then exhausted again
	Use coping strategies for first time to fill 6-month gap (migration, collection of wild foods)	In-built safety net used (mobility exploited)
4. Moderate rainfall: harvest supplies 9 months' food	Second year of coping strategies to fill 3-month gap: borrow 3 months' supply from kin	In-built safety net still functioning. Reciprocity called on
5. Rainfall returns to normal: 18 months' food	Repay 3-month loan. 12 months' consumption; 3 months' stock	Reciprocity repaid; security partially recovered
6. Second normal year: 18 months' food	12 months' consumption; 9 months' stock	
	Invest 3 months' stock in cattle, balance 6 months	Reinvest surplus
7. Third normal year: 18 months' food	12 months' consumption; 12 months' stock	Security fully recovered

The example of cultivators has been chosen for the sake of simplicity, but the model applies to all five livelihood systems, albeit in slightly modified forms. For dual livelihood systems and transhumant fishers, people had added security in that harvest failure did not necessarily coincide with pastoral drought or a failed fishing campaign. This enabled

Graph 7.1 Drought/recovery curve in secure livelihood systems

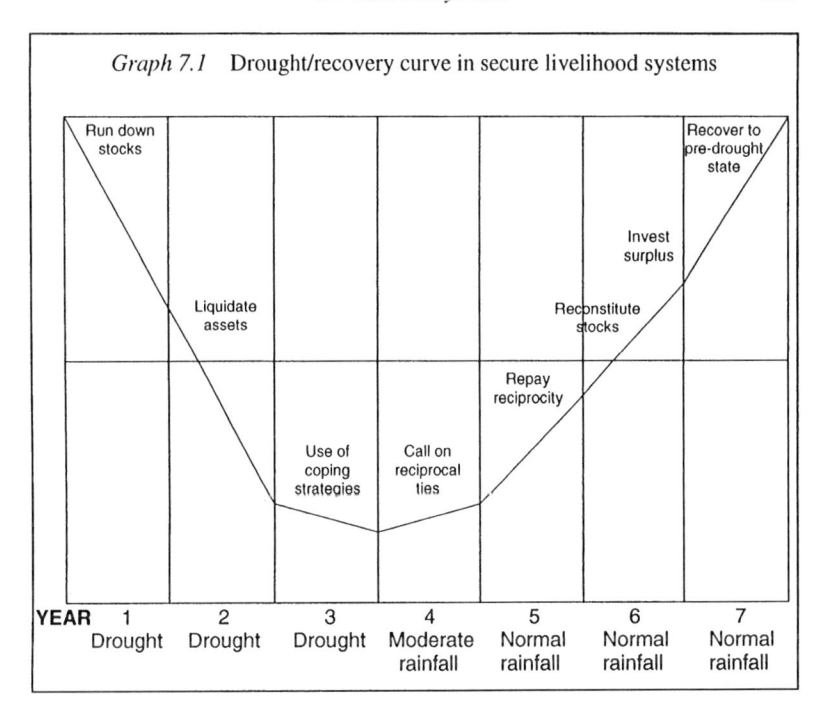

```
Run down                                                    Recover to
 stocks                                                     pre-drought
                                                             state
                                          Invest
                                          surplus
            Liquidate                  Reconstitute
             assets                      stocks

                                 Repay
                                 reciprocity
                  Use of    Call on
                  coping    reciprocal
                  strategies  ties

YEAR  1       2        3        4         5        6         7
    Drought Drought Drought Moderate  Normal   Normal    Normal
                             rainfall  rainfall rainfall  rainfall
```

them to switch productive activities and sometimes capital (e.g. by extra investment in fishing equipment or livestock) into the unaffected sector. With generalised drought and low flood levels, in the sequence of running down stocks followed by asset liquidation they continued to juggle resources between both main activities.

Transhumant pastoralists, notoriously vulnerable to prolonged cycles of drought and restricted in their ability to bounce back owing to the particular vulnerability of their capital store (livestock), nevertheless fit into a modified form of the model. Although some assets would have been liquidated (i.e. animals sold or died), most were able to retain the seed of herds to enable reconstitution. Further, for this group, reciprocal calls on cultivators' cereal stores were central to survival in periods of drought, even if cultivators had lost or sold their cattle entrusted to the pastoralists.

To sum up, the traditional livelihood systems of the Delta and Seno were all resilient and insensitive to food insecurity in that they could not only withstand periods of food stress but also bounce back to normal patterns of activity and security afterwards. Transhumant fishers and diversified agro-pastoralists and agro-fishers were perhaps the most

152   *Adaptable Livelihoods*

secure, but classifying livelihood systems according to a hierarchy of vulnerability or security fails to recognise the interdependence of different livelihood systems. Further, there were rich and poor producers within each livelihood system, which would directly influence the degree of *household* resilience and sensitivity to food stress.

THE TRANSITION FROM SECURITY TO VULNERABILITY

Understanding how livelihood systems guaranteed security in the past is a means of demonstrating how current systems have changed. There is no fixed date at which these systems ceased to function in the manner described, nor indeed did all members of each livelihood system undergo the transition at the same moment or speed. Broadly speaking, these secure systems functioned until the cycle of drought in the early 1970s, after which they moved into a period of transition, partially but never fully recovering in the decade up to the drought cycle of the early to mid-1980s, after which the transition from security to vulnerability was complete. There is little documented evidence to explain why these systems failed to recover after 1973. Clearly, their security must already have been eroded to some extent prior to the particularly severe drought cycle of the early 1970s. The slow and partial recovery from this in turn made systems more vulnerable to the subsequent cycle which began less than ten years later, thereby hastening the process of increased vulnerability. The overall impoverishment of producers resulting from wider macroeconomic stagnation – often made worse not better by government policies – further contributed to their decline (Chapter 5). Underlying this process is the changing natural-resource base, undermined by lower rainfall and flood levels and increasingly intensive exploitation of those resources which are available and which facilitate the spreading of risk. Livelihood systems which emerged from the 1980s drought cycle were fundamentally altered in their capacity to provide food security: not only were they more sensitive to the shock of drought, but they had also lost their capacity to bounce back. It is to these systems that we now turn.

THE PRESENT: FOOD INSECURITY IN LIVELIHOOD SYSTEMS TODAY

Whereas all five livelihood systems were resilient and insensitive to periods of stress in the past, results of the SADS monitoring system since

1987 demonstrate that they are now all, to a greater or lesser degree, vulnerable to food stress and have lost their capacity to bounce back. This means not only that each bad year (and for some producers, certain seasons in every year) threatens household food security, but also that livelihood systems are in a permanent state of flux as they adapt to each period of stress. In contrast to secure systems, vulnerable ones do not bounce back to their pre-stress state, but evolve into increasingly weakened systems over time. People do not stand still in the face of these changes and constantly adapt their livelihoods to the extent possible. This section outlines the changes in each livelihood system, both in terms of reduced resilience and increased sensitivity to food insecurity and ways in which people have altered their activities to confront this.

Cultivators

Harvest season. The main changes in this system today are, firstly, that the security of harvest levels meeting food needs for at least twelve months has disappeared. Even in an exceptionally good year, rice cultivators expect to harvest no more than a year's supply and millet cultivators about nine months' worth at best. Consequently, cultivators enter the harvest season short of food and need to continue to collect wild grains before the harvest and afterwards if the harvest itself is poor. Alternatively, as soon as one harvest is completed, millet cultivators will move in search of work on rice harvests and *vice versa*. Increasingly, however, these traditional labour exchanges are under stress, both because there is less demand with lower harvests and because the supply of labour is higher, as more households need to supplement their own inadequate production. On the other hand, in exceptionally good years like 1988–9, there is insufficient labour to harvest the bumper crop as reciprocal linkages have broken down and many long-term migrants do not return, despite the good harvest. Barter continues in good years, but decreases in bad ones and people turn to the market, principally because cash needs have to be met, rather than diversifying food needs. Added to this is the increased burden of debt repayment: the classic poverty trap where, in order to cultivate and feed the household during the hungry season, levels of debt, almost exclusively with private traders based in Mopti, via their local agents, must be incurred which account for much of the subsequent year's harvest. Finally, taxes imposed by the government are always collected with vigour during or immediately after the harvest, as are numerous informal payments in kind to local officials.

Cold season. This period has come to be known as the dead season in Mali (*la saison morte*), but this belies the often feverish activity that people are forced to engage in to meet household food requirements. True, the cultivation of counter-season crops in flood-retreat pools is less practised now than it was, principally because of lack of water, but this is the moment when strategies to cope with the projected household food deficit are planned for and embarked upon until the next harvest. These include gathering of communally held resources for resale, movement into adjacent livelihood systems in search of work (e.g. in fishing camps), and playing the markets by juggling between cereals and livestock. Migration to Bamako and the coastal states, and even to the gold mines of Burkina Faso, has come to characterise this period particularly for farmers and agro-pastoralists in Douentza and in the drylands surrounding the Delta. Whereas in the past, such seasonal migration was not unknown, the motivation for it was different: young men in particular would leave to accumulate savings with which to marry and establish 'independent' households. Today, expectations of remittances of any sort are low. The principal reason for leaving is to remove a mouth to feed from the family grain store.

Dry season. This is now the hungry season proper, brought forward by at least three months; in bad years, it has already been under way since the cold season. The options for coping strategies implemented in the cold season diminish as the Sahel dries out and as food prices begin to rise. Dependence on the market intensifies, for both credit and food: activities are informed by the need to generate cash income, to buy both food and seed for the following agricultural campaign. Labour is a constraint on all such activities: household members may be absent on migration and, in a bad year, increasingly delay their return until the harvest rather than helping with work in the fields. The available family labour has to be divided between preparing the fields and meeting daily food needs. Some opportunities exist for paid work in the fields of wealthier families, but these are rare. More often, impoverished kin are 'taken on', to be fed first and to work second, by households which can ill afford additional demands on household food supplies. Wild foods become an increasingly important supplement to diets.

Rainy season. The hungry season continues throughout the rains, broken only by the ripening of the first millet in September. Wild foods (*fonio*, wild water melons, *kalsireri*) are more abundant than during the dry season, most ripening in mid-August. Apart from these, families are almost entirely dependent on the market for food supplies. Fewer fields tend to be cultivated in particularly severe years, thereby setting in train the vicious circle of low production, irrespective of rainfall levels. Further, if the early rains fail, and rice cultivators in particular need to re-sow, constraints on seed availability can mean that production from later rains is less.

Vulnerability to food insecurity. Tables 7.8 and 7.9 summarise the seasonal activities of dry and wetland cultivators today. Activities are divided into 'traditional' and 'adaptive' categories. Given that these diagrams represent a normal year, the adaptive strategies are just that and not coping strategies in the sense of being fall-backs in the event of unusual disruptions to expected levels of production. The principal difference in these calendars compared with Tables 7.1 and 7.2 is the relative lack of importance of traditional activities (i.e. those which, in the past, were primary activities – millet and rice cultivation). Harvest times are shorter and the time available for cultivation is reduced by the need to find cash income to buy or time to gather food. Obviously not all family members can perform all the activities listed: the household division of labour has thus intensified, particularly in the dry and rainy seasons, to meet subsistence and primary activity needs. For small households, or those with high dependency ratios, this can mean either going hungry in the short term or sacrificing next year's harvest. Usually, it is a combination of the two.

Agro-pastoralists

In the 1984–5 drought, many cultivators who had entrusted their cattle to transhumant herders lost all their animals. Since then, a tendency under way since 1973 has intensified and both cultivators and agro-pastoralists increasingly invest in goats in preference to cattle. Goats not only reproduce more quickly, but are also better suited to drier conditions and can be converted into cash for cereals in smaller units. In recent years, therefore, this category of producers has become a great mixture. It includes the traditional black Fulani, many of whom now herd their own goats locally rather than departing on transhumance with cattle, as well as those who still have cattle and follow more traditional household divisions of labour. A further group of agro-pastoralists on the drylands are cultivators who have switched from entrusting their cattle to the Fulani and now herd goats themselves in addition to cultivation. Finally, impoverished transhumant pastoralists who can no longer sustain their households from livestock have resorted to cultivation to make up the deficit. The success of agro-pastoral strategies hinges to a large extent on their ability to maximise returns from timely sales of livestock to purchase grains, depending on the terms of trade between the two (Chapter 9).

Table 7.8 Dryland cultivators: present-day seasonal activity calendar

Activities	Harvest			Cold			Dry			Rainy		
	O	N	D	J	F	M	A	M	J	J	A	S
Sale of personal goods										▓		
Few migrants return									■			
Search for work on others' fields								▓	▓	▓	▓	
Millet cultivation						■	■	■	■	■	■	■
Search for credit for food, seed								▓	▓	▓		
Sale of small-stock								▓	▓	▓		
Cereals purchased on market(a)					▓	▓	▓	▓	▓	▓		
Wood cutting for sale to buy food			■	■	▓	▓	▓	▓				
Some bartering of millet for milk		▓	▓	▓								
Harvesting wild foods			■	■	▓							
Migration to south for subsistence					▓	▓	▓					
Early departure for off-farm rice harvest	■											
Own millet harvest	▓	▓										

Key: ■ Traditional activities   ▓ Adaptive activities

Note: (a) The moment when market purchase begins obviously depends on the year in question. It is rare that millet is not being bought by April.

Table 7.9 Wetland cultivators: present-day seasonal activity calendar

Activities	Seasons											
	Harvest			Cold			Dry			Rainy		
	O	N	D	J	F	M	A	M	J	J	A	S
Sale of personal goods												
Few migrants return												
Search for work on others' fields		▒	▒									
Rice cultivation		■	■					■	■	■	■	■
Search for credit for food, seed		▒	▒									
Daily activities to earn cash												
Cereals purchased on market(a)												
Wood cutting for sale to buy food												
Collecting cow dung for sale												
Casual labour in fishing camps												
Bartering rice for fish/milk/millet			■	■	■	■	■					
Migration to south for subsistence			▒	■	■							
Own rice harvest		▒										
Harvesting wild foods												
Early departure for off-farm millet harvest												■

Key: ■ Traditional activities   ▒ Adaptive activities

Note: (a) The moment when market purchase begins obviously depends on the year in question. It is rare that millet is not being bought by April.

Harvest season. Like cultivators, those agro-pastoralists who have diversified from cultivation into a dual livelihood system now meet a much smaller proportion of their food needs from cereal production than in the past. Far from investing surplus cereals in livestock, the harvest season is now the time when they must make projections about the balance between storing their food in livestock or in cereals. Livestock herds can become almost non-existent after heavy sales in the preceding dry and rainy seasons. For those with herds, some bartering of milk for cereals still takes place, as a way of constituting stocks.

Cold season. Whilst broadly in the same position as cultivators, agro-pastoralists are now rarely able to use this season as a period of consolidation for their herds, selling surplus cereals to invest in cattle. Instead, they continue to juggle existing herds with inadequate stocks of food and to judge the best timing of sales of animals to buy food. Those with very few remaining animals seek work herding other people's and as intermediaries moving animals from one place to another. They will also migrate to the south if no local pastoral work is available. Bartering milk for cereals continues for those with herds, but on a much reduced scale.

Dry season. As with cultivators, the hungry season for agro-pastoralists begins in the dry season, if not before. They depend on sales of animals for the purchase of food, as stocks from their own cereal production rarely last this long. If browse is scarce, they may also need to purchase fodder to feed their small ruminants. In a dry year, animal deaths will also be high at this time, and milk yields (always low in this season) can dry up. Sales of livestock are now at their height, when the terms of trade between millet and goats are least favourable.

Rainy season. The hungry season continues into the rains. Household labour is particularly stretched at this time, needing not only to cultivate and herd animals, but also, in bad years, to generate extra income from coping strategies. Milk availability (especially for those with cattle) does, however, mitigate food insecurity.

Vulnerability to food insecurity. Table 7.10 shows the present-day seasonal calendar of agro-pastoralists. For those who were formerly cultivators entrusting their cattle to the Fulani, but who now herd their own goats, the pastoral side to main activities has become a means of filling the cereal deficit rather than a combination of this with long-term accumulation of surplus. Those who have taken up agro-pastoralism because they live on the margin for millet cultivation, and who traditionally maximised their food security by diversifying activities, are now doubly vulnerable: not only has millet production declined, but they also have far smaller herds of which they have to liquidate a much greater proportion

Table 7.10 Agro-pastoralists: present-day seasonal activity calendar

Activities	Harvest			Cold				Dry				Rainy	
	O	N	D	J	F	M	A	M	J	J	A	S
Rice cultivation[a]	T	T						T	T	T	T	T
Millet cultivation[a]					A						A	A
Migration to south if no pastoral activities			A	A	A	A						
Harvesting wild foods		A										
Herding other people's animals				A	A	A	A	A				
Sale of last animals?				A	A	A	A	A				
Market dependence to maximise livestock/cereals terms of trade				A	A	A	A	A				
Herding own animals (much reduced; goats not cattle)	T	T	T	T	T	T						
Some bartering of milk/cereals		T	T	T								
Investment in animals?				T								
Rice harvest[a]	T	T										
Millet harvest[a]			T									T

Key: ■ Traditional activities   ▒ Adaptive activities
Note: [a] One or the other.

every year. The new category of agro-pastoralists (former pure pastoralists who are now forced into cultivation because of declining herd size) are also doubly vulnerable, unless they manage to reconstitute herds to return to pastoralism (to bounce back). In keeping with the shift from a secure to a vulnerable system, few are able to do this. In contrast, post-drought investment in livestock by merchants and civil servants has created a demand for a shepherding class (i.e. herding animals for another owner). Transhumant pastoralists have always done this in conjunction with their own herds, and agro-pastoralists who have lost their herds have sought to move in on this market.

Agro-fishers

Harvest season. Like their pastoral counterparts, agro-fishers now have to rely increasingly on their fishing activities to make up the deficit in household food needs from cereal production. As with all cultivators, the role of wild foods in their diet becomes central in the period prior to the harvest and thereafter, particularly if the harvest is poor. If the rice harvest fails, the entire family will fish from the start of the campaign in contrast to the traditional division of labour up to the end of the harvest. As more and more strangers come to the traditional fishing grounds of the sedentary agro-fishers in the middle and northern Delta, pressure on declining fish stocks, often leading to conflict, characterises fishing campaigns.

Cold season. Again, like agro-pastoralists, agro-fishers are increasingly obliged to depend on their non-agricultural activity (fishing) for subsistence rather than for accumulation, as they did in the past. Instead of returning to their villages after the fishing campaign in traditional territories close to their villages, agro-fishers now continue downstream and join the camps of transhumants, where conflict between them intensifies as fish become increasingly scarce. As fishing seasons become shorter (with the flood height less and the retreat starting sooner) and as more and more strangers come into the Delta, while indigenous agro-fishers increase their dependence on fish, yields are falling. To augment income, they sell *bourgou* to agro-pastoralists for fodder, and collect cow dung for sale to transhumant fishers for smoking fish.

Dry season. Fishing reserves, traditionally left until this season, are increasingly violated earlier on in the fishing campaign, thereby removing the dry season safety net. Moreover, collective fisheries are not as productive as they were, and no longer represent a guaranteed opportunity for capital accumulation. Thus, agro-fishers become increasingly indebted to the traders who supply their equipment as well as cereals when their stocks are exhausted. As the fishing campaign draws to an end, movements between camps become ever more intense, all fishers eventually congregating in the last remaining productive fisheries. In addition to these fishing activities, they also need to start rice cultivation for the next campaign, and this puts a strain on family labour.

Rainy season. Fish production ceases in July, though it rises for a short time with the new flood and the *kolaki*, or first of the new season, in Youvarou,[3] which briefly interrupts the hungry season. Thereafter, fishing is suspended until November. There is no longer any wildlife to hunt during this season. Agro-fishers are now preoccupied with rice cultivation, and they face the same constraints as wetland cultivators. Credit is needed both for seed and for next year's fishing equipment, but few agro-fishers are able to repay their existing debts, thereby increasing the cost of new credit and eventually making it unavailable on any terms. When this happens, their fishing is limited to using existing and/or traditional equipment or the ability to borrow from kin.

Vulnerability to food insecurity. Table 7.11 summarises the present-day activities of agro-fishers. This calendar differs from its traditional counterpart (Table 7.4) less than is the case for other sedentary producers: the intensification of fishing does not show up on the calendar. Agro-fishers have more options than undiversified cultivators and the terms of trade between fish and millet tend to be more favourable than those between goats and millet, thereby protecting fishers' food entitlements better than for other sedentary groups. They are, however, caught to a far greater degree in a debt trap: credit is now required for fishing equipment, cereals and seed (rather than just for equipment as in the past), and the means of repayment is both declining (fewer fish and more fishers), and required to meet subsistence needs. Few – if any – agro-fishers ever manage to repay one year's debt and so the credit terms become successively more arduous.

Transhumant fishers

Harvest season. The traditional transhumance routes and the timing of movements downstream have been disrupted in recent years by declining rice production in the zones of origin of these fishers, as well as by falling fish stocks. This makes credit increasingly hard to find in this season, and there is invariably a backlog of unpaid debt from previous years. Transhumant fishers move northwards at a much faster rate than in the past as the flood retreat is earlier, and they often settle in the lake zone of Walado and Debo for most of the campaign. Wild foods (wild rice, *bourgou* grains and water-lilies) supplement their cereal stocks.

Table 7.11 Agro-fishers: present-day seasonal activity calendar

Activities	Harvest			Cold				Dry		Rainy		
	O	N	D	J	F	M	A	M	J	J	A	S
Rice cultivation		■								■		■
Collecting *bourgou*, cow dung		▒	▒	▒	▒	▒						
Fishing more intensively			■	■	■	■	■	■	■			
Some bartering of fish/rice for millet/fish	▒	▒										
Harvesting wild foods				■						▒	▒	
Own rice harvest		■	■									
Early departure for off-farm millet harvest												■

Key: ■ Traditional activities ▒ Adapative activities

Cold season. Whereas transhumant fishers' food entitlements during the fishing campaign were habitually guaranteed by stocks of cereals from their villages of origin, they are now forced to buy or barter cereals for fish. Like agro-fishers, they face the same shortening of the fishing campaign and rising numbers of people dependent on fish for subsistence rather than accumulation. Increasingly intensive forms of fishing are practised, including senne nets with small meshes and monofilament nets which are theoretically illegal; the use of illegal equipment inevitably incurs formal fines and informal pay-offs to local forestry agents who police the fishing campaign. Nevertheless, the transhumant group remains relatively favoured as their advanced techniques enable them to catch substantial quantities of fish for sale to exporters. But their lines of credit are now stretched in two directions – for fishing equipment as well as for cereals, making repayment in full virtually impossible.

Dry season. As rights of access to the collective fisheries become increasingly conflictual, transhumant fishers have established their own camps in the last productive areas of Lake Debo. Fish catches still generally exceed daily consumption in this period, but are by no means adequate for debt repayment, let alone accumulation. Both agro-fishers and cultivators now congregate in the camps habitually dominated by transhumants in this period, all in search of some form of cash with which to buy cereals. Thus, whereas the transhumants remain relatively secure, this season is no longer a period of abundance for them.

Rainy season. The tendency is for transhumant fishers to stay in the fisheries of Lake Debo for longer and longer and even cultivate rice locally, some never returning home for the agricultural campaign. As agro-fishers specialise in fishing, the number of effective transhumants rises. Those who do return south begin their journey back up the Delta as early as the end of July/August. Either way, they are no longer able to reconstitute stocks, to invest in new fishing equipment or to pay back old loans, even though in food-security terms they do not experience a hungry season in the same way as other groups. Their cereal needs, like every other market transaction, are met by the fish traders but on increasingly expensive terms. At the end of the season, *bourgou* grains and other wild foods can be gathered to supplement food stocks.

Vulnerability to food insecurity. Table 7.12 summarises the present-day seasonal activities of transhumant fishers which, at a glance, have changed much less than the calendars of other systems. Transhumant fishers have intensified existing activities rather than diversifying into new ones. Fishing remains one of the more secure sources of productive entitlements, as evidenced by the increasing numbers of people fishing. But,

Table 7.12 Transhumant fishers: present-day seasonal activity calendar

Activities	Harvest			Cold			Dry			Rainy		
	O	N	D	J	F	M	A	M	J	J	A	S
Rice cultivation at home		■									▒	▒
Inability to repay credit												
Some bartering of fish for cereals			▒	▒								
Fishing more intensively							■	■	■	■		
Harvesting wild foods			▒	▒								
Search for credit for equipment			▒	▒								
Own rice harvest at home				■								

Key: ■ Traditional activities   ▒ Adaptive activities

although transhumant fishing remains one of the more secure livelihood systems, its security has been undermined like all others, particularly in the longer term. Falling fish stocks, rising numbers of fishers, increasingly abusive practices and a rising debt burden all undermine resilience and increase sensitivity.

Transhumant pastoralists

Harvest season. Increasingly dry conditions in the drylands around the Delta (the Mema to the north-west and the Seno to the east) exert pressure on the system of controlled access to dry season pastures: herders seek to enter the 'waiting zones' and the Delta itself earlier and to leave later. If milk yields are low and/or the harvest is poor, they are no longer able to build up stocks of cereals for the dry season through barter and have to purchase on the market. In this and the following season, the Fulani expect to recoup rents for herding animals and for those rented to cultivators. In bad years, these reciprocal links break down.

Cold season. The food security of transhumant pastoralists during this and the next season is determined by pasture availability and their success in amassing stocks of cereals through barter and, increasingly, purchase. Even if local pastures are reasonable, successive dry years in the northern regions of Gao and Tombouctou have meant increasing numbers of strangers competing for the pastures of the Delta and Seno. Entry into the Delta and movement through the different pasturing territories was traditionally controlled by a system set up under the *Dina*, the Fulani theocratic state which controlled the Delta in the nineteenth century. The present pressure makes the regulated movements of herds through the Delta ever more difficult to maintain and pastures that habitually had enough pasture for the dry season are now exhausted much earlier. Equally, if the previous rainy season has been poor, some transhumant herders (like their fishing counterparts) do not leave the dry season pastures at all. Inadequate pasture means lower milk production, both for consumption and barter. Also, if the harvest was poor, cultivators by now have little surplus to barter. Herders are thus forced to fall back on animal sales to meet cereal needs via the market.

Dry season. When pastures are scarce, this season is a constant struggle to find sufficient pasture and water for the animals. The Fulani adopt a strategy of spending one day finding pasture, the next water, and so on. When dry season pastures run out, herders fall back on vetiver grass, found particularly in the *leydi* (traditional Fulani pasturing territory) of Woro Ngia, near Toguéré. Barter with cultivators of milk for cereals no longer exists in this season: all producers depend on the market, selling animals to raise the money. Cattle prices tend to hold their value relative to cereals better than goats, but the latter are the preferred unit of sale as they are smaller in value. In drought years, this is the moment when cattle die.

Rainy season. As soon as the rains begin, transhumant pastoralists start on rainy season transhumance routes. If they remain too long in dry season pastures, the regenerative capacity of the pasture for the following year is considerably reduced. If the rains fail, many herds will stay in or near the dry season pastures; at best they will make short sorties into the drylands in search of pasture and water, but near enough to be able to return to the relative safety of permanent water points. Subsistence is largely milk-based for those family members who transhume with the animals, supplemented by some cereals if stocks have been accumulated. If the pasture is poor, milk production and human consumption inevitably decline. Families remaining around villages with milk herds are equally dependent on milk yields and their ability to barter or sell milk for cereals. In bad years, this is increasingly rare, and pastoralists, like all other livelihood systems, are obliged to resort to the market.

Vulnerability to food insecurity. Table 7.13 summarises the present-day seasonal activity calendar for transhumant pastoralists. Their choice of strategy depends to a very large extent on the year in question. If they have sufficient animals and the pasture is good, they can revert to a more or less traditional pattern. One important caveat to this is that bartering for cereals and more general reciprocal links with sedentary producers become increasingly strained, due to lack of surplus household cereal production. Increasingly, therefore, pastoralists are forced to resort to the market for the constitution of cereal stocks. If it is a bad year, however, and transhumance patterns are radically altered, the result is pressure on pastures with permanent water points, low milk yields and animal deaths. The strategies adopted by herders are closer to genuine coping strategies than the adaptive strategies seen in other livelihood systems, because they can be abandoned in good years. Nevertheless, in most years during and since the 1984–5 drought, transhumant pastoral activity calendars have been much closer to the bad year cycle than the good one, implying that the system is undergoing adaptation rather than just short-term coping.

CHARACTERISTICS OF PRESENT-DAY VULNERABLE LIVELIHOOD SYSTEMS

In response to changes in natural-resource availability and increasing vulnerability, not all livelihood systems have adapted in the same way, nor

Table 7.13 Transhumant pastoralists: present-day seasonal activity calendar

Activities	Seasons											
	Harvest			Cold			Dry			Rainy		
	O	N	D	J	F	M	A	M	J	J	A	S
Continue to sell animals if rains fail	▒	▒								▒	▒	▒
Purchase of cereals on market/sale of animals						▒	▒	▒	▒	▒		
Families left with insufficient stocks		▒	█						▒	▒		
Only limited transhumance or no departure									█	█	█	█
Search for other herds to shepherd throughout cycle												
Reciprocal ties with cultivators breaking down					▒	▒						
Entry into Delta/early arrival in dry season pastures							█	█	█			
Need to buy cereals on market to build up stocks			█	█	█	█	█					
Some bartering of milk for cereals												
Early arrival in waiting zones on edge of Delta												█

Key: █ Traditional activities   ▒ Adaptive activities

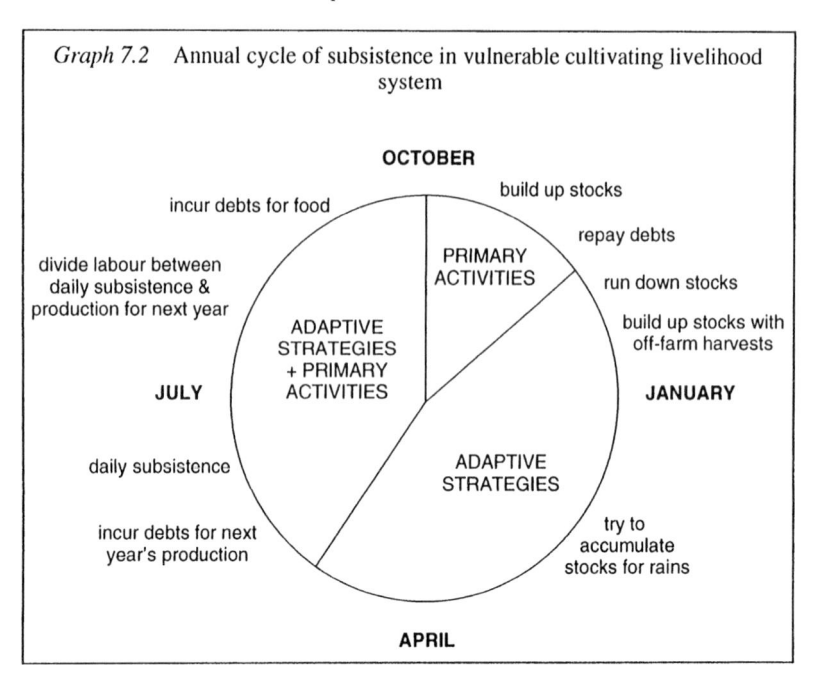

168   Adaptable Livelihoods

Graph 7.2 Annual cycle of subsistence in vulnerable cultivating livelihood system

```
                              OCTOBER
                                 |
        incur debts for food  /     \  build up stocks
                             /       \  repay debts
    divide labour between   /  PRIMARY \
    daily subsistence &    / ACTIVITIES \ run down stocks
    production for next year             \
                       ADAPTIVE            build up stocks with
                       STRATEGIES          off-farm harvests
                       + PRIMARY
         JULY          ACTIVITIES          JANUARY

       daily subsistence  \    ADAPTIVE  /
                           \  STRATEGIES/
        incur debts for next\           / try to
        year's production    \         /  accumulate
                              \       /   stocks for rains
                                APRIL
```

are they all equally vulnerable. There are, nevertheless, a number of common characteristics in the process of becoming more vulnerable to food stress, represented schematically in Graph 7.2 for cultivating livelihood systems. In contrast to Graph 7.1, which showed how high resilience/low sensitivity systems enabled producers to weather cycles of drought and to recover, in the low resilience/high sensitivity cultivating system represented in Graph 7.2, each year is a cycle of shortfall, subsistence and recovery or collapse.

The principal difference in livelihood systems in the Delta and Seno today, compared with the past, is that primary and secondary activities can no longer guarantee annual food needs in most years. The ability of livelihood systems to accumulate in good years, and the sequential options this provided for meeting successive dry years and recovering from them, has been replaced by a cycle of subsistence and coping in each year, such that accumulation is rarely possible and food stocks are restricted to a few months' supply at best.

Second, what were used as coping strategies in the past *only* in the trough of the drought/recovery curve, are now part of the normal seasonal calendar of activities. As such, they are adaptive rather than coping strategies. The overall effect of this shift from security to vulnerability has been to concertina the sequential options pursued in the past over an entire cycle of drought and recovery into a single year. The only option producers have when drought hits this system is to intensify existing behaviour.

Third, the systems are far less flexible because of the constant struggle to meet food needs. As a result, there is not only less time available for primary and secondary activities but also little residual time for meeting longer-term needs. If these are to be met, short-term food needs must be sacrificed. In the case of cultivation, in particular, producers consistently report a decline in areas cultivated. In 1988, for example, people argued that conditions were good enough to have produced two years' worth of cereals, but because the preceding year had been so poor, they were unable to cultivate sufficient land. As most cultivators have relied on manual labour rather than animal traction since the 1982–5 drought (having sold ploughs and/or lost traction animals), labour is an increasing constraint on production. Conversely, for dual livelihood systems, more time is devoted to the non-agricultural primary activity (fishing or herding). This is also true of transhumant fishers. In certain seasons of the year, particularly the dry and rainy seasons, the total amount of time spent working has increased in an effort to meet daily subsistence needs as well as to cultivate for the following year. But the vicious circle of subsistence and coping (i.e. adaptation) means that most producers are unable to benefit even from good years. Consequently, the options for intensifying existing behaviour in bad years are very limited.

Fourth, there is no evidence of new activities being introduced into the cycle. Instead, those resources which are most productive in certain seasons (e.g. fisheries) are exploited more intensively by more people, both directly (e.g. in the case of agro-fishers now going on transhumance rather than fishing only in their immediate locality) and indirectly (e.g. in the search for casual labour by cultivators in fishing camps). This creates forced mobility between different activities and places, intensifying the household division of labour.

Fifth, and related to this, is a forced diversification of activity for all livelihood systems, but particularly those which are agriculturally based. This is partly to spread risk (e.g. investment where possible in a few goats), but also because of the extreme seasonality of resource availability. Whereas, in the past, diversification beyond primary activities was used to accumulate and act as a safety net, it is now the basis of subsistence.

Sixth, whereas in the past – with the exception of transhumant fishers and at times transhumant pastoralists – livelihood systems were largely not reliant on the market for subsistence, nowadays all groups depend on the market to supply both cereals and credit (often by the same trader). The extreme seasonality of the terms of trade of the different resources on which producers depend makes this strategy highly risky. As Chapter 9 will demonstrate, it can be very lucrative or very costly, depending on the flexibility of timing of sales and purchases. Invariably, vulnerable people have little such flexibility. Those who cannot optimise their terms of trade are further impoverished.

Seventh, although traditional reciprocal relations still exist, these are coming under increasing strain. In the past, it was through reciprocal exchanges of labour and goods that specialist producers were able to diversify their subsistence base, store assets and, in hard times, call on claims and loans. Nowadays, the market fulfils this function to an increasing degree: bartering of cereals, milk and fish is declining; demand for reciprocal labour exchanges during harvest time is much less in bad years (although supply can be insufficient in exceptionally good ones such as 1988), as are transfers of assets between livelihood systems for the purposes of accumulation (e.g. cultivators entrusting their animals to herders). People also report that, within villages, traditional loans of seed and labour between households have diminished, forcing them to seek credit with merchants.

The determinants of high resilience and low sensitivity of traditional food-security systems were summarised in Table 7.7. Table 7.14 presents the determinants of low resilience and high sensitivity in present-day systems. Buffers against periods of drought no longer exist, as these are used for subsistence in each year. It is in this context that the role of coping strategies must be considered: clearly, they perform a very different role in secure livelihood systems and in vulnerable ones, even if it is the same activity which is being pursued.

Barriers to re-entry which block recovery are implicit in the systemic characteristic of low resilience. As has been seen in the descriptions above of how livelihood systems have changed, adaptive strategies are specific to each livelihood system. The barriers to re-entry which lock these systems in a constant state of vulnerability, irrespective of the year in question, are similarly system-specific. High sensitivity increases the height of these barriers, because, after each shock, the system has more ground to recover. Table 7.15 summarises the principal barriers to re-entry in each of the five vulnerable livelihood systems. It is these barriers which need to be tackled if the systemic vulnerability of livelihood systems is to be reversed.

Table 7.14 Characteristics of vulnerable livelihood systems

Sources of calls on entitlement	Low resilience	High sensitivity
Production	1. Structural food gap (primary activity does not meet annual consumption requirements) 2. Secondary activities to fill food gap (i.e. for subsistence)	1. No buffer against failure of primary activity 2. No buffer
Exchange	3. Food gap means high market dependence 4. Local economy is open to national supply and demand – including access to multiple resources	3. Immediate exposure to rises in cereal prices 4. Sensitivity is widespread, pressure on multiple resources intensifies
Assets	5. No capacity for accumulation 6. Uncertain mobility between agro-ecological zones for lower and less sure return	5. No assets to liquidate or rapid liquidation of those few that are available 6. Mobility between agro-ecological zones is necessity; cannot spread risk
Adapting	7. Coping strategies used every year (i.e. adaptive strategies)	7. Coping strategy use can only be intensified (limited opportunities for this)
Claims	8. Breakdown of reciprocal ties and claims which persist are increasingly exploitative	8. Either no claims to call on or calls on claims erode other people's basis of subsistence
Livelihood protection	9. No surplus to invest (diversification only possible by diverting capital or labour away from subsistence production)	9. Either no diversification of production, hence failure in one sector disastrous; or diversification at the expense of subsistence, reducing returns from all activities

172   Adaptable Livelihoods

Table 7.15 Barriers to re-entry in vulnerable livelihood systems

Livelihood system	Adaptive strategy	Barriers to re-entry
Cultivators	Seek work in other livelihood systems Long-term migration	Inability to accumulate to invest in own production Inability to diversify production to spread risk, exploit range of resources
Agro-pastoralists	Shift from cattle to goats Livestock sold to meet immediate consumption needs	Risk of cattle too great with threat of drought Inability to build up substantial goat herds because of low cereal production
Agro-fishers	Intensification of fishing	Chronic indebtedness because of low cereal production Declining fish production
Transhumant fishers	Intensification of fishing	Chronic indebtedness Declining crop yields upstream Declining fish production
Transhumant pastoralists	Shift from cattle to goats	Risk of cattle too great with threat of drought Insufficient capital to reconstitute large herds Other livelihood systems no longer entrust cattle for herding

CONCLUSIONS: INFORMATION NEEDS FOR INDICATORS OF FOOD STRESS

This section considers the season- and livelihood system-specific indicators which were derived from the monitoring process. These are a combination of standard EW indicators (covering flood and rainfall data, agricultural, pastoral and fish production data, pest infestation) and detailed socio-economic indicators (concerning markets, migration, employment opportunities, gathering, bartering, asset depletion, credit availability, tax collection and consumption), which inform about livelihood security rather than just food security.

Indicators were initially derived from questions to producers about the critical factors in each season in their access to food which cover far more than usual food-security indicators. Some of the indicators are used in most EWS which collect socio-economic data (e.g. the terms of trade between cereals and small-stock), whereas others are much less frequently used, being concerned with the context in which people take decisions about the mix of activities they will pursue in the coming months (e.g. availability of household labour, robustness of reciprocal claims in local communities).

The precise mix of indicators tracked by the monitoring system varies depending on what has happened in the previous season and in the year in question. If, for example, large departures on migration are cited after the harvest, particular attention will be paid to the ability of those remaining behind to subsist and to the timing of returning migrants to cultivate, as well as to opportunities for casual labour in recipient zones. Equally, if it is seen that reserves of small-stock have been run down and reinvestment was not possible after the harvest, the focus shifts to other assets which might be liquidated in place of goats. If the fishing campaign is relatively productive and the agricultural sector has suffered a drought, emphasis shifts to the capacity of the fishing sector to absorb cultivators. Collection of information is, therefore, an iterative process between expected signals of food and livelihood stress on the one hand, and actual patterns of activities and choices in a given year on the other.

The obvious drawback of this approach is that it has none of the elegance of a streamlined handful of key indicators which can apparently be monitored to convey what the overall food-security situation is. There are a number of reasons why habitual key EW indicators alone will not suffice to monitor food security in this area, such that they have to be supplemented with information about multiple resource use, constant adaptation, migration (in its widest sense) and calls on entitlement, as well as the more usual attention to sources of entitlement.

Multiple resource use. The key to survival in the area is the ability to move between productive resources in different seasons of the year. This has always been a characteristic of livelihood systems, but in the post-drought period the demarcation between livelihood systems dependent on particular resources and the reciprocal links between them to diversify sources of income and food has become blurred, such that nowadays almost all producers will move temporarily into positions where they can exploit particular productive resources for part of every year. This is either directly (e.g. in the case of cultivators seeking to keep some small-stock themselves rather than entrust cattle to transhumant pastoralists), or indirectly (as in the case of cultivators seeking casual employment in fishing camps). The absorptive capacity of different livelihood systems, and the ways in – and terms under – which these movements and exchanges take place, are of central importance to the extent of insecurity in a given year. Further, many of these resources are managed under systems of communal property, making the monitoring of availability of and access to CPRs essential. Only by tracking movements between livelihood systems, and between the availability of resources in different areas, held under a variety of management regimes, is it possible to assess whether food insecurity will be a widespread phenomenon, affecting all sectors, or whether more productive sectors will be able to take up the slack created by, for example, a failed harvest.

Constant adaptation. Lacking the capacity to weather periods of stress with pre-planned safety nets (genuine coping strategies) or to bounce back to a normal pattern of activity thereafter, as secure systems can, vulnerable livelihood systems are constantly adapting to changing conditions. In the years 1987–8 to 1990–1, a pattern of 'normality', in the sense of the mix of activities repeating itself in any consistent fashion, has not been established. There are common threads, which the information collected reflects, and the range of options for adaptive strategies has been determined. But the ways in which these are selected requires information on the motivation for and the intensity and effectiveness of their use, not simply monitoring whether or not they are adopted. Consequently, it is necessary to know what factors are influencing producer uptake of particular activities, and, as has been demonstrated, these factors are not simply determined by immediate food-security needs.

Migration. Migration patterns within and out of the zone are far more complex than a simple question of out-migration once harvests fail. Producers opt for phased migration, balancing available family labour between local rural–rural migration, more distant rural migration and migration to nearby and distant urban centres. Migration between livelihood systems also occurs, albeit at times within the same locality. Finally, for the transhumant livelihood systems, modification of habitual transhumance routes is central to adaptation. The mere fact of migrating gives no clear indication of the food-security status of the populations concerned. It is necessary not simply to be able to monitor migration, but also to be able to distinguish between different types of migration and the reasons for it (whether, for example, it is habitual migration, whether remittances are expected or to what extent recipient zones or systems will be able to absorb the migrants).

Calls on entitlement. The ability of the state to extract taxes and fines, of the private commercial sector to levy high interest rates on credit, and of increasingly stretched traditional exploitative relations to intensify demands for payment of dues and to invent new ones, all combine to compromise household food security in both the short and longer term. The state, for example, in collecting back taxes when cereal prices are at their lowest in good years, not only reduces household resources for consumption but also wipes out the ability to accumulate. Traditional systems of control, by extracting particularly high rents for access to resources when they are scarce, increase the cost of coping. The terms and conditions under which people gain access to food and other resources through credit mechanisms are also critical determinants of their capacity to produce (in the case of credit for seed or fishing equipment), as well as of their future access to markets for their produce (as in the case of transhumant fishers). These are all calls on household resources which would otherwise be directed into acquiring food or other livelihood needs and, as such, need to be monitored as critical determinants of overall food and livelihood security.

We return to these issues in the following chapters, which look at particular groups of entitlements in greater detail: production (Chapter 8); exchange (Chapter 9) and coping and adapting (Chapter 10). Chapter 11 concludes by identifying a streamlined list of indicators which can monitor livelihoods and food security within them.

8 Production Entitlements

INTRODUCTION

This chapter examines regional and household data on the production entitlements derived from cereals (millet and rice), livestock and fisheries. The importance of different sources of production entitlement is first examined for each livelihood system. As Chapter 7 has shown, for all sedentary producers, cereal production was habitually the main source of production entitlements, with pasturing and fishing revenue being a source of accumulation and wild food consumption reserved as a safety net for bad years. As livelihood systems become more vulnerable, secondary sources of production entitlements (herding and fishing) become increasingly central in meeting subsistence requirements (either directly, or through sales to purchase cereals) and thus move from secondary to primary sources of entitlement. Equally, tertiary sources of entitlement (e.g. wild foods), traditionally reserved for periods of food stress, are now regularly exploited in most years. Table 8.1 summarises the different categories of production entitlements for each livelihood system, under secure and vulnerable conditions. The importance of different sources of production entitlements for market dependence is discussed in Chapter 9.

REGIONAL PRODUCTION

Cereals. Total cereal production in the 5th Region averaged 236 400 tons between 1975 and 1990, but if the exceptional year 1988–9 (when production peaked at 495 200 tons) is excluded, average production was only 219 200 tons, falling to a low of 99 800 in 1984, indicating the extreme variability of production from one year to the next.

Graph 8.1 disaggregates production into millet and rice. Rice production figures include irrigated rice produced in the ORM polders, data from which are notoriously unreliable. Millet accounts for an average of 76 per cent of total cereal production. This proportion rises above 90 per cent only in two years: 1984–5 (95 per cent) and 1987–8 (92 per cent), both regarded as bad years overall. This 90 per cent threshold is a good, early (i.e. after initial estimates of the rice harvest) rule of thumb indicator of cereal production entitlements in the 5th Region. Although rice

Table 8.1 Sources of production entitlements by livelihood system

Source of production entitlement	Cultivators	Agro-pastoralists	Agro-fishers	Transhumant fishers	Transhumant pastoralists
Secure livelihood system					
Cereals	subsistence accumulation	subsistence	subsistence	subsistence	
Livestock	accumulation	subsistence accumulation	accumulation		subsistence accumulation
Fish			accumulation	accumulation subsistence	
Wild foods	safety net	safety net	safety net		
Vulnerable livelihood system					
Cereals	subsistence (accumulation)	subsistence	subsistence	subsistence	
Livestock	subsistence	subsistence (accumulation)	subsistence (accumulation)		subsistence (accumulation)
Fish	subsistence		subsistence (accumulation)	subsistence (accumulation)	
Wild foods	subsistence	subsistence	subsistence		

Note: Words in brackets refer to the use of the source of entitlement if still available, once subsistence needs have been met.

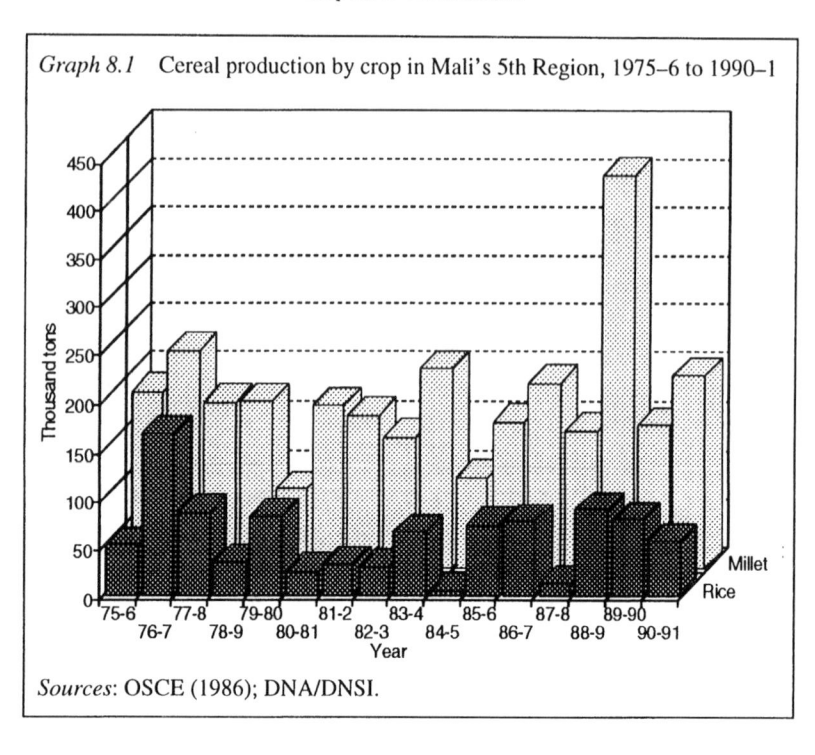

178 Adaptable Livelihoods

Graph 8.1 Cereal production by crop in Mali's 5th Region, 1975-6 to 1990-1

[Bar chart showing Millet and Rice production in thousand tons from 75-6 to 90-91]

Sources: OSCE (1986); DNA/DNSI.

producers are generally regarded as being more food-secure than their millet-cultivating counterparts, in dry years they are proportionately more vulnerable to declines in cereal production. Whereas millet is entirely dependent on local rainfall levels, rice depends on local rainfall plus the flood level, itself determined by rainfall in the Futa Jallon mountains in Guinea where the River Niger rises.[1] Where the flood no longer reaches (the drier edges of the Delta), millet is increasingly cultivated. No systematic data are available to show that producers in the Delta are shifting from rice to millet, but anecdotal evidence from village interviews confirms this trend on the drier borders of the Delta.

Using the census data presented in Chapter 6 for the 5th Region, Graph 8.2 shows *per capita* cereal production over the same period. This exceeds minimum requirements (167 kg/person/year) in only three of the sixteen years (i.e. 19 per cent of the time). It falls to less than half the minimum requirements in only one year (1984) and to less than two-thirds of minimum requirements in a further three years. If these especially good and bad years are excluded, production averaged 144 kg/person, or 86 per cent of minimum requirements, in the nine years in question. Thus, over-

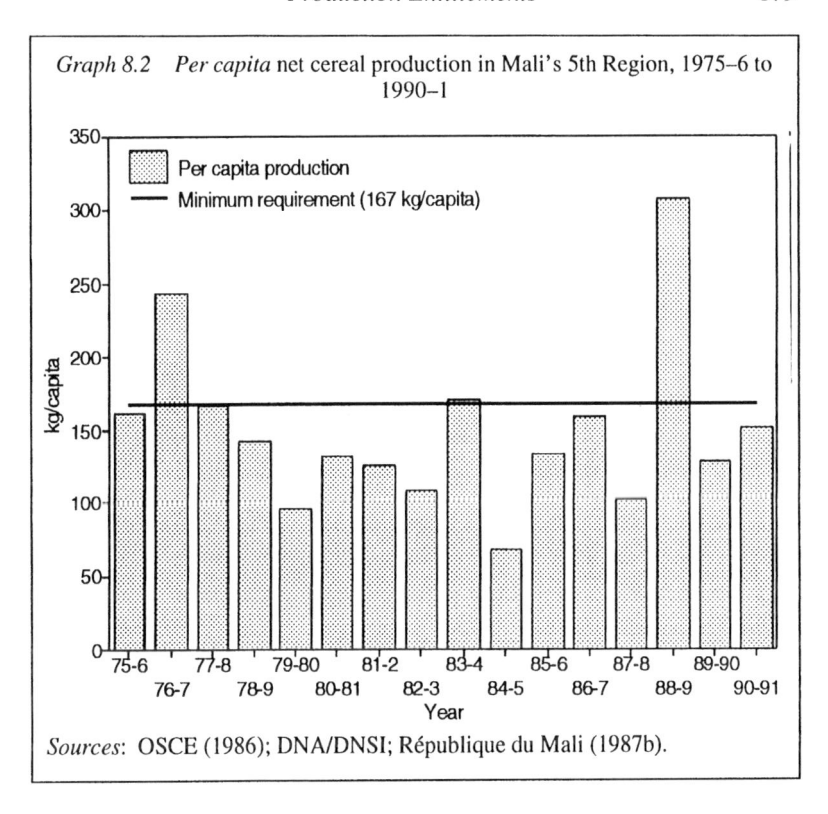

Graph 8.2 *Per capita* net cereal production in Mali's 5th Region, 1975–6 to 1990–1

[Bar chart showing per capita production in kg/capita from 1975-6 to 1990-1, with a minimum requirement line at 167 kg/capita]

Sources: OSCE (1986); DNA/DNSI; République du Mali (1987b).

all, producers in the 5th Region experience a structural cereal gap in most years and this falls to critical levels in at least one in four years. Population growth in the Region averaged only 1.07 per cent between 1976 and 1987, so this cannot fully explain declining (excluding the exceptional year 1988–9) *per capita* production. Graph 8.2 also shows that inter-annual variation in production has increased significantly since the mid-1980s drought. Taking the last seven years shown (1984–5 to 1990–1), the food gap ranged from 55 per cent below the average for the period (in 1984–5), to 105 per cent above it (in 1988–9).

Entitlements derived from cereal production thus result in a food gap in most years, and are characterised by increasing variability from one year to the next, both of which entail greater risk and vulnerability to food insecurity. In the past, as shown in Chapter 7, people expected to harvest at least twelve months' supply of food and often as much as two years: in other words, cereal (or primary) production entitlements guaranteed food security, freeing up other sources of entitlement for different needs (accu-

180   *Adaptable Livelihoods*

mulation, etc.). Primary production entitlements today, in contrast, can only partially fulfil annual consumption requirements, thereby forcing producers to use secondary and coping/adaptive sources of entitlement to fill the food gap. In so doing, they must also seek to diversify sources of entitlement, to minimise the risk inherent in inter-annual fluctuations in cereal production.

Livestock. Livestock is the principal secondary source of productive entitlements for most people, the exception being transhumant pastoralists, for whom it is, of course, the main source. Fishing livelihood systems, whilst having greater opportunities to diversify than the others, nevertheless invest in some livestock to diversify their productive base.

Estimating production entitlements derived from livestock is far more problematic than for cereals. Data for cattle in the 5th Region are highly incomplete and surveys are rarely directly comparable. Those conducted by ODEM only take account of livestock which are raised extensively. Figures are based on estimates at the *arrondissement* level, but as these are used as a basis for calculating the head tax on livestock, they are invariably inaccurate. Stall-fed sheep and goats are also excluded from the estimates, an important omission, as cultivators and agro-pastoralists are increasingly turning to this method of intensive livestock raising to diversify household sources of income. For households with a labour constraint, stall-feeding a few sheep (and, less often, goats) is a more secure option than allocating a proportion of family labour to extensive pasturing. Attempts to estimate the number of animals owned by households met with little success, not least because household livestock holdings are closely guarded secrets both within the community and especially from the tax-collecting administration. Relative livestock holdings within villages could be identified using wealth-ranking techniques, but monitoring the disposal of livestock to buy cereals is more problematic. Sales of livestock were, however, identified in household budget surveys.

Given these caveats, Graph 8.3 summarises available regional-level data on livestock for the 1980s, showing the decline in livestock numbers during the drought of the mid-1980s and the partial post-drought recovery. This was characterised by a dramatic shift in the composition of herds from cattle to goats (mainly) and sheep. By 1987, cattle holdings had reached only 79 per cent of 1981 levels, whereas goat and sheep numbers had increased six-fold, from 27 per cent of total livestock in the Region in 1981 to 73 per cent by 1987. RIM (1987), conducting post-drought aerial surveys, estimated a 38 per cent reduction in the cattle population of the Delta, but a 66 per cent increase in small ruminants. These figures must, however, be treated with caution. Levels of post-drought 'recovery', in

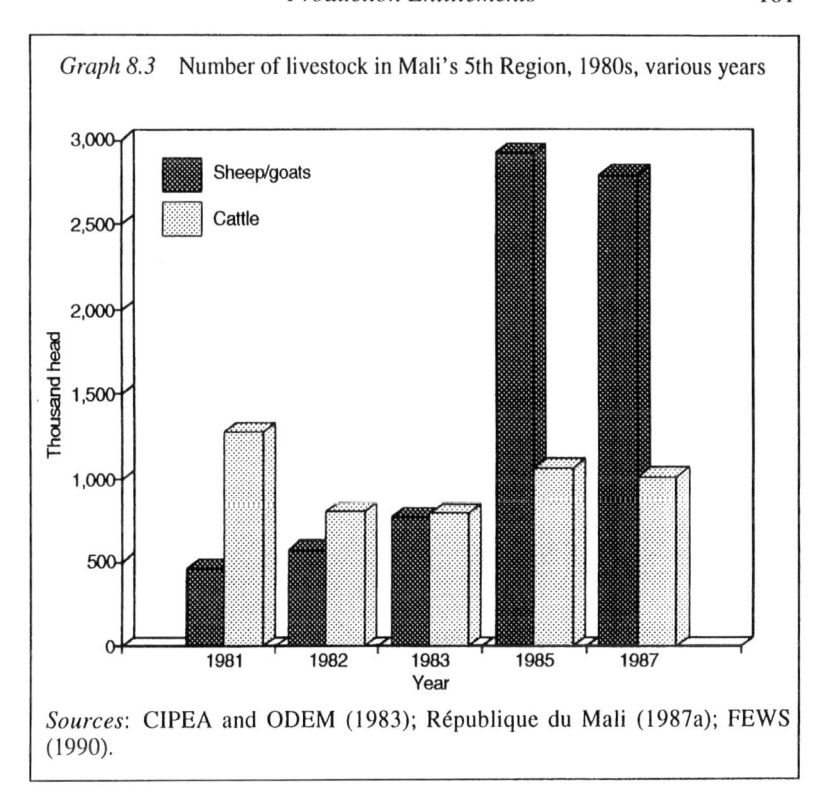

Graph 8.3 Number of livestock in Mali's 5th Region, 1980s, various years

Sources: CIPEA and ODEM (1983); République du Mali (1987a); FEWS (1990).

particular, are partly explained by influxes of animals from the 6th and 7th Regions in search of pasture.

This trend indicates two dimensions of adaptation: first, the greater resilience of goats to drier conditions makes them preferred animals, despite their increased sensitivity to disease; second, because goats are nowadays used by cultivators and agro-pastoralists as stores of value to liquidate over quite short time periods to purchase cereals, their much lower unit cost than cattle makes them more appropriate. In the past, cattle were used by these groups for longer-term saving, and entrusted to transhumant herders for care (Chapter 7).

Fisheries. Agro-fishers and transhumant fishers are distinct from other livelihood systems in that they have always been more integrated into marketing networks, to sell their fish. Nevertheless, most fishing households would habitually have expected to meet all or most of their annual cereal requirements through their own production, whilst revenue from fishing was a source of savings and only marginally used for immediate consumption. But, as with other livelihood systems, fishers have experienced a reduction in *per capita* cereal production. They have turned to fishing to fill the food gap, but here too production has declined. Production of fish has fallen dramatically with declining flood and rainfall levels, as Graph 8.4 shows. Whereas annual production averaged 83 000 tons in the 1970s, this fell to 64 000 in the 1980s. This drop in production, accompanied by a decline in the diversity of species caught (carp are now the main catch), is perhaps the most graphic illustration of the declining natural-resource base in the Delta and the concomitant downward pressure on production entitlements for people. Further, as more and more fishers (both indigenous to the Delta and strangers from downstream – the transhumants) have to fill increasingly large food gaps, the decline in *per capita* production is even greater. Moorehead (1991: 66) estimates that by the mid-1980s, approximately 100 000 people relied on fishing as a principal occupation.

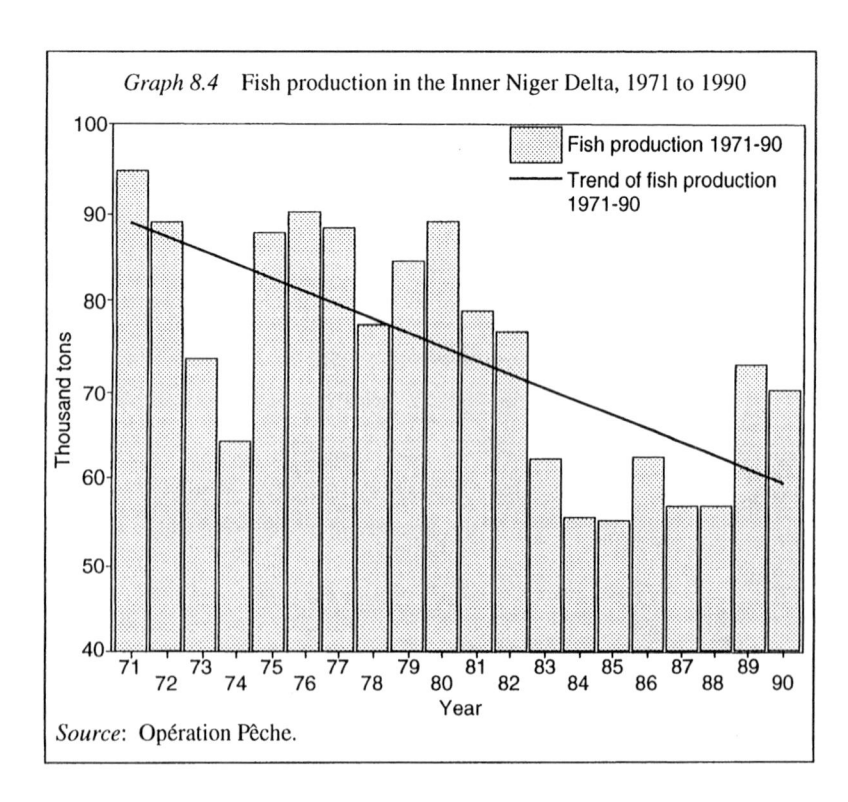

Graph 8.4 Fish production in the Inner Niger Delta, 1971 to 1990

Source: Opération Pêche.

HOUSEHOLD FOOD AVAILABILITY

Declining sources of primary and secondary productive entitlements at regional level are confirmed at the household level. This section presents household data on cereal production and purchase in the Delta.[2] As explained in Chapter 4, these data are purely indicative owing to the small sample size. Data are analysed first for all households in the sample, and then by the three sedentary livelihood systems in the area (cultivators, agro-pastoralists and agro- fishers).

The food gap. Production data are shown for 1989–90, an overall satisfactory year according to the general indicators summarised at the end of Chapter 7. As such, it is representative of an 'average' year in the Region, although the idea of average belies the extreme inter-annual variability in cereal production. All data are presented on a *per capita* basis. Millet and rice production are combined and have been converted into net weights. Purchases of cereals are included in the overall estimates of household food availability, but sales and gifts are not, as data on these proved to be unreliable. Accurate estimates of wild foods collected and cereals acquired through participating in other people's harvests were not obtained. Moorehead (1991: 115) has estimated that wild foods supplied an average of 85 days' worth of household food availability in the Delta in 1985–6 (23 per cent of annual minimum requirements)[3] and that cereals acquired from participating in other people's harvests added a further 35 days (10 per cent). These two sources of food thus account for about a third of total household food availability. This figure is higher than partial estimates for 1989–90 suggest and may be explained by the especial dependence on these sources of food immediately after the drought of the mid-1980s. Further, demand for outside labour to harvest crops has fallen consistently since the drought (with the exception of 1988, when there was a labour shortage, owing to the bumper harvest). An average of 91 days (25 per cent) of food from these two sources combined has been added to the estimates of total household food availability. These sources of entitlement effectively fill the residual gap between own harvests plus purchases, and annual minimum requirements.

The proportion of annual *per capita* food needs met by own cereal production amounted to an average of around 66 per cent of consumption requirements, with a further 26 per cent of needs met by purchases. Household production estimates are lower than regional estimates, explained by the uneven distribution of productive capacity in the Region (the southern *cercles* of Koro and Bankass are much more productive than elsewhere). Overall, producers meet 91 per cent of minimum requirements through production and exchange entitlements.

When disaggregated by livelihood system, these data tell a rather different story. Graph 8.5 shows that cultivators meet the average (67 per cent rather than 66 per cent of requirements) from their own cereal production and are able to increase this by only 16 per cent via market purchases, leaving an overall food gap of 61 days, possibly to be filled by wild food collection and/or off-farm harvests. In sharp contrast, agro-pastoralists not only produce more food (79 per cent of requirements), but also purchase similar quantities to cultivators on the market. Their ability to acquire more food than cultivators, without recourse to the safety net of wild food collection and off-farm harvests, is explained mainly by the fact that the agro-pastoralists in the part of the Delta where the survey was carried out are relatively wealthy producers, having kept up livestock holdings, whilst also maintaining relatively high agricultural production. Further, pastoral conditions in 1989–90 had been satisfactory to good for four consecutive years. This result would not hold for the drylands, where agro-pastoralists are as vulnerable as undiversified cultivators. Fishers are habitually much more dependent on the market for cereals than other producers, as they sell fish to purchase cereals. Agro-fishers produce the least amount of cereals of all sedentary livelihood systems (51 per cent of

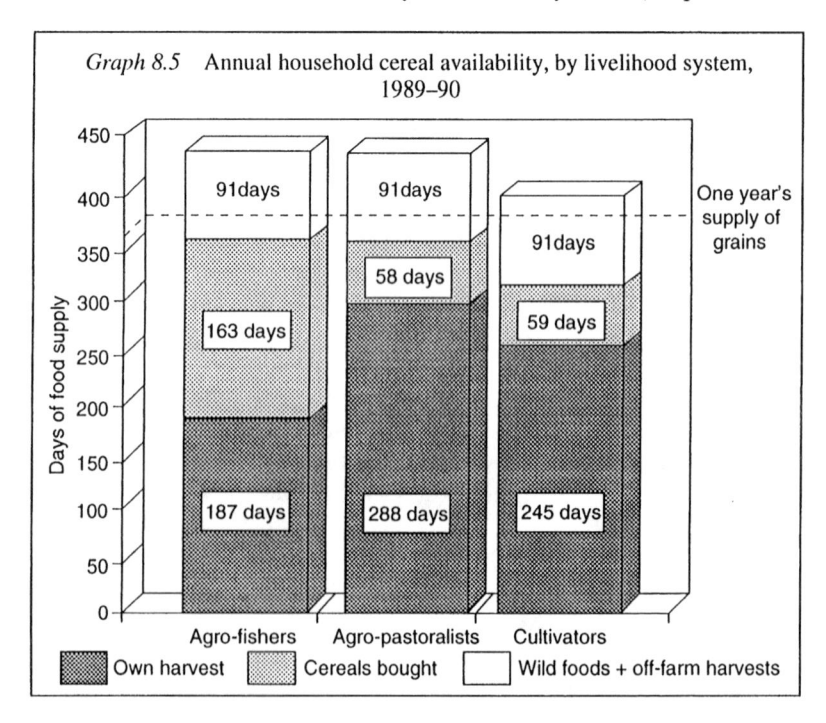

Graph 8.5 Annual household cereal availability, by livelihood system, 1989–90

Livelihood system	Own harvest	Cereals bought	Wild foods + off-farm harvests
Agro-fishers	187 days	163 days	91 days
Agro-pastoralists	288 days	58 days	91 days
Cultivators	245 days	59 days	91 days

(One year's supply of grains = dashed line at ~365 days)

requirements) but purchase far more than the other two on the market (45 per cent of requirements). Overall, they meet the highest proportion of cereal needs through production and exchange entitlements (96 per cent).

FILLING THE FOOD GAP

In cultivating livelihood systems, cereal production does not meet annual food needs. Additional food is acquired via direct consumption of fish, milk and meat. For all but transhumant pastoralists (for whom milk is a staple food), these foods represent important sources of protein, but not of calories. It is more economic to sell them and buy cheaper cereals. Producers are thus dependent on the market to fill the food gap. Market dependence as an indicator of vulnerability is measured in two ways: first, the proportion of cereal needs met from the market (the 'cereals bought' box in Graph 8.5) and second, the proportion of cash income spent on buying these cereals.

In secure livelihood systems, if food needs are met through primary productive entitlements, market dependence is low, in terms of both the proportion of cereals acquired on the market and the proportion of total income spent on food. Secondary productive entitlements (livestock, fisheries) provide the resources for accumulation and savings, spreading of risk, diversification and investment in future production. In vulnerable systems, a high proportion of cash income spent on acquiring cereals makes these kinds of livelihood-securing strategies impossible.

Decisions about investments to enhance sources of production entitlements fall into two categories: (a) production-enhancing investment (e.g. wells, ploughs, fishing equipment), and (b) risk-reducing investment (e.g. stores of food, gold, animals and investments in kinship networks – for example, by lending to kin in order to be able to borrow at a later date, or by investing in marriages that will cement these networks). In the past, people could make choices about the balance between the two, safe in the knowledge that their food needs would be met in most years. Nowadays, they must juggle between an increased need for risk-reducing investments, given the increased variability in cereal production, and the necessity of enhancing production to meet food needs. It is not surprising that category (a) investments which can if necessary be easily converted into category (b) investments are the preferred choice. The clearest example of such 'fungibility' is goats, which can be sold on an as-needed basis to buy food, whilst at the same time providing a potential source of accumulation if they can be retained. Another example is the redivision of household labour, so that some members are more or less permanent migrants, often far afield: if they find employment, they can supplement household incomes; if they do not, at least they are not

186   *Adaptable Livelihoods*

a drain on household resources. But, as will be seen in subsequent chapters, it is precisely the fungibility of certain choices which makes them risky.

Expenditure. In order to see how households meet cash needs to buy food, and the kinds of trade-off they make between different types of investment, household budget data were collected in 1989–90, as explained in Chapter 4. Data were only available for the Delta and, again, are indicative rather than statistically representative. Items of household expenditure have been grouped according to the following categories: cereals; essential food; non-essential food; other non-food; productive investment; and fiscal and miscellaneous calls on entitlement.

Taking all households together, half of all household income is spent on acquiring food, of which cereals and other essential foods account for 91 per cent. The balance of household expenditure is divided more or less equally between productive investment (15 per cent), fiscal and other calls on entitlement (16 per cent) and other (miscellaneous) items of expenditure (17 per cent). It is interesting to note that the equivalent of two-thirds of household expenditure on cereals is spent on state and other calls on entitlement (16 per cent compared with 27 per cent).

Graph 8.6 shows expenditure on food and non-food items, by livelihood system. Total annual *per capita* expenditure (in FCFA) for each livelihood system is as follows: cultivators 23 764; agro-pastoralists 18 725; and agro-fishers 28 874. Agro-fishers thus earn over 50 per cent more *per capita* than agro-pastoralists. There is no significant variation in the amount spent on food items between cultivators and agro-pastoralists: both spend around a quarter of total cash income on cereals and negligible amounts on non-essential foods (less than 8 per cent). Agro-fishers, whilst spending about the same on essential foods and non-essential foods, spend nearly twice as much on cereals as other producers.

Graphs 8.7 to 8.9 further disaggregate these data by livelihood system, showing the proportion of expenditure on different items. Food expenditure as a proportion of total expenditure is 46 per cent for cultivators; 60 per cent for agro-pastoralists; and 51 per cent for agro-fishers. For expenditure on non-food items, agro-fishers understandably show the highest proportion of total expenditure on productive equipment (21 per cent). Such expenditure is very low for agro-pastoralists (9 per cent) and only slightly higher for cultivators (14 per cent). For agro-pastoralists and agro-fishers, calls on entitlements by the state are around 15 per cent of expenditure, rising to 22 per cent for cultivators. This latter figure is surprising, given that agro-pastoralists, and agro-fishers in particular, tend to be most liable to fines, given their mix of their productive activities (they are fined for browsing goats in illegal places, and cutting wood for smoking fish, and pay taxes on boats).

Graph 8.6 Expenditure on food and non-food items, by livelihood system, 1989–90

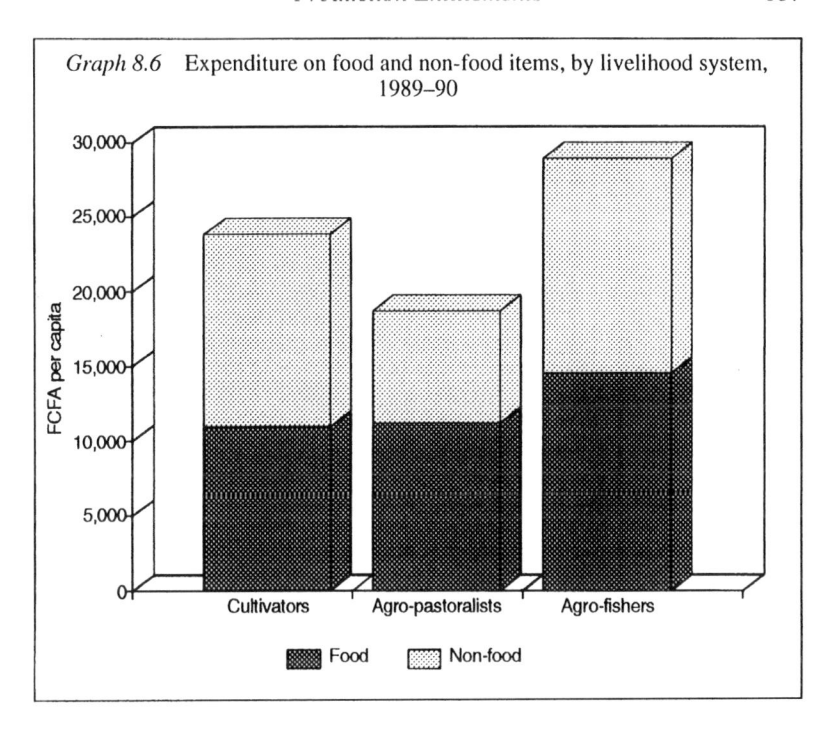

Graph 8.7 Cultivators: proportion of expenditure on food and non-food items, 1989–90

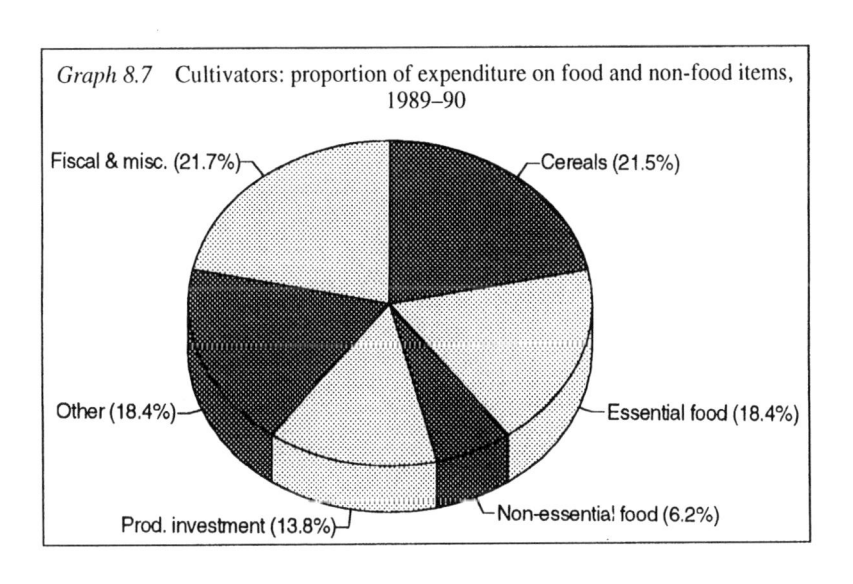

Graph 8.8 Agro-pastoralists: proportion of expenditure on food and non-food items, 1989–90

- Fiscal & misc. (15.1%)
- Cereals (26.1%)
- Other (15.9%)
- Prod. investment (8.6%)
- Non-essential food (8.0%)
- Essential food (26.3%)

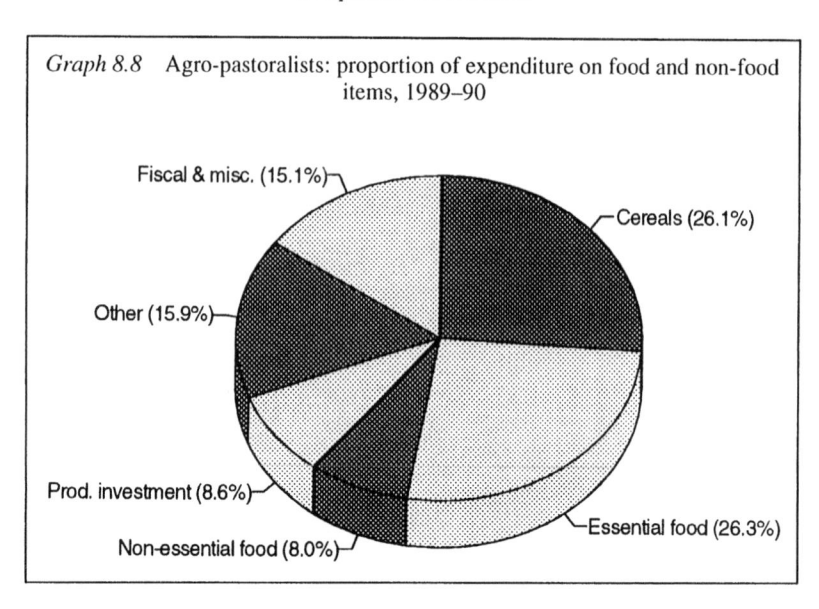

Graph 8.9 Agro-fishers: proportion of expenditure on food and non-food items, 1989–90

- Fiscal & misc. (12.8%)
- Cereals (30.7%)
- Other (16.3%)
- Prod. investment (20.5%)
- Essential food (14.4%)
- Non-essential food (5.4%)

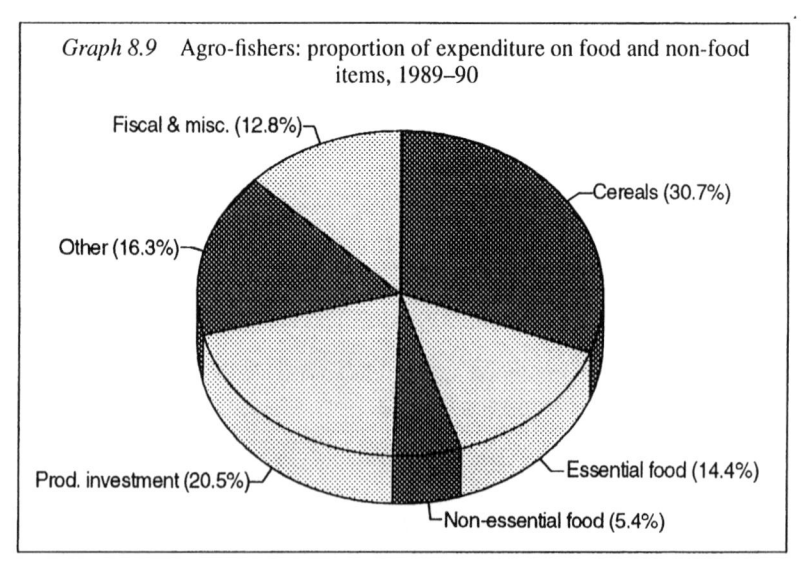

Cash Income. The need for cash income rises as what was subsistence production in the past becomes more and more commercialised and market dependence increases. Wood, for example, is now sold by cultivators to raise cash whereas in the past it was collected for domestic fuel;

Production Entitlements

and agro-fishers sell more fish than in the past. Cash income does not include the value of the cereal harvest, or of fish or animal products which are produced and consumed directly. Further, data are not available on wild foods, game and off-farm harvests which would have added to cash income if sold. Income from remittances was only sporadically reported and almost certainly does not reflect the full level of transfers (Chapter 4). In considering the cash income of households, the objective is to see to what extent they rely on secondary sources of production entitlements (livestock and fish) and coping/adaptive sources of entitlement to meet cereal expenditure needs. Put another way, this section seeks to estimate how much income can be generated from secondary and coping/adaptive (tertiary) activities with which to fill the food gap.

The mix of cash income from primary and secondary activities obviously depends on the livelihood system in question; diversified systems have always been more dependent than undiversified ones on livestock or fishing for cash income. In secure systems, it will be recalled, sedentary producers who habitually received a guaranteed annual cereal supply from cultivation relied on secondary activities for accumulation and risk spreading. As systems have become more vulnerable, secondary activities (especially fishing) have become increasingly important sources of income, such that they may contribute more to total income than cereal production (were it sold rather than consumed). This is because it is more efficient (i.e. the returns to labour are greater, so long as credit is available for equipment) to convert fish into cereals via the market than to try and increase cereal production at the expense of fishing. Whether or not the lion's share of total income comes from secondary activities, the key difference between secondary activities in conditions of security and vulnerability is the disposal of income derived from them. They no longer represent assured sources of accumulation and capacity to spread risk, but instead are used in the first instance to meet subsistence requirements, with only the residual income (if any) being reserved for accumulation.

Secondary activities are distinct from coping/adaptive ones because they have habitually been part of activity patterns for mixed livelihood systems in every year, even in secure systems. In contrast, coping strategies were reserved in secure systems for periods of food stress. As the proportion of cash income from coping/adaptive activities increases over time (in good and satisfactory, as well as bad, years), *within each livelihood system*, the argument that these activities are adaptive and not coping strategies is substantiated. Hence, the higher the proportion of income derived from coping/adaptive strategies, the more adaptive they are, and the fewer the options reserved for bad years.

Clearly, the categories are not water-tight; wood cutting for example (classified as adapting/coping) has always been pursued by certain groups (the poorest, particularly undiversified cultivators) in every year, but it has never represented a principal source of accumulation and saving, or a means of spreading risk, in the way that diversification into livestock or fishing has. Equally, seeking casual labour on the fields of richer neighbours has always been pursued by poorer households, but this was often to cement reciprocal ties or to repay debt in kind, in this sense a poor household's best option for risk spreading (but not for accumulation). The point about this classification is not to argue that income from activities in the coping/adaptive category was never generated in non-crisis years by anyone, but rather to indicate the overall shift towards these activities as regular and essential sources of household income for subsistence. The precise mix of activities pursued by a given household is chosen according to a complex range of livelihood criteria (Chapter 10).

In the cycle of subsistence and adaptation, producers move into the market to acquire food as vulnerability intensifies. They do not necessarily reduce their market dependence in good years, because of the myriad of cash needs; in 1988, for example, cereal sales to repay debts and back taxes were high in the harvest season and people were buying cereals again by the rainy season. There is, of course, no way of knowing what would happen if drought disappeared. There is no guarantee that everything would return to normal, because drought is only one variable in the process of evolving livelihood systems. Nevertheless, in vulnerable systems, even though market dependence for subsistence may fall off in good years, the ability to accumulate and to break out of the annual cycle of subsistence and coping is highly restricted because of the longer-term effects of vulnerability (Chapter 7).

Taking all households together, not surprisingly very few cereals are sold (on average 9 per cent), although this does not take account of gifts and other informal transfers. Cereals are sold to meet cash needs immediately after the harvest (debts, taxes). By far the most significant source of cash income comes from secondary sources of productive entitlements, animals and milk (33 per cent) and fish (23 per cent); followed by wage labour (19 per cent), accounting for well over half of all income not derived from either primary or secondary productive entitlements. Gathered products provide only 5 per cent of income. Miscellaneous sources of income are twice as significant (12 per cent), and it should be noted that this category includes value-added gathered products (e.g. mats, blankets, etc.).

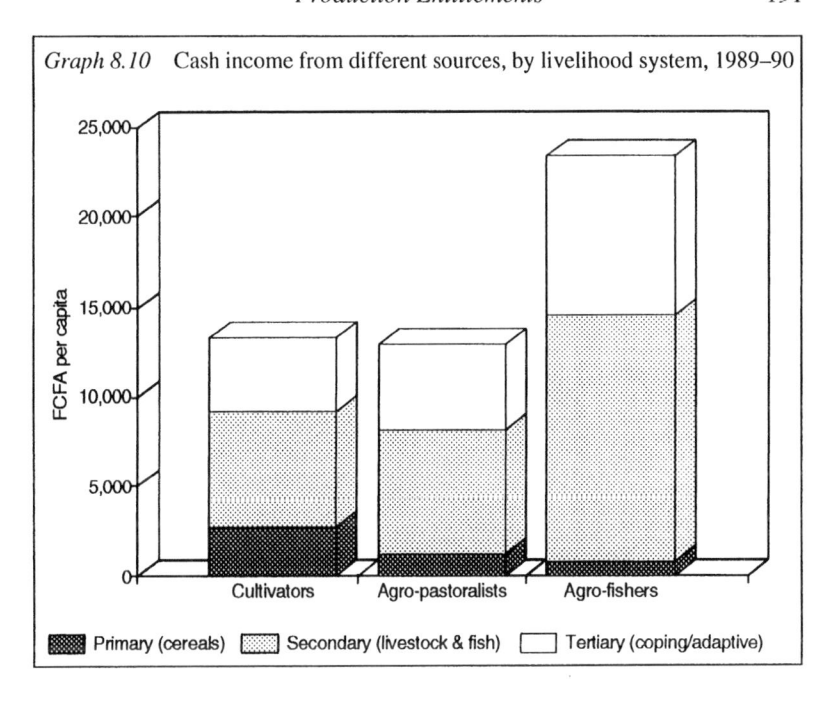

Graph 8.10 Cash income from different sources, by livelihood system, 1989–90

[Bar chart showing FCFA per capita for Cultivators, Agro-pastoralists, and Agro-fishers, with segments for Primary (cereals), Secondary (livestock & fish), and Tertiary (coping/adaptive).]

Graph 8.10 shows total cash income from primary, secondary and coping/adaptive activities, by livelihood system. Variation in sources and levels of cash income is greater than variation in items of expenditure. Total *per capita* cash income for each livelihood system (in FCFA) is as follows: cultivators 13 359; agro-pastoralists 13 000; and agro-fishers 23 394. Again, agro-fishers spend significantly more (over 75 per cent) than other producers.

Graphs 8.11 to 8.13 disaggregate these data, showing the proportions of cash income from different sources for each livelihood system. Agro-fishers, who purchase the most cereals, also have the highest incomes, most of which comes from fish (40 per cent). Cultivators also acquire some income from fish (11 per cent), indicating diversification into inhabitual activities. Income from animals and milk is significant across all livelihood systems, accounting for 53 per cent of agro-pastoralists' income, 38 per cent of cultivators' income and 19 per cent of agro-fishers' income. As would be expected, cultivators are forced to rely on selling cereals for the highest proportion of cash income (20 per cent), whilst the others are able to rely on fish or milk to a much higher extent.

Graph 8.11 Cultivators: proportion of cash income from different sources of entitlement, 1989–90

- Miscellaneous (12.0%)
- Cereals (19.8%)
- Labour (15.0%)
- Gathering (4.4%)
- Fish (11.1%)
- Animals & milk (37.7%)

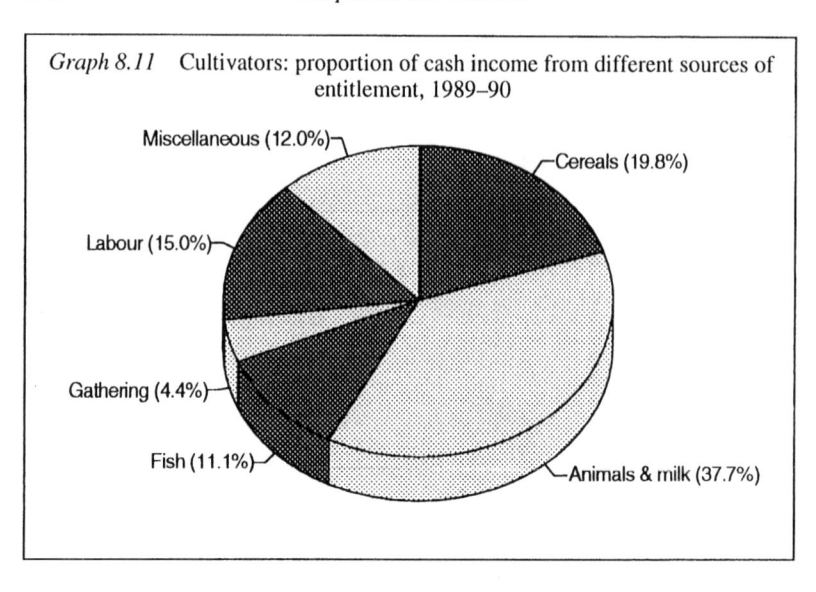

Graph 8.12 Agro-pastoralists: proportion of cash income from different sources of entitlement, 1989–90

- Miscellaneous (11.9%)
- Cereals (9.0%)
- Labour (11.1%)
- Gathering (13.6%)
- Fish (1.1%)
- Animals & milk (53.3%)

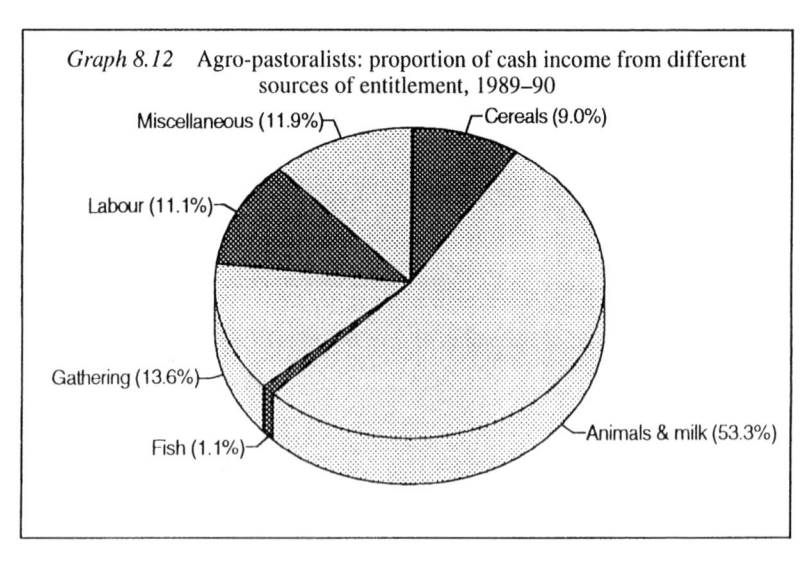

Turning to sources of cash income from coping/adaptive sources of entitlement, agro-fishers again have the highest incomes by far, most of which (26 per cent of total income) comes from wage labour. This compares with 11 per cent for agro-pastoralists and 15 per cent for cultivators. Income from gathering is significant only for agro-pastoralists (14 per

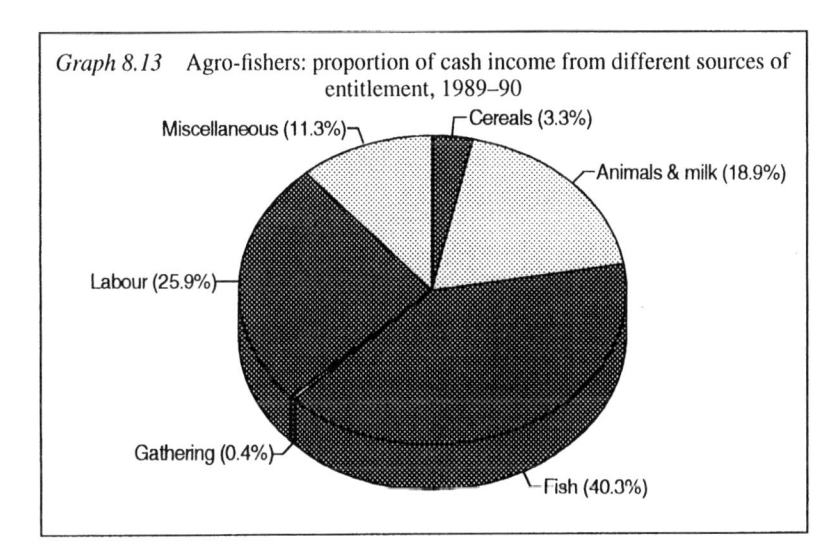

Graph 8.13 Agro-fishers: proportion of cash income from different sources of entitlement, 1989–90

- Miscellaneous (11.3%)
- Cereals (3.3%)
- Animals & milk (18.9%)
- Labour (25.9%)
- Gathering (0.4%)
- Fish (40.3%)

cent), although the miscellaneous category includes goods based on gathered products (e.g. mats). This accounts for around 12 per cent of income for all systems.

Cash income/expenditure balances. In the cycle of subsistence and coping, people move into the market to acquire food as their livelihoods become more insecure and out of it again as the situation improves. As all livelihood systems spend around half their cash income on buying food in a satisfactory (or average) year, they are obviously highly market-dependent, particularly in bad years. Even though market dependence for subsistence may fall off dramatically in good years, the ability to accumulate and save is very limited because of the longer-term effects of vulnerability. Here we are considering the seasonality of households' cash balance, to see when and whether they are trading at a profit or a loss during the year. It is to be expected that the moments of food insecurity would coincide with seasons in which people are spending more than they are earning.

All three livelihood systems show an overall annual deficit, with cultivators by far the worst-off. Each year, on a *per capita* basis, they spend on average a third more than they earn. This is only partly explained by under-recording of income (Chapter 4): producers in all livelihood systems are increasingly indebted.

Graphs 8.14 to 8.16 show the seasonal income and expenditure balances for each of the three systems. Cultivators have the largest overall deficit,

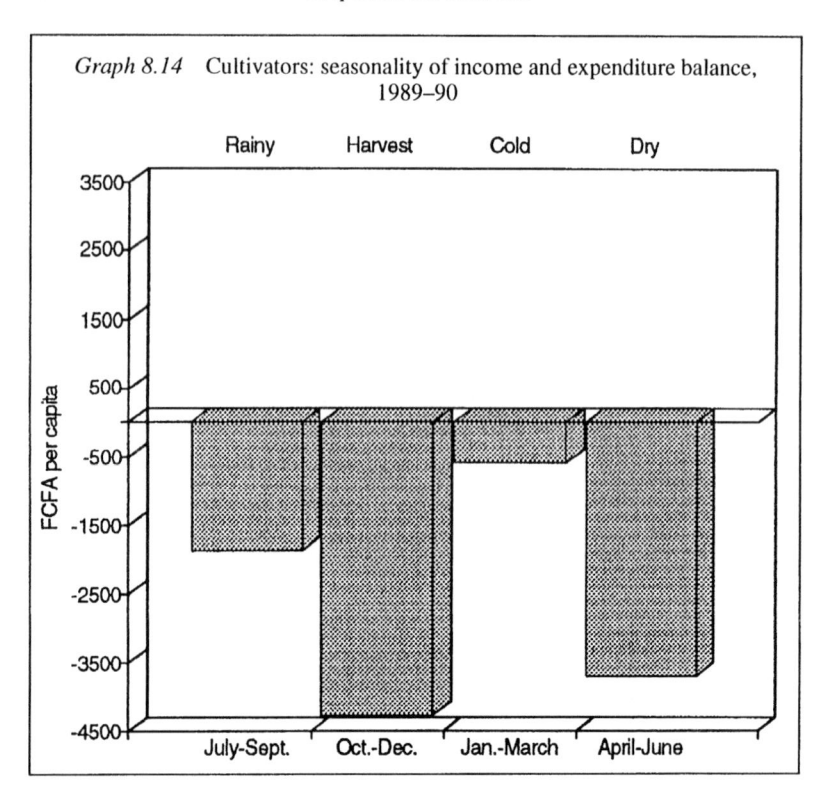

Graph 8.14 Cultivators: seasonality of income and expenditure balance, 1989–90

but, apart from the cold season when households had food stocks, this is lowest in the rainy season, explained by the fact that this came at the end of the exceptional year of 1988–9, when all livelihood systems had adequate cereal production, even though substantial quantities had to be sold to meet debt repayments. Further, wild foods were in good supply in the rainy season of 1989, leading to a reduction in the need for cash to purchase cereals on the market. Agro-pastoralists and agro-fishers have negligible cash deficits in this season. Fish prices are high at this time, although availability is low. In more normal years, this would be the season of highest over-expenditure, especially for cultivators. It is interesting to note, however, that a single good year did allow producers at least to meet most of their cash needs through the hungry season, because of a guaranteed source of food (their own harvest), which freed up cash income for other items of expenditure. Cultivators have the highest shortfall in the harvest season, due to the fact that rice cultivators do not harvest their crop until the end of the period (December/January). For millet cultivators in the sample, this could be explained by poor harvests in 1989, at a time of high cash needs to

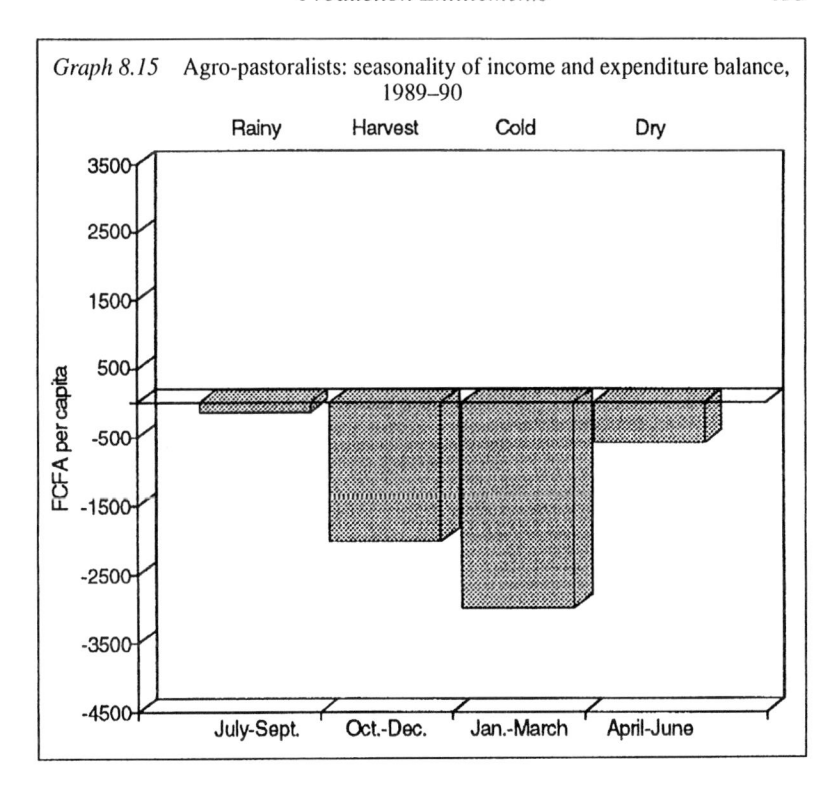

Graph 8.15 Agro-pastoralists: seasonality of income and expenditure balance, 1989–90

[Bar chart showing FCFA per capita across four seasons: July-Sept. (Rainy), Oct.-Dec. (Harvest), Jan.-March (Cold), April-June (Dry). All bars show deficits, with the largest deficit in Jan.-March.]

meet outstanding claims both from private traders and from the state, and with prices at their lowest. The cultivators' deficit shrinks after the rice harvest, to rise again sharply in the dry season. Agro-pastoralists, on the other hand, continue to show a large deficit in the cold season, when they are subject to high levels of fiscal demand and are purchasing animals to build up herds. By the dry season, these purchases have ceased. Agro-pastoralists' much smaller food gap (see above) explains the lower deficit in the dry season. Agro-fishers show a different pattern: they more or less balance their income and expenditure in all but the dry season. It is of note that no surplus is shown during the fishing campaign (November to February), when traditionally they would have expected to build up surpluses.

CONCLUSIONS: INDICATORS OF PRODUCTION ENTITLEMENTS

The primary characteristic of vulnerable livelihood systems is a structural cereal gap, or the inability to meet annual food requirements through primary production entitlements. This in turn engenders insecurity,

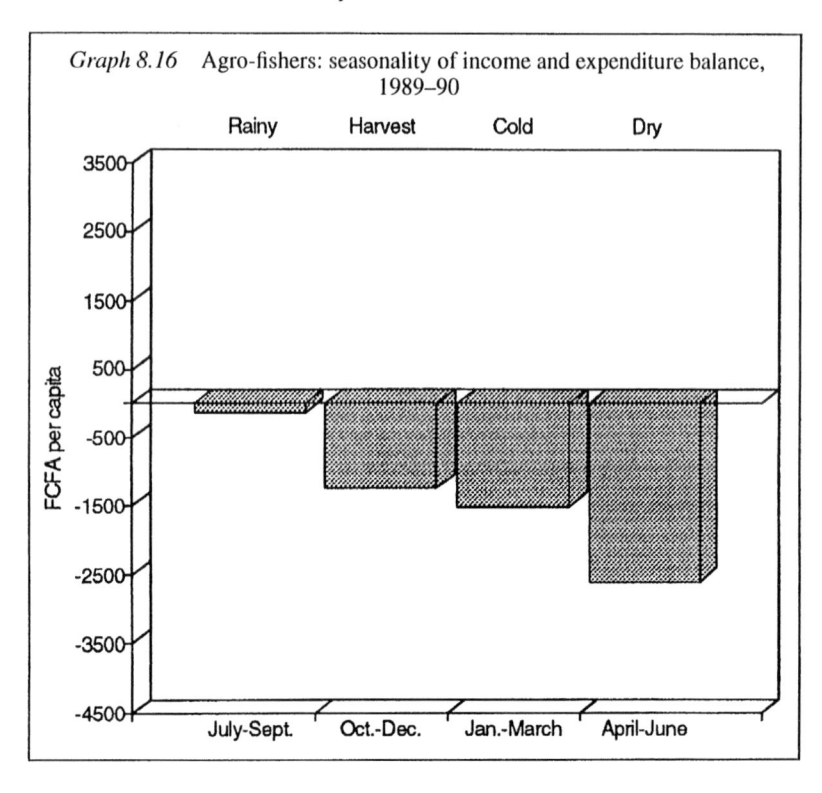

Graph 8.16 Agro-fishers: seasonality of income and expenditure balance, 1989–90

instability and high risk. A food gap is confirmed at both regional and household level across the three livelihood systems examined. Further, it is clear from regional level data that the variability in cereal-derived production entitlements has increased since the drought of the mid-1980s. But unlike conventional balance-sheet analyses of food security, this food gap is not the end of the story. Two sets of strategies are used to fill the gap. First, sources of production entitlements for subsistence are diversified into livestock and, for some systems, fisheries. Whereas in the past, for sedentary producers, these sources of entitlement were reserved for accumulation, they are now central to meeting annual consumption needs. In so far as livestock is concerned, the most striking feature of the post-drought period is the shift from cattle to goats. For fisheries, total production is falling and the numbers of people reliant on fisheries for their livelihoods is rising. Data are not available for additional sources of food (off-farm harvests, barter, wild food collection) but, taken together, these probably meet up to 25 per cent of requirements.

The second, linked strategy is dependence on the market: all households purchase significant quantities of food, but insufficient to meet minimum requirements. Cash income to purchase food comes both from the sale of sources of production entitlements (principally fish and livestock), and also from coping and adaptive activities. These latter sources of income are not reserved for bad years, but are relied on to fill the food gap in average ones. All three livelihood systems finish the year with an overall cash deficit, indicating that productive sources of entitlement are inadequate to meet calls. The vulnerability of the systems is confirmed by their inability to balance sources of and calls on entitlement and to accumulate and the need to use coping/adaptive strategies to fill the food gap in every year.

The key production entitlement indicators of food insecurity examined in this chapter are the existence of an annual food gap and, critically, the ways in which this gap is filled. To track food insecurity on this basis, the following indicators are required:

- the size of the annual cereal gap (the difference between sources of primary production entitlement and minimum consumption requirements);
- the amount of food acquired via non-market channels (from barter, off-farm harvests and wild food collection);
- the amount of food acquired via the market;
- the effectiveness of diversifying sources of entitlement, either by secondary productive entitlements or coping/adaptive sources;
- the terms of trade between different sources of entitlement, and between sources of and calls on entitlement (e.g. goats being sold to purchase cereals for consumption).

9 Exchange Entitlements

INTRODUCTION

Market prices for staple cereals (and, in the case of pastoralists, for livestock) are widely recognised as important indicators of food security. Food prices tend to be the socio-economic indicator most frequently monitored by EWS, not least because of the relative simplicity of their collection. Price data are a simple way of following changes in purchasing power, one aspect of food entitlement decline. Monitoring the prices of goods which food-insecure people are *selling*, as well as the cereals they must buy, enables more accurate tracking of exchange entitlements over time. The supply of cereals on markets is also monitored by EWS as an indication of food availability decline.

Unlike EWS which rarely collect more than staple food price data on urban markets, the SADS system used a wider range of variables including: the role of the market in the process of adaptation to increasing vulnerability; the key seasonal terms of trade between the range of goods bought and sold by different producers and what happens to these in particularly bad years; and the costs to producers forced to trade on rural rather than urban markets. Monthly market surveys covered ten rural markets and the market in Mopti (as well as the neighbouring livestock market in Fatoma). This chapter examines the data collected in these surveys and addresses the following issues: the nature of market dependence in vulnerable livelihood systems; what market data can indicate about changes in exchange entitlements from season to season and year to year in these systems; the extent to which the market enables producers to adapt to increasing vulnerability to food insecurity; which market indicators can most usefully be monitored to track changes in levels of food insecurity and how these need to be interpreted.

MARKET DEPENDENCE IN VULNERABLE LIVELIHOOD SYSTEMS

As Table 9.1 shows, the terms of trade which producers face in the market have fundamentally changed as livelihood systems have moved from security to vulnerability. Millet is used throughout this chapter as a proxy

Table 9.1 Key seasonal terms of trade in secure and vulnerable livelihood systems

Livelihood system	Key seasonal market relationships (terms of trade)			
	Harvest	Cold	Dry	Rainy
Secure				
Cultivators	Millet for cattle, gold, milk	Millet for cattle, fish	Cattle for gold	–
Agro-pastoralists	Millet for cattle, (goats)	Millet for cattle, (goats)	Millet for cattle, gold Goats for cattle	–
Agro-fishers	Gold for equipment	Millet, fish for equipment	Fish for cattle, gold	–
Transhumant fishers	Gold for equipment	Fish for milk, cattle, gold	Fish for cattle, gold	–
Transhumant pastoralists	Milk for millet, fish[a]	Milk for millet, fish	Milk for millet, fish Cattle for cattle[b]	–
Vulnerable				
Cultivators	Millet for cash (Millet for milk)[c]	(Millet for milk, fish)[d] Millet for cash, (goats)	Cash for millet	Cash for millet
Agro-pastoralists	Millet for goats	Millet for goats	Goats for millet	Goats for millet
Agro-fishers	Credit for equipment[e]	Credit for equipment Fish for debt repayment	Fish for millet, debt repayment	Fish for millet, debt repayment
Transhumant fishers	Credit for equipment	Credit for equipment Fish for debt repayment, millet, (milk)	Fish for millet, debt repayment	Fish for millet, debt repayment
Transhumant pastoralists	Milk for millet	Milk for millet (Animals for millet)	Animals for millet	(Animals for millet)[f]

Table 9.1 (*continued*)

Notes: (a) Delta transhumant pastoralists only.
(b) Exchanging unproductive animals for productive ones.
(c) Millet is now only exchanged for milk in this season in a good year.
(d) Millet for milk (and for fish in the Delta) would be the preferred exchange and does take place in years of good harvests. Millet for cash is, however, the most important exchange, reflecting the need to sell cereals after the harvest to meet cash needs (repayment of debt, taxation, etc.). In a bad year, this may be reversed at the end of the cold season (i.e. cash for millet).
(e) Ideally, fishers buy equipment, but invariably today they are forced to acquire it on credit, to be repaid with the subsequent fish catch.
(f) Distress sales in time of drought.

for all cereals, though in the case of wetland farmers the exchange would in fact be rice. 'Gold' is used as a proxy for accumulation: such exchanges actually cover a range of reasons for exchange including savings and social expenditures (e.g. on marriage), which were seen as a form of accumulation as they cemented reciprocal ties or secured future claims on kin, often called on in time of stress. 'Cash' is used as shorthand for the need to purchase cereals on the market without directly exchanging a different source of production entitlement. Most obviously, this would be via the sale of labour, but also by means of the coping strategies discussed in Chapter 10. When cereals are sold after the harvest to meet cash needs, these terms of trade are reversed. The terms of trade in parentheses in the table are of secondary importance.

What clearly emerges from the table is that the key market relationships for each group of producers are significantly different both from each other and from season to season, in secure and vulnerable systems. For *cultivators*, market exchange is now limited to the need to sell cereals to meet cash needs after the harvest and to re-enter the market as buyers at the end of the cold or in the dry season (depending on household stocks). In the past, cultivators did not exchange during the rainy season, relying on household stocks for food until the following harvest. Exchanging millet for milk and fish, to diversify diet, now occurs only in years of abundance, whereas in the past this was a major reason for bartering between livelihood systems. Traditional exchanges of millet for cattle and gold, to diversify production and accumulate, no longer occur. In years of abundance, the preferred strategy now is to diversify into goats, but, as Chapter 7 has shown, in the recent good year of 1988–9, the capacity of cultivators to invest in livestock was in fact extremely limited. As undiversified producers, cultivators are thus caught in the classic trap of having to sell cheap after the harvest and to buy back at high prices later in the year. To this extent, they are the least well-placed of all producers to be able to optimise exchange entitlements. Their best option is to try and become agro-pastoralists by investing significantly in goats.

Agro-pastoralists retain broadly the same strategy in vulnerable systems as in secure ones in the harvest and cold seasons: diversifying by selling millet to acquire livestock. Whereas in the past they invested in cattle, nowadays they buy cheaper goats, which are more easily liquidated later in the year. In secure systems, the dry season was a period of accumulation, upgrading goats to cattle, exchanging non-productive for productive animals, or accumulating savings held in other forms (gold). Like cultivators, they did not participate in the market during the rainy season, using stocks and their own milk production for food. In the dry and rainy seasons, they now reverse their strategy, selling off goats in order to purchase cereals. As part of this process, they have become more sedentary.

Agro-fishers in secure systems sold millet and rice in order to purchase fishing equipment, their cereal needs having been met by their own production. Again, the dry season was a period of accumulation, investing the profits from fishing in cattle (to diversify production) and in fishing equipment or gold; little market activity took place in the rainy season, as household stocks and fishing met food requirements. Today, they are caught in a double bind: first, they must borrow in the harvest and cold seasons in order to acquire equipment to fish, and second, in the dry and rainy seasons they must purchase cereals to meet food needs, as well as having to repay debts incurred for equipment. Merchants are often horizontally stratified in providing fishing equipment and cereals, making large profits from sales to groups of fishers who are tied to them by debt.

Transhumant fishers are in a similar position to the more sedentary agro-fishers. In the past, they began to accumulate at the height of the fishing campaign (in the cold and dry seasons), trading fish for cattle (to diversify production) and gold (for accumulation), as well as for milk to diversify diets. Nowadays, they too must use fish sales to repay credit for equipment and to meet subsistence needs, right up until the following harvest.

Transhumant pastoralists depended on the market in the past principally as a means of diversifying diet and exchanging expensive protein (livestock products) for larger quantities of cheaper calories (cereals). In the dry season, they upgraded their herds by exchanging non-productive animals for productive ones. Again, their market activity in the rainy season was minimal, not least because they were far away from markets at the time. In today's vulnerable system, they still rely on the market to convert milk into cereals, but in most years are required to sell animals in the cold and particularly the dry season to meet cereal needs, as herds are too small to provide sufficient quantities of milk. In drought years, they may also be forced to sell livestock in the rainy season. Of all livelihood systems in the Delta and Seno, they have been the most successful in retaining favourable terms of trade, although they own fewer and fewer of the animals they herd. Transhumant pastoralists also still rely on barter to a greater extent that other livelihood systems, due both to the persistence of some reciprocal ties with their former cultivating slaves and the need to exchange milk on a more or less daily basis when it is most abundant.

Table 9.2 summarises the shifts in the reasons for market participation between secure and vulnerable livelihood systems, confirming that

Table 9.2 Differences in market relationships between secure and vulnerable livelihood systems

Livelihood system	Seasonal reasons for market exchange			
	Harvest	Cold	Dry	Rainy
Secure				
Cultivators	Diversify production Accumulation Diversify diet	Diversify production Accumulation Diversify diet	Accumulation	—
Agro-pastoralists	Diversify production (Upgrade herd)	Diversify production (Upgrade herd)	Accumulation Upgrade herd	—
Agro-fishers	Invest in production	Invest in production	Accumulation Diversify production	—
Transhumant fishers	Invest in production	Invest in production Diversify diet	Accumulation Diversify production	—
Transhumant pastoralists	Diversify diet	Diversify diet	Diversify diet Invest in production Upgrade herd Accumulation	—
Vulnerable				
Cultivators	(Diversify diet)	Subsistence	Subsistence	Subsistence
Agro-pastoralists	Insurance	Insurance	Subsistence	Subsistence
Agro-fishers	Credit to produce	Credit to produce Repayment of debt	Subsistence Repayment of debt	Subsistence
Transhumant fishers	Credit to produce	Credit to produce Repayment of debt	Subsistence Repayment of debt	Subsistence
Transhumant pastoralists	(Diversify diet)	(Diversify diet) Subsistence	Subsistence	(Subsistence)

vulnerable systems are characterised by short-term cycles of subsistence and exchange, whereas secure ones permitted longer-term accumulation and diversification of primary activities as well as the capacity to insure against the risk of particularly bad years. In secure systems, the role of the market was restricted to meeting longer-term livelihood needs, including social expenditures that cemented long-term alliances between and within livelihood systems. The only immediate need to be met by the market was to diversify diet. Producers were not dependent on the market for survival, whereas nowadays they are unable to subsist without recourse to the market.

THE SAMPLE OF MARKETS

The markets monitored were divided between listening posts as follows: Mopti (the central market in the town plus the neighbouring regional livestock market at Fatoma); Youvarou (the district capital market, Gatie Luomo on the drylands on the edge of the Delta and Attara on the main river north of the major floodplain); Tenenkou (the district capital market, Diafarabé at the southern-most tip of the Delta, and Diondiori and Toguéré Koumbé on the floodplain); Douentza (the district capital market, N'Gouma in the Sahelian north of the district and Hombori to the east near the border with the 7th Region). Only four markets are included in the analysis (see Map 4 in Chapter 6): Mopti as the regional market, treated as representative of an urban market and for which wholesale prices have been analysed; Douentza, treated as a representative dryland market for the Seno; and Toguéré Koumbé and Youvarou, where data have been aggregated in seasonal complementarity to provide one representative wetland market, the former of key significance from October to January and the latter an important area of concentration during the dry season.

Urban market: Mopti. Situated on three linked islands in the Delta, Mopti is joined to the 'mainland' by a causeway to the town of Sévaré, 13 km away, which is on the only metalled road in the north of the country, connected to San, Ségou in the south-west, Bamako, and Douentza and Gao in the east. There are several daily markets in the town, feeding an urban population of around 65 000 people. Data for this survey were gathered at the main Thursday market in the port and at the livestock market at Fatoma.

Mopti is the hub through which the Delta and surrounding drylands' imports and exports pass. The regional office of OPAM, the state cereal marketing board, is in Sévaré. Prior to market liberalisation, this was the regional centre for the very partial control of cereal markets; nowadays, it is responsible for the storage and distribution of food aid in the event of concessional imports to the Region. Mopti is also the hub of credit mechanisms in the 5th Region, particularly for the fishing sector. Its central importance as a transit zone for the Region's imports and exports, as well as for financial services, makes it an excellent barometer of regional economic activity. The strategies pursued by cereal merchants prior to and during the harvest, for example, are a good and early indication of the regional food balance; any rupture of cereals supply to rural markets is signalled at an early stage in Mopti.

Wetland markets. Delta market activity and prices are highly seasonally determined by the movement of the flood through the Delta and the seasonal resource availability to which it gives rise. Thus a composite market has been constructed from average prices on those markets actually used by producers throughout the year, as they move between resources.

The small town of Toguéré Koumbé, in the *cercle* of Tenenkou, is completely surrounded by water during the high water season. It is the most important market on the north-western shore of the Delta, and the one most influenced by the seasonal productivity of the zone. Between February and June (depending on water levels), an important cattle market takes place on the outskirts of the town. From the onset of the rains (June/July) until the start of the fishing campaign (November), market activity shrinks to almost nothing. The market in Toguéré is fed, according to the season, from two different areas: while river transport is possible (August/January) goods are brought from the south of the Delta, via Diafarabé and Tenenkou, using the main waterway of the Diaka; between January and July, merchants come mostly overland from Mopti. For a number of weeks in January/February, access is impossible from Mopti, when there is insufficient water for boats and too much for vehicles. Local merchants congregate in Toguéré, particularly during the fishing campaign, and many operate on a circuit between Diafarabé, Tenenkou, Diondiori and Toguéré (see Map 3 in Chapter 6).

With a population of about 4500, Youvarou is the administrative capital of the *cercle*. Situated on the northern shore of Lake Debo, it straddles the floodplains to the south and the drylands to the north and, during the dry season, is on the main dirt road linking Mopti to Tombouctou and the north, via Diré and Niafunké. Like Toguéré, it has no direct link to Bamako, and in the high water season access to Mopti (and the paved road to the south) is possible only by boat. Whereas the traders of Toguéré operate on circuits of exchange between the markets of the southern Delta, Youvarou is on the circuit of those in the northern Delta (Attara) and the drylands to the west (Gatie Luomo), these latter being centres of exchange of contraband goods from Mauritania. As market activity in Toguéré declines, so trade in fish and livestock in Youvarou picks up. The fishing campaign on Lake Debo is at its height from January to March, and livestock spend the dry season in and around the pastures of Lake Debo.

Dryland market. Douentza, on the main paved road joining Bamako to the capital of the 7th Region (Gao), is the administrative capital of the *cercle*. The market takes place on a Sunday, and has historically been an important cross-roads between northern Arab and Tuareg pastoral peoples and cultivators and agro-pastoralists to the south. Nowadays, caravans from the north continue to exchange salt from Taodeni for cereals from Bankass to the south of Douentza (Hesse and Thera, 1987, citing Gallais, 1975).

The road linking Douentza to Mopti and Gao, first established by the French in colonial times and metalled in 1985–6 between Sévaré and Gao, shifted trade on a more west/east axis. The main supply routes are from Mopti, Koro, Bankass, San, Sikasso and Bamako, bringing cereals and manufactures in exchange for livestock, mats, wood and market garden products. Being on the main road means that Douentza market never experiences ruptures in supplies of cereals, whereas outlying dryland markets do have periodic seasonal breaks in supply, with a relatively poorly developed internal marketing system, due principally to inaccessible roads in the rainy season. (Unlike the wetland markets, poor roads cannot be compensated for by riverine transport.) Douentza is also an important livestock market, with exporters coming seasonally from Niger, Burkina Faso and the coastal West African states. However, recent regional unrest and changes in trading regimes (Nigeria's closing of its frontier to livestock; the shift by Côte d'Ivoire to importing beef from Argentina and the EC; and the brief Mali/Burkina Faso war) have seriously reduced the importance of Douentza.

ANALYSIS OF DATA

Price data were collected for the following items: wholesale and retail prices for millet, rice, paddy, sorghum, and for smoked, dried and fresh fish; other cereals, subject to availability (e.g. maize); young goats, sheep and heifers; fresh and soured milk; gathered products, including wild *fonio*, water-lily tubers and grains, *bourgou* grains and grass, and wood, and goods derived from them (charcoal and mats); a basket of condiments representing the standard ingredients of the daily sauce; and tea and sugar, which although not essential foods, are regularly consumed by all households. In addition, the number of sellers was plotted as a proxy for the level of market activity. Qualitative information was also recorded including: patterns of movements of goods and prices between markets; who was buying and selling and the reasons for exchange; and origins of goods. The methodology used for collecting these data has been explained in Chapter 4. As already noted, for the purposes of this analysis millet is used as the cereal in all instances.

General price trends are analysed to consider relative values between strategic goods which rural producers exchange. Inflation has not been taken into account in the analysis. The regional urban market of Mopti represents the most favourable terms of trade in the area; retail prices on the representative rural wetland and dryland markets generally reflect the least favourable terms of trade. Within the two extremes are wholesale terms of trade on rural markets (more favourable than retail ones, less favourable than urban wholesale ones) and retail terms of trade on urban markets (less favourable than wholesale ones, more favourable than rural wholesale ones). These intermediate levels of prices have been excluded from the analysis for the sake of simplicity. Data were gathered on wholesale and retail prices in all markets, and confirm the pattern of least to most favourable from rural retail to urban wholesale prices for most goods. Exceptions are indicated in the analysis below. Milk is not traded wholesale, so the urban retail price has been used.

General price trends are calculated for each of the following goods: millet (retail prices for dryland and wetland markets, wholesale prices for the urban one); goats; heifers (used as a proxy for all cattle); milk (soured not fresh, as the latter is infrequently sold on markets); fish (for which an average wholesale price has been calculated, using smoked and dried prices);[1] and condiments (for which a typical basket of condiments used in the preparation of the daily meal has been calculated).[2] These are the key goods bought and sold by different producers in vulnerable livelihood systems, identified in Table 9.1. Although price data were collected on a monthly basis, prices are aggregated by season in all instances. The period covered is the harvest season of 1987 to the rainy season of 1991 (four agricultural years, 1987–8 to 1990–1). Price trends are analysed in order to consider: the movement of prices over the four-year period; differences in prices between dryland, wetland and urban markets; and the seasonality of price swings.

For the purposes of comparison, 1987–8 has been used as the representative bad year and 1988–9 as the representative good one. None of the three bad/satisfactory years in the sample were crisis years on a par with

1984–5, although 1987–8 was the next worst since then, particularly given that in the intervening period there had not been a really good harvest in the area. By way of illustration, Graph 9.1 compares millet prices on the markets of Youvarou and Toguéré Koumbé in the hungry seasons of 1984–5 (i.e. January to September 1985) with the same months in 1987–8.

The key terms of trade identified in Table 9.1 for vulnerable livelihood systems are then calculated for the goods over the four years, and analysed and compared in the context of each system in good and bad years. The key terms of trade are as follows: cultivators – cash for millet[3] and goats for millet; agro-pastoralists – goats for millet; agro-fishers and transhumant fishers – fish for millet; transhumant pastoralists – milk, cattle and goats for millet.

Cultivators and agro-pastoralists are treated together. As pointed out in Chapter 7, cultivators seek to invest in goats if they can and agro-pastoralists effectively become undiversified cultivators when their herds are entirely liquidated. The same terms of trade are therefore relevant to both livelihood systems. Equally, all fishers are grouped together as both

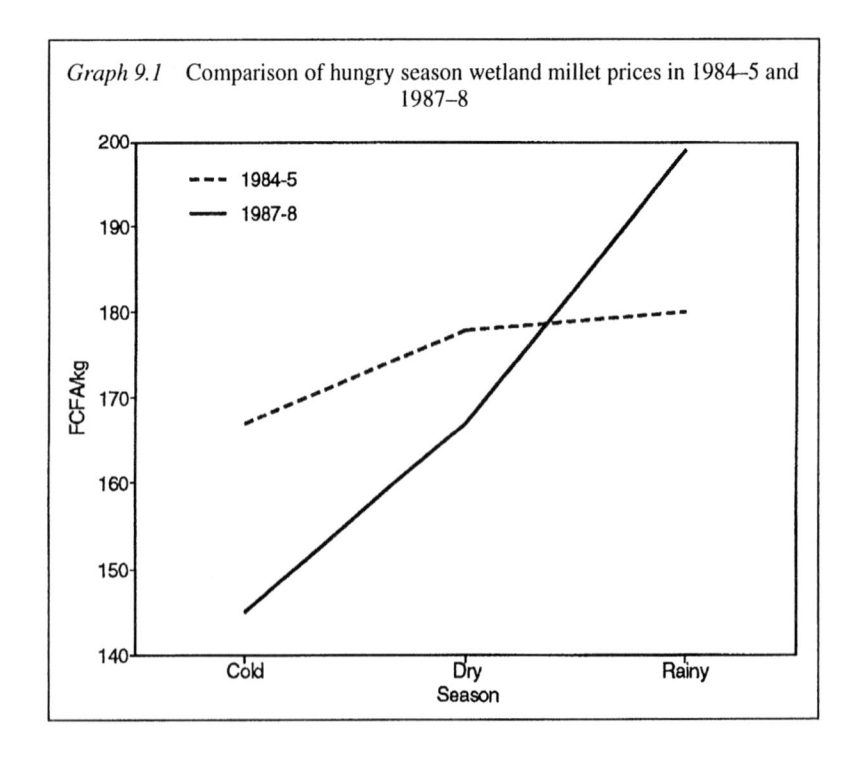

Graph 9.1 Comparison of hungry season wetland millet prices in 1984–5 and 1987–8

Exchange Entitlements 209

systems depend on the fish for millet exchange. Credit for fishing equipment and subsequent fish for debt repayment were also identified in Table 9.1 as being key exchanges for these producers, but despite attempts to gather data on the costs of both credit and equipment, no reliable figures were collected. This is due to the oligopolistic structure of the fish trade in Mopti. Such data as were gathered did not accurately reflect the actual terms of trade under which fishers exchange for credit and equipment, and have therefore been excluded from the analysis. Transhumant pastoralists are treated on their own for cattle for millet and milk for millet exchanges. The terms of trade between goats and millet are, however, relevant to them as well as to cultivators and agro-pastoralists, as there is a tendency for all herders to switch from cattle to goats under conditions of increasing vulnerability.

PRICES

Millet. In both dryland and wetland markets, the seasonality of millet prices is clear: in bad years, prices do not fall significantly after the harvest, whereas in good and satisfactory ones they do. This drop occurs in the drylands before the wetlands, as the latter depend on the later rice harvest in December/January to break the hungry season. New season millet does not arrive on wetland markets until November/December. Prices rise consistently throughout the year, dropping in the rainy season if the rains are good and if farmers (usually in the south rather than in the immediate area) have carry-over stocks which they release on to the market before the post-harvest price drop. In the wetlands, during a good year there is almost no seasonal price swing, indicating the low demand for millet (and adequate household rice supplies). A dramatic fall in millet prices at the end of 1987–8 signalled the promise of good rice harvests. In contrast, in bad years, seasonal price rises mirror those of the drylands. For dryland markets the difference between urban (wholesale) and rural (retail) prices is a reflection of whether the drylands are in surplus: if they are, local prices fall below those of the urban market; if not, prices are considerably higher. As millet is not produced in the wetlands (although it is on the surrounding drylands), prices on these markets are less sensitive to changes in local supply, always remaining significantly higher than urban prices.

Goats. Prices for goats generally show the opposite trend to those for millet: falling steeply in bad years as cultivators and agro-pastoralists liquidate their stock to acquire cereals, and rising strongly in good years as they seek to reconstitute their herds up to levels that will provide them with insurance in future periods of stress. Prices are generally higher on the wetlands than the drylands, which may reflect periodic scarcity value. The value of goats is falling over time, due to saturation of the market as confirmed by the marked difference in urban and rural prices. As explained in Chapter 6, it has been estimated that the number of goats in the 5th Region has increased by 66 per cent since 1982, whereas cattle numbers have fallen from 1.2 million to 600 000 (RIM, 1987). The bottom appears to be falling out of the goat market, making the strategy of diversifying into goats as an insurance against high cereal prices less and less effective over time and especially in bad years.

Cattle. The seasonality of cattle prices follows broadly the same pattern as that of goats. What is striking is the contrasting movement of prices in the dry and cold seasons of the first three years. These are the times of the year when herders are most closely connected with the market both because they are concentrated in the Delta and around permanent water points in the Seno, and because they are increasingly obliged to sell livestock and livestock products to purchase cereals. Low prices at the end of 1989–90 and 1990–1 reflect poor climatic conditions, but may also be the result of a slump in the demand for Sahelian beef on Côte d'Ivoire markets, as imports of subsidised EC frozen meat undercut prices of animals imported from Mali. As with goats, the increased difference between urban and rural prices towards the end of the period indicates that, for rural producers, trading in cattle on local markets is becoming less profitable over time.

Milk. The seasonality of milk prices is determined by the availability of good pasture and the proximity of markets. In the rainy season and continuing in the period of high water in the Delta (i.e. through the harvest and cold seasons), milk production is high because of the availability of green pasture, and prices fall; in the dry season, milk production is very low and prices rise.

Fish. Fish prices are conditioned by the flood level, transport constraints in the Delta and the level of national and international demand on the Mopti market. The cold and dry seasons are the most productive when traders from Ghana, Côte d'Ivoire, Burkina Faso and Bamako appear on the scene. Prices rise, because of the presence of effective demand and the ease of transport in the Delta. There is, however, a general trend downwards, which may reflect an overall fall in demand from international markets; traditional West African coastal importers are rapidly developing their own marine fisheries. Rural fish prices are consistently lower than urban ones, and fishers receive on average 76 per cent less for their catch on local markets than if they were selling in Mopti (although these prices take no account of transport costs). Differences between rural and urban fish prices are more stable from year to year than for other products, due to the highly controlled urban fish market. The difference increased significantly in 1990–1, indicating not only a poor fishing campaign but also saturated rural markets and increasingly oligopolistic urban ones.

Prices in good and bad years

This section considers the first two years of data discussed under overall price trends as indicative of good (1988–9) and bad (1987–8) years, in order to establish what happens to exchange entitlements when food insecurity threatens.

Millet. Graph 9.2 shows a clear inverse relationship between years, with prices rising through the seasons in bad years and falling in good ones. For cultivators this means that in bad years, they will be obliged to sell (for fiscal reasons, amongst others) when prices are comparatively low and buy

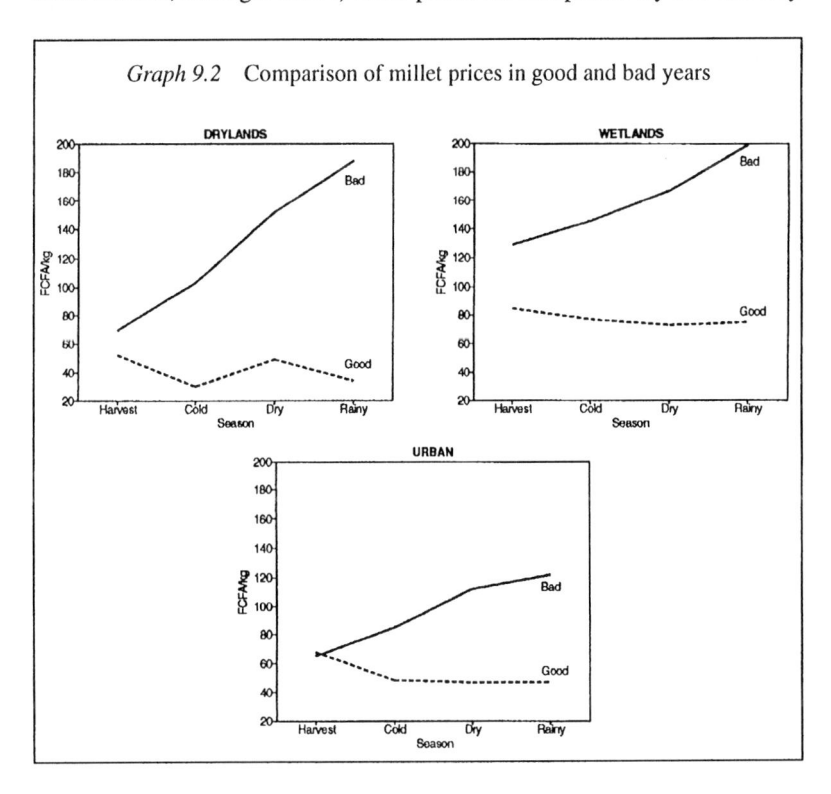

Graph 9.2 Comparison of millet prices in good and bad years

later (to meet their cereal needs) when they are high. In good years, when they have sufficient cereals for most of their own consumption and may have enough to diversify their investments, they face a falling or static market. For agro-pastoralists, bad years and high millet prices imply a total reliance on the sale of their animals to provide their cereal needs, especially in the dry and rainy seasons. In good years, their crops will suffice for their subsistence and they can concentrate on building up their herds. For transhumant pastoralists, the degree to which they have to sell animals will depend crucially on the price of livestock and dairy products (see below), whilst in good years, access to cereals should be relatively easy. For agro-fishers and transhumants, the price of fish will be crucial for their access to cereals in bad years; in good years, their own production will suffice for most of their needs, especially during the fishing campaign, leaving them free to invest in equipment and other goods for insurance against bad years.

Comparing urban and rural millet prices in good and bad years, wetland (retail) prices are higher than urban (wholesale) ones in all years. Urban prices remain more stable in good years than rural ones, the latter falling as people sell millet locally. Millet sales in the wetlands are much lower than in the drylands because of rice production, and the comparatively high density of population, especially in the cold and dry seasons, keeps demand buoyant even in the good year. Dryland producers lose when they are selling (in the harvest and cold seasons of the good year) when prices are 42 per cent lower than on urban markets, and have to pay 45 per cent more than urban (wholesale) prices when they are buying (in the dry and rainy seasons of the bad year).

Goats. Graph 9.3 shows the dynamic of livestock movements into and out of the Delta at different seasons: when goats are in dryland pastures during the rainy and harvest seasons they are cheaper there and more expensive in the Delta, and when they have moved onto the floodplains in the cold and dry seasons, their wetland price falls while their dryland price rises. The data generally confirm that in good years prices of livestock rise, as producers try and regenerate their herds, either through natural increase or acquisition. Cultivators evidently face adverse terms of trade in good years when they are looking to invest in livestock, especially in view of the price of cereals in good and bad years. Agro-pastoralists benefit in good years from the high prices their animals command, but face severely adverse terms of trade in bad years. Although agro-fishers and transhumants seek to diversify by investing in goats in secure livelihood systems, they have few opportunities to do this in present-day vulnerable ones. In most seasons on both rural markets,

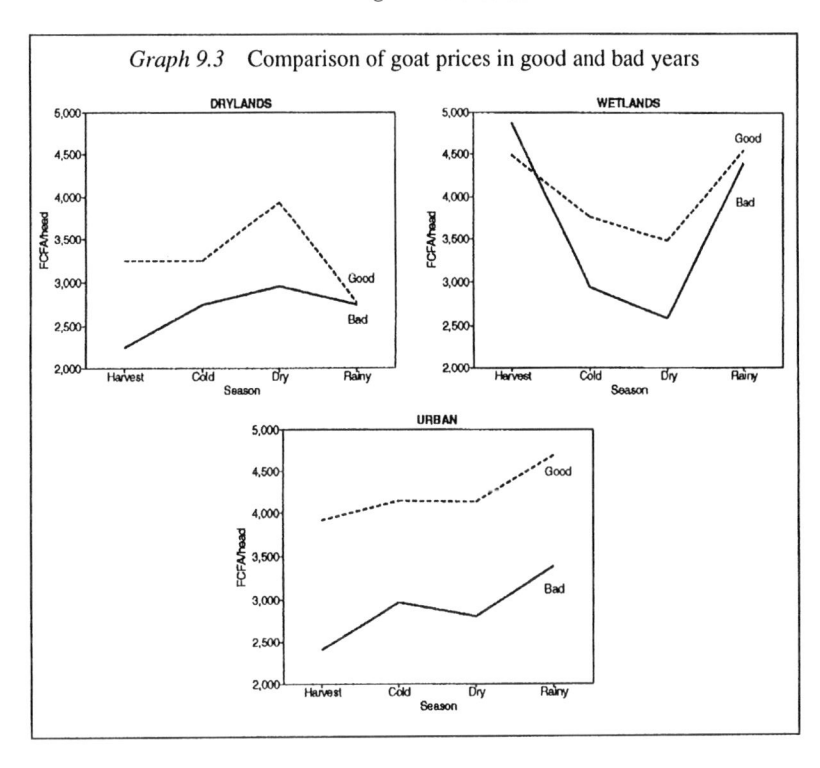

Graph 9.3 Comparison of goat prices in good and bad years

prices are lower than on urban ones. The exception is wetland markets in bad years, when prices are higher than or equivalent to urban ones, indicating that selling goats on those rural markets remains a relatively favourable exchange. This is also true in the harvest season of the good year in wetland markets. In dryland markets in bad years, rural goat prices are on average 93 per cent of urban ones and this falls to 78 per cent in the good year. The figures for wetland markets are 128 per cent in the bad year and 96 per cent in the good one.

Cattle. Graph 9.4 shows that in bad years cattle prices rise in the harvest and cold seasons and then fall off sharply in the dry and rainy ones. The harvest and cold seasons are the times of the year when cereals are relatively plentiful, and pastoralists can obtain them largely by bartering milk, meaning that few animals come on to the market. In 1987–8 it was not in fact a bad year for cattle owners as pasture production was average; the fall in prices in the dry season and during the rains reflects the need to sell animals and buy cereals. In good years the pattern reverses; prices fall in

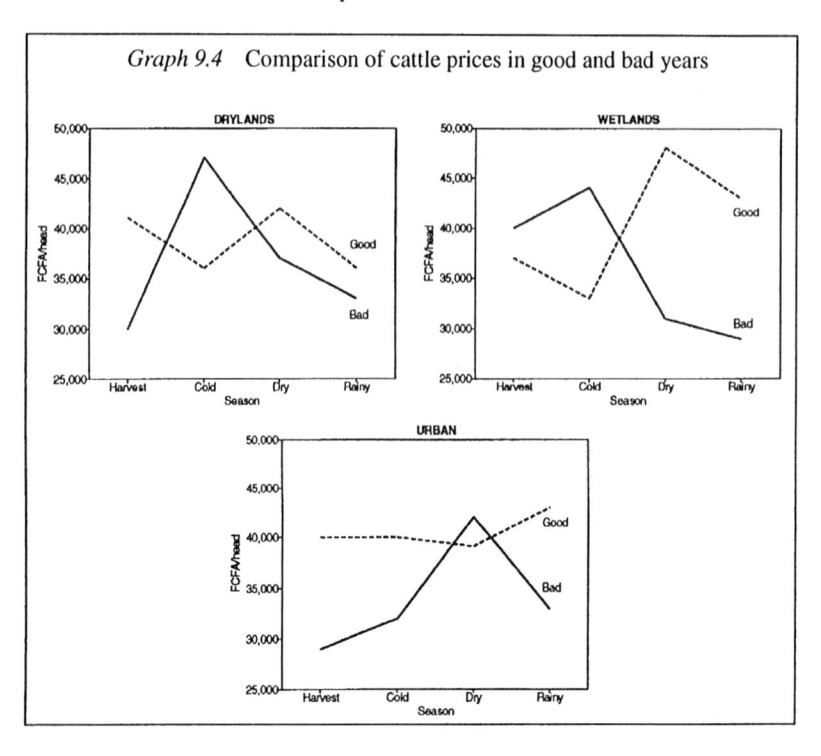

Graph 9.4 Comparison of cattle prices in good and bad years

the harvest and cold seasons because more animals come on to the market, as herders see the rate of reproduction of their herds will be higher. In the dry season, they will have sold enough animals, and bartered enough cereals for dairy products, not to have to sell their animals, so prices rise. Finally, prices fall in the rainy season as animals (and traders) move to distant markets. In the drylands, rural cattle prices peak in the cold season of the bad year and fall thereafter, when distress sales begin and animals depart on transhumance with the onset of the next year's rains. In the wetlands, cattle prices are highest in the dry season of the good year when there are no sales of any significance, whereas they fall in the same season of the bad year during distress sales. In urban markets, prices do not fall in the bad year until the onset of the rains (when sales drop off). For herders, 1987–8 was not a particularly bad year, as confirmed by no sign of large-scale urban distress sales in the dry season. In good years, prices do not rise as high on urban markets as on rural ones, increasing only in the rains when animals are scarce. This may be due to reduced international demand, discussed above.

Milk. Graph 9.5 shows that in both drylands and wetlands, milk prices are better in good years than bad, reflecting the extent to which they depend on disposable income. Prices are low in the harvest season when milk is plentiful, as well as in the rains; as production declines in the cold and dry seasons, so prices rise to their highest point, just before the animals leave on transhumance. Urban milk prices show no significant difference in good and bad years, possibly because dairy herds are now stationed around Mopti all year round to meet urban demand, fuelled by the setting up of *Kossam* Mopti, a milk retailing venture, at the beginning of 1989. Transhumant pastoralists' response to this guaranteed source of demand has been to expand the size of the milk herd (*dounti*) which stays in the Delta, whilst the bulk of the herd (*garti*) goes on transhumance in the rainy season.[4] Milk herds are tended by women who are shifting their activities away from bartering milk in villages (and, in the case of agro-pastoral houscholds, cultivating), towards supplying milk to the urban market. This results in much larger concentrations of herds around Mopti all year round than in the past. This tendency has been further exacerbated

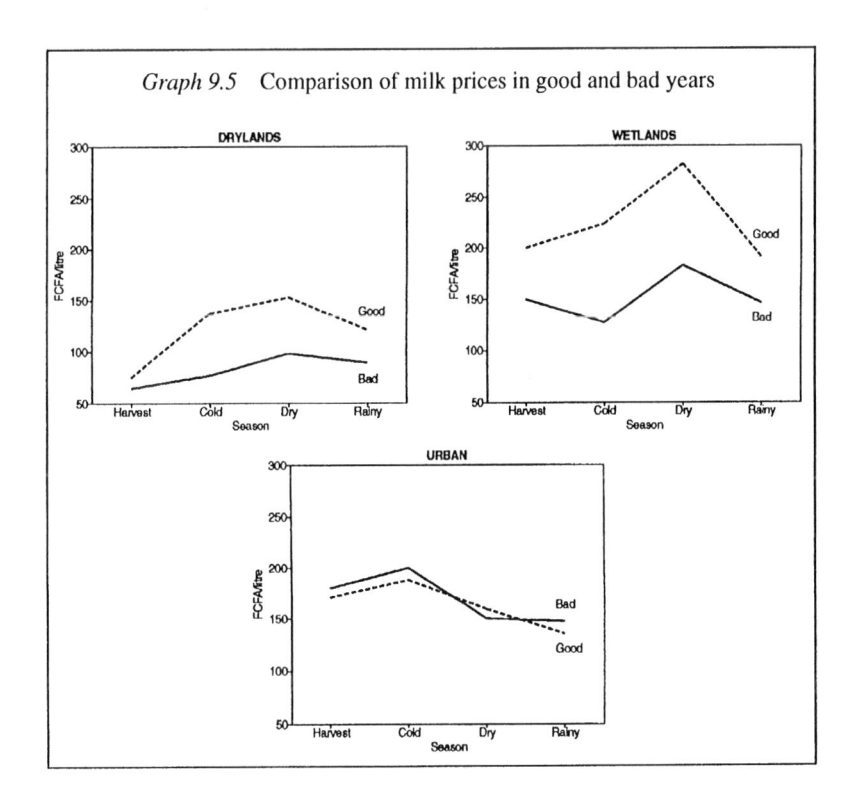

Graph 9.5 Comparison of milk prices in good and bad years

since 1990 by the insecurity in the drylands around the Delta, which has discouraged herders from leaving on transhumance.

Fish. Fish is the only product *sold* by producers which increases in value in a bad year, particularly in those seasons when fish is plentiful (at the end of the harvest season, and during the cold and dry ones). Graph 9.6 shows that in the bad year prices fall from the dry to rainy season in wetland markets, possibly reflecting the fact that many more people turn to fishing in bad years in order to get access to cereals, and that agro-fishers in particular, seeing their crop is likely to fail, intensify their fishing effort. On urban markets prices rise throughout the year, but less sharply in the bad year than in the good. *Per capita* fish production is lower in bad years than good (both because overall fish production is lower and because more people turn to fishing in bad years), which offsets the apparent gains of the bad year. Rural fish prices are consistently lower than urban ones, averaging 65 per cent of urban ones (not taking account of transport costs) in both the bad and the good year, indicating that fishing is a robust strategy in bad years as rural–urban terms of trade do not decline. Urban prices are almost double those in the wetlands by the rainy season of the bad year, due to the difficulties in transporting fish from the Delta to Mopti at this time.

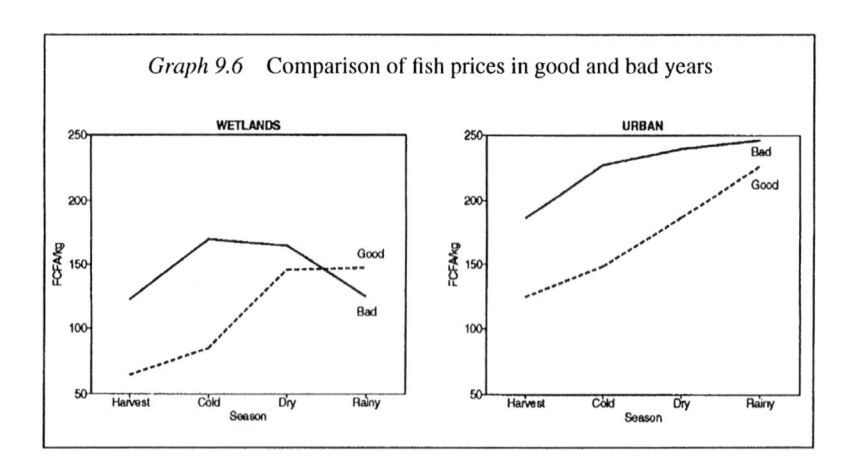

Graph 9.6 Comparison of fish prices in good and bad years

TERMS OF TRADE

This section looks at the terms of trade on which different producers depend over the four-year period. It is these, rather than actual prices, which dictate the exchange entitlements of producers. The exception to this is the 'cash/millet' exchange on which undiversified producers depend, as they have no choice but to earn cash to purchase cereals or to sell millet to meet cash needs (e.g. when repaying debts after the harvest). All terms of trade are calculated on the basis of the number of kilograms of millet which can be purchased for the sale of one unit (kilogram of fish; litre of milk; or head of livestock). It will be recalled from Table 9.1 that, at certain moments in the year (e.g. after the harvest), the exchange may be reversed (i.e. the sale of millet to purchase other goods).

Cultivators and agro-pastoralists. In addition to millet/cash exchanges, these producers depend on millet for goat exchanges for their food security. Graph 9.7 graphically illustrates the pattern of the four-year period of a bad year followed by one good one and two satisfactory/bad ones. In the drylands, the terms of trade peaked in the cold season of 1988–9 at 108.3 kg of millet for one goat and were lowest in the rainy season of 1987–8 at 14.6. The equivalent figures for the wetland market are 60.3 in the rainy season of 1988–9 and 12.4 in the rainy season of 1989–90, followed by 15.5 in the dry season of 1987–8. The overall trend confirms the declining effectiveness of the strategy of investing in goats as

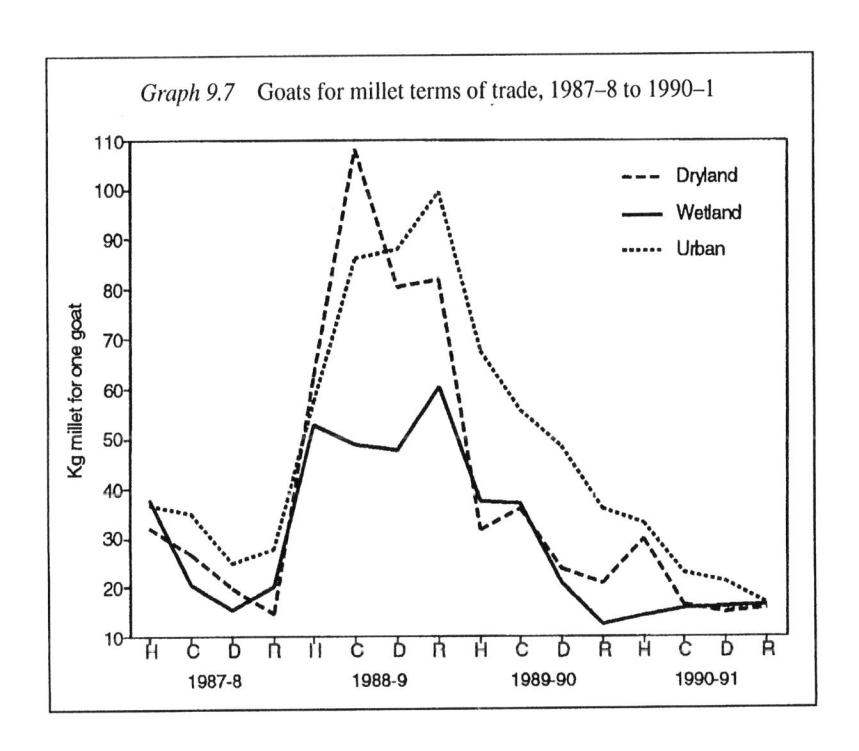

Graph 9.7 Goats for millet terms of trade, 1987–8 to 1990–1

an insurance against high millet prices in a bad year. For, although 1987–8 was universally accepted as being a worse year than 1990–1, this strategy was on average 16 per cent less profitable at the end of the period on dryland markets, and 34 per cent less profitable on wetland ones. Goats for millet terms of trade are consistently lower in rural markets than in urban ones: over the four-year period, 37 per cent lower on average in wetland markets and 19 per cent lower in dryland markets. Average urban terms of trade are lowest in 1990–1, having declined by an average of 24 per cent over the four years.

Transhumant pastoralists. Transhumant pastoralists rely on a combination of milk for millet exchanges and, when these fail to fill the food gap, cattle for millet ones. In both cases, for drylands and wetlands, the peak of the good year is apparent from Graph 9.8 (cattle for millet) and Graph 9.9 (milk for millet). Cattle for millet terms of trade peaked at 1200 kg of millet for one heifer in the cold season of 1988–9 in the drylands and at 657.5 in the dry season of 1988–9 in the wetlands. The low point in the drylands was 169 in the dry season of 1990–1, and 145.7 in the wetlands during the rainy season of 1987–8. It should, however, be recalled that pastoralists make cattle for millet exchanges only in crisis

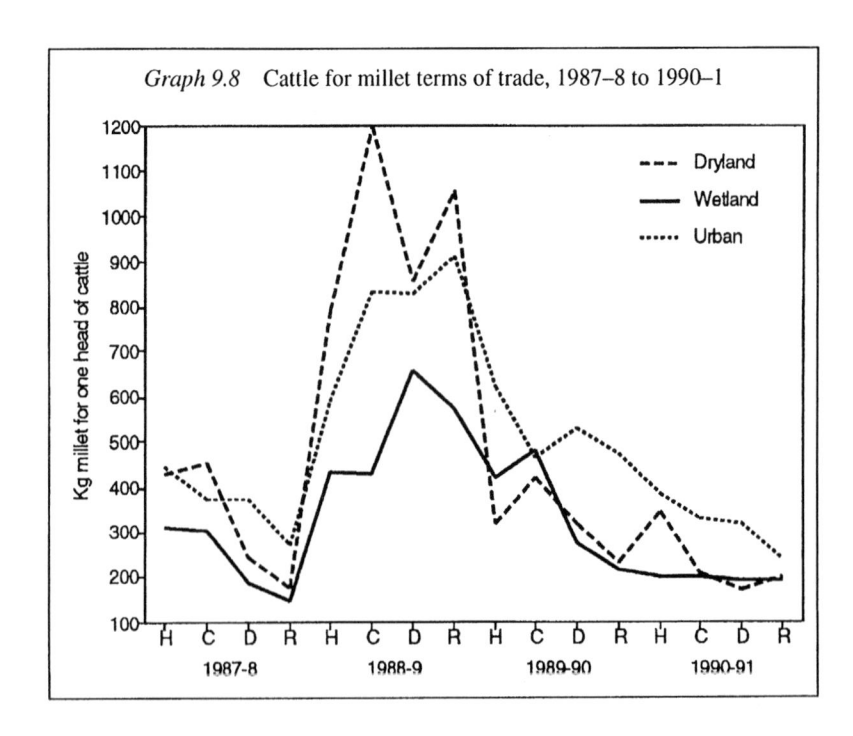

Graph 9.8 Cattle for millet terms of trade, 1987–8 to 1990–1

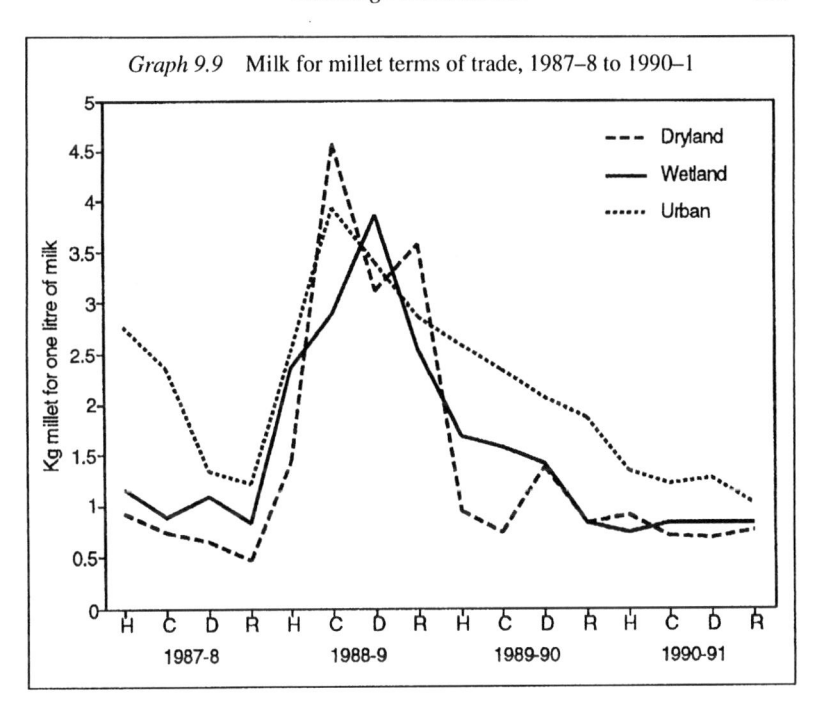

Graph 9.9 Milk for millet terms of trade, 1987–8 to 1990–1

y-axis: Kg millet for one litre of milk

Legend: Dryland (dashed), Wetland (solid), Urban (dotted)

x-axis categories: H C D R for each year 1987-8, 1988-9, 1989-90, 1990-91

years, which neither 1987–8 nor 1990–1 were for the pastoral economy. Dryland terms of trade are higher than urban ones in 1988–9, but otherwise rural exchanges are almost always less favourable than urban ones. Over the four-year period, the terms of trade are, on average, 25 per cent lower on wetland markets than on urban (wholesale) ones and 13 per cent lower on dryland ones. As with goats for millet exchanges undertaken by agro-pastoralists and cultivators, cattle for millet terms of trade for transhumant pastoralists were significantly worse in 1990–1 than in 1987–8, with average annual terms of trade 29 per cent lower at the end of the period in the drylands, 18 per cent lower in the wetlands and 14 per cent lower on urban markets. The lower exchange values at the end of the period can be explained by insecurity in the drylands surrounding the Delta, which meant that normal transhumance routes were disrupted; stranger herds did not move into the Delta in the dry season and indigenous Delta herders did not venture far into the drylands during the rains. Further, as explained above, the advent of *Kossam* Mopti in 1989 has encouraged a concentration of herds around the town, leading to a glut on local markets, and reduced demand in the coastal West African states for Sahelian beef has depressed local markets. Taken together, these elements

220   *Adaptable Livelihoods*

indicate the increasing vulnerability of the livestock economy in the Region.[5]

Milk is traded in significant quantities only in the harvest and cold seasons. The peaks occurred in the cold season of 1988-9 at 4.57 kg of millet for 1 litre of milk in the drylands, and 2.90 in the wetlands. The lowest points were 0.70 in the cold season of 1990-1 in the drylands and 0.73 in the harvest season of the same year in the wetlands, but these were only marginally lower than at the same time in 1987-8 in the drylands. In the wetlands, however, terms of trade were nearly a third lower in the harvest and cold seasons of 1990-1 than at the same time in 1987-8, implying that for wetland herders, the terms of market dependence were significantly worse by the end of the period, despite better overall conditions (in both years, pastoral conditions were satisfactory rather than bad). The factors affecting cattle for millet exchanges have had a similarly depressing effect on wetland milk for millet ones. *Kossam* Mopti, in particular, has altered patterns of supply and demand in the Delta, to the detriment of those pastoralists who still seek to trade in the wetlands rather than stationing themselves around the town, though even there, they are adversely affected. Over the four years, urban terms of trade are on average about 50 per cent more favourable than rural exchanges, but the profitability of urban milk for millet exchanges has declined by nearly 40 per cent over the period, again due to the effects of *Kossam* Mopti. More stable exchanges in the drylands can be explained by fewer changes to established patterns of local supply and demand for milk. Beyond Douentza, where dryland prices were collected, the local herding economy had been severely disrupted by conflict by the end of the period.

Agro-fishers and transhumant fishers. All fishers rely principally on fish for millet exchanges. Graph 9.10 shows that the critical months are the cold and dry seasons; wetland terms of trade peaked in the dry season of 1988-9 at 2 kg of millet for 1 kg of fish and were lowest in the dry season of 1990-1 at 0.69, compared with a low of 0.99 in 1987-8. As with other products, over the four-year period, the strategy of exchanging fish for millet has not resulted in improved or stable terms of trade. The downward trend coupled with falling *per capita* fish catches indicates that, although fish for millet exchanges are profitable in good years, as a strategy for bad years they are decreasingly so, as more and more people turn to fishing. Over the four-year period, the rural terms of trade are, on average, less than half those on urban markets (not taking account of transport costs). Selling on rural rather than urban markets cost fishers nearly twice as much in 1990-1 as in 1987-8, indicating the tightening debt-induced grip of the Mopti fish traders and their agents in rural markets, as well as the increasingly oligopolistic structure of large-scale fish trading in Mopti.

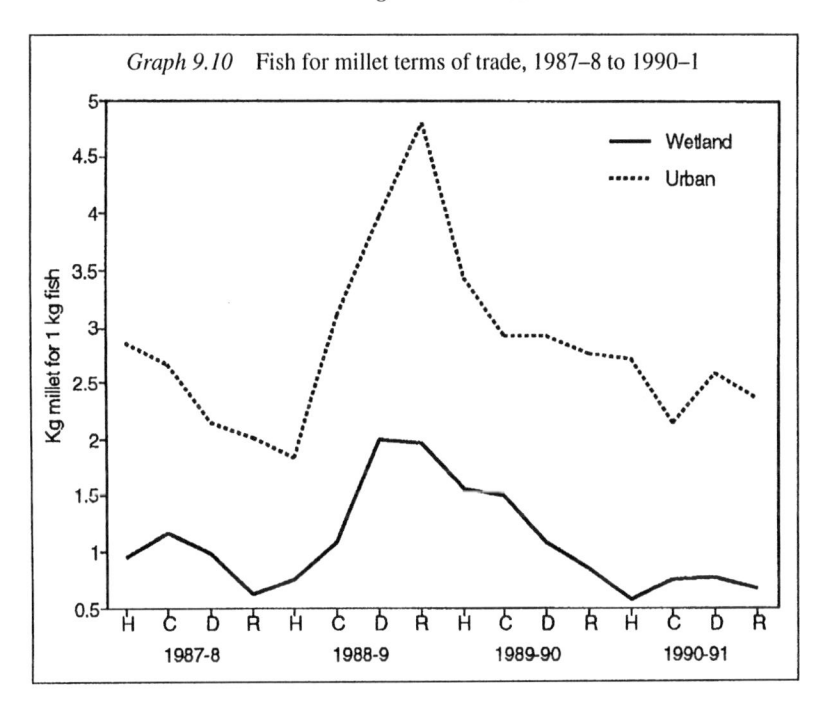

Graph 9.10 Fish for millet terms of trade, 1987–8 to 1990–1

Terms of trade in good and bad years

This section re-examines the above data by comparing terms of trade in good (1988–9) and bad (1987–8) years. Even though the preceding section has argued that the worst year from a terms of trade point of view was 1990–1, in terms of overall food-security conditions based on a range of indicators 1987–8 remains the worst year (Chapter 7). The declining value of key terms of trade over the period nevertheless indicates that, in the event of a very bad year now, the tendencies shown for 1987–8 would be greatly intensified.

Cultivators and agro-pastoralists. Exchanging goats for millet is the key market exchange for cultivators and agro-pastoralists in bad years. Graph 9.11 shows the high cost of this strategy, given that, in the good year, the objective is to reverse the transfer and sell millet in order to buy goats. These exchanges take place in the harvest, cold and dry seasons when, for dryland producers in particular, the terms of trade are consistently unfavourable. Thus when acquiring millet in the bad year, a goat will only provide 19.5 kg of millet in the dry season; when trying to regain this goat the following year in the cold season, 108.3 kg of millet must be sold. Wetland producers benefit from much lower adverse swings in good

Graph 9.11 Comparison of goats for millet terms of trade in good and bad years

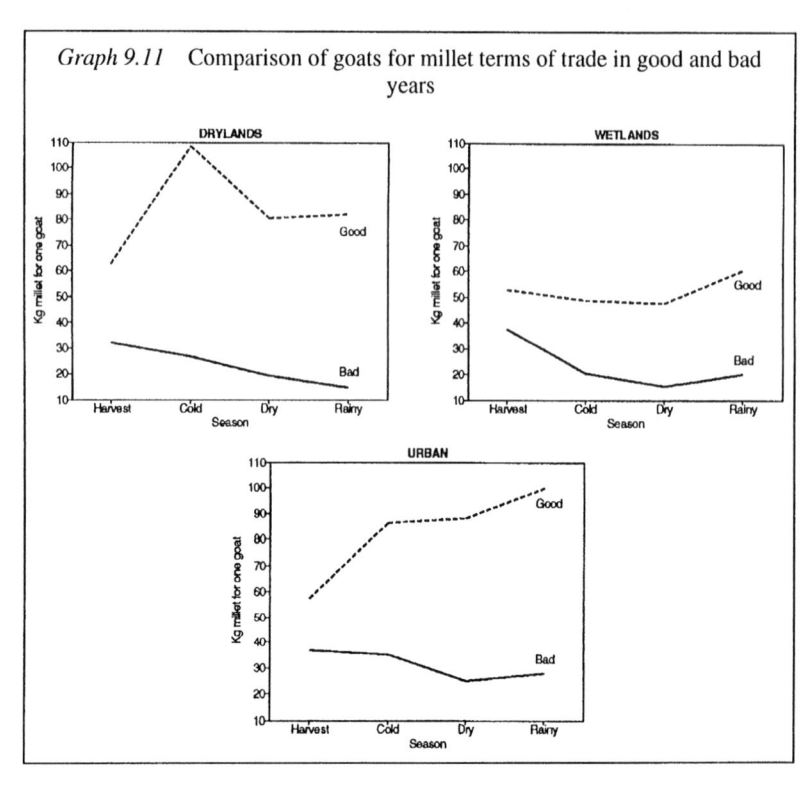

years (the terms of trade average about 50 kg of millet for one goat when they are restocking), whereas in bad years the terms of trade are comparable in both markets. For dryland producers, the terms of trade become increasingly unfavourable on rural markets compared with urban ones as the bad year progresses. In contrast, in the good year when they are trying to buy goats to accumulate (in the harvest and cold seasons) rural terms of trade swing against them. They are consequently disadvantaged by trading on rural markets in both good and bad years. Wetland producers are also always better-off trading in urban markets: for them prices rise in both good and bad years to near parity with urban ones at harvest time (when they are, in fact, exchanging rice for goats). Later on in the dry and cold seasons, when they need to sell goats to buy the cheapest staple (millet), trading on rural markets costs them 67 per cent more in the bad year than urban trade, compared with 81 per cent more in the good year.

Transhumant pastoralists. Graph 9.12 shows that in a bad year, sales of cattle would be highest in the cold and dry seasons, only escalating in the rainy season if the subsequent rains fail. In the two years in question, the

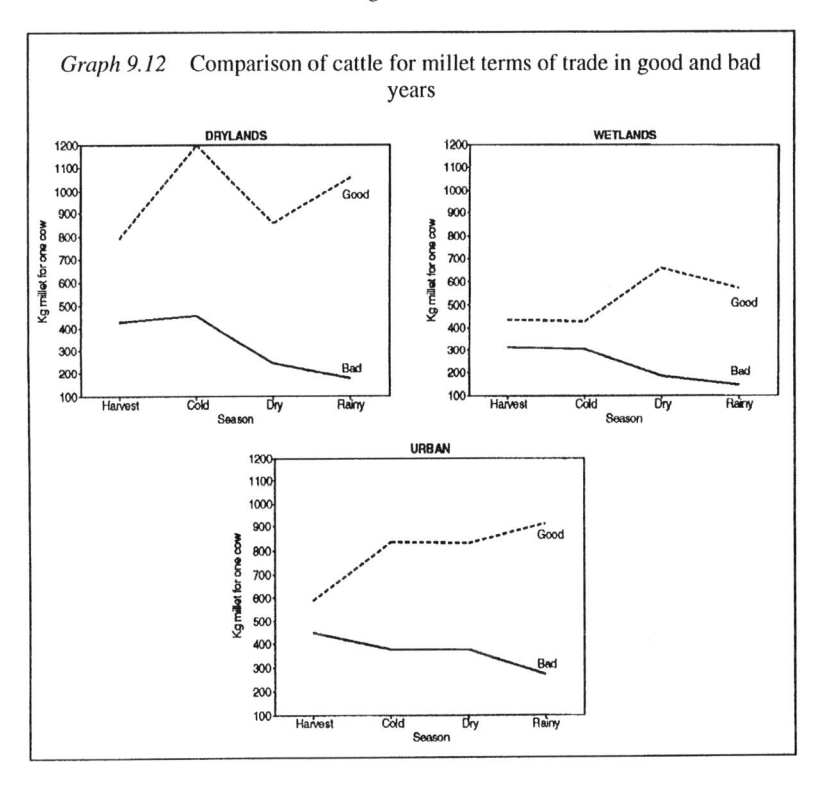

Graph 9.12 Comparison of cattle for millet terms of trade in good and bad years

middle rainy season (i.e. at the end of the bad year) was in fact excellent. In dryland markets, the terms of trade peak in the cold season of the good year at 1200 kg of millet for one heifer, and fall to a low of 243.4 kg in the dry season of the bad year when herders are destocking to acquire millet. The continuing fall at the end of the bad year is explained not by distress sales, but by inactive markets when animals are on transhumance. The pattern for the bad year is similar on wetland markets but, as in the case of goats, the terms of trade do not move so adversely against pastoralists in the good year. Wetland terms of trade thus peak at 657.5 kg in the dry season of the good year, and fall to a low of 185.6 kg in the dry season of the bad year. Given that in practice they do not exchange cattle for millet in good years, this is less significant than in the case of goats. Comparing rural and urban markets, for dryland pastoralists exchanging on rural markets in bad years is marginally less profitable than urban trade, but in good years they are nearly 25 per cent better-off exchanging on rural markets. When pasture conditions are good, rural markets in the drylands thus work to the advantage of herders; the trouble is, they do not tend to sell animals at this time. Wetland herders, in contrast, are always better-off trading on the urban market.

Turning to the terms of trade between milk and millet, Graph 9.13 demonstrates a similar pattern of terms of trade moving in the same direction in dryland and wetland markets in bad years, but being more favourable for dryland pastoralists in good years than for wetland ones. Again, pastoralists do not switch from selling to buying milk, so the terms of trade are highly favourable in good years. In the drylands, the terms of trade peak in the cold season of the good year. They are lowest in the rainy season of the bad year, explained by the good 1987–8 rains (and hence abundant milk supplies), coupled with high millet prices. Pasture conditions at the end of 1988–9 were not as good (hence there was less milk) and millet was cheaper. Comparing the terms of trade for the strategic seasons in which milk is exchanged for millet (harvest and cold), the terms of trade were three and a half times more favourable in the good year than the bad on dryland markets and two and a half times better on

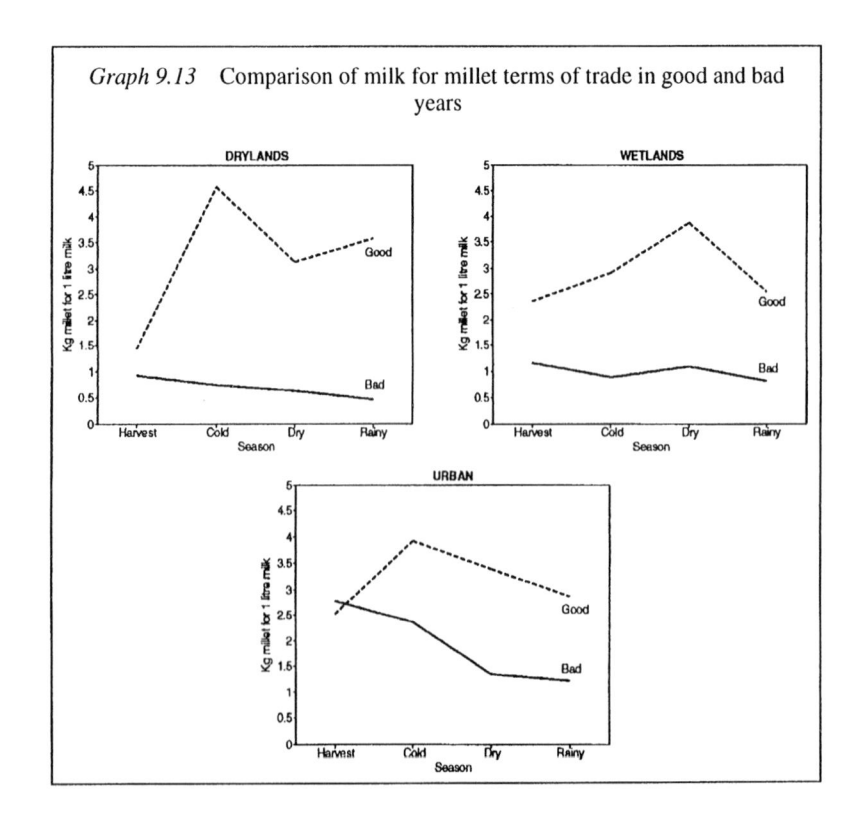

Graph 9.13 Comparison of milk for millet terms of trade in good and bad years

wetland ones. Differences on urban markets are less marked, with an increase of around 25 per cent in the good year. Urban terms of trade are 22 per cent higher than on wetland markets in the good year and more or less the same on dryland ones. In contrast, in the bad year, the urban terms of trade are more than two and a half times those on wetland markets and nearly four times those on dryland ones, indicating that, in bad years, dryland producers in particular can benefit greatly from selling on urban markets. This strategy is especially difficult where milk is concerned, because it cannot be stored for long periods and pastoralists need to sell milk close to where animals are herded.

Agro-fishers and transhumant fishers. The key terms of trade for fishers are fish for millet, shown in Graph 9.14. The key months are November to March. It is thus late harvest and especially cold and dry season prices which determine fishers' access to food. The fish for millet terms of trade vary less between good and bad years than for other products, increasing by around 45 per cent on both wetland and urban markets in good years. This is because, as explained above, fish is more expensive in bad years, in contrast to the other goods which people sell to acquire millet. Actual revenue from fishing is lower, however, because the quantity of fish caught falls in a bad year. The difference in trading on rural rather than urban markets hardly varies between good and bad years, in contrast to other key terms of trade, with rural terms of trade remaining at around 44 per cent of urban ones. Demand for fish in good and bad years alike is determined by the presence of fish exporters in Mopti, whose trading strategies are based much less on local conditions than those of other urban traders.

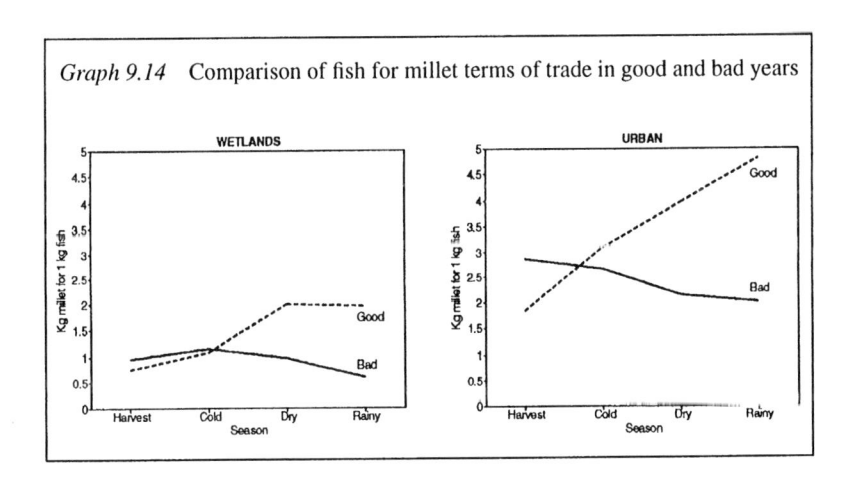

Graph 9.14 Comparison of fish for millet terms of trade in good and bad years

CONDIMENTS

Condiments, whilst not primary products and hence not part of the key terms of trade, nevertheless constitute an essential item of food expenditure and provide vital vitamins and minerals for local diets. Prices were collected for a representative basket of condiments necessary to make the sauce eaten with either millet or rice (salt, oil, baobab leaves and *soumbala*, a local ingredient made of dried onions and leaves), plus tea and sugar. Fish and meat are not included in the index as, in times of food shortage, sauce would be made without either. Urban retail not wholesale condiment prices are analysed, because rural producers buy at retail prices on urban markets to resell in rural markets as a coping strategy (i.e. diversifying into small-scale commerce). They rarely have the capital to buy large quantities from wholesalers.

Dryland condiment prices over the four-year period are, on average, 11 per cent higher than urban ones, and wetland prices 33 per cent higher, reflecting transport costs. Condiment prices fluctuate much less than other goods between years, possibly because of the increase in the number of very small-scale traders on local markets, with the result that margins are falling as competition increases. This coping strategy, often pursued by women and already guaranteeing only very small profit margins, is becoming less profitable over the period. The difference in price between buying on urban markets for resale on dryland ones declined from an average of 20 per cent in 1987-8 to 5 per cent in 1990-1 and in wetland markets from 39 per cent to 25 per cent. Again, these margins do not take account of transport costs, which further reduce margins.

Prices in good and bad years. Graph 9.15 shows that on urban markets, prices rise sharply in the dry and rainy seasons of the bad year and fall to a stable but higher level in the good year. This sharp rise may be explained by an increase in the demand for urban condiments for resale in retail markets as a coping strategy in the bad year. On dryland markets, there is a similar rise in the dry season of the bad year, but this stabilises for the rest of the period thereafter, with one season (cold in the good year) going against the trend. In wetland markets, the pattern is much more stable in both years, after an initial rise in the cold season of the bad year. In both dryland and wetland markets, price rises in the bad year coincide with high staple food prices and an early start to the hungry season; at the beginning of the bad year condiment prices were significantly higher than in urban markets, but as more condiments were purchased on local markets for resale, the difference declines until the end of the year, recovering slightly at the beginning of the good year but overall remaining lower than at the

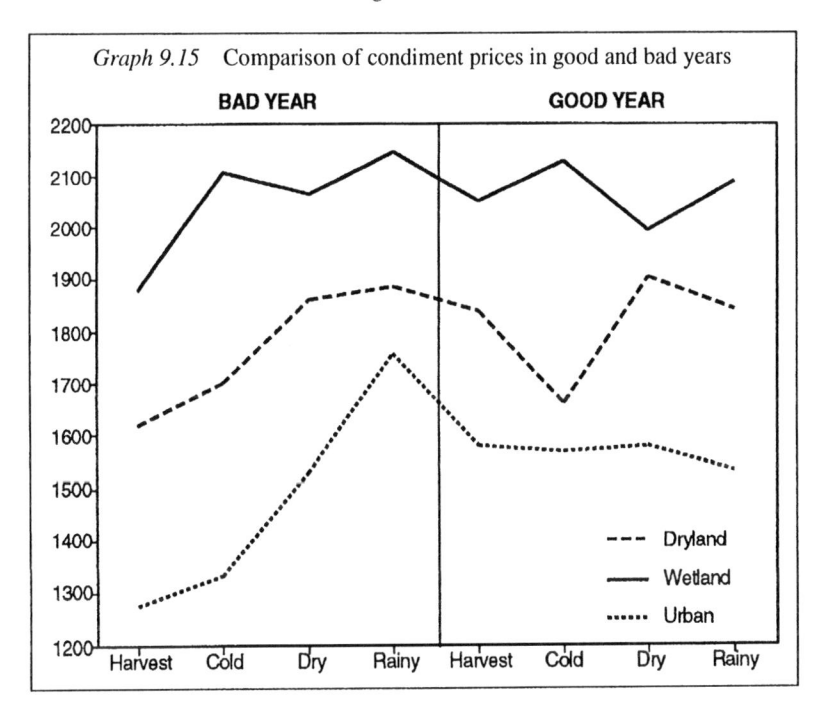

Graph 9.15 Comparison of condiment prices in good and bad years

beginning of the period. This suggests that the increase in small-scale retail trade in the dry and rainy seasons of the bad year continued in the good year, albeit at a reduced level, but above that of the beginning of the period. This has the effect of reducing the margin of profitability for retailers. For those buying condiments for subsistence, the cost of buying on rural rather than urban markets averaged 20 per cent more in the bad year on dryland markets and 39 per cent more on wetland ones, compared with 16 per cent and 32 per cent in the good year. For those attempting to subsist on a daily basis, these apparently quite small differences are significant. In times of extreme food stress, the staple is consumed without sauce.

OTHER PRODUCTS

Data were collected on a number of other products to see if monitoring their presence and price on the market would be good indicators of the effectiveness of coping mechanisms. Table 9.3 shows the frequency with which wild foods appeared on markets in good and bad years, by season,

Table 9.3 Frequency with which wild foods appear on markets

Market/wild food	Bad year (1987–8)				Good year (1988–9)			
	Harvest	Cold	Dry	Rainy	Harvest	Cold	Dry	Rainy
Wetland markets								
Fonio		▓	▓					
Water-lilies[a]		▓	▓	▓	▓	▓	▓	
Bourgou[b]				▓	▓			
Dryland markets								
Fonio	▓							

Notes: [a] Not available in dryland areas.
[b] Grains and grass, depending on the season.

Exchange Entitlements 229

and indicates that in both dryland and wetland markets, only the number of sellers or the quantity of such foods could differentiate between good and bad years. The exception to this is the absence of *fonio* in wetland markets in the bad year, explained by the shortage in the drylands leading to an insufficient surplus to sell on wetland markets. No consistent pattern emerged on the number of sellers of wild foods. Equally, prices either shadowed the price of millet (in the case of *fonio*) or did not fluctuate substantially, the only exception being *bourgou* grass, which increased significantly in value in the bad year when it was purchased by agropastoralists and transhumant pastoralists for fodder.

Price data were also collected for mats woven from doum palm, as an indicator of the most frequently sold artisanal manufacture, particularly in times of food stress. At the beginning, mat prices were more or less the same in dryland and wetland markets, but over the four years, wetland prices rose on average 28 per cent above dryland prices, reflecting demand from the fishing trade which purchases large quantities for packing fish. In dryland markets, the average price fell by 52 per cent over the period, but by only 3 per cent on wetland markets (although this latter figure disguises inter-annual variations). For dryland producers in particular, this is becoming an increasingly uneconomic activity and for wetland ones, it is dependent on high demand from the fish trade. On dryland markets, prices are on average 11 per cent higher in good years than bad, but in wetlands the difference is 47 per cent, reflecting the increased demand in a good fishing campaign.

Graph 9.16, comparing mats for millet terms of trade over the four years, shows that the strategy is least effective when it is most needed. At the beginning of the period, dryland terms of trade averaged 2.77, compared with 1.96 in the wetlands, but by 1990–1 both averaged 1.79, principally explained by the saturation of the mat market in the drylands.

Graph 9.17 compares the terms of trade in good and bad years, to see the effectiveness of making mats to sell in order to purchase millet as a coping strategy. The terms of trade swing strongly against producers in bad years on both dryland and wetland markets, falling to an average of only 1.9 in the dry and rainy seasons of the bad year (the moment when millet purchases are highest). For wetland mat sellers the greatest demand comes during the fishing campaign, when the terms of trade averaged 6.1 in the good year, compared with only 1.9 in the bad one. Although the terms of trade recover dramatically in a good year, particularly in the wetlands, mats are a highly labour-intensive activity, not pursued if other coping strategies are available.

230   *Adaptable Livelihoods*

Graph 9.16 Mats for millet terms of trade, 1987–8 to 1990–1

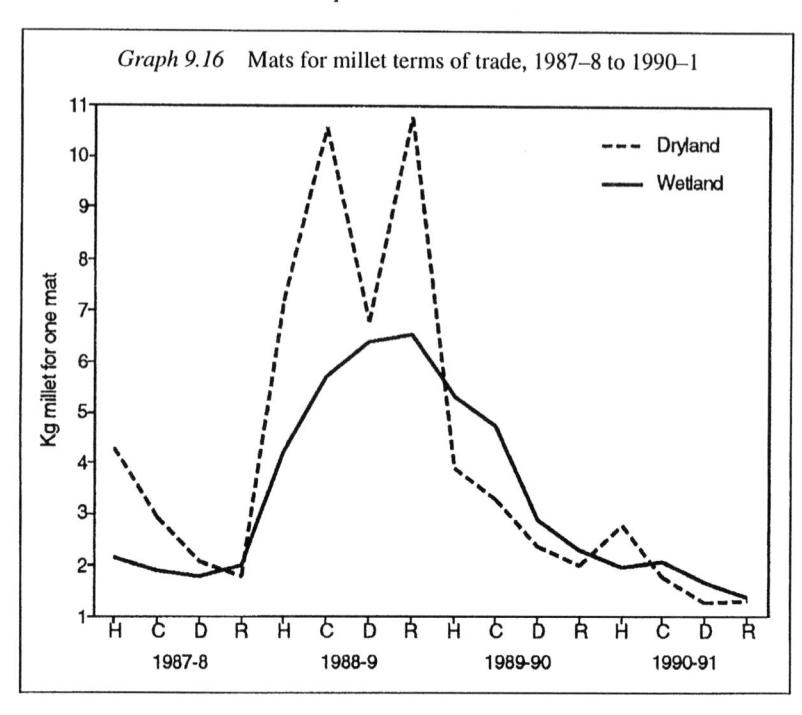

Graph 9.17 Comparison of mats for millet terms of trade in good and bad years

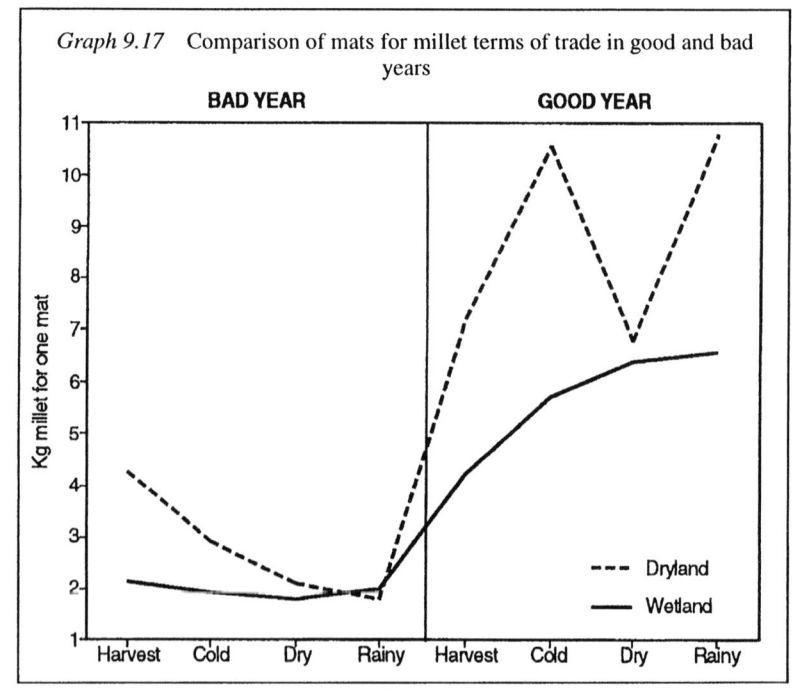

LEVELS OF MARKET ACTIVITY

This section considers data for the number of traders by sector on rural markets, which serve as partial indicators of levels of market activity. Data are available for three years (1988–9 to 1990–1); the indicative bad year used is 1990–1. The number of traders clearly indicates only one side of the level of market activity: it was not possible to estimate numbers of people attending the market. 'Market activity' throughout the section therefore refers only to the number of traders, but includes inhabitual traders, producers who were temporarily moving into petty commerce as a coping strategy. This group is principally represented in the category of wood and condiment sellers.

In the dryland market, the number of traders increased by over 50 per cent over the period, whereas in wetland markets it declined by about 30 per cent. The dramatic increase in the size of Douentza market may be due to more easterly markets being disrupted by conflict. Wetland markets, in contrast, have shrunk as the Delta has become more insecure, particularly in the low water seasons when access from the drylands is easier. Wetland market figures include fish traders, accounting for 23 per cent of traders at the beginning of the period and 19 per cent at the end.

Levels of market activity in good and bad years

Graph 9.18 shows the number of traders by category (cereals; livestock, butchers and fish; and wood and condiments) and season in dryland and wetland markets in good and bad years respectively. The livestock/butchers/fish category indicates the demand for goods derived from secondary activities, supply of which increases in years when the cereal harvest fails. The wood/condiments category indicates the level of coping strategy-based sales: it is producers turning to small-scale commerce which swell this category.

Cereal traders. In the dryland market, the number of cereal traders remains more or less stable throughout the good year, but in the bad year is both higher overall (by 108 per cent) and increases by 18 per cent as the year progresses. The higher level of activity in a bad year is explained by constant cereal purchases throughout the year, rising as the hungry season progresses. There is no evidence of supply collapsing on the basis of this indicator. The stability of cereal traders in the good year may be explained by post-harvest sales, including the need to sell to pay fiscal dues,

232 Adaptable Livelihoods

Graph 9.18 Comparison of number of traders in good and bad years

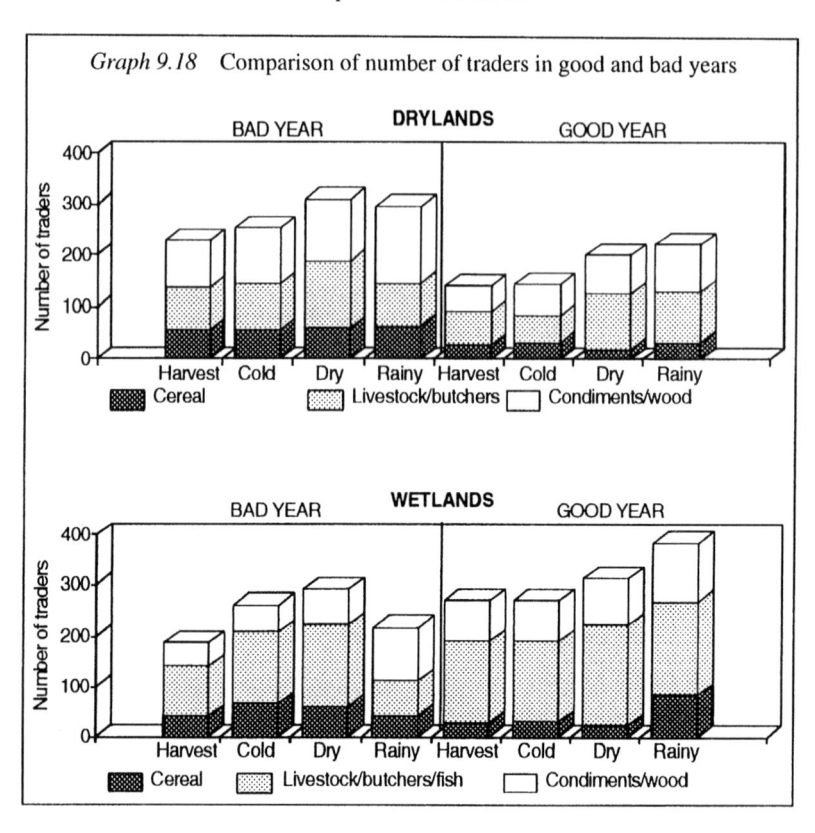

DRYLANDS — BAD YEAR / GOOD YEAR; categories: Harvest, Cold, Dry, Rainy; series: Cereal, Livestock/butchers, Condiments/wood.

WETLANDS — BAD YEAR / GOOD YEAR; categories: Harvest, Cold, Dry, Rainy; series: Cereal, Livestock/butchers/fish, Condiments/wood.

balanced by purchases later in the year. In the wetland market, the number of cereal traders is less stable than in the drylands. At the end of the good year, it increases significantly, explained by traders coming into the Delta from the south to sell millet from stocks liquidated before the next harvest. In the bad year, numbers are highest in the cold and dry seasons, falling off in the rainy season, when supplies from the south do not increase as stocks have already been exhausted, and when transport becomes difficult and expensive. Nevertheless, as in dryland markets, there is no indication of a breakdown in supply. It is worth recalling that in the wetlands, fish traders also sell cereals as part of their vertically integrated strategies.

Livestock traders, butchers, and fish traders. In dryland markets, overall levels of livestock traders and butchers are 15 per cent higher in the bad year than in the good one, but this masks seasonal variations. In the bad year, the number of traders rises sharply in the cold season (80 per cent higher than in the good year) and is 20 per cent higher in the dry season, indicating early distress sales to purchase cereals and possibly a lack of goats left to sell by the dry season. In the good year, the number of traders increases in the dry season and remains high in the rainy season, indicating restocking in a good year and reflecting the satisfactory (rather than good) rains at the end of the good year. In wetland markets, there is evidence of high levels of market activity at the beginning of the good year, when producers were able to invest surplus in livestock. Numbers of traders increase again sharply in the dry season, as in the drylands, falling back in the rains. In the bad year, numbers of traders rise later in the cold season and peak in the dry one but at a lower level than in the good year, falling to almost nothing in the rains. This year appears to go against the expected trend, explained almost certainly by the disruption of livestock transhumance routes and marketing circuits by conflict in the area in 1991. Overall, the number of traders is 31 per cent less in the bad year than in the good one, due to reduced overall levels of livestock trading caused by disrupted markets.

Fish traders are also included in this category in wetland markets, where there were nearly twice as many in the good year as the bad one. There is little seasonality in the presence of local fish traders (in contrast to Mopti, where exporters come specifically for the fishing campaign), due to the intensification of fishing for longer and longer periods in the wetlands, as well as the multiple functions which fish traders fulfil: when they are not buying fish, they are supplying cereals and credit, and still collecting repayment of the latter.

Condiment and wood traders. Increases in the number of condiment sellers are an indication of producers engaging in a coping strategy. The same is true for wood traders, although in wetland markets this is also conditioned by demand for wood to smoke fish at the height of the fishing campaign (from the late harvest season until the dry season). In dryland markets, there were 71 per cent more condiment and wood sellers in the bad year than in the good one, all of them selling condiments not wood. A decline in wood sales may be explained by people cooking less, and certainly because they were gathering their own fuel rather than purchasing it. On wetland markets, the reverse is true: there were 33 per cent more condiment and wood sellers in the good year than the bad. This difference is entirely accounted for by a fall in wood traders, as numbers of condiment sellers remained more or less constant. The drop may be due to reduced demand with a poor fishing campaign. Unlike in the drylands, condiment selling does not appear to be an important strategy for wetland producers in bad years, although, again, market disruptions may explain the low figure in the bad year.

CONCLUSIONS: INDICATORS OF EXCHANGE ENTITLEMENTS

On the basis of the results presented, there can be little doubt of the utility of collecting market data from which to derive indicators of food stress in vulnerable livelihood systems, where increasing market dependence means that producers are forced to turn to the market to subsist. By collecting price data continuously for the key primary and secondary goods produced and traded, on those rural markets on which most rural people exchange, reliable indicators of food stress can be derived. Analysis of these indicators can provide vital insights into both short- and long-term changes in the value of vulnerable people's market exchanges. Short-term changes can be detected by comparing the year in question with recent baseline good and bad years, for which there are clear patterns in the movement of prices and the terms of trade, as well by analysing the seasonal significance of price swings within a given type of year. Longer-term changes can be detected by looking at prices and the terms of trade over time. To this extent, these results confirm the importance attached to market data by most EWS.

The analysis presented here hinges critically on *the terms of trade* in which producers engage, rather than actual prices. The assumption of many EWS that most food-insecure groups exchange cash for the food staple in order to meet food needs, does not adequately reflect the role of the market in vulnerable rural livelihood systems. Exchanging cash for millet is in fact rather an exceptional exchange in rural areas, undertaken only by cultivators who have no goats left to sell or by other producers who have exhausted their other sources of production entitlements. In other words, cash for millet exchanges only occur when cash from income-generating coping strategies is available. Monitoring the price of the food staple is thus potentially a rather late indicator of food stress, whereas monitoring the terms of trade under which most producers exchange can be a much earlier indicator of changes in access to food. Terms of trade can also say much more about the costs to future productive capacity of acquiring food in the short term. If market data are to be early indicators of food stress, and to be at all sensitive to the different levels of vulnerability of distinct livelihood systems and intensification of this, it is essential that the key terms of trade for a given area be identified and that the necessary products are tracked over time. Because key terms of trade shift, particularly from one season to another but also over time, as livelihood systems become increasingly vulnerable, it is vital to know what the *preferred* terms of trade are for producers and the extent to which these are compromised by structural vulnerability (as shown in Table 9.1) and by proximate vulnerability in a particularly bad year, as indicated by the analysis of good and bad years.

Other market indicators monitored produced less clear-cut results. Monitoring mat prices as an indicator of one of the gathered products (doum palm) which people convert into a product for which there is a strong local demand in the Delta (for packing fish), is a useful indicator of the effectiveness of this coping strategy. Other gathered products could not be accurately tracked: wood prices, for example, were hard to monitor accurately, not least because it is the weight of a pile of wood, rather than its price, that is varied.[6] Wild food prices presented no consistent pattern, and even their appearance on markets did not vary significantly in good and bad years. Whilst providing interesting supplementary data to the key terms of trade in so far as their consumption is likely to drop if prices rise sharply and vital vitamins and minerals will therefore be cut from local diets, condiment prices do not constitute a main source of fluctuation in exchange entitlements for rural people.

Measuring the number of traders on local markets can provide a partial indication of levels of market activity, but can say little about how actively local people are buying and selling particular goods. Attempts to estimate the overall level of market activity proved too time-consuming, especially as markets last for most of the day. Numbers of traders were principally a useful indicator of the number of producers turning to small-scale commerce as a coping strategy.

Levels of non-livestock asset disposal have not been analysed here because systematic data on such disposals yielded no discernible pattern of results. This is possibly because many of the kinds of assets habitually handled on markets had already been liquidated in the 1984–5 drought and were not reconstituted by the time data presented here were collected. Further, no year in the study period was a crisis year, which might have seen large-scale disposal of unusual remaining assets. Examples of this (e.g. selling burial urns and important family ornaments) were widespread in 1984–5.

The approach of the SADS system was to monitor the maximum possible number of market indicators, in order to arrive at a more manageable list of indicators. Table 9.4 summarises the data sources and derived indicators which have been analysed in this chapter. Those shown in italics are the most important. These indicators are based on data collected for a relatively small number of prices, although considerably more than in most standard EWS market surveys which tend to concentrate on the prices of staple foods. Data have been analysed for: prices of urban and rural primary and secondary sources of production entitlements (millet,

Table 9.4 Summary of indicators of exchange entitlements

Market data	Indicator
Prices of rural (retail) primary and secondary sources of production entitlements	*Changes in key terms of trade over time* *Key terms of trade in good and bad years* *Seasonal changes in key terms of trade* Changes in prices over time Prices in good and bad years Seasonal price changes
Prices of urban (wholesale) primary and secondary sources of production entitlements	*Changes in urban vs rural key terms of trade over time* *Urban vs rural key terms of trade in good and bad years* *Seasonal changes in urban vs rural key terms of trade* Changes in urban vs rural prices over time Rural vs urban prices in good and bad years Seasonal differences in urban vs rural prices
Rural and urban condiment prices	Prices in good and bad years
Rural gathered product prices	*Changes in terms of trade between gathered products and millet over time* *Terms of trade between gathered products and millet in good and bad years*
Number of traders	*Increase in small-scale trade*
Disposal of other assets	*Unusual asset disposal in bad years*

goats, cattle, milk and fish), condiment prices and gathered product prices; and levels of market activity. Crucially, the interpretation of these data is dependent upon additional information collected at livelihood-system level concerning the critical seasonal terms of trade between different products for each system. Prices do not stand alone, but rather are sensitive indicators if analysed in the context of who is doing what when.

The significance of actual prices and the terms of trade between them varies according to the livelihood system in question and the moment of the year when producers are exchanging. As shown in Table 9.1, the key determinants of market exchange (both actual prices and terms of trade) have altered for producers in the transition from secure to vulnerable livelihood systems. Further, as Table 9.2 showed, the *reasons* for market exchange have also shifted, such that producers have become increasingly market-dependent for their subsistence rather than for the purposes of investment in production, accumulation, and diversification of productive activities and of diet. In this climate of increasing market dependence, the critical exchanges which different livelihood systems engage in on the market are direct indicators of their ability to use exchange entitlements to improve access to food.

Finally, what are the implications of the analysis for the food and livelihood security of vulnerable people? Increased market dependence, whilst enabling them partially to fill the food gap left by shortfalls in their own production (and, in the case of fishers and transhumant pastoralists, to convert expensive protein into cheaper calories), nevertheless incurs high risks in bad years and is becoming more risky over time. Being wholly reliant on millet leaves producers supremely vulnerable in both a bad year (when they must purchase millet) and a good one (when they must sell it to repay debts and meet other cash needs). Diversification of sources of entitlement is thus essential to maximise exchange entitlements. Yet diversification is itself problematic, even assuming that the capital can be found to diversify production entitlements. There are indications from cattle, goat and milk terms of trade with millet that the local livestock economy is under increasing stress. As a favoured means of diversifying and spreading risk, investment in livestock offers less insurance against bad times now than in 1987–8 (although the recent devaluation of the FCFA has had the effect of raising livestock prices due to increased competitiveness in export markets). Intensification of fishing is apparently a more robust means of diversification, because fish retains its value relative to millet in bad years better than other products and because the price of fish is rising over time. But this strategy too is constrained, because of declining *per capita* production, due both to more people fishing and to falling fish stocks. Furthermore, it is an option only available to wetland producers who can get access to fisheries. Other options for diversification, notably from gathered products, may enable people to stand still or get by in bad years, but cannot offer much in the way of increased security. Exchange entitlements, whilst central to survival in vulnerable livelihood systems, are under stress and offer little in the way of sustainably reducing sensitivity or increasing resilience in the long term.

10 Coping and Adaptive Entitlements

INTRODUCTION

This chapter examines the entitlements derived from coping strategies, that is, the tertiary activities pursued by people to survive when their habitual primary and secondary activities cannot guarantee a livelihood. Production and exchange entitlements are the central planks of subsistence in any year, as well as enabling accumulation in a good year (increasingly difficult in vulnerable livelihood systems). Coping strategies, in contrast, are reserved for periods of unusual stress, often resulting in food insecurity. As argued in Chapter 3, these same activities become adaptive strategies when they are used in every year to fill the food gap left once production and exchange entitlements have failed to meet minimum food requirements.

THE CHANGING USE AND MIX OF STRATEGIES

All coping strategies are treated as a distinct set of sources of entitlement in the livelihood entitlements matrix elaborated in Chapter 2. But the *reasons why* people pursue certain strategies need to be distinguished from the *sources of* those strategies. Most strategies are inevitably derived from the same agro-ecological and socio-economic conditions as production and exchange entitlements. Consequently, each coping strategy is itself *derived from* one of the sources of entitlement in the matrix (production, exchange and assets), although all such strategies are *used to* cope and/or adapt and hence to increase overall entitlements. Coping strategies are not hermetically sealed from habitual activities and the entitlements to which they give rise; but rather, are extensions or adaptations of such activities. By way of illustration, diversification into small-scale commerce is derived from exchange entitlements, but does not form part of the principal exchange entitlements of any livelihood system analysed in Chapter 9. Similarly, some coping strategies rely on the same entitlements which condition production, but, again, they are distinct from habitual productive activities. Reciprocally-based strategies are classified under assets or

Coping and Adaptive Entitlements 239

claims and may be mediated by membership of a livelihood system or the moral economy. In addition to production, exchange and asset-based strategies, there are three further sub-categories of bases from which coping strategies are derived: labour, migration and CPRs. The first two can be considered under the 'exchange' category, and the exploitation of CPRs can relate to production, exchange or assets. Calls on entitlement (consumption, claims and livelihood protection) similarly offer the potential for coping if drains on resources can be reduced. Thus cutting consumption is a common coping strategy and, when necessary, forfeiting livelihood protection is.

It is of note that the state does not feature in any of the strategies pursued. As argued in Chapter 3, the inclusion of state interventions (free food aid distributions, for example) in the category of coping strategies, clouds the concept to the point of obscurity. Whereas such distributions certainly fit into the livelihood entitlements matrix, they represent increased assets mediated by the state, but not an option open to producers in the face of insecurity. The state may reinforce or undermine coping strategies, but cannot initiate them.

This dual classification of coping strategies (what they are used for, as well as the entitlement base from which they are derived) is significant because it is precisely those constraints and opportunities which exist in productive, exchange and asset-based entitlements which also condition the potential of and obstacles to coping strategies. There is an iterative process between habitual entitlements and coping/adaptive ones: if the former are under strain, coping and adaptive entitlements will also be. This has implications for the effectiveness of coping strategies in cushioning households against food stress. In vulnerable livelihood systems, as the following data will show, such strategies are centrally important to subsistence in every year, whilst at the same time offering limited and uncertain cushions against food and livelihood stress. Critically, many are characterised as being unsustainable, in an economic as well as an environmental sense (what De Waal, 1989, has called 'erosive' coping strategies); in other words, the strategies themselves are likely to become less effective over time.

The full range of different strategies identified by the monitoring system is summarised in Table 10.1. These are classified, first, according to the entitlement base from which they are derived and, secondly, according to whether they are pursued to offset potential risk (insurance strategies) or as deficit-management strategies, employed once productive and exchange entitlements have failed to meet expected requirements in a given year. Some strategies (e.g. tapping internal credit mechanisms or herding other

Table 10.1 Classification of coping/adaptive strategies by entitlement base and type of strategy

Entitlement base	Insurance strategy	Deficit-management strategy
Production-based:		
• mixture of late and early maturing seed	■	
• diversify into market gardening for sale	■	
• switch from cattle to goats	■	
• exploit other skills[a]	■	■
Common property resource-based:		
• collection of wild foods		■
• cutting of *bourgou* for sale as fodder/own use		■
• wood-cutting		■
• mat-making from palms for sale to fishers		■
• intensify fishing[b]	■	■
• increase size of milk herd staying in pastoral safety nets	■	■
• shepherd other people's animals	■	■
Reciprocally-based:		
• increase collection of traditional services/dues		■
• reduce payment of traditional dues		■
• intensify claims on kin		■
• work on richer households' land		■
• internal credit mechanisms[c]	■	■
• internal self-help mechanisms[d]		■
Asset-based:		
• liquidation of stocks of food		■
• sale of animals		■
• sale of gold		■
• sale of domestic goods		■
• sale of productive assets[e]		■
Labour-based:		
• redivision of household labour	■	■
• longer working day	■	■
Exchange-based:		
• trade with traders in place of barter		■
• establish/increase credit and repayment links	■	■
• very small-scale retailing	■	■
• exploit informal economy[f]		■
• act as intermediary in exchanges of livestock		■

Table 10.1 (continued)

Entitlement base	Insurance strategy	Deficit-management strategy
Migration-based:		
• work in neighbouring livelihood system[g]		■
• migrate to urban centres and stay away longer	■	■
• intensify habitual rural-rural migration		■
• alter transhumance routes[h]	■	■
Consumption-based:		
• reduce intake[i]		■
• migrate to reduce household consumption		■

Notes:
[a] e.g. artisanal work.
[b] Equipment, time spent.
[c] e.g. for seed stocks.
[d] e.g. for restocking.
[e] e.g. ploughs.
[f] e.g. transport by boat.
[g] e.g. fishing camps.
[h] Stay in traditional safety nets.
[i] e.g. number of meals, condiments.

people's animals) can fall into both categories, depending on the point at which they are used in the annual productive cycle.

Production-based strategies. Once habitual production entitlements have failed to meet expected requirements, there are few production-based strategies which can be used for deficit management. This is primarily due to the single growing season in the Sahel, but also demonstrates the inability – and unwillingness – of people to grow counter-season crops in this zone. In traditional secure livelihood systems, cultivation of flood-retreat crops and of counter-season crops in permanent marsh pools was a means of increasing income and diversifying diets after the main harvest. Cekan (1991) has identified these as a principal source of coping in less arid parts of present-day Mali, but in the Sahel and even in the Delta such diversification is no longer practised on any scale. This is because of declining and uncertain flood levels; the changing arrival and departure of the flood; fewer permanent water pools in the drylands; and greater movement after the harvest season, making cultivation, which requires that households stay put, a less attractive option than other activities.

Recent development initiatives to promote market gardening of non-traditional crops (such as vegetables) for sale have met with limited enthusiasm from rural people. In addition to the need to remain sedentary, other obstacles they cite against this practice are: the cost of seed; high labour inputs (especially for watering); consumer dislike of some of them; and above all, the uncertainty of market demand, particularly in bad years. Such market gardening tends to be concentrated around larger urban centres (Mopti) where there is more stable demand from expatriates and wealthier urban consumers, and is often practised by relatively secure peri-urban producers who have access to the required inputs. In Douentza, a project was set up to encourage mothers of children in feeding centres to market garden, as a means of diversifying the diets of undernourished children. This met with limited success: some of the food was at least consumed, but sale of the surplus remained a problem. In Gao, a highly drought-prone area outside the SADS zone, numerous small-scale market gardening projects were set up as part of the rehabilitation projects for pastoralists displaced by the 1984 drought and, by 1986, piles of rotting lettuces could be seen in the market.

Using a mixture of early and late maturing seed has always been practised in the zone. Its importance as an insurance strategy, if there are no household stocks, is that early maturing varieties break the hungry season a month or more before the main harvest. Against this, yields are lower for these varieties, so that overall production is less. In years when producers have to purchase seed, their flexibility to mix early and late maturing varieties is much reduced, although inter-household exchanges can mitigate this.

CPR-based strategies. Exploiting CPRs is the backbone of many deficit-management strategies, both in respect of intensifying use of those CPRs on which secondary activities are based (fisheries and pasture),[1] and of exploiting additional ones (wild food, wood, *bourgou*). Their significance for coping behaviour in vulnerable livelihood systems is that investment in private property is so risky as to fail to guarantee livelihood security. Consequently, reciprocal access to other resources is needed when local production fails. The terms on which this access is gained (whether the resources are genuinely common property – that is, managed communally according to a set of agreed rules – or open access, with no agreed rules), is central to the potential for particular resources to enhance the entitlement base of particular groups of producers. Claims on entitlements can, for example, rise sharply in a bad year if local resource managers raise the costs of access to strangers.

Data from elsewhere show that, as people become more vulnerable to food insecurity, their dependence on CPRs increases (Jodha, 1985, 1990). Moorehead (1991), in a detailed study of CPR management in the Delta, has shown, for example, that 24 per cent of household food needs in

1985–6 came from wild foods, and that most of the income to buy the 41 per cent of cereals purchased on the market came from exploiting CPRs (*ibid.*: 347). He identifies a number of implications of this dependence, which undermine the ability of CPRs to fulfil the role of sustainable coping strategies: increased conflict over access to these resources, both between communities and between them and the state; resulting extraction of fines and other payments from producers by the state (i.e. increased calls on entitlement); degradation of the resource base as use intensifies; and, as more and more people exploit CPRs, increase of abusive practices and erosion of traditional management systems.

Under existing management systems, the future of CPR-based coping strategies is therefore glum: there will be fewer of them, and access to them will be controlled by outsiders, whose interests are not to manage the resources in a sustainable manner but to maximise the extraction of surplus from them in the short term. Moorehead (1991) refutes classic tragedy-of-the-commons arguments in the context of the Delta, arguing instead that their management is governed by 'structural chaos', in which state and conflicting local interests combine to create the conditions under which resources are degraded. Nowhere in this process is the centrality of CPRs to coping strategies given priority.

Reciprocally-based strategies. These too appear to be important ways of coping, principally in terms of deficit management. People, however, repeatedly report the breakdown of those traditional reciprocal arrangements which were essentially welfarist (provision of credit and loans in kind, employment creation by wealthier households, and loans of animals, stocks of food and seed). Bartering arrangements break down when there is little surplus, as do demands for labour; in the past these sometimes represented reciprocal exchanges to benefit poorer households. In contrast, extractive reciprocal ties have intensified: those in positions of authority to extract dues within the community do so with greater vigour than in the past.

The growing dependence on the market discussed in Chapter 9 is testimony to the collapse of reciprocal ties: the private sector now provides credit and, in the case of fisheries in particular, purchases production. The costs of this credit to producers are high, and repayment in kind is a particularly effective means of extracting high interest rates. People become caught in a debt trap from which they cannot escape. The shift from intra-community reciprocity to market dependence means that people are often forced to exchange on the basis of existing debt burdens rather than actual prices.

Asset-based strategies. As noted in Chapter 2, De Waal (1989) cites evidence from Sudan indicating that people will preserve assets in preference to meeting immediate food needs, by choosing to go hungry in the short term in order to be able to produce in the future. Results from the SADS system indicate that, whereas this linear sequence model may be the *preferred* choice, it nevertheless oversimplifies the role of assets in choices of coping behaviour, for the following reasons. First, those assets traditionally associated with production which cultivators seek to preserve (ploughs, traction animals) were largely liquidated during the mid-1980s, as were non-productive traditional stores of value (gold). In conditions of increasing vulnerability, these have not been reconstituted, even in the highly productive year 1988-9, underlining vulnerable livelihood systems' incapacity to accumulate, or only sporadically and with great difficulty. Second, assets now tend to be held in livestock, particularly goats. These are more easily liquidated than other assets and permit producers to sell and restock over relatively short periods (often in one annual cycle), depending on food and cash needs and on the terms of trade between goats and millet (Chapter 9). Third, one of the principal reasons for liquidating assets is repayment of debt and taxation: both money-lenders and the state insist on collection immediately after the harvest when producers have stocks of cereals to sell. Producers therefore have little choice, either about going hungry to preserve assets or about having to sell them at the moment when they are least valuable.

Labour-based strategies, which are distinct from reciprocal labour exchanges or migrating in search of paid employment, are universally adopted by households coping with food shortages. In contrast to conventional wisdom that there is a *saison morte* (dead season) after the harvest these days, in the absence of cultivation of counter-season crops, family labour both increases the time it works and intensifies the division of labour. In Phase 3 of the SADS monitoring system, one of the objectives was to measure the amount of time spent on coping strategies to substantiate this argument, made repeatedly by producers (see below). The critical constraint to local labour-based strategies, however, is demand for labour. Reciprocal labour exchanges have declined in rural areas and the urban sector offers few employment opportunities.

Exchange-based strategies. Such is the extent of market dependence nowadays, that few, if any, forms of exchange can now be entirely classified as a coping strategy. The terms and conditions under which trade takes place to some extent still mirror the multiple functions of traditional (non-market) exchange relations in so far as single traders provide a multiplicity of services. What has changed is the fact that the terms on which producers now exchange are dependent rather than reciprocal. Progressive liberalisation of the cereal market in Mali since 1982 (Chapter 5) has not meant that most producers have unconditional access to a free market. Instead, they are locked into systems of credit (often granted in kind) with traders, whom they repay in kind later in the year. Despite the cost of these closed circuits, rural people are generally reluctant to break them (for example, by seeking credit from alternative sources such as banks or development projects, on the rare occasions when such avenues are available), because of the security local private credit systems offer in the sense of future credit being guaranteed, if only to pay back the interest on the capital outstanding. Genuine exchange-based coping strategies (which are not central to livelihood systems) include (very) small-scale commerce, practised mainly by women, and acting as intermediaries in exchanges of fish and livestock in particular (principally men).

Migration-based strategies. Rural–rural migration was traditionally part of the reciprocal exchanges between livelihood systems and between different agro-ecological zones. Whereas demand for seasonal labour on other people's farms, during cultivation (the dry and rainy seasons) and at harvest time, has declined as harvests themselves are smaller, new forms of rural–rural migration have evolved to maximise the exploitation of seasonally-specific resources: seeking work in fishing or herding camps; moving in search of wild foods; extending existing periods of transhumance and altering transhumance routes to minimise risk; and more important, movements to productive areas in bad years.

Migration to urban centres, particularly in the coastal West African states, has always been part of the activities of rural people but this was habitually to accumulate savings, especially for young men prior to marriage, and thereafter to send back remittances to supplement household incomes. Nowadays, people report that remittances are rare and, indeed, not expected; the principal motivation is to reduce calls on limited household cereal stores, by finding a basis of individual subsistence elsewhere. A further trend in migration patterns is that the length of stay increases: whereas prior to the 1980s drought cycle, migrants departed seasonally for a maximum of six months between the harvest and the start of the next agricultural campaign, they frequently remain away for several years now. This imposes strains on labour demands at harvest time when the harvest is good, as in 1988; but ideally families manage migration, such that labour needs at home are balanced against the benefit to be gained from cutting household consumption.

One way of intensifying the pattern is for whole families to migrate, often separately, men going to the coast, while women seek work in neighbouring rural areas or local urban centres. Seasonal migration into Mopti is now an established pattern, such that permanent camps of displaced persons swell in the months after the harvest and decline again as the new agricultural campaign begins. The population of the town nearly doubles in the dry season every year.

Consumption-based strategies. Almost all producers report reductions in the composition of dietary intake in the months running up to the harvest, particularly of protein in the sauce served with the cereal staple. Reduction in the number of meals a day is also widespread in this period in most years.

THE SEASONALITY OF COPING STRATEGIES

People's ability to map out their choice and timing of coping strategy use is constrained not only by the seasonality of resource availability, but more critically by factors of hidden seasonality, which limit the mix of options available at any one time and can severely reduce the real returns to pursuing a given strategy. Table 10.2 shows the seasons of the year in which available coping strategies can be used. Those based on production and seasonally available CPRs (e.g. fisheries, dryland pasture, wild foods) are the most seasonally specific. Those which appear to show no seasonality (based on reciprocity, assets, labour and consumption) do, of course, have hidden seasonality. For asset liquidation, seasonal fluctuations in the terms of trade mean that the timing of disposals is critical to maximise returns, although the need to raise cash invariably does not coincide with the best time to sell. Equally, local demand for labour is highly seasonally specific and, although urban labour demand is more stable (though weak), household labour requirements themselves fluctuate seasonally, thereby reducing the apparent flexibility of this strategy. Exchange-based strategies suffer from the seasonality of terms of trade, as shown in Chapter 9. Consumption-based strategies have the hidden seasonality of the costs of low intake being particularly detrimental in terms of labour productivity and increased health risks at particular times (especially in the rainy and harvest seasons).

COPING AND ADAPTIVE STRATEGIES IN THE INNER NIGER DELTA AND SAHEL

Data collected on coping strategies presented a number of analytical difficulties, summarised as follows:

Table 10.2 Seasonality of coping/adaptive strategies

Strategy	Harvest	Cold	Dry	Rainy
Production-based:				
• mixture of late and early maturing seed				■
• diversify into market gardening for sale		■		
• switch from cattle to goats	■	■	■	■
• exploit other skills		■	■	■
Common property resource-based:				
• collection of wild foods	■		■	■
• cutting of *bourgou* for sale as fodder/own use	■	■		
• wood-cutting	■	■	■	■
• mat-making from palms for sale to fishers	■	■		
• intensify fishing	■	■	■	
• increase size of milk herd staying in pastoral safety nets			■	
• shepherd other people's animals			■	■
Reciprocally-based:				
• increase collection of traditional services/dues	■	■	■	■
• reduce payment of traditional dues	■	■	■	■
• intensify claims on kin	■	■	■	■
• work on richer households' land	■			■
• internal credit mechanisms	■	■	■	■
• internal self-help mechanisms	■	■	■	■
Asset-based:				
• liquidation of stocks of food	■	■		
• sale of animals	■	■	■	■
• sale of gold	■	■	■	■
• sale of domestic goods	■	■	■	■
• sale of productive assets	■	■	■	■
Labour-based:				
• redivision of household labour	■	■	■	■
• longer working day	■	■	■	■
Exchange-based:				
• trade with traders in place of barter	■	■		
• establish/increase credit and repayment links	■	■	■	■
• very small-scale retailing	■	■	■	■
• exploit informal economy	■	■	■	■
• act as intermediary in exchanges of livestock	■	■	■	

248   Adaptable Livelihoods

Table 10.2 (continued)

Strategy	Seasons in which strategy can be exploited			
	Harvest	Cold	Dry	Rainy
Migration-based:				
• work in neighbouring livelihood system	■	■		
• migrate to urban centres and stay away longer	■	■	■	■
• intensify habitual rural–rural migration	■	■		
• alter transhumance routes			■	■
Consumption-based:				
• reduce intake	■	■	■	■
• migrate to reduce household consumption	■	■	■	■

- tremendous variation in patterns of activity between different livelihood systems and communities and households within them;
- lack of consistent trends in the timing of uptake of particular strategies, over and above the seasonality between good and bad years identified above;
- an inability to gain reliable information on the motivation for pursuing a particular strategy (e.g. was it habitual behaviour, or pursued only in bad years) and, again, wide intra-community variation in this;
- the impossibility of deriving changes in patterns of behaviour from one year to the next, because of the complexity of responses within and between livelihood systems.

Consequently, this section provides illustrations of the kinds of strategies pursued, and the effectiveness of or returns to such behaviour, without making any claims to representativity. The aim is to demonstrate how collecting information about coping strategies can provide invaluable contextual information which can subsequently be used to interpret indicators. Whether indicators can themselves be derived from this context of coping – or, more precisely, adapting – is discussed at the end of the chapter.

Production-based strategies. One of the most critical constraints to production following a drought year is the ability to acquire seed for the subsequent agricultural campaign, particularly for rice cultivators. Table 10.3 shows the cost of having to buy paddy prior to the agricultural cam-

Table 10.3 The cost of acquiring paddy in good and bad years

Market	Bad year June 1988		Good year June 1989		% increase between good and bad year
	FCFA/kg	Cost of sowing 1 ha[a]	FCFA/kg	Cost of sowing 1 ha[a]	
Youvarou	206	17 510	43	3 655	+479%
Tenenkou	120	10 200	51	4 335	+235%
Toguéré	113	9 605	51	4 335	+222%
Mopti	117	9 945	70	5 950	+167%

Note: [a] Calculated at 85 kg paddy per hectare.

paign in 1988 (i.e. the end of a bad year) and in 1989 (the end of a good year, when most rice cultivators had managed to preserve a stock of seed). With the exception of Mopti (where rice cultivators are generally wealthier urban inhabitants), the difference in price is between two and nearly five times. A range of strategies are pursued to overcome this, including borrowing seed from kin (repaid in kind), and renting fields from wealthier neighbours with a surplus of seed, then dividing the harvest between the owner and the cultivator. For those who are forced to buy paddy, credit is either sought from traders or assets (e.g. traction animals) are sold, although by the late 1980s, there were few of these left in all but the most productive areas. The purchased paddy is then bartered locally to acquire a mix of late and early maturing varieties. In Toguéré Koumbé in 1990, a traction bullock was bartered for 120 kg of paddy in May, equivalent to a selling price of 8000 FCFA (compared with a market value of over 30 000 FCFA), indicating the desperate need for paddy at this time of the year and its shortage of supply.

Diagram 10.1 illustrates the vicious circle in which cultivators in vulnerable livelihood systems are caught, unable to find sufficient seed, labour or food for subsistence during the period of cultivation. The first example is taken from habitual cultivating practices, the second from 1988–9, an exceptionally good year, illustrating how many cultivators were unable to maximise the opportunities presented by the good rains of 1988.

CPR-based strategies. In addition to the intensification of fishing and herding discussed in Chapter 7, the collection of wild foods is one of the most practised of these. Wild foods are not only numerous, but also have different qualities which determine their use. Those that are regularly collected have become incorporated into the normal cycle of activities.

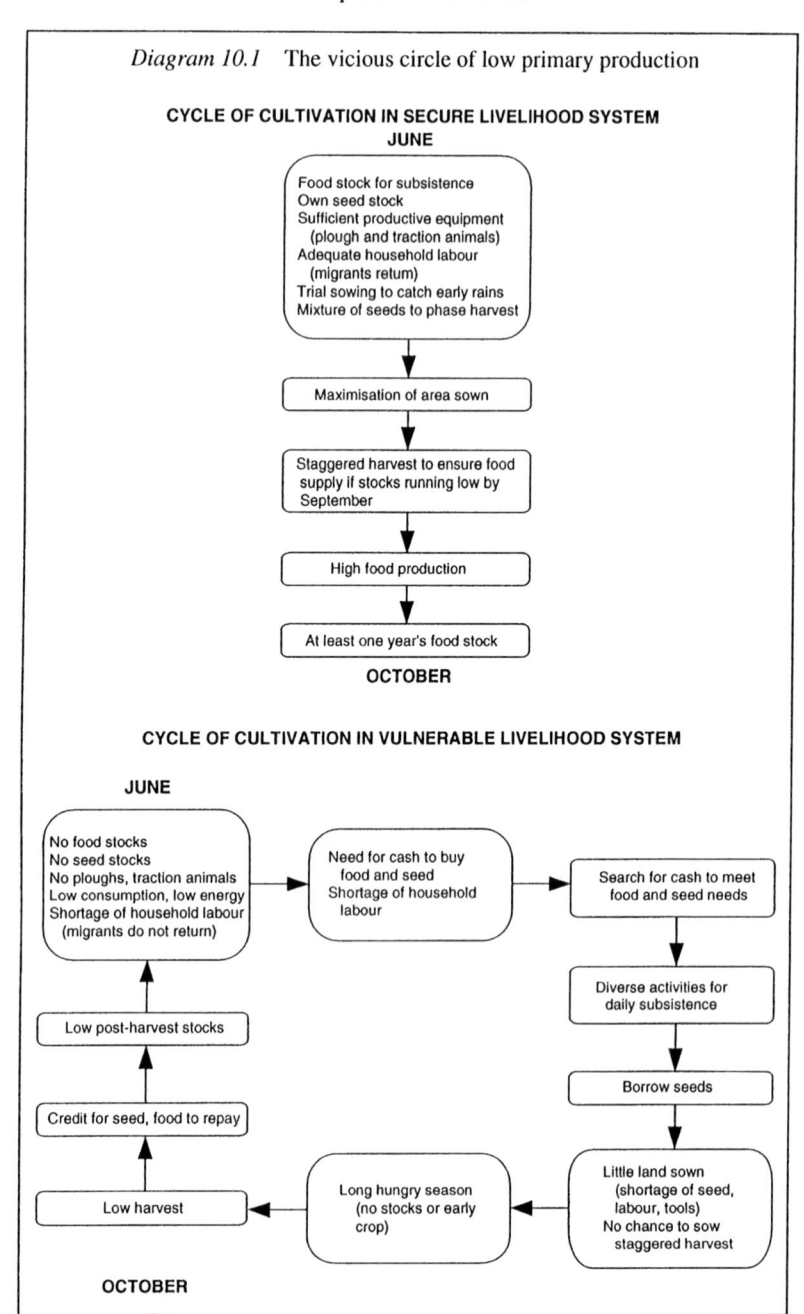

250 *Adaptable Livelihoods*

Diagram 10.1 The vicious circle of low primary production

CYCLE OF CULTIVATION IN SECURE LIVELIHOOD SYSTEM
JUNE

- Food stock for subsistence
- Own seed stock
- Sufficient productive equipment (plough and traction animals)
- Adequate household labour (migrants return)
- Trial sowing to catch early rains
- Mixture of seeds to phase harvest

↓

Maximisation of area sown

↓

Staggered harvest to ensure food supply if stocks running low by September

↓

High food production

↓

At least one year's food stock

OCTOBER

CYCLE OF CULTIVATION IN VULNERABLE LIVELIHOOD SYSTEM
JUNE

- No food stocks
- No seed stocks
- No ploughs, traction animals
- Low consumption, low energy
- Shortage of household labour (migrants do not return)

→ Need for cash to buy food and seed; Shortage of household labour

→ Search for cash to meet food and seed needs

↓

Diverse activities for daily subsistence

↓

Borrow seeds

↓

Little land sown (shortage of seed, labour, tools); No chance to sow staggered harvest

← Long hungry season (no stocks or early crop)

← Low harvest

↑ Credit for seed, food to repay

↑ Low post-harvest stocks

OCTOBER

Others are gathered in most years, while a third category, collected only in bad years, are those least preferred by consumers. There are, however, some groups (e.g. displaced persons around Douentza, *Bella*) who rely on these foods for part of every year and who have become specialised in gathering and bartering or selling them.

Reciprocally-based strategies. Labour exchanges between rice- and millet-growing areas tend to decline in bad years, as lower harvest levels mean reduced demand. Equally, in exceptionally good years, such as 1988–9, there was a marked shortage of labour for both the millet and the rice harvest as fewer strangers arrived than required due, in part, to the failure of long-term migrants to return to their villages despite the good agricultural campaign. This strategy is therefore most effective in satisfactory years and is determined by the absorptive capacity of neighbouring livelihood systems, rather than by demand for coping options. In 1991, the average pay for work in the rice harvest was three to six sacks of paddy (255–510 kg). In 1988, when labour was in short supply, the average was ten sacks or 850 kg, sufficient to meet the annual cereal requirements of 2.6 adults. For those who can find the work, it therefore makes a significant contribution to household grain stores, particularly if the paddy is resold in order to purchase millet.

Asset-based strategies. Disposal of productive assets is avoided where possible because of the adverse effects on future production. When producers are ultimately forced to sell, prices are invariably depressed. In March 1991, for example, bullocks were being sold for a quarter of their normal value, gold was sold for about 1000 FCFA a gram, whereas it normally reflects the world price.

Assets also have to be liquidated to meet calls on entitlements. After the 1988 harvest, the first good one in Douentza since the onset of the drought cycle of the mid-1980s, producers owed several years' back taxes, amounting to an average household bill of 30–40 000 FCFA, and collection was pursued when prices were at their lowest for many years. People were obliged to sell a ton of millet (priced at 40 FCFA/kg), or the equivalent of annual cereal requirements of nearly six people. Had they been able to delay payment until the following June, they would have needed to sell 300 kg (by which time the price had risen again to 133 FCFA/kg). This is one of the principal reasons why rural producers are unable to accumulate or to invest in productive activities in good years.

Labour-based strategies are constrained by the limited opportunities for casual labour outside the rural sector; and the low and highly seasonally-specific demand within the rural economy in bad years. In Mopti, in January 1990, following an average to poor harvest, daily *per capita* wages were less than 1000 FCFA, compared with over 2000 FCFA in January 1988. These figures are based on the earnings of a group of six men, clubbing together to hire a cart to transport sacks of cereals. In a bad year, the number of sacks they can hope to transport declines significantly owing to surplus labour. Moreover, because the price of millet is so much higher in a bad year, they can only expect to purchase 16 kg for a day's labour, compared with 48 kg in a good year. The opportunities for individual employment are considerably fewer in a bad year, and wage rates are approximately halved.

Exchange-based strategies. Bartering usually declines in bad years when there is little surplus. Although it picked up noticeably in 1988–9, there were strong indications that the degree of producer integration into the market was such that the barter terms of trade were based on current market prices, whereas traditional barter exchanges seek to iron out seasonal fluctuations between exchanging livelihood systems. An example from the fishing camp of Dentaka illustrates, however, that by bartering fish for millet, producers were able to exchange at the equivalent wholesale rather than retail price on the nearby market of Youvarou.

Incurring debt is intimately bound up with exchange-based strategies, as the creditor is invariably a merchant who will extract repayment in cash or kind. For example, in the 1989–90 fishing campaign, fish merchants set prices for repayment of credit for equipment when the credit was taken out, at a rate of 200 FCFA/kg for dried fish. The average market price for dried fish in Youvarou between February and July 1990 was 600 FCFA/kg. On a loan of 10 000 FCFA, to be paid back in kind over six months, this amounted to a rate of interest of 200 per cent.

A further example of the cost of credit comes from the need to borrow 200 kg of millet in July 1988, when the retail price was 200 FCFA/kg in both Youvarou and Douentza (i.e. a loan to the value of 40 000 FCFA). This had to be repaid in cash after the harvest, when the millet price dropped to 63 FCFA/kg in Youvarou and 49 FCFA/kg in Douentza. In order to repay the loan, the Youvarou producer was forced to sell 634 kg of millet and the Douentza one 816 kg.

Migration-based strategies. As noted earlier, migration by whole families to different agro-ecological zones, as well as to urban areas, can enable them to subsist over a year when the harvest has produced only four months of food. Traditional transhumance routes are also modified as part of the portfolio of coping strategies. Herders, for example, transhume on much shorter axes from dry season pastures and water points in a bad year, not risking to venture too far into the Sahel.

Consumption-based strategies are typically the reduction of the number of meals in a day, but as noted above, there are also a number of choices that can be made about consumption of wild foods, some of which, such as *fonio* and wild rice and even *cram-cram*, are now considered to be normal parts of the diet in certain seasons, while others are still seen as foods of last resort.

An example of a household of 17 people (nine of whom are active) in Toguéré Koumbé illustrates the kinds of consumption strategies pursued. In order to cultivate in 1988, the household sold one of its three traction animals for 75 000 FCFA to buy paddy. They also had to buy food to last them through to the harvest and therefore cut consumption to one meal a day in order to be able to buy six sacks of paddy (not the nine they had hoped for). They bartered some of the paddy they had bought in order to get a mixed variety of seeds, but much of the rice was flooded too early, leaving them after the harvest with only eight sacks of paddy, four of which were set aside for seed for the following year. In order to increase household consumption, they harvested wild water-lilies and acquired 70 kg of millet from labour in harvests elsewhere and a milk cow from kin. The women in the household engaged in small-scale commerce and the men cut straw, but to get them through the following hungry season they cut consumption again to one meal a day, rather than sell another traction animal.

ALLOCATION OF HOUSEHOLD TIME AS AN INDICATOR OF COPING STRATEGY USE

Results from Phase 2 of the SADS system suggested that household labour was no longer used solely – or perhaps primarily – for primary and secondary activities every year. Household labour was an important contribution to food security, enabling households to diversify sources of entitlement by pursuing a range of coping/adaptive strategies. This section presents the results of household data on time budgets collected in Phase 3. As with other household data, these results should be regarded as purely indicative. The reasons for collecting this information were, first, to see whether 'coping' strategies have become incorporated into the normal cycle of household activities. Data were collected at the end of a good year (the rainy season of 1988–9), and during a satisfactory – or normal – year (1989–90). A related question was whether there was scope for intensifying existing coping behaviour in bad years, given that household labour availability remains more or less constant irrespective of the year in ques-

254   *Adaptable Livelihoods*

tion (the only option is for individuals to spend more time working). Labour allocation was analysed by season to see whether there were particular seasonal constraints. Finally, the objective was to see what differences there were between female and male labour allocation, and whether the burden of coping/adapting was shared evenly between the sexes.

Activities recalled by people were divided into primary and secondary activities; coping/adaptive activities; and non-revenue-generating activities.[2] This last category was excluded from the analysis. For women, domestic and child-care duties average about 30 hours per week and show no significant variation either between livelihood systems or seasonally. Within the category of coping/adaptive activities, exchange and migration are distinguished from 'habitual' or 'other' coping strategies (gathering, cutting wood, weaving, construction, casual labour), but the sum of these three sets of activities are treated as coping/adaptive activities. As was argued in the categorisation of cash income (Chapter 8), these categories are not watertight. Some secondary activities are central to certain livelihood systems (e.g. pastoralism to transhumant pastoralists) and coping/adaptive activities may be partially habitual. It is thus conceivable, for example, that a certain amount of gathering may be part of primary activities, or that agricultural labour on other people's fields may have been considered as primary agricultural activity rather than adaptive behaviour by producers. Equally, some exchange is central to primary and secondary production, but not coping behaviour. Nevertheless, the majority of these activities were classified by producers as not being habitually part of their normal productive activities. By dividing household activities in this way, an indication can be gleaned of the amount of time devoted to adaptive behaviour.

Labour allocation between own food production and other activities

Graph 10.1 shows the number of hours per week spent on the three categories of activity, by livelihood system. Average recorded labour on these activities (excluding non-revenue-generating tasks) was 32.3 hours per week, probably reflecting some under-recording of work. Taken together, all households spend over half their time (55 per cent) on coping/adaptive activities (migration, exchange, other coping). The balance of their time is divided more or less equally between primary and secondary activities.

Graphs 10.2 to 10.4 disaggregate the proportion of time spent on each type of activity by livelihood system. Migration, referring only to those household members who migrated during the course of the year in question

Graph 10.1 Number of hours per week spent on primary, secondary and coping/adaptive activities, by livelihood system, 1989–90

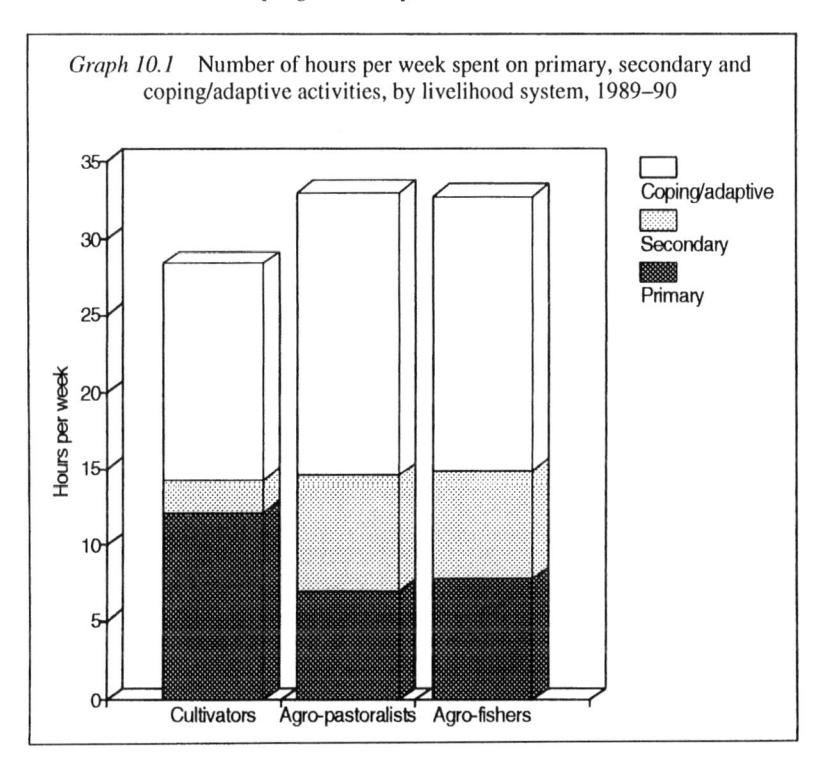

Graph 10.2 Cultivators: proportion of time spent on primary, secondary and coping/adaptive activities, 1989–90

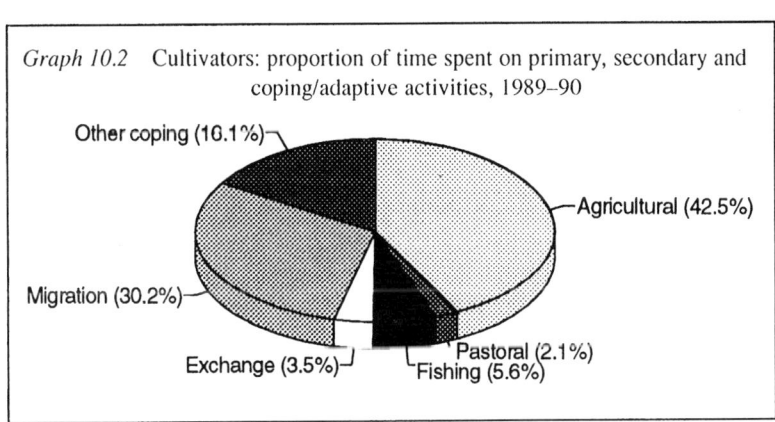

(i.e. short-term migrants), and excluding those who were absent for more than twelve months, accounted for between half and two-thirds of the time spent on coping/adaptive activities. Agro-pastoralists are the most reliant

Graph 10.3 Agro-pastoralists: proportion of time spent on primary, secondary and coping/adaptive activities, 1989–90

Other coping (23.3%)
Agricultural (20.9%)
Migration (26.4%)
Pastoral (23.0%)
Fishing (0.3%)
Exchange (6.1%)

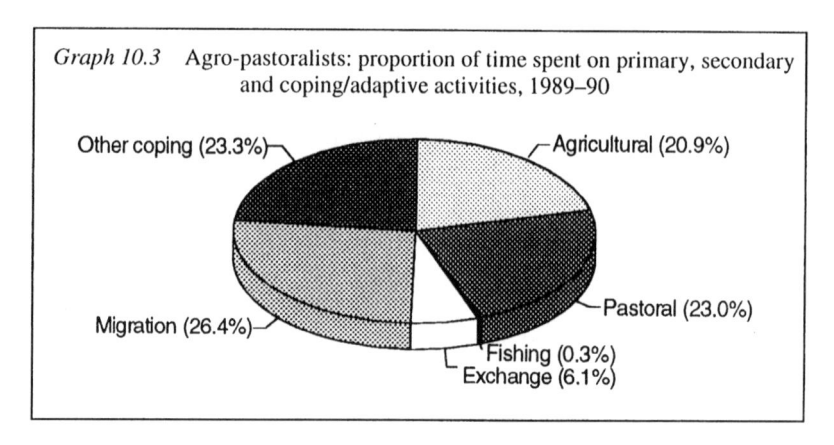

Graph 10.4 Agro-fishers: proportion of time spent on primary, secondary and coping/adaptive activities, 1989–90

Other coping (12.8%)
Agricultural (23.5%)
Migration (39.1%)
Fishing (22.0%)
Exchange (2.4%)

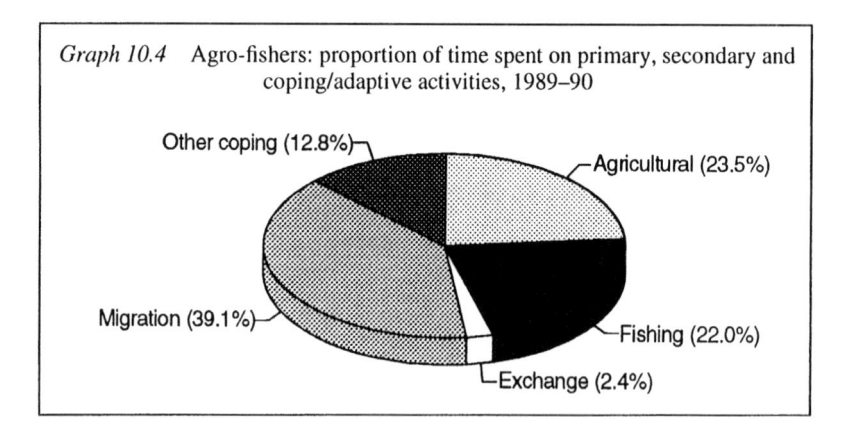

on other coping/adaptive activities, which account for 23 per cent of their total time, compared with 16 per cent for cultivators and 13 per cent for agro-fishers. The latter's most common adaptive strategy – intensifying fishing – is hidden under secondary activities and, to an even greater extent, under the category of migration (39 per cent). Extensive migration to more distant fisheries, it will be recalled from Chapter 7, was not habitually part of agro-fishers' (as opposed to transhumant fishers') activity calendars. Now, nearly twice as much time is spent fishing away from home as locally. Cultivators, somewhat surprisingly, spend only 8 per cent of their time on pastoral and fishing activities – or half as much time as on other coping activities – indicating little capacity for diversification into these sectors. Again, however, time spent migrating disguises work in these sectors away from home, especially in fishing camps. Exchange occupies only a fraction of time in all livelihood systems.

Seasonal allocation of time between activities

Graphs 10.5 to 10.7 show that coping/adaptive strategies form a significant part of labour use in all seasons for all livelihood systems, confirming that their use is neither restricted to particularly bad years nor to the traditional hungry season, but that adaptive behaviour is most intense when the opportunities for these activities are greatest. Thus, cultivators spend most time on these activities in the cold season, when work in neighbouring livelihood systems is most available (in fishing camps, working on off-farm rice harvests), and least time in the dry season, when, although the need for cash or other sources of entitlement is greatest, opportunities are most limited. For agro-pastoralists, coping/adaptive strategies are pursued more uniformly throughout the year, decreasing only in the rainy season.

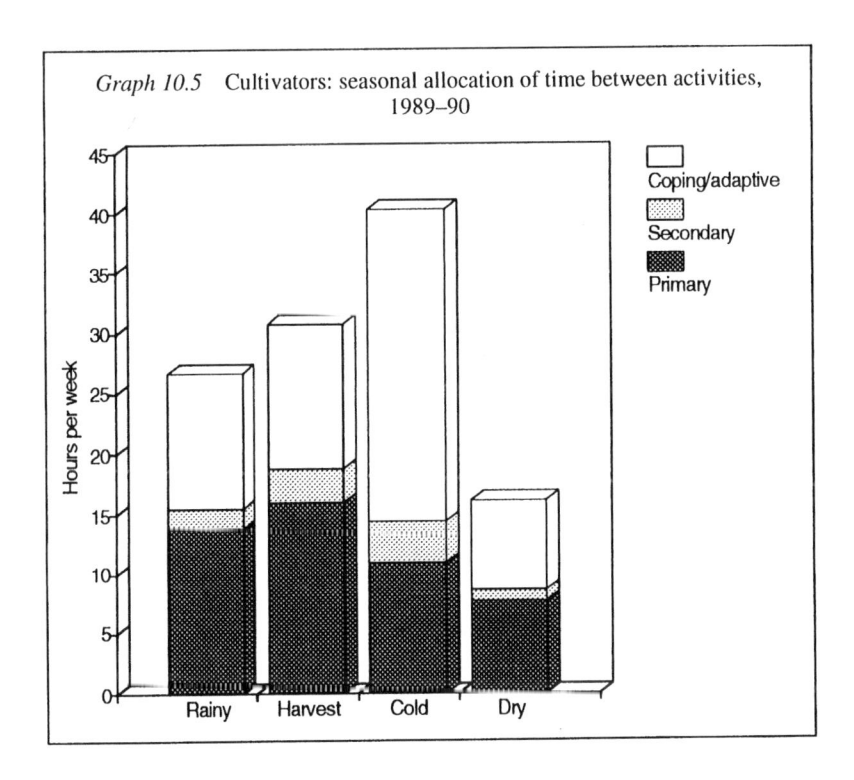

Graph 10.5 Cultivators: seasonal allocation of time between activities, 1989–90

Graph 10.6 Agro-pastoralists: seasonal allocation of time between activities, 1989–90

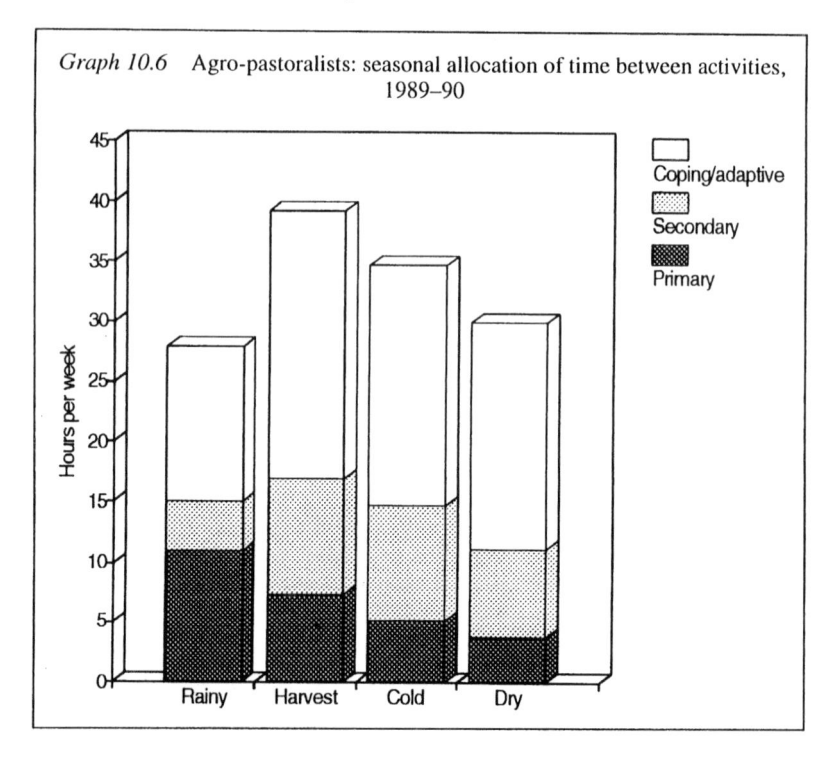

It should be noted, however, that for all three systems labour expenditure is surprisingly low in the rainy season, due to the fact that this was the end of the exceptionally good year of 1988, when unusually most households had adequate stocks of food prior to the harvest. Both agro-pastoralists and agro-fishers were busiest in the harvest season, principally because of additional work on secondary activities. Agro-fishers show the least seasonality in their pursuit of coping/adaptive strategies, indicating that they migrate for as long as possible in search of fish (in the harvest and cold seasons). Fishing more or less ceases during the dry season until the new flood arrives. Their coping/adaptive time in the dry season was principally taken up with collecting wild foods and wood-cutting.

Labour allocation by gender

Graph 10.8 shows the number of hours per week spent on productive activities by type of activity, by gender and by livelihood system. Female labour (including domestic and child-care tasks) averages 50 hours a week, compared with 45 hours for men. There are no significant dif-

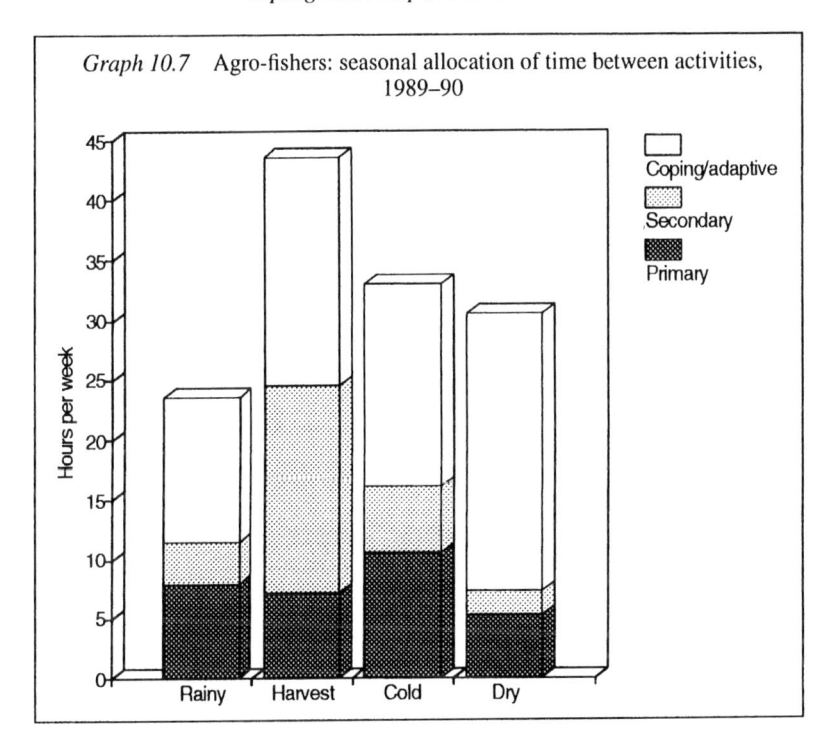

Graph 10.7 Agro-fishers: seasonal allocation of time between activities, 1989–90

ferences between livelihood systems, with the exception of male agro-fishers (50 hours per week) and female cultivators (44 hours per week).

Women spend an average of 17 hours a week on coping/adaptive activities, compared with 18 for men. Of this, women spend on average three times as long as men on activities such as gathering, wood-cutting, weaving, construction and casual labour; for agro-pastoralist women, this rises to four times as long. Graphs 10.9 to 10.11 show the proportional allocation of men's and women's labour between the three categories of activity, confirming that women in all livelihood systems spend *proportionally* more time than men on coping/adaptive activities. To some extent these data are distorted by consistent under-reporting of women's time spent on primary and secondary activities, but they nevertheless show that the burden of coping – especially other coping activities – is carried out equally, or more by women than men. Gathering is traditionally a female activity, as well as some exchange, but this alone does not explain the intensification of women's labour in these activities. It appears that as livelihood systems become more vulnerable and hence as coping strategies become adaptive, demands on female labour intensify.

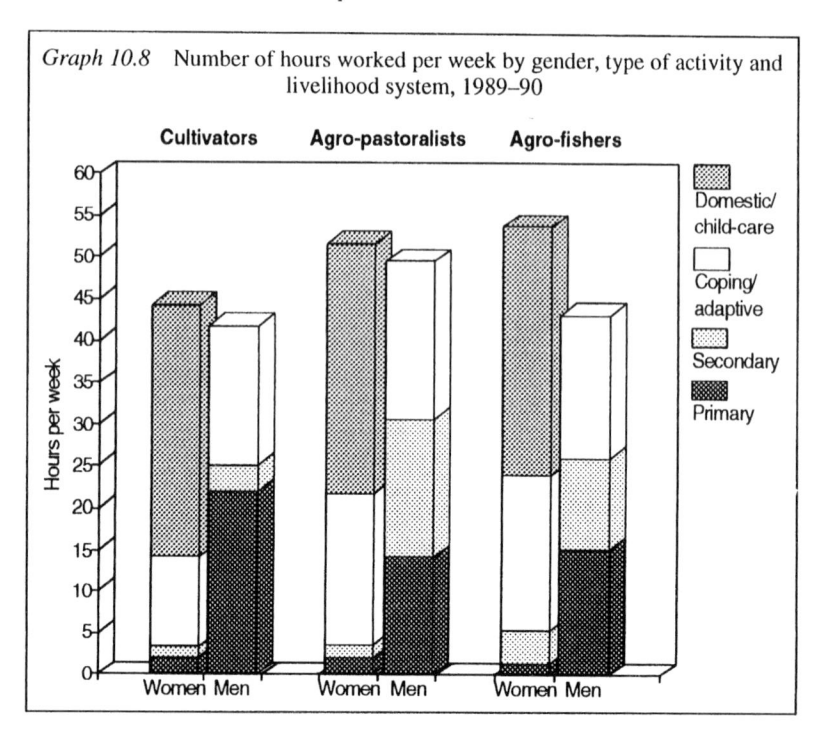

Graph 10.8 Number of hours worked per week by gender, type of activity and livelihood system, 1989–90

COPING OR ADAPTING?

The overwhelming characteristic of these strategies is that they offer, without exception, uncertain, piecemeal and poorly remunerated means of filling the annual food gap. There is, for example, no established labour market in accessible urban centres, nor the certainty of market demand for

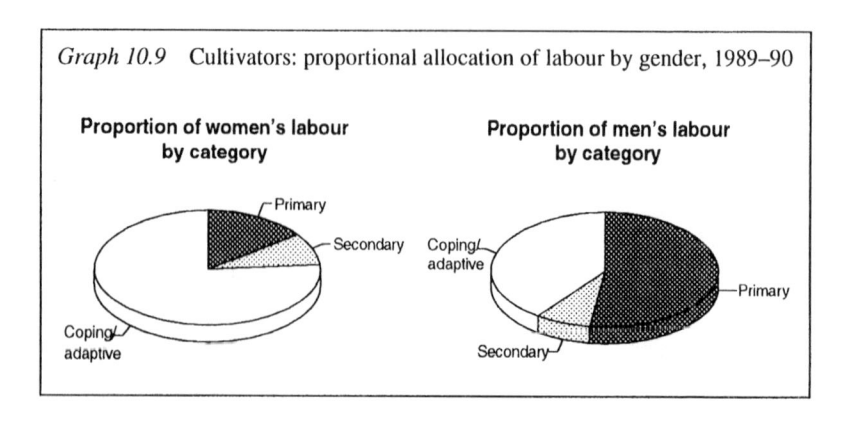

Graph 10.9 Cultivators: proportional allocation of labour by gender, 1989–90

Graph 10.10 Agro-pastoralists: proportional allocation of labour by gender, 1989–90

Proportion of women's labour by category

Proportion of men's labour by category

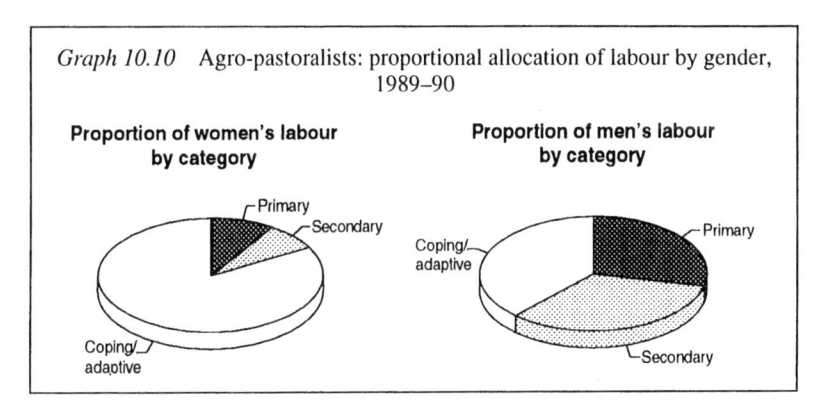

Graph 10.11 Agro-fishers: proportional allocation of labour by gender, 1989–90

Proportion of women's labour by category

Proportion of men's labour by category

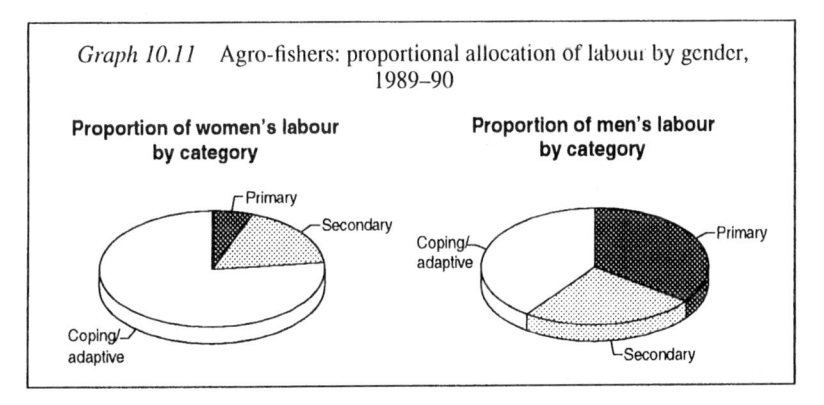

counter-season crops. Further, as more and more producers seek to exploit these strategies for longer periods, the resource base from which they are derived comes under increasing pressure. The greatest opportunities are found in the Delta which, as a traditional safety net within the Sahelian zone, becomes a magnet for producers from an ever wider radius to the north and east. Nevertheless, these activities are central to subsistence in all years, as a comparison between bad (1987–8) and good (1988–9) years shows.

In 1987–8, there was an agricultural drought in the SADS zone, following a reasonably good year in 1985–6 (after the drought cycle of 1982–3 to 1984–5) and a satisfactory/bad year in 1986–7. Millet and rice harvests in 1987–8 met between two and four months of food needs, according to producers' own estimates. Pastoral conditions were much better, and the fishing campaign was averagely productive. All groups of producers, however, used coping strategies to some extent, the greatest uptake being amongst millet cultivators, followed by rice cultivators.

262 *Adaptable Livelihoods*

Agro-pastoralists fell back on their pastoral resources and agro-fishers on the fisheries. In 1988–9, when harvests, as well as pastoral and fishing conditions, were the best since 1980, there was nevertheless significant use of coping strategies by all livelihood systems. A principal reason for this was that people were forced to meet substantial calls on entitlements – selling cereals to repay outstanding tax bills and debts – despite adequate food production to meet annual requirements. As Chapter 7 has shown, the conditions in 1988–9 did not recur in the study period. In 1989–90, conditions were satisfactory, and in 1990–1, drought prevailed once more. The 1987–8 pattern is therefore more representative of the post-drought period than that of 1988–9, although good years do occur periodically.

Table 10.4, comparing the use of coping strategies in a bad year (1987–8) characterised by drought but not famine conditions, with an exceptionally good one (1988–9),[3] shows that coping strategies are used by all producers in some seasons of some years, and by some producers in some seasons of all years. The principal differences are in the timing of uptake (e.g. when migration occurs) and in terms of the options available (e.g. cereal stocks could not be sold in the bad year because there were none; other assets – with the exception of animals – were sold in neither year because they had been liquidated in the mid-1980s). Clearly, there are differences (e.g. the timing of wild food collection), but many so-called coping strategies are either hardly used at all (e.g. internal self-help mechanisms) or are used in both years (e.g. increasing collection of traditional services and dues).

How justified, then, is the use of the term 'coping strategy', which, as argued in Chapter 3, needs to be defined quite precisely if it is to have any analytical use, particularly as a tool for monitoring changes in vulnerability to food insecurity? The definition proposed was that coping strategies are activities which are reserved for periods of unusual food stress, which permit people to cope with disruptions in their normal bundle of entitlements, such that they can minimise the degree of disruption (sensitivity) and maximise bounce back (resilience) to their habitual pattern of activities once the period of food stress is over. Clearly, from these data, what are nowadays interpreted by outsiders as coping strategies were indeed so in the past, but since the drought of the mid-1980s, when they failed to permit producers to bounce back, they have become part of the normal cycle of activities. Their use is *reduced* – but not altogether suspended – in *abnormally good* years. In *abnormally bad* years, the only option is for producers to *intensify* existing normal activities and not to resort to coping strategies reserved as safety nets. Household data indicate that the scope for intensifying the use of coping strategies is itself limited,

Table 10.4 Coping strategies used in a good and bad year

Strategy	Cultivators		Agro-pastoralists		Agro-fishers		Transhumant fishers		Transhumant pastoralists	
Year:	Bad	Good	Bad	Good	Bad	Good	Bad	Good	Bad	Good
Seasons: (Harvest, Cold, Dry, Rainy)	HCDR	HCDR	HCDR	HCDR	HCDR	HCDR	HCDR	HCDR	HCDR	HCDR
Production-based:										
• mixture of late and early maturing seed	■	■								
• diversify into market gardening for sale										
• switch from cattle to goats	■	■	■■	■■					■	■
• exploit other skills			■■	■■						
Common property resource-based:										
• collection of wild foods	■	■	■	■	■	■				
• cutting *bourgou* for sale as fodder/own use	■■		■							
• wood-cutting	■	■								
• mat-making from palms for sale to fishers	■	■								
• intensify fishing					■	■	■	■		
• increase size of milk herd staying in pastoral safety nets			■	■	■	■			■	■
• shepherd other people's animals										

263

Table 10.4 (continued)

Strategy	Cultivators		Agro-pastoralists		Agro-fishers		Transhumant fishers		Transhumant pastoralists	
Year:	Bad	Good	Bad	Good	Bad	Good	Bad	Good	Bad	Good
Seasons: (Harvest, Cold, Dry, Rainy)	HCDR	HCDR	HCDR	HCDR	HCDR	HCDR	HCDR	HCDR	HCDR	HCDR
Reciprocally-based:										
• increase collection of traditional services/dues										
• reduce payment of traditional dues										
• intensify claims on kin										
• work on richer households' land										
• internal credit mechanisms										
• internal self-help mechanisms										
Asset-based:										
• liquidation of stocks for food										
• sale of animals										
• sale of gold										
• sale of domestic goods										
• sale of productive assets										
Labour-based:										
• redivision of household labour										
• longer working day										

Table 10.4 (continued)

Strategy	Cultivators		Livelihood system and seasonal use							
			Agro-pastoralists		Agro-fishers		Transhumant fishers		Transhumant pastoralists	
Year:	Bad	Good	Bad	Good	Bad	Good	Bad	Good	Bad	Good
Seasons: (Harvest, Cold, Dry, Rainy)	HCDR	HCDR	HCDR	HCDR	HCDR	HCDR	HCDR	HCDR	HCDR	HCDR
Exchange-based:										
• trade with traders in place of barter										
• establish/increase credit and repayment links										
• very small-scale retailing										
• exploit informal economy										
• act as intermediary in exchanges of livestock										
Migration-based:										
• work in neighbouring livelihood system										
• migrate to urban centres and stay away for longer										
• intensify habitual rural-rural migration										
• alter transhumance routes										
Consumption-based:										
• reduce intake										
• migrate to reduce household consumption										

as they already account for a significant proportion of household labour in a normal year. Coping strategies as short-term one-off responses to isolated periods of food insecurity have thus been replaced by a process of adaptation, using the same activities but for very different reasons.

CONCLUSIONS: INDICATORS OF COPING AND ADAPTIVE ENTITLEMENTS

It was pointed out in Chapter 3 that the use of coping strategies as indicators of food stress and impending crisis presupposed that the livelihood systems in question were secure: coping strategies were therefore distinct activities, used only in particular circumstances for relatively short periods of time. From the data presented here it is evident that these conditions do not hold in the SADS zone: some coping strategies are used by certain groups throughout all years, and others in some seasons of all years. Chapter 3 also demonstrated how monitoring coping strategies in order to predict famine is based on the premise that there is a sequential uptake of these activities, which seeks to preserve assets for future production, whilst at the same time meeting minimum consumption requirements. The dual objectives are, therefore, to prevent death by starvation and to prevent destitution. According to this model, death by starvation – or migration to emergency feeding camps to prevent death – only occurs when people have failed to avoid destitution. If people avoid destitution, they may go hungry but they will be able to continue to subsist once conditions return to normal.

If strategies are used as part of a process of adaptation, rather than as short-term, one-off responses to isolated periods of food stress, there are a number of implications for their use as indicators of food stress. Above all, the notion of repeatable sequential uptake is untenable for the following reasons:

- The mere fact of *using* a particular strategy, or sequence of strategies, can indicate nothing about food stress, because some people use them all the time and others do so for part of every year. It is hard to know in advance what the sequence of use will be and who will use which strategies.
- The *timing* of use will change depending on how evolved the process of adaptation is, echoing Mortimore's (1989) argument, that one person's coping strategy is another's livelihood. What may signal an alarm at a given point in one year or drought cycle will not necessarily indicate the same thing the next time round.

Coping and Adaptive Entitlements 267

- The *reasons* for uptake will depend on the mix of adaptive strategies available to particular livelihood systems and households within them. This mix is determined by: the characteristics of the strategy in question; where the household is in the process of adaptation; and other constraints and opportunities offered by the overall livelihood system (see below). It is very difficult to monitor the motivation for the use of coping strategies.

- The *effectiveness* of particular strategies in mitigating food insecurity is even more difficult to discern predictively, particularly if the reasons for pursuing a particular strategy are themselves uncertain. Generally, the effectiveness of coping strategies is used to explain retrospectively why famines did not occur, or why some people survived.

Whereas it is possible to monitor coping strategies, what they reveal is by no means clear. Even when monitored directly, as in the SADS system (or indirectly as advocated by Eele, 1987, for example), interpretation of the results remains elusive. It is not enough to monitor the uptake or pursuit of coping strategies in isolation from other factors. Most so-called coping strategies are, in fact, adaptive strategies and if these are to be useful indicators of food stress, what counts is the *intensity* of their use (how dependent households are on such strategies in a given season/year); their *sustainability* when this intensity increases (in both an economic and an environmental sense); the *motivation* for their use (coping or adapting) and the range of options open to particular households or livelihood systems; and their *effectiveness* in meeting food and livelihood needs, or the costs and benefits of particular strategies. This analysis is a formidable task. Motivation can be assessed by constructing retrospective activity calendars as a basis for comparison with current activity patterns (Chapter 7). Examples of the returns to coping – or their effectiveness – have been given, indicating that it is possible to estimate in a crude way how much a particular strategy will provide. Sustainability is much harder to assess, although it is clear that many strategies are economically unsustainable, especially without outside investment or reinforcement. In the latter case, there are risks of overkill: few strategies have robust enough results to sustain widespread reinforcement. The environmental costs of some – but not all – strategies are also likely to be high, particularly if they are pursued with intensity over a long period, which is inevitable once they have become adaptive strategies. One proxy indicator for the intensity of their use has been demonstrated here: the amount of time spent on particular activities. But all these indicators have substantial information-collection requirements, especially if changes over time are to be tracked,

268   *Adaptable Livelihoods*

which are far beyond the scope of local food monitoring or famine EW systems.

How, then, can indicators be developed to encapsulate the complexity of vulnerable livelihood systems without being unduly complex and infeasible? The first step in analysing adaptive as opposed to coping strategies is to reclassify them, not simply according to the entitlements from which they are derived, the seasons in which they can be used, or the priority with which they are (hypothetically) taken up, but on the basis of livelihood criteria. These reflect the range of factors which households have to weigh up in selecting their mix of adaptive strategies and include: the balance between risk and expected return; availability in good and bad years; labour requirements, including whether they are gender-specific and require particular household divisions of labour; whether they have high or low barriers to entry (e.g. requiring particular skills, high start-up capital); whether they are dependent on neighbouring livelihood systems or on traditional access rights; whether they incur debt and health risks; and whether they are sustainable. Table 10.5 classifies the coping strategies identified above according to livelihood criteria, which in turn influence how useful they will be as adaptive strategies, to particular kinds of producers and households.

A number of points emerge from the table:

- Strategies are roughly evenly divided between the four categories of risk and return, with, not surprisingly, marginally more being high-risk, low-return. These categories are not cast in stone and depend on the circumstances in which strategies are pursued. Disposal of assets, for example, is classified as being high-risk, low-return on the assumption that assets are probably being liquidated as distress sales when their terms of trade with cereals are unfavourable. The risk to future livelihood security is high. On the other hand, collection of wild foods is a low-risk strategy because it is dependent on household labour availability. Low-risk, high-return strategies are obviously the most attractive, but are also the least numerous. More important, they have other constraints, such as being dependent on the absorptive capacity of other households or livelihood systems, or of being highly seasonally specific.
- Exploitation of most strategies can be intensified in drought years, but only for certain seasons within them. Most are not, however, sustainable in the short term, meaning that, in successive years of drought, the strategies will become exhausted (e.g. assets can only be liquidated once, demand for labour in neighbouring livelihood sys-

269

Table 10.5 Classification of coping/adaptive strategies according to livelihood criteria

Livelihood criteria
(see key at end of table)

Coping/adaptive strategy	A	B	C	D	E	F	G	H	I	J	K	L	M	N	O	P	Q	R	S
Production-based																			
• mixture of late and early maturing seed		■																	
• diversify into market gardening for sale			■		■					■							■	■	
• switch from cattle to goats			■							■						■ ■		■	
• exploit other skills	■		■							■									
Common property resource-based:																			
• collection of wild foods					■	■ ■	■	■	■ ■			■		■ ■	■	■ ■	■ ■	■	
• cutting *bourgou* for sale as fodder/own use			■		■ ■	■	■ ■		■ ■	■	■ ■	■ ■		■	■	■ ■	■ ■	■	
• mat-making from palms for sale			■			■ ■	■ ■									■		■	
• wood-cutting						■	■ ■			■	■	■ ■		■ ■		■ ■		■	
• intensify fishing							■												
• increase size of milk herd staying in pastoral safety nets								■					■	■	■				
• shepherd other people's animals				■					■ ■	■ ■	■	■ ■	■	■ ■		■ ■	■		
Reciprocally-based:																			
• increase collection of traditional services/dues																			
• reduce payment of traditional dues		■							■ ■	■ ■	■	■		■		■ ■	■	■	
• intensify claims on kin				■						■						■	■		
• work on richer households' land	■		■							■									
• internal credit mechanisms	■									■									
• internal self-help mechanisms										■									

Table 10.5 (continued)

Coping/adaptive strategy	Livelihood criteria (see key at end of table)																		
	A	B	C	D	E	F	G	H	I	J	K	L	M	N	O	P	Q	R	S
Asset-based:																			
• liquidation of stocks for food																	■■		
• sale of animals				■■													■		
• sale of gold			■■																
• sale of domestic goods				■■															
• sale of productive assets																			
Labour-based:																			
• redivision of household labour		■■				■■	■■	■■									■■		■
• longer working day						■	■	■											
Exchange-based:																			
• trade with traders in place of barter	■					■■	■■	■							■■	■■■			
• establish/increase credit and repayment links				■		■	■								■■	■■■			
• very small-scale retailing	■					■				■	■	■■	■	■			■		
• exploit informal economy		■				■	■			■	■	■■	■	■			■		
• act as intermediary in exchanges of livestock	■					■	■	■						■					
Migration-based:																			
• work in neighbouring livelihood system		■		■	■	■	■			■	■	■	■	■			■		■
• migrate to urban centres and stay away for longer					■	■				■				■			■		
• intensify habitual rural–rural migration														■			■		
• alter transhumance routes			■			■	■		■	■				■		■			

270

271

Table 10.5 (continued)

Coping/adaptive strategy	Lvelihood criteria (see key at end of table)																		
	A	B	C	D	E	F	G	H	I	J	K	L	M	N	O	P	Q	R	S
Consumption-based:																			
• reduce intake																			■
• migrate to reduce household consumption				■ ■		■ ■	■ ■	■									■ ■		

Key:
- A low-risk, low-return
- B low-risk, high-return
- C high-risk, high-return
- D high-risk, low-return
- E seasonally specific
- F can intensify use in drought years
- G sustainable in short term
- H sustainable in long term
- I requires traditional access rights
- J livelihood system-specific
- K contingent on recipient livelihood system
- L high labour requirement
- M gender-specific
- N requires redivision of household labour
- O requires start-up capital
- P other high barriers to entry
- Q low barriers to entry
- R incurs debt, fines or dues (high potential calls on entitlement)
- S incurs health risks

tems will dry up in periods of dearth). Equally, some are not sustainable in the long term, because of the deleterious effects on the natural-resource base. The number of strategies which can support producers in both the short term under drought conditions and the longer term is very limited.

- Intensification of exploitation of CPRs is central to many responses to periods of food stress, yet these strategies are constrained by the fact that they are often high-risk (in the sense of incurring fines or dues), dependent on having traditional access rights (or having to pay for them), and seasonally specific. Moreover, because they depend upon exploitation of resources managed under increasingly chaotic conditions, they are unsustainable in the long term.
- Switching from cattle to goats is also related to CPR-based strategies, because goat herding (particularly on a small scale) tends to be carried out around villages on CPRs or protected browse on which fines for misuse are levied. So, although this is one of the most practised strategies precisely because it is so effective, it is not sustainable in the long term, particularly as more and more people take it up. Further, as Chapter 9 has shown, such is the intensity of use of this strategy that the bottom is falling out of the goat market.
- Those strategies which are contingent on recipient livelihood systems are only as robust as the resource base of the system in question. Whereas in years when drought is not universal (e.g. in 1987, when there was an agricultural but not a pastoral or fishing drought), they can be extremely effective, in periods of total drought, they break down. Furthermore, as systems become increasingly vulnerable, their absorptive capacity of people from outside declines. Cultivators employ less and less casual labour, both for cultivation and for harvesting.
- The labour requirements of coping strategies are, of course, central to household decision-making. Large households with high dependency ratios and small households have fewer choices and less ability to spread risk than large ones with low dependency ratios. The fact that many resources on which coping strategies depend are seasonally specific to some extent mitigates the need to choose between one strategy and another. It is possible, for example, to work on other people's fields at the end of the dry and beginning of the rainy season, and thereafter to collect wild foods. But both will limit the time available for the producer's own cultivation. Migration, particularly if it is driven by the need to reduce calls on household stocks rather than the opportunity of remittances, has

Coping and Adaptive Entitlements 273

severe consequences for the flexibility of those left behind. Both redivision of household labour (e.g. women taking over all home-based productive tasks whilst men migrate) and lengthening of the working day are central to the adaptive process.

- Some strategies have high barriers to entry, including the need for particular skills or (privileged) membership of a particular livelihood system and the assets associated with it. Few require start-up capital, for the reason that this is rarely available, so that options falling into this category tend to be primary activities rather than adaptive mechanisms. Most are classified as having low barriers to entry, because it is these kinds of activities which people in vulnerable systems are *able* to pursue.
- The risk of incurring debt, state fines or dues to other producers is high for many strategies, particularly those derived from CPRs and those which are dependent upon establishing credit and repayment relations with traders. These are double-edged strategies: the cost in fines, if caught, may wipe out any benefit from the activity. Equally, they may improve access to food in the short term, but increase vulnerability in the medium term.
- Strategies which incur health risks are also double-edged if they increase consumption but also the risk of infection, which in turn will have an adverse effect on nutritional status. Longer working hours may also reduce resilience to disease. The epidemiological consequences of migration are well-known. In this area, the spread of malarial parasites to which there is no local immunity is particularly problematic; and people from drier areas migrating into the Delta during the high and falling water seasons are exposed to acute malarial conditions. Division of families and migration to urban centres is also associated with the spread of AIDS and other sexually transmitted diseases.

The classification of adaptive strategies in Table 10.5 is not meant to be hard and fast, and there may well be dispute about the choice of category in particular cases. The mix of strategy characteristics will also change over time and according to the year in question. The point is not to establish a fixed typology of strategies, but to demonstrate an approach which reflects the kinds of issues which households confront during the process of adaptation. In stark contrast to the model of sequential uptake discussed in Chapter 3, there is no consistent set of strategies which meets all food, let alone livelihood, security needs and which is available to all households.

274 *Adaptable Livelihoods*

As argued in Chapter 2, the choices which households make about food security are situated within wider livelihood security considerations. The same strategy or mix of strategies will not suit everyone in a given area. Large households, for example, can opt for household divisions of labour to spread risk say between high-return, high-risk strategies and some low-return, low-risk ones. Small households will have to choose between one strategy or another. Certain livelihood systems (e.g. cultivators) are much more dependent on the absorptive capacity of neighbouring systems than others (e.g. transhumant fishers). Some households will have traditional access rights to resources which they can both exploit and charge rents for (e.g. local 'masters of the water', 'masters of the land' or *dioros*, the heads of Fulani pasturing clans),[4] whilst others will have to pay for these rights. Still others may be wealthy enough to overcome high barriers to entry, whilst poorer households are excluded from those strategies requiring start-up capital. The mix of strategies chosen is therefore dependent on membership of a given livelihood system, household size and relative wealth, being a stranger or a founding family, and the strength of kinship links to traditional resource managers.

Given these reservations, Table 10.6 grades the use of coping strategies at livelihood-system level to provide an overall assessment. Obviously, such grading of strategies is dependent on local conditions. High motivation/intensity indicates that the strategy is already pursued by many people and is thus perceived by them to be the best option available; motivation and intensity of use are treated together in the table, as their assessment will only differ in a given year. High effectiveness means that returns to pursuing that particular strategy are more likely than others to assist in filling the food gap. High economic sustainability means that these strategies can be pursued over time, and high environmental sustainability, that they do not have deleterious effects on the natural-resource base. Not surprisingly, very few strategies score highly in all, or most, respects. Finally, it must be stressed that the overall assessment would need to be updated regularly, to reflect the changing opportunities afforded by different strategies over time.

Unpacking adaptive strategies in this way is a first step towards meeting the requirements for monitoring adaptation, by identifying the kinds of factors which will influence the motivation for and the intensity and effectiveness of coping/adaptive strategies, as well as their economic and environmental sustainability. Ideally, strategies would be assessed at household level, as indicated in Table 10.5. Realistically, only system-level assessment is likely to be feasible for a local monitoring system, although household-level constraints must be borne in mind, especially

Table 10.6 Grading of coping/adaptive strategies according to use

Strategy	Motivation/intensity	Effectiveness	Sustainability
Production-based			
• mixture of late and early maturing seed	high	high	econ. high
• diversify into market gardening for sale	low	low	econ. low
• switch from cattle to goats	high	high	env. high; econ. med.
• exploit other skills	med.	med./low	econ. low
Common property resource-based:			
• collection of wild foods	high	med./high	econ. high; env. high
• cutting *bourgou* for sale as fodder/own use	high	med./high	env. low; econ. med.
• wood-cutting	high	med.	env. low; econ. med.
• mat-making from palms for sale to fishers	med.	low/med.	econ. low/ med.
• intensify fishing	high	high	env. low; econ. med.
• increase milk herd staying in pastoral safety nets	high	med.	env. low; econ. med.
• shepherd other people's animals	med.	low/med.	econ. low/med.
Reciprocally-based:			
• increase collection of traditional services/dues	high	med.	econ. med.
• reduce payment of traditional dues	high	low	econ. low
• intensify claims on kin	med.	low	econ. low
• work on richer households' land	med./low	low/med.	econ. low
• internal credit mechanisms	med.	med.	econ. med.
• internal self-help mechanisms	low	low	econ. low
Asset-based:			
• liquidation of stocks for food	high	med.	econ. low
• sale of animals	high	med.	econ. low/med.
• sale of gold	low	high/med.	econ. low
• sale of domestic goods	med.	med.	econ. low
• sale of productive assets	med.	med.	econ. low

Table 10.6 (continued)

Strategy	Use of strategy		
	Motivation/ intensity	Effectiveness	Sustainability
Labour-based:			
• redivision of household labour	high	med./high	econ. high
• longer working day	high	high	econ. high
Exchange-based:			
• trade with traders in place of barter	high	med.	econ. med.
• establish/increase credit and repayment links	high	med./low	econ. low
• very small-scale retailing	med.	med./low	econ. med.
• exploit informal economy	med.	med.	econ. med.
• act as intermediary in exchanges of livestock	low	med./low	econ. med./low
Migration-based:			
• work in neighbouring livelihood system	high/med.	med.	econ. med.; env. low/med.
• migrate to urban centres and stay away for longer	high	med.	econ. med./low
• intensify habitual rural-rural migration	med./high	med./low	econ. low/med.; env. low/med.
• alter transhumance routes	high	med.	env. low
Consumption-based:			
• reduce intake	high	low/med.	econ. med./low
• migrate to reduce household consumption	high	med.	econ. med./low

Table 10.7 Examples of indicators to monitor the use of coping/adaptive strategies

Strategy	Motivation	Intensity	Effectiveness	Sustainability
Production-based:				
• exploit other skills (e.g. artisanal work)		Appearance of goods on market	Terms of trade goods/millet	Demand for goods
Common property resource-based:				
• collection of wild foods	Carried out every year or unusually?	Timing of collection Pressure on foods Availability on market	No. of weeks of food supply	
Reciprocally-based:				
• internal credit mechanisms	To buy food or invest in production?	Price and availability of credit	Price of credit (compared with formal channels)	Availability of credit
Asset-based:				
• sale of animals	Distress sales or habitual disposals?	Price of livestock	Terms of trade livestock/millet	Type of animals sold (seed of herd?)
Labour-based:				
• redivision of household labour	To subsist or to protect livelihood?	Who is doing what compared with habitual seasonal activities?	No. of weeks of food supply from unusual activities	

Table 10.7 (continued)

Strategy	Indicator of strategy use			
	Motivation	Intensity	Effectiveness	Sustainability
Exchange-based:				
• very small-scale retailing	To subsist or to protect livelihood?	No. of traders on markets	Margins on trade	Saturation of market for small-scale trade?
Migration-based:				
• work in nearby livelihood system	Habitual or unusual migration?	No. of people looking for work in productive zones	Rates and type of remuneration	
Consumption-based:				
• reduce intake	To protect assets or last resort?	Timing of reduction (relative to hungry season)		Health of population

when considering who will benefit from the reinforcement of a given strategy. The next step is to derive indicators from Tables 10.5 and 10.6, which can reasonably be tracked over time. Table 10.7 gives examples of the kinds of indicators which can monitor these factors. Similar indicators could be derived for other strategies, based on the above examples. It is of note that some of these indicators are the same as those used to monitor exchange entitlements, thereby reducing the implicit information requirements.

What we have to do now is to develop a simple methodology using indicators which genuinely serve as proxies for the overall complexity of livelihood systems. It is to this issue that we now turn in the final chapter.

11 Tracking and Tackling Food Vulnerability

INTRODUCTION

There are four steps in famine prevention: detection, preparedness, intervention and rehabilitation. This study has focused on the first of these, comprising monitoring and prediction or assessment. This final chapter considers its implications for the other steps and proposes a way of integrating the four stages within an information and policy-making framework, thus forging what has been described as the 'missing link' between famine EW and response (Buchanan-Smith and Davies, in press). It explores the conclusions that can be drawn for the development of sustainable and appropriate methodologies for monitoring vulnerability to food insecurity, and the uses to which such information can be put by planners and policy-makers.

SUMMARY OF FINDINGS

Famine is not the principal problem in the Sahel in most years, but instead chronic food insecurity, which creates the conditions under which famine can strike in exceptional times. Most EWS are concerned with famine and the failure of food systems; more precisely, with predicting such failure in order to intervene in a timely manner to mitigate the effects of system failure on immediate food consumption. This study has challenged conventional approaches to famine EWS, on the grounds that they do not work (they fail to prevent famine) and that preoccupation with food *crises* diverts attention away from the increasing structural vulnerability of Sahelian livelihoods, thereby increasing the likelihood of widespread famine in the future. An experimental local food monitoring system – the SADS – sought to develop a framework within which vulnerability to food insecurity could be tracked and tackled. The starting point for reconsidering famine EW is to concentrate on how people feed themselves, rather than on how they fail to do so.

Sahelian livelihood systems are becoming more vulnerable with successive episodes of drought. There are two dimensions to increased vulnerability: reduced resilience (the capacity to bounce back after a shock) and increased sensitivity (the intensity of impact of a given shock). Food security is but one objective people seek to realise in the wider context of the livelihood systems they rely on to subsist. Continual trade-offs are made to optimise meeting immediate consumption needs and preserving future assets: to reduce sensitivity and increase resilience. This is a process of adaptation which people struggling to survive within vulnerable livelihood systems undertake, and it is the potential of, and limits to, this process which must be central to a policy of famine prediction and prevention.

Taking the nature and intensity of vulnerability (or its opposite, security) as a starting point, a livelihood entitlements framework has been elaborated as a means of identifying appropriate indicators of food stress. This framework identifies not only sources of but also calls on entitlement, the balance between the two being the entitlement bundle available in a given year. Membership of a livelihood system determines the bundle of entitlements to which people have access. Differences in food-security status within communities need to be tracked according to the livelihood systems practised within them. Although structural individual or household vulnerability (e.g. being under five or part of a female-headed household) contributes to food insecurity, it is not the optimum focus for monitoring *changes* in vulnerability from one season or year to another in an area where all livelihood systems are structurally vulnerable. To monitor such changes, the focus must be on proximate livelihood-system vulnerability. By developing a set of indicators based on sources of and calls on entitlements, capable of monitoring both proximate livelihood-system vulnerability and the ability to cope and adapt, not only can the collapse of food security be predicted for particular productive groups, but means of reinforcing livelihoods to make them sustainably less food-insecure can also be identified.

The ability to cope – or take up tertiary activities – is endemic to Sahelian livelihood systems, and people's coping strategies must be tracked to monitor changes in levels and intensity of food insecurity. The SADS system set about monitoring coping strategies, on the assumption that they would be robust and sensitive indicators of food stress, and would facilitate the identification of appropriate and timely responses. There are a number of shortcomings to this approach, indicating that the idea of coping strategies needs to be treated with caution. First, they can be defined so broadly as to be indistinguishable from general patterns of decision-making at the individual, household and community level. Second, they can be based on the false assumption that people *do* cope and that food insecurity is a transitory phenomenon, thus masking the collapse of livelihood security and overestimating people's ability to survive. Third, if coping strategies and their reinforcement were to become the centre-piece of household food-security monitoring and interventions, there is a further risk of poor people remaining locked into a vicious circle of subsistence and coping, exacerbated by interventions designed to support coping strategies which are neither economically nor environmentally sustainable; they can enable people to stand still but not to move forward. Fourth, the idea of coping strategies being cast in stone and of people following an identifiable and repeatable pattern of uptake in times of stress, ignores the fact that one person's coping strategy is another's livelihood, making the identification and monitoring of repeated patterns of coping behaviour more or less impossible for representative groups. Finally, the very complexity of coping strategies makes for potentially huge difficulties in data collection and interpretation. To address these issues, it is necessary to differentiate between coping and adaptation: whereas the former is a characteristic of structurally secure livelihood systems, vulnerable systems are characterised by adaptation. Coping strategies as short-term, temporary responses to declining food entitlements are distinct from adaptive strategies which are long-term permanent changes in the mix of activities, necessary to reduce the vulnerability of livelihood systems to collapse.

The methodology used by the SADS system was based on two objectives: first, to establish a baseline of habitual sources of and calls on food entitlements (using the livelihood entitlements framework), against which temporary deviations or permanent changes could be measured. This baseline was defined in terms of when people last felt secure in their livelihoods (prior to the drought cycle of the early 1970s). The second aim was to develop a set of indicators capable of predicting whether or not people would achieve immediate food and livelihood security relative to this baseline, in a given season or year as well as over the longer term. These indicators needed to address three issues: whether primary and secondary activities could guarantee food security; if not, how people would cope with food insecurity; and finally, how and whether people would recover from episodes of food insecurity or adapt to permanent changes in their food-security status. A simplified version of this methodology is summarised in the next section.

Data from the SADS system have been analysed within the context of food and famine policy in Mali. In the 1980s, this policy was characterised by two extremes. At the macroeconomic level, cereal market liberalisation preoccupied donors and government alike, as part of a wider programme of structural adjustment. The drought of the mid-1980s interrupted this process, and in the aftermath of untimely and often inappropriate emergency relief, a number of famine EWS were set up. These two arms came together at the beginning of the 1990s, when the donor/government programme responsible for cereal market restructuring (the PRMC) assumed responsibility both for the national EWS (the SAP) and for a programmed response mechanism to ensure that SAP warnings were translated into managed free food distributions, furnished by the national security stock. This policy has been notably more successful than attempts elsewhere in the Sahel and Horn of Africa to translate EW of food shortages into timely response, and the restructuring of cereal markets has been a necessary but insufficient precondition for more fundamental adjustment of the food sector. But taken together, these two branches of policy – between which there is a gaping hole of inaction or inappropriate intervention – do not tackle the fundamental problems facing food-insecure people in Mali. Famine is in fact quite a rare event, even in the Sahelian north, and nationally the country moves between surplus and deficit depending on the year in question. Nowhere in the pursuit of NFS objectives (outlined in 1982) has the increasing structural vulnerability of Sahelian livelihood systems been systematically addressed. The implicit assumption has been either that people are at risk of the threat of famine, or that they simply require better market incentives to produce more.

Taking the 5th Region of Mali as a case study, the worsening structural vulnerability of livelihood systems is shown to be due to a combination of lower rainfall and flood levels (in the Inner Niger Delta), a declining natural-resource base, and greater exploitation of those resources which are relatively plentiful in dry seasons and years. This process has been exacerbated by inappropriate and extractive state policies. The intensification of vulnerability is due less to natural population growth (which is only 1.07 per cent a year in the 5th Region) than to the fact that the seasonal floodplain of the Inner Niger Delta in the midst of the Sahelian drylands, which has always been a safety net in times of stress, has now become central to the subsistence of increasing numbers of people in every year, as they migrate in search of wetland resources. Indigenous Delta inhabitants are, in turn, also becoming more impoverished. It was this safety net which was the focus of the SADS monitoring system, as the Delta is the place to which food-insecure people move when their primary sources of entitlement fail.

The diversity and seasonality of natural resources in the Delta and the surrounding drylands together give rise to local livelihood systems, which in turn determine how food security is achieved. On the drylands, three principal systems are found: millet cultivators, agro-pastoralists and transhumant pastoralists. On the wetlands, there are rice cultivators and, in addition to both types of pastoralist, agro-fishers and transhumant fishers. All these livelihoods have traditionally depended on seasonally specific exploitation of natural resources and linked labour exchanges between livelihood systems. In the period between the two drought cycles of the 1970s and the mid-1980s, these systems underwent a transition from security – so defined by practitioners of the livelihoods concerned – to vulnerability. Not only have they become more sensitive to the shock of drought or a low flood, but they are also less and less able to bounce back to a pre-shock state. Data collected over a four-year period since the drought of the mid-1980s covering production, exchange and coping/adaptive entitlements for all five livelihood systems in the Delta and surrounding drylands, confirm this transition to structural vulnerability. Barriers to re-entry into more secure livelihood systems lock poor people in a constant state of structural vulnerability, irrespective of the year in question. Buffers against periods of stress no longer exist: the only option is to intensify the adaptive strategies already pursued, and the opportunities for so doing are highly constrained. The scene is therefore set for widespread crisis for the next cycle of drought. If this scenario is to be tackled – or the threat of famine mitigated – it is the barriers to re-entering secure livelihood systems which are resilient to drought which must be addressed. The nature and intensity of this transition vary between livelihood systems and within them, but broad characteristics of the change can be identified and indicators to predict food and livelihood insecurity derived from them.

The principal difference is that primary and secondary activities (cultivating, fishing and herding) can no longer guarantee annual food needs in most years. Whereas, in the past, all livelihood systems not only met annual food needs but also had a series of buffers against production failure, a structural food gap now engenders insecurity, instability and high risk. This is filled by a combination of the use of traditional sources of investment and accumulation for more immediate consumption needs, and the pursuit of adaptive strategies. The capacity to accumulate in good years, and the sequential options this provided for meeting successive dry years and recovering from them, has been replaced by a cycle of subsistence and coping in each year, such that accumulation is rarely possible. Further, there is little flexibility in present-day livelihood systems: people operate a fine balancing act, trading-off short-term food needs against longer-term livelihood protection. Livelihood systems have become more diversified to spread risk, but diversification is itself becoming less effective.

All livelihood systems are much more market-dependent than in the past, and have few guaranteed sources of income (in the case of undiversified cultivators), and face declining terms of trade (for those with pastoral or fishing incomes). People are thus ill-equipped to participate in the market. The increasing strain under which reciprocal exchanges and ties operate further promotes dependence on the market: as livelihoods become more vulnerable, reciprocal ties either break down or become increasingly exploitative. In the past, most exchange was for the purpose of diversifying diets or accumulating or investing to spread risk. Nowadays, exchange is central to subsistence. As market dependence increases, successful optimisation of exchange entitlements becomes ever more central to reducing vulnerability. It is the terms of trade between the different goods traded by each livelihood system, which vary from season to season, rather than prices alone, which indicate the degree of food insecurity in a given year. Key terms of trade for subsistence have changed in the transition from secure to vulnerable systems. All producers are able to partially fill the food gap by relying on the market, but this is at the cost of accumulation and is a highly risky strategy. In bad years, the key terms of trade swing sharply and adversely against them. Furthermore, as calls on entitlements intensify, the need to raise cash – usually when what they are selling has little value – means that market dependence is further increased at a high cost.

Reliance on a complex range of adaptive strategies to try and generate cash income for market purchases, or increase sources of entitlement in kind (e.g. by collection of wild foods, seeking work paid in kind in neighbouring livelihood systems), now characterises all livelihood systems. What were traditionally (and are still commonly perceived to be) coping strategies employed exclusively in periods of food stress are now adaptive strategies that have become incorporated into the normal pattern of activities and make up a significant proportion both of cash income and of household labour allocation. The overwhelming characteristic of the strategies pursued is that they offer – without exception – uncertain, piecemeal and poorly remunerated means of filling the annual food gap. There is not, for example, a known and guaranteed labour market in accessible urban centres, nor the certainty of market demand for counter-season crops: many strategies are economically unsustainable, as seen in the collapse of goat prices as more and more people invest in them as an insurance against crop failure or pastoral drought. Further, as more and more people seek to exploit these strategies for longer periods, the natural-resource base from which they are derived comes under increasing pressure. The greatest opportunities for seasonal exploitation of resources are found in the Delta which, as a traditional safety net within the Sahelian zone, becomes a magnet for people from an ever wider radius to the north and east.

Indicators to track food vulnerability in a given year include: the size of the annual food gap (the difference between sources of primary production entitlement and minimum consumption requirements); the amount of food acquired via non-market channels (from barter, off-farm harvests and wild food collection); the amount of food acquired via the market; the returns to diversifying sources of entitlement, either from secondary productive entitlements or coping/adaptive sources; and the terms of trade between different sources of entitlement, and between sources of and calls on entitlement.

If coping strategies are used as part of a process of adaptation, rather than as short-term, often one-off responses to isolated periods of food stress, there are a number of implications for their use as predictive indicators of that stress. Above all, the notion of repeatable sequential uptake is untenable, firstly, because the mere fact of *using* a particular strategy, or sequence of strategies, can indicate nothing about food stress, because some people use them all the time and others do so for part of every year. It is very hard to know in advance what the sequence of use will be and who will use which strategies. Second, the *timing* of use will change depending on how evolved the process of adaptation is, because one person's coping strategy is another's livelihood. What may signal an alarm at a given point in one year or drought cycle will not necessarily indicate the same thing the next time around. Third, the *reasons* for uptake will depend on the mix of adaptive strategies available to particular livelihood systems and households within them. This mix is determined by the characteristics of the strategy in question; where the household is in the process of adaptation; and other constraints and opportunities offered by the overall livelihood system. It is very difficult to monitor the motivation for the use of coping strategies. Finally, the *effectiveness* of particular strategies in mitigating food insecurity is even more difficult to discern predictively, particularly if the reasons for pursuing a given strategy are themselves uncertain. Generally, the effectiveness of coping strategies is used to explain retrospectively why famines did not occur, or why some people survived.

Given that adaptive strategies cannot be monitored as indicators of food stress according to the model of a repeatable sequential uptake of strategies, it is the motivation for and the intensity and effectiveness of their use, as well as their economic and environmental sustainability, which would have to be tracked over time, if they are to be useful indicators.

This is a substantial task. Moreover, because adaptive strategies are only part of livelihood systems, and in vulnerable systems the mix of adaptation and primary and secondary activities shifts continuously from one season and one year to the next, indicators are required which cover a much wider range of entitlements and food availability than are habitually considered by EWS. Particularly important gaps, even in multiple indicator EWS, which must be monitored are the process of constant adaptation and its dependence on multiple resource use (i.e. not simply cereal production), as well as migration in its widest sense and calls on entitlement. On the basis of analysis of present-day production, exchange and coping/adaptive entitlements, the key indicators derived from the system are summarised within the livelihood entitlements framework, in Table 11.1.

A SIMPLIFIED METHODOLOGY FOR MONITORING LIVELIHOODS

This section sketches out a simplified methodology for monitoring vulnerable livelihoods, based on the lessons learnt from the SADS system. Built into the system is the identification of a range of responses. The aim is preventive, to detect the process of increasing vulnerability rather than only the catastrophe of famine, so as to trigger timely and appropriate response (which may or may not involve distributions of emergency food aid). The methodology further enables evaluation of the impact of interventions on the vulnerability of recipient groups.

The proposed methodology is designed to track changes in food insecurity, and indicators have been developed accordingly. The approach could, however, be modified to address other aspects of livelihood vulnerability, such as more general monitoring of poverty or the consequences of declining natural-resource availability. The objective is twofold: first, to track changes in livelihood vulnerability/security over time, in order to identify the nature of structural vulnerability and the longer-term interventions needed to enable people to regain security in their livelihoods. Second, the system can also function as a more conventional famine EWS, predicting short-term collapse of entitlements. In the event of an exceptionally bad year, tracking of crisis indicators would be stepped up, but these are not the *raison d'être* of the system. Further, the system permits the identification of flexible response options, for both crisis and non-crisis years. To this end, it could be the basis both of a contingency plan and of a longer-term planning exercise to address the underlying causes of food and livelihood vulnerability.

Table 11.1 Summary of indicators in the livelihood entitlements matrix

Sources of and calls on entitlements			Mediators of entitlement		
	Natural	Individual/ household	Livelihood system	Moral economy	Market	State

Sources

Production	Rainfall and flood levels. Levels of pest damage. Assessment of pastoral, fishing reserves.	Number of months of annual food gap.	Number of months of annual food gap.	Number of months of food from off-farm harvests.		
Exchange		Number of months of food acquired via the market.	Number of months of food acquired via the market.	Number of months of food acquired through reciprocal ties. Level of barter.	Adverse movements in key seasonal terms of trade.	
Assets			Level of diversification of sources of entitlement.	Level of asset disposal through kin	Level of asset disposal via the market (and terms of trade of asset with millet).	

Table 11.1 (continued)

Sources of and calls on entitlements	Mediators of entitlement					
	Natural	Individual/ household	Livelihood system	Moral economy	Market	State
Coping/ adaptation	Availability of wild foods and other gathered products. Changes in traditional transhumance routes.		Number of months of food from wild foods. Absorptive capacity of neighbouring livelihood systems.[a]	Intensification of exploitation of reciprocal ties to increase coping.[b]	Effectiveness of coping strategies relative to price of millet.[c] Demand for artisanal goods and gathered products (and terms of trade with millet).	Promotion or inhibition of coping strategies
Calls						
Consumption		Declining nutritional status. Reduction in number of meals.	Early start to hungry season.			

Table 11.1 (continued)

Sources of and calls on entitlements	Mediators of entitlement				
	Natural	Individual/ household	Livelihood system	Moral economy	State
Claims				Intensification of claims on kin. Claims erode the basis of subsistence of the debtor.	Levels of state tax collection. Levels and targets of fining and licensing.
Livelihood protection	Intensification of abusive pasturing, fishing, wood-cutting.	Reduction in land area cultivated.	Reduction in land area cultivated. Reduction in sources of entitlement.(d)		Increase in state fining for environmental degradation.

Notes: (a) e.g. employment opportunities.
(b) e.g. level of rural-rural migration.
(c) e.g. price of day's casual labour.
(d) e.g. no more animals, no more credit for fishing equipment.

Adapting Drèze and Sen's (1989) distinction between entitlement protection and entitlement promotion, interventions resulting from the proposed methodology fall into three categories:

- *entitlement provision* (or relief), required in crisis years when livelihood systems are unable to provide adequate food on any terms and so to respond to proximate vulnerability;
- *entitlement protection* (or mitigation), relevant in both normal years and early on in crisis years to support existing sources of entitlement and reduce calls on these, thereby addressing both proximate vulnerability and potential future structural vulnerability;
- *entitlement promotion* (or rehabilitation and development), needed to increase sources of entitlement and reduce calls on them in a sustainable manner and so to facilitate recovery and address structural vulnerability.

The methodology has 11 stages or steps which cover detection (monitoring and assessment/prediction); the three types of intervention; and evaluation of their impact. Step 1 is the preliminary groundwork undertaken before monitoring can take place. Steps 2 to 6 are the monitoring parts of the system, conducted annually. Steps 7 to 10 cover annual prediction and interventions, whilst the final Step 11 suggests one-off rehabilitation measures as well as longer-term development interventions. The methodology seeks to do five things: to find out what people normally do; to see what options they have when conditions are abnormal; to assess how effective these options will be; to identify and trigger what can be done to make them more effective both in the short and longer term; and to evaluate the impact of short- and longer-term interventions on reducing vulnerability and improving household food and livelihood security. Table 11.2 indicates how data collection, analysis and response would be phased, in the Sahel, assuming a single rainy season from June to September. The flooded rice harvest in the Delta in January is not included, but could be added where relevant.

Step 1: livelihood entitlements matrix. The starting point for the methodology is building a local livelihood entitlements matrix. This initial step must be carried out prior to monitoring and takes one calendar year to take account of seasonal variations. Information collection is at community (village or transhumant camp) level, supplemented by random household interviews to cross-check collective information. This could be shortened by using PRA techniques, particularly for recalling habitual seasonal activity calendars and how they have changed. Constructing a

Table 11.2 Methodology for livelihood vulnerability monitoring and entitlement enhancement

Steps in methodology	O	N	D	J	F	M	A	M	J	J	A	S
Year 1												
Step 1: livelihood entitlements matrix (detection)												
Classification of local livelihood systems	①	①	①	①	①	①	①	①	①	①	①	
Draw up activity calendars for each livelihood system	①	①	①	①	①	①	①	①	①	①	①	
Construct livelihood entitlements matrix for each livelihood system							①				①	
Indicator identification for subsequent phases												①
Subsequent years												
Step 2: production entitlements (detection)												
Pre-harvest study			②									
Post-harvest study			②									
Pasture availability assessment							②					
Fishing campaign assessment		②										
Step 3: exchange entitlements (detection)												
Seasonal market surveys	②	③	③	②	③	③	③	③	③	③	③	③
Step 4: asset-based entitlements (detection)												
Post-harvest coping strategy map			②									
Seasonal market surveys	②	③	③	②	③	③	③	③	③	③	③	③
Step 5: coping/adaptive entitlements (detection/assessment)												
Post-harvest coping strategy map			②	④								
Assessment of coping effectiveness			④	④			⑤			⑤		

Table 11.2 (continued)

Steps in methodology	O	N	D	J	F	M	A	M	J	J	A	S
Step 6: calls on entitlement (detection)												
Post-harvest estimate of calls			❷									
Step 7: short-term prediction (assessment)												
Initial alarm if bad year			❹	❹							❺	❺
Assessment of overall calls vs sources							❺	❻	❻	❺		
Step 8: entitlement provision (response)				❻	❻	❻	❻	❻	❻	❻	❻	❻
Step 9: entitlement protection (response)				❼	❼	❼	❼	❼	❼	❼	❼	❼
Step 10: long-term assessment (assessment)								❹				
Step 11: entitlement promotion (response)	❽	❽	❽	❽	❽	❽	❽	❽	❽	❽	❽	❽

Key: Detection: ❶ – background;
                   ❷ – in all years;
                   ❸ – additional in crisis years.
      Assessment: ❹ – in all years;
                   ❺ – additional in crisis years.
      Response: ❻ – entitlement provision;
                   ❼ – entitlement protection;
                   ❽ – entitlement promotion.

livelihood entitlements matrix involves classification of livelihood systems in the area, based on identification of what different people do to acquire food and livelihood security (the construction of activity calendars); the completion of a livelihood entitlements matrix for the area to be monitored (what the potential sources of and calls on entitlements are); and the derivation of indicators from this. Identification of local livelihood systems may be relatively straightforward, either if existing work has already done this, or if the area is more homogenous than the SADS zone. It is, however, important to cross-check existing classifications through the construction of activity calendars, especially in areas where livelihoods have undergone rapid changes with recent periods of drought.

Activity calendars must include an assessment of whether the livelihood systems in question are secure or vulnerable. This can be done using the characteristics of high-resilience/low-sensitivity livelihood systems in Table 7.1 and low-resilience/high-sensitivity ones in Table 7.2. These characteristics will need to be adapted to local conditions, but using the matrix for indicators of the transition from high resilience/low sensitivity to low resilience/high sensitivity shown in Table 2.8, appropriate indicators can be developed. By way of illustration, Table 11.3 shows such indicators for the study area. Crudely, the process amounts to counting the number of 'buffers' which a given livelihood system has against the threat of food and livelihood insecurity. The greater the number of buffers, the less its sensitivity to disturbance and the greater its capacity to recover, as Table 11.3 shows. It is worth recalling that, in vulnerable livelihood systems, local people's definitions of food insecurity and famine change as their livelihood systems evolve. For this reason, any monitoring system needs to be dynamic enough to reflect these changed perceptions. Obviously, some standardisation of what constitutes a crisis is required for planning purposes, but over time, indicators and what they mean will need to be updated to reflect what is happening on the ground.

In constructing activity calendars, key seasonal terms of trade for market-dependent livelihood systems need to be identified, as shown in Table 9.1. These are the basis for identifying exchange entitlement indicators, as shown in Table 9.4. Once the seasonal pattern of the normal disposal of goods has been established, indicators of unusual disposals (i.e. assets) can also be picked up. Finally, on the sources side of the matrix the range of coping strategy options open to producers in the area needs to be identified and classified. Ideally, this would be according to the livelihood criteria suggested in Table 10.5; more easily, they can be graded at livelihood-system level as indicated in Table 10.6. These are the tools which are subsequently used in the monitoring process, Steps 2 to 6.

Table 11.3 Indicators of the transition from security to vulnerability

Sources of and calls on entitlements	Sustainability of entitlements			
	Security		Vulnerability	
	High resilience	Low sensitivity	Low resilience	High sensitivity
Sources				
Production	More than 1 year's food needs met by primary production. Capacity to accumulate, invest from secondary production.	Up to 1 year's buffer against primary productive failure (1st buffer). Diversification into and savings from secondary production (2nd buffer).	Structural food gap. Secondary production to fill food gap.	No buffer against primary productive failure. No buffer against secondary productive failure.
Exchange	Low market dependence or guaranteed purchasing power. Favourable terms of trade.	Limited vulnerability to rising cereal prices (3rd buffer).	High market dependence, no guaranteed purchasing power. Unfavourable terms of trade.	Highly vulnerable to rising cereal prices.
Assets	Capacity for accumulation.	Ability to liquidate assets progressively (4th buffer).	No capacity for accumulation.	No claims, or calls on claims erode others' basis of subsistence.
Coping	Coping strategies used only in times of food stress.	Coping strategies are bottom-line safety nets (5th buffer).	Coping strategies used every year.	Coping strategy use cannot be intensified.

Table 11.3 (continued)

Sources of and calls on entitlements	Sustainability of entitlements			
	Security		Vulnerability	
	High resilience	Low sensitivity	Low resilience	High sensitivity
Adaptation	Little or no adaptation.	Adaptation could be pursued (*6th buffer*).	Adaptation is intense.	No, or very limited, options for intensifying adaptation.
Calls				
Consumption	Adequate annual consumption (good nutritional status, sufficient intake all year).	Good health, adequate nutritional status at start of crisis (*7th buffer*).	Inadequate annual consumption (low nutritional status, regularly reduced intake).	Poor health, low nutritional status at start of crisis.
Claims	Extensive reciprocal ties.	Calls on claims are for others' surplus, not basis of subsistence (so likely to be met when needed) (*8th buffer*). State calls can be met easily (*9th buffer*).	Reciprocal ties have broken down or are exploitative.	Calls on claims erode the basis of others' subsistence. State calls cannot be met without increasing vulnerability.
Livelihood protection	Investment in future security.	Future security (*10th buffer*).	Limited or no investment in future security.	Future vulnerability

Calls on entitlements must also be estimated: consumption is notoriously difficult to estimate, but claims and the potential for livelihood protection derived from the sum of sources and calls are less problematic (see Step 6 below).

Step 2: production entitlements. Indicators of production entitlements need to detect how much food is available once all sources of and calls on production have been settled. Two rounds of survey are required: a pre-harvest survey to detect whether it is an exceptionally poor year, and a post-harvest survey to calculate the balance of sources of and calls on production entitlements. In areas with pastoral and fishing livelihood systems, additional assessments covering these activities are required. The pre-harvest survey is based on producers' own assessments of the forthcoming crop and their estimate of the size of the food gap (whether it is normal, or more or less than the norm and by how many months). Over time, correlations between producers' pre-harvest and post-harvest assessments can be made (e.g. whether they tend to over- or under-estimate during the growing season). Similar methods can be used to assess other resources, based on a simple scale of whether resource availability will meet normal entitlement levels, or be substantially below or above this. Data from more formal surveys (e.g. national production estimates, rainfall and flood levels) can be used to cross-check and substantiate producers' estimates. The post-harvest survey needs to assess both sources of and calls on production entitlements: producers' estimates of household stocks once all calls have been met. Calls can be expressed in terms of the number of weeks or months of household food supply they will require to be settled, under prevailing market conditions.

Step 3: exchange entitlements. Monitoring exchange entitlements is based on the key terms of trade for each livelihood system, identified in Step 1. In normal years, seasonal market monitoring will suffice, but if a crisis year is indicated, monthly monitoring is necessary to track the consequences of unmanageable market dependence. A further indicator of exchange entitlements relates to levels of barter. Data indicate that barter declines as market dependence increases, but is responsive to short-term changes in the vulnerability of livelihood systems: barter tends to return when conditions improve, albeit temporarily. As such, levels of barter can confirm data from other indicators as to the severity of the year in question. They can also indicate whether reciprocal ties are operating to subsidise or extract rents from particularly vulnerable households or livelihood systems.

Step 4: asset-based entitlements. Asset-based entitlements can be indirectly monitored by market surveys: most obviously via the disposal of livestock, but also by the sale of productive equipment (e.g. ploughs) and other assets. Again, in the event of a crisis year being signalled, market surveys need to extend their remit to monitor for asset disposal. Asset disposal is further indicated by the coping strategy maps drawn up in Step 5.

Step 5: coping and adaptive entitlements. At the same time as the post-harvest survey, coping strategy options for the coming year need to be mapped out: what activities people intend to pursue with a given food gap, and how intended activity patterns differ from normal years (i.e. the motivation for pursuing particular activities). These 'coping strategies' are understood within the context of adaptation, identified in Step 1. Thus, instead of all tertiary activities being regarded as coping behaviour, annual mapping will show which activities are being *unusually* undertaken. In vulnerable livelihood systems, those strategies mapped out annually as coping options will not be distinct from normal behaviour, but rather an intensification of normal activity calendars. Thus, once key coping activities have been identified for the year in question, crude indicators of coping and adaptive entitlements need to detect two things: the intensity of use in a given area (how many people will be pursuing a given strategy), and the likely effectiveness of such a strategy in meeting food needs (e.g. the number of days of wild food collection in a month). Methods for doing this have been indicated in Chapter 10: most obviously, the terms of trade between selling particular goods in order to purchase food, but also rough calculations of, for example, the profit from transporting goods or engaging in small-scale commerce or the local availability of wild food. Such a task is not as unmanageable as it first appears, given that each year there is a selection of the proposed strategies to be intensified, so that not all potential strategies have to be examined each year. The effectiveness of those strategies undertaken every year also needs to be estimated, but this can be done as part of Step 1 and only updated as necessary. Over time, sustainability of use of particular strategies can be monitored. Economic sustainability can be detected by monitoring the effectiveness of a given strategy over time. Environmental sustainability is more problematic, and it is unlikely that a monitoring system set up to detect food insecurity would prioritise it. Nevertheless indicators of coping strategy use which was detrimental in the medium term would provide a basis for developing a means of monitoring their environmental sustainability.

Step 6: calls on entitlements. At the same time as coping strategies for the year are mapped out, an estimate of calls on entitlements can be made. Claims can be directly estimated (e.g. levels and timing of taxation, outstanding debts to traders and other producers, and the cost of meeting these from selling cereals). Livelihood protection calls can be detected from coping strategy mapping (whether resources are being diverted to this end rather than to immediate consumption). Actual consumption can be monitored, albeit very imprecisely, in a bad year using the indicator of number of meals consumed.

Step 7: short-term predictions. Once all actual and potential sources of entitlement, as well as calls on these, have been estimated, short-term predictions can be made, to inform of impending crisis and to suggest what level of monitoring is required in subsequent months. The balance of entitlement availability for each livelihood system can be expressed in two ways: first, the estimated size of the food gap, and second, the cost to future security of meeting the gap. A prediction might, therefore, indicate a three-month food gap for agro-pastoralists, with liquidation of most animals, or, alternatively, a six-month gap with the preservation of the seed of the herd. This two-track approach indicates not only the scale of food insecurity, but also suggests the kinds of intervention which would be appropriate to simply meeting immediate food needs on the one hand, or protecting future livelihoods on the other. In the event of the pre-harvest survey indicating an especially poor year, an earlier initial prediction can be made in August–September, to be subsequently substantiated by the post-harvest assessment.

Step 8: entitlement provision. In crisis years, entitlement provision interventions will be required: food or cash to meet immediate consumption requirements, on the basis of predictions that indicate either that the food gap cannot be filled at any price, or that it can only be met at an unacceptably high cost to future productive capacity. This, of course, is the habitual response of almost all famine EWS. Yet certainly in the study area, and in other comparable zones where livelihoods are vulnerable but adaptation is highly evolved, entitlement provision is likely to be indicated relatively infrequently (one or two years in ten).

Step 9: entitlement protection. Whereas most EWS stop at the point of entitlement provision – and often resort to emergency food aid distributions, for want of alternative options, even when they are inappropriate – entitlement protection is far more likely to be indicated. This centres on interventions which seek to enhance existing sources of entitlement or to reduce calls. It is intimately bound up with the trade-off that producers make to meet immediate consumption needs, whilst at the same time protecting future livelihoods. On the sources side, it might involve low-interest credit based on using livestock as collateral to prevent untimely distress sales to purchase cereals; market interventions to support livestock prices; provision of seed for cultivators; or seasonal off-farm employment (possibly generated by public works) at the time of the year when producers' own coping strategies were unremunerative and household labour was available (i.e. labour would not have to be diverted away from investment in future production). On the calls side, it might include delaying tax collection until the terms of trade to producers were more favourable, or providing short-term credit to spread debt repayment to the private sector. These kinds of interventions could be used in conjunction with entitlement provision. Entitlement provision, like entitlement protection, addresses proximate vulnerability. Protection also has the potential to reduce the worsening of structural vulnerability, by facilitating bounce back.

Step 10: longer-term assessment. The final step in detection is longer-term assessment, carried out at the end of the dry season and beginning of the rains. The point of this exercise is to assess the future vulnerability of livelihoods, as well as to evaluate interim entitlement provision and protection measures undertaken thus far during the year, thereby predicting post-crisis outcomes in the event of a bad year. This assessment needs to address four questions: Has productive capacity been preserved? Are calls on entitlement likely to compromise future production? How effective have interim entitlement provision and protection measures been? And what further measures are needed?

Step 11: entitlement promotion. Entitlement promotion refers to both immediate one-off rehabilitation measures and longer-term development interventions to address structural vulnerability (reducing sensitivity and increasing resilience). Rehabilitation measures would include income transfers (rather than credit) to reconstitute productive assets (e.g. livestock, ploughs) and cash or cereals to sustain households until the next harvest, based on the results of Step 10. Identification of longer-term development interventions will rely on analyses of obstacles faced by livelihood systems (the characteristics of low resilience and high sensitivity that they exhibit) and assessment of: which coping/adaptive strategies have the potential for reinforcement, such that they can offer economically and environmentally sustainable increases in entitlements (e.g. promoting seasonally appropriate off-farm employment); how production entitlements can be increased (e.g. by investments to improve yields or area sown, or by diversifying the productive base); and whether exchange entitlements can be enhanced (e.g. by promoting production that will enable producers to benefit from optimal terms of trade). Equally, interventions can address the reduction of calls on entitlements, especially if these are particularly seasonally detrimental (e.g. not collecting back taxes when cereal prices are lowest or providing seasonal malaria prophylaxis). These kinds of interventions indicate that the monitoring system is far more widely applicable to a range of planning tasks than simply famine prevention, mitigation and rehabilitation.

Implementing the methodology

The information needs of the proposed methodology are not as overwhelming as they may at first appear. Five elements require clarification: sampling; regularity of information collection; sources of information; qualitative versus quantitative data; and methods of data collection. Sampling will depend to a large extent on the diversity of livelihood systems in the area in question: the greater the number, the more complex the sample. As suggested in Chapter 4, once local livelihood systems have been identified, a one-off census of the local population to determine membership of identified systems is recommended, to enable crude quantification of the numbers involved in subsequent predictions. Thereafter, the methodology does not advocate systematic statistically viable samples, but rather selection of sentinel villages (and in the case of transhumants, key herding groups or fishing camps) which are broadly representative of the different agro-ecological zones in the area and the livelihood systems represented within them. Choosing a traditional safety net, such as the Inner Niger Delta, permits the monitoring of a far greater number of people than situating the monitoring system in areas which people tend to leave once primary production fails. The initial task of identifying patterns of such movement (included within activity calendars) will pay off in subsequent years of monitoring.

Phasing of monitoring, after the initial year, is seasonal (i.e. a maximum of four passages a year) and often carried out only once a year (as in the case of coping strategy mapping, for example). The number of rounds can be stepped up in a particularly poor year if small changes in circumstances are likely to be significant, or if the impact of seasonal interventions needs to be evaluated.

The utility of qualitative versus quantitative data in famine EW and planning more generally is a long-standing debate (see Davies *et al.*, 1991). Clearly, it is not possible to quantify all elements in the proposed methodology; nor is it necessary. The principal need for quantified data is driven by the restricted response options which national planners face (how many people require how many tons of food aid). In a decentralised system, where response options are flexible and aiming to address issues of entitlement protection and promotion as well as provision, relative values will normally suffice. The initial census to classify the numbers of people in each livelihood system will enable crude quantified estimates of the numbers of people requiring interventions in a given year. Furthermore, by converting calls on and sources of entitlements into comparable measures (e.g. number of months of food availability), assessments can be roughly quantified. Critically, the approach has an in-built capacity to weight the importance of particular factors, by considering the range of sources of and calls on entitlement and estimating their likely contribution to food and livelihood protection needs. Again, coping strategy effectiveness can be calculated very roughly as demonstrated in Chapter 10. Finally, over time, qualitative data can be given quantitative 'values' relative to previous years.

Sources of information are principally people in sentinel villages (and transhumant camps) with directed interviews conducted at village level, supplemented by household interviews when necessary (e.g. if there is little consensus as to annual coping strategy maps, or if livelihood criteria are indicated as being household-specific, as in the case of coping strategies requiring high labour inputs). Estimates of *per capita* post-harvest stocks need to be based on a sample of households in sentinel villages, substantiated by national rainfall, flood and production data. Other sources of information are key informants (e.g. traders, local community chiefs) and existing data (e.g. rainfall and flood levels, national production estimates). Table 11.4 gives examples of possible sources of information.

Finally, the methods used to collect data are a combination of RRA, PRA techniques[1] and more conventional surveying. Thus coping strategy maps can be drawn up by local people, whereas market surveys would be conducted by field agents, as described in Chapter 4. There is an important caveat to the use of RRA and PRA techniques: if the objective is monitoring rather than appraising, the question of sustainability of these often time-consuming exercises (for local people) is central, as well as their willingness to continue to participate if benefits do not accrue. In this respect, PRA is likely to be more effective than RRA. RRA is a one-off exercise usually with a predetermined output in mind (e.g. project identification), using particular techniques and methods to extract information from villagers. PRA, in contrast, is a process (possibly initiated by RRA) which continues over a number of years and involves not simply gathering information but also using the information to initiate action and evaluate the impact of that action on the problems identified. If narrow famine EW is the objective, PRA is almost impossible to sustain: if no famine is indicated, no action ensues. Further, it is especially difficult to undertake in communities under stress, where conflicts over resources are central to survival and where EWS tend to be seen to represent access to emergency relief alone. By locating famine EW within a wider pro-

Table 11.4 Examples of sources of information for livelihood monitoring

Entitlement to be monitored	Indicator	Sources of information
Production	Size of annual food gap	Village estimates National production data Rainfall and flood data
	Intensified fishing	Local government fisheries agents Traditional chiefs of fisheries
	Pasture availability	Pastoral associations Traditional chiefs of pasturing territories
Exchange	Terms of trade	Market surveys Local traders Urban (wholesale) traders and transporters
Assets	Asset disposal	Market surveys Local traders
	Levels of remittances sent from migrants	Demand for and price of labour in recipient zones Money transfers by post or via local transporters
Coping/adaptation	Unusual migration	Producers in highly productive areas (recipient zones) Local government administrators, transporters Local specialists in gathering (e.g. certain ethnic groups, the long-term displaced) Herders in distant pastures
	Increased wild food collection	Forestry and pastoral local government agents

Table 11.4 (continued)

Entitlement to be monitored	Indicator	Sources of information
Consumption	Low nutritional status	Increased incidence of under-nutrition/illness in health centres
Claims	High state claims	Local government administrators (tax collectors, agents with powers to fine, e.g. forestry officials) National taxation administration
	High levels of debt repayment	Local traders and money-lenders Richer households
Livelihood protection	Intensification of abusive wood-cutting Over-fishing	Levels of fines levied by local government agent

gramme of livelihood monitoring and famine mitigation (or livelihood security enhancement), the scope for PRA increases because, even if famine is not indicated, in vulnerable livelihood systems (those which merit continuous monitoring anyway) both entitlement protection and entitlement promotion will be necessary. Linking monitoring to interventions, via sub-national contingency plans (see below), offers the opportunity of sustaining a local monitoring system. Monitoring with no directly identified response will not work, however participatory the methods of information extraction may be.

POLICY IMPLICATIONS: SAVING LIVES, SAVING LIVELIHOODS

Most famine EWS are concerned with saving lives. The proposed methodology, in contrast, aims to save livelihoods. Clearly the remit of the different types of interventions suggested – entitlement provision, protection and promotion – extends far beyond narrow famine prevention. Three elements are implicit in the idea of saving livelihoods: first, contingency planning which enables the information/prediction/response system to trigger pre-planned responses to the specific problems identified (which includes options for entitlement provision, promotion and protection); second, within this, the linking of development and emergency interventions; third, and related to this linkage, multi-purpose monitoring which can be used both to warn of crisis and as a planning tool in every year. These three elements imply that food-security planning needs to be decentralised to be sufficiently flexible to respond to local conditions. Further, the monitoring system itself can only realistically operate on a decentralised basis, which does not preclude the possibility of a common methodology being used in several localities, to facilitate aggregation of comparable indicators to construct a national level picture. Decentralisation of commonly agreed methodologies can help to optimise the inevitable trade-off between standardisation of information and its quality.

These three elements require radical shifts in both donor and government thinking with respect to famine EW and mitigation, and in the division of responsibility between them. Such a shift presupposes a benevolent state, in the sense that state policy seeks to reduce rural poverty and the threat of famine. This cannot, of course, be taken as a given, especially where state policies have traditionally sought to extract wealth from rural areas and, in more extreme instances, where donors and government alike have used tardy response to food crises as a political weapon (see Buchanan-Smith and Davies, in press). No EWS can be conceived in isolation from the political context within which it must operate. But a system which seeks to link emergency and development assistance before the onset of a crisis, has the potential to mitigate some of the high political stakes which invariably operate in times of crisis.

Contingency planning. Contingency planning refers to pre-designed responses, triggered by pre-agreed signals from a monitoring system. Pioneered in local-level famine EW in Turkana district, northern Kenya (see Turkana Drought Contingency Planning Unit, 1992; Swift, 1989b), it represents a means of linking information provision and prediction to response, rather than leaving this to identification, negotiation and chance in each cycle of drought. If the range of interventions proposed here is to be available when needed, contingency planning is essential, given the complexity of response options. In such a contingency plan, there is a need to go with the endemic variability of vulnerable livelihood systems in Sahelian agro-ecological areas, rather than seeking solely to minimise the effect of it. Interventions thus require a combination of reducing risk and maximising income to confront such risks. The contingency plan would be elaborated as a function of the first and subsequent years of monitoring. It would consist of a set of entitlement provision, protection and promotion measures, as well as pre-established plans and – critically – resources for their implementation. Ideally, these would need to be prepared for each livelihood system, although this may not be possible in highly agro-ecologically diverse areas. Triggering particular types of intervention according to signals from the monitoring system can also be part of the plan. Such triggers would need to be identified in the context of the particular area in question. Over time, the effectiveness of interventions can be fed back into the contingency plan to substantiate the sensitivity of particular indicators and the appropriateness of response.

Multi-purpose monitoring and planning. Contingency planning which addresses entitlement protection – and especially entitlement promotion – has a far wider remit than simply famine prevention. The implication of the proposed methodology is that the information provided can be used for a range of development objectives designed to address the numerous facets of livelihood insecurity and rural poverty. Clearly, to address all needs, additional monitoring or information collection would be required (e.g. incidence of morbidity for health planning); but the inference is that food-security planning needs to be situated within the context of livelihood security planning, if it is to address causes rather than symptoms alone. In the first instance, the focus can be food security, but over time the system has the potential to be developed for a multiplicity of planning tasks.

Linking relief and development. If livelihood vulnerability monitoring becomes the focus of information collection, planning and response, the artificial distinction between emergency relief and rehabilitation and development can be broken down. Current practices, within both donor agencies and government ministries, tend to treat emergency relief and development interventions as bureaucratically distinct entities. This is inconsistent with the ways in which local people respond to food insecurity, especially in vulnerable livelihood systems where the process of adaptation is highly evolved. Planning and interventions need to reinforce the trade-off which vulnerable people make between short-term consumption and longer-term livelihood protection, rather than separating the two and so making the trade-off less rather than more effective.

Decentralisation of food-security planning. All this implies that planning itself needs to be decentralised, based on the principle of subsidiarity. Subsidiarity refers to the allocation of policy-making decisions and implementation tasks to the lowest possible administrative level. This does not imply mandatory decentralisation of all decision-making and tasks, but that these should be carried out as close to the user or beneficiary as is feasible (Swift, 1994). Highly centralised state bureaucracies are ill-equipped to respond flexibly; however good local information may be, it is often put to one side as being irrelevant to the pressing decisions about allocation of scarce resources (invariably emergency food aid) which national-level planners and donors need to make. If response to food shortages shifts away from uniform preoccupation with emergency food aid (invariably negotiated on a case-by-case basis each year) towards a range of development and emergency options, the need to concentrate power and decision-making at the centre can decline. A core element in this is the need to decentralise resources as well as decision-making, on which both donors and government would need to act.

The case for decentralisation of food and livelihood-security planning needs to be assessed on a country-by-country basis. It is unlikely, for example, that such an initiative would be acceptable in state structures which are otherwise highly centralised. In the case of Mali, however, decentralisation is now a general policy objective. Further, regional-level SAP representatives and the relatively decentralised level of information collection already in place offer an opportunity to build a regional planning and response capacity along the lines outlined. This route is fraught with difficulties, not least because, certainly until the overthrow of the Traoré regime in 1991, the Malian state was principally associated in local people's minds with disentitlement (essentially through direct and indirect taxation, the benefits of which do not return to local people: see

Moorehead, 1991), not entitlement provision, protection and promotion. In the post-Traoré political climate, the government – whilst too bankrupt to be benevolent – is moving towards curbing some of the past excesses of disentitlement. With donor support, there is scope for developing the base established by the SAP and the SADS along the lines proposed here, particularly in the current political climate of greater accountability and less centralisation of resources and power. What is clear is that continued inaction in tackling the increasing structural vulnerability of livelihoods will undoubtedly incur high costs to the state and donors in the future, whether through an inability of local people to pay taxes, or through the ever more frequent need for emergency relief.

CONCLUSIONS: SO WHAT?

Is the approach advocated too complex, costly and cumbersome to be feasible or desirable? Is such an approach, as critics will argue, a luxury in the climate of scarce resources (especially for prevention) and calls for ever greater simplification of EW indicators? How appropriate is the demand for more comprehensive information collection for planning purposes? There is a trade-off to be made between what is feasible and what is necessary or desirable. In making this trade-off, it must be recognised that information will always be used for a variety of purposes and cannot be reserved only for the purpose for which it was intended. There is thus a strong argument to be made for making information widely applicable and relevant at the outset. Further, decision-makers will take decisions irrespective of the quality and quantity of information available. The challenge is to make the information as accessible and accurate as possible and to tie it into the decision-making process so that decisions are taken in as informed an environment as possible. Decentralised contingency planning is essential to this process.

The case for the proposed approach rests on four points. First, there is little evidence that existing methods of famine EW and response work. Lives may be saved, but invariably late in the day; and livelihoods are ruined, thereby setting in motion a vicious circle of increased vulnerability for the future, the human and economic costs of which will certainly be high.

Second, famine that grips headlines in the North is in fact quite a rare event in much of Africa (and increasingly associated with war as much as drought). What does not filter through is the increasing vulnerability of livelihoods in areas which are not affected by conflict, as well as those that are time bombs ticking away to explode into future destitution on an unprecedented scale. Prediction needs to address this issue first, and famine when appropriate, but not to be driven by disasters (which increasingly arise out of war) and so ignore the structural vulnerability which ultimately gives rise to them. A preventive rather than curative approach is thus needed. Emphasising coping strategies in isolation from the ways in which their use changes in conditions of vulnerability, implicit in which is the notion that people *do* cope, further obscures the threat of increasing structural vulnerability, or the inability to cope when crisis hits.

Third, isolating food security from wider livelihood security and poverty issues, whilst useful as an initial means of setting priorities (especially when response is late and crisis has already taken hold), risks subsuming development objectives under an imposed and misconceived hierarchy of meeting food needs first and in preference to all other needs, notably future security. Food-insecure people do not do this, but instead make finely balanced trade-offs between short- and longer-term needs. Both emergency and development interventions need to reinforce these trade-offs if they are to succeed. The continuum of entitlement promotion, protection and – only when these two have failed – provision, is a far closer reflection of how local people confront vulnerability than the current stop–go practice of emergency or development assistance in hermetically sealed boxes.

Fourth, the approach necessitates decentralisation of planning: it is based on recognising the location-specific nature both of vulnerability and of likely solutions to it. National-level planning, whilst essential for overall resource allocation, cannot address vulnerability in anything but a mechanistic way. Decentralisation is a necessary prerequisite for feasible contingency planning and flexible and appropriate response.

Four areas of policy change are thus indicated. First is the adoption of a methodology along the proposed lines, which integrates livelihood vulnerability monitoring with famine EW, and systematically links monitoring to a range of pre-planned response options as well as to the capacity to evaluate the impact of those responses. Second, contingency plans must be drawn up to service this process of detection and assessment. Third, a shift in planning behaviour and attitudes is required, both to remove the artificial distinction between the role of emergency relief and development aid, and also to integrate famine EW better with tracking increasing structural vulnerability. Finally, to meet these needs, food-security planning – and by implication livelihood-security planning – requires decentralisation of both planning and resource allocation, if locally relevant policies are to be identified and implemented.

Sahelian livelihoods are under increasing threat. Although it cannot be known what would happen in the Sahel if drought were to disappear, there is no guarantee that everything would return to normal, not least because drought is only one variable in the process of evolving and increasingly vulnerable livelihood systems. Structural vulnerability is here to stay and intensifies with each cycle of drought and the failure to recover from it. Yet, this is not entirely a story of gloom. It is possible to find out what is happening in a comparatively cheap and straightforward way, a process which then indicates that there are a number of relatively simple things which can be done to reduce the threat to livelihoods of proximate vulnerability and to stem the advance of increasing structural vulnerability. But there are no short cuts. If these livelihoods are to be saved, finding out about how they are evolving and what local people, who are themselves expert in saving their livelihoods, do to confront vulnerability, and thus what can be done to assist in making them more secure, is not a luxury, but a necessity if widespread hunger on a hitherto unseen scale is not to be the future of the Sahel and other parts of famine-prone rural Africa.

Notes

1 Introduction

1. The project (*Projet Information Alimentaire*) on which this book is based was conceived and funded by Save the Children Fund (UK), with technical assistance from the Food Emergencies Research Unit of the London School of Hygiene and Tropical Medicine. In the aftermath of the African famines of the mid-1980s, the aim of the project was to find more effective ways of predicting famines, in order to assist NGOs to intervene earlier in the cycle of famine, destitution and death. The book covers the initial years of the monitoring system set up by the project, known as the *Suivi Alimentaire Delta Seno* (SADS). From 1987 to 1989, SCF collaborated with the International Union for the Conservation of Nature and Natural Resources (IUCN) and OXFAM (UK) in establishing the SADS. IUCN's 'Project for the Conservation of the Environment in the Inner Niger Delta' had been carrying out research in the Delta since 1984 and its work on the socio-economy of Delta livelihood systems was of central importance to the development of the SADS. OXFAM's work on the causes of famine in Douentza also provided much information. SADS remains part of SCF's *Projet Suivi Alimentaire Delta Seno*, which continues to operate in Mali and has since diversified beyond information provision, into local-level interventions (*Projet d'Appui Villageois*) and regional food-security planning.
2. See Buchanan-Smith *et al.* (1991) for a description of EWS in the Sahel and Horn of Africa.
3. Important exceptions are the Agricultural Planning Unit in Darfur, Sudan, and the Turkana Drought Contingency Planning Unit in Kenya (see Buchanan-Smith *et al.*, 1991).

2 Security and Vulnerability in Livelihood Systems

1. This section is based on Davies in Maxwell and Smith (1992).
2. See Handy (1985: 30), citing Maslow.
3. Report of the Advisory Panel on Food Security, Agriculture, Forestry and Environment to the World Commission on Environment and Development, cited in Chambers (1988: 1).
4. For a review, see Davies *et al.* (1991).
5. Maxwell (1986: 66) summarises the principles of farming systems research in what he calls a 'quintessential five step procedure' – to classify; diagnose; recommend; implement; and evaluate.
6. Monitoring intra-household variations was beyond the scope of the information system.

3 Coping and Adapting

1. Corbett considers *inter alia* Cutler's (1986) sequence from Red Sea Province, Sudan in 1984; Rahmato's (1987) sequence from Wollo Province, Ethiopia in 1984–5; and De Waal's (1989) sequence from Darfur, Sudan in 1984.
2. There is, in addition, a range of intra-household factors which will further differentiate options, but it is beyond the scope of almost all EWS to monitor at this level.
3. Longhurst (1986), for example, notes that in communities with land holding and income inequalities, household responses will differ. Watts (1988) also describes how wealthier households can benefit from the distress sales (of livestock, assets or labour) at depressed prices by poorer members of the community.
4. These livelihood systems are, in turn, often found in areas which are of low resilience and high sensitivity in natural-resource terms.

4 Monitoring How People Feed Themselves

1. Primary activities are the main activities of a livelihood system (e.g. cultivation for cultivators, pastoralism for transhumant pastoralists). Secondary activities are those into which producers *normally* diversify (see Chapter 7).
2. See Davies and Thiam (1987).
3. Village chiefs are the most local level of administrator, below the *arrondissement*.
4. Mali does not have a university as such, but *Ecoles Normales*, the level of which is approximately equivalent at graduation to first or second year university education.
5. Due to personnel constraints it was not possible to cover the remaining *arrondissements* of the *cercle* of Tenenkou – Dioura, Sossobé, Diafarabé – in any systematic fashion. Sossobé is similar to Toguéré Koumbé and the market at Diafarabé was monitored on a monthly basis. The drylands of Dioura were not dissimilar to the *arrondissement* of Gatie Luomo to its north, covered by the Youvarou listening post.
6. In theory, this is quite comprehensive and includes, for example, estimates of cereal production, fish production, numbers of livestock, rainfall and flood data. In practice, such data collection is sporadic and although almost always quantified, is often based on very rough estimates calculated with little ground-truthing. Local government agents also provide information for the official EWS, the SAP (see Chapter 5). Although SAP data collection has improved dramatically over time, at the outset (when SADS was also beginning) information supplied to the SAP system was highly variable in quality. By way of illustration, in some *arrondissements*, local agents had no means of transport with which to visit villages and consequently estimated conditions without leaving the *chef lieu d'arrondissement*.
7. Data were reliable for only 38 of the 50 households in the wetland sample. In the original sample, ten transhumant pastoral and ten transhumant fishing households were identified.

5 Drought, Food Insecurity and Early Warning in Mali

1. In 1959, Mali exported 20 000 tons of millet and 5000 tons of rice. Even then, the North had a deficit, but was able to satisfy food requirements from livestock, fisheries, etc. (Lecaillon and Morrisson, 1986: 46).
2. Livestock numbers are estimated to have increased by 50 per cent between 1945 and 1959, exports rising from 20 000 to 100 000 head by 1959. 12 000 tons of fish were exported in 1959 (Lecaillon and Morrisson, 1986: 22).
3. Amongst the Tuareg in the Inner Niger Delta, for example, a study in 1981–2 found that calories derived from cereals accounted for only 45 per cent to 67 per cent of total intake (Wagenaar-Brouwer, 1985). In northeastern Mali, where, unlike the Delta, cereals are not cultivated, a study in 1983 found that 68 per cent of calories came from milk, 24 per cent from cereals and 8 per cent from meat (Sidibe, 1985). Such estimates need to be treated with caution, however, as they are highly seasonally specific.
4. The European Community (EC), for example, will not contribute food aid in kind to Mali for non-emergency purposes, arguing that the country does not have a structural deficit.
5. The WFP has had an accord with the GRM since 1968 to provide food aid for food-for-work projects. Development initiatives – usually identified by Local Development Committees – are supported by the programme, in the following sectors: training; rural roads; upgrading productive capacity; forestry protection; and general livelihood security support.
6. WFP, Belgium, Canada, EC, France, Germany, the Netherlands and United States.
7. Estimates of household stocks are now incorporated into *Direction Nationale de la Statistique et de l'Informatique* (DNSI) surveys.
8. Donor funding for many ODRs has been withdrawn since the early 1990s, with the result that they have largely ceased to function.
9. The food strategy document was prepared by the GRM, in collaboration with the *Fonds d'Aide et de Coopération de France* and the United States Agency for International Development (USAID), after consultation with the World Food Council. The *Commission d'Elaboration de la Stratégie Alimentaire* was set up to draft the original food strategy document from June 1981 to April 1982.
10. The CNAUR has since ceased to exist as an independent structure and is now part of the *Cellule d'Appui au Développement à la Base* (CADB).
11. The devaluation of the FCFA in January 1994 has had the effect of raising prices for agricultural commodities (meat and fish in particular), thus helping rural surplus producers at the expense of (urban) consumers.
12. For a discussion of GIEWS and FEWS, see Buchanan-Smith *et al.* (1991), and Davies (1992).
13. The 7th Region was divided into two, forming the 8th Region of Kidal, following the Accord of Tamanrasset signed between the GRM and Tuareg in 1991.

14. According to Trine (1990), although it is not clear if this figure includes recurrent costs incurred by the Malian administration.
15. The *Cellule d'Etudes et de Recherche* was set up in 1991, in order to analyse data in more detail, without the constraint of monthly bulletin preparation. This development has met with little success and has been criticised in some quarters, as it is seen to go beyond the SAP's mandate.
16. The USA, Canada and France contribute food aid which is all sold and converted into counterpart funds; the EC donates the equivalent value of food aid in cash; and the Canadian International Development Agency and the Dutch also contribute money. This all goes into a common fund. The *Deutsche Gesellschaft für Technische Zusammenarbeit GmbH* (GTZ) also provides technical assistance to OPAM.
17. An evaluation of the SAP is being undertaken by the PRMC in 1995, in order to review its role.
18. Ironically, this is also seen as a strength of the SAP in that 'the project is situated between the two principal centres of decision-making about food aid' (Egg and Teme, 1990: 40).
19. 'For the population, a distribution that is not controlled is a gift to the local administration.' See Davies (1992) for a summary of these evaluations and the problems associated with food aid reaching intended beneficiaries.
20. This is certainly true of the SADS, which bases its market prices on key trader informants for large quantities and actual purchases from traders for retail prices (Chapter 4).
21. These were prepared with support from the United Nations Development Programme. For the 5th Region, see République du Mali (1985).

6   Livelihood Safety Nets: The Inner Niger Delta in the Sahel

1. The new government is considering the abolition of *arrondissement*-level administration, but has so far met with fierce opposition from the civil service. This is to be replaced with *Communes Rurales* as part of a wider process of decentralisation. Although the law on decentralisation has been passed, it awaits a presidential decree before it can be implemented.
2. For millet, the *Opération de Développement du Mil dans la Région de Mopti*; for rice, the *Opération de Développement du Riz dans la Région de Mopti* (ORM); for livestock, ODEM; and for fisheries, OPM.
3. The River Niger is navigable as far as Gao from November to January and to Tombouctou until February.
4. Somadougou in the south-east of the Delta is the second major entry point for animals coming from the direction of Bandiagara.

7   Livelihood Systems

1. The preliminary results of Phases 1 and 2 of the project were written up in a continuous manner as data were collected, in the quarterly Bulletins of the SADS system, *Stratégies Vivrières* (SADS, quarterly). The project also published a number of research reports at the end of two years of monitoring to provide a picture of the overall seasonal pattern of results (Davies *et al.*,

Notes 315

1990a, 1990b, 1990c, and 1990d). This chapter draws on these documents, as well as on unpublished data from the monitoring system collected between 1987 and 1989.
2. See Chapter 6 for how these seasons correspond to rising and falling water seasons in the Delta.
3. This is not practised further upstream in Toguéré because the water flows too fast.

8 Production Entitlements

1. Rice production, it will be recalled from Chapter 6, is contingent upon the flood level and its timing relative to rainfall.
2. As explained in Chapter 4, comparable data for the drylands are not available.
3. That is, 23 per cent of 365 days. Moorehead (1991) calculates total household food availability to be 354 days or 97 per cent of minimum requirements.

9 Exchange Entitlements

1. Wholesale prices for fish are used throughout as this is the way fish is sold by fishers. Dried and smoked fish have also been converted into equivalent wet fish weights, using the following coefficients: for smoked fish 0.50; and for dried fish 0.25 (i.e. 1 kg of smoked fish is equivalent to 2 kg of fresh fish and 1 kg of dried fish is equivalent to 4 kg of fresh fish).
2. This comprises: 1 kg of salt; 1 litre of oil; 1 kg of baobab leaves; 1 kg of *soumbala*; 100 gm of tea and 1 kg of sugar.
3. This, it will be recalled, is not strictly speaking a terms-of-trade relationship, but the price of millet. When producers are forced to sell millet after the harvest to meet cash needs, the exchange is reversed.
4. The milk herd during the cold and dry season is called the *benti*.
5. It should, however, be noted that the 50 per cent devaluation of the FCFA in January 1994 dramatically increased the competitiveness of Sahelian livestock exports. As a result, their value doubled in some markets.
6. Wood can, of course, be weighed to arrive at a unit price; but this is much more difficult than weighing other products (which can be done with hand-held scales).

10 Coping and Adaptive Entitlements

1. Pasturing is a primary activity for transhumant pastoralists; and fishing, in conjunction with cultivation in their zones of origin, is for transhumant fishers (see Chapters 7 and 8).
2. **Primary activities**: *agricultural* – cultivation, weeding, harvesting, threshing.
Secondary activities: *pastoral* – animal husbandry, cutting straw, herding, milking, milk processing, transhumance; *fishing* – fishing, fish processing, maintaining equipment.

Coping/adaptive activities: *exchange* – gone to market, small-scale trade; *migration* – travel, absent; *other coping* – gathering wild foods, cutting wood, other gathering, artisanal work, construction, casual labour.
Non-revenue-generating activities: *domestic* – cooking, housework, child care; *other* – illness.

3. See Table 6.3 in Chapter 6 for rainfall, flood and production data for these years.
4. See Moorehead (1991) for a detailed description of how traditional management regimes operate in the Delta.

11 Tracking and Tackling Food Vulnerability

1. See, for example, Mascarenhas *et al.* (1991) for a detailed description of such methods.

References

Amin, S. (1965) *Trois Expériences Africaines de Développement: le Mali, la Guinée et le Ghana*, Presses Universitaires de France, Paris.
Autier, P., J. D'Altilia, J. Delamalle and V. Vercruysse (1989) 'The Food and Nutrition Surveillance Systems of Chad and Mali: The "SAP" After Two Years', *Disasters*, vol. 13, no. 1, pp. 9–32.
Bâ, A.H., and J. Daget (1962) *L'Empire Peul du Macina (1818–1853)*, Les Nouvelles Editions Africaines, Abidjan.
Bayliss-Smith, T. (1991) 'Food Security and Agricultural Sustainability in the New Guinea Highlands: Vulnerable People, Vulnerable Places', *IDS Bulletin*, vol. 22, no. 3, pp. 5–11.
Blaikie, P., and H.C. Brookfield (1987) *Land Degradation and Society*, Methuen, London and New York.
Borton, J., and J. Shoham (1991) 'Mapping Vulnerability to Food Insecurity: Tentative Guidelines for WFP Offices', Study commissioned by the World Food Programme, RDI, London, March, mimeo.
Buchanan-Smith, M., S. Davies and R. Lambert (1991), 'Guide to Famine Early Warning Systems in the Sahel and Horn of Africa. A Review of the Literature: Volume 2', *IDS Research Report*, no. 21.
Buchanan-Smith, M., S. Davies and C. Petty (1994) 'Food Security: Let them Eat Information', *IDS Bulletin*, vol. 25, no. 2, pp. 69–80.
Buchanan-Smith, M. and S. Davies (in press) *Famine Early Warning and Response: The Missing Link*, Intermediate Technology Publications, London.
Campbell, D.J. (1990) 'Strategies for Coping with Severe Food Deficits in Rural Africa: Review of the Literature', *Food and Foodways*, vol. 4, no. 2, pp. 143–62.
Cannon, T. (1991) 'Food Systems and Marginal Lands: Avoiding Environmental Determinism in Explaining Hunger', School of Humanities, Thames Polytechnic, London, mimeo.
Cekan, J. (1991) 'Counter-seasonal Coping Strategies in Rural Mali', mimeo.
Chambers, R. (1988) 'Sustainable Rural Livelihoods: A Key Strategy for People, Environment and Development', in C. Conroy and M. Litvinoff (eds), *The Greening of Aid*, Earthscan, London.
Chambers, R. (1989) 'Editorial Introduction: Vulnerability, Coping and Policy', *IDS Bulletin*, vol. 20, no. 2, pp. 1–7.
CIPEA and ODEM (1983) 'Recherche d'une Solution aux Problèmes de l'Elevage dans le Delta Intérieur du Niger au Mali', *Rapport de Synthèse*, vol. 5, Bamako, Mopti and Addis Ababa, mimeo.
Corbett, J.E.M. (1988) 'Famine and Household Coping Strategies', *World Development*, vol. 16, no. 9, pp. 1009–1112.
Cutler, P. (1986) 'The Response to Drought of Beja Famine Refugees in Sudan', *Disasters*, vol. 10, no 3, pp. 181–8.
Daget, J. (1954) 'Les Poissons du Niger Supérieur', *Mémoires de l'Institut Fondamental d'Afrique Noir*, no. 36, IFAN, Dakar.

Davies, S. (1992) 'Famine Early Warning and Response: the Missing Link? – Case Study No. 4 – Mali'. Paper presented at the conference 'Predicting and Preventing Famine: an Agenda for the 1990s', 4–6 November, 1992, IDS, Brighton and SCF, London, mimeo.

Davies, S., and A. Thiam (1987) 'The Slow Onset of Famine: Early Warning, Migration and Post-drought Recovery. The Case of Displaced Persons in Gaoville', SCF Early Warning Project, Report No. 1, Bamako, mimeo.

Davies, S., A. Thiam, M. Bangaly, M. Karambe, A. Ag Hatalaya and M. Coulibaly (1990a) 'Elements à Suivre: Indicateurs Saisonniers de la Situation Alimentaire', *Document de Référence SADS*, PIA/SCF, Mopti and IDS, Brighton.

Davies, S., A. Thiam, M. Bangaly, M. Karambe, A. Ag Hatalaya and M. Coulibaly (1990b) 'Calendriers d'Accès à la Nourriture', *Document de Référence SADS*, PIA/SCF, Mopti and IDS, Brighton, mimeo.

Davies, S., A. Thiam, M. Bangaly, M. Karambe, A. Ag Hatalaya and M. Coulibaly (1990c) 'Stratégies d'Adaptation contre l'Insécurité Alimentaire', *Document de Référence SADS*, PIA/SCF, Mopti and IDS, Brighton, mimeo.

Davies, S., A. Thiam, M. Bangaly, M. Karambe, A. Ag Hatalaya and M. Coulibaly (1990d) 'Calendriers Saisonniers d'Activités', *Document de Référence SADS*, PIA/SCF, Mopti and IDS, Brighton, mimeo.

Davies, S., M. Buchanan-Smith and R. Lambert (1991) 'Early Warning in the Sahel and Horn of Africa: The State of the Art. A Review of the Literature: Volume 1', *IDS Research Report*, no. 20.

De Waal, A. (1989) *Famine that Kills: Darfur, Sudan, 1984–1985*, Clarendon Press, Oxford.

Downing, T.E. (1988) 'Climatic Variability, Food Security and Smallholder Agriculturalists in Six Districts of Central and Eastern Kenya', unpublished Ph.D. Dissertation, Clark University.

Downing, T.E. (1990) 'Assessing Socio-economic Vulnerability to Famine: Frameworks, Concepts and Applications', Final Report to USAID FEWS Project, *FEWS Working Paper*, no. 2.1, Washington D.C., March (draft).

Drèze, J., and A. Sen (1989) *Hunger and Public Action*, WIDER, Oxford University Press, Oxford.

D'Souza, F. (1985) 'Anthropology and Disasters', *Anthropology Today*, vol. 1, no. 1, pp. 18–19.

Duffield, M. (1990a) 'Sudan at the Cross-roads: From Emergency Procedures to Social Security', *IDS Discussion Paper*, no. 275, IDS.

Duffield, M. (1990b) 'War and Famine in Africa', Exploratory Report for OXFAM, Oxford, November, mimeo.

Eele, G. (1987) 'Data Sources for Timely Warning in Nutritional Surveillance', in 'Figures for Food in Africa', Proceedings of the Workshop on Statistics in Support of African Food Policies and Strategies, Brussels, 13–16 May, 1986, *Eurostat News*, Special Edition.

Egg, J. and Teme, B. (1990) 'Rapport de Mission d'Evaluation du Projet "Système d'Alerte Précoce" (SAP) au Mali', Programme de Restructuration du Marché Céréalier du Mali, INRA Montpellier and IER Bamako, mimeo.

ENDA (1985) 'La Vie Pastorale au Sahel', *Initiation aux Sociétés Pastorales Sahéliennes*, no. 1, ENDA, Dakar.

FAO (1990) Annex 9, 'Use of Food Balance Sheets for the Estimation of Deficits and Surpluses', *Strengthening National Early Warning and Food Information Systems in Africa*, FAO Workshop, Accra, Ghana, 23–26 October 1989.

Farrow, R.A. (1975) 'The African Migratory Locust in its Main Outbreak Area of the Middle Niger: Quantitative Studies of Solitary Populations in Relation to Environmental Factors', *Locusta*, no. 11, OICMA.

FEWS (1990) *Vulnerability Assessment*, FEWS/Washington for USAID, Bureau for Africa, Washington D.C., June.

Frankenberger, T.R. (1992) 'Indicators and Data Collection Methods for Assessing Household Food Security', in S. Maxwell and T. R. Frankenberger, *Household Food Security: Concepts, Indicators, Measurement*, UNICEF, New York, and IFAD, Rome, pp. 73–134.

Frankenberger, T.R., and D.M. Goldstein (1990) 'Food Security, Coping Strategies and Environmental Degradation', *Arid Lands Newsletter*, vol. 30, Office of Arid Lands Studies, University of Arizona, pp. 21–7.

Frankenberger, T.R., and C.F. Hutchinson (1991) 'Sustainable Resource Management Based on a Decentralised Food Security Monitoring System', Discussion Paper, Office of Arid Lands Studies, College of Agriculture, University of Arizona, Tucson, April, mimeo.

Gallais, J. (1957) 'La Région du Diaka: Mission d'Etude et d'Aménagement du Niger', *Etudes de Géographie Humaine*, Travaux Publiques de la République Soudanaise, Dakar.

Gallais, J. (1958) 'La Vie Saisonnière au Sud du Lac Debo: Mission d'Etude et d'Aménagement du Niger', *Enquêtes Géographiques*, no. 2, Service de l'Hydraulique de l'Afrique Occidentale Française, Dakar.

Gallais, J. (1967) 'Le Delta Intérieur du Niger: Etude de Géographie Régionale', *Mémoires de l'Institut Fondamental d'Afrique Noir*, no. 79 (2 volumes), IFAN, Dakar.

Gallais, J. (1975) *Pasteurs et Paysans du Gourma*, Mémoire du Centre d'Etudes de Géographie Tropicale, Bordeaux, Editions Centre National de Recherche Scientifique, Paris.

Gallais, J. (1984) *Hommes du Sahel*, Collections Géographiques, Flammarion, Paris.

Gore, C. (1992) 'Entitlement Relations and "Unruly" Social Politics: A Comment on the Work of Amartya Sen', IDS, Brighton, mimeo.

Hall, R.E. (1991) 'Taking Conflict into Consideration: Implications for Famine Mitigation Activities', Office of Arid Lands Studies, College of Agriculture, University of Arizona, Tucson, mimeo.

Handy, C.B. (1985) *Understanding Organisations*, Penguin Business, Harmondsworth.

Hesse, C. (1987) 'Livestock Market Data as an Early Warning Indicator of Stress in the Pastoral Economy', *Pastoral Development Network Discussion Paper*, no. 24f, ODI.

Hesse, C., A. Thiam, C. Fowler and J. Swift (1984) 'A Fulani Agro-Pastoral Production System in the Malian Gurma', CIPEA, Arid and Semi-arid Zone Programme, Bamako, June.

Hesse, C., and S. Thera (1987) 'Production Systems and Famine Risk in the Cercle of Douentza, Mali', draft report prepared for OXFAM (UK), Bamako, mimeo.

Holling, C.S. (1973) 'Resilience and Stability of Ecological Systems', *Annual Review of Ecology and Systematics*, vol. 4. pp. 1–23.
Holling, C.S. (1978) *Adaptive Environmental Assessment and Management*, John Wiley, Chichester.
IRRT (1984) *Les Stratégies Alimentaires dans Quatre Pays d'Afrique: une Etude sur la Politique Alimentaire – Formulation et Mise en Oeuvre au Kenya, Mali, Rwanda et en Zambie*, préparée pour la Commission des Communautés Européennes, Amsterdam, January.
IUCN (1986) 'Projet de Conservation dans le Delta Intérieur du Niger', *Rapport Semestriel*, no. 1, MRNE, Direction Nationale des Eaux et Forêts, Mopti and IUCN, Gland, mimeo.
IUCN (1987a) 'Conservation de l'Environnement dans le Delta Intérieur du Fleuve Niger: Document de Synthèse', Projet de Conservation dans le Delta Intérieur du Niger, *Rapport Technique*, no. 3, MRNE, Direction Nationale des Eaux et Forêts, Mopti and IUCN, Gland, mimeo.
IUCN (1987b) 'Evaluation des Projets de Développement – Youvarou, Projet de Conservation dans le Delta Intérieur du Niger', *Rapport Technique*, MRNE, Direction Nationale des Eaux et Forêts, Mopti and IUCN, Gland, mimeo.
IUCN (1989a) *Rapport sur l'Economie de la Région de Mopti (Mali) 1970–1985*, (draft), Programme Sahel, IUCN, Gland, mimeo.
IUCN (1989b) *The IUCN Sahel Studies: 1989*, IUCN and NORAD, Gland.
IUCN (1989c) 'Analyse des Investissements Hydrauliques dans le Cercle de Youvarou', Projet de Conservation dans le Delta Intérieur du Niger, *Rapport Technique*, MRNE, Direction Nationale des Eaux et Forêts, Mopti and IUCN, Gland, mimeo.
IUCN (1989d) 'Les Structures d'Encadrement des Programmes de Développement: Le Cas du Cercle de Youvarou', Projet de Conservation dans le Delta Intérieur du Niger, *Rapport Technique*, MRNE, Direction Nationale des Eaux et Forêts, Mopti and IUCN, Gland, mimeo.
Jodha, N.S. (1985) 'Social Science Research in Rural Change: Some Gaps', International Crops Research Institute for the Semi-Arid Tropics, India, mimeo.
Jodha, N.S. (1990) 'Rural Common Property Resources: A Growing Crisis', *Gatekeeper Series*, no. 24, IIED.
Kabeer, N., and S. Joekes (1991), 'Editorial: Researching the Household: Methodological and Empirical Issues', *IDS Bulletin*, vol. 22, no. 1, pp. 1–4.
Lalau-Keraly, A., and G. Winter (1988), 'Rapport de Mission d'Evaluation du Projet Système d'Alerte Précoce au Mali', OSCE, Bamako, November mimeo.
Lecaillon, J., and C. Morrisson (1986) 'Economic Policies and Agricultural Performance: The Case of Mali, 1960–1983', *OECD Development Centre Papers*, Paris.
Lipton, M. (1983) 'Poverty, Undernutrition and Hunger', *World Bank Staff Working Paper*, no. 597, World Bank, Washington D.C.
Lipton, M., and C. Heald (1984) 'African Food Strategies and the EEC's Role: An Interim Review', *IDS Commissioned Study*, no. 6.
Longhurst, R. (1986) 'Household Food Strategies in Response to Seasonality and Famine', *IDS Bulletin*, vol. 17, no. 3, pp. 27–35.
McCracken, J., J. Pretty and G. Conway (1988) *An Introduction to Rapid Rural Appraisal for Agricultural Development*, IIED, London.

McLean, W. (1987) 'Assessment of the Food Emergency in Mali 1983–5', paper presented at the 5th IDS Food Aid Seminar, IDS, Brighton, April, mimeo.
Mascarenhas, J., P. Shah, S. Joseph, R. Jayakaran, J. Devavaram, V. Ramachandran, A. Fernandez, R. Chambers and J. Pretty (1991) 'Proceedings of the February 1991 Bangalore PRA Trainers' Workshop', *RRA Notes No. 13*, IIED, London, and Myrada, Bangalore.
Maxwell, S. (1986) 'Farming Systems Research: Hitting a Moving Target', *World Development*, vol. 14, no. 1, pp. 65–77.
Maxwell, S. (1991) 'Food Security in Developing Countries: Issues and Options for the 1990s', *IDS Bulletin*, vol. 21, no. 3, pp. 2–13.
Maxwell, S., and M. Smith, with contributions from S. Davies, A. Evans, S. Jaspars, J. Swift and H. Young (1992) 'Household Food Security: A Conceptual Review', in S. Maxwell and T.R. Frankenberger, *Household Food Security: Concepts, Indicators, Measurement*, UNICEF New York and IFAD, Rome, pp. 1–72.
Moorehead, R.M. (1991) 'Structural Chaos: Community and State Management of Common Property in Mali', unpublished D.Phil. Thesis, IDS, University of Sussex.
Mortimore, M.J. (1989) *Adapting to Drought: Farmers, Famines and Desertification in West Africa*, Cambridge University Press, Cambridge.
OSCE (1986) *Statistiques de Base; Céréales et Elevage*, Office Statistique des Communautés Européennes, Bamako, May.
Pirzio-Biroli, D. (1988) 'Mali Cereals Policy and Food Sector Work: Institutional Structure and Efficiency of Emergency Food Aid and Early Warning Systems', Mission to Mali Report, mimeo.
Rahmato, D. (1987) 'Famine and Survival Strategies: A Case Study from North East Ethiopia', *Food and Famine Monograph Series*, no. 1, Institute of Development Research, Addis Ababa University, Addis Ababa, May.
Reardon, T., and P. Matlon (1989), 'Seasonal Food Insecurity and Vulnerability in Drought-Affected Regions of Burkina Faso', in D.E. Sahn (ed.), *Seasonal Variability in Third World Agriculture: The Consequences for Food Security*, Johns Hopkins University Press, Baltimore and London.
République du Mali (1982) *Elaboration de la Stratégie Alimentaire*, Commission d'Elaboration de la Stratégie Alimentaire, Ministère de l'Agriculture and CILSS/Club du Sahel, OCDE, Bamako, July.
République du Mali (1985) *Diagnostic de la Région de Mopti*, Comité Régional de Développement, Mopti, March.
République du Mali (1987a) *Evaluation de la Situation Alimentaire, Nutritionnelle et Socio-sanitaire en 1987 au Mali et Perspectives pour 1988*, Rapport Final, Cellule de Prévision, d'Evaluation et d'Appui, CNAVS, Ministère de l'Administration Territoriale et du Développement à la Base, Bamako, November.
République du Mali (1987b) *Recensement Général de la Population et de l'Habitat: Résultats Provisoires*, Ministère du Plan and Ministère de l'Administration Territoriale et du Développement à la Base, Bamako, July.
République du Mali (1991a) *Rapport de Mission: Contrôle des Opérations de Transport et de Distributions Alimentaires Gratuites dans la Région de Mopti (1991)*, CADB, MATDB, Bamako, July.

République du Mali (1991b) *Rapport de Mission: Contrôle des Opérations de Transport et de Distributions Alimentaires Gratuites dans les Cercles de Diré et Niafunké (1991)*, CADB, MATDB, Bamako, September.

République du Mali (1991c) *Rapport de Mission: Contrôle des Opérations de Transport et de Distributions d'Aide Alimentaire dans la Région de Koulikoro (1991)*, CADB, MATDB, Bamako, December.

République du Mali (1992) *Rapport de Mission Conjointe CNAUR/USAID de Suivi et Evaluation des Distributions Alimentaires Gratuites (Visite Présidentielle) dans la Région de Kayes (1991)*, CADB, MATDB, Bamako, December.

Riely, F. (1991) 'Household Responses to Recurrent Drought: A Case Study of the Kababish Pastoralists in Northern Kordofan, Sudan', *Famine and Food Policy Discussion Papers*, no. 6, International Food Policy Research Institute.

RIM (1987) 'Refuge in the Sahel: Livestock Populations and Production Systems in the Mali Fifth Region. A Rapid Assessment of Current Resources by Low Level Aerial Survey and Complementary Ground Studies', République du Mali, MRNE, Bamako and Resource Inventory and Management Ltd, St Helier, Jersey.

SADS (quarterly) 'Stratégies Vivrières', *Rapport Saisonnier du Suivi Alimentaire Delta Seno*, PIA/SCF, Mopti, Mali.

SADS (1989) 'Que Faire? Recommandations d'Action du Suivi Alimentaire Delta Seno', PIA/SCF, Mopti, mimeo.

SADS (1992) 'Evaluation du Projet d'Appui Villageois, Youvarou, Avril 1991–Mars 1992', SADS, SCF (UK), Mopti, mimeo.

Sen, A.K. (1981) *Poverty and Famines: An Essay on Entitlement and Deprivation*, Clarendon Press, Oxford.

Sen, A.K. (1983) 'Development: Which Way Now?', *Economic Journal*, vol. 93, pp. 745–62.

Sidibe, S. (1985) 'Développement Rural et Auto-suffisance Alimentaire: Etude de Modifications Intervenues dans les Modes d'Alimentation et leurs Répercussions sur l'Auto-suffisance Alimentaire au Mali', Rapport de Consultation, Bamako, August, mimeo.

Simmons, E.B. (1987) 'Policy and Structural Reform of Grain Markets in Mali', paper presented at ODI conference on 'The Design and Impact of Adjustment Policies on Agriculture and Agricultural Institutions', London, September, mimeo.

Speirs, M. (1986) 'Aid Policies and Food Strategies in Africa: The European Community and Mali', Copenhagen, July, mimeo.

Sundberg, S. (1988) 'An Overview of the Food Consumption and Nutrition Situation in Mali', Report submitted to USAID/Mali, Agricultural Development Office, Bamako, March, mimeo.

Swift, J. (1989a) 'Why are Rural People Vulnerable to Famine?', *IDS Bulletin*, vol. 20, no. 2, pp. 8–15.

Swift, J. (1989b) 'Planning Against Drought and Famine in Turkana: A District Contingency Plan', in T.E. Downing, K.W. Gitu and M.K. Crispin (eds), *Coping with Drought in Kenya*, Lynne Rienner, Boulder and London.

Swift, J. (1994) 'Dynamic Ecological Systems in the Administration of Pastoral Development', in I. Scoones (ed.), *Living with Uncertainty: New Directions in Pastoral Development in Africa*, Intermediate Technology Publications, London.

Trine, F. (1990) 'Famine Early Warning Systems and Food Security', unpublished M.Phil. thesis, IDS, mimeo.

Turkana Drought Contingency Planning Unit (1992) 'Turkana District Drought Manual: Version 2', Lodwar, mimeo.

Turton, D. (1977) 'Response to Drought: The Mursi in Ethiopia', in J.G. Garlick and R.W.J. Keays (ed.), *Human Ecology in the Tropics*, Taylor & Francis, London.

Wagenaar-Brouwer, M. (1985) 'Preliminary Findings on the Diet and Nutritional Status of Some Tamasheq and Fulani Groups in the Niger Delta of Central Mali', in A.G. Hill (ed.), *Population, Health and Nutrition in the Sahel: Issues in the Welfare of Selected West African Communities*, Routledge & Kegan Paul, London, pp. 226–52.

Watts, M. (1983) *Silent Violence, Food, Famine and Peasantry in Northern Nigeria*, University of California Press, Berkeley.

Watts, M. (1988) 'Coping with the Market: Uncertainty and Food Security among Hausa Peasants', in I. De Garine and G.A. Harrison (eds), *Coping with Uncertainty in Food Supply*, Clarendon Press, Oxford, pp. 260–90.

WFP (1986) 'Evaluation of World Food Programme Emergency Response in West Africa 193–85 – Country Report: Mali', WFP, Rome.

WFP (1989) 'Review of Food Aid Policies and Programmes: Anti-Hunger Strategies of Poor Households and Communities: Roles of Food Aid', Report No. WFP/CFA:27/ P/INF/1 Add.1, WFP, Rome.

World Bank (1986) *Poverty and Hunger: Issues and Options for Food Security in Developing Countries*, World Bank Policy Study, Washington D.C.

World Bank (1989) *Sub-Saharan Africa: From Crisis to Sustainable Growth: A Long-Term Perspective Study*, World Bank, Washington D.C.

World Bank (1990) *Poverty: World Development Report 1990*, World Bank and Oxford University Press, Oxford and New York.

Index

absorptive capacity, 1, 63, 173, 251, 268, 272, 274
access, 10, 74, 242, 274
    to fisheries, 163, 237
    to food, 2, 4, 5, 13, 15, 16, 19, 40, 48–9, 55, 60, 61, 71, 81, 99, 106, 107, 110, 120, 121, 139, 148, 175
    to market, 175, 245
    to pasture, 63, 145, 148, 165
accumulation, 48, 53, 57, 89, 126, 128, 130, 133–6 *passim*, 139, 154, 160, 168, 170, 176, 185, 189, 190, 193, 196, 201, 202, 204, 238, 284, 285, 295
adaptation, 1, 3, 4, 13, 45–59 *passim*, 66, 138, 153, 155–69 *passim*, 174, 266–8, 274, 282, 287, 296, 298
    definition, 55
    motivation, 174
adjustment, structural, 90–3 *passim*, 99, 106, 283
administration, 69, 91, 117–24 *passim*, 314ch6n1
agriculture, 79–83, 88–90 *passim*, 96, 98, 106, 127, 135, 163, 173, 248, 255, 256
    see also individual headings
agro-fishing/fishers, 33, 63, 99, 109, 123, 126, 143–5, 151–2, 160–3, 169, 172, 177, 181–2, 184, 186–96 *passim*, 202, 203, 208, 209, 212, 216, 220–1, 225, 237, 255–6, 258, 259, 261–5 *passim*, 284
agro-pastoralism/pastoralists, 33, 34, 40–1, 62–3, 109, 122, 123, 139, 142–3, 151–2, 154, 155, 158–60, 172, 177, 180, 181, 184, 186–8, 191, 192, 194, 195, 199, 201–3, 206, 208–10, 212, 217–18, 221–2, 255–9, 261–5 *passim*, 284, 299
aid, 91, 309
    food, 2, 3, 5–7, 11–14 *passim*, 19, 37–9 *passim*, 46, 54, 64, 69, 76, 84, 86, 91, 92, 94–6 *passim*, 98, 99, 102–7 *passim*, 119, 120, 205, 239, 287, 299, 301, 307, 313ch5n4,5,314ch5n16
AIDS, 273
Amin, S., 79
Argentina, 206
assessment, 13, 300
assets, 18, 20, 23, 35–44 *passim*, 51, 62, 74–5, 97, 127, 149, 170, 239, 243–4, 264, 270, 275, 277, 288, 292, 295, 297–8, 300
    liquidation of, 20, 36–8, 47–50 *passim*, 71, 74, 126, 151, 172, 235, 236, 244, 246, 249, 251, 253, 262, 268, 270, 275, 277, 288, 297–8, 303, 312ch3n3
    preservation of, 40, 46, 50, 243, 266, 281
    redistribution of, 50
Associations Villageoises, 102, 105
Attara, 204, 205
Autier, P., 98
availability
    food, 4, 21, 37, 55, 58, 61, 71, 73, 75, 77, 81, 89, 183–5, 198, 287
    pasture, 63, 165, 210

Bâ, A.H., 65
balance, food, 5, 81–7
Bamako, 119, 122, 123, 154, 204–6 *passim*, 210
Bani River, 63, 83, 111, 122
Bankass, 111, 122, 183, 206
banks, 245
barriers, to entry, 268, 273, 274
    to re-entry, 170, 172, 284
barter, 41, 42, 63, 68, 74, 75, 127–30 *passim*, 134, 139, 143, 148, 153, 158, 163, 165, 166, 170, 172, 196, 197, 201, 202, 213–15 *passim*, 243, 249, 252, 253, 286, 297
Bayliss-Smith, T., 25
Bella, 51, 137–8, 251

Blaikie, P., 25, 31–2
blankets, 190
border controls, 123
borrowing, 47, 185, 202, 249, 252
  see also loans
Borton, J., 6
bourgou, 117, 130, 145, 160, 161, 163, 206, 229, 242, 247
Brookfield, H.C., 25, 31–2
browse, 158, 272
Buchanan-Smith, M., 12, 48, 103, 280, 305
buffers, 28, 29, 43, 170, 284, 294, 295
bureaucracies, 10, 89, 103, 307
  see also civil service
Burkina Faso, 122, 123, 127, 154, 206, 210

calendars, activity, 21, 70, 139–48, 156–68, 256, 267, 294, 298, 301
Campbell, D.J., 45
Canada, 314ch5n16
Cannon, T., 22
capacity to produce, 18, 23, 175, 183, 244
capital, 88, 172, 235, 268, 273, 274
cash, 20, 69, 139, 185–95 *passim*, 201, 217, 234, 237, 246, 257, 285, 300
cattle, 63, 71, 79, 114, 133, 134, 151, 155, 166, 172, 180, 181, 196, 199, 201, 202, 205–10 *passim*, 213–14, 218–19, 222–3, 236, 237, 272
Cekan, J., 241
cercles, 121–4
  see also individual headings
cereals, 20, 38, 40, 47, 63, 71, 74, 75, 77, 79, 81–6, 90–5 *passim*, 99, 102, 104, 105, 120, 122, 124, 128–32 *passim*, 138, 143, 148, 151, 158, 163, 166, 169, 170, 176–80, 183–5, 189–93, 198, 201, 202, 206, 212, 231–2, 244, 283, 300
  see also individual headings
Chambers, R., 18, 21, 22
charcoal, 206
chiefs, 67, 69, 73, 302, 312ch4n3
child care, 77, 254, 258
children, 84, 242
  see also under-fives

CILSS, 96
CIPEA, 65
civil service, 89, 93, 119–21, 160
claims, 20, 35–44 *passim*, 51, 57, 133, 135, 149, 170, 171, 201, 239, 242, 290, 296, 298
climate, 7, 79, 123, 210
  see also rainfall
CNAUR, 91, 92, 96, 97, 103, 313ch5n10
COC, 91, 92, 102
collapse, livelihood, 61, 72
collectivisation, 80–1, 120
commerce, 71, 76, 226, 231, 238, 245, 253, 298
competitiveness, 104, 105, 237
condiments, 71, 206, 207, 226–7, 233–6 *passim*
conflict, 8–9, 88–9, 131, 220, 230, 233, 243
construction, 128, 254, 259
consumption, 5, 17, 18, 29, 35, 36, 38, 39, 41, 43, 57, 73, 74, 83–4, 88, 89, 130, 133, 135, 172, 180, 183, 196, 239, 241, 246, 265, 266, 271, 276, 278, 281, 284, 289, 296, 298–9, 307
  reduction, 47, 166, 239, 243, 245, 253
coping strategies, 1–4, 11–13 *passim*, 16, 18, 20, 21, 25, 34, 35, 38, 39, 41–59 *passim*, 61, 66, 70–3, 77, 89, 127, 139, 143, 145, 148, 154, 166, 168–71 *passim*, 174, 189, 201, 226, 233, 234, 238–79, 281–2, 285, 294, 298, 300, 309
  asset-based, 239, 240, 243–4, 246, 247, 251, 264, 270, 275, 277
  consumption-based, 239, 241, 246, 248, 253, 265, 271, 276, 278
  CPR-based, 239, 240, 242–3, 246, 247, 249, 251, 263, 269, 275, 277
  definition, 55, 262, 281
  effectiveness, 4, 52–6, 58, 235, 248, 267, 274–8, 286, 289, 298, 302
  erosive/non-erosive, 54, 239
  exchange-based, 239, 240, 244–7 *passim*, 252, 254, 265, 270, 276, 278

intensity of, 130, 133, 134, 267, 272, 274–8, 298
labour-based, 239, 240, 244, 246, 247, 251–2, 264, 270, 276, 277
migration-based, 239, 241, 245–6, 248, 252, 254, 265, 270, 276, 278
motivation, 49, 54, 56, 58, 238, 248, 267, 274–8, 286, 298
production-based, 239–42, 246–9 *passim*, 263, 269, 275, 277
reciprocally-based, 238–9, 240, 243, 246, 247, 251, 264, 269, 275, 277
reinforcement of, 267, 282, 300
uptake, 38, 47–51 *passim*, 55, 56, 59, 73, 248, 261, 262, 266, 267, 273, 282, 286
Corbett, J.E.M., 29, 45, 47, 49
Côte d'Ivoire, 122, 206, 210
cotton, 80, 81, 90, 116
counterpart funds, 84, 94, 95, 102, 314ch5n16
counter-season crops, 139, 154, 241, 244, 260, 285
CPRs, 130, 154, 174, 239, 242–3, 246, 263, 269, 272, 273, 275, 277
credit, 51, 73, 74, 76, 81, 89–91 *passim*, 102, 104, 105, 122, 126–8 *passim*, 130, 145, 154, 161, 163, 170, 172, 174, 175, 189, 199, 205, 209, 233, 239, 243, 245, 249, 273, 299, 300
cultivation/cultivators, 29, 32, 33, 81–3, 109, 126, 127, 129–31 *passim*, 138–9, 150, 153–7, 172, 177, 181, 186–8, 191–5 *passim*, 199, 201, 203, 208–12 *passim*, 217–18, 221–2, 234, 249, 255–7 *passim*, 260, 263–5
dryland, 47, 61–3, 109, 138–40, 154–6 *passim*
wetland, 62, 63, 109, 138, 139, 141, 145, 157, 161, 201, 284
cycles, 26, 29, 50, 55, 57, 61, 124–31 *passim*, 135–6, 139, 150, 152, 168, 169

Daget, G., 65, 117

dairy products, 212, 214
see also milk
dams, 63
data collection, 9, 10, 12, 52, 59, 63–70, 73–8, 96–8, 121, 282, 301, 312ch4n6
Davies, S., 5, 12, 70, 102, 280, 301, 305
death, 1, 23, 266
Debo, Lake, 115, 123, 124, 145, 161, 163, 205, 206
debt, 33, 36, 73–5 *passim*, 126, 129, 135, 153, 160, 161, 165, 172, 220, 243, 252, 268, 273, 298
repayment, 120, 129, 145, 153, 161, 163, 190, 194, 202, 209, 217, 233, 243–5, 252, 262, 273, 300, 304
decentralisation, 64, 107, 117, 305, 307–9 *passim*, 314ch6n1
deficits, cash, 77, 193–7
food, 7, 81, 83, 84, 87, 90, 102, 104, 105, 154, 160
management of, 239, 241–3 *passim*
degradation, resource base, 36, 42, 243
Delta, Inner Niger, 1–2, 7–9, 62–3, 73, 84, 108–75, 183–5, 202, 205, 212, 261, 283, 286, 291, 301
dependency ratios, 36, 37, 272
destitution, 1, 10, 23, 29, 46, 47, 53, 57, 70, 72, 266, 308
devaluations, 90, 123, 237, 313ch5n11, 315ch9n5
development, 11, 32, 65, 69, 117–20 *passim*, 135, 245, 300, 305–7 *passim*, 309
CRDs, 117, 199
Local – Committees, 67–8, 117–19 *passim*, 313ch5n5
De Waal, A., 29, 38, 54, 88, 239, 243
Diagnostics Régionales, 107, 119
Diafarabé, 124, 145, 204, 205
Dina, 165
Diondiori, 67, 204, 205
disease, 30, 181, 273
displaced, 23, 63, 68–70 *passim*, 122, 137, 245–6, 251
disruptions, 55, 155, 262
distribution, food, 88, 90, 94, 105

diversification, 34, 48, 76, 77, 89, 90, 139, 143, 145, 153, 158, 163, 169, 173, 180, 185, 190, 191, 196, 197, 201, 202, 204, 210, 237, 238, 241, 256, 284, 288
DNA, 98
DNSI, 98
donors, 2, 11–14 passim, 84, 91, 94, 95, 97, 99, 102–4 passim, 107, 305, 307, 308
Douentza, 62, 63, 65, 66, 70, 71, 73, 111, 114, 122–3, 126, 129, 130, 154, 204, 206, 230, 242, 251, 252
Downing, T.E., 22, 47
Drèze, J., 36, 291
droughts, 1–4, 8–10 passim, 17, 24, 26, 30, 34, 36, 40, 46, 50, 56, 57, 69, 83, 84, 94–6 passim, 105, 106, 109, 122, 126, 128, 135–8 passim, 143, 150–2 passim, 190, 242, 261, 262, 272, 283, 284, 309–10
post-, 4, 69, 107, 137, 148, 160, 173, 180, 183, 248, 262
drylands, 1, 8, 60, 62, 73, 109, 111, 114, 116, 117, 123, 126–8, 135–9 passim, 154, 165, 166, 184, 283–4
markets, 204–6 passim, 209, 210, 212–32 passim
D'Souza, F., 45
Duffield, M., 9, 53
dung collection, 130, 160
dykes, 119

early warning systems, 2–7 passim, 9, 11–13, 16–18, 20–2 passim, 30, 37–9 passim, 42, 46–9 passim, 56, 60, 61, 72, 92, 96, 99, 102, 103, 107, 121, 172, 173, 198, 234, 280, 283, 287, 299, 301, 302, 305, 308, 309
see also individual headings
EC, 90, 91, 96, 206, 210, 313ch5n4,314ch5n16
education, 53, 65, 312ch4n4
Eele, G., 48, 267
Egg, J., 96, 98, 99, 102, 103
emergency, 12, 88, 95, 105, 106, 305, 307
relief, 11, 12, 32, 88, 91, 99, 106, 283, 291, 302, 207–9 passim

employment, 52, 68, 75, 81, 89, 122, 126, 130–1, 154, 158, 169, 172, 243, 244, 252, 285, 299, 300
see also labour
ENDA, 8
entitlements, 20–1, 23, 33, 35–45, 51, 60, 71, 239, 281
calls on, 11, 15, 36–45 passim, 60, 61, 69, 121, 137, 149, 173–5, 197, 239, 243, 251, 262, 281, 282, 285–91 passim, 293, 294, 296–302 passim
exchange, 35–43 passim, 60, 71, 72, 76, 132–4 passim, 149, 171, 198–237, 239, 244–7 passim, 252, 254, 288, 292, 295, 297, 303
food, 10, 13, 15, 20, 34, 36, 37, 45, 50, 55–6, 60, 61, 69, 81, 143, 161, 163, 198, 282
livelihood, 3, 4, 11, 21, 23, 33–6, 41–4 passim, 60, 71, 238, 239, 242, 281, 282, 288–93;
matrix, 3, 21, 35–7 passim, 39, 41, 43, 45, 238, 239, 291–4 passim
production, 20, 23, 37, 43, 131–4, 163, 176–97, 201, 238–41, 292, 297, 300, 303
promotion, 291, 293, 300, 301, 305–7 passim, 309
protection, 291, 293, 299–301, 305–7 passim, 309
provision, 291, 293, 299–301, 305–7 passim, 309
sources of, 11, 35–45 passim, 61, 66, 69, 137, 149, 173, 180, 183, 197, 237, 281, 282, 285–91, 294–7 passim, 299, 301, 302; diversification, 180, 197, 237, 253, 286
environment, 274, 298
equipment, 75, 127, 129, 186
fishing, 77, 122, 126, 145, 151, 160, 161, 163, 175, 185, 189, 199, 202, 209, 212, 252
Ethiopia, 38, 312ch3n1
exchange, 20, 35–43 passim, 60, 68, 71, 72, 76, 77, 132–4, 149, 170, 171, 198–237, 239, 244–7, 254–7

passim, 265, 270, 276, 278, 284, 285, 288, 292, 295, 297, 303
  labour, 50, 109, 129, 153, 170, 244, 251, 284
expenditure, household, 74, 76, 77, 186–8
exporters, foreign, 145, 163, 225, 233
exports, 79–81 *passim*, 122, 204, 205, 237, 313ch5n1,2
extension, 89–91 *passim*

failure, food system, 5, 6, 8, 12, 13, 16, 45, 61, 280
  harvest, 9, 46, 51, 104, 126, 143, 150, 174
fall-back strategies, 34, 46, 55, 76, 134
families, founding, 74, 274
famine, 1, 2, 5, 7–9, 11, 20, 22, 23, 28, 29, 45, 53, 88, 107, 135, 138, 280, 287, 294, 302, 308
FAO, 5, 96
farming systems research, 22, 55, 311ch2n5
Fatoma, 71, 122, 198, 204
FCFA zone, 90
feeding centres, 9, 266
FEWS, 96, 102
field agents, 2, 64–6 *passim*, 70, 76, 302
fines, 36, 37, 120, 163, 174, 186, 243, 272, 273, 304
fish, 71, 75, 79, 109, 114, 117, 121, 122, 126, 127, 130–4 *passim*, 160, 161, 163, 170, 177, 182, 189–92 *passim*, 194, 197, 199, 201, 202, 206, 207, 209–11 *passim*, 216, 220–1, 225, 233, 236, 237, 245, 252, 315ch9n1
fishers/fishing, transhumant, 33, 34, 63, 83, 98, 99, 109, 123, 126–8 *passim*, 145–6, 150–2, 160, 161, 163–5, 169, 172, 177, 182, 199, 202, 203, 208, 209, 212, 220–1, 225, 237, 256, 263–5, 274, 284
fisheries sector, 83, 98, 99, 106, 119, 120, 124, 126–31, 143–5 *passim*, 150–1, 154, 160–5, 169, 173, 176, 180–2, 185, 189, 190, 196, 202, 205, 216, 229, 237, 242, 245, 246, 249, 252, 255, 256, 258, 261–2, 284, 285, 297
flexibility, 7, 25, 34, 95
floodplains, 111, 114, 116, 117, 138, 212
flood-retreat crops, 114, 116, 154, 241
flood, 79, 83, 111, 114–16 *passim*, 124, 126, 128, 130, 131, 138, 143, 148, 151, 152, 160, 161, 172, 178, 182, 205, 210, 241, 283, 284, 288, 302
fodder, 158, 160
fonio, 83, 117, 154, 206, 229, 253
food-first approach, 18–20 *passim*
food-for-work, 33, 313ch5n5
forecasts, crop, 20, 297
forestry agents, 120, 163
forests, 109, 117, 119
France, 314ch5n16
Frankenberger, T.R., 18, 45, 46, 48–50 *passim*
Fulani, 62–3, 139, 155, 158, 165, 274
functionaries, 67

Gallais, J., 65, 111
Gao, 10, 122, 123, 165, 206, 242
gap
  cereal, 179, 195, 197
  food, 43, 56, 72, 76, 77, 134, 171, 179–80, 182–97 *passim*, 237, 238, 260, 284–6 *passim*, 288, 297, 299, 303
gardening, market, 139, 241–2, 247
gathering, 120, 143, 172, 190, 192–3, 235, 236, 254, 259
Gatie Luomo, 204, 206
gender issues, 36, 42, 254, 258–61 *passim*
Germany, 314ch5n16
Ghana, 210
GIEWS, 96
gifts, 69, 74, 183, 190
goats, 63, 71, 114, 129, 155, 158, 161, 166, 169, 172, 173, 180, 181, 185, 196, 197, 199, 201, 202, 206–13 *passim*, 217, 221–2, 233, 234, 236, 237, 244, 272, 285
gold, 75, 185, 199, 201, 202, 244, 251
Goldstein, D.M., 18, 45, 48
Gore, C., 40, 55

grasses, 117, 206
grazing, 120–1
groundnuts, 80, 81, 116
growth, economic, 53

Hall, R.E., 9
harvest, off-farm, 75, 139, 183, 184, 189, 196, 197, 257, 286, 288
Heald, C., 90, 94
health, 52, 246, 268, 273, 296, 306
herders/herding, 63, 139, 155, 158, 160, 165, 166, 176, 181, 209, 210, 216, 221, 224, 239, 245, 249, 252, 272, 284
Hesse, C., 62, 65
Holling, C.S., 25, 26
Hombori, 204
Horn of Africa, 5, 7–9 *passim*, 12, 14, 48, 56, 283
households, 15, 51–8, 62, 72–7, 183–97, 248, 253–60, 272–4, 286
   budgets, 76, 180, 186–97
   composition, 51, 74
   division of labour, 73, 76, 139, 143, 154, 155, 160, 169, 185, 244, 254, 268, 273, 274
   female-headed, 4, 23, 37–8, 281
   food systems, 15-17 *passim*, 36, 183–95
   gender mix, 36, 42
   status, 51, 74
   time budgets, 244, 253–60
hunger, 2, 6, 12, 22, 50, 127, 243, 266, 310
hungry season, 48, 56, 77, 88, 97, 121, 127, 128, 153, 154, 158, 161, 163, 194, 208, 209, 226, 231, 242, 257, 289
hunting, 120, 161, 172, 189
Hutchinson, C.F., 46, 48

illness, 17, 23, 36
imports, 5, 11, 19, 38, 81, 84, 86, 90, 122, 204–5
impoverishment, 1, 8, 53, 88, 109, 123, 152
incentives, producer, 89, 95, 283
income, 45, 48, 62, 69, 74, 76, 77, 79, 90, 93, 139, 180, 185, 186, 188–95, 197, 243, 285, 300, 306, 313ch4n8
   off-farm, 17
indicators, 10, 13, 16, 18, 20, 21, 34–7, 39–41, 48–50, 57, 59–61 *passim*, 70–1, 74–6, 131–5, 172–5, 197, 235–6, 248, 268, 277–9, 282, 286–305 *passim*
inflation, 207
information, 2, 9–13 *passim*, 16, 21, 49, 52, 57, 61, 65–6, 78, 96, 98, 104–7, 110, 119, 121, 172–5, 218, 301–6, 308, 312ch4n6,7
   see also monitoring
infrastructure, 10, 119
inputs, 32, 33, 81, 89–91 *passim*, 105, 242
insecurity, food, 2–4 *passim*, 7–9, 12, 15, 21, 22, 30–2, 35, 37, 44, 46, 53, 55, 59–65 *passim*, 72, 73, 87–9, 98, 105, 137, 152–66, 174, 197, 211, 281–2, 284, 285, 286, 287, 294, 299
   chronic, 3, 7, 16, 17, 20, 24, 53, 55, 88, 280
   transitory, 12, 16, 17, 20, 53, 55, 282
insecurity, political, 216, 219, 230
institutions, 81, 89, 91
   see also individual headings
insurance mechanisms, 47–8, 51, 54, 56, 93, 204, 210, 212, 218, 237, 239, 242, 285
interest rates, 174, 243, 252
International Monetary Fund, 90, 91
interventions, 3, 9, 13, 21, 30–3 *passim*, 37, 38, 40, 44, 46, 55, 57, 59, 61, 64, 72, 73, 81, 102, 107, 239, 280, 282, 287, 291, 299, 300, 305, 306, 309
   development, 11
   village-level, 13, 65, 78
investments, 20, 40, 54, 68, 75, 77, 79, 89, 90, 93, 119, 123, 129, 135, 139, 143, 148, 151, 160, 169, 185, 186, 202, 208, 217–18, 233, 284, 285
   fungibility, 185–6
irrigation, 32, 79, 93, 119
IRRT, 81

IUCN, 8, 62, 65, 66, 114, 117
  Project, 62, 65

Jodha, N.S., 242
Joekes, S., 72

Kabeer, N., 72
Keita, Modibo, 80, 120
KéMacina, 111, 145
Kenya, 306, 311ch1n3
kin, 36–7, 47, 68, 69, 73, 74, 124, 154, 161, 185, 201, 249, 274
Koro, 111, 122, 183, 206
Kossam Mopti, 215, 219, 220

labour, 21, 32, 51, 68, 73, 76, 77, 124, 130, 158, 161, 169, 173, 180, 239, 242, 244, 253–60, 264, 268, 270, 272, 276, 277, 285
  casual, 68, 69, 75, 128, 169, 173, 190, 251, 254, 259, 272
  demand/supply, 21, 38, 68, 69, 128, 138, 153, 183, 243–6 *passim*, 251, 268
  division of, 73, 139, 143, 154, 155, 160, 169, 185, 244, 254, 268, 273, 274
  exchanges of, 50, 109, 129, 153, 170, 244, 251, 284
  market, 260, 285
  returns to, 189
  sale of, 20, 47, 139, 155, 165, 192, 193, 197, 201
  shortage, 126–8 *passim*, 131, 143, 153, 154, 169, 183, 245, 251
Lalau-Keraly, A., 102
land, 25, 31–2, 34, 47, 109
landless, 22, 23, 38
Lecaillon, J., 79, 80
liberalisation, market, 88, 91–5 *passim*, 102, 120, 204, 244, 282–3
licences, 120
Lipton, M., 36, 90, 94
listening posts, 10, 63–6, 121–4, 204
livelihood systems, 1–4 *passim*, 7, 8, 10, 13, 15–44, 51, 52, 55, 56, 58, 61–4, 66–70, 73, 88, 106, 108, 111–17, 121, 123, 137–97, 273, 274, 281, 283–306 *passim*

  diversity of, 7, 10, 15, 33–5, 106, 108, 123, 284
  traditional, 138–48
  see also individual headings
livestock, 20, 24, 32, 38, 47, 53, 62, 63, 69, 74–5, 77, 83, 91, 99, 119, 121–3, 128, 139, 143, 148, 151, 155, 158, 176, 177, 180–1, 185, 189–93, 196, 201, 206, 212–13, 218–20, 231–3, 237, 243, 244, 300, 313ch5n2
  small stock, 34, 47, 121, 127, 158, 173, 180
  see also individual headings
loans, 36, 47, 91, 170, 243
  repayment, 74, 75, 163
location, 7, 9–10
Longhurst, R., 45, 47, 312ch3n3

maize, 82, 84, 206
malaria, 273, 300
management, 25, 31, 32, 243
market dependence, 17, 37, 41, 51, 76, 77, 89, 126–8, 130, 145, 154, 166, 170, 184, 185, 188, 190, 193, 197–204, 234, 237, 243, 244, 285, 294, 295, 297
marketing system, 51, 81, 90, 93–5, 104, 206
markets, 4, 35, 37–42 *passim*, 50, 67, 69, 71, 75, 88, 90–2, 95, 102–5 *passim*, 122, 124, 145, 153, 170, 172, 175, 181, 198, 201, 202, 204–37, 242, 244, 245, 283, 288–90
  labour, 260, 285
  parallel, 94
MATDB, 96, 103
Matlon, P., 46
mats, 71, 190, 193, 206, 229–31, 235
Mauritania, 206
Maxwell, S., 15, 16, 22, 25, 55
McCracken, J., 49
McLean, W., 96
meals per day, 69, 74, 130, 246, 253
Mema, 111, 165
migration/migrants, 9, 10, 21, 23, 46, 47, 50, 68, 70, 74, 75, 84, 89, 109, 114, 121–3, 126–31 *passim*, 139,

Index

153, 154, 158, 172–4 *passim*, 185, 239, 241, 244–6, 248, 252, 254–6, 258, 262, 265, 270, 272–3, 276, 278, 283, 287, 303
   return from, 40, 69, 127, 173
   rural–rural, 21, 122, 124, 128, 130, 153, 174, 245
   rural–urban, 9, 21, 23, 69, 81, 121, 127, 174, 245, 252, 273
   seasonal, 69, 73, 122, 123, 154, 245
milk, 24, 71, 75, 127, 143, 148, 158, 165, 170, 190–3 *passim*, 199, 201, 202, 206–10 *passim*, 213, 215–16, 218, 220, 224–5, 236, 237
   Kossam Mopti, 215, 219, 220
millet, 62, 63, 81–3 *passim*, 104, 109, 114, 116, 119, 122, 127–30, 132, 134, 138, 153, 154, 158, 161, 176, 178, 194–5, 199, 201, 202, 206–12, 217–31 *passim*, 234, 236, 237, 244, 251, 252, 261, 284
minerals, 84, 235
mobility, 7, 9, 10, 34, 51, 63, 76, 84, 89, 131, 154, 169, 171, 241
modernisation, 120
moneylenders, 47, 244
monitoring, 3, 6–14 *passim*, 17, 20–2, 34, 35, 42, 45, 47, 56, 58, 103, 104, 110, 121, 173, 267, 280, 287–305, 309
   SADS, 1–3 *passim*, 6, 9–11, 13, 14, 20, 21, 30, 35, 42, 47, 52, 59–78, 104, 107, 110, 121, 135, 152, 198, 235, 244, 266, 280–2 *passim*, 308, 311ch1n1
Moorehead, R.M., 8, 111, 115–17, 119–21 *passim*, 136, 182, 183, 242, 243, 307
Mopti, 9, 10, 65, 68–70 *passim*, 111, 114, 119, 121–2, 127–35, 145, 198, 204–5, 207, 209–11 *passim*, 215, 216, 219, 220, 225, 233, 242, 245, 249, 251–2
moral economy, 35–7, 39–42 *passim*, 50, 51, 55, 239, 288–90
Morrisson, C., 79, 80
Mortimore, M.J., 26–8 *passim*, 46, 50, 266
multiple resource use, 173–4, 287

National Food Strategy, 89–93 *passim*, 95, 105–7 *passim*, 283
needs, 18, 22, 38, 43, 58, 65, 72, 76, 77, 169, 185, 202, 244, 281, 284, 299, 309
NGOs, 2, 11, 13, 14, 67, 76, 95, 106, 117
N'Gouma, 204
Niger, 206
Niger River, 63, 79, 83, 111, 122, 178, 314ch6n3
Nigeria, 47, 50, 123, 206
normality, 10–11, 174
nutritional status, 5, 38, 39, 52, 273, 289, 296, 304

ODEM, 65, 98–9, 180
ODRs, 67, 89, 119, 313ch5n8
Office du Niger, 79–80, 89, 122, 126
officials, government, 68, 69, 98
old and infirm, 23, 52
OPAM, 93–4, 119, 204–5, 314ch5n16
OPM, 99
options, 13, 17, 31, 36, 45, 49–54 *passim*, 56, 161, 168, 169, 174, 189, 237, 239, 246, 262, 267, 291, 294, 298
ORM, 119, 176
output, 20, 57, 79, 83, 84, 88, 90
OXFAM, 62, 65, 66

paddy, 206, 248–9, 251, 253
parastatals, 81, 93, 120
pastoralism/pastoralists, transhumant, 23, 24, 29, 32, 33, 36, 53, 61, 63, 83, 99, 106, 109, 120, 122–4, 126–8 *passim*, 130, 131, 138, 139, 145, 147–8, 151, 160, 165–7, 172, 177, 181, 185, 199, 202, 203, 206, 208, 209, 212, 213, 218–20, 222–5, 237 242, 252, 254–6 *passim*, 261, 263–5, 284, 285, 297
pasture, 34, 36, 83, 98–9, 109, 117, 123, 124, 126–8 *passim*, 131, 132, 143, 145, 148, 165, 166, 210, 223, 224, 242, 246, 252
pests, 37, 129, 172
Pirzio-Biroli, D., 84
Pisani Plan, 90

planning, 2, 3, 11–13 *passim*, 21, 64, 69, 83, 89–108, 117–21, 287, 300, 301, 305–9 *passim*
  contingency, 287, 305, 306, 208, 309
  regional, 107, 119
ploughs, 185, 244, 297, 300
political factors, 8, 9, 81, 91, 99, 103, 305–8 *passim*
politicians, 67
population, 5, 9, 10, 64, 84, 85, 89, 110–111, 137
  density, 84, 212
  growth, 17, 53, 81, 84, 89, 90, 110, 179, 283
poverty, 22, 34, 53, 83, 106, 153, 287, 305, 306, 309
PRA, 70, 74, 291, 302
prediction, famine, 1, 2, 5, 11, 12, 23, 38, 41, 47, 72, 266, 280, 281, 291, 293, 308
pregnancy, 36
prevention, famine, 1, 11, 12, 44, 47, 54, 72, 88, 280, 281, 300, 305, 306
prices, 5, 16, 17, 20, 34, 37, 38, 40, 57, 71, 81, 89, 94, 96, 99, 104, 105, 120, 124, 126–34 *passim*, 154, 166, 194, 198, 206–29, 234–7 *passim*, 249, 251, 252, 285, 300
  producer, 80, 81, 88, 90, 94
  retail, 207, 212
  urban/rural, 198, 207, 209–16 *passim*
  wholesale, 207, 212
pricing policy, 90, 94
PRMC, 84, 91, 92, 94–6, 102–8 *passim*, 283, 314ch5n17
private sector, 51, 91, 94, 102, 104, 105, 174, 243, 300
production, food, 5, 12, 17, 20, 22, 23, 35–43 *passim*, 50, 51, 55, 57, 60, 68, 69, 73–7, 81–3, 88, 90, 93, 95, 104, 126–34, 139–48, 171, 172, 176–97, 241, 242, 246, 248–50, 263, 269, 275, 277, 288, 292, 295, 297, 300, 302
productivity, 17, 46, 79, 126, 246
Projet d'Appui Villageois, 13, 78
protection, livelihood, 21, 29, 35, 36, 38–43 *passim*, 149, 171, 239, 284, 290, 296, 298, 299, 302, 307

protein energy malnutrition, 84
public works, 299
purchases, food, 63, 69, 143, 155, 176, 181, 183–6 *passim*, 191, 197, 201, 202, 210, 217, 243

questionnaires, 71, 74, 96, 98, 119

rainfall, 5, 8, 20, 24, 31, 32, 37, 39, 60, 79, 80, 88, 95, 111, 114, 124, 126–31 *passim*, 138, 143, 148, 152, 154, 155, 166, 172, 178, 182, 209, 215, 233, 283, 288, 302
Reardon, T., 46
reciprocal links, 37, 48, 50, 75, 129, 139, 145, 148, 151, 153, 166, 170, 171, 173, 190, 201, 202, 243, 245, 264, 269, 275, 277, 285, 289, 296, 297
recovery, 25, 26, 29, 55, 56, 60, 61, 106, 148, 151, 152, 180, 282, 291
reform, 89–90, 93–106
rehabilitation, 242, 291, 300, 307
remittances, 75, 154, 174, 185, 189, 245, 303
renting/rents, 165, 175, 249, 274, 297
République du Mali, 65, 89, 90, 103, 104, 119
research, 22, 75, 91
reserves, 18, 127, 160
  see also stocks
resilience, 1, 2, 4, 15, 21, 25–9 *passim*, 34, 42–4 *passim*, 54, 56, 57, 59, 66, 93, 137, 148–66 *passim*, 170, 171, 237, 281, 294–6, 300
responses, 7, 13, 14, 17, 21, 24, 30, 33, 34, 41, 46, 47, 50–2, 56, 59, 72, 92, 95–9 *passim*, 150, 248, 280, 281, 287, 301, 309, 312ch3n3
  programmed, 102–5, 283
restructuring, *see* PRMC
revenue, 62, 76, 120
rice, 62, 63, 79, 81–4 *passim*, 109, 114, 116, 119, 124, 126–30 *passim*, 138, 143, 145, 153, 155, 160, 161, 176, 178, 194, 195, 201, 202, 209, 212, 248–9, 251, 253, 261, 284, 315ch8n1
Riely, F., 50

RIM, 180
Rimaïbe, 139
risk, 18, 21–3 *passim*, 33, 34, 169, 172, 179, 180, 237, 239, 268–72, 274, 284, 306
  avoidance, 34, 54, 139, 143
  management, 45, 48, 152, 185, 189, 190
  roads, 88, 122, 123, 204, 206
RRA, 49, 70, 302

SADS, *see* monitoring
safety nets, 1, 9, 10, 40, 51, 73, 76, 95, 109–36, 139, 143, 148, 169, 174, 261, 283, 286, 301
sampling, 204–6, 301
SAP, 12, 65, 92, 96–105, 119, 283, 307, 308, 314ch5n17
saving, 54, 76, 90, 139, 154, 181, 182, 185, 190, 193, 201, 245
seasonal factors, 7, 24, 33, 34, 49, 56, 63, 66, 88, 110, 114, 137, 154–5, 158, 169, 170, 193, 198, 199, 209–16, 220–4 *passim*, 227, 233, 246–8 *passim*, 254, 257–9, 268, 272
  'dead season', 128, 154, 244
security
  food, 1–5, 11–22 *passim*, 32–6 *passim*, 43, 45, 46, 54, 58, 60, 61, 65, 66, 69, 70, 72, 87–93, 108–10 *passim*, 119, 124–35, 137–52, 173, 237, 281, 282, 305, 309
  livelihood, 1, 12, 16, 18–24 *passim*, 33, 46, 61, 109, 139, 237, 268, 274, 291, 307, 309
sedentarisation, 37
seed, 32, 127, 128, 131, 154, 155, 161, 170, 175, 242, 243, 248–9, 299
self-sufficiency, food, 81, 89, 90
Sen, A.K., 20, 36, 291
Seno, 111, 114, 122, 128, 138, 145, 148, 151, 167, 168, 202, 210
sensitivity, 4, 15, 25–34, 42–4 *passim*, 54, 56, 57, 61, 66, 137, 148, 149, 152, 165, 170, 171, 237, 281, 294–6, 300
Sévaré, 119, 204, 206
sheep, 71, 114, 180, 206

shocks, 3, 16, 17, 21, 22, 26, 27, 29, 31–3 *passim*, 55, 58, 148
Shoham, J., 6
shortages
  food, 1, 7, 12, 15, 34, 46, 47, 88, 96, 109, 127, 138, 153, 244, 283, 307
  labour, 126–8 *passim*, 131, 143, 153, 154, 158, 169, 183, 245, 251
  seed, 127, 128, 131
  traction animals, 130
Sidibe, S., 313ch5n3
SIM, 102, 104
Simmons, E.B., 95
slaves, former, 51, 137–9 *passim* 148, 202
Smith, M., 15, 16, 25
sorghum, 81, 82, 84, 104, 116, 216
Speirs, M., 81, 91
starvation, 23, 29, 88, 266
state policies, 17, 37–9 *passim*, 41, 42, 44, 51, 152, 239, 283, 288–90, 305
  see also adjustment; reform
stocks, 5, 53, 68, 73–5 *passim*, 87, 89, 96, 109, 126–32 *passim*, 134, 138, 148, 151, 158, 161, 165, 166, 168, 194, 201, 202, 209, 243, 297, 302
SNS, 94, 102, 104, 119, 283
storage, 91, 94, 205
stores, 20, 35, 40, 51, 109, 151, 170, 181, 185
strangers, 51, 67, 69, 109, 110, 123, 130, 131, 160, 165, 182, 219, 251, 274
straw collection, 130, 253
stress, food, 1, 4, 9, 13, 14, 20, 22, 24, 34, 40, 41, 45, 46, 49–59 *passim*, 61, 63, 71, 73, 143, 151, 153, 172–5, 189, 234, 239, 266, 267, 272, 281, 286
subsidies, 80, 88, 91, 94
subsistence, 8, 18–20 *passim*, 24, 29, 43, 50, 53, 54, 59, 62, 70, 76, 77, 81, 130, 160, 163, 166, 168–70 *passim*, 176, 189, 190, 196, 237–9 *passim*, 282, 285
success, system, 13, 16, 45, 46
Sudan, 53, 243
  Darfur, 38, 54, 311ch1n3, 312ch3n1
  Kordofan, 50

sugar, 71, 206
Sundberg, S., 84
supervisors, 64, 65
supply, food, 25, 45, 48, 75
surplus, 80, 87, 195
surveys, household, 65, 72–7, 97
  livelihood system, village-level, 66–70
  market, 70, 71, 198–237, 297–8, 302
  nutrition, 96–7
survival, 10, 16, 18, 28, 29, 45, 54
sustainability, 18, 19, 24–6 *passim*, 29, 33, 44, 53, 54, 103, 267, 268, 274–8, 295–6, 298
Swift, J., 23, 36, 306, 307

targeting, 6, 103, 119, 121
taxation, 36, 37, 51, 76, 93, 120, 126, 129, 153, 172, 174, 175, 180, 186, 190, 244, 251, 262, 298, 300, 304, 307, 308
tea, 71, 206
technical assistance, 103
technology, 91
Teme, B., 96, 98, 99, 102, 103
Tenenkou, 67, 71, 109, 115, 123–35, 204, 205
Thera, S., 62, 65
threshold, coping/adaptation, 58
time budgets, 74, 76, 77, 169, 244, 253–60, 267
timing, 54, 56, 58, 246, 262, 266, 286
Toguéré Koumbé, 66, 123–4, 126–35, 204, 205, 208, 249, 253
Tombouctou, 10, 122, 165
Tons Villageois, 120
traction animals, 130, 169, 244, 249, 253
trade, 71, 104, 121–3, 127, 244
  rural–urban, 207, 218–20 *passim*, 222, 223, 225, 227
  terms of, 20–1, 24, 41, 42, 49, 90, 99, 127, 128, 133, 134, 155, 158, 161, 170, 173, 197–9 *passim*, 202, 207–9 *passim*, 212, 216–31, 234–6, 244, 246, 252, 268, 285, 286, 294, 297, 298, 300, 303

traders, market, 47, 68, 71, 74, 89, 91, 94, 102, 104, 105, 119, 145, 153, 160, 170, 202, 205, 210, 220, 226, 230–6 *passim*, 244, 245, 249, 252, 273, 298, 302, 304
tragedy of the commons, 243
training, 53, 65
transfers, 20, 21, 47, 74, 76, 189, 190, 300
transhumance, 63, 74, 145, 155, 160, 161, 165, 166, 169, 174, 216, 219, 245, 252
  see also fishers; pastoralists
transport, 102, 104, 105, 122, 123, 128, 145, 205, 210, 216, 252, 298
Traoré, President, 91, 99, 307
Trine, F., 314ch5n14
Tuareg, 89, 131, 138, 206, 313ch5n3,13
Turton, D., 38

UDPM, 91, 99, 120
uncertainty, 27, 28, 56, 131, 242
  'as norm/aberration', 28
under-fives, 5, 23, 30, 37, 39, 281
unemployed, 22, 23
urbanisation, 81, 88
USA, 314ch5n16
USAID, 96

vaccination, livestock, 119
vitamins, 84, 235
vulnerability, 1, 3, 4, 10, 11, 15, 17, 21–6, 44, 66, 72, 77, 110, 152, 155, 158, 160, 161, 163, 166, 168, 169, 179, 185, 190, 197, 198, 244, 280–310
  differential, 23, 24, 30
  proximate, 4, 23, 24, 26, 29–30, 33, 38, 42, 43, 52, 61, 235, 281, 291, 300, 310
  structural, 4, 23–6 *passim*, 29, 33, 42, 47, 52, 61, 72, 235, 280, 283, 284, 287, 291, 300, 309, 310

Wagenaar-Brouwer, M., 313ch5n3
wages, 68, 69, 190, 192, 193, 251, 252
Walado, Lake, 115, 123, 124, 161

war, civil, 9, 53
  Mali/Burkina Faso, 206
water, 99, 123, 128, 154, 165, 166, 210, 252
Watts, M., 45, 47, 312ch3n3
weaving, 254, 259
wells, 119, 185
wetlands, 1, 62, 63, 73, 83, 109–36 *passim*, 283, 284
  markets, 204–7 *passim*, 209, 210, 212–33 *passim*
wild foods, 33, 47, 50, 69, 71, 75, 111, 117, 120, 126–32 *passim*, 138, 139, 145, 153, 154, 160, 161, 163, 176, 183, 184, 189, 190, 194, 196, 197, 206, 227–9, 235, 237, 242, 243, 245–9 *passim*, 251, 253, 262, 268, 285, 286, 289, 298, 303
Winter, G., 102
women, 36, 52, 68, 76, 77, 215, 226, 245, 253, 254, 258–61 *passim*, 273

wood, 71, 111, 120, 130, 138, 186, 188, 190, 206, 233, 235, 242, 254, 259, 304
World Bank, 15, 16, 53, 79, 91
World Food Programme, 48, 53, 54, 94, 96, 313ch5n5
Woro Ngia, 165

Youvarou, 62, 66, 71, 109, 115, 123, 126, 129, 130, 161, 204–6, 208, 252

zones, agro-ecological, 6, 50, 51, 73, 79, 245, 301
  Sahelian, 79, 88, 114
  Sahelian–Saharan, 79, 83
  Sahelian–Sudanic, 79, 88
  Sudanic, 79
  Sudanic-Guinean, 79